MISES:

An Annotated Bibliography

MISES:
An Annotated Bibliography

A comprehensive listing of books and articles
by and about Ludwig von Mises

Compiled by
Bettina Bien Greaves
and
Robert W. McGee

The Foundation for Economic Education, Inc.
Irvington-on-Hudson, New York 10533

1993

ABOUT THE FOUNDATION

The Foundation for Economic Education (FEE) is the oldest economic research organization dedicated to the preservation of individual freedom and the private property order. It was established in 1946 by Leonard E. Read (1898-1983), and is guided by the principles of its adviser, Ludwig von Mises (1881-1973). Both men served FEE until their deaths.

Throughout the years, FEE's mission has not changed. Its goal is to study the moral and intellectual foundation of a free society and share its knowledge with individuals everywhere. Its principal publication is the monthly journal, *The Freeman*. FEE avoids political controversies and remains a purely educational organization. It takes inspiration from the statement of Ludwig von Mises at the conclusion of his great work on socialism:

> Everyone carries a part of society on his shoulders; no one is relieved of his share of responsibility by others. And no one can find a safe way for himself if society is sweeping towards destruction. Therefore, everyone, in his own interests, must thrust himself vigorously into the intellectual battle. None can stand aside with unconcern; the interests of everyone hang on the result. Whether he chooses or not, every man is drawn into the great historical struggle, the decisive battle into which our epoch has plunged us.

This bibliography is an updated and much-expanded version of the bibliography compiled by Bettina Bien Greaves: *The Works of Ludwig von Mises*. Irvington-on-Hudson, N.Y.: Foundation for Economic Education, Inc., 1970.

ISBN 0-910614-79-2

TABLE OF CONTENTS

PREFACE

My late husband, Professor Ludwig von Mises, has been described as "the greatest economist of his generation, one of the great social thinkers of our age, a powerful and original mind [which] saw economics not as some narrow specialty, but as a study of not less than the whole realm of human action, human decision." Those are the words of Henry Hazlitt, noted economist and author of the best-selling *Economics in One Lesson,* when he spoke at the October 16, 1973, Memorial Service in Professor Mises' honor.

Bettina Bien Greaves first heard my husband speak in 1951, at a *Freeman* seminar at Washington Square. She took shorthand notes of his lectures and distributed her notes to the attendees. Learning this, my husband said to her with a half smile on his face, "Next time, young lady, you had better write your own book!"

In the following 18 years she attended every one of Professor Mises' New York University graduate economic seminar lectures, always taking notes. In the evenings she read, not only his books, but also those of scholars who did not agree with his opinions about freedom and the free market. Maybe, without being conscious of it, my husband's words laid the groundwork for the present bibliography.

Bettina possesses not only copies of all the books, papers, essays and monographs which Professor Mises ever wrote, but she also owns prints of almost every photograph that has ever been taken of him. By listing the Professor's works and works about him, she hopes to help students see him and his contributions in perspective.

Because Bettina has studied Professor Mises' writings line by line, word for word, she is able to discuss the pros and cons of his work with the most learned scholars. Certainly her serious studies have enabled her to make this bibliography *the* definitive listing of his works and the most complete listing now available of books and articles about him. It should be of tremendous help to future students and scholars, when they write not only about economics, but also about philosophy and other social sciences. It will introduce them to a great deal of material for their writings and doctoral dissertations.

Margit von Mises

April 16, 1989

INTRODUCTION

*"Where there is no free market, there is no pricing system; without
a pricing system, there is no economic calculation."*
Economic Calculation in the Socialist Commonwealth (1920)

With these words, Professor Ludwig von Mises dismissed the possibility of economic calculation in a socialist society where the government owns or controls all factors of production. In a socialist society, there are no exchanges, no sales or purchases of factors of production. Without exchanges there is no real market; without a market, there are no real prices. Without prices derived through competition on the market, there is no way to compare the relative values of the various factors of production. Thus, in a socialist society without prices, there can be no economic calculation. Pointing this out is one of Mises' major contributions to economic theory.

Some early socialists noted Mises' criticism of their doctrine and tried to answer. In 1936, Oskar Lange, a Marxist economics professor, later the Polish Ambassador to the United States and then to the United Nations and a member of the Polish Politburo at the time of his death in 1965, even proposed that the socialists erect a statue of Dr. Mises. "For it was his powerful challenge that forced the socialists to recognize the importance of an adequate system of economic accounting to guide the allocation of resources in a socialist economy."[1] Although no socialist government has as yet adopted Professor Lange's suggestion to honor Dr. Mises,[2] he has long been constructing his own "monument" — his writings — a much more important and useful monument than any marble statue. Moreover, they will serve as guideposts to show future generations the road to economic understanding, peace and prosperity.

---

[1] "On the Economic Theory of Socialism," published in the book of the same title. Benjamin E. Lippincott, ed. (Minneapolis: University of Minnesota Press, 1938) p.57.

[2] In September 1990, George Koether presented to the University of Warsaw in Poland a bronze head of Mises, created by the sculptress Nellie Erickson. It was installed in the University Library, next door to the Oskar Lange room.

Dr. Mises' long career as a writer started in 1902. In that year, when he was only 21 years old, his first book was published, an historical study of the peasant in Galicia, a section of Austria-Hungary where Mises was born, now within the borders of Ukraine. Mises' early writings were primarily historical. However, the bulk of his later work was in economic theory, especially on the epistemological fundamentals of the science of economics. It is generally recognized that he made three major contributions.

Mises' first significant contribution was in monetary theory. In 1912, he applied to money the marginal utility (subjective value) theory developed by his predecessors in the "Austrian School of Economics," notably Carl Menger and Eugen von Böhm-Bawerk. By analyzing money and credit on the basis of subjective value theory, Mises developed a logically consistent explanation of the economic booms and busts which have appeared periodically in modern hampered-market economies. This explanation, with which Mises' name is associated, is known as the "monetary theory of the trade cycle."

Mises' second great accomplishment was in pointing out, in 1920, that economic calculation is not possible without free market pricing. His reasoning has certainly been illustrated by the experience of the U.S.S.R. Attempts to plan production and allocate resources within socialist countries so as to reduce economic malproduction have resulted in shoddy merchandise, noticeable malinvestments, and production bottlenecks. In the effort to reduce such economic imbalances in the mid-1960s, Yevsei G. Liberman and others urged the nation's economic planners to improvise a quasi profit-and-loss system. However, they failed to comprehend the essence of Mises' position, namely that profits and losses cannot be known in the absence of private ownership and competitive bidding for the factors of production. As Liberman and his colleagues clung to the communist principle of government ownership and control of productive facilities, their "reforms" could not succeed in reducing economic malproduction, as a free market would have.

His third major contribution was in the 1920s and 1930s as he explained that economics was a unified praxeological (human action) science, developed by reason and logic from *a priori* truths or axioms.

Mises was largely ignored by academicians during his lifetime. When he wasn't ignored he was often misunderstood, misinterpreted and even maligned. Mises realized that later generations would come to understand his teachings better, build on his work, reject some of the theories he presented, and go beyond. That is the way of science; some theories form the basis for the future development of knowledge; other doctrines that are accepted as truths today are shown to be errors tomorrow. Since Mises' death, the number of books and articles about him has been mushrooming. Many people are learning about him for the first time; many others are gaining a better understanding of his teachings; and, as a result, he is beginning to gain some much deserved recognition.

Mises spent a great deal of time and effort in explaining the epistemology on which economic theories are based. Step by logical step he demonstrated that the fundamentals on which he reasoned stem from the undeniable fact that man acts. Man acts, decides, chooses, consciously, purposively, in the attempt to attain various needs, wants, values, goals. Men's needs, wants, values, and goals are personal, subjective. But the fact that men act is objective. Philosophers and economists may consider the actions of men and their consequences with *Wertfreiheit*, that is without making value judgments themselves as to the merits of the actions, decisions, and choices of other men. Thus the reasoning of economists may be "value free" and the conclusions to which their logic leads them on the basis of this objective fact are *not* matters of opinion. Mises' epistemology, therefore, is logical, scientific and factual.

Methodological individualism and the subjective, marginal utility theory of value were at the root of all Mises' work. As he refined his understanding of economic theory, this understanding of subjectivism made him increasingly critical of macroeconomics. He pointed out that economic phenomena are the outcomes of individual actions, decisions, and choices; everything in the market is always changing; there are no constants that can be measured. It must be admitted that Mises sometimes used the term "price level" in his early writings, but he was adamant in his later years that there can be no price *level*. Prices, the statistician's usual unit of measurement, are expressions of momentary exchange ratios among the subjective values of individuals, each acting at a particular time and place. The significance of a price is lost when it is treated as a quantity of money and added to other quantities of money to form economic aggregates or averages.

Mises was careful to explain that he was not an anarchist. He considered government necessary to protect life and property and to assure the conditions under which persons could engage in voluntary cooperation without being at the mercy of those who would disrupt peaceful social cooperation.

Mises distinguished, on the one hand, between profit (and loss) on the market and "monopoly gain" on the other hand. Profits (and losses) are market phenomena, arising out of the superior (inferior) alertness of the entrepreneur, i.e. rewards (penalties) for his success (or failure) in anticipating consumer wants and producing below (above) the prices consumers are willing to pay for his contributions. A "monopoly gain" *may* arise on the market in those rare instances when the owner of a good or service, who enjoys complete right of disposal over its total supply, happens to be in a position to increase his total income by selling fewer units at a higher price per unit. Although no monopolist can ever be sure whether his return from sales is a "monopoly gain" or a "profit" in the market sense, "monopoly gain" is a theoretical possibility on the market and, as such, Mises considered it worth describing as the only case on the market when consumer demands were not supreme. A government-created or government-protected monopoly, which of course Mises did not sanction, is something very different from a market monopoly. A government-protected monopoly is, of course, a threat to the market. Any income generated by such a monopoly is neither profit (nor loss) in the market sense. Moreover, it is not a "monopoly gain" by Mises' definition either; some of it may be pay for services rendered, as in the case of government mail delivery, trash collection, or highways, but part of it is tribute exacted forcefully by means of the government agency's privileged position.

Mises advocated free market money and free banking. Given a free market and voluntary exchange, traders would in time select as their medium of exchange, i.e., as money, the most marketable commodity in their trading community. Under the conditions of his day Mises said money would be gold. Over time, the demand for money will inevitably induce entrepreneurs to experiment with devices or innovations to economize the use of the market's commodity money, to use gold more efficiently. They will develop such gold saving devices as clearing agencies, tokens, money certificates, banknotes, checking accounts, credit cards, and the like. Insofar as these devices facilitate and promote market transactions, or hamper and hinder them, they will prove useful and helpful on the one hand, or hurtful and detrimental on the other. In either case, however, they will not be part of the stock of money proper. Rather they will remain money substitutes, near money, and the like. Such money substitutes would, of course, affect the market value per unit of the commodity money, but they would not themselves be money proper.

Mises held that market competition would *tend* (for there is no guarantee on the market) to keep money honest, and to keep the banks from issuing banknotes on the basis of fractional, or non-existent, reserves. Such banknotes would have nothing more behind them than the fractional reserves and/or the deposits of clients who had access to them on demand themselves, or evidences of liability, i.e., someone else's or some agency's promise-to-pay. As soon as a private bank issued more promises-to-pay than it could redeem it would be over-extended and courting disaster. A private, commercial bank that issued such banknotes could not keep them "redeemable on demand" indefinitely without some sort of subsidy or special privilege, in which case they would no longer be completely private banks. Under free banking, Mises maintained, banks should comply with the common law, fulfill their contracts as agreed upon, and apply truth-in-labeling to their banknotes. However, advocacy of free banking would not call for legislation *compelling* the banks to retain certain reserves. As a matter of fact, Mises considered it dangerous to empower legislatures to specify a bank's required reserves, even a 100% gold reserve. *Empowering the legislature to fix reserve requirements at any level, even 100%, would imply also the authority to revise (that is, to raise or to lower) them.*

*   *   *

From 1902, when Professor Mises' first book appeared, until his death, he was a persistent and consistent writer. He was a prolific author. And yet, when he wrote he always had something worthwhile to say. Although his many books and articles often covered the same fields, there is surprisingly little serious repetition.

Throughout his early career, Mises wrote and lectured in German, although he had an English-language article published as early as 1909. For a time, when he was in Switzerland, he wrote and lectured in French — Mrs. Mises says that his French pronunciation was better than his English ever became. Even before he came to this country in 1940, he had a good knowledge of English acquired largely through reading. However, when he immigrated, he realized he would have to improve his English still more. For several years, a private tutor, Arthur Goddard, helped him. Economist Henry Hazlitt, who became a very close friend, went over his first books published in this country: *Bureaucracy, Omnipotent Government*, both issued in 1944, and also *Human Action,* which came out in 1949. In time, Mises became fluent in English, although he always spoke with an accent. He developed a remarkable vocabulary and English became his language of choice when dealing with economics.

Mises was a strong advocate of studying languages. Generally speaking, he was suspicious of translations. He believed that few translators were familiar enough with the two languages in which they were working, as well as with the ideas being translated, to produce a faithful translation of the original. Thus, Mises maintained that the best way to read any work was in its original language. Even so, he realized that most people would not learn additional languages well enough to read books in their original tongues. Therefore, he sanctioned translations of his several books, for which we must be grateful.

Mises' full name was "Ludwig Edler von Mises." "Edler von" indicated the particular rank of nobility to which he was entitled under the old Austro-Hungarian Empire. His name appeared as "Ludwig von Mises" on his books and articles published in Austria-Hungary before 1919. After World War I, all Austrian titles of nobility were abolished by law. As a result, his writings published in Austria between the two World Wars list him simply as "Ludwig Mises." After he left Vienna, however, he again wrote under the name "Ludwig von Mises," as he did in Switzerland when he published his *Nationalökonomie* (1940). After he became an American citizen he no longer used the title prefix, "von," in his personal life, although he continued to write and publish, as he had at the start of his career, under his full name, "Ludwig von Mises." He hoped this would make it unnecessary to answer individually the letters of librarians and bibliographers as to whether or not he was the same author whose works had been published under that name before 1919. Yet confusion continues. Library cataloguers and indexers are not always consistent; references to his works may be found alphabetized under either "von" or "Mises." "Mises" is preferred.

In Vienna, Mises' influence was due in large part to his official positions with the University of Vienna, the Austrian government's Chamber of Commerce, and the economic research institute which he founded. In addition to teaching at the University, he also held in his Chamber of Commerce office a private seminar which was attended over the years by important intellectuals, industrialists, young economists, and occasional foreign visitors. Mises continued this seminar tradition in the United States, teaching at New York University until his retirement in 1969, at the age of 87.

Since Mises' death in 1973, references to him in the literature have proliferated. Many are hearing about him and his contributions for the first time. Many others are becoming more appreciative of his teachings. Even some who ignored Mises for decades and stood for all he opposed are beginning to pay him heed. As Robert Heilbroner, the outspoken Keynesian, has admitted, "It turns out, of course, that Mises was right.... [S]etting prices became a hopeless problem [in the Soviet system] . . . . In all likelihood, then, the direction in which things are headed is some version of capitalism, whatever its title may be." (*The New Yorker*, September 10, 1990). To the extent that Mises is now being recognized as having been "right" all along, it is due to his persistence and his prodigious production over the years. His influence as the leading spokesman for the "Austrian School of Economics" will undoubtedly continue to grow.

Bettina Bien Greaves

ACKNOWLEDGMENTS

This bibliography has had a long history. It could be said that it was actually begun in 1951, when I first started attending Mises' seminars. From that time on, I collected and read everything of Mises I could find and soon began keeping a record of his works.

Mises' early files and records disappeared when his personal library in Vienna was ransacked shortly after Hitler's army invaded Austria in 1938. Thus, it would have been extremely difficult, if not impossible to locate his early writings and to construct a bibliography that was anywhere near complete without the list the Professor gave me long ago, compiled by his faithful, long-time Vienna secretary, Mrs. Theresia Thieberger. During the years when my husband, Percy L. Greaves, Jr., and I attended Mises' graduate seminar at New York University Graduate School of Business Administration (1950-1969), Mises gave us copies of articles he wrote as they appeared in print. We had a chance to see his library one summer when my husband and I, at Mrs. Mises' request, catalogued his books. After he died, we went over his correspondence and pamphlet files in his New York apartment and I have since gone through his papers at Grove City College (Grove City, Pennsylvania) where they are now lodged.

A preliminary typed bibliography was presented to Mises in 1961 on the occasion of his 80th birthday. This was an open-ended bibliography as the Professor was still working and writing. In 1970, the Foundation for Economic Education (FEE) published an up-dated version. But I was soon dissatisfied with it, especially after Professor Mises' death when I looked through his papers and discovered quite a few articles that had not been included. I determined to revise the bibliography "some day." That "some day" might never have come if it hadn't been for Dr. Robert W. McGee. Bob kept after me and finally agreed to work with me in bringing out a new and revised bibliography, which we would make as complete as possible. Thus, *this* bibliography was born. It might never have appeared if it hadn't been for Bob McGee. And it couldn't have appeared in its present form without my files and collection of Misesiana.

Bob brought his computer, which had the diacritical marks necessary to list foreign language titles, to my office and spent many a day searching FEE's library and mine, as well as my private file folders, for anything by or about Mises. When he encountered a mention of Mises in a footnote or bibliography that we could not find in FEE's files, I would visit one of the large libraries in the vicinity to locate the references cited. Bob then entered the data on his computer.

Bob and I soon became overwhelmed by the extent and complexity of the project; it almost seemed to acquire a life of its own. Unfortunately, Bob's studies and his many activities as Professor of Accounting (Seton Hall University), editor of a tax newsletter, and so on, allowed him little time to convert the raw data to final form. Unfortunately also, the computer on which the entries had been made was not compatible with any of the Foundation's word processors. So FEE purchased a new computer that could handle Bob's entries and the bibliography was completed in-house.

Several possible arrangements were considered. We finally decided to group entries under three major categories: (1) books, monographs, and articles, *by* Mises, (2) reviews of Mises' books, and (3) books and articles *about* him. To give Mises credit for his pioneering contributions, his books and articles are listed chronologically by date of their original appearance, with data describing various editions and translations following. Most of Mises works were published originally in English or German. However, persons interested in reading his writings in other languages will find one or several translated into Chinese, Czech, Dutch, French, Greek, Hebrew, Hungarian, Italian, Japanese, Polish, Portuguese, Spanish and Swedish. Translations into Icelandic, Lithuanian, and Russian are in the works. The compilers believe they have included all editions and translations of Mises' major published works, although it is possible that a few may have escaped them. They welcome news of any omissions or errors.

Some of Mises' articles appeared in little-known, ephemeral periodicals and have not been readily available. Fortunately, quite a few of these have just recently been assembled in two new anthologies, *Money, Method and the Market Process* (B-28) and *Economic Freedom and Interventionism* (B-29). Many references cited are practically impossible to locate, but are listed here for the benefit of students, usually with annotations or quotes. Some reviews of Mises' books were supplied him by clipping services hired by his publishers; many articles that mention him were found among his papers at Grove City College; still others have been located and collected by the compilers over the years. This bibliography also includes obituaries.

The two compilers had intended to bring the section of "abouts" down to the present time, but the bibliography was becoming unwieldy, especially as Mises citations have mushroomed since his death in 1973. Therefore, they finally decided to close down the "abouts" as of 1981, the 100th anniversary of Mises' birth. Post-1981 "abouts" will have to await a follow-up volume.

In addition to Mrs. Thieberger, with whose Viennese-compiled bibliography we started, several other persons provided special assistance. Our thanks to:

Professor Israel Kirzner, who helped identify several Hebrew translations;

Ms. Friederike Zeitlhofer of the Austrian Institute in New York City, who located in the Institute's fine collection of works by Austrian authors some sources we were seeking;

Ms. Diane Grundy, Librarian, Grove City College, who kindly had copies made from the Library's Mises collection of several articles I had overlooked during my visit;

Professor Toshio Murata, translator into Japanese of Mises' *Human Action,* who located in Japan several articles about Mises and summarized or translated them into English;

and last but not least,

John Batalana and Richard Ebeling who directed us to many Mises citations they had discovered in the course of their extensive reading, which we wouldn't have found otherwise.

A few notes on format. Initial articles (a, an, the) are ignored in alphabetizing titles. The two compilers have tried to make the entries as accurate, complete, and consistent as possible. However, inconsistencies occur because quoted passages, taken from many different sources published over decades, have been copied verbatim — except for correcting obvious typographical errors. Also, "von" has been rendered consistently in lower case, except at the start of a sentence. If the source, date, or author of an entry cannot be determined, that is noted; "n.d." means no date was indicated; a date followed by (?) represents the compilers' best guess. When no translator is credited with a translation, it was the work of Bettina Bien Greaves.

BBG

October 1992

VITA

1881   Born September 29 to Arthur Edler and Adele (Landau) von Mises, at Lemberg, in the Austro-Hungarian Empire. After World War I, Lemberg became "Lwow," a part of Poland; after World War II, "Lvov," a part of Ukraine in the U.S.S.R.; then in December 1991, "Lviv," in the newly independent republic of Ukraine. Ludwig's father, educated at Zürich Polytechnic, was a construction engineer employed in the Austrian Railroad Ministry. Ludwig was the oldest of three boys; one died as a child; Richard became well known as a mathematician.

       Attended a private elementary school, then the public Akademische Gymnasium in Vienna (1892-1900).

1900   First visit to Switzerland.

1900-1902   Attended Universität Wien (University of Vienna).

1902   *"Die Entwicklung des gutsherrlich-bäuerlichen Verhältnisses in Galizien (1772-1848)"* [The Development of the Relationship between Peasant and the Lord of the Manor in Galicia, 1772-1848]. A monograph about the decline of serfdom in Mises' native Galicia.

1903   Mises' father died.

1906   February 20: Awarded Dr. Jur. degree, Doctor of both Canon and Roman Laws, from the Universität Wien [University of Vienna]. When Mises attended the University, it had no separate economics department; the only path to studying economics in those days was through law.

1904 (?) -1914 Attended seminar of Eugen von Böhm-Bawerk at the Universität Wien.

1910   Completed compulsory military service, consisting of three 4-week periods of duty, one each year for three years.

1906-1912   Taught economics to seniors of the Wiener Handelsakademie für Mädchen [Viennese Commercial Academy for Girls].

1907-1908   Began working at the Kammer für Handel, Gewerbe und Industrie [Austrian Chamber of Commerce], "Handelskammer" for short, an official advisory agency of the Austrian government.

1912   *Theorie des Geldes und der Umlaufsmittel* [Theory of Money and Credit], Mises' first important theoretical work.

1913   Appointed Privatdozent (unsalaried lecturer) at the University of Vienna.

1914-1918   Called back to active duty when World War I started. He left Vienna in the summer of 1914 to go to war, on the same day and on the same train on which he had planned to leave to teach a seminar in Silesia. He served as a captain with the artillery in the Austro-Hungarian cavalry, primarily on the Eastern front in the Carpathian Mountains, Russian Ukraine, and Crimea. During the latter part of the war, he worked on economic problems with the Army's General Staff in Vienna.

VITA

1918-1919	Taught a class of officers seeking to return to civilian life at the Wiener Exportakademie [Viennese Export Academy], later the Hochschule für Welthandel [Institute for World Trade].
1918-1920	Director, League of Nation's Austrian Abrechnungs Amt [Reparations Commission].
1918-1934	Returned to the University of Vienna as a Privatdozent (unsalaried lecturer); invested May 18, 1918, with the title of "Professor Extraordinary."
	After World War I, Mises helped to revive the Nationalökonomische Gesellschaft [Economic Society], publisher of the quarterly, *Zeitschrift für Nationalökonomie.*
1918-1938	Resumed position with the Handelskammer, the Austrian Chamber of Commerce.
1919	*Nation, Staat und Wirtschaft: Beiträge zur Politik und Geschichte der Zeit* [Nation, State, and Economy: Contributions to the Politics and History of Our Time].
1920	"Die Wirtschaftsrechnung im sozialistischen Gemeinwesen" [Economic Calculation in the Socialist Commonwealth]. Paper presented to the Nationalökonomische Gesellschaft, later published in the *Archiv für Sozialwissenschaft und Sozialpolitik* (1920).
1919-1933	Active member, Verein für Sozialpolitik [Association for Social Policy].
1920-1934	Conducted a private seminar [Privatseminar] in his office on alternate Friday evenings. Participants: University Ph.D.s and guests, by invitation only.
1922	*Die Gemeinwirtschaft: Untersuchungen über den Sozialismus* [Socialism: An Economic and Sociological Analysis].
1923	*Die geldtheoretische Seite des Stabilisierungsproblems* [Stabilization of the Monetary Unit, from the Viewpoint of Theory].
1924	*The Theory of Money and Credit*, 2nd German edition.
1926	Lecture tour of U.S. universities, under sponsorship of Laura Spelman (Rockefeller) Foundation.
1927-1938	January 1, 1927: The Oesterreichisches Institut für Konjunkturforschung [Austrian Institute for Business Cycle Research], established by Mises, began operations. Mises became its Acting (Executive) Vice President; F. A. Hayek served as manager until 1931; when Hayek migrated to London, Oskar Morgenstern took over.
1927	*Liberalismus* [Liberalism]. First English translation published 1962 as *The Free and Prosperous Commonwealth.*
1928	*Geldwertstabilisierung und Konjunkturpolitik* [Monetary Stabilization and Cyclical Policy].
1929	*Kritik des Interventionismus: Untersuchungen zur Wirtschaftspolitik und Wirtschafts-ideologie der Gegenwart* [Critique of Interventionism: Inquiries into Present Day Economic Policy and Ideology].
1931	Visited the United States for the Congress of the International Chamber of Commerce.

VITA

1931	*Die Ursachen der Wirtschaftskrise: Ein Vortrag* [The Causes of the Economic Crisis: A Lecture].
1932	*Socialism,* 2nd German edition.
1933	*Grundprobleme der Nationalökonomie* [Epistemological Problems of Economics].
1934	English translation of *Theorie des Geldes und der Umlaufsmittel* [The Theory of Money and Credit].
1934-1940	Professor of International Economic Relations, Institut Universitaire des Hautes Études Internationales [Graduate Institute of International Studies], Geneva, Switzerland. Even though he had left Vienna to accept this position in Switzerland, Mises retained his association with the Austrian Chamber of Commerce on a part-time basis until the *Anschluss,* Hitler's annexation of Austria in March 1938.
1936	English translation of *Die Gemeinwirtschaft* [Socialism].
1937	Mises' mother died in Vienna.
1938	July 6: Married Margit (née Herzfeld) Sereny in Geneva.
1940	*Nationalökonomie: Theorie des Handelns und Wirtschaftens* [Economics: Theory of Action and Exchange].
	Migrated to the United States, arriving in New York on August 2.
1940-1944	Wrote reminiscences of his life in Vienna, translated and published posthumously as *Notes and Recollections* (1978).
	Rockefeller Foundation and National Bureau of Economic Research grants enabled Mises to write two books, *Omnipotent Government* and *Bureaucracy,* both published in 1944.
1942	January and February: 2-month appointment in Mexico as Visiting Professor at the Universidad Nacional Autónoma de México, Escuela Nacional de Economía [National University of Mexico, School of Economics].
1945-1969	Visiting Professor, New York University, Graduate School of Business Administration. Gave two courses, Monday evening lecture (February 1945-Spring 1964), Thursday evening seminar (Fall 1948-Spring 1969).
1946	Member, Economic Principles Commission, National Association of Manufacturers. As such, consulted in the preparation of *The American Individual Enterprise System*, 2 vols. (McGraw Hill, 1946), the product of "the consensus of judgment among the Commission members."
	Acquired U. S. citizenship.
	July 26 to September 4: Visiting Professor in Mexico, lecturing for the Escuela de Economía [School of Economics] of the Asociación Mexicana de Cultura [Mexican Cultural Association].

VITA

1946-1973	Adviser, Foundation for Economic Education, Inc. (Irvington-on-Hudson, N.Y.).
1947	*Planned Chaos.*
	Instrumental in the founding, with F. A. Hayek, of the Mont Pèlerin Society, an international society of businessmen, economists, and other intellectuals.
1949	July 30 to August 28: lectured in Mexico for the Escuela de Economía [School of Economics] of the Asociación Mexicana de Cultura [Mexican Cultural Association].
	Human Action: An Economic Treatise.
1950	March 31 to April 16: Lecture tour of Peru, at the invitation of the Banco Central de Reserve (Central Reserve Bank), Pedro Beltrán, Chairman.
1951	*Socialism* - New U. S. edition of English translation, enlarged with *Planned Chaos* (1947) as its epilogue.
1952	*Planning for Freedom: And Other Essays and Addresses.* Later enlarged editions published 1962, 1974, and 1980.
1953	*The Theory of Money and Credit.* New U. S. edition of English translation, enlarged with a new essay on "Monetary Reconstruction."
	Richard von Mises, Ludwig's brother, the mathematician, dies.
1954-1955	January 1954 to April 1955: Adviser to National Association of Manufacturers.
1956	February 20: Mises' Doctorate renewed and commemorated by the Universität Wien [University of Vienna] on the 50th anniversary of the date on which it was awarded.
	Festschrift published on the occasion of the Fiftieth Anniversary of Mises' Doctorate, February 20, 1956, *On Freedom and Free Enterprise: Essays in Honor of Ludwig von Mises* (Mary Sennholz, editor).
	The Anti-Capitalistic Mentality.
1957	Distinguished Service Award of the Fellowship of Former Overseas Rotarians.
	June 8: Granted Honorary Degree, Doctor of Laws, Grove City College, Grove City, Pennsylvania.
	Theory and History.
1958	September 19 to September 28: Visited Mexico under sponsorship of the Instituto de Investigaciones Sociales y Económicas [Institute for Social and Economic Investigations] to participate in a seminar with several other members of the Mont Pèlerin Society.
1959	June 2 to June 15: Invited to Buenos Aires, Argentina, by the Centro de Difusión de la Economía Libre [Center for the Promotion of the Free Economy], later the Centro de

4

VITA

Estudios sobre la Libertad [Center for the Study of Freedom]. Delivered six lectures, published posthumously as *Economic Policy: Thoughts for Today and Tomorrow* (1979).

1960   English translation of *Grundprobleme der Nationalökonomie* [Epistemological Problems of Economics].

1962   *The Ultimate Foundation of Economic Science.*

English translation of *Liberalismus* [Liberalism] under the title of *The Free and Prosperous Commonwealth.*

October 20: Awarded Österreichisches Ehrenzeichen für Wissenschaft und Kunst [Austrian medal of honor for science and the arts] in recognition of his "distinguished activities as a scholar and teacher and for his internationally recognized work in the fields of political science and economics."

1963   June 5: Awarded Honorary Degree, Doctorate of Laws, by New York University, "for his exposition of the philosophy of the free market, and his advocacy of a free society."

Human Action, 2nd ed., revised.

1964   July 28: Granted Honorary Degree, Doctor Rerum Politicarum [Doctor of Political Science] by the University of Freiburg, Breisgau, Germany.

1966   *Human Action*, 3rd edition.

1965-1971   Visiting Professor, Plano University, Plano, Texas.

1969   September: Cited by the American Economic Association as "Distinguished Fellow" of the year.

1971   September 29: Festschrift published in honor of Mises' 90th birthday: *Toward Liberty: Essays in Honor of Ludwig von Mises on the Occasion of his 90th Birthday* (2 volumes).

1973   October 10: Mises dies at St. Vincent's Hospital in New York City.

For purposes of this bibliography, in referring to Mises' books, monographs and anthologies, each has been assigned a number according to the date of its first publication. Thus, Mises' very first book (no translation available), *Die Entwicklung des gutsherrlich-bäuerlichen Verhältnisses in Galizien: 1772-1848* (1902) is B-1; Mises' fourth book, *Socialism* (first published in 1922 as *Die Gemeinwirtschaft*), is referred to as B-4. And so on.

A detailed publication history of each book, arranged chronologically under the heading of each first edition, is included in the "Books and Monographs" section.

The "Book Review" section cites and quotes from book reviews of each book. There the books are listed alphabetically by their English-language title, or by their original title if no English translation is available.

As an aid to locating a specific book by title or by number, here is a listing of Mises' books in order of publication, each with its Book Number and the several titles under which it has appeared.

B-1.   *Die Entwicklung des gutsherrlich-bäuerlichen Verhältnisses in Galizien: 1772-1848*   [The Development of the Relationship between Peasant and Lord of the Manor in Galicia: 1772-1848] (1902). No English translation available.

B-2   *Theorie des Geldes und der Umlaufsmittel* (1912).
The Theory of Money and Credit (English).
Teoría del Dinero y del Crédito (Spanish).
Kahei oyobi Ryūtūshudan no Riron (Japanese).
Chinese translation also.

B-3   *Nation, Staat und Wirtschaft* (1919).
Nation, State, and Economy (English).

B-4   *Die Gemeinwirtschaft* (1922).
Socialism (English).
El Socialismo (Spanish).
Le Socialisme (French).
Socialismo (Italian).

B-5   *Die geldtheoretische Seite des Stabilisierungsproblems* (1923).
Stabilization of the Monetary Unit -- From the Viewpoint of Theory (English); included in B-24.

B-6   *Liberalismus* (1927).
The Free and Prosperous Commonwealth (English, 1st ed.).
Liberalism (English, 2nd & 3rd eds.).
Liberalismo (Spanish).
Kapitalism och Socialism (Swedish).
Liberalismo (Portuguese).
Liberalizm w Klasycznej Tradycji (Polish).

B-7   *Geldwertstabilisierung und Konjunkturpolitik* (1928).
       Monetary Stabilization and Cyclical Policy (English); included in B-24.
       *La Stabilizzazione del Potere d'acquisito della Moneta e la Politica della
           Congiuntura* (Italian).

B-8   *Kritik des Interventionismus* (1929).
       A Critique of Interventionism (English).
       Uma Crítica ao Intervencionismo (Portuguese).

B-9   *Die Ursachen der Wirtschaftskrise* (1932).
       The Causes of the Economic Crisis (English); included in B-24.
       De Oorzaken van de Economische Crisis (Dutch).
       Las Causas de la Crisis Económica (1986).

B-10   *Grundprobleme der Nationalökonomie* (1933).
       Epistemological Problems of Economics (English).
       Problemi Epistemologici dell'economia (Italian).

B-11   *Nationalökonomie* (1940).   German-language predecessor to *Human Action*
           (B-16).   No English translation available.

B-12   *Omnipotent Government* (1944).
       Omnipotencia Gubernamental (Spanish).
       Le Gouvernement Omnipotent de l'État Totalitaire à la Guerre Total
           (French).
       See also B-25.

B-13   *Bureaucracy* (1944).
       Burocracia (Spanish).
       La Bureaucratie (French).
       Greek translation also.

B-14   *Planned Chaos* (1947); included as the epilogue to *Socialism* (B-4, 1951 and later
           editions).

B-15   *Observations on the Cooperative Movement* (1947).

B-16   *Human Action* (1949, rev., 1963, 1966).
       La Acción Humana (Spanish).
       L'Action Humaine (French).
       L'Azione Umana (Italian).
       Ação Humana (Portuguese).
       Ningen-Koi-Gaku (Japanese).
       Chinese translation also.

B-17   *Profit and Loss* (1951).
       Las Ganancias y las Pérdidas   (Spanish, as included in Spanish translation of B-18).

B-18   *Planning for Freedom* (1952, 1962, 1974, 1980, with various addenda).
       Planificación para la Libertad (Spanish).

B-19   *The Anti-Capitalistic Mentality.* (1956).
Die Wurzeln des Anti-Kapitalismus (German).
La Mentalidad Anticapitalista (Spanish).
A Mentalidade Anticapitalista (Portuguese).
Den antikapitalistika mentaliteten (Swedish).
La Mentalitá Anticapitalistica (Italian).
Mentalnosc Antykapitalistyczna (Polish)

B-20   *Theory and History* (1957).
Teoría e Historia (Spanish).
Chinese translation also.

B-21   *The Historical Setting of the Austrian School of Economics* (English, 1969).
El Establecimiento Histórico de la Escuela Austriaca de Economía (Spanish, 1962).

B-22   *The Ultimate Foundation of Economic Science* (1978).
Keizai Kagaku no Kontei (Japanese).
Chinese translation also.

POSTHUMOUS PUBLICATIONS

B-23   *Notes and Recollections* (written 1940, translated and published 1978).
Erinnerungen (German).

B-24   *On the Manipulation of Money and Credit* (1978; includes translations of B-5, B-7 and B-9).

B-25   *Im Namen des Staates: oder Die Gefahren des Kollektivismus* [In the name of the State or the Dangers of Collectivism] (1978). Preliminary version of *Omnipotent Government* (B-12). No English translation available.

B-26   *The Clash of Group Interests and Other Essays* (1978).

B-27   *Economic Policy: Thoughts for Today and Tomorrow* (1979).
Vom Wert der Besseren Ideen (German).
Seis Lecciones Sobre el Capitalismo (Spanish).
Politique Économique (French).
As Seis Liçöes (Portuguese).
Ekonomia I Polityka (Polish).
Japanese translation; title of which translates into English as "*Decision for Freedom.*"
Greek translation also.

B-28   *Money, Method, and the Market Process* (1990).

B-29   *Economic Freedom and Interventionism* (1990).

Arranged chronologically by dates of first editions. For complete information about articles included in anthologies see the Articles Section. *viz.,* "Interventionismus" (1926) listed with other articles in *A Critique of Interventionism* (B-8) as Article 26.5.

B-1   *Die Entwicklung des gutsherrlich-bäuerlichen Verhältnisses in Galizien: 1772-1848.* [The Development of the Relationship between Peasant and Lord of the Manor in Galicia: 1772-1848]. According to Mises (B-23, *Notes and Recollections,* p. 6), this study about the disappearance of serfdom in Mises' native Galicia was the result of an assignment by his college professor. Galicia, now part of Poland and Ukraine, had been the site of a bloody peasant uprising against the nobility in 1846. Mises was not proud of this work because it was "more a history of government measures than economic history."

   1902   *Die Entwicklung des gutsherrlich-bäuerlichen Verhältnisses in Galizien: 1772-1848.* [The Development of the Relationship between Peasant and Lord of the Manor in Galicia, 1772-1848]. Vienna & Leipzig: Franz Deuticke, 1902. vi: 144pp. (Series: *Wiener Staatswissenschaftliche Studien.* 4:2). No English translation available.

B-2   *The Theory of Money and Credit.* A detailed sophisticated explanation of the quantity theory of money based on the subjective, marginal utility theory. Explains money's origin, the development and nature of banking, the cause and consequences of inflation and credit expansion, the differences in the value of different moneys, as well as the reason for "cyclical" economic fluctuations.

   1912   First edition published in German: *Theorie des Geldes und der Umlaufsmittel.* Munich & Leipzig: Duncker & Humblot, 1912. xi: 476pp.

   1924   Second revised edition published in German: *Theorie des Geldes und der Umlaufsmittel.* New introduction by Ludwig Mises. Munich & Leipzig: Duncker & Humblot, 1924. xv: 420pp.

   1934   English translation of the second (1924) German edition: *The Theory of Money and Credit.* Translated by H. E. Batson. Introduction by Lionel Robbins. London: Jonathan Cape, 1934. 445pp. index.

   1935   U. S. edition: *The Theory of Money and Credit.* Translation by H. E. Batson. Introduction by Lionel Robbins. N.Y.: Harcourt, Brace & Co., 1935. 445pp. index.

   1936   Spanish translation of the second (1924) German edition: *Teoría del Dinero y del Crédito.* Translated by Antonio Riaño. Madrid: M. Aguilar, 1936. 490pp.

   1949   Japanese translation of the second (1924) German edition: *Kahei oyobi Ryütü-shudan no Riron.* Translated by Yoneo Azuma. Tokyo: Jitsugyo no Nipponsha, 1949.

1953   Reprint of the English language translation (1934) of the second (German) edition: *The Theory of Money and Credit*. Translated by H. E. Batson. New edition, enlarged with an essay on Monetary Reconstruction. New Haven: Yale University Press, 1953. 493pp. index.

1961   Spanish translation of the English language enlarged (1953) edition: *Teoría del Dinero y Crédito*. Translated by José Ma. Claramunda Bes. Spanish translation edited by Hermilo Larumbe Echávarri. Barcelona: Ediciones Zeus, 1961. 546pp.

1961   Spanish translation by Gustavo R. Velasco of the 1953 essay, "Monetary Reconstruction," in *Revista Bancaria*. 4:2 (July-August 1953) 418-429. Reprinted as a separate booklet: *Reconstrucción Monetaria*. Buenos Aires: Centro de Estudios sobre la Libertad, 1961. 91pp.

1969   Chinese translation: Translated by H. P. Yang. Taiwan (Republic of China): Taiwan Bank, Economic Research Department, 1969. 403pp.

1971   Reprint of 1953 English language edition: *The Theory of Money and Credit*. New edition, enlarged with an essay on Monetary Reconstruction. Translated from the German by H. E. Batson. Irvington-on-Hudson, N.Y.: The Foundation for Economic Education, Inc., 1971. 493pp. index.

1980   Reprint of 1953 English language edition: *The Theory of Money and Credit*. Translated from the German by H. E. Batson. With a new foreword by Murray N. Rothbard. Indianapolis: Liberty Fund, 1980. 541pp. index.

1980   Reprint of 1949 Japanese translation: *Kahei oyobi Ryütüshudan no Riron*. Translated by Yoneo Azuma. Tokyo: Nihon Hyöron-Sha, 1980.

B-3   *Nation, State and Economy*. A discussion of the respective influences of the nation (the ideological/cultural unit), the state (the political/legal institution) and the economy (the product of market relationships). An analysis of the statist trends in Austria and Germany that were the ultimate causes of their economic and military ruin in World War I.

1919   First edition published in German: *Nation, Staat und Wirtschaft: Beiträge zur Politik und Geschichte der Zeit*. Vienna & Leipzig: Manzsche Verlags- und Universitäts-Buchhandlung, 1919. 182pp.

1983   English translation: *Nation, State, and Economy: Contributions to the Politics and History of Our Time*. Translated by Leland B. Yeager. (© Institute for Humane Studies). New York: New York University Press, 1983. xxv:231pp. index.

B-4   *Socialism: An Economic and Sociological Analysis*. A detailed analysis and devastating critique of all aspects -- economic, cultural, social, etc. -- and of all varieties of socialism. Here Mises explained why economic calculation would be impossible in a completely controlled socialistic society, a problem even the socialists have acknowledged and tried (unsuccessfully) to refute.

1922   First edition: *Die Gemeinwirtschaft: Untersuchungen über den Sozialismus*. Jena: Gustav Fischer, 1922. viii:503pp.

1932   Second revised edition: *Die Gemeinwirtschaft: Untersuchungen über den Sozialismus.* Jena: Gustav Fischer, 1932. xx:500pp. index. Appendix: Excerpt from "Neue Beiträge zum Problem der sozialistischen Wirtschaftsrechnung" (Article 23.6)

1936   English translation of the second German (1932) edition: *Socialism: An Economic and Sociological Analysis*. Translated by J. Kahane. London: Jonathan Cape, 1936. 528pp. index. Includes several alterations and additions by Mises to Part II, chapter 2, section 4.

1936?   U.S. edition: *Socialism: An Economic and Sociological Analysis.* New York: Macmillan Co., n.d. 528pp. index. Reprint of Jonathan Cape 1936 edition.

1938   French translation of second German (1932) edition: *Le Socialisme: Étude économique et sociologique.* Translated from the German by Paul Bastier, André Terrasse, and François Terrasse. Preface by François Perroux. Paris: Librairie de Médicis, 1938. 626pp. index. Incorporates Mises' revisions and additions for the English (1936) translation.

1951   Reprint of the English translation (1936), enlarged: *Socialism: An Economic and Sociological Analysis*. Translated by J. Kahane. New edition, enlarged with an Epilogue. New Haven: Yale University Press, 1951. 599pp. index. NOTE: Epilogue first included in this edition originally published in 1947 as *Planned Chaos* (B-14).

1961   Spanish translation of the second German (1932) edition plus the 1951 Epilogue: *El Socialismo: Análisis Económico y Sociológico.* Translated by Luis Montes de Oca. Foreword by Gustavo R. Velasco dated August 1959. Mexico: Editorial Hermes, 1961. xxiv:621pp. index. Included is an evaluation (pp.xvii-xxiv) of Mises and the "Austrian School"; although unsigned, this was undoubtedly translated from a manuscript provided by Mises himself.

1968   Reprint of the Spanish (1961) translation by Luis Montes de Oca: *El Socialismo: Análisis Económico y Sociológico.* 2nd edition. Buenos Aires: Centro Naval, Instituto de Publicaciones Navales, 1968. 613 pp. Type reset.

1969   Reprint of the 1951 English language edition as enlarged: *Socialism: An Economic and Sociological Analysis.* London: Jonathan Cape, 1969. 599pp. index.

1981   Reprint of English language 1951 edition: *Socialism: An Economic and Sociological Analysis.* Translated by J. Kahane. Indianapolis: Liberty Fund, 1981. 569pp. indexes. The type in this new oversized (7" x 10") reprint was completely reset. It contains a Publisher's Preface, a new Foreword by F. A. Hayek, an Index to works cited, Indexes to subjects and names, Publisher's Notes explaining the significance of abstruse references and English translations of all foreign terms and quotations. For ease of reference, paging of the earlier 1951 English translation is also shown in the margin.

1981   Reprint of the 1932 German edition: *Die Gemeinwirtschaft: Untersuchungen über den Sozialismus.* With a new foreword by Christian Watrin. Munich: Philosophia Verlag, 1981. xx:500pp. index. As this edition was photo-offset, it does *not* include Mises' revisions for the 1936 English, 1938 French and later editions, nor the Epilogue, first included in the 1951 edition.

1989   Spanish language reprint: *Socialismo: Análisis Económico y Sociológico.* 3rd Spanish edition. Translation of Luis Montes de Oca. With a new Preface by Alberto Benegas Lynch. New York: Western Books Foundation, n.d. [1989]. Published under the auspices of the Centro de Estudios sobre la Libertad (Buenos Aires). xxxii:621pp. index.

[1989]   A down-sized reprint (6" x 9") of the Liberty Fund (1981) edition. Indianapolis: Liberty Fund, n.d. [1989]).

1990   Italian translation: *Socialismo: Analisi Economica e Sociologica.* Edited by Dario Antiseri. Preface by Dario Antiseri. Milan: Rusconi, 1990. 666pp. index. Translation of the English-language Liberty Fund (1981) edition, including Hayek's Introduction.

1990   Unabridged audiotape version: *Socialism.* Read by Bernard Mayes. Ashland, Ore.: Classics on Tape, 1990. 18 cassettes.

IN PROCESS: Russian translation.

B-5   *Stabilization of the Monetary Unit -- From the Viewpoint of Theory.* An analysis of inflation and its consequences.

1923   First edition: *Die geldtheoretische Seite des Stabilisierungsproblems.* Munich & Leipzig: Duncker & Humblot, 1923. 37pp. Published in conjunction with an essay by Franz Klein on the legal aspect of the stabilization problem in the series *Schriften des Vereins für Sozialpolitik.* 164:2.

1978   English translation by Bettina Bien Greaves: "Stabilization of the Monetary Unit -- from the Viewpoint of Theory" in *On the Manipulation of Money and Credit,* 1978 (B-24).

B-6   *Liberalism* or *The Free and Prosperous Commonwealth.* A forceful restatement of the role of government under classical liberalism. Mises defines the role of government and explains what it should and should not do to foster peace, freedom and prosperity.

1927   First edition: *Liberalismus.* Jena: Gustav Fischer, 1927 iv:175pp.

1930   Swedish translation: *Kapitalism och Socialism.* Stockholm, 1930. Entry based on listing of Mises' books in *Nationalökonomie* (B-11).

1962   English translation: *The Free and Prosperous Commonwealth: An Exposition of the Ideas of Classical Liberalism.* Translated by Ralph Raico.

Edited by Arthur Goddard. With a Preface to the English-language Edition by Ludwig von Mises. Princeton: D. Van Nostrand, 1962. x:207pp. index.

1964   French translation of Chapter I (pp. 18-46, 52-59) and Chapter II (pp.60-104): "L'Économie Libérale: Ses Fondements, Ses Conditions" [The Liberal Economy: Its Foundations, Its Conditions] in *Les Essais: Cahiers Trimestriels, #20*. (Series: *Contributions à la Nouvelle Pensée Économique 1)*. Paris: L'Imprimerie du Delta, 1964-1965. pp. 47-157.

1977   Spanish translation: *Liberalismo*. Translated by Joaquin Reig Albiol from the English (1962). Madrid: Union Editorial, 1977 [©1975]. 240pp.

1978   Second English-language edition, reprint of 1962 version: *Liberalism: A Socio-Economic Exposition*. Translated by Ralph Raico. Edited by Arthur Goddard. Foreword by Louis M. Spadaro. ©Institute for Humane Studies. Kansas City [Mission, Kans.]: Sheed Andrews & McMeel [later under New York University Press imprint]. 1978 . xviii:207pp. index.

1982   Reprint of 1977 (©1975) Spanish translation by Joaquin Reig Albiol: *Liberalismo*. 2nd ed. Buenos Aires: Centro de Estudios sobre la Libertad, 1982. 247pp.

1985   Third English-language edition, reprint of 1978 version: *Liberalism: In the Classical Tradition*. Translated by Ralph Raico. Preface by Bettina Bien Greaves. Foreword by Louis M. Spadaro. Published jointly by Cobden Press (San Francisco) and the Foundation for Economic Education (Irvington-on-Hudson, N.Y.). xviii:206pp. index.

1987   Portuguese translation from the 1985 English edition: *Liberalismo: Segundo a Tradição Clássica*. Translated by Haydn Coutinho Pimenta. Rio de Janeiro: José Olympio/Instituto Liberal, 1987. xxii:200pp.

1989   Polish translation from the 1985 English-language edition: *Liberalizm w Klacycznej Tradycji: System Spoleczno-Ekonomiczny*. Translated by Jozef, Emil i Helena. Oswiaty Kageniec, 1989. 174pp.

1991   Unabridged audiotape version: *Liberalism*. Read by Nadia May. Ashland, Ore.: Classics on Tape, 1991. 6 cassettes.

IN PROCESS: Russian translation.

B-7   *Monetary Stabilization and Cyclical Policy*. An analysis of credit expansion and its consequences, with special reference to the doctrines of Irving Fisher.

1928   First edition: *Geldwertstabilisierung und Konjunkturpolitik*. Jena: Gustav Fischer, 1928. 84pp.

1935   Italian translation: *La Stabilizzazione del Potere d'acquisto della Moneta e la Politica della Congiuntura*. Translated from the German by Jenny Griziotti

Kretschmann.   In *Mercato Monetaria* (Nuova Collana di Economisti, Stranieri e Italiani, Vol. 8) Turin, 1935. pp.23-90.

1978   English translation by Bettina Bien Greaves: "Monetary Stabilization and Cyclical Policy" in *On the Manipulation of Money and Credit*, 1978 (B-24).

B-8   *A Critique of Interventionism.* A compilation of essays, some previously published, on economic issues under discussion in Europe in the 1920s. Mises' critiques of European interventionist programs of that day -- Marxism, price controls, nationalized banking, etc. -- are still pertinent.

1929   First edition: *Kritik des Interventionismus: Untersuchungen zur Wirtschaftspolitik und Wirtschaftsideologie der Gegenwart.* [Critique of Interventionism: Inquiries into Present Day Economic Policy and Ideology]. Jena: Gustav Fischer, 1929. iv:136pp. Includes "Interventionismus" [Interventionism] (26.5), "Gebundene Wirtschaft" [The Hampered Market Economy] (new), "Sozialliberalismus" [Social Liberalism] (26.4), "Antimarxismus" [Anti-Marxism] (25.4), and "Theorie der Preistaxen" [Theory of Price Controls] (23.5).

1976   Reprinted in German: *Kritik des Interventionismus: Untersuchungen zur Wirtschaftspolitik und Wirtschaftsideologie der Gegenwart* [Critique of Interventionism: Investigations into Present Day Economic Policy and Ideology]. With an Introduction to the new edition by F. A. Hayek. Darmstadt: Wissenschaftliche Buchgesellschaft, 1976. 146pp. Also included in this new edition is "Verstaatlichung des Kredits?" [The Nationalization of Credit?] (Article 29.3), inadvertently omitted from the 1929 German edition (see *Notes and Recollections*, B-23, pp. 113-114).

1977   English translation: *A Critique of Interventionism.* Translated by Hans F. Sennholz. New Rochelle, N.Y.: Arlington House. 164pp. Includes the five essays in the 1929 German edition plus "The Nationalization of Credit?" (Article 29.3), which Mises had intended to have included in the 1929 German edition.

1987?   Portuguese translation from the English: *Uma Crítica ao Intervencionismo.* Translated by Arlette Franco. Rio de Janeiro: Nordica: Instituto Liberal, n.d. 184pp.

B-9   *The Causes of the Economic Crisis.* A lecture before an assembly of German industrialists (Deutscher Hauptverband der Industrie) at Teplitz-Schönau, Czechoslovakia, February 28, 1931.   An explanation of the reasons why the "great depression" persisted.

1931   *Die Ursachen der Wirtschaftskrise: Ein Vortrag.* [The Causes of the Economic Crisis: A Lecture]. Tübingen: J. C. B. Mohr (Paul Siebeck), 1931.   34pp. Originally published in two installments in *Mitteilungen des Deutschen Hauptverbandes der Industrie.* (31.1).

1933   Dutch translation by A. J. Bergsma: *De Oorzaken van de Economische Crisis* (The Hague: Mouton & Co., 1933. 28pp.). Foreword by the translator.

1978   English translation by Bettina Bien Greaves: *The Causes of the Economic Crisis,* included (pp.175-203) in *On the Manipulation of Money and Credit,* 1978 (B-24).

1986   Spanish translation of English translation from B-24: "Las causas de la crisis económica." *Libertas.* 3:5 (October 1986) 213-239. Buenos Aires: La Escuela Superior de Económica y Administración de Empresas (ESEADE), 1986. Excerpt of Spanish translation in two parts. First installment not available. Continuation: *Negocios y Bancos.* 75 (June 15, 1989) 24-25.

B-10   *Epistemological Problems of Economics.* A compilation of essays, many reprinted from European economic journals, on subjective value theory, *a priori* theorems, the science of human action, the methodology of economics, and so on.

1933   First edition: *Grundprobleme der Nationalökonomie: Untersuchungen über Verfahren, Aufgaben und Inhalt der Wirtschafts- und Gesellschaftslehre.* Jena: Gustav Fischer, 1933. xiv: 216pp. index. Included are "Soziologie und Geschichte" (29.2), "Begreifen und Verstehen" (30.1), "Vom Weg der subjektivistischen Wertlehre" (31.2), "Bemerkungen zum Grundproblem der subjektivistischen Wertlehre" (28.2), "Die psychologische Wurzeln des Widerstandes gegen die nationalökonomische Theorie" (31.3), "Der Streit um die Wertlehre" (33.4), and "Das festangelegte Kapital" (31.4) – plus some new material.

1960   English translation: *Epistemological Problems of Economics.* Translated by George Reisman. With a Preface to the English-language Edition by Ludwig von Mises. Princeton: D. Van Nostrand Co., Inc., 1960. xxiii:239pp. index. Included are "Sociology and History" (29.2), "Conception and Understanding" (30.1), "Remarks on the Fundamental Problem of the Subjective Theory of Value" (28.2), "The Psychological Basis of the Opposition to Economic Theory" (31.3), "The Controversy Over the Theory of Value" (33.4), "Inconvertible Capital" (31.4), plus "The Task and Scope of the Science of Human Action" (written for inclusion in the 1933 anthology, B-10).

1981   Reprint of 1960 English translation: *Epistemological Problems of Economics.* With a new Foreword by Ludwig M. Lachmann (© Institute for Humane Studies, 1976). New York: New York University Press, 1981. xxxi:239pp.

1988   Italian translation of the 1981 English edition: *Problemi Epistemologici dell'economia.* Translated by Elda Guglielmetti. Edited by Lorenzo Infantino. Rome: Armando, 1988. 251pp. index. (Series: I classici dell'epistemologia).

B-11   *Nationalökonomie: Theorie des Handelns und Wirtschaftens* [Economics: Theory of Action and Exchange]. An overall praxeological treatment of economics. The German-language predecessor of *Human Action,* 1949 (B-16). No English translation available.

    1940   *Nationalökonomie: Theorie des Handelns und Wirtschaftens.* Geneva: Éditions Union, 1940. xvi:756pp. index. In December 1944, Mises wrote: "My objective in writing the treatise *Nationalökonomie: Theorie des Handelns und Wirtschaftens,* was to provide a comprehensive theory of economic behaviour which would include not only the economics of a market economy (free-enterprise system) but no less the economics of any other thinkable system of social cooperation, viz., socialism, interventionism, corporativism and so on. Furthermore I deemed it necessary to deal with all those objections which from various points of view -- for instance: of ethics, psychology, history, anthropology, ethnography, biology -- have been raised against the soundness of economic reasoning and the validity of the methods hitherto applied by the economists of all schools and lines of thought. Only such an exhaustive treatment of all critical objections can satisfy the exacting reader and convince him that economics is a science both conveying knowledge and able to guide conduct." (As quoted in Margit von Mises, *My Years with Ludwig von Mises,* 1976 edition, p.105; 2nd 1984 edition, pp. 101-102).

    1980   Reprint of the 1940 edition: *Nationalökonomie: Theorie des Handelns und Wirtschaftens.* Munich: Philosophia Verlag, 1980. xvi:756pp. index. (The International Carl Menger Library Series). This book, originally published in Geneva, Switzerland, in 1940, when much of Europe was under the sway of anti-capitalistic Nazism, was practically unknown at that time in the German-speaking world. Now once again, it is available in German.

B-12   *Omnipotent Government: The Rise of the Total State and Total War.* A history and analysis of the events and conflicts in Europe that led to both world wars. As indicated by the book's subtitle, Mises illustrates how, unless ideas change, pro-interventionist ideas transform a "liberal" society -- "liberal" in the classical sense -- into a totalitarian one. He uses the Nazi (National Socialist) regime of Hitler's Germany and the rise of economic nationalism to illustrate this thesis.

    1944   First edition: *Omnipotent Government: The Rise of the Total State and Total War.* New Haven: Yale University Press, 1944. ix:291pp. index.

    1946   Spanish translation: *Omnipotencia Gubernamental.* Translated by Pedro Elgoibar. Mexico: Editorial Hermes, n.d. 452pp.

    1947   French translation: *Le Gouvernement Omnipotent de l'État Totalitaire à la Guerre Total.* Translated by M. de Hulster. Paris: Librairie de Médicis, 1947. 408pp.

    1969   Reprint of the 1944 edition: *Omnipotent Government: The Rise of the Total State and Total War.* New Rochelle, N.Y.: Arlington House, 1969. ix:291pp. index.

1978   German version: See *Im Namen des Staates, oder Die Gefahren des Kollektivismus* (B-25)

1985   Reprint of 1944 edition: *Omnipotent Government: The Rise of the Total State and Total War.* Spring Mills, Penna.: Libertarian Press, 1985. xii:291pp. index.

B-13   *Bureaucracy.*   An explanation in fairly simple language of the basic difference between bureaucratic management and profit-and-loss management. Bureaucracy has a legitimate role to play in governmental affairs. However, there are significant and important distinctions between *bureaucratic* management, which is appropriate in government, and *profit-and-loss* management, which is essential for the successful operation of business.

1944   *Bureaucracy.* New Haven: Yale University Press, 1944. viii:125pp.

1945   British edition: *Bureaucracy.* London: W. Hodge, 1945. 148pp.

1946   French translation: *La Bureaucratie*. Translated by R. Florin & P. Barbier. Paris: Librairie de Médicis, 1946. 136pp.

1951   Spanish translation: *La Burocracia*. Caracas: Universidad Central de Caracas, Instituto de Economía, 1951.

1962   Paperback reprint of 1944 edition, with a new preface: *Bureaucracy.* New Haven: Yale University Press, 1962. viii:125pp.

1969   Spanish translation by Dalmacio Negro Pavón.

1969   Reprint of 1944 edition, including both 1944 and 1962 prefaces, plus an index: *Bureaucracy.* New Rochelle, N. Y.: Arlington House, 1969. 128pp. index.

1974   Reprint of 1969 Dalmacio Negro Pavón's Spanish translation: *Burocracia.* Madrid: Unión Editorial; Guatemala: Editorial Universidad Francisco Marroquín, 1974. 165pp.

1983   Reprint of 1969 edition: *Bureaucracy.* Cedar Falls, Iowa: Center for Futures Education;   distributed by Libertarian Press, Spring Mills, Penna., 1983. xii:128pp.

1988   Greek translation by Sotirios Papasotiriou. Published for E.K.O.M.E. (Society for Social and Economic Studies) by Euroekdotiki, 1988. 144 pp.

1989   Unabridged audiotape version: *Bureaucracy.* Read by Robert Morris. Ashland, Oregon: Classics on Tape, [1989]. 4 cassettes.

IN PROCESS: Italian translation.
                    Russian translation.

B-14   *Planned Chaos*. Forceful critique of the leading -isms -- Interventionism, Socialism, Communism, Nazism, and Fascism. Written for inclusion in the Spanish-language 1961 edition of *Socialism* (B-4); incorporated as the Epilogue in the English-language (1951 and later) editions of *Socialism*.

      1947   *Planned Chaos*. Foreword by Leonard E. Read. Irvington-on-Hudson, N. Y.: Foundation for Economic Education, 1947. 90pp. Many printings.

      1956   French translation: *Le Chaos du Planisme*. Translated by J.-P. Hamilius. Paris: Éditions Génin, Librairie de Médicis, 1956. 136pp.

     IN PROCESS: Dutch translation.

B-15   *Observations on the Cooperative Movement*. Part I of *Cooperatives in the Petroleum Industry*, a report prepared for the Empire State Petroleum Association and the Illinois Petroleum Marketers Association. "Favoritism harms those favored no less than those at whose expense the favors are granted." Cooperatives, being the beneficiaries of special privileges, have not had to think first of consumers. "Business is not an end in itself. It exists and operates for the benefit of the public . . . . The cooperative type of business organization can justify its existence only by renouncing the privileges which it enjoys today. Only as far as the cooperatives are able to hold their own without the support of tax exemptions, cheap government credit and other favors can cooperativism be considered as a legitimate method of doing business in a free society."

      1947   *Observations on the Cooperative Movement*. New York: Petroleum Industry Research Foundation, 1947. 61pp.

      1990   Reprinted in *Money, Method, and the Market Process* (B-28).

B-16   *Human Action: A Treatise on Economics*. A comprehensive and systematic treatise on economics, social philosophy, and the social sciences, Mises' major economic treatise, his *magnum opus*. A survey of the science of human action, its epistemology (methodology), its theories derived by reasoning logically from *a priori* axioms, and their application to specific economic phenomena.

      1949   *Human Action: A Treatise on Economics*. New Haven: Yale University Press, 1949. xv:889pp. index.

      1949   British edition: *Human Action: A Treatise on Economics*. London: W. Hodge & Co., 1949. 889pp. index.

      1954   Index, *Human Action* (1949) by Vern [Vernelia] Crawford. Irvington-on-Hudson, N.Y.: Foundation for Economic Education, [1954]. [20pp.]

      1959   Italian translation: *L'Azione Umana: Trattato di Economia*. Translated and edited by Tullio Bagiotti. Turin: Unione Tipografico, Editrice Torinese, 1959. xix:861pp. index.

1960   Spanish translation: *La Acción Humana: Tratado de Economía.* Translated by Joaquín Reig Albiol. Valencia: Fundación Ignacio Villalonga, 1960. 2 vols., 601pp. & 673pp. index.

1963   Second edition, revised and enlarged: *Human Action: A Treatise on Economics.* New revised edition. New Haven: Yale University Press, 1963. xix:907pp. Index prepared by Vernelia A. Crawford. Notable revisions include Chapter 15:6 on freedom and government, 16:6 on monopoly, and 27:6 on corruption. NOTE: Unfortunately, this second edition contains serious typographical errors; an "Errata" sheet was issued, noting the more flagrant typos. See Henry Hazlitt's "Mangling a Masterpiece," *National Review.* 16:18 (May 5, 1964), 366-367, and Chapter 8 in Margit von Mises, *My Years with Ludwig von Mises* (New Rochelle, N.Y.: Arlington House, 1976; 2nd enlarged ed., Cedar Falls, Iowa: Center for Futures Education, 1976).

1966   Third edition: *Human Action: A Treatise on Economics.* 3rd revised edition. Chicago: Henry Regnery, 1966. xvii: 907pp. index. A new and corrected printing of the 2nd edition, incorporating Mises' 1963 revisions.

1968   Second Spanish-language edition, incorporating Mises' second and third edition changes and additions: *La Acción Humana: Tratado de Economía.* Translation by Joaquín Reig Albiol. Madrid: Editorial Sopec, 1968. 1070pp.

1976/7   Chinese translation by Tao-Ping Hsia. 2 vols. 15:489pp; 491-903pp.

1978   Reprint of third revised edition (1966): *Human Action: A Treatise on Economics.* 3rd revised edition. Chicago: Contemporary Books, [1978]. xvii:907pp. index.

1980   Third Spanish language edition; translation made from 3rd (1966) English language edition: *La Acción Humana: Tratado de Economía.* Madrid: Unión Editorial, 1980. 1302pp. Index based on Crawford's 1954 index; translator's notes of certain terms based on Percy L. Greaves, Jr's. *Glossary to Human Action: Mises Made Easier* (Dobbs Ferry, N.Y.: Free Market Books, 1976; 2nd ed., Irvington, N.Y.: Free Market Books, 1990).

1985   French translation of the third revised edition: *L'Action Humaine: Traité d'Économie.* Translated by Raoul Audouin. Paris: Presses Universitaires de France, 1985. xi:942pp. index.

1985   Contemporary Books reprint (3rd revised ed.): *Human Action.* With a new preface by Margit von Mises. Issued in a special limited leatherbound edition (200 copies) by Laissez Faire Books (New York).

1986   Fourth Spanish edition, paperback. Reprint of third (1980) edition: Madrid: Union Editorial, 1986. 1302pp.

1990   Contemporary Books paperback reprint (3rd revised ed.): (San Francisco & New York: Laissez Faire Books). 907pp. index.

1990   Portuguese translation of 3rd revised ed.: *Ação Humana: um Tratado de Economia*. Translated by Donald Stewart, Jr. Rio de Janeiro: Il Instituto Liberal, 1990. [xvi]: 872+4pp. index of names.

1990   Unabridged audiotape version: *Human Action*. Read by Bernard Mayes. (Ashland, Ore.: Classics on Tape, 1990). 30 cassettes.

1991   Chinese translation by Tao-Ping Hsia (1976/7) revised by Hui-Lin Wu. Taipei, Taiwan: Yuan Liu Publishing Co., 1991. (Nos. 1 & 2 in series of famous books on liberalism). 2 vols., 1-506; 507-1074pp.

1991   Japanese translation: *Ningen-Kōi-Gaku*. Translated by Toshio Murata. Tokyo: Shunjü Sha, Inc., 1991. 995pp. index.

B-17   *Profit and Loss.* Paper presented at the Mont Pèlerin meeting, Beauvallon, France, September 1951. "[P]rofit and loss are generated by success or failure in adjusting the course of production activities to the most urgent demand of the consumers." Profits emerge from the difference between the values of factors of production and the value of these factors when they are converted into finished consumers goods; profits disappear as soon as this maladjustment disappears.

1951   *Profit and Loss.* South Holland, Ill.: Consumers-Producers Economic Service, 1951. 53pp.

1952   Included in *Planning for Freedom* (B-18).

B-18   *Planning for Freedom, and Other Essays and Addresses*. A collection of articles and addresses (1945-1958), each a brief and fairly easy to understand explanation of some aspect of economics or government intervention. This compilation includes "Planning for Freedom" (45.2), "Middle-of-the-road Policy Leads to Socialism" (50.4), "Laissez Faire or Dictatorship" (49.1), "Stones into Bread, the Keynesian Miracle" (48.2), "Lord Keynes and Say's Law" (50.7), "Inflation and Price Control" (45.4), "Economic Aspects of the Pension Problem" (50.3), "Benjamin M. Anderson Challenges the Philosophy of the Pseudo-Progressives" (50.2), "Profit and Loss" (B-17), "Economic Teaching at the Universities" (52.3), "Trends Can Change" (51.2), and "The Political Chances of Genuine Liberalism" (51.3). The 1951 essay, "Profit and Loss," makes a real contribution to economic theory.

1952   First edition: *Planning for Freedom, and Other Essays and Addresses*. South Holland, Ill.: Libertarian Press, 1952. 174pp.

1962   Second edition: *Planning for Freedom, and Other Essays and Addresses*, enlarged. South Holland, Ill.: Libertarian Press, 1962. 184pp. Includes all essays in the 1952 first edition as listed above, plus "Wages, Unemployment and Inflation" (58.2).

1974   Third (memorial) edition: *Planning for Freedom, and Twelve Other Essays and Addresses*. Memorial Edition (3rd). South Holland, Ill.: Libertarian Press, 1974. xii:194pp. Essays in the 1962 plus various addenda : "An honor for a philosopher," *Wall Street Journal* editorial (June 17, 1963), Henry Hazlitt's "Salute to von Mises: For 92 Years He Has Fought the Good Fight" (*Barron's*, October 1, 1973), Gottfried Haberler's "Mises' Private Seminar" and Albert Hunold's "How Mises Changed My Mind," both from *The Mont Pèlerin Quarterly*, October 1961, and "Ludwig von Mises, Distinguished Fellow, 1969" (American Economic Association citation).

1980   Fourth edition: *Planning for Freedom and Sixteen Other Essays and Addresses*. South Holland, Ill.: Libertarian Press, 1980. xii:280pp. In addition to the essays and various addenda in the 1974 edition, includes four more Mises essays -- "My Contributions to Economic Theory" (40.2), "The Gold Problem" (65.3), "Capital Supply and American Prosperity" (52.4), "Liberty and Its Antithesis" (60.2) -- and "The Essential von Mises" by Murray N. Rothbard (1973).

1986   Spanish translation: *Planificación para la Libertad y Otros Dieciséis Ensayos y Conferencias*. Translated and edited by Alberto Benegas Lynch from the 4th (1980) English edition, with addenda. Buenos Aires: Centro de Estudios Sobre la Libertad, 1986. 350pp.

B-19   *The Anti-Capitalistic Mentality.* Mises' theory as to why capitalism is so widely misunderstood nowadays and, hence, feared and rejected. He argues that disgruntled intellectuals who fail to attain their ambitions envy successful entrepreneurs and blame capitalism for their frustrations. Economic theory is interwoven with Mises' interpretation and value judgment based on his understanding.

1956   *The Anti-Capitalistic Mentality*. Princeton: D. Van Nostrand Co., 1956. vi:114pp. index.

1956   British edition. *The Anti-Capitalistic Mentality*. London: Macmillan, 1956. 120pp.

1957   Swedish translation: *Den antikapitalistika mentaliteten*. Translated by Lennart Thureson. Stockholm: Natur och Kultur, 1957. 117pp.

1957   Spanish translation: *La Mentalidad Anticapitalista*. Translated by J. Reig. Valencia: Fundación Ignacio Villalonga: Biblioteca de Estudios Económicos, 1957. 166pp. index. "Estudio preliminar" [Introductory Discussion] (pp. 15-59) by J. Reig.

1958   German translation: *Die Wurzeln des Anti-Kapitalismus* [The Roots of Anti-capitalism]. Translated by Stephen Frowen. Frankfurt am Main: Fritz Knapp, 1958. 125pp.

1961 (?)   Argentine reprint of 1957 Spanish translation: *La Mentalidad Anticapitalista*. Buenos Aires: Fundación Bolsa de Comercio, n.d..

1966   Reprinted in full (pp. 323-383) in *Omnibus Volume 6*. New Rochelle, N.Y.: Conservative Book Club, n.d.

1972   Reprint of 1956 edition: *The Anti-Capitalistic Mentality*. South Holland, Ill.: Libertarian Press, 1972. 134pp. index. Also included in this edition: "The Major Writings of Ludwig von Mises," "Major Writings of Mises' Predecessors in the 'Austrian Neo-Classical School'," "Ludwig von Mises" by Bettina Bien Greaves (*Human Events,* September 25, 1971), and "Publisher's Remarks on Significance of Writings of Ludwig von Mises."

1979   Second edition of 1958 German translation: *Die Wurzeln des Anti-Kapitalismus.* New foreword by Peter Muthesius. Frankfurt am Main: Fritz Knapp, 1979. 125pp.

1988   Portuguese translation: *A Mentalidade Anticapitalista.* Translated by Carlos dos Santos Abreu. Rio de Janeiro: José Olympio: Instituto Liberal, 1988. ix:113pp.

1988   Italian translation: *La Mentalità Anticapitalistica.* Translated by Elda Guglielmetti. Edited by Lorenzo Infantino. Rome: Armando, 1988. 102pp. index.

1990   *The Anti-Capitalistic Mentality.* Spring Mills, Penna.: Libertarian Press, 1990. vi:114pp. index. Contains Mises' text only; omits addenda to 1972 edition.

1991   Polish translation: *Mentalnosc Antykapitalistyczna.* Translated by Jan M. Malek. Warsaw: Wydawnictwa Niepodleglosc, 1991. 108pp.

IN PROCESS: Russian translation.

B-20   *Theory and History: An Interpretation of Social and Economic Evolution.* A critique of ideas of Karl Marx, his philosophy of history and his dialectical materialism. An examination of the methodological differences between economics (praxeology), based on reason and logic, and history, based on "understanding."

1957   *Theory and History: An Interpretation of Social and Economic Evolution.* New Haven: Yale University Press, 1957. ix:384pp. index.

1964   Spanish translation: *Teoría e Historia.* Translated by Jorge Gómez de Silva. Mexico: Ediciones Colofón, 1964. viii:396pp.

1969   Reprint of 1957 edition: *Theory and History: An Interpretation of Social and Economic Evolution.* New Rochelle, N.Y.: Arlington House, 1969. ix:384pp. index.

1971   Chinese translation by K. C. Kan. Taipei, Taiwan: Lion Book Co., 1971.

1975   Spanish translation: *Teoría e historia.* Translated by Rigoberto Juárez-Paz. Madrid: Unión Editorial. 330pp.

1984 Reprint of 1957 edition: *Theory and History: An Interpretation of Social and Economic Evolution.* New York and London: Garland Publishing, 1984. 384pp. index. (Series: History and Historiography, edited by Robin Winks).

1985 Reprint of 1957 Yale edition: *Theory and History: An Interpretation of Social and Economic Evolution.* With a new Preface by Murray N. Rothbard. Auburn, Ala.: Ludwig von Mises Institute, 1985. [xvi]:384pp. index.

B-21 *The Historical Setting of the Austrian School of Economics.* A brief review of the development of Austrian economic theory.

1962 First published in Spanish translation: *El Establecimiento Histórico de la Escuela Austriaca de Economía.* (Colección Investigaciones No. 43) Universidad Nacional de la Plata (Argentina), Facultad de Ciencias Económicas, 1962. pp. 691-727.

1969 *The Historical Setting of the Austrian School of Economics.* New Rochelle, N.Y.: Arlington House, 1969. 45pp.

1984 Reprint of 1969 version: *The Historical Setting of the Austrian School of Economics.* Auburn, Ala.: Ludwig von Mises Institute, 1984. 45pp.

1989 Published in Spanish by Centro de Estudios en Economía y Educación (Mexico) as part of an introductory economics book.

1992 Italian translation by Lorenzo Infantino. *La Collocazione Storica della Scuola Austriaca di Economia.* Rome: Libera Università Internazionale degli Studi Sociali. 44pp.

B-22 *The Ultimate Foundation of Economic Science: An Essay on Method.* Mises' last book, written and published when he was over 80 years old. Mises explains the basic (*a priori*) suppositions from which economic theories are developed logically, step by step. Some fundamental observations on the nature of human action and praxeology. An epistemological study of economics and critique of positivism.

1962 *The Ultimate Foundation of Economic Science: An Essay on Method.* Princeton: D. Van Nostrand, 1962. xi:148pp. index.

1969 Japanese translation: *Keizai Kagaku no Kontei.* Translated by Toshio Murata. Serialized in *Keizai Rondan* (Tokyo: Keizai Rondan Sha) August 1968 to August 1969.

1969 Chinese translation by D. P. Hsia. Taiwan: Taiwan Bank, Economic Research Department, 1969. 129pp.

1978 *The Ultimate Foundation of Economic Science: An Essay on Method.* With a new Foreword by Israel M. Kirzner. (©Institute for Humane Studies). Kansas City [Mission, Kans.]: Sheed Andrews & McMeel, 1978. xvii:148pp. index.

IN PROCESS: Spanish translation.

Posthumous Compilations and Publications
of Previously Unpublished Works

B-23   *Notes and Recollections*. Mises' reminiscences and reflections describing his life and activities in Vienna. An intellectual autobiography written by Mises in German shortly after his arrival in the United States in 1940. After Mises' death, his widow discovered the manuscript among his papers and had it translated. Mises describes his economic and political ideas and his role as a political activist in Austria in the years before the Nazi takeover in 1938.

       1978 *Notes and Recollections*. Foreword by Margit von Mises. Translation by Hans F. Sennholz of 1940 German-language manuscript. Postscript (September 12, 1976) by Sennholz. South Holland, Ill.: Libertarian Press, 1978. 181pp. index.

       1978 German version: *Erinnerungen* [Reminiscences]. With a Foreword by Margit v. Mises and an Introduction by Friedrich August von Hayek. Stuttgart: Gustav Fischer, 1978. xvi:112pp. index. Includes bibliography of Mises' works.

B-24   *On the Manipulation of Money and Credit*. An elaboration of Mises' theories of money, inflation, credit expansion, index numbers, the balance of payments doctrine, and the trade cycle. Includes "Stabilization of the Monetary Unit -- From the Viewpoint of Theory," 1923 (B-5), "Monetary Stabilization and Cyclical Policy," 1928 (B-7), and "The Causes of the Economic Crisis" 1931 (B-9). Also included is a translation of "Der Stand und die nächste Zukunft der Konjunkturforschung," [The Current Status of Business Cycle Research and Its Prospects for the Immediate Future] (33.3), and "The Trade Cycle and Credit Expansion" (46.2).

       1978 *On the Manipulation of Money and Credit*. Translated from the German by Bettina Bien Greaves. Edited by Percy L. Greaves, Jr. Dobbs Ferry, N.Y.: Free Market Books, 1978. liv:296pp. indexes. Includes Translator's Preface, Editor's Introduction, and several articles by the editor.

B-25   *Im Namen des Staates: oder Die Gefahren des Kollektivismus* [In the Name of the State: or the Dangers of Collectivism]. Written in Geneva in 1938/39. German language version of several chapters (I-IV, VI, VII, IX, and XII) of *Omnipotent Government*, 1944 (B-12) plus an additional chapter VII. In his 1978 foreword, Alfred Müller-Armack writes: "The book, completed in the spring of 1939 and supplemented in the fall by another chapter, was not published at that time. In 1940, Mises migrated to the United States. The basic ideas it contained were included in his first successful English-language book, *Omnipotent Government*. One can only surmise why the author did not publish it later. Possibly the favorable impression he received of the German Republic in the course of his several visits there after 1945 persuaded him not to publish a book noticeably pervaded by traces of anti-Germanism, an attitude which was understandable due to the state of affairs when he wrote." (Translated from the German)

1978　*Im Namen des Staates: oder Die Gefahren des Kollektivismus* [In the Name of the State: or the Dangers of Collectivism] Stuttgart: Bonn Aktuell, 1978. 262 pp. index.

B-26　*The Clash of Group Interests and Other Essays.* A pamphlet consisting of several Mises articles not previously available in English. In addition to the title essay (45.3), this monograph includes "The Myth of the Failure of Capitalism" (32.2) translated from the German by Jane E. Sanders, "The Freedom to Move as an International Problem" (35.6) translated from the German by Bettina Bien Greaves, and "Karl Menger and the Austrian School of Economics" (29.1) translated from the German by Albert Zlabinger.

　　1978　*The Clash of Group Interests and Other Essays.* Occasional Paper Series #7. Richard M. Ebeling, ed. Preface by Murray N. Rothbard. New York: The Center for Libertarian Studies, June 1978. 28pp.

B-27　*Economic Policy: Thoughts for Today and Tomorrow.* Six lectures delivered in June 1959 at the University of Buenos Aires. A series of lectures presented in Argentina, transcribed from tapes, were edited by Margit von Mises and George Koether. Fairly simple presentations on capitalism, socialism, interventionism, inflation, foreign investment, and policies and ideas.

　　1979　*Economic Policy: Thoughts for Today and Tomorrow.* Foreword by Margit von Mises. South Bend, Ind.: Regnery/Gateway, 1979. ix:106pp. Several printings.

　1979/1980　*Economic Policy: Thoughts for Today and Tomorrow.* Serialized chapter by chapter, in *The Freeman*, December 1979 to May 1980.

　　1980　Japanese translation: *Decision for Freedom*. Translated by Toshio Murata. Tokyo: Kobunsha, n.d. [1980 ?]. 170pp.

　　1981　Serialization scheduled in the *Independent* (Western Australia) to start Sunday, July 5, 1981.

　　1981　Spanish translation: *Seis Lecciones Sobre el Capitalismo*. Translated by Joaquín Reig Albiol. Madrid: Instituto de Economía de Mercado/Unión Editorial, 1981. 107pp.

　　1983　French translation: *Politique Économique: Réflexions pour Aujourd'hui et pour Demain.* Translated by Raoul Audouin. Paris: Institut Économique de Paris, 1983. xv:111pp.

　　1983　German translation: *Vom Wert der Besseren Ideen: Sechs Vorlesungen über Wirtschaft und Politik* [Concerning the Value of Better Ideas: Six Addresses on Economy and Policy]. Translated by Hertha Bosch. Edited by Margit von Mises. Stuttgart: Poller/Bonn Aktuell, 1983. 117pp. index.

1984   Greek translation by Yannis Loverdos. Published through the initiative
        of A. Andrianopoulos by Euroekdotiki, 1984. 146pp.

1985   Portuguese translation: *As Seis Lições*. Translated by Maria Luiza X.
        de A. Borges. Rio De Janeiro: José Olympio: Instituto Liberal, 1985.
        xi:98pp.

1988   Polish translation: *Ekonomia I Polityka: Rozwazania na Dzis i Jutro*.
        Translated by Jósef Emil. Publisher unknown, 1988. 74pp.

IN PROCESS: Icelandic translation.
            Lithuanian translation.

B-28   *Money, Method, and the Market Process.* A collection of essays, some previously
        unpublished, on a wide range of topics -- methodology, socialism, inflation, trade,
        cooperatives, and so on. Reprinted in this collection is "Observations on the
        Cooperative Movement" (B-15). Also 20 additional essays including "The
        Disintegration of the International Division of Labor" (38.5), "Epistemological
        Relativism in the Sciences of Human Action (61.8), "On Equality and Inequality" (61.2),
        "Capitalism versus Socialism" (69.1), "A Hundred Years of Marxian Socialism" (1967,
        previously unpublished) and "The Role of Doctrines in Human History" (undated and
        previously unpublished).

   1990   *Money, Method, and the Market Process: Essays by Ludwig von Mises.*
           Selected by Margit von Mises. Edited with an introduction by Richard M.
           Ebeling. Auburn, Ala.: Praxeology Press of the Ludwig von Mises Institute;
           Norwell, Mass.: Kluwer Academic Publishers, 1990. xxiv:325pp. index.

B-29   *Economic Freedom and Interventionism: An Anthology of Articles and Essays.* A
        collection of 47 articles by Mises not previously collected in book form, written and
        published after he came to the United States in 1940. They deal in relatively simple
        terms with private property, savings, investment, profit-and-loss, government,
        intervention and inflation. Among them are "The Economic Foundations of Freedom"
        (60.1), "The Elite under Capitalism" (61.11), "Inequality of Wealth and Incomes"
        (55.2), "The Agony of the Welfare State" (53.2), "The Plight of Business Forecasting"
        (56.2), "On the International Monetary Problem" (67.1), "Small and Big Business"
        (61.7), "Economics as a Bridge to Interhuman Understanding" (47.3), and "Economic
        Freedom in the Present-Day World" (58.1).

   1990   *Economic Freedom and Interventionism: An Anthology of Articles and Essays.*
           Selected and edited by Bettina Bien Greaves. Irvington-on-Hudson, N.Y.:
           Foundation for Economic Education, 1990. xiii:250pp. index.

(Arranged chronologically by date of first appearance)

Some of these articles have been reprinted many times in many different periodicals and/or translated into several different languages. To track down and list every such reprint would be practically impossible. However, we have listed all we have been able to locate. Anthologies of Mises' works in which an article or essay is included are indicated by Book Number, i.e., B-8, *A Critique of Interventionism,* B-18, *Planning for Freedom,* etc. See *Books* section for details. English translations of foreign language titles appear in square brackets. The numbers at the left indicate the year of publication and entry number. For example, Article 24.3 is the third Mises article listed for 1924. Significant events in Mises' life are inserted in bold typeface.

Mises wrote quite a few newspaper articles in the 1920s and 1930s. If no city is indicated, it may be assumed they were published in Vienna.

1904

04.1   "Zur Frage der Altersversorgung der Arbeiter" [Concerning Workers' Old Age Pensions]. *Zeitschrift für Volkswirtschaft, Sozialpolitik und Verwaltung.* 13 (1904) 463-465.

1905

05.1   "Zur Geschichte der österreichischen Fabriksgesetzgebung" [On the History of Austrian Factory Legislation]. *Zeitschrift für Volkswirtschaft, Sozialpolitik und Verwaltung.* 14 (1905) 209-271. Describes Austrian legislation on the limitation of child labor in industry. According to Mises, it was published against the advice of his Professor Grünberg. See *Notes and Recollections* (B-23) p. 6.

1906   Awarded the Doctor of both Canon and Roman Laws

1907

07.1   "Die wirtschaftspolitischen Motive der österreichischen Valuta-regulierung" [The Economics of Austrian Foreign Exchange Controls]. *Zeitschrift für Volkswirtschaft, Sozialpolitik und Verwaltung.* 16 (1907) 561-582.

1908

08.1   "Neuere Schriften über Geld- und Bankwesen" [Recent Writings on Money and Banking]. *Zeitschrift für Volkswirtschaft, Sozialpolitik und Verwaltung.* 17 (1908) 660-674.

1909   Becomes Economic Adviser, Austrian Chamber of Commerce

09.1   "Das Problem gesetzlicher Aufnahme der Barzahlungen in Österreich-Ungarn" [The Problem of the Legal Resumption of Gold Payments in Austria-Hungary]. *Jahrbuch für Gesetzgebung, Verwaltung und Volkswirtschaft (Schmollers Jahrbuch).* 33:3 (1909) 985-1037.

09.2   "The Foreign Exchange Policy of the Austro-Hungarian Bank." *The Economic Journal.* 19 (June 1909) 201-211.

1910

10.1   "La Réforme financière en Autriche" [Financial Reform in Austria]. *Revue Économique Internationale.* 7:4 (October 1910) 39-59.

10.2   "Zum Problem gesetzlicher Aufnahme der Barzahlungen in Oesterreich-Ungarn: Ein Schlusswort gegenüber Walther Federn" [Concerning the Problem of the Legal Resumption of Gold Payments in Austria-Hungary: A Reply to Walther Federn]. *Jahrbuch für Gesetzgebung, Verwaltung und Volkswirtschaft* (Schmollers Jahrbuch). 34:3-4 (1910) 1877-1884. Federn wrote two articles in 1909 criticizing Mises' Article 09.1 (listed above); see "Books and Articles About Mises: 1909" for details.

10.3   "Neue Literatur über Geld- und Bankwesen" [New Literature on Money and Banking]. *Zeitschrift für Volkswirtschaft, Sozialpolitik und Verwaltung.* 19 (1910) 385-395.

1912

12.1   "Die Reform der österreichischen Versicherungsgebühren" [Reform of Austrian "Social Security" Taxes]. *Österreichische Zeitschrift für öffentliche und private Versicherung.* 3 (1912) 265-274.

12.2   "Das vierte Privilegium der Österreichisch-Ungarischen Bank" [The Fourth Privilege of the Austro-Hungarian Bank]. *Zeitschrift für Volkswirtschaft, Sozialpolitik und Verwaltung.* 21 (1912) 611-624.

12.3   "Neue Literatur über Geld- und Bankwesen" [New Literature on Money and Banking]. *Zeitschrift für Volkswirtschaft, Sozialpolitik und Verwaltung.* 21 (1912) 669-676.

12.4   "Entgegnung" [Rejoinder]. *Zeitschrift für Volkswirtschaft, Sozialpolitik und Verwaltung.* 21(1912) 753-756. A reply to W. Federn's criticism (unavailable) of Mises' Article 12.2 listed above. Mises writes that he "considers it fruitless to continue any longer the polemic with Federn."

12.5   Three short book reviews: *Archiv für Sozialwissenschaft und Sozialpolitik.* 35:1 (July 1912) 241-242, 251-252, and 252-253, respectively:
         Andreas Walther's *Geldwert in der Geschichte: Ein methodologischer Versuch* [Monetary Value in History: A Methodological Attempt] (1912);

Otto Heyn's *Erfordernisse des Geldes: Ein Beitrag zur Geldtheorie* [The
Prerequisites of Money: A Contribution to Monetary Theory] (1912);
Paul Stiassny's *Der österreichische Staatsbankerott von 1811* [The 1811
Bankruptcy of the Austrian Government] (1912).

1913   Appointed Privatdozent, University of Vienna

13.1   "Die allgemeine Teuerung im Lichte der theoretischen Nationalökonomie" [The General
Rise in the Cost of Living, from the Viewpoint of Economic Theory]. *Archiv für
Sozialwissenschaft und Sozialpolitik.* 37 (1913) 557-577.

1914 - 1918   World War I. Called to Active Service.

14.1   "Die Störungen im Wirtschaftsleben der österreichisch-ungarischen Monarchie während der
Jahre 1912/1913" [Economic Disturbances in the Austro-Hungarian Monarchy, 1912-
1913]. *Archiv für Sozialwissenschaft und Sozialpolitik.* 39 (1914/1915) 174-186.

1916

16.1   "Vom Ziel der Handelspolitik" [The Goal of Trade Policy]. *Archiv für Sozialwissenschaft
und Sozialpolitik.* 42:2 (December 1916) 561-585.

1918   Returns to the University of Vienna. Invested with the title "Professor Extraordinary." Resumes position at the Austrian Chamber of Commerce. Becomes Director, League of Nations' Austrian Reparations Commission.

18.1   "Zur Klassifikation der Geldtheorie" [Concerning the Classification of Monetary Theory].
Archiv für Sozialwissenschaft und Sozialpolitik. 44 (1917/1918) 198-213. Incorporated,
with minor deletions and additions in the second edition (1924) of the German-language
Theory of Money and Credit (B-2) and as "Appendix A" of the English translations.

18.2   "Die Quantitätstheorie" [The Quantity Theory]. *Mitteilungen des Verbandes
österreichischer Banken und Bankiers.* 1:3/4 (1918) 37-40.

18.3   "Zur Währungsfrage" [The Question of the Monetary Standard]. *Mitteilungen des
Verbandes österreichischer Banken und Bankiers.* 1:5/6 (1918) 1-6. Includes comments by
others on Mises' "Die Quantitätstheorie" (18.2 above), as well as Mises' response (pp.2-4)
to their comments.

18.4   "Über Kriegskostendeckung und Kriegsanleihen" [On Covering the Costs of War and of War
Loans]. No.2 (Vienna: Phoebus, 1918) 3-14. A lecture transcribed from notes, not edited
by Mises.

1919

19.1 Reviews of three books in *Archiv für die Geschichte des Sozialismus und der Arbeiterbewegung.* 1:1 (undated) 89-99:
    Gustav Cassell's *Theoretische Sozialökonomie* [Theoretical Social Economics] (1918);
    Karl Diehl's *Theoretische Nationalökonomie* [Theoretical National Economics] (1916);
    W. Gelesnoff's *Grundzüge der Volkswirtschaftslehre* [Principles of Economic Theory] (1918).

19.2 "Der Wiedereintritt Deutsch-Österreichs in das Deutsche Reich und die Währungsfrage" [The Re-entry of German-Austria into the German Reich (Empire) and the Currency Question]. *Wirtschaftliche Verhältnisse in Deutsch-Österreichs: Schriften des Vereins für Sozialpolitik.* 158 (1919) 147-171.

19.3 "Zahlungsbilanz und Devisenkurse" [Balance of Payments and Foreign Exchange Rates]. *Mitteilungen des Verbandes österreichischer Banken und Bankiers.* 2:3/4 (1919) 39-46. English translation of about one-third of this article included in *On the Manipulation of Money and Credit* (B-24) 50-54.

19.4 "Einstellung der Notenvermehrung oder Devisenverordnungen: Bemerkungen zum vorstehenden Artikel des Finanzrates Dr. Franz Bartsch" [Suspension of Note Expansion or Foreign Exchange Regulations: Remarks on the Foregoing Article by Treasury Officer Dr. Franz Bartsch]. *Mitteilungen des Verbandes österreichischer Banken und Bankiers.* 2:5/6 (April 22, 1919) 1-2.

19.5 "Geldentwertung und Staatshaushalt" [Monetary Devaluation and the Government's Budget]. *Neues Wiener Tagblatt.* 273 (October 5, 1919) 15-16.

19.6 "Richard Lieben als Nationalökonom" [Richard Lieben as Economist]. *Neue Freie Presse.* #19835 (November 14, 1919) 3.

19.7 "Stadt und Land in der direkten Besteuerung" [Direct Taxation in City and Province]. *Neues Wiener Tagblatt.* In two parts: 324 (November 27, 1919) 8; 326 November 29, 1919) 8.

19.8 "Die Wiedereinführung des börsenmässigen Valutahandels" [The Reintroduction of Exchange Rates Transactions on the Stock Exchange]. *Neue Freie Presse.* #19872 (December 23, 1919) 2-3.

1920

20.1 Review of Walter Huth's *Die Entwicklung der deutschen und französischen Grossbanken im Zusammenhange mit der Entwicklung der Nationalwirtschaft* [The Development of Large German and French Banks in Relation to Economic Development] (1918). *Weltwirtschaftliches Archiv* (Kiel). 15 (July-April 1919-1920) 128.

20.2   "Ernste Rückgänge der Valuta" [Severe Declines in Foreign Exchange]. *Neue Freie Presse.* #19907 (January 28, 1920) 1.

20.3   "Zu Karl Mengers Achtzigstem Geburtstag" [On Carl Menger's 80th Birthday]. *Neues Wiener Tagblatt.* 52 (February 22, 1920) 2.

20.4   "Die Abschaffung des Geldes in Russland" [The Abolition of Money in Russia]. *Neue Freie Presse.* #20195 (November 17, 1920) 9.

20.5   "Die Politischen Beziehungen Wiens zu den Ländern im Lichte der Volkswirtschaft" [Vienna's Political Ties to the Provinces from the Economic Viewpoint]. *Jahrbuch der Gesellschaft Österreichischer Volkswirte.* (1920) 1- 22. A lecture, December 2, 1919.

20.6   "Die Wirtschaftsrechnung im Sozialistischen Gemeinwesen" [Economic Calculation in the Socialist Commonwealth]. *Archiv für Sozialwissenschaft und Sozialpolitik.* 47 (1920) 86-121. This article launched the lively economic calculation debate that continues to this day. Translated into English by S. Adler and reprinted in *Collectivist Economic Planning* (1935). See Article 35.1 for further details.

1921

21.1   "Wie könnte Oesterreich gerettet werden? Ein wirtschaftspolitisches Programm für Oesterreich" [How Can Austria Be Rescued? A Politico-Economic Program for Austria]. *Die Börse.* (February 17, 1921).

21.2   "Die Ansprüche der Noteninhaber bei der Liquidation der Bank" [The Claims of Noteholders upon the Liquidation of the Bank]. *Neue Freie Presse.* In two parts: #20293 (February 25, 1921) 9; #20294 (February 26, 1921) 10-11.

21.3   "Karl [Carl] Menger." *Neues Wiener Abendblatt.* 55:56 (February 26, 1921) 1-2. An obituary; Menger had died that morning.

21.4   "Die Wiener Industrie und die Luxuswarenabgabe" [Viennese Industry and Taxes on Luxury Goods]. *Neues 8 Uhr Blatt.* 1987 (May 13, 1921) 4.

21.5   "Die Arbeit im sozialistischen Gemeinwesen" [Labor in the Socialist Commonwealth]. *Zeitschrift für Volkswirtschaft und Sozialpolitik.* N.F. [New Series] 1 (1921) 459-476. Incorporated in the first German edition (1922) of *Socialism* (B-4) and, with some new material added, in the second German edition (1932). See pp.163-181 of the 1938, 1951 and 1969 English language editions, pp. 142-159 of the 1981 Liberty Fund edition.

1922

22.1   "Inflation und Geldknappheit: Gegen eine weitere Verwendung der Notenpresse" [Inflation and the Shortage of Money: Against the Continued Use of the Printing Press]. *Neue Freie Presse.* #20666 (March 11, 1922) 2.

22.2   "Das österreichische Währungsproblem vor 30 Jahren und heute: ein Gedenkblatt" [The Austrian Monetary Problem Thirty Years Ago and Today: A Commentary]. *Neue Freie Presse.* #20672 (March 17, 1922) 2.

22.3   Review of Wm. F. Spalding's *Eastern Exchange, Currency and Finance* (3rd ed., 1920). *Zeitschrift für Volkswirtschaft und Sozialpolitik.* N.F. [New Series] 2:1-3 (1922) 169-170.

22.4   Review of Hugo C. M. Wendel's *The Evolution of Industrial Freedom in Prussia, 1845-1849* (1921). *Zeitschrift für Volkswirtschaft und Sozialpolitik.* N.F [New Series] 2:4-6 (1922) 367.

22.5   "Die alte und die neue Notenbank" [The Old and the New Bank of Issue]. *Österreichische Revue.* (December 25, 1922).

1923

23.1   "Das österreichische Problem" [The Austrian Problem]. *Neue Freie Presse.* #20977 (February 5, 1923) 5. A review of Siegfried Strakosch's *Der Selbstmord eines Volkes: Wirtschaft in Oesterreich* [The Suicide of a People: Economy in Austria].

23.2   "Carl Mengers 'Grundsätze' in zweiter Auflage" [Carl Menger's *Principles*, 2nd ed.]. *Neues Wiener Tagblatt.* (February 26, 1923).

23.3   "Wilhelm Rosenbergs politische Wirksamkeit" [Wilhelm Rosenberg's Political Effectiveness]. *Neues Freie Presse.* #21038 (April 6, 1923) 3.

23.4   A review of Waldemar Mitscherlich's *Der Nationalismus Westeuropas* (The Nationalism of Western Europe). *Weltwirtschaftliches Archiv.* 19 (1923) 302-303.

23.5   "Preistaxen: I. Theorie" [Price Controls: I. Theory]. *Handwörterbuch der Staatswissenschaften*, 4th ed. (Jena: Gustav Fischer, 1923). 6:1055-1062. Reprinted in *Critique of Interventionism* (B-8).

23.6   "Neue Beiträge zum Problem der sozialistischen Wirtschaftsrechnung" [New Contributions to the Problem of Socialist Economic Calculation]. *Archiv für Sozialwissenschaft und Sozialpolitik.* 51 (December 1923) 488-500. Incorporated in part as the "Appendix" of the second edition (1932) of *Socialism* (B-4). Includes comments by Mises on articles by A. W. Cohn (1920), Karl Kautsky (1922) and O. Leichter (1923). See annotations of their articles under "Books and Articles About Mises: 1920, 1922, 1923."

1924

24.1   Review of Gustav Seibt's *Deutschlands kranke Wirtschaft und ihre Wiederherstellung* [Germany's Sick Economy and Its Recovery] (Bonn, 1923). *Jahrbuch für Gesetzgebung, Verwaltung und Volkswirtschaft (Schmollers Jahrbuch).* 48:1 (1924) 334-335.

24.2 "Über Deflationspolitik" [On Deflationary Policy]. *Mitteilungen des Verbandes Oesterreichischer Banken und Bankiers*. 6:1/2 (1924) 13-18. Incorporated in the second German-language edition (1924) of *The Theory of Money and Credit* (B-2), Part 2, Chapter 7; Chapter 13:4 of Liberty Fund (1980) edition.

24.3 "Die Rückkehr zur Goldwährung" [The Return to the Gold Standard]. *Mitteilungen des Verbandes österreichischer Banken und Bankiers*. 6 (1924) 106-122.

24.4 "Eugen v. Böhm-Bawerk: Zu seinem 10. Todestag" [The Tenth Anniversary of Eugen von Böhm-Bawerk's Death]. *Neue Freie Presse*. #21539 (August 27, 1924) 9.

24.5 "Finanz- und währungspolitische Fragen in der Gegenwart" [Present-day Questions of Financial and Monetary Policy]. *Mitteilungen des deutschen Hauptverbandes der Industrie* (Teplitz-Schönau). 5:12 (March 20, 1924) 201-209. A lecture presented March 15, 1924, in Czechoslovakia to German industrialists.

1925

25.1 Review of Karl Helfferich's *Das Geld* [Money] (6th ed., rev. Leipzig, 1923). *Zeitschrift für Volkswirtschaft und Sozialpolitik*. N.F. [New series] 4 (1924-1925) 160.

25.2 Transcript of remarks at the Stuttgart (September 24-26, 1924) meeting of the Verein für Sozialpolitik. *Verhandlungen* [Proceedings]: *Theorie des Klassenkampfes, Handelspolitik, Währungsfrage* [Theory of the Class Struggle, Trade Policy, and the Currency Question]. *Schriften des Vereins für Sozialpolitik*. (Munich & Leipzig: Duncker & Humblot, 1925) Vol. 170:225-328. Index. Mises' remarks appear on pp. 275-280 and 313-315. An excerpt follows: "Three years ago a colleague from the German Reich, who is here in this hall today, visited Vienna and participated in a discussion with some Viennese economists. Everyone was in complete agreement concerning the destructiveness of inflationist policy. Later, as we went home through the still of the night, we heard in the Herrengasse [a main street in the center of Vienna] the heavy drone of the Austro-Hungarian Bank's printing presses which were running incessantly, day and night, to produce new banknotes. Throughout the land, a large number of industrial enterprises were idle; others were working part-time; only the printing presses stamping out notes were operating at full speed. Let us hope that industry in Germany and Austria will once more regain its pre-war volume and that war- and inflation-related industries, devoted specifically to the printing of notes, will give way to more useful activities." (Translated from the German)

25.3 "Die Goldkernwährung" [The Gold Exchange Standard]. *Deutsche Allgemeine Zeitung* (Berlin). (February 24, 1925). A review of Fritz Machlup's *Die Goldkernwährung* (Halberstadt, 1925). Reprinted in *H.M.B.-Blätter*. (July/August 1926) 54-58.

25.4 "Antimarxismus" [Anti-Marxism]. *Weltwirtschaftliches Archiv*. 21:2 (April 1925) 266-293. Reprinted in *Critique of Interventionism* (B-8).

25.5 "Die Goldwährung" [The Gold Standard]. *Neues Wiener Tagblatt*. 101 (April 12, 1925) 19-20.

1926   Tours U.S.   Lectures at Universities.   Establishes Austrian Institute for Business Cycle Research.

26.1   "Eugen von Philippovich." *Neue österreichische Biographie, 1815-1918.*   Part 1:3 (Vienna, 1926) 53-62.

26.2   "Vorwort" [Foreword] to Siegfried Strakosch's *Das sozialdemokratische Agrarprogramm in seiner politischen und volkswirtschaftlichen Bedeutung* [The Political and Economic Meaning of the Social-Democratic Agricultural Program]. (Vienna, 1926) 3-4.

26.3   "The Economic Prospects of Austria." *Proceedings of the Academy of Political Science in the City of New York* (May 10-16, 1926). 12:1 (July 1926) 271-272.

26.4   "Sozialliberalismus" [Social Liberalism]. *Zeitschrift für die gesamte Staatswissenschaft.* 81:2 (1926) 242-278. Reprinted in *Critique of Interventionism* (B-8).

26.5   "Interventionismus" [Interventionism]. *Archiv für Sozialwissenschaft und Sozialpolitik.* 56 (1926) 610-653. N.B. This article is *not* the same as the 1979 and 1980 articles of the same title.

        Reprinted in *Critique of Interventionism* (B-8).

        Reprinted also in *Grundtexte zur sozialen Marktwirtschaft: Zeugnisse aus 200 Jahren ordnungspolitischer Diskussion* [Basic Texts on the Market Economy: Witnesses to 200 Years of Discussion of the Political Order]. (Stuttgart: Gustav Fischer, 1981) 213-220; and in English-language version, *Standard Texts on the Social Market Economy: Two Centuries of Discussion* (Gustav Fischer, 1982) 177-182.

        Portuguese translation: "O Intervencionismo." Translated by José Joaquim Teixeira Ribeiro. (Coimbra) 1944. 55pp.

        Spanish translation: "Intervencionismo." Translated by Eduardo L. Suárez, in *Ludwig von Mises: Infatigable Luchador Contra la Economía Ficticia* [Ludwig von Mises: Indefatigable Fighter Against False Economics]. (Mexico: Centro de Estudios en Economía y Educación, 1983) 71-104.

26.6   "Wandlungen in der Amerikanischen Wirtschaftspolitik" [Changes in American Economic Policy]. *Industrieller Klub* (Vienna). 342 (1926) 10-15. An address given November 18, 1926.

26.7   Review of F. Y. Edgeworth's *Papers Relating to Political Economy* (London, 1925). *Jahrbuch für Gesetzgebung, Verwaltung und Volkswirtschaft (Schmollers Jahrbuch).* 49:6 (1926) 1400-1401.

1927

27.1   Review of Hereward T. Price's *Volkswirtschaftliches Wörterbuch. Part 1: Eng.-Deutsch* [Economic Dictionary: Part 1, English-German] (1926). *Archiv für Sozialwissenschaft und Sozialpolitik.* 58:1 (1927) 213-215.

27.2   "Das Ende des Laissez-Faire, Ideen zur Verbindung von Privat- und Gemeinwirtschaft" [The End of Laissez-Faire: Ideas for Combining the Private and Public Economy]. *Zeitschrift für die gesamte Staatswissenschaft*. 82 (1927) 190-191. A review of a lecture given by John M. Keynes in Berlin.

27.3   Review of Carl Rodbertus-Jagetzow's *Neue Briefe über Grundrente, Rentenprinzip und soziale Frage an Schumacher* [New Letters to Schumacher on Land Rent, Income and Social Questions]. *Zeitschrift für die gesamte Staatswissenschaft*. 82:3 (1927) 628-629.

27.4   "Amerika und der Wiederaufbau der europäischen Wirtschaft" [America and the Reconstruction of the European Economy]. *Mitteilungen des Hauptverbandes der Industrie* (Teplitz). 8 (1927) 5-7.

27.5   "Die Vereinigten Staaten von Europa" [The United States of Europe]. *Weltwirtschaft*. 15 (1927) 147-148.

1928

28.1   "Die Lehre vom Gelde" [The Theory of Money]. *Forschungen und Fortschritte* (Berlin). (February 1928).

28.2   "Bemerkungen zum Grundproblem der subjektivistischen Wertlehre" [Remarks on the Fundamental Problem of the Subjective Theory of Value]. *Archiv für Sozialwissenschaft und Sozialpolitik*. 59:1 (February 1928) 32-47. In this essay, Mises says, he "sought to eliminate the distinction between economic and noneconomic action." *Notes and Recollections* (B-23), p.122.
    Reprinted in *Epistemological Problems of Economics* (B-10), German version (1933), English translation (1960).

28.3   "Neue Schriften zum Problem der sozialistischen Wirtschaftsrechnung" [New Papers on the Problem of Economic Calculation under Socialism]. *Archiv für Sozialwissenschaft und Sozialpolitik*. 60 (1928) 187-190. A critique of several articles on this subject. For Mises' comments on each, see "Books and Articles About Mises" as follows: Marschak (1923), Neurath and Cassau (1925), and Horn, Brutzkus, and Adolf Weber (1928).

28.4   Review of Eduard Heimann's *Die sittliche Idee des Klassenkampfes und die Entartung des Kapitalismus* [The Ethical Idea of the Class Struggle and the Decline of Capitalism]. *Zeitschrift für die gesamte Staatswissenschaft*. 85(1928) 167-168.

28.5   "Währung und Finanzen des Bundesstaates Oesterreich" [The Currency and Finances of the Federal State of Austria]. *Deutsche Wirtschafts-Zeitung*. 25:38/39 (September 20, 1928) 913-915.

1929

29.1   "Karl [Carl] Menger und die österreichische Schule der Nationalökonomie" [Carl Menger and the Austrian School of Economics]. Anlässlich der Enthüllung des Denkmals in der Universität [Upon the Occasion of the Unveiling of a Memorial in Menger's Honor at the University of Vienna]. *Neue Freie Presse*. In two parts: #23123 (January 29, 1929) 2-3; #23124 (January 30, 1929) 2.

English translation by Albert Zlabinger: "Karl [Carl] Menger and the Austrian School of Economics." *The Clash of Group Interests and Other Essays* (Occasional Paper #7). New York: Center for Libertarian Studies, June 1978.

29.2   "Soziologie und Geschichte: Epilog zum Methodenstreit in der Nationalökonomie" [Sociology and History: Epilogue to the Methodological Controversy in Economics]. *Archiv für Sozialwissenschaft und Sozialpolitik.* 61:3 (1929) 465-512. Included in *Epistemological Problems* (B-10). In referring to the science of human action, Mises later came to prefer the term "praxeology" instead of "sociology," which he used here. However, he sanctioned the use of "sociology" in the English translation (1960) of *Epistemological Problems* (B-10); see his preface, p.viii; also *Notes and Recollections* (B-23), p. 123.

29.3   "Verstaatlichung des Kredits?" [Nationalization of Credit?]. *Zeitschrift für Nationalökonomie.* 1:3 (1929) 430-439. Mises intended to have this essay included in the 1929 edition of *Critique of Interventionism* (B-8), but it was inadvertently omitted. However, it was included in the 1976 German-language reprint and also in the 1977 English translation. See *Notes and Recollections* (B-23), pp.113-114.

        English translation by Louise Sommer: "The Nationalization of Credit," in *Essays in European Economic Thought.* Princeton: Van Nostrand. (1960) 106-119.

        Spanish translation by Gustavo R. Velasco: "La Estatización del Crédito," in *El Universal* (Mexico, n.d.). Reprinted in *Temas Contemporáneos* (Mexico: Instituto de Investigaciones Sociales y Económicas). 17:206 (December 15, 1971) 1-16.

        Spanish translation by Eduardo L. Suárez: "¿La Nacionalización de la Banca y el Crédito?" in *Ludwig von Mises: Infatigable Luchador Contra la Economía Ficticia* [Ludwig von Mises: Indefatigable Fighter Against False Economics]. (Mexico: Centro de Estudios en Economía y Educación). (1983) 107-117.

29.4   Remarks at a meeting (Zürich, September 1928) of the Verein für Sozialpolitik. *Verhandlungen des Vereins für Sozialpolitik* [Proceedings of the Society for Social Policy]. 175 (Munich & Leipzig) 1929. On this occasion, according to F. A. Hayek, Mises "not only admitted but indeed emphasized the fact that monetary causes can only act by producing a 'lag' between various prices, wages and interest rates." (Hayek, *Monetary Theory and the Trade Cycle*, London, 1933, p.124n)

29.5   Review of Ernst Grünfeld's *Das Genossenschaftswesen volkswirtschaftlich und soziologisch betrachtet* [Guilds Considered Economically and Sociologically]. *Zeitschrift für Völkerpsychologie und Soziologie.* 5:4 (December 1929) 467-468.

1930

30.1   "Begreifen und Verstehen" [Conception and Understanding]. *Jahrbuch für Gesetzgebung, Verwaltung und Volkswirtschaft (Schmollers Jahrbuch).* 54:2 (1930) 331-343. Included in *Epistemological Problems* (B-10).

        French translation of Parts I-III, by P. Roubier and H. Mankiewicz. "Entendre et Comprendre" in *Recueil d'Études en l'honneur d'Edouard Lambert* (date ?).

30.2   "Das Wirtschaftssystem des Interventionismus" [The Interventionist Economic System]. *Mitteilungen des Deutschen Hauptverbandes der Industrie* (Teplitz-Schönau). 11:31 (July 31, 1930) 569-571.

30.3   "The Suitability of Methods of Ascertaining Changes in Purchasing Power for the Guidance of International Currency or Banking Policy." League of Nations. (October 10, 1930) 28 pp. mimeo. Included in *Money, Method, and the Market Process* (B-28).

30.4   "Anpassung der öffentlichen Ausgaben an die Tragfähigkeit der Wirtschaft" [Adjustment of Public Spending to Economic Productivity]. *Industrieller Klub.* 351 (December 10, 1930) 12pp. A lecture given in Vienna, December 1, 1930.

1931

31.1   "Die Ursachen der Weltwirtschaftskrise" [Causes of the Economic Crisis]. *Mitteilungen des Deutschen Hauptverbandes der Industrie* (Teplitz-Schönau). In two parts: 12:10 (March 12, 1931) 157-160; 12:11 (March 19, 1931) 171-174. A lecture, presented February 28, 1931, at Teplitz-Schönau, Czechoslovakia, before German industrialists. Later published as a separate monograph and translated into English, Spanish and Dutch. See B-9.

31.2   "Vom Weg der subjektivistischen Wertlehre" [On the Development of the Subjective Theory of Value]. *Probleme der Wertlehre*, Part I. Ludwig Mises and Arthur Spiethoff, eds. *Schriften des Vereins für Sozialpolitik.* 183 (Munich & Leipzig: Duncker & Humblot, 1931) 73-93. Included in *Epistemological Problems of Economics* (B-10).

31.3   "Die psychologischen Wurzeln des Widerstandes gegen die nationalökonomische Theorie" [The Psychological Basis of the Opposition to Economic Theory]. *Probleme der Wertlehre*, Part I. Ludwig Mises & Arthur Spiethoff, eds. *Schriften des Vereins für Sozialpolitik.* 183 (Munich & Leipzig: Duncker & Humblot, 1931) 275-295. Included in *Epistemological Problems of Economics* (B-10).

31.4   "Das festangelegte Kapital" [Inconvertible Capital]. *Economische Opstellen: Aangeboden aan Prof. Dr. C. A. Verrijn Stuart* [Economic Essays: Presented to Prof. C. A. Verrijn Stuart]. (Haarlem: De Erven F. Bohn N.V., 1931) 214-228. Included in *Epistemological Problems of Economics* (B-10).

31.5   "Unrentabilität als Prinzip" [Unprofitability as a Principle]. *Allgemeiner Tarifanzeiger* [General Price Reports]: *Sonderausgabe aus Anlass des L. Jahrganges der Zeitschrift* [Special 50th Anniversary Edition of the Periodical]. (1931) 67-68.

31.6   "Die bankpolitischen Lehren der Krisis" [The Banking Theories of the Crisis]. *Allgemeiner Tarifanzeiger.* 31 (August 1, 1931) 1000-1001.

31.7   "Die Krise und der Kapitalismus" [The Crisis and Capitalism]. *Neue Freie Presse*. #24099 (October 17, 1931) 13.

31.8   "Die Goldwährung und ihre Gegner" [The Gold Standard and Its Enemies]. *Neue Freie Presse*. In two parts: 24168 (December 25, 1931) 24; 24171 (December 30, 1931) 11.

1932

32.1   "Die Stellung des Geldes im Kreise der wirtschaftlichen Güter" [The Role of Money in the Realm of Economic Goods]. Published in Volume II of a 4-volume Festschrift honoring Friedrich von Wieser. *Die Wirtschaftstheorie der Gegenwart.* Hans Mayer, ed. (Vienna, 1931/2). 309-318.
         English translation in *Money, Method, and the Market Process* (B-28).

32.2   "Die Legende vom Versagen des Kapitalismus" [The Myth of the Failure of Capitalism]. *Der internationale Kapitalismus und die Krise.* Festschrift for Julius Wolf, April 20, 1932. (Stuttgart, 1932) 23-29.
         Polish translation: "Legenda o selnáni kapitalismu" in *Hospodárska Politika* (21) 27 kvetna (1933) 402-404.
         English translation by Jane E. Sanders in *The Clash of Group Interests and Other Essays,* 1978 (B-26) 13-18.

32.3   "The Great German Inflation." *Economica.* 12:36 (May 1932) 227-234. A review of Frank D. Graham's *Exchange, Prices and Production in Hyperinflation: Germany, 1920-1923* (Princeton University Press, 1930). Reprinted in *Money, Method, and the Market Process* (B-28).

32.4   "Der Kampf um die englische Handelspolitik" [The Controversy over English Trade Policy]. *Neue Freie Presse.* 449 (June 25, 1932) 17. A review of the German translation of an anthology edited by William Beveridge.

32.5   Review of Rudolph Sieghart's *Die Letzten Jahrzehnte einer Grossmacht: Menschen, Völker und Probleme des Habsburger-Reichs* [The Last Decades of a Great Power: The People, the Local Inhabitants and the Problem of the Habsburg Empire] (Berlin, 1932). *Economica.* Vol. 38 (November 1932) 477-478. A review in English of a German language book.

1933

33.1   "Planwirtschaft und Sozialismus" [Economic Planning and Socialism]. *Neues Wiener Tagblatt.* 78 (March 19, 1933) 2-3.

33.2   "Senior's Lectures on Monetary Problems." *Economic Journal.* 43:171 (1933) 525-530. A review of Nassau W. Senior's lectures (Nos. 3, 4 and 5 in the series of *Reprints of Scarce Tracts in Economic and Political Science.* London School of Economics and Political Science). Reprinted in *Money, Method, and the Market Process* (B-28).

33.3   "Der Stand und die nächste Zukunft der Konjunkturforschung" [The Current Status of Business Cycle Research and its Prospects for the Immediate Future]. *Festschrift für Arthur Spiethoff* (Munich: Duncker & Humblot, 1933) 175-180.
         English translation by Joseph R. Stromberg: "From Crank-Up to Crack-Up," *The Libertarian Forum* (New York). (June 1975) 3-5.
         English translation by Bettina Bien Greaves: "The Current Status of Business Cycle Research and Its Prospects for the Immediate Future" in *On the Manipulation of Money and Credit,* 1978 (B-24) 207-213.

33.4   "Mündliche Aussprache über die Wertlehre im theoretischen Ausschuss des Vereins für Sozialpolitik" [Discussion of Value Theory in the Committee on Theory of the Association for Social Policy], September 30, 1932, Dresden. *Probleme der Wertlehre* [Problems of Value Theory] Part II. L. Mises & Arthur Spiethoff, eds. *Schriften des Vereins für Sozialpolitik.* 183:2 (Munich & Leipzig: Duncker & Humblot, 1933) 1-12, 37 & 116-120. Excerpt, "Der Streit um die Wertlehre" [The Controversy over the Theory of Value], included in *Epistemological Problems of Economics* (B-10).

1934 Accepts a position as Professor of International Economic Relations at the Graduate Institute of International Studies, Geneva, Switzerland, while retaining a part-time association with the Austrian Chamber of Commerce in Vienna.

34.1   "Grundsätzliches zur Frage der Geldwertstabilisierung" [Fundamental Considerations With Respect to Monetary Stabilization]. *Welt Wirtschaftswoche* (Vienna). (April 1, 1934).

34.2   "Die österreichische Nationalökonomie" [The Austrian Economy]. *Der Wirtschafter.* (April 27, 1934) 316-317.

34.3   "Bilanz des XIX Jahrhunderts" [The 19th Century on Balance]. *Wiener Wirtschaftswoche.* 3 (December 25, 1934) 51-53.

34.4   "Das Währungsproblem" [The Monetary Problem]. *Mitteilungen des Verbandes österreichischer Banken und Bankiers.* 16:10/11 (November 1934) 271-277. Written to be incorporated as the Preface to the English translation (1934) of *The Theory of Money and Credit* (B-2).

1935

35.1   "Economic Calculation in the Socialist Commonwealth." *Collectivist Economic Planning:Critical Studies of the Possibilities of Socialism.* F.A. Hayek, ed. (London: Routledge & Kegan Paul, 1935) 87-130. English translation by S. Adler of Article 20.6. This article, substantially revised by Mises, included in *Socialism* (B-4).
        Published as a separate pamphlet. (London: George Routledge & Sons, Ltd., n.d.) pp.87-130.
        Reprinted (1990) as a separate monograph: "Foreword" by Yuri N. Maltsev; "Introduction" by Jacek Kochanowicz; "Postscript" by Joseph T. Salerno. (Auburn, Alabama: Ludwig von Mises Institute). 74pp.
        Reprinted in *Austrian Economics, III.*, Stephen Littlechild, ed. (Aldershot, Hants, England; Brookfield, Vermont: Edward Elgar, 1990) 251-294.
        Excerpt in *Socialist Economics.* Alec Nove and D. M. Nuti (eds.). (Baltimore: Penguin Books, 1972), 75-91. This Novi-Nuti anthology includes Oskar Lange's "answer" to other authors who were struggling to solve the problem of calculation and planning in socialist economies.
        The 1935 anthology reviewed in several journals, including:
        The Financial News (February 11, 1935).
        New Statesman and the Nation (February 23, 1935).
        Sir Josiah Stamp, "Simply Priceless," *Time and Tide* (March 9, 1935).

The Scotsman (March 14, 1935).

Time and Tide (March 16, 1935).

Labour (April 1935) 185.

The Economist (April 20, 1935) 907.

Tablet (May 25, 1935).

The Times (London Literary Supplement: June 20, 1935).

Spanish translations of excerpts:

"El Cálculo Económico en la Comunidad Socialista," *Temas Contemporáneos* (Instituto de Investigaciones Sociales y Económicas, Mexico). 15:186 (April 15, 1970);

"Empresas Públicas y Gestión Empresarial" [Public Enterprises and Entrepreneurship]. *Resumen* (Mexico). 83 (November 1972) 81-82;

Orientación Económica (Caracas, Venezuela). 31 (November 1969) 22;

Tópicos de Actualidad (Centro de Estudios Económico-Sociales, Guatemala). 12:238 (January 15, 1971) 13-16.

35.2   "Der Weg der österreichischen Finanzpolitik" [The Course of Austrian Financial Policy]. *Wirtschaftliche Nachrichten*, 1935. 18:1 (January 10, 1935) 38-39. NOTE: This issue of *Wirtschaftliche Nachrichten* also includes articles by Gottfried Haberler and Oskar Morgenstern, both of whom were then associated with Mises in the Oesterreichisches Institut für Konjunkturforschung.

35.3   "Neue Ausgabe der Werke Carl Mengers" [New Edition of Carl Menger's Works]. *Neues Wiener Tagblatt*. 124 (May 5, 1935) 27. Announcement of two volumes, now published in German in photostat reproductions, of a projected collection of Menger's works by the London School of Economics. Includes an English-language introduction by F. A. Hayek.

35.4   Review of T. E. Gregory's *The Gold Standard and its Future* (3rd ed., 1934). *Economica*. (May 1935) 229-232.

35.5   "Der Kultus des Irrationalen" [The Cult of the Irrational]. Published in Hungarian translation: "Ami értelemmel fel nem fogható." *Cobden* (Budapest). (January 1935) 4-5.

35.6   "Freizügigkeit als internationales Problem" [The Freedom to Move as an International Problem]. *Wiener Wirtschaftswoche*. 4:51-53 (Christmas 1935).

English translation by Bettina Bien Greaves in *The Clash of Group Interests and Other Essays*, 1978 (B-26).

1936

36.1   "Ein neuer Band der Gesammelten Werke Carl Mengers" [A New Volume of the Collected Works of Carl Menger]. *Neues Wiener Tagblatt.* (January 3, 1936). A short announcement of the publication of Volume III of the London School of Economics edition of Menger's works.

36.2   "Londoner Ausgabe der Schriften von Karl [Carl] Menger" [London Edition of the Writings of Carl Menger]. *Neues Wiener Tagblatt.* (November 29, 1936) 19-20. A review; Volume IV of the London School of Economics German-language edition of Menger's collected works had just appeared. Only Hayek's introduction is in English.

36.3   "Memorandum on New Technical Arguments for Postponing Stabilization" inThe *Improvement of Commercial Relations Between Nations and the Problems of Monetary Stabilization* (Volume II of a 2-volume study). (Paris: International Chamber of Commerce, Joint Committee of the Carnegie Endowment and the ICC, 1936) 156-163.

36.4   "Memorandum on Exchange Stabilization and the Problem of Internal Planning" in *The Improvement of Commercial Relations between Nations and the Problems of Monetary Stabilization* (Volume II of a 2-volume study). (Paris: International Chamber of Commerce, Joint Committee of the Carnegie Endowment and the ICC, 1936) 187-190.

36.5   "Wirtschaftsordnung und politische Verfassung" [Economic Order and Political Government]. *Wiener Wirtschaftswoche.* 5 (1936) 51-53.

36.6   "La Théorie dite Autrichienne du Cycle Économique" [The Austrian Theory of the Trade Cycle]. *Bulletin Périodique,* Société Belge d'Études et d'Expansion. 35:103 (December 1936) 459-464.

         Spanish translation: "La Política Bancaria en las Depresiones Económicas," [Journal] Universidad de Panama, Centro de Investigaciones Sociales y Económicas. 10 (November 1937) 11-19.

         English translation by David O'Mahony and J. Huston McCulloch: "The 'Austrian' Theory of the Trade Cycle" in *The Austrian Theory of the Trade Cycle and Other Essays* (Occasional Paper 8). New York: Center for Libertarian Studies. (September 1978). 44pp. Preface by Richard M. Ebeling. Includes also Gottfried Haberler's "Money and the Business Cycle"

         (1932), Murray N. Rothbard's "Economic Depressions: Their Cause and Cure" (1969), and Friedrich A. Hayek's "Can We Still Avoid Inflation?" (1970). This monograph reprinted by The Ludwig von Mises Institute (Auburn University, Auburn, Ala., 1983).

         English translation by Mahony and McCulloch reprinted in *Austrian Economics, II.* Stephen Littlechild, ed. (Aldershot, Hants, England; Brookfield, Vt.: Edward Elgar, 1990) 291-296.

1937

37.1   "Autarkie -- der Weg ins Elend: Internationale Arbeitsteilung ist Grundlage der europäischen Kultur" [Autarky: The Road to Misery: International Division of Labor is the Foundation of European Civilization]. *Der Europäer.* 3:3 (March 1937) 3.

37.2   "Der Völkerbund und das Rohstoffproblem" [The League of Nations and the Problem of Raw Materials]. *The New Commonwealth Quarterly.* 3:1 (London: New Commonwealth Institute, June 1937) 15-25.

37.3   "The Logical Character of the Science of Human Conduct." Travaux du IXe Congrès (Paris, August 1-6, 1937) International de Philosophie, Congrès Descartes [Proceedings of the Ninth International Philosophical Congress, Descartes Congress]. *Actualités Scientifiques et Industrielles.* (Paris: Hermann, 1937). pp.V.49-V.55.

37.4   "Introduction" to A. S. J. Baster's *The Twilight of American Capitalism: An Economic Interpretation of the New Deal* (London: P. S. King & Son, 1937) v-vi.

French translation of Introduction to Baster in French version of the book, *Le Crépuscule du Capitalisme Américain: Étude Économique du New Deal*. Paris: Librairie de Médicis. (date ?).

1938   **Anschluss. Hitler occupies Austria. Mises' ties to Vienna severed. Marriage to Margit (née Herzfeld) Sereny in Switzerland.**

38.1   "Or et Inflation" [Gold and Inflation]. *Aujourd'hui*. 1:4 (February 15, 1938) 153-161.

38.2   Review of Stefan Th. Possony's *Die Wehrwirtschaft des totalen Krieg* [The Defense (or Military) Economy in Total War] (1938). *Paneuropa: R. N. Coudenhove-Kalergi* (Zürich/Vienna: Pan Europa Verlag). 14:3 (March 1938) 95-96.

38.3   Remarks at Le Colloque [Conference] Walter Lippmann, August 26-30, 1938. (Paris: Librairie de Médicis, 1938). See pp. 31, 36-38, 41-42, 52-53, 60-61, 74, 88-90 and 109 of the published proceedings.

38.4   "Économie Dirigée et Démocratie" [The Controlled Economy and Democracy]. *Aujourd'hui*. 1:10 (October 15, 1938) 495-499.

38.5   "The Disintegration of the International Division of Labour." *The World Crisis* by the Professors of the Graduate Institute of International Studies. London, New York and Toronto: Longmans, Green. (1938) 245-274.

   French translation by M. Romain Godet: "La Crise de la Division Internationale du Travail." *La Crise Mondiale*. Paris: Librairie du Recueil Sirey, S.A. (1938) pp. 267-301. Reprinted separately under same title, Éditions Polygraphiques (Zurich, 1938); also reprinted in French translation as "Les Illusions du Protectionnisme et de l'Autarcie." by Librairie de Médicis (Paris, 1938).

   Spanish translation: "Las Ilusiones del Proteccionismo y de la Autarquía." *Investigación Económica*.(Escuela Nacional de Economía, Universidad Nacional Autónoma de México). 2:1 (First Quarter, 1942). 28-54.

   Reprinted in *Money, Method, and the Market Process* (B-28).

Reviews and comments:

English edition of *The World Crisis* reviewed in several publications, including:

   The (Edinburgh) Scotsman (March 28, 1938).

   Church Times (March 18, 1938). "More interesting is the essay on the decay of international trade. The conclusion of the author, Ludwig v. Mises, is that the poor results obtained by the League of Nations, the World Economic Conferences, and more special conferences and negotiations between smaller groups of nations, are due to the fact that the world lacks to-day the desire for peaceful co-operation and is under the rule of militarist ideas."

French edition of the book, *La Crise Mondial,* reviewed by R.P. in *Journal de Genève*. 33 (February 3, 1938) 1.

The New York Times editorialized on Mises' essay (May 29, 1938): "[T]he new, like the old, arguments for protectionism and autarchy are primarily not economic but political and military . . . . Autarchy, it is important to remember, is never an isolated phenomenon. It is always found as part of a wider policy, itself the result of the general philosophy of the ruling Government. That philosophy is the antithesis of liberalism. Liberalism is a philosophy of peace and international cooperation. Autarchy is primarily militaristic in aim."

38.6 "Les Équations de l'Économie Mathématique et le Problème du Calcul Économique en Régime Socialiste" [The Equations of Mathematical Economics and the Problem of Economic Calculation in a Socialist Order]. Translated from the German mss. by Gaston Leduc. *Revue d'Économie Politique.* Paris: Librairie du Recueil Sirey. (1938) 1055-1062.

38.7 "The Non-Neutrality of Money." Unpublished manuscript of a talk found among Mises' papers, probably given in Paris in 1938. Reprinted in *Money, Method, and the Market Process,* 1990 (B-28).

1939

39.1 "Les Hypothèses de Travail dans la Science Économique" [Theories of Labor in Economic Science]. *Cournot nella economia e nella filosofia.* Padua: Cedam. 17 (1939) 97-122. Lecture delivered at the Independent Faculty of Economics, Venice.

1940   Migration to the United States

40.1 "L'autarcie et la Guerre" [Autarky and War]. *La Revue Danubienne.* 1:7 (May 6, 1940).

40.2 "My Contributions to Economic Theory." Talk before the New York University economics faculty, November 20, 1940. 6pp. mimeo. Included in 4th (1980) edition of *Planning for Freedom* (B-18).

1941

41.1 "Productive Capitalism vs. Distributive Socialism: America's Advantages in Postwar Reconstruction." *Trusts and Estates.* 72 (January 1941) 41-45. Remarks at a Symposium on Public Control and Private Enterprise (pp.28-32 in Symposium reprint).

41.2 "Grandfather Willcke" (unsigned editorial). *The New York Times.* (March 22, 1941). In *My Years with Ludwig von Mises* (1976 edition, pp. 87-88; 1984 edition, p. 84) Margit von Mises lists titles and dates of editorials and Letters to the Editor by Mises that appeared in *The New York Times* between March 28, 1942 and July 31, 1943. Every title she lists plus payment vouchers ($10 per editorial) have been located among Mises' papers on file at Grove City College (Grove City, Penna.). Although this title was not included, authorship is verified by *New York Times* payment voucher to Mises.

41.3 "American Credits for Europe?" *The Voice of Austria.* 1:3 (August 1941) 9.

41.4 Review of Maxine Y. Sweezy's *The Structure of the Nazi Economy* (Harvard University Press, 1941). *Journal of Central European Affairs.* University of Colorado. (date ?).

1942

42.1   Review of Karl Robert's (pseud.) *Hitler's Counterfeit Reich: Behind the Scenes of Nazi Economy* (New York: Alliance Book Corp. 1941). *Journal of Central European Affairs* University of Colorado. (date ?).

42.2   "Social Science and Natural Science." *Journal of Social Philosophy & Jurisprudence.* 7:3 (April 1942) 240-253.
        Reprinted in *Money, Method, and the Market Process* (B-28).

42.3   "Inflation and You." *The American Mercury.* 55:223 (July 1942) 66-71.
        Reprinted in *Economic Freedom and Interventionism* (B-29).

42.4   "Ideas sobre la Política Económica de la Postguerra" [Ideas About the Postwar Political Economy]. *Cuadernos Americanos.* 4:4 (July-August 1942) 87-99. No known English or German version.

42.5   "Hitler's Achilles Heel" (unsigned editorial). *The New York Times* (March 20, 1942). Mises' authorship verified by *New York Times* payment voucher found among his papers.

42.6   "Comenius" (unsigned editorial). *The New York Times* (March 28, 1942) 16C. On the 350th anniversary of the birth of Jan Amos Komensky (Comenius), Czech fighter against intolerance, oppression and injustice, "his hopes and longings are alive in the hearts of millions of Czechs." No payment voucher found among Mises' papers, but this unsigned editorial attributed to Mises on the strength of its subject matter, writing style, and date in Mrs. Mises' listing (*My Years with Ludwig von Mises*, 1976 ed., p.87; 1984 ed, p.84).

42.7   "The Nazis Under Blockade" (unsigned editorial). *The New York Times* (March 30, 1942). Mises' authorship verified by *New York Times* payment voucher found among his papers.

42.8   "Germany's Transport Problem" (unsigned editorial). *The New York Times* (April 13, 1942). Mises' authorship verified by *New York Times* payment voucher found among his papers.

42.9   "Reich Gets Big Shock: New Securities Ordinance Viewed as Blow at System." Letter to the Editor, *The New York Times* (June 21, 1942).

42.10   "Economic Nationalism and Peaceful Economic Cooperation." MSS found among Mises' papers, apparently written in early 1942.
        Reprinted in *Money, Method, and the Market Process* (B-28).

1943

43.1   "Super-National Organization Held No Way to Peace: Radical Change in Political Mentalities and Social and Economic Ideologies Viewed as Necessary in Order to Eradicate Economic Nationalism." Letter to the Editor. *The New York Times* (January 3, 1943) E-8. Listed in Margit von Mises' *My Years with Ludwig von Mises* (1st ed., p. 88; 2nd ed., p. 84) by the title of the typed manuscript, "The Problems of a Postwar Union of the Democratic Unions."
        Digest of this letter, "Post-War Viewpoints." *Washington News Digest.* (May 1943) 15-17.

43.2   "Socialism *versus* European Democracy." *The American Scholar*. 12:2 (Spring 1943) 220-231.

43.3   "A 'New' World Currency?" (unsigned editorial). *The New York Times* (March 30, 1943) p.20L. Mises' authorship verified by *New York Times* payment voucher.
Reprinted in *Austrian Economics Newsletter*. Auburn, Ala.: Ludwig von Mises Institute. 9:3 (Spring/Summer 1988) 7.

43.4   "Autarky and Its Consequences." Manuscript dated May 5, 1943. Included in *Money, Method, and the Market Process* (B-28).

43.5   "Industrial 'Empires'" (unsigned editorial). *The New York Times* (June 18, 1943). Mises' authorship verified by *New York Times* payment voucher.

43.6   "Inflation and Money Supply" (unsigned editorial). *The New York Times* (June 20, 1943) 12E. Mises' authorship of this editorial verified by *New York Times* payment voucher.

43.7   "British Post-War Problems" (unsigned editorial). *The New York Times* (July 25, 1943) p.10E. Mises' authorship verified by *New York Times* payment voucher.

43.8   "Another Risorgimento!" (unsigned editorial). *The New York Times* (July 31, 1943) p.12C. The new American Committee for Italian Democracy recalls the hopes of great Italians of the past who sought democracy and freedom. "Dictatorships have failed. The one in Italy could not even wage war efficiently . . . . It is men's hearts that are stirred today, in Italy by the vision of a restored freedom worth more than all the tattered rags of empire." Although no payment voucher was found among Mises' papers, this unsigned editorial attributed to Mises on the strength of its subject matter, writing style, and date included in Mrs. Mises' listing (*My Years with Ludwig von Mises*, 1976 ed., p.87; 1984 ed, p.84).

43.9   "'Elastic Expectations' and the Austrian Theory of the Trade Cycle." *Economica*. New Series. 10:39 (August 1943) 251-252. Comments on L. M. Lachmann's article in *Economica*, February 1943.

43.10   Review of Adolf Sturmthal's *The Tragedy of European Labor, 1918-1939* (Columbia University Press, 1943). *The American Economic Review*. 33:3 (September 1943) 702-705.

43.11   Review of Egon Ranshofen-Wertheimer's *Victory is Not Enough! The Strategy for a Lasting Peace* (Norton, 1942). *Economica*. New Series. 10:40 (November 1943) 318-319.

43.12   "The German Supply Problem" (unsigned editorial). *The New York Times* (December 26, 1943). According to the editorial, clues reach the U.S. occasionally through German newspaper stories as to why German technical experts reportedly "warned Hitler against a Russian campaign." The editorial cites the dreadful state of transport, the demolished roads and bridges, the need to construct thousands of miles of new highways and railroads with slave labor, 80% female, etc. Although no payment voucher for this editorial was found, it is attributed to Mises on the basis of subject matter, writing style, plus the fact that a copy dated in Mises' hand was found among his papers at Grove City College (Grove City, Penna.).

1944

44.1 "Big Business and the Common Man: High Living Standards in U.S. Came from Big Mass Production Enterprise." *Barron's*. 24:9 (February 28, 1944) 3.

44.2 "The Treatment of 'Irrationality' in the Social Sciences." *Philosophy and Phenomenological Research*. 4:4 (June 1944) 527-545.
Reprinted in *Money, Method, and the Market Process* (B-28).

44.3 Review of S. Leon Levy's *Nassau W. Senior: The Prophet of Modern Capitalism* (Bruce Humphries, 1943). *American Economic Review*. 34.2 (June 1944) 359-361.

44.4 "Causes of War." *Santa Ana* (California) *Register* (October 18, 1944) 4, 14. Text of October 17, 1944 lecture, not edited by Mises. For more information on this lecture, see Hoiles, "Books and Articles About Mises: 1956."

1945 Becomes Visiting Professor at New York University's Graduate School of Business, a position he maintained until his retirement in 1969.

45.1 Review of *A Challenge to Peacemakers: Conflicting National Aspirations in Central and Eastern Europe*. Joseph S. Roucek, editor. (Philadelphia: American Academy of Political and Social Science). *Annals 232* (1944). *The American Journal of International Law* (January 1945) 151-152.

45.2 "Planning for Freedom," an address, March 30, 1945, before the American Academy of Political Science in Philadelphia. Published, together with a speech by Rufus S. Tucker before the same audience, in a 24-page pamphlet: *Economic Planning* (New York: Dynamic America, 1945) 3-12.
       Included in the Mises anthology, *Planning for Freedom* (B-18).
       Reprinted in *Vital Speeches of the Day*. 11:14 (May 1, 1945) 441-444.
       Reprinted by Register Publishing Company (Santa Ana, California).
       Reprinted as "The Myth of the Mixed Economy." *American Affairs* (National
           Industrial Conference Board). 7:3 (July 1945) 169-174.
       Reprinted in *Freedom*. New York: Dynamic America. (March 1946) 1-14.
       Reprinted as "Interventionism and the Free Market." *Basic Economics: A Book of
           Readings*. Arthur D. Gayer, C. Lowell Harriss and Milton H. Spencer, eds.
           (Englewood Cliffs, N.J.: Prentice-Hall, 1951) 605-610.
       Spanish translation: "Planificar para la Libertad." *Tres Mensajes*. Buenos Aires:
           Centro de Difusión de la Economía Libre. (1959) 51-71.
       Spanish translation: "Planificar para la Libertad." *Temas Contemporáneos*. Mexico:
           Instituto de Investigaciones Sociales y Económicas. 5:68 (August 1, 1960).
       Spanish translation: "Planificación para la Libertad." *Tópicos de Actualidad*
           Guatemala: Centro de Estudios Económico-Sociales. 7:120 (February 15,
           1966).
       Spanish translation by Eduardo L. Suárez: "Planeación Para la Libertad." *Ludwig
           von Mises: Infatigable Luchador Contra la Economía Ficticia* [Ludwig von
           Mises: Indefatigable Fighter Against False Economics]. Mexico: Centro de
           Estudios en Economía y Educación. (1983) 55-67.

45.3   "The Clash of Group Interests." *Approaches to National Unity*, Fifth Symposium. New York: Conference on Science, Philosophy and Religion in their Relation to the Democratic Way of Life. (1945) 148-160.
> Included in monograph, *The Clash of Group Interests and Other Essays* (B-26).
> Included in *Money, Market, and the Market Process* (B-28).

45.4   "European Experiences with Price Control." *The Commercial and Financial Chronicle*. 162:4448 (December 20, 1945) 1ff.
> Included as "Inflation and Price Control" in *Planning for Freedom* (B-18).
> Reprinted as a separate 12-page pamphlet: "Inflation and Price Control." Irvington, N.Y.: Foundation for Economic Education, 1970.
> Inserted by Congressman John H. Rousselot in the *Congressional Record* as "Inflation -- Cause and Effect." 117:170 (Extension of Remarks, 92nd Congress, 1st session, November 10,1971) E12058.
> Last two sections published as "Price-Wage Freeze BAD, Says Economist," *Applied Christianity* (January 1973). 45-47.
> Spanish translation by Salvador Abascal Carranza: "Inflacion y Control de Precios," published in pamphlet form. Mexico: Instituto de la Integración Iberoamericana, 1982.

1946   Acquires U.S. citizenship. Appointed part-time staff member of the Foundation for Economic Education. Member, Economic Principles Commission of the National Manufacturers' Association and as such consulted in the preparation of *The American Individual Enterprise System*, 2 vols. (McGraw-Hill, 1946), the product of "the consensus of judgment among the Commission members."

46.1   "Business Under German Inflation." *The Commercial and Financial Chronicle*. 163:4470 (March 7, 1946) 1ff.

46.2   "The Trade Cycle and Credit Expansion." Memorandum (April 24, 1946) prepared for a committee of businessmen for whom he served as consultant.
> Included in *On the Manipulation of Money and Credit* (B-24).

1947   **Mont Pèlerin Society Founded**

47.1   "Le Capitalisme a-t-il fait faillite? [Has Capitalism Failed?]. *France-Amérique*. No. 80 (November 23, 1947) 1, 7.

47.2   "We Must Control Credit." Contribution to a symposium, "Can an Economic Depression be Avoided?" *The New York Times Magazine*. (April 13, 1947) 7, 71-75.

47.3   "Economics as a Bridge for Interhuman Understanding." Prepared for the Sixth Conference (1945) on Science, Philosophy and Religion, *Approaches to Group Understanding*." New York: Harper & Bros. (1947) 303-318. See also Mises' footnote to Moritz J. Bonne paper in this symposium, p.236.
> Included in *Economic Freedom and Interventionism* (B-29).

1948

48.1   "The Objectives of Economic Education." March 1, 1948. 14pp. mimeographed.
> First published in Spanish translation: "Los Objetivos Inmediatos de la Educación
> Económica." *Carta Mensual.* Mexico: Asociación de Banqueros). 3:27/28
> (July and August 1948) 92-103.
> Spanish translation by Lic. Gustavo R. Velasco, with Prologue by the translator,
> reprinted in pamphlet form. Mexico: Instituto Tecnológico de México,
> Asociación Mexicana de Cultura. (n.d.) 23 pp.
> Reprinted: *Temas Contemporáneos.* Mexico: Instituto de Investigaciones Sociales
> y Económicas. 6:72 (December 1, 1960).
> Reprinted as a booklet. Buenos Aires: Centro de Estudios Sobre la Libertad. (1960)
> 29pp.
> Major portion of original mimeographed version included in *Economic Freedom
> and Interventionism* (B-29) and in *The Freeman.* 41:4 (April 1991) 148-152.

48.2   "Stones into Bread, the Keynesian Miracle." *Plain Talk.* 2:6 (March 1948) 21-27.
> Included in *Planning for Freedom* (B-18).
> Included in *Critics of Keynesian Economics.* Henry Hazlitt, ed. Princeton, N.J.:
> Van Nostrand, 1960. 305-315.

48.3   "Should We Return to a Gold Standard?" Remarks in a Symposium, *Studies in Business
> Economics.* No. 17 (52pp.) New York: National Industrial Conference Board. (1948) 43.

1949

49.1   "Laissez Faire or Dictatorship." *Plain Talk.* 3:4 (January 1949) 57-64.
> Included in *Planning for Freedom* (B-18)
> Reprinted in *The Classical Liberal.* Caldwell, Idaho: Center for the Study of
> Market Alternatives. New Series. 2:1 (February 1992) 1-7.
> Dutch translation: "Laissez faire of dictatuur." *Vraagstukken van heden en morgen.*
> Comité ter Bestudering van Ordeningsvraagstukken. No.10.
> Spanish translation by Gustavo R. Velasco: "El Significado del Laissez Faire." *El
> Foro.* Mexico: Órgano de la Barra Mexicana, Colegio de Abogados). Second
> Series. 6:2 (June 1949) 81-92.
> Reprinted: *Temas Contemporáneos.* Mexico: Instituto de Investigaciones Sociales
> y Económicas. 7:78 (June 1, 1961).
> Reprinted: "Laissez Faire o Dictadura." *Tópicos de Actualidad.* Guatemala: Centro
> de Estudios Económico-Sociales. 7:161 (November 1, 1967).

49.2   "The Why of Human Action." *Plain Talk.* 3:12 (September 1949) 6-10. Prior to the
publication of Mises' *Human Action,* he was asked by *Plain Talk* why he wrote the book:
"Economics does not allow of any breaking up into special branches . . . . All economic
facts condition one another mutually. Each of the various economic problems must be
dealt with in the frame of a comprehensive system assigning its due place and weight to
every aspect of human wants and desires . . . . To provide such a comprehensive analysis is
the task of my book, *Human Action: A Treatise on Economics. "*
> First three paragraphs reprinted as "Economists and Politicians." *The Freeman*
> 6:3 (March 1956) 45.
> Included in *Economic Freedom and Interventionism* (B-29).

1950

50.1   *A Reading List for the Alert Citizen.* Irvington-on-Hudson, N.Y.: Foundation for Economic Education, 1950. 20pp. multilithed. A bibliography, with brief annotations, of 113 books.

50.2   "Benjamin M. Anderson Challenges the Philosophy of the Pseudo-Progressives." *Plain Talk.* 4:5 (February 1950) 51-58. A review of B. M. Anderson's *Economics and the Public Welfare* (Van Nostrand, 1949).
  Included in *Planning for Freedom* (B-18).
  Included in *Plain Talk: An Anthology from the Leading Anti-Communist Magazine of the 40s.* Isaac Don Levine, ed. (New Rochelle: Arlington House, 1976) 375-379.

50.3   "Economic Aspects of the Pension Problem." *The Commercial and Financial Chronicle.* 171:4884 (February 23, 1950) 793 (1)ff.
  Included in *Planning for Freedom* (B-18).

50.4   "Middle-of-the-Road Policy Leads to Socialism." *The Commercial and Financial Chronicle.* 171:4904 (May 4, 1950) 1ff. Address given at the University Club, New York, April 18, 1950.
  Reprinted as a pamphlet: South Holland, Illinois: Consumers-Producers Economic Service, January 1951.
  Included in *Planning for Freedom* (B-18).
  Discussed in *Faith and Freedom* (March 1952).
  Reprinted in *The Capitalist.* Brigham Young University, Young Conservative Club. 2::22 (March 17, 1964) 1-4.
  Reprinted as a booklet: South Holland, Illinois: Libertarian Press, 1965.
  Excerpt: "How Price Control Leads to Socialism." *The Freeman.* Irvington, N.Y.: Foundation for Economic Education. 16:6 (June 1966) 23-25.
  Two long excerpts in Mark Skousen's *Playing the Price Controls Game.* New Rochelle, N.Y.: Arlington House, 1977. 121-124.
  French translations of portions of this article plus excerpts from Article 51.3: "La Chaîne sans Fin des Interventions Économiques." *Angoisses et Espoirs de la Civilisation Occidentale* [Despair and Hope for Western Civilization]. Paris: Editions SEDIF. (1952) 7-17.
  Included in *L'Informateur* (*circa* January 23, 1975).
  Spanish translation in *Mercurio* (Buenos Aires).
  Reprinted from *Mercurio:* "La Cadena sin Fin de las Intervenciones Económicas." *Temas Contemporáneos.* Mexico: Instituto de Investigaciones Sociales y Económicas. 4:46 (October 1, 1958).
  Spanish translation: "El Camino del Medio Nos Lleva al Socialismo." Bogota, Colombia: Fundación para Estudios sobre la Libertad, n.d.
  Spanish translation: "El Intervencionismo Conduce al Socialismo." *Tres Mensajes.* Buenos Aires: Centro de Difusión de la Economía Libre, 1959. 7-27.
  Reprinted from Argentine translation: "El Intervencionismo Conduce al Socialismo." *Temas Contemporáneos.* Mexico: Instituto de Investigaciones Sociales y Económica. 8:96 (October 15, 1962).
  Spanish translation by Héctor Esteves H: "La Política del Camino del Centro Conduce al Socialismo." *Temas Contemporáneos.* Mexico: Instituto de Investigaciones Sociales y Económicas. 15:181 (November 15, 1969).

Reprinted: "El Intervencionismo Conduce al Socialismo." *Tópicos de Actualidad*
Guatemala: Centro de Estudios Económico-Sociales. 4:52 (January 1, 1963).

Reprinted: "Las Terceras Posiciones Conducen al Socialismo." Guatemala: Camara
de Comercio de Guatemala. 4 (October 1974) 86-92.

Spanish translation: "El Camino del Medio Nos Lleva al Socialismo." Bogota,
Colombia: Fundación para Estudios Sobre la Libertad, (1963 ?).

Spanish translation by Salvador Abascal Carranza from Libertarian Press edition of
Planning for Freedom: "La Política de Economía Mixta Conduce al
Socialismo." Mexico: Instituto de la Integración Iberoamericana, January
1983.

Included in *Resource Book on Agriculture*. Economics in Argumentation. Irvington,
N.Y.: Foundation for Economic Education, 1986-1987. Section 5.

Reprinted with "Liberty and Property" (Article 58.3). Foreword by Thomas J.
DiLorenzo. Auburn, Ala: Praxeology Press/Ludwig von Mises Institute,
[1992].

50.5   "The Alleged Injustice of Capitalism." *Faith and Freedom*. 1:7 (June 1950) 5-8.
Included as Part 3, Chapter 4, in *The Anti-Capitalistic Mentality* (B-19).
Reprinted in *Reflections on Faith and Freedom*. Los Angeles: Spiritual
Mobilization, 1952. 39-45.

50.6   "The Idea of Liberty is Western." *American Affairs*. 12 (October 1950) 207-211.
Included as Chapter 4, Sections 4 & 5 in *The Anti-capitalistic Mentality* (B-19).
Included in *Money, Method, and the Market Process* (B-28).

50.7   "Lord Keynes and Say's Law." *The Freeman*. New York. 1:3 (October 30, 1950) 83-85.
Included in *Planning for Freedom* (B-18).
Reprinted in *The Critics of Keynesian Economics*, Henry Hazlitt, ed. Princeton,
N.Y.: Van Nostrand, 1960. 315-321.

50.8   "The Economics of War." Chapter XXXIV of *Human Action* (B-16) published in booklet
form by *Christian Economics*. New York, 1950.
Abridgement of Chapter in *Plain Talk*. 4:1 (October 1949) 39-44.
Abridged version also in *Ideas on Liberty* Irvington, N.Y.: Foundation for
Economic Education. No.3 (November 1955) 59-65; reprinted in *Essays on
Liberty, III*. (Foundation for Economic Education, 1958) 385-396; also in
Free Trade: The Necessary Foundation for World Peace, Joan Kennedy
Taylor, ed. (Foundation for Economic Education, 1986. 77-83.
Spanish translation of excerpt, "Las Políticas de la Paz" [The Politics of Peace].
Resumen, Suplemento Mensual. Mexico. No. 14 (February 1967) 41.

1951

51.1   "True German History." *The Freeman*. New York. 1:8 (January 8, 1951) 250-251. A
review of Erich Eyck's *Bismarck and the German Empire* (Macmillan, 1950).

51.2   "Trends Can Change." *The Freeman*. New York. 1:10 (February 12, 1951) 300-301.
Included in *Planning for Freedom*, 1952 (B-18).
Spanish translation: "Las Tendencias Pueden Cambiar." *Civis*. Buenos Aires. 3
(December 1954).

51.3   "The Political Chances of Genuine Liberalism." *Farmand*. Oslo, Norway. February 7, 1951.

        Included in *Planning for Freedom* (B-18).

        French translation of portions of this article, plus excerpts from Article 50.4: "La Chaîne sans Fin des Interventions Économiques" (1952); see 50.4 above.

        Reprinted in French: *L'Informateur* (*circa* January 23, 1975).

        Spanish translation of extract: *Mercurio*. Buenos Aires; reprinted as "La Cadena Sin Fin de las Intervenciones Económicas."*Temas Contemporáneos*. Mexico: Instituto de Investigaciones Sociales y Económicas. 4:46 (October 1, 1958).

51.4   "Inflation: An Unworkable Fiscal Policy!" *The Commercial and Financial Chronicle*. 173:5006 (April 26, 1951) 1ff. Transcript of remarks at University of Chicago Law School Conference on Economics of Mobilization (April 6-8, 1951).

        Reprinted in *Defense, Controls and Inflation*. Aaron Director, ed. (University of Chicago Press, 1952) 107-110, 115-116 and 331-334.

        Reprinted in *New York University Alumni News* (November 1962).

        Included in *Economic Freedom and Interventionism* (B-29).

51.5   "Inflation: How Government Generates It and Then Endeavors to Shift Responsibility." *New York World Telegram and Sun*. (May 7, 1951). Written as guest columnist for Lawrence Fertig.

        Included in *Economic Freedom and Interventionism* (B-29).

51.6   "The Symptomatic Keynes." *The Freeman*. New York. 1:19 (June 18, 1951) 604-605. A review of R. F. Harrod's *The Life of John Maynard Keynes* (Harcourt, Brace & Co., 1951).

        Reprinted in *Christian Economics*. New York. 3 (August 28, 1951) 1, 4.

        Included in *Economic Freedom and Interventionism* (B-29).

51.7   *Ludwig von Mises' Seminar (June 25-July 6, 1951)*. Lecture notes transcribed by Bettina Bien, edited by Percy L. Greaves, Jr., not edited by Mises. Irvington, N.Y. : Foundation for Economic Education, 1951. 66 pp. multilithed.

51.8   "Inflation [misprinted "Injection" in some editions] Must End in a Slump." *New York Journal American*. (August 28, 1951). Written as guest columnist for Merryle Rukeyser.

        Included in *Economic Freedom and Interventionism* (B-29).

51.9   "The Trade Cycle." *The Freeman*. New York. 1:26 (September 24, 1951) 828-829. A review of Alvin H. Hansen's *Business Cycles and National Income* (New York: Norton, 1951).

        Included in *Economic Freedom and Interventionism* (B-29).

1952

52.1   "India's Economic Problem." *The Freeman*. New York. 2:8 (January 14, 1952) 250-252. A short review of four books:

        Clare and Harris Wofford, Jr.'s *India Afire* (John Day, 1951);

        George Catlin's *In the Path of Mahatma Gandhi* (Henry Regnery, 1950);

        Jawaharlal Nehru's *Independence and After: A Collection of Speeches, 1946-1949* (John Day, 1950); and

        John Ely Burchard, ed. *Mid-Century: The Social Implications of Scientific Progress* (Technology Press and Wiley, 1950).

52.2 "On the Confiscation of Rent and 'Man's Power to Reason'." *Henry George News.* 15 (February 1952) 8. Brief summary of Mises' lecture remarks, November 14, 1951.

52.3 "Our Leftist Economic Teaching." *The Freeman.* New York. 2:14 (April 7, 1952) 425-428. Review of Paul M. Sweezy's textbook on socialism (Harvard University's Economics Handbook Series). Included as "Economic Teaching at Our Universities" in *Planning for Freedom* (B-18).

> Excerpt in Walter Block, "Farm price controls, African famine and higher education: A combination that doesn't feed people." *Grainews* (Canada). (July 1983) 44.

52.4 "Capital Supply and American Prosperity." Address at the University Club of Milwaukee, October 13, 1952. Published by the author.

> Spanish translation: "La Existencia de Capital y la Prosperidad Americana." *Tres Mensajes.* Buenos Aires: Centro de Difusión de la Economía Libre, 1959. 29-50.
>
> Spanish translation: "La Afluencia de Capital y la Prosperidad Americana." *Tópicos de Actualidad.* Guatemala: Centro de Estudios Económico-Sociales. 2:22 (March 1, 1961).
>
> Included in the 4th (1980) edition of *Planning for Freedom* (B-18).
>
> Reprinted in *Perspectives on Public Policy.* Washington, D.C.: Council for a Competitive Economy, n.d.

52.5 "The Individual in Society." Extracted from *Human Action* (B-16). Published as *In Brief* Irvington, N.Y.: Foundation for Economic Education. 8:1 (January 1952).

> Included in *Essays on Liberty, I.* Foundation for Economic Education, 1952. 76-87.
>
> Spanish translation in *Mercurio* (Buenos Aires).
>
> Reprinted as "El Individuo en la Sociedad." *Temas Contemporáneos.* Mexico: Instituto de Investigaciones Sociales y Económicas. 3:37 (January 1, 1958).
>
> Reprinted in *The Freeman.* Irvington, N.Y. 21:6 (June 1971) 349-356 and 28:10 (October 1978) 624-631.
>
> Reprinted in *Free Market Economics: A Basic Reader.* Bettina Bien Greaves, compiler. Irvington, N.Y.: Foundation for Economic. 1975. 6-9.
>
> Reprinted in *When We Are Free.* 1st ed. [not 2nd], Lawrence W. Reed and Dale M. Haywood, eds. Midland, Mich.: Northwood Institute Press,1981. 79-86.
>
> Dutch translation of excerpt: "Vrijheid door Markteconomie." *Burgerrecht.* 7:273 (October 18, 1952) 9.
>
> Excerpt published as "A Page on Freedom." *The Freeman.* Irvington, N.Y. 35:3. (March 1985) 131.
>
> Included in *Economic Freedom and Interventionism* (B-29).

1953

53.1 "Freedom is Slavery." *The Freeman.* New York. 3:12 (March 9, 1953) 410-411. A review of Robert L. Hale's *Freedom Through Law, Public Control of Private Governing Power* (Columbia University Press, 1952).

> Spanish translation: "Libertad es Esclavitud." *Ideas Sobre la Libertad.* Buenos Aires: Centro de Estudios Sobre la Libertad. 1:3 (August 1959) 15-18.

53.2 "Agony of the Welfare State," *The Freeman.* New York. 3:16 (May 4, 1953) 555-557.

> Reprinted in *Free Economic Review* (India). (July 1953) 5, 12.
>
> Included in *Economic Freedom and Interventionism* (B-29).

53.3   "Economics Too Exciting." *The Freeman*. New York. 3:17 (May 18, 1953) 602. A review of R. H. Tawney's *The Attack and Other Papers* (Harcourt, Brace & Co., 1953).

53.4   "Free Port of the World." *The Freeman*. New York. 3:20 (June 29, 1953) 702. A review of Luis Montes de Oca's collection of essays (Mexico: Informador Económico).

53.5   "Gold versus Paper." *The Freeman*. New York. 3:21 (July 13, 1953) 744-746.
         Spanish translation: "Oro contra Papel." *Ideas Sobre la Libertad*. Buenos Aires: Centro de Estudios Sobre la Libertad. 1:1 (December 1958) 49-53.
         Included in *Economic Freedom and Interventionism* (B-29).

53.6   "Bemerkungen über die mathematische Behandlung nationalökonomischer Probleme" [Comments about the Mathematical Treatment of Economic Problems]. *Studium Generale*. Berlin-Goettingen-Heidelberg: Springer Verlag. 6:11 (December 1953) 662-665.
         English translation by Helena L. Ratzka: "Comments About the Mathematical Treatment of Economic Problems." *Journal of Libertarian Studies*. Oxford (England): Pergamon Press. 1:2 (1977) 97-100.

53.7   "Why Read Adam Smith Today?" Introduction to Adam Smith's *An Inquiry into the Nature and Causes of the Wealth of Nations: Selections* (1776). Chicago: Henry Regnery, Gateway Edition, 1953) iii-vi or v-x. (The page numbers differ in some editions.)
         Included in *Economic Freedom and Interventionism* (B-29).

1954

54.1   "Myrdal's Economics." *The Freeman*. New York. 4:14 (April 5, 1954) 496. A review of Gunnar Myrdal's *The Political Element in the Development of Economic Theory* (London: Routledge & Kegan Paul, 1953).

54.2   "Preface" to U.S. edition of W. H. Hutt's *The Theory of Collective Bargaining*. Glencoe, Illinois: The Free Press, 1954. 9-11.

54.3   Letter (May 24, 1954) to Mr. René A. Wormser, General Counsel for the Special Committee to Investigate Tax-Exempt Foundations. *Tax Exempt Foundations: Hearings before the Special Committee to Investigate Tax-Exempt Foundations and Comparable Organizations. Part II*. 945-1241. House of Representatives, 83rd Congress, 2nd Session (U. S. Government Printing Office, 1954), 1192. The full text of Mises' letter follows:

     Dear Mr. Wormser:
     Referring to your letter of May 13, 1954, I should like to submit the following remarks:
     I have in my books and articles critically analyzed the epistemological and political prepossessions that are responsible for the scientific sterility of the present-day academic treatment of the problems of human action, in this country as well as abroad. I think that the fanatical dogmatism prevailing in many faculties and the virtual boycott of all dissenters are among the most alarming symptoms of the actual crisis of western civilization.
     It is a fact that the intolerant practices of many university departments of the social sciences are lavishly financed by some rich foundations. These foundations are uncritically committed to the epistemological ideas and the political bias prevalent in the university faculties. But it was not foundations

that inaugurated this tendency and converted the professors to their own tenets. It was, on the contrary, the universities that converted the foundations to their opinions. The trustees and the staffs of the foundations were convinced that the best method they could choose was to put their trust in the professors. They were deluded by the prestige that the name universities enjoyed. They adopted the professor worship current in some European countries.

In the reports of the foundations and in the public utterances of their leading functionaries one does not discover any propositions about methods and techniques of social studies that would not be stereotyped repetitions of the slogans coined by the self-styled "unorthodox" professors long before American foundations began to spend money for these studies.

My answer to each of the three questions you formulate in the second paragraph of your letter is emphatically yes. For a justification of my point of view [concerning empirical studies] I refer to my publications.

With kindest regards,

Sincerely yours,
Ludwig von Mises

1955

55.1   "Government vs. Liberty." *The Freeman.* Irvington, N.Y.. 5:9 (March 1955) 394, 396. A review of Philip Cortney's *The Economic Munich* (Philosophical Library, N. Y., 1949).

55.2   "Inequality of Wealth and Incomes." *Ideas on Liberty, No.1.* Irvington, N.Y.: Foundation for Economic Education. (May 1955) 83-88.
> Reprinted in *Essays on Liberty, III.* Irvington, N.Y.: Foundation for Economic Education, 1958). 123-131.
> Spanish translation: "Desigualdad de riquezas e ingresos." *Ideas Sobre la Libertad* Buenos Aires: Centro de Estudios Sobre la Libertad. 2:6 (October 1960) 5-9; also in *Tópicos de Actualidad.* Guatemala: Centro de Estudios Económico-Sociales. 2:31 (November 1, 1961).
> Reprinted: "For a Free Economy."*The Washington World* (September 11, 1962) 8-9.
> Included in *Economic Freedom and Interventionism* (B-29).

55.3   "The Green-Eyed Monster." *The Freeman.* Irvington, N.Y. 5:17 (November 1955) 745-747. A review of William E. Rappard's *The Secret of American Prosperity* (Greenberg, 1955). Mises was incensed by the title given his review by the editor; he considered it a slur on Rappard, his friend and former colleague, director of the graduate institute in Geneva where Mises had taught.
> Included in *Economic Freedom and Interventionism* (B-29).

55.4   "Explodes Unification Fallacy." *Christian Economics.* New York. 7:20 (November 15, 1955) 3. Review of Hans F. Sennholz's *How Can Europe Survive?*" (Van Nostrand, 1955).
> Included in *Economic Freedom and Interventionism* (B-29).

55.5   "Ein Brief an den Herausgeber" [Letter to the Editor]. *Monatsblätter für Freiheitliche Wirtschaftspolitik.* 7 (November 1955) 392-393. Editor Muthesius had asked permission to reprint the chapter on cartels and monopoly in *Liberalism* (B-6). In reply Mises wrote: "What I was able to say on the subject in that book in 1927 represented only one stage in my efforts . . . . A complete treatment of the essence of monopoly is feasible only within the realm of comprehensive economic theory. This I tried to offer in my book *Human*

Action (B-16) .... There I believe I said everything that was to be said on this problem. If policy did not lay the basis for what is called in the United States 'conspiracy in restraint of trade,' there would be no monopoly problem. The politicians conduct a crusade against cartels while at the same time they are doing all they can to make cartelization possible .... The demagogy of the Department of Justice was revealed in the clearest light a few years ago when an enterprise which purchased foods for its numerous branches was investigated. The firm's return on these commodities nationwide was 7% and has been declining steadily in recent years. What it was rebuked for by the majority was that it *undersold* other domestic grocers. That must certainly appear unforgivable in the eyes of the government, whose pricing policy it is to raise the prices of all farm products considerably." Mises declined to express an opinion as to whether or not Germany should enact cartel legislation; all that was needed, he said, was to repeal protective tariffs and other interventions with market transactions. (Translated from the German)

1956   Fiftieth Anniversary of Mises' Doctorate.

56.1   "Luxuries into Necessities." *Newsletter.*   New York University Graduate School of
Business Administration. 1:4 (Spring 1956) 3.
   Slightly edited version in *The Freeman.* Irvington, N.Y. 6:8 (August 1956) 31.
   Spanish translation: "Lujos Que Se Convierten en Necesidades." *Hoja de*
      Información Económica. Mexico: Instituto de Investigaciones Sociales y
      Económicas. 12:288 (May 15, 1967); reprinted in *Mercurio* (Buenos Aires);
      also in *Espejo.* Mexico: Instituto de Investigaciones Sociales y Económicas.
      1:7 (September 15, 1960) 56-57.
   Included in *Economic Freedom and Interventionism* (B-29).

56.2   "The Plight of Business Forecasting." *National Review.* 1:20 (April 4, 1956) 17-18.
   Reprinted in *National Review Reader* (Bookmailer, N. Y., 1957).
   German translation: "Falsche Propheten." *Monatsblätter für freiheitliche*
      Wirtschaftspolitik. 7 (July 1956) 398-401.
   Included in *Economic Freedom and Interventionism* (B-29).

56.3   "Freedom and Government." *The Freeman.* Irvington, N.Y. 6:11 (November 1956) 62-64.
   Reprinted in *Colorado Springs Gazette Telegraph* (November 28, 1956) 28.

56.4   "Facts about the 'Industrial Revolution'." Extract from *Human Action* (B-16). 1st ed.,
613-619; 2nd ed., 618-624, 3rd ed. 617-623.
   Reprinted in *The Freeman.* Irvington, N.Y. 6:2 (February 1956) 48-55; also in
      Essays on Liberty, IV. Foundation for Economic Education, 1958. 158-170.
   Spanish translation: "Hechos Acerca de la Revolución Industrial." *Mercurio*
      (Buenos Aires); also in *Temas Contemporáneos.* Mexico: Instituto de
      Investigaciones Sociales y Económicas. 4:45 (September 1, 1958).
   Reprinted in *Free Market Economics: A Basic Reader.* Bettina Bien Greaves, comp.
      Irvington, N.Y.: Foundation for Economic Education, 1975) 257- 261.
   Also in *Free Markets or Famine.* V. Orval Watts, ed. Midland, Mich.: Ford Press,
      1967. 107-114; revised ed. (1975) 117-124.
   Portuguese translation: "A Verdade Sôbre a Revolução Industrial." São Paulo
      (Brazil): Instituto de Pesquisas e Estudos Sociais, [1964]. 15pp.
   Spanish translation: "Consideraciones en Torno a la más Popular Interpretación de
      la 'Revolución Industrial'." *Clásicos Contemporáneos* (Centro de
      Divulgación del Conocimiento Económico, Caracas). 1 (June 1985).

1957

57.1   "Der Sparer als Wahler" [The Saver as a Voter]. *Zeitschrift für das gesamte Kreditwesen.* 10:1 (January 1, 1957) 24-25.
       English translation by Bettina Bien Greaves in *Economic Freedom and Interventionism* (B-29).

57.2   "Vollbeschäftigung und Währungspolitik" [Full Employment and Monetary Policy]. *Schweizer Monatshefte.* 36:10 (January 1957) 745-751.
       English translation: *National Review.* 3:25 (June 22, 1957) 589-591.
       Reprinted in *Indian Libertarian* (Research Department, R. L. Foundation). 5:14 (September 15, 1957) A-C as Supplement No. 7.
       Included in *Economic Freedom and Interventionism* (B-29).

57.3   "Die Rolle der Vorstellung vom Volkseinkommen in der Weltpolitik" [The Role of the National Income Concept in World Policy]. *Wirtschaftsfragen der freien Welt: Festgabe zum 60. Geburtstag von Bundeswirtschaftsminister Ludwig Erhard.* [The Free World's Economic Problems: Festschrift on the Occasion of the 60th Birthday of West German Economic Minister Ludwig Erhard]. Erwin von Beckerath, Fritz W. Meyer, Alfred Müller-Armack, eds. Frankfurt/M: Fritz Knapp Verlag, 1957. 502-506.

57.4   "Die Wahrheit über den Interventionismus" [The Truth About Interventionism]. *Monatsblätter für Freiheitliche Wirtschaftspolitik.* 3:10 (October 1957) 599-607.
       Norwegian translation: "Den økonomiske frihet i våre dager." *Farmand.* 62:51-52 (December 21, 1957) 31-39.

57.5   "Het Staatsingrijpen Interventionisme en zign Gevolgen" [Government Interventionism and its Consequences]. *Burgerrecht* (September 21 & 28, 1957) 6-7, 8, respectively. Dutch translation of Mises' Amsterdam (September 16, 1957) address.
       Reprinted (pp.5-22), together with Dutch translation of Article 58.2 (pp.23-37) in a pamphlet. Amsterdam: Civitas Humana, [1959].

1958

58.1   "Economic Freedom in the Present Day World." *USA: An American Magazine of Fact and Opinion.* New York. 5:1 (January 17, 1958) 1-5. In 1938 at the instigation of French philosopher Professor Louis Rougier, a conference was held on economic freedom. Later meetings were prevented by World War II. In 1957, Centre Paul Hymans' chairman Paul Hatry proposed a similar conference. French economist Jacques Rueff queried the 1938 participants planning to attend the 1957 gathering. This article is Mises' response.
       First published in French: "La liberté économique dans le monde actuel." *Travaux du Colloque International du Libéralisme Économique*, Ostend, September 10-13, 1957 (Brussels: Éditions du Centre Paul Hymans) 267-278.
       Condensed in *Christian Economics.* New York. 10:19 (October 14, 1958) 1, 3.
       Spanish translation: "La Libertad Económica en el Mundo Actual" Buenos Aires: Centro de Difusión de la Economía Libre, 1959) 25pp.; reprinted in *Revista Defensa Nacional.* Buenos Aires. 1:2 (May-August 1962) 42-47; also in *Espejo.* Mexico: Instituto de Investigaciones Sociales y Económicas. 8:65 (May-June 1967) 25-37.
       Included in *Economic Freedom and Interventionism* (B-29).

58.2   "Wages, Unemployment and Inflation." *Christian Economics.* 10:5 (March 4, 1958) 1, 3.
            Reprinted as "The Economics and Politics of My Job: Wages, Unemployment, and
                Inflation." *The Freeman.* Irvington, N.Y. 8:5 (May 1958) 15-22, and as a
                pamphlet. Foundation for Economic Education, [n.d.]. 14pp.
            Reprinted in *Essays on Liberty, V.* Foundation for Economic Education, 1958.
                25-37.
            Included in *Planning for Freedom,* 2nd (1960) & later eds. (B-18).
            Reprinted in *Christian Economics.* New York. 19:19 (October 17, 1967) 1, 4.
            Reprinted again in *The Freeman.* Irvington, N.Y. 25:9 (September 1975) 529-536.
            Reprinted as part of Manufacturing Studies Course MFG 105: "Corporate Problems
                in the National Economy" (General Electric). pp. A-25 - A-28.
            Reprinted in *Free Market Economics: A Basic Reader.* Bettina Bien Greaves, comp.
                Irvington, N.Y.: Foundation for Economic Education, 1975) 122-125.
            Spanish translation: "Implicaciones Económicas y Políticas del Empleo: Salarios,
                Desempleo, Inflación." *Temas Contemporáneos.* Mexico: Instituto de
                Investigaciones Sociales y Económicas. 4:52 (April 1, 1959).
            Spanish translation: "Implicaciones Económicas y Políticas de Salarios, Desempleo
                e Inflacion." *Topicos de Actualidad.* Guatemala: Centro de Estudios
                Económico-Sociales. 1:4 (January 15, 1960); reprinted, *Topicos de
                Actualidad.* 21:459 (April 1, 1980) 43-53.
            Spanish translation: "Salarios, Desocupación e Inflacion." *Ideas sobre la Libertad*
                Buenos Aires: Centro de Studios Sobre la Libertad. 2:5 (June 1960) 6-13.
            Spanish translation: "Salarios, Desocupación e Inflación." Bogota: Fundación para
                Estudios sobre la Libertad, n.d.
            Also reprinted as "Salarios, Desempleo e Inflación." *Ideas Sobre la Libertad*
                Buenos Aires: Centro de Estudios Sobre la Libertad. 18:32 (June 1976) 25-
                32.
            Dutch translation: "Lonen, Werkloosheid en Inflatie," in a pamphlet, together with
                Dutch translation of Mises' address (Article 57.5). Amsterdam: Civitas
                Humana, [1959].
            Dutch translation reprinted later: *Burgerrecht.* 16:724 (November 25, 1961) 3.

58.3   "Liberty and Property." *The Commercial and Financial Chronicle.* 188:1675 (October 23,
            1958). Paper presented at Mont Pèlerin Society, September 8, 1958 (Princeton, N.J.).
            Italian translation: "Libertà e Proprietà." *Rivista Internazionale di Scienze
                Economiche e Commerciali.* 5:11 (1958).
            Spanish translation: "Libertad y Propiedad." *Ideas Sobre la Libertad.* Buenos Aires:
                Centro de Estudios Sobre la Libertad. 1:2 (April 1959) 13-26.
            Dutch translation of excerpt: "Vrijheid en Welvaart" [Freedom and Welfare].
                Burgerrecht. 16:728 (December 30, 1961) 7.
            Excerpt: *The Free Market Reader.* Llewellyn H. Rockwell, Jr., ed. Auburn, Ala.:
                Ludwig von Mises Institute, 1988. 56-61.
            Reprinted as a pamphlet. Auburn, Ala.: Ludwig von Mises Institute, 1988.
            Excerpts: *The Free Market.* Auburn, Ala: Ludwig von Mises Institute (October
                1987). 1-2, 6-7.
            Reprinted, with "Middle-of-the-Road Policy Leads to Socialism" (Article 50.4).
                Foreword by Thomas J. DiLorenzo. Auburn, Ala.: Praxeology Press/Ludwig
                von Mises Institute, [1992]).

58.4   "Prólogo." Gustavo R. Velasco's *Libertad y Abundancia.* Mexico: Editorial Porrua, 1958.
            xv-xviii.

1959

59.1 "Undeveloped Countries." *The Mont Pèlerin Quarterly.* 1:1 (April 1959) 19-21. Remarks at the September 13, 1958 session of the Mont Pèlerin Society (Princeton, N. J.).

59.2 "Capital and Interest: Eugen von Böhm-Bawerk and the Discriminating Reader." *The Freeman.* Irvington, N.Y. 9:8 (August 1959) 52-54. A review of the English translation by Hans F. Sennholz and George D. Huncke of the 1922 edition of Eugen von Böhm-Bawerk's 3-volume *Capital and Interest* (South Holland, Illinois: Libertarian Press, 1959).
  Reprinted in *The Exploitation Theory of Socialism-Communism.* 3rd rev. ed.
    South Holland, Illinois: Libertarian Press, 1975. Appendix.
    N.B. *The Exploitation Theory* . . . is an extract from Böhm-Bawerk's
    Capital and Interest (Libertarian Press, 1959).
  Included in *Economic Freedom and Interventionism* (B-29).

59.3 Comments in a "Symposium on Keynes." *Christian Science Monitor.* Second Section, (September 11, 1959) 9.

59.4 "The Soviet System's Economic Failure." *New York World-Telegram and Sun* (October 5, 1959) 31, 34. Written as guest columnist for Lawrence Fertig.
    Spanish translation: "Fracaso Económico del Sistema Soviético." *Ideas Sobre la
      Libertad.* Buenos Aires: Centro de Estudios Sobre la Libertad. 2:4
      (December 1959) 16-18.
    Dutch translation: "De mislukking van Rusland's economische politiek."
      Burgerrecht: Special edition, 1959-1960. 13:630 (December 31, 1959) 19.
    Included in *Economic Freedom and Interventionism* (B-29).

59.5 "Bemerkungen über die ideologischen Wurzeln der Währungskatastrophe von 1923" [Remarks on the Ideological Roots of the 1923 Monetary Catastrophe]. *Freundesgabe zum 12. Oktober 1959 für Albert Hahn.* [Friendly presentation on occasion of Hahn's 70th birthday]. Frankfurt am Main: Fritz Knapp Verlag, 1959. 54-58.

59.6 "Liberalismus: (II) Wirtschaftlicher Liberalismus" [Economic Liberalism]. *Handwörterbuch der Sozialwissenschaften..* Stuttgart: Gustav Fischer, 1959. No. 23. 596-603.

59.7 "Markt" [The Market]. *Handwörterbuch der Sozialwissenschaften.* Stuttgart: Gustav Fischer, 1959. No. 27. 131-136.

59.8 "The Plight of the Underdeveloped Nations." n.d. MSS found among Mises' papers, possibly written in connection with the September 1958 Mont Pèlerin meeting at Princeton, N.J. when Mises spoke briefly on the subject. See 59.1 above.
    First published in *Money, Method, and the Market Process* (B-28).

59.9 Six lectures (June 1959) presented in Argentina under the auspices of the Centro de Difusión de la Economía Libre (later the Centro de Estudios sobre la Libertad). Newspaper accounts about his lectures were published at the time in the Argentine press, see *La Prensa,* "Books and Articles About Mises: 1959." The lectures themselves were published posthumously as *Economic Policy: Thoughts for Today and Tomorrow* (B-27).

1960

60.1   "The Economic Foundations of Freedom." *Christian Economics.* New York. 12:2 (January 26, 1960) 1-2.

> Reprinted in *The Freeman.* Irvington, N.Y. 10:4 (April 1960) 44-52.
>
> Reprinted in *Essays on Liberty, VII..* Foundation for Economic Education, 1960. 36-49.
>
> Dutch translation in 2 parts: "De economische grondvesten van recht en vrijheid" [Economic Fundamentals of justice and freedom] and "Welvaaret bedreigd door staatsinmenging" [Prosperity threatened by government interference]. *Burgerrecht.* 15:657/659 (July 16/30, 1960) 19 & 5 respectively.
>
> Reprinted in the *Indian Libertarian;* excerpts in *The Plain-Speaker* (London). 1:2 (May & June 1965) 15; and in *Intelligence Survey.* Melbourne (Australia). 14:10 (August 1965) 6.
>
> Included in *Economic Freedom and Interventionism* (B-29).

60.2   "Liberty and Its Antithesis." *Christian Economics.* New York. 12:15 (August 1, 1960) 1, 3. A review of F.A. Hayek's *The Constitution of Liberty* (Chicago: University of Chicago Press, 1959).

> Reprinted in *Planning for Freedom,* 4th (1980) edition (B-18).
>
> Included in *Economic Freedom and Interventionism* (B-29).

60.3   "Socialism, Inflation and the Thrifty Householder." *Christian Economics.* 12:19 (October 18, 1960) 1, 3.

> Included in *Economic Freedom and Interventionism* (B-29).

60.4   "Foreword." Israel Kirzner's *The Economic Point of View.* Princeton, N.J.: D. Van Nostrand, 1960. vii-viii.

> Included in *Economic Freedom and Interventionism* (B-29).

1961   Mises' 80th Birthday.   Honored by Mont Pèlerin Society.

61.1   "Foreign Spokesmen for Freedom." *The Freeman.* Irvington, N.Y. 11:3 (March 1961) 14-15.

> Included in *Economic Freedom and Interventionism* (B-29).

61.2   "On Equality and Inequality: The Low Estate of the 'Common Man' in the Philosophy of the Left." *Modern Age.* Chicago. 5:2 (Spring 1961) 139-147.

> Spanish translation: "Igualdad y Desigualdad." *Ideas Sobre la Libertad.* Buenos Aires: Centro de Estudios Sobre la Libertad. 2:8 (October 1961) 4-14.
>
> German translation: "Gleichheit und Ungleichheit." *Monatsblätter für freiheitliche Wirtschaftspolitik.* 7:10 (October 1961) 597-605.
>
> Included in *Modern Age: The First Twenty-Five Years: A Selection.* George A. Panichas, ed. Indianapolis: LibertyPress, 1988. 94-102.
>
> Included in *Money, Method, and the Market Process* (B-28).

61.3   "Unemployment and the Height of Wage Rates." *Christian Economics* (New York). 13:8 (April 18, 1961) 1, 3.

> Included in *Economic Freedom and Interventionism* (B-29).

61.4   "The Marxian Theory of Wage Rates." *Christian Economics*. New York. 13:11 (May 30, 1961) 1, 3. Part One of address at Spring 1961 meeting of the Christian Freedom Foundation.

        Reprinted in *The Exploitation Theory of Socialism-Communism* (Extract from Eugen Böhm-Bawerk's *Capital and Interest*). South Holland, Illinois: Libertarian Press, 1975. 145-151.

        Included in *Economic Freedom and Interventionism* (B-29).

61.5   "The Marxian Class Conflict Doctrine." *Christian Economics*. New York. 13:18 (October 3, 1961) 1, 3. Part Two of address at Spring 1961 meeting of the Christian Freedom Foundation.

        Included in *Economic Freedom and Interventionism* (B-29).

61.6   "Niet hinken op twee gedachten" [Do Not Hesitate Between Two Doctrines]. *Burgerrecht* 16:715 (September 23, 1961) 6-7. Dutch language translation of Mises' comments on "full employment," credit expansion, price and wage controls.

61.7   "Small and Big Business" (excerpts). *U.S.A.: An American Magazine of Fact and Opinion*. New York. 8:19 (September 22, 1961) 7-8. Remarks at Mont Pèlerin Society (Turin, Italy) meeting, September 1961.

        Reprinted in *Il Politico*. Milan: University of Pavia. 27:2 (1962) 264-278.

        Included in *Economic Freedom and Interventionism* (B-29).

61.8   "Epistemological Relativism in the Sciences of Human Action." *Relativism and the Study of Man*. Helmut Schoeck & James W. Wiggins, eds. Princeton, N.J.: Van Nostrand, 1961. 117-134. Paper prepared for Symposium on Relativism and the Study of Man, Emory University, September, 1959.

        Included in *Money, Method, and the Market Process* (B-28).

61.9   "Kapitalbildung und die Lehre vom Wachstum" [Capital Creation and the Theory of Growth]. *Wirtschaft, Gesellschaft und Kultur, Festgabe für Alfred Müller-Armack* [Economy, Society and Culture: Festschrift for Alfred Müller-Armack]. Franz Greiss & Fritz W. Meyer, eds. Berlin: Duncker & Humblot, 1961. 159-165.

61.10   "Foreword." Louis Baudin's *A Socialist Empire: The Incas of Peru*. Princeton, N.J.: Van Nostrand, 1961. v-xi.

        Spanish translation: "Reflexiones Sobre el Imperio Socialista de los Incas" [Reflections on the Socialist Empire of the Incas]. *Orientación Económica*. Caracas (Venezuela); reprinted in *Topicos de Actualidad*. Guatemala: Centro de Estudios Economico-Sociales. 10:192 (February 15, 1969) 13-19.

61.11   "The Elite Under Capitalism." First published in Italian translation as "L'Elite Nella Società Capitalistica." *Rivista Internazionale di Scienze Economiche e Commerciali* . 8:7 (1961).

        First English-language publication: *The Freeman*. Irvington, N.Y. 12:1 (January 1962) 3-11.

        Excerpt: *The South Australian Farmer*. Adelaide. April 13, 1962.

        Reprinted in *The Freeman*. Irvington, N.Y. 20:6 (June 1970) 367-375; also in *Essays on Liberty, IX*. Foundation for Economic Education, 1962. 76-89.

        French translation of excerpt: "Les fruits du capitalisme" [The Fruits of Capitalism]. *L'Informateur des Chefs d'Entreprises Libres*. Lyon & Paris. (January 15, 1966) 2.

Reprinted in *Free Markets or Famine.* V. Orval Watts, ed. Midland, Mich.: Ford
Press, 1967. 95-104; 105-114 in revised (1975) edition.

Reprinted in *Free Market Economics: A Basic Reader.* Bettina Bien Greaves,
compiler. Irvington, N.Y.: Foundation for Economic Education, 1975.
85-89.

Reprinted in *The Federalist Papers, No. 86.* James Ervin Norwood, George W.
Nilsson & Joseph L. Call, eds. Waco, Tex.: Friends of Freedom Publishers,
1988. 113-126.

Included in *Economic Freedom and Interventionism* (B-29).

1962   **Awarded Austrian Medal of Honor for Science and the Arts**

62.1   "Freedom Has Made a Comeback: Breaking the Spell of Conformity." *The New Guard.* 2:3
(March 1962) 15. Remarks at Young Americans for Freedom (Madison Square Garden, New
York) Freedom Rally. (March 7, 1962).

Reprinted in *Economic Freedom and Interventionism* (B-29).

62.2   "A Dangerous Recommendation for High School Economics." *Christian Economics.* New
York. 14:7 (April 3, 1962) 1, 3. A review of the National Task Force Report on Economic
Education (1961) of the Committee for Economic Development and American Economic
Association.

Included in *Economic Freedom and Interventionism* (B-29).

62.3   "A New Treatise on Economics." *New Individualist Review.* University of Chicago. 2:3
(Autumn 1962) 39-42. A review of Murray N. Rothbard's *Man, Economy and State*
(Princeton, N.J.: D. Van Nostrand, 1962).

Spanish translation: "Un Nuevo Tratado de Economia." *Ideas Sobre la Libertad* .
Buenos Aires: Centro de Estudios Sobre la Libertad. 5:19 (December 1964)
60-64.

Included (pp. 323-326) in *New Individualist Review.* Indianapolis: Liberty Fund,
1981). Bound volume complete (April 1961 through Winter 1968 inclusive)
containing all issues of the *Review* ever published).

Included in *Economic Freedom and Interventionism* (B-29).

62.4   "Un episodio significativo" [A Significant Incident]. *Il Maestro dell'Economia di Domani*
[The Master of Tomorrow's Economy]. Edizioni di "Via Aperta." Verona: Casa Editrice
l'Economista, 1962. 27-28. A posthumous tribute of several authors to Luigi Einaudi,
President of the Republic of Italy 1948-1955, who had helped control Italy's post-World
War II inflation. Unable to contribute an article because he was recovering from minor
surgery, Mises wrote a letter to Angelo Charles Casteli (March 19, 1962) which was
printed as his tribute to Einaudi. A translation from the published Italian version follows:

"I am sorry that my health does not permit me to pay tribute as I would
have liked to the memory of Luigi Einaudi, great scientist, Italian patriot and one
of the most illustrious economists and statesmen of our time. It was an honor to
be his friend.

"I shall limit myself today to reporting one incident, which seems
indicative of the character of the man.

"In 1926, thanks to Laura Spelman Rockefeller, I met Einaudi for the
first time. I was traveling in the United States for several months in the company
of the Dutch historian Huizinga, the ethnologist Malinowski, and several other
noted scholars. At the end of our trip, the group of professors met with the

economic faculty of Harvard University. There a heated debate developed, presided over by F. W. Taussig, concerning the economic situation. As a result of this analysis, forecasts for the future were pessimistic.

"Einaudi contributed little to the discussion. But later, as we were returning to the hotel, he addressed me with these few words: 'There are certainly reasons for being pessimistic; but I believe we should remember the words of Lincoln, "It is not possible to fool all of the people all of the time".' It was only this observation by Einaudi that enabled my hopes for Italy and the rest of the world to revive once more.

"The future proved him right and permitted him to play a decisive role in the recovery of his country from the horrors of tyranny and war. His contributions belong to history."

62.5   "Wage Earners and Employers." Remarks recorded for broadcast on the U.S. Steel Concert Hour, May 17, 1962. A transcript of the broadcast appeared in *The Freeman.* 38:5 (May 1988) 172-173. Mises addressed the question: "Are the interests of the American wage earners in conflict with those of their employers, or are the two in agreement?" He concluded: "In fact, good profits and high real wages go hand in hand."

Included in *Economic Freedom and Interventionism* (B-29).

62.6   "Tribute to F.A. von Hayek." Written for a banquet in Hayek's honor in Chicago, May 24, 1962, which Mises was unable to attend due to his busy schedule and his age. Published in Margit von Mises' *My Years with Ludwig von Mises*. Appendix One in 1st ed. (New Rochelle, N.Y.: Arlington House, 1976); Appendix Two in 2nd ed. (Cedar Falls, Iowa: Center for Futures Education, 1984).

1963

63.1   "The Economic Role of Saving and Capital Goods." *The Freeman.* Irvington, N.Y. 13:8 (August 1963) 28-33.

         Reprinted in *The Construction News.* 29 (September 23, 1963) 4-5, 15.

         Reprinted in *Essays on Liberty, XI..* Foundation for Economic Education, 1964. 116-124.

         Spanish translation: "El Papel de Los Ahorros y Bienes de Capital." *Ideas Sobre la Libertad* . Buenos Aires: Centro de Estudios Sobre la Libertad. 10:27 (November 1970) 13-18.

         Reprinted in *Free Market Economics: a Basic Reader.* Bettina Bien Greaves, compiler. Foundation for Economic Education, 1975. 74-76.

         Reprinted in *World Research INK.* San Diego. 1:8 (May 1977) 6, 11.

         Included in *Economic Freedom and Interventionism* (B-29).

63.2   "Siegfried von Strakosch (1867-1933)." *Neue Oesterreichische Biographie ab 1815: Grosse Oesterreicher* [New Austrian Biographies from 1815: Noted Austrians]. Vienna: Amalthea-Verlag. Vol.15 (1963) 160-165.

1964

64.1   "Zukunft des Dollar, Zukunft der Demokratie" [The Future of the Dollar, the Future of Democracy]. *Zeitschrift für das gesamte Kreditwesen.* 17:1 (January 1, 1964) 14-15.

64.2   "Professor Hutt on Keynesianism." *The Freeman.* Irvington, N. Y. 14:1 (January 1964) 57-59. A review of W.H. Hutt's *Keynesianism: Retrospect and Prospect* (Chicago: Henry Regnery, 1963).
         Included in *Economic Freedom and Interventionism* (B-29).

64.3   "A New Primer on Economics." *The Individualist.* Philadelphia: Intercollegiate Society of Individualists. 3:1 (January 1964) 5. A review of Faustino Ballvé's *Essentials of Economics: A Brief Survey of Principles and Policies.* Translated by Arthur Goddard from the Spanish: *Diez Lecciones de Economía* (1956). (Princeton: Van Nostrand, 1963).

64.4   "Deception of Government Intervention." *Christian Economics.* New York. 16:3 (February 4, 1964) 1, 3.
         Included in *Economic Freedom and Interventionsim* (B-29).

64.5   "Wage Interference by Government." *Christian Economics.* New York. 16:9 (April 28, 1964) 1, 3.
         Reprinted in *Human Events.* Washington, D.C. 24:20 (May 16, 1964) 6.
         Included in *Economic Freedom and Interventionism* (B-29).

64.6   "Das Eigentum in der Marktwirtschaft" [Property in the Market Economy]. *Monatsblätter für freiheitliche Wirtschaftspolitik.* 10:12 (December 1964) 725-729. Part I of July 1964 lecture, Freiburg, Germany: "Eigentum an Produktionsmitteln in der Marktwirtschaft" [Private Ownership of the Means of Production in the Market Economy]. See 65.1 for Part II.

64.7   "A National Policy for Peace." *The Freeman.* Irvington, N.Y. 14 (August 1964) 17-19. Excerpt from *Human Action.* 1st ed.(1949) 682-684; 2nd ed. (1963) 686-688; 3rd ed. (1966) 685-688.
         Included in *Free Trade: The Necessary Foundation for World Peace.* Joan Kennedy Taylor, ed. Foundation for Economic Education, 1986. ix-xi.

1965   Appointed Visiting Professor at Plano University (Texas).

65.1   "Monopole--Dichtung und Wahrheit" [Monopoly -- Fiction and Truth]. *Monatsblätter für freiheitliche Wirtschaftspolitik.* 11:1 (January 1965) 40-47. Part II of July 1964 lecture, Freiburg, Germany: "Eigentum an Produktionsmitteln in der Marktwirtschaft" [Private Ownership of the Means of Production in the Market Economy]. See 64.6 for Part I.

65.2   "Ein Wort zum Monopolpreisproblem" [A Word on the Monopoly-Price Problem]. *Vom Sinn der Konzentration: Beiträge aus Wissenschaft und Praxis. Volkmar Muthesius zum 65. Geburtstag am 19. März 1965.* [On the Meaning of Concentration: Contributions to Theory and Practice. To Volkmar Muthesius on his 65th Birthday, March 19, 1965]. Frankfurt am Main: Fritz Knapp Verlag, 1965. 31-35.
         Reprinted in *Monatsblätter für freiheitliche Wirtschaftspolitik.* 11:5 (May 1965) 270-272.

65.3   "The Gold Problem." *The Freeman.* Irvington, N.Y. 15:6 (June 1965) 3-8.
  Spanish translation: "El Problema del Oro." *Tópicos de Actualidad* . Guatemala:
   Centro de Estudios Económico-Sociales. 6:109 (September 1, 1965).
  Reprinted in *Free Market Economics: A Basic Reader.* Bettina Bien Greaves,
   compiler. Foundation for Economic Education, 1975. 136-139.
  Reprinted in *Planning for Freedom,* 4th ed., 1980 (B-18).
  Included in *Freedom and Money* (pamphlet). Irvington, N.Y.: Foundation for
   Economic Education, [1988].

1966

66.1   "Wilhelm Roepke, RIP." *National Review.* New York. 18:10 (March 8, 1966) 200.
  Spanish translation: "Descanse en Paz Wilhelm Roepke." *Espejo.* Mexico. 7:60
   (July-August 1966) 12-14.
  Spanish translation: "Wilhelm Roepke R.I.P." *Ideas Sobre la Libertad.* Buenos
   Aires: Centro de Estudios Sobre la Libertad, 7:23 (October 1966) 4-5.

66.2   "Observations on the Russian Reform Movement." *The Freeman.* 16:5 (May 1966) 23-29.
  Included in *The Libertarian Alternative: Essays in Social and Political Philosophy.*
   Tibor R. Machan, ed. (Chicago: Nelson-Hall, 1974) 343-349.
  Included in *Money, Method, and the Market Process* (B-28).

66.3   "The Supremacy of the Market." *The Freeman..* New York. 16:10 (October 1966)17-20.
Excerpt from *Planned Chaos* (B-14) 27-34.

66.4   "The Outlook for Saving and Investment." *Farmand.* Oslo (Norway). Anniversary issue
(February 12, 1966) 24-25.
  Spanish translation: "Perspectivas del Ahorro y la Inversión." *Orientación*
   Económica. Caracas: Instituto Venezolano de Análisis Económico y Social.
   29 (November 1968) 29-30.
  Spanish translation by Gustavo R. Velasco: "Perspectivas del Ahorro y la
   Inversion." *Hoja de Información Económica* . Mexico: Instituto de
   Investigaciones Sociales y Económicas. 15:354 (February 15, 1970).
  Reprinted in Spanish: *Boletin Semanal.* Colombia. 5:222 (October 5-12,1970) 14.
  Reprinted in Spanish: *Espejo.* Mexico. 13:98 (November-December, 1972), 44-47.
  Included in *Economic Freedom and Interventionism* (B-29).

66.5   "Some Observations on Current Economic Methods and Policies." Unpublished 16-page
manuscript, dated June 14, 1966, found among Mises' papers. First published in *Money,*
Method, and the Market Process (B-28).

1967

67.1   "On the International Monetary Problem." *American Opinion.* Belmont, Mass. 10:2
(March 1967) 23-28.
  Spanish translation: "Consideraciones sobre el Problema Monetario Internacional."
   Ideas Sobre la Libertad. Buenos Aires: Centro de Estudios Sobre la Libertad.
   9:25   (November 1968) 8-16.
  Included in *Economic Freedom and Interventionism* (B-29).

67.2   "El Práctico." *Espejo.* Mexico. 8:68 (November-December, 1967) 33-35. Spanish translation of an unidentified excerpt.

67.3   "Hundred Years of Marxian Socialism." Unpublished 29-page manuscript found among Mises' papers after his death. Written for presentation at the University of Chicago, January 24, 1967. Mises was unable to attend due to illness. This manuscript first published in *Money, Method, and the Market Process* (B-28).

67.4   "On Some Atavistic Economic Ideas." First published in French: "Du Caractère Atavique de Quelques Idées Économique." *Les Fondements Philosophiques des Systèmes Économiques.* Festschrift for Jacques Rueff upon the occasion of his 70th birthday. Paris: Payot, 1967. 317-319.
    Included in *Economic Freedom and Interventionism* (B-29).

1968

68.1   "Wirtschaft und Staat" [The Market and the State]. *Schweizer Monatshefte.* 48:1 (April 1968) 13-16. German translation of an English-language manuscript, "The Market and the State."
        English-language version: *Medical Student: Family Doctor: Citizen.* N. M. Camardese, ed. Ashland, Ohio: Smail Creative Printing, 1972. 205-209.
        German-language version: "Wirtschaft und Staat." *Monatsblätter für freiheitliche Wirtschaftspolitik.* 14:6 (June 1968) 354-357.
        Excerpt: "The Market and the State." (A Page on Freedom #27). *The Freeman.* Irvington, N.Y. 36:1 (January 1986) 4.
        Spanish translation: "El Mercado y el Estado." *Comercio e Industria.* San Salvador. 1:48 (December 1989) 70; *La Prensa.* Honduras. (March ?, 1990); *Temas* New York. 40:465 (December 30, 1989) 37; and *Libre Empresa.* 1:3 (March-April 1990) 2.
    Included in *Economic Freedom and Interventionism* (B-29).

1969   Cited by the American Economic Association as "Distinguished Fellow of the Year." Retires as Visiting Professor at New York University.

69.1   "Capitalism versus Socialism." *The Intercollegiate Review.* Bryn Mawr, Penna.: Intercollegiate Studies Institute. 5:3-4 (Spring 1969) 133-139.
        Included in *Money, Method, and the Market Process* (B-28).

69.2   "On Current Monetary Problems." Lansing, Mich.: Constitutional Alliance, 1969. 30-page minibook. Interview of Mises by Percy L. Greaves, Jr.
        Spanish translation: "Sobre los Problemas Monetarios Actuales." *Temas Contemporáneos.* Mexico: Instituto de Investigaciones Sociales y Económicas. 20:238 (August 15, 1974).
    Included in *Economic Freedom and Interventionism* (B-29).

1973

73.1   "Foreword" (dated September 16, 1970) to Percy L. Greaves, Jr's. *Understanding the Dollar Crisis*. Belmont, Mass.: Western Islands, 1973; 2nd ed., Dobbs Ferry, N.Y.: Free Market Books, 1984. xi-xiii.
        Included in *Economic Freedom and Interventionism* (B-29).

1973   **October 10**   **Mises dies in New York City at age 92.**

*   *   *

Posthumous Publications

1979

79.1   "Interventionismus" [Interventionism]. *Monatsblätter für freiheitliche Wirtschaftspolitik.* 25 (1979) 64-71. Excerpt from Chapter 3, Sections v, vi and vii, pp. 82-94 of *Im Namen des Staates oder Die Gefahren des Kollektivismus* (B-24). This article is *not* the same as Mises' two other articles called "Interventionism," 26.5 (1926) or 80.2 (1980).

79.2   "Capitalism." *The Freeman.* Irvington, N.Y. 29:12 (December 1979) 707-717. The first of Mises' June 1959 lectures in Argentina; Chapter 1 of *Economic Policy: Thoughts for Today and Tomorrow* (B-27).
        Inserted by Congressman Ron Paul in *Congressional Record*, Extension of
            Remarks (December 6, 1979) E5970-5973.

1980

80.1   "Socialism." *The Freeman.* Irvington, N.Y. 30:1 (January 1980) 35-49. Mises' second June 1959 lecture in Argentina; Chapter 2 of *Economic Policy* (B-27).
        Spanish translation by Julio Cole: "El Socialismo." *Tópicos de Actualidad.*
            Guatemala: Centro de Estudios Económico-Sociales. Part 1, 21:460 (April
            15, 1980) 54-62; Part 2, 21:461 (May 1, 1980) 63-72.
        Reprinted in *The Morality of Capitalism.* Mark W. Hendrickson, ed. Irvington,
            N.Y.: Foundation for Economic Education, 1992. 45-56.

80.2   "Interventionism." *The Freeman.* Irvington, N. Y. 30:2 (February 1980) 84-96. Mises' third June 1959 lecture in Argentina; Chapter 3 of *Economic Policy* (B-27). This is *not* the same as Mises' two other articles called "Interventionism," 26.5 and 79.1.
        Reprinted in *Immigrants in Search of Freedom, 1683-1983.* Camarillo, Calif.: The
            Tricentennial Committee of 300 Years of German Immigration to the USA,
            1683-1983. 71-82.
        Spanish translation: "El Intervencionismo." *Temas Contemporáneos.* Mexico.
            27:320 (June 15, 1981) 3-18.

80.3   "Inflation." *The Freeman.* Irvington, N.Y. 30:3 (March 1980) 151-163. Mises' fourth June 1959 lecture in Argentina; Chapter 4 of *Economic Policy* (B-27).

80.4   "Foreign Investment." *The Freeman.* Irvington, N.Y. 30:4 (April 1980) 240-251. Mises' fifth lecture in Argentina; Chapter 5 of *Economic Policy* (B-27).

80.5   "Politics and Ideas." *The Freeman.* Irvington, N.Y. 30:5 (May 1980) 289-298. Mises' sixth June 1959 lecture in Argentina; Chapter 6 of *Economic Policy* (B-27).

1981

81.1   "The Wisdom of Ludwig von Mises." *The Freeman.* Irvington, N.Y. 31:9 (September 1981). Memorial issue in honor of the 100th anniversary of Mises' birth, consisting almost entirely (pp.518-572) of quotations from *Human Action* selected by George Koether, arranged alphabetically by topics in dictionary format. Also includes "*Human Action* Reappraised" (pp.573-576) by John Chamberlain.

     South African reprint. Durban: Philip H. Moore, 1981. 28pp

     Spanish translation: "La Sabiduría de Ludwig von Mises." *Ideas sobre la Libertad*

         Buenos Aires: Centro de Estudios sobre la Libertad. 23:41 (April 1982).

AUDIOTAPES

As far as the compilers have been able to determine, only three talks by
Mises were audiotaped and made available to the public on cassettes.

1958   "Liberty and Property." Talk given at the opening session of the Mont Pèlerin Society
        meeting, Princeton, N.J., September 8, 1958. See Article 58.3.   Audio-Forum cassette
        #400, 44 minutes.

1962   "Austrian School of Economics." Talk given at New York University Faculty Club, May 2,
        1962. Introduction by William H. Peterson. Mises speaks of the intellectual life in Vienna
        between the two World Wars and the contributions to the "internationalization of science and
        teaching" made by the participants in his private seminar. Audio-Forum casette #900. 35
        minutes.

1970   "Socialism vs. Free Market Exchange." Talk in Seattle, Wash., May 2, 1970. Also sold
        under the title of "Why Socialism Always Fails." Introduction by Norbert Einstein. Written
        questions from the audience, read aloud by Percy L. Greaves, Jr., answered by Mises.
        Socialism is popular because people are convinced that it will be *their* ideas and *their* plans
        which will prevail; socialism fails because conflicts arise as the members of one faction try to
        force others to conform; the market has succeeded because it enables persons with *different*
        ideas and *different* plans to divide the labor, specialize, cooperate and trade. Audio-Forum
        cassette #155-9; Laissez Faire Books cassette #LV0095. 86 minutes.

                              *   *   *

                Three books by Mises have been reproduced on audiotape.

B-4   *Socialism.*   Unabridged audiotape version. Read by Bernard Mayes. Ashland, Ore.: Classics
        on Tape, 1990. 18 cassettes.

B-13   Bureaucracy. Unabridged audiotape version.   Read by Robert Morris.   Ashland, Oregon:
        Classics on Tape, [1989].   4 cassettes.

B-16   *Human Action.*   Unabridged audiotape version.   Read by Bernard Mayes. Ashland, Ore.:
        Classics on Tape, 1990. 30 cassettes.

Many excerpts from Mises books have been published separately and in anthologies of works by various authors. He is often quoted. The dividing line between articles he wrote as separate pieces, excerpts from his works, and articles *about* him is not always easy to draw. Several excerpts from his writings have been listed in this bibliography as "Articles." For instance:

> 50.6 - The Idea of Liberty is Western
> 50.8 - The Economics of War
> 52.5 - The Individual in Society
> 56.4 - Facts About the 'Industrial Revolution'
> 64.7 - A National Policy for Peace.

Generally speaking, quotation books and articles with Mises' quotes have been included among the *Abouts*. Here are the *Excerpts* that we have located; undoubtedly there are many others that we have missed.

Excerpts from Mises' books are arranged alphabetically according to the English-language title of the books from which they were taken; excerpts from articles are listed alphabetically by the title under which they were published. To avoid confusion due to different paging in different editions, excerpts are identified by chapter and section, rather than by pages.

EXCERPTS FROM BOOKS

The Anti-capitalistic Mentality (B-19)

"The Alleged Injustice." *The Capitalist Reader.* Lawrence S. Stepelevich, ed. New Rochelle, N. Y.: Arlington House, 1977. 152-157. (Chapter 4, Section 3).

"The Anti-Capitalistic Mentality." *Client's Quarterly Newsletter.* Lakewood, Colorado: Al V. Barr, public accountant. 3 (March 1983) 17-23. (Introduction and Chapter 1, Sections 1-4).

"Der Antikapitalismus der Intellektuellen" [The Anticapitalism of the Intellectuals]. *Industriekurier.* Dusseldorf. 52 (April 4, 1959). (Chapter 1, Sections 5 & 6, of the 1958 German translation).

"Extracts" selected by Tarleton Winchester. *Shorelines.* U. S. Lines, European Organisation News. 1:6 (December 1956) 10-12.

"El Fanatismo de la Gente de Pluma" [The Bigotry of the Literati]. *Tópicos de Actualidad.* Guatemala: Centro de Estudios Económico-Sociales. 13:266 (March 15, 1972) 23-30. (Chapter 3, Section 6).

"El Frente Anticapitalista" [The Anti-capitalistic Front]. *Tópicos de Actualidad.* Guatemala: Centro de Estudios Económico-Sociales. 13:264 (February 15, 1972) 15-18. (Chapter 2, Section 2).

"The Idea of Liberty is Western." See Article 50.6

"Jedermanns Sozialphilosophie" [Everyman's Social Philosophy]. *Deutsche Zeitung und Wirtschafts Zeitung.* 8 (January 26, 1957) 4. (Chapter 2).

EXCERPTS

"La Libertad de Prensa" [The Freedom of the Press]. *Tópicos de Actualidad.* Guatemala: Centro de Estudios Económico-Sociales. 13:265 (March 1, 1972) 19-22. (Chapter 3, Section 4).

"Liberty and Western Civilization." *The Truth Seeker.* 117:1 (Spring 1990) 50. Mistakenly identified as an excerpt from *Economic Policy* (B-27). (Chapter 5, section 5 opening paragraphs).

"La Literatura en el Capitalismo" [Capitalistic Literature]. *Hoja de Información.* Mexico: Instituto de Investigaciones Sociales y Económicas. 3:53 (August 1, 1957). (Chapter 3, Sections 1 & 2).

"Materialismo" [Materialism]. *Tópicos de Actualidad.* Guatemala: Centro de Estudios Económico-Sociales. 14:300 (August 15, 1973) 130-134. (Chapter 4, Section 2).

"The Resentment and the Anti-Capitalistic Bias of American Intellectuals." *The Intellectuals: A Controversial Portrait.* George B. de Huszar, ed. Glencoe, Ill.: The Free Press, 1960. 365-370. (Chapter 1, Sections 4, 5 & 6).

"El Teatro y las Novelas de Tesis 'Social'" [The "Social" Novels and Plays]. *Tópicos de Actualidad.* Guatemala: Centro de Estudios Económico-Sociales. 13:267 (April 1, 1972) 31-35. (Chapter 3, Section 6)

"True Capitalism." *The Capitalist Reader.* Lawrence S. Stepelevich, ed. New Rochelle, N. Y.: Arlington House, 1977. 72-81. (Chapter 2, Section 1, & Chapter 5).

"What's Behind the War on Business." *U. S. News & World Report.* (October 19, 1956) 156-175. (Substantial portion of the entire book).

"Why 'Intellectuals' Hate Capitalism." *Human Events.* Washington, D.C.. 14:11 (March 16, 1957). (Chapter 1, miscellaneous quotes from Sections 4-6 & Section 9).

Bureaucracy (B-13)

"Bureaucratic Management." *Fundamentals of Health Care.* George B. De Huszar, ed. Caldwell, Idaho: Caxton Printers, 1962. 128-143. (Chapter 2).

"Market versus Bureaucratic Planning." *The Libertarian Reader.* Tibor R. Machan, ed. Totowa, N.J.: Rowman & Littlefield, 1982. 147-163. (Chapter 1, Sections 2, 3, & 4; plus Chapter 2, Sections 3, 4, & 5).

"La Organización Burocrática de las Empresas del Estado" [Bureaucratic Management of State Enterprises]. *Temas Contemporáneos.* Mexico: Instituto de Investigaciones Sociales y Económicas. 17:201 (July 15, 1971) 20pp. (Chapters 3 & 4 of Spanish translation).

Hebrew translation:*Enterprise* (Hebrew language periodical). Exact dates and pages not available, but one of the 16 installments was published during the Hebrew month that spanned December 1949 to January 1950. As nearly as we can determine, the excerpts from *Bureaucracy* in each installment are as follows: #2: pp.81-87; #3: pp.22-30; #4: pp.93-101; #5: pp.53-56; #6: pp.74-76; #8: pp.110-113; #9: pp.105-108. See below for excerpts from *Planned Chaos* (B-14).

EXCERPTS

Epistemological Problems (B-10)

"The Science of Human Action." *Philosophy and Economic Theory.* Frank Hahn & Martin Hollis, eds. London: Oxford University Press, 1979. 57-64. (Chapter 1, Sections 5 & 6).

Human Action (B-16)

"Acerca de Impuestos" [Concerning Taxes]. *Tópicos de Actualidad.* Guatemala: Centro de Estudios Económico-Sociales. 21:472 (October 15, 1950) 141-148. Reprinted in *Clásicos Contemporáneos.* Caracas: Centro de Divulgación del Concocimiento Económico. 1 (June 1985) 5. (Chapter 32, Sections 1 & 3).

"Consideraciones en Torno a la Decadencia de la Civilización Clásica" [Observations on the Causes of the Decline of Ancient Civilization]. *Tópicos de Actualidad.* Guatemala: Centro de Estudios Económico-Sociales. 11:228 (August 15, 1970) 103-107. (Chapter 30, Section 2's Excursus).

"The Economics of War." See Article 50.8.

"Facts About the 'Industrial Revolution'." See Article 56.4.

"Importancia de la Economía en la Educación" [The Importance of Economics in Education]. *Hoja de Información Económica*. Mexico: Instituto de Investigaciones Sociales y Económica. 23:552 (May 15, 1978). (Chapter 38, Sections 6 & 7).

"Construcción Imaginaria de una Sociedad Socialista" [The Imaginary Construction of a Socialist Society] and "Imposibilidad del Cálculo Económico en un Régimen Socialista" [The Impossibility of Economic Calculation Under Socialism]. *La Ciencia Económica ante la "Inutilidad" del Socialismo* [Economic Science as Opposed to the "Disutility" of Socialism]. Translated by José Vicente Torrente Secorún. Valencia: Fundación Ignacio Villalonga, 1959. 85-133. (Chapters 25 & 26).

"The Impossibility of Economic Calculation under Socialism." Polish translation by Ewa Rurarz, in *Solidarnosc z Wolnoscie* [Solidarity with Liberty]. Don C. Lavoie, ed. Washington, D.C.: Cato Institute, 1982. (Chapter 26).

"The Individual in Society." See Article 52.5.

"Interference with the Structure of Prices." *ISI Essay Series.* Philadelphia: Intercollegiate Society of Individualists. 3:10 (n.d.). (Chapter 30).

"La Limitación de la Descendencia" [The Limitation of Offspring]. *Tópicos de Actualidad.* Guatemala: Centro de Estudios Económico-Sociales. 14:292 (April 15, 1973) 54-65. (Chapter 24, Section 2).

"The Market." *Economics: A Reader.* Kenneth Elzinga, ed. New York: Harper & Row, 1971(?). Mises gave reprint permission and publication was scheduled, but book not seen by compilers. (Chapter 15, Section 4).

El Mercado [The Market]. Translated by Joaquín Reig. Guatemala: Centro de Estudios Económico-Sociales, 1972. 111pp. (Chapter 15). Excerpts published separately:
    Section 5: "La Competencia" [Competition]. *Tópicos de Actualidad.* Guatemala: Centro de Estudios Económico-Sociales. 14:307 (December 1, 1973) 195-206;
    Section 6: "La Libertad" [Freedom]. *Tópicos de Actualidad.* Guatemala: Centro de Estudios Económico-Sociales. 14:305 (November 1, 1973) 173-186; also reprinted in *Resumen.* .Mexico: Instituto de Investigaciones Sociales y Económicas. (February 1974) 412-415.
    Section 13: "La Propaganda Comercial" [Commercial Advertising]. *Hoja de Información Económica.* Mexico: Instituto de Investigaciones Sociales y Económicas. 16:377 (February 1, 1971); and *Tópicos de Actualidad.* Guatemala: Centro de Estudios Económico-Sociales. 14:304 (October 15, 1973) 168-172.

O Mercado [The Market]. Translated by Donald Stewart, Jr. Serie Pensamento Liberal No.4. Rio de Janeiro: Instituto Liberal, 1987. 151pp. (Chapter 15, Portuguese translation).

"More on Human Action." *American Opinion.* Belmont, Mass. 8:10 (November 1965) 87-101. (Chapter 6, Section 15).

"A National Policy for Peace." See Article 64.7.

"La Práctica de l'Acción Humana" [The Practice of Human Action]. *Mundo Empresario.* Santa Cruz, Bolivia: Cámara de Industria y Comercio y El Mundo. 96 (July 23, 1989) 3. ("Introduction" of 1st ed., 1949; from Spanish language translation of "The Wisdom of Ludwig von Mises," see below).

"The Objectives of Currency Devaluation," *Viewpoints.* Rockland-Atlas, National Bank of Boston. (August 1959). (Chapter 31, Section 4).

"The Socialist Society," "The Socialist Planner," "Socialism's Unique Problem," "Socialism in Disguise," *Wall Street Journal.* (December 12, 13, 14, & 15, 1949, respectively). (Miscellaneous excerpts from the newly-published *Human Action*).

"De Sprookjes van de Welvaartsschool" [The Myths of the Welfare State]. *Burgerrecht.* Amsterdam. (September 17, 1957) 3. (Chapter 35, from Section 3).

"Why Advertising Should Not be Restricted." *Advertising Agency and Advertising & Selling.* (February 1950). 70. (Chapter 15, Section 13).

"The Wisdom of Ludwig von Mises." *The Freeman.* Irvington, N.Y.: Foundation for Economic Education. 31:9 (September 1981). Practically the entire issue (pp.518-572) consists of short excerpts from *Human Action*, selected by George Koether and arranged alphabetically in dictionary format. See Article 81.1.
    South African reprint: Durban: Philip H. Moore, 1981. 28pp.
    Spanish translation: "La Sabiduría de Ludwig von Mises." *Ideas sobre la Libertad.* Buenos Aires: Centro de Estudios sobre la Libertad. 23:41 (April 1982).

Im Namen des Staates oder die Gefahren des Kollektivismus (B-25):

> "Interventionismus" [Interventionism]. *Monatsblätter für freiheitliche Wirtschaftspolitik.* 25 (1979) 64-71. (Chapter 3, Sections 5, 6 & 7). N.B. See Article 79.1; this is *not* the same as either Article 26.5 or Article 80.2 of the same title.

> "Irrwege des Interventionismus" [Interventionism's Wrong Path]. *Der Unternehmer.* 6/79. Vienna. 5.

Liberalism [or *The Free and Prosperous Commonwealth*] (B-6)

> "Der Liberalismus und das Kartellproblem" [Liberalism and the Cartel Problem]. *Monatsblätter für freiheitliche Wirtschaftspolitik.* 7 (November 1955) 406-411. (Chapter 2, Section 7).

> "A Note on Bureaucracy." *Regulation: AEI Journal on Government and Society.* Washington, D.C.: American Enterprise Institute. 9:5 (September/October 1985) 44-45. (Chapter 2, Section 8).

> "Private Property and the Government" and "The Impracticability of Socialism." *The Market Economy: A Reader.* James L. Doti & Dwight R. Lee, eds. Los Angeles, Calif.: Roxbury Publishing Co., 1991. 85-90. (Chapter 2, Sections 3 & 4).

Nationalökonomie (B-11)

> "Die Goldwährung" [The Gold Standard]. *Neue Zürcher Zeitung.* No.767 (May 26, 1940) Handelsteil [Business Section]. (Chapter 4, Part 4, Section 19).

Notes and Recollections (B-23)

> "Excerpts from the Memoirs of Ludwig von Mises." *Libertarian Review.* San Francisco. (January/February 1978) 13-17.

Omnipotent Government (B-12)

> "Etatism" *The Wisdom of Conservatism.* 4 vols. Peter Witonski, ed. New Rochelle, N.Y.: Arlington House, 1971. Vol.3:1629ff. (Chapter 3, Selections).

> "Etatismo y Proteccionismo" [Statism and Protectionism] *Espejo.* Mexico: Instituto de Investigaciones Sociales y Económicas. 1:8 (October 15, 1960) 38-41. (Chapter 3, Section 7)

Planned Chaos (B-14). See also excerpts below from epilogue to 1951 and later editions of *Socialism*.

"The Supremacy of the Market. *The Freeman*. Irvington, N.Y. 16:10 (October 1966) 17-20. See Article 66.3. (Chapter 2, miscellaneous paragraphs, pp.25-28, 34).

Hebrew translations: *Enterprise*. (Hebrew language periodical). Exact dates and pages not available, but one of the 16 installments was published during the Hebrew month that spanned December 1949 to January 1950. As nearly as we can determine, the excerpts in each installment from *Planned Chaos* are as follows: #1: Chapter 1; #7: pp.32-34; #10) pp.80-86; #11: pp.48-55; #12: Chapter 2; #13: Chapter 3; #14: pp.28-31; #15: pp.27-28; and #16: Chapter 6. For excerpts from *Bureaucracy* (B-13), see above.

Socialism (B-4):

"From the 'Preface' to the Second German Edition of *Socialism* in 1932." *Notes from FEE*. Irvington, N.Y.: Foundation for Economic Education. March 1982.

"Economic Calculation in Socialism." *Comparative Economic Systems: Models and Cases*. rev. ed. Morris Bornstein, ed. Homewood, Ill.: Richard D. Irwin, 1969. 61-67. (Parts of Section 3 in Chapter 1 of Part 2, Yale/Jonathan Cape eds. [Chapter 5 of Liberty Fund, 1981 ed.] plus Section 4 of Chapter 2 in Part 2, Yale/Jonathan Cape eds. [Chapter 6 of Liberty Fund, 1981 ed.]).

"El Cálculo Económico en la Comunidad Socialista" [Economic Calculation in the Socialist Community]. *Temas Contemporáneos*. Mexico: Instituto de Investigaciones Sociales y Económicas. 15:186 (April 15, 1970) 3-15. (Sections 2, 3, & 4 of Chapter 2 in Part 2, Yale/Jonathan Cape eds. [Liberty Fund, 1981 ed., Chapter 6]).

"La Decadencia de la Cultura" [The Cultural Decline]. *Hoja de Información Económica*. Mexico: Instituto de Investigaciones Sociales y Económicas. 12:282 (February 15, 1967). (Section 7 of Chapter 2 in Part 3, Yale/Jonathan Cape eds. [Chapter 18, Liberty Fund, 1981 ed.]).

"El Fracaso del Intervencionismo" [The Failure of Interventionism]. *Tópicos de Actualidad*. Guatemala: Centro de Estudios Económico-Sociales. 692 (December 15, 1989) 128-137. Reprinted in *Comercio e Industria*. El Salvador. 49 (January-February 1990) 25-31. (Epilogue's "Introductory Remarks" & Section 1).

"Die Idee des Sozialismus" [The Socialist Idea]. *Marktforum*. Vienna: Carl Menger Institut. 1:1 (June 1987) 20. (From *Die Gemeinwirtschaft*, 1981 reprint of 2nd German-language edition).

"Mistakes in Socialist Theory." *Facts Forum News*. Dallas: Facts Forum, Inc. 4:2 (February 1955) 9-13. (Parts of Sections 3, 7, of Chapter 4 in Part 3, Yale/Jonathan Cape eds. [Chapter 20, Liberty Fund 1981 ed.] plus Epilogue's "Introductory remarks" & Section 1).

"El Nazismo" [Nazism]. *Tópicos de Actualidad*. Guatemala: Centro de Estudios Económico-Sociales. 16:336 (February 15, 1975) 21-24. (First five paragraphs, Section 8 of Epilogue).

"El Práctico" [Practice]. *Espejo.* Mexico: Instituto de Investigaciones Sociales y Económicas. 8:68 (November/December 1967) 33-35. (Last 6 paragraphs of Spanish translation of Mises' "Preface").

"Socialism -- A Critical Review." *Freeman Digest.* Provo, Utah. (July 1, 1979) 103-116. (Epilogue, excerpts).

"Sozialismus oder Vernunft?" [Socialism or Chicanery?]. *Die Brücke.* Hans Ilau, compiler. Frankfurt a. M. (n.d.; introduction dated October 1946). (Miscellaneous excerpts).

Theory and History (B-20):

"El Bienestar Commun Frente a los Intereses Especiales" [Common Weal versus Special Interests]. *Espejo.* Mexico: Instituto de Investigaciones Sociales y Económicas. 8:67 (September/October 1967) 59-61. (Chapter 2, Section 2).

"Las Tendencias Actuales y el Futuro" [Present-Day Trends and the Future]. *Temas Contemporáneos.* Mexico: Instituto de Investigaciones Sociales y Económicas. 10:127 (May 15, 1965) 2-16. (Chapter 16, Sections 1, 2, & 3)

The Theory of Money and Credit (B-2):

Reconstrucción Monetaria [Monetary Reconstruction]. Translated by Gustavo R. Velasco. Buenos Aires: Centro de Estudios sobre la Libertad, 1961. 93pp. (1953 epilogue).

The Ultimate Foundation of Economic Science (B-22)

"A Perfect System of Government?" *The Freeman.* Irvington, N.Y. 22:12 (December 1972) 747-752. (Chapter 5, Section 10).
Dutch translation: "Is er een Volmaakkt Regeringsstelsel mogelijk?" 2 installments, *Burgerrecht.* 17:777 (December 29, 1962) 13; 18:778 (January 5, 1963) 2.

"La Mente Humana" [The Human Mind]. *Orientación Económica.* Caracas, Venezuela. 13 (July 1964) 24-34. (Chapter 1).

EXCERPTS FROM ARTICLES

"Economic Calculation in the Socialist Commonwealth." *Socialist Economics: Selected Readings*. Alec Nove & D. M. Nuti, eds. Baltimore: Penguin Books, 1972. pp.75-91. (Excerpt from "Economic Calculation in the Socialist Commonwealth, Article 35.1).

"Empresas Públicas y Gestión Empresarial" [Public Enterprises and Entrepreneurship]. *Orientación Económica*. Caracas, Venezuela. 31 (November 1969) 22. (Spanish translation of excerpt from "Wirtschaftsrechnung im Sozialistischen Gemeinwesen," Article 20.6)
    Reprinted, *Resumen* (Mexico). 83 (November 1972) 81-82.

"El fracaso de las leyes del salario mínimo y la coerción sindical" [The breakdown of minimum wage laws and labor union coercion]. *La Prensa.* Honduras. (March 27, 1990) 7. Reprinted in *La Hora* . Guatemala. (June 15, 1990). (Spanish translation of excerpt from "The Gold Problem," Article 65.3).

"Vrijheid en Welvaaart" [Freedom and Welfare]. *Burgerrecht.* Amsterdam.16:728 (December 30, 1961) 7. (Dutch translation of excerpts from "Liberty and Property," Article 58.3).

BOOK REVIEWS

Mises books are listed here alphabetically by their English titles. If no English translation is available, they appear here alphabetized by their original title.

Reviews of each book are listed alphabetically by the name of the reviewer or, if unsigned, by the name of the periodical in which they appeared.

Reviews of a book that has appeared in several editions are arranged here in a single listing. For instance, reviews of *The Theory of Money and Credit* (B-2; 1st German edition, 1912; 2nd German edition, 1924; English-language editions, 1934, 1953, 1971, 1980) are all assembled in one alphabetical listing, irrespective of date or language, according to the name of the reviewer or, if anonymous, by the name of the publication. Thus, reviews of this book on money, in various languages -- by Rudolf Hilferding (1912), and Albert Hahn (1924), both in German, and by R. G. Hawtry (1934), and Henry Hazlitt (1953), both in English -- all appear in close proximity in this section.

The Anti-Capitalistic Mentality (B-19)

E.S.A. "Anti-Capitalistic Mentality Probed, Scored in New Book." *Standard Times*. (November 1956). "In a well-expressed analysis, Dr. Mises predicts that this effort [on the part of those who oppose, not communism, but only a communist system they do not themselves control], being 'purely negative' must fail inevitably; he buttresses his beliefs with a clear definition of capitalism, its benefits and advantages. The author has succeeded admirably in presenting in simplest terms a subject of formidable and complex dimension."

Åkerman, Johan. "Adam Smiths världsbild--och Lenins" [Adam Smith's world view, or Lenin's]. *Farmand*. Oslo, Norway. No. 36 (September 7, 1957) 23-27. Comments on Hoff's several comments (see below).

Albert, Dr. "Recht der Arbeit" [The Right to Work]. *Zeitschrift für die Wissenschaft und Praxis des gesamten Arbeitsrechts*. 12:1 (January 1959). A review of the German translation of the book. "We find here discussions of consumer sovereignty, the vicarious role of the entrepreneur, the best possible satisfaction of consumer needs, the rise of the most capable through competition, pay according to one's contribution to production, the impossibility of the 'mixed' economy under which all of us are actually living today, and the impossibility of economic calculation in the planned economy. Through scientific discussion over the last 30 years, all these themes have been shown to be untenable or misleading, tautological or circular reasoning . . . . Ludwig von Mises has undoubtedly performed a service in calling attention to the possibility of economic calculation in the planned economy and for having given this view a decided impetus. However, that by no means justifies his extreme opinion." (Translated from the German)

Albert, Hans. "Einzelbesprechungen" [Specific Reviews]. *Jahrbücher für Nationalökonomie und Statistik*. 170:4 (1958). This book "is strongly polemical and simply written . . . . Ludwig v. Mises has long been trying to prove that extreme laissez-faire liberalism was the quintessence of economics. The ideological criticism of the last 30 years has evidently changed his comprehension no more than has the course of the debate, which he sparked earlier, on economic calculation in the planned economy . . . . Surely very few will accept the political [pro-laissez faire] conclusion he reaches at the close of his book." (Translated from the German)

All American Books. "Why They Bite the Hand That . . . " New Rochelle, N.Y.: America's Future. 3:1 (Spring 1957) 12. "There is no secret about the fact that many people dislike capitalism . . . . What has been the mystery is why so many want to throw out a system that far outdistances any other in providing a high living standard for 'all the people'. ¶Ludwig von Mises thinks he knows -- and perhaps he does . . . . ¶Von Mises says it's almost entirely a matter of jealousy, plus a lack of understanding of economic laws . . . . ¶If von Mises does not, in the end, tell us what to do about this situation he at least gives us a diagnosis. The search for a remedy is always advanced by identification of the cause of the illness."

American Banker. (December 10, 1956). "Professor von Mises examines critically the anti-capitalistic sentiments of the intellectuals, the writers and the literati and exposes their fallacies and misconceptions."

Bert, Erik. *Daily Worker* (New York). (March 20, 1957) 7. Reviewed in conjunction with two other books: "Even though he [Mises] comes to us after long years of teaching at the University of Vienna, he can show Madison Avenue a few things . . . . ¶Von Mises sounds the tocsin for 'open and unrestricted support of laissez-faire capitalism.' ¶Among its worst enemies are the 'anti-communist liberals' who are aiming at Communism' but call it 'planning' or the 'welfare state.' If the capitalists who are paying for the 'people's capitalism' hokum ever read von Mises, they will raise the very devil with the P.C. advertising copy-writers, probably hire Prof. von Mises and dump the lot of them. And well they deserve it."

R.A.C. [Roy A. Childs]. "The Anti-capitalistic Mentality." *Books for Libertarians.* Washington, D.C. [Dec. 1972/Jan. 1973]. "While Mises' analysis here is welcome indeed, he does not, in my opinion, take it far enough. He does not discuss the fact that there has not been, until our own time, a philosophical, consistent, non-contradictory defense of capitalism, particularly from the perspective of ethics -- but in this regard Mises himself is 'part of the problem'."

Castellano, Pablo. "La Mentalidad Anticapitalista" [The Anticapitalistic Mentality]. *Temas Contemporáneos* Mexico: Instituto de Investigaciones Sociales y Económicas. 3:26 (June 1, 1957) [8 pp.]. "Von Mises studies the 'anticapitalistic mentality,' i.e., the mental attitude of many enemies of capitalism. Does that mean the communists? The socialists? The syndicalists? The revolutionaries? No. He doesn't treat the open enemies of the economic regime of the neighboring country, but the less obvious enemies, those who oppose the capitalistic system out of personal laziness or for purely individual reasons." (Translated from the Spanish)

Chamber of Commerce of the U. S., Economic Research Department. "Congratulations: von Mises." *Economic Intelligence.* 100 (November 1956). "*The Anti-Capitalistic Mentality* by Ludwig von Mises may do for America what Karl Marx did for Europe and much of the world, but in reverse. It is the most devastating analysis of the corrosive forces undermining capitalism that has come to our attention."

_____. "Neglect of the Market." *Economic Intelligence.* 101 (December 1956). "Dr. Ludwig von Mises . . . . attempts to explain the Western world's paradoxical hostility to that system of economic organization which has most improved living conditions and material well-being, by giving scope to individual freedom and initiative."

Chamberlain, John. "A Reviewer's Notebook." *The Freeman.* Irvington, N.Y. 6:11 (November 1956) 55-58. "Like Dr. Mises' other books, *The Anti-Capitalistic Mentality* makes the incontestable point that the West owes its tremendous economic development, its machine technology, its inventiveness, its high standards of living, its many amenities, its surging populations, its low death rates, its good medical care and its nonfatalistic outlook to the rise of laissez faire capitalism . . . . The strange thing about it, however, is that the more capitalism succeeds in augmenting the individual's blessings, the more it is libeled and hated . . . . According to Dr. Mises, the chief reason why capitalism is hated is that it deprives incompetents of easy excuses for their failures."

_____. "Dissecting the Prejudices Of the Anti-Capitalist Mind." *The Wall Street Journal.* (October 23, 1956). "Since there aren't enough psychiatrists or psychoanalysts in the world to cure the huge number of people who parade their enmities, their jealousies and their pernicious infantilism through Dr. Mises' pages, *The Anti-Capitalistic Mentality* might be set down as the work of a thoroughly disillusioned fatalist . . . But more sanguine people would put a different gloss on a lot of it. ¶Isn't it possible, for example, that many of the people whom Dr. Mises regards as hopelessly jealous incompetents are merely guilty of short-term thinking and defective training in logic . . . . ¶Paradoxically enough, if it were not for the phenomenon of men like Ludwig von Mises one would be entirely justified in writing off capitalism as a lost cause. But Dr. Mises' own career is evidence enough that the 'anti-capitalistic mentality' is no longer as pervasive as it used to be . . . . ¶Dr. Mises and his school are, as the saying goes, 'not without influence'. . . . The work already accomplished by Dr. Mises and his followers does much to negate the pessimistic conclusions of his latest book."

Clark, Fred G. and Richard Stanton Rimanoczy. "Freedom Furnishes No Alibis." *The Economic Facts of Life* New York: American Economic Foundation. 9:12 (December 1956). "For the last 20 years, during which the authors have been working at the job of interpreting America's economic system to Americans, we have been receiving a substantial and persistent flow of letters attacking us for defending that system and exhibiting a degree of hatred, venom and spleen that has continued to amaze us because we could see no logic or reason behind the attacks. Even more puzzling was the fact that most of these people seemed to be well educated and include many who would be considered thought leaders. Because of our interest in finding a rational explanation, it was only natural that when Ludwig von Mises finished his new book *The Anticapitalist Mentality*, we were among the first to stand in line to buy a copy."

The Cotton Trade Journal. "Unabashed Approval of Capitalism." (February 15, 1957). "How refreshing and stimulating it is to find one of our most prominent economists has written a book which is a frank, unabashed, and even proud defense of capitalism . . . . Mr. von Mises' very readable volume analyzes briefly the social characteristics of capitalism and the ordinary man's social philosophy."

L.D. "Die Wurzeln des Antikapitalismus" [The Roots of Anticapitalism]. *La Revue de la Banque.* Brussels. 22:9-10 (1958) 738-739. A review of the German (1958) translation. "Von Mises, skillful and fiery polemicist, is the author of an important scientific work, important because collectivism of all forms has pervaded the modern world . . . . ¶One may dispute the author's doctrine and approve a mixed economic system. Yet every cultivated person should read this remarkable work which offers interesting testimony to the contemporary mentality." (Translated from the French)

De Bruyne, Hektor. "Het Liberalisme van Ludwig von Mises" [The Liberalism of Ludwig von Mises]. *Economisch Tijdschrift en Sociaal.* Antwerp. 3 (July/August 1960) 191-194. A review of the German (1958) translation.

Dickson, Harald. "Antikapitalistisk mentalitet och liberalistisk propaganda" [Anticapitalistic mentality and liberal propaganda]. *Samtid och Framtid: Tidskrift för idépolitik och kultur.* Stockholm. 14:2 (1957) 81-82.

The Economist. London. "Liberalism in Caricature: The Anti-Capitalist Mentality." (April 13, 1957) 135. "This is a sad little book, from which admirers of its author -- and these are many, even among those who radically disagree with his political conclusions -- should be warned away. Professor von Mises has a splendid analytical mind and an admirable passion for liberty; but as a student of human nature he is worse than null and as a debater he is of Hyde Park standard . . . . To find an equal dogmatism coupled with an equally *simpliste* view of the springs of conduct, an equal propensity for propping up dummies and knocking them down, an equal contempt for human facts coupled with an equally vituperative style, one would have to turn to the less sophisticated Marxists . . . . The case for freedom needs making and re-making, tirelessly and ingeniously; but its cause is ill served by such stuff as this."

Efron, Edith. *The Objectivist Newsletter.* New York: Ayn Rand & Nathaniel Branden. 1:5 (May 1962) 17-18.

Faulhaber, R. W. *Books on Trial..* Chicago: Thomas More Assn. 15:4 (December 1956) 2. "This is evidently an important book if one judges by the number of prominent and favorable reviews given it in many national periodicals . . . . Indeed there are masses of men who do not consider capitalism the greatest invention of man since the wheel. Von Mises is not one of them . . . . ¶Now it would seem that one who defends a system which is assumed perfect -- laissez-faire capitalism in this case -- can only conclude that its critics are irrational. And such is very much the content of von Mises explanation of the anti-capitalistic mentality."

Fertig, Lawrence. "Anti-Capitalism: Dr. von Mises Probes Reason Why It Infects Many Important Groups." *New York World Telegram and Sun.* (October 22, 1956). "Above all, Dr. von Mises is a passionate advocate of freedom and human progress. He is just as contemptuous of the society of 'status' which existed in the past as he is of restrictive socialism which threatens to be the society of the future. He writes with a vigorous and at times vitriolic pen in defense of a system where consumers are supreme." The reviewer cites Robert L. Heilbroner's *The Quest for Wealth* as a "good example of the anti-capitalism Dr. von Mises is talking about." Portions of this review in *Fortnight* (December 1956, January 1957).

The Free Press. Burlington, Vermont. (November 30, 1956). "What makes the many feel unhappy under capitalism, says Professor Mises, is precisely the fact that capitalism grants to each the opportunity to obtain the most desirable positions -- positions which, of course, can only be obtained by a few. In such a society each man whose ambitions have not been fully satisfied is looking for a scapegoat whom he could make responsible for his own shortcomings. He blames the existing social order."

General Electric Company. *Plant Community Relations Review.* 5:11 (November 1956) 6. "In his new book Dr. von Mises makes a devastating analysis of the anti-business bias in America and examines its roots and consequences in American life."

Greaves, Percy L., Jr. "Capitalism and the Tenth Commandment." *Christian Economics.* New York. 8:19 (October 30, 1956) 1, 3. "In a free society, it is primarily a person's own fault, if he does not rise to a position of leadership . . . . Men, being what they are, often try to find a scapegoat for their own failures . . . . They blame the system . . . . There is much food for thought in this little volume . . . . Too much of what passes for the thinking of our generation has been formed by the mouthings and the writings of irresponsible babblers totally unfamiliar with the great teachings of economics, the science of human action . . . . As Professor Mises has written, 'The ideas of the revolutionaries and reformers found approval with the immense majority of ignorant people exclusively driven by the most powerful human passions of envy and hatred'."

Grimes, William H. "No Dirty Word: Thinking Things Over." *The Wall Street Journal.* (October 23, 1956). "Time was not so long ago when capitalism was a dirty word . . . . Well, times do change. Now it appears that capitalists are coming out of the caves where they have been hiding. Not only that, some of them are wearing buttons announcing that they are capitalists . . . . On this page today John Chamberlain reviews a book, *The Anti-Capitalistic Mentality,* by Prof. Ludwig von Mises. Dr. Mises finds that part of the anti-capitalistic propaganda comes from what he calls the intellectuals . . . . If the capitalistic system in the United States is in danger today, it is not the danger from a frontal attack. It is the danger that it will be loaded with so many forms of government intervention that it will no longer be able to perform its function."

Gross, Herbert. "Fehldeutungen der Marktwirtschaft" [Mistaken Interpretations of the Market Economy]. *Neue Literatur.* 139 (November 23, 1956) 19. "Mises warns sharply against those intellectuals who preach in anti-communist garb. 'To be sure, they appear to reject communism, but they still use the jargon of Marx or Lenin. In short: They pretend to fight communism, while they seek to return the people to the ideas of the Communist Manifesto.' ¶Even the economically-minded reader will be frightened at first by the many formulations Mises uses, with remorseless clarity, to express the basic elements of freedom and welfare. However, a document like this of incorruptible and broad intellect, is badly needed today. We need a compass to guide us along the right path and to help us understand exactly why the welfare of the West has improved so remarkably since the end of the war." (Translated from the German)

Hamilius, J. P. "The Anti-Capitalistic Mentality." *Letzeburger Journal.* Luxembourg. (December 7, 1957) 12. "This work offers a profusion of thoughtful and new ideas to the economist as well as to anyone else who is interested in 'capitalism' and closely related problems. One should not pass up von Mises' publications. What is especially notable is the extremely clear and comprehensible presentation that enables even those who are not at home in economics to understand the most important parts." (Translated from the German)

_____. "La Mentalité Anticapitaliste." *L'Echo de L'industrie.* Revue Luxembourgeoise de la Vie Économique et Sociale, Fédération des Industriels Luxembourgeois. 36:15 (April 12, 1958) 15. "In his new work, he [Mises] exposes and analyzes in detail the essential aspects of the anti-capitalistic mentality as it is encountered in the United States. Although concerned with false beliefs held by American intellectuals, most of his observations and conclusions apply to Europe as well." (Translated from the French)

Handelsblatt. Düsseldorf. November 20/21, 1959. "A clever, psychological study . . . . One should not take the book to be an explanation of liberal theory. On that account, although it is very readable, it is a book more for specialists who can compensate for the inevitable objections and limitations. But for them it is a stimulating and amusing book." (Translated from the German)

Hanson, Agnes O. *Library Journal.* 81 (November 1, 1956) 2604. "This civilized presentation, by a world renowned libertarian economist, is clarifying and stimulating reading for all who are concerned with individual freedom and a sound economy."

Harper's. (January 1957). "Ludwig von Mises, author of *The Anti-Capitalistic Mentality,* is sure that society is going to hell in a hack (government-owned) because it has abandoned the pure capitalism of the middle of the nineteenth century . . . . Under pure capitalism the market was a place where every man was rewarded exactly as he deserved to be rewarded . . . . ¶One area, however, in which von Mises does not accept the verdict of the market is economics. His own theories of economics happen not to have fared very well in either the commercial or the intellectual marketplace . . . . But von Mises rejects the market decision on his work not because he is envious of his betters as the rest of us do, but because sound economics is the victim of conspiracy ('propaganda and indoctrination has well succeeded in enforcing its taboos')."

Hausdorfer, Walter. *Library Journal.* 81 (September 15, 1956) 1991. "In attempting to explain the psychological attitude of the anti-capitalists, the author, a well-known economist, shows that the basis of success of big business, adjustment to mass demand, has in itself antagonized those less successful in understanding the essential democracy of the market. He believes that this resentment carries through the professions, white collar workers, intellectuals, and the so-called 'cousins', or less fortunate heirs of capitalists, and that a fallacy in the common man's social philosophy lies in his basic ignorance of economics, a condition which persists among the literati, who fail to understand the nature of the literary market. Non-economic objections likewise are discussed. Recommended for public and college libraries."

Hazlitt, Henry. "Why Anti-Capitalism?" *Newsweek.* (October 15, 1956) 110. "Why? Why, at the very moment when capitalism has brought the greatest material and scientific progress known to history should it be meeting with its greatest disparagement and opposition? This is the question Prof. Ludwig von Mises has set himself to answer in a short book called *The Anti-Capitalistic Mentality* . . . . Many readers will question whether the envy and frustration that Mises describes constitute a sufficient explanation of today's anti-capitalist mentality . . . . But Mises is much too good a logician not to recognize that the arguments against capitalism cannot be answered merely by an *ad hominem* retort that they spring from discreditable motives. In his great works, *Human Action* and *Socialism,* he has spelled out in full the real arguments for capitalism and against Socialism. And he restates them here in summary form."

Heilbroner, Robert L. "Economic Paradox." *The New York Times Book Review.* (November 18, 1956) 20. "Without a doubt the 'anti-capitalistic mentality' is a peculiar and fascinating problem of our day . . . . To analyze such a paradoxical state of affairs takes a variety of gifts. One must have sufficient grounding in history to appreciate that the theme of protest is not limited to our times but runs through much of Western civilization . . . . Secondly, one must have the ability to identify with the critics as well as with the partisans of each society . . . . Neither of these qualities of objectivity are to be found, unfortunately, in Ludwig von Mises' *The Anti-Capitalistic Mentality.*"

Hoff, Trygve J.B. Comments on opinions concerning *The Anti-Capitalistic Mentality* were published in the Swedish journal, *Samtid och Framtid.* (See below). According to Trygve J. B. Hoff, editor of *Farmand,* one Cabinet member and three university professors "condemned the book so severely," that Hoff "got irritated and wrote . . . in protest." (Personal letter to B.B.G. from Hoff, October 19, 1957):
      "Den unaturlige 'jamnstellingen'." *Farmand* . Oslo. (January 26, 1957).
      "Den unaturlige 'jamnstellingen' II." *Farmand.* Oslo. 5 (February 2, 1957) 25-31.
      "Den anti-kapitalistiske mentalitet." *Farmand.* Oslo. 24 (June 15, 1957) 17-23.

"Anti-kapitalistisk mentalitet, II." *Farmand*. Oslo. 29 (July 20, 1957) 21-25.

"Kapital og kapitalisme." *Farmand*. Oslo. 33 (August 17, 1957) 17-18.

_____. "Hvorfor motstand mot kapitalismen?" *Farmand* (Oslo). 37 (September 14, 1957) 17-23. Response to Åkerman (see above).

Hoiles, R. C. "War on Business." Two part article plus an unsigned editorial, "Overcoming 'Literary Reluctance'." *Colorado Springs Gazette Telegraph*. (October 25, 1956) 34; (October 26, 1956) 17. Comments on the substantial excerpts reprinted in *U.S. News & World Report*, October 19, 1956. After reading Ludwig von Mises' *Socialism* and *Human Action*, the reviewer invited the Professor to California to lecture. "In all my reading," the reviewer writes, "I have never found a man who could more clearly and logically show the fallacies of socialism and how it means poverty and misery to the masses than Dr. Ludwig von Mises. ¶And if citizens are perturbed about the trends toward socialism and want to help reverse the trend, the best thing they can do is to improve the understanding of one individual -- and that's oneself. And the quickest and easiest way to do that is to read such books as this new book, *The Anti-Capitalistic Mentality*."

Hoja de Información Económica. "Dos Libros Extraordinarios" [Two Extraordinary Books]. Mexico: Instituto de Investigaciones Sociales y Económicas. 3:66 (February 15, 1958). Spanish (1957) translation reviewed in conjunction with Faustino Ballvé's *Diez Lecciones de Economía* (English-language translation, *Essentials of Economics,* 1963). "In brief, Professor Mises' thesis is that in a society in which equal opportunity for all citizens is legally recognized and freedom of initiative is respected, the most apt and the most capable will win out. As a result, those who do not attain fortune and success feel frustrated." (Translated from the Spanish)

Human Events. 13:50 (December 15, 1956). "In 'pre-capitalistic' (or 'status') societies, where rank is ordained by birth, the 'lower orders' accept their humble station because they hold it through no failing of their own. The main characteristic of *laissez faire* capitalism, on the other hand, is that society operates on a 'contract,' rather than a 'status' basis, and rank (as represented by wealth) is determined by merit (service rendered to consumers). In such a society, those at the bottom . . . . blame the 'system' . . . . ¶While this is the theme of his book, Dr. Mises' great learning does not allow him to limit himself merely to the psychological aspects of capitalism. *The Anti-Capitalistic Mentality* is also a lucid introduction to Dr. Mises' thought and the economics of the free market in general."

International Review of Social History. Amsterdam. 2 (1957) 296.

Ives, C. P. "Anti-Anti-Capitalists." Found among Dr. Mises' Grove City College papers, source unknown. (December 21, 1956?). "For forty years or more Prof. Ludwig von Mises, a Viennese economist of the classic stamp, has been hammering at the enemies of the free market, which is to say the almost unanimous body of *chic* and fashionable opinion of the time. And now in a brief book he summarizes his position in one of the most hilariously contemptuous pieces of economic polemics in quite a while."

Jaquemet, Gaston. "Die Abneigung gegen den Kapitalismus" [The Aversion to Capitalism]. *Schweizer Monatshefte*. 36:12 (March 1957) 1012-1013. "The comprehensive knowledge of the author and his firm grasp of world affairs enable him to create a brilliant essay; one can only deplore that it is not available in German, for one would then give this book with enthusiasm to his friends who entertain contrary ideas." (Translated from the German)

Landers, Marian. "Why Is Capitalism the Scapegoat?" A syndicated review: "In this book Mises displays the unusual ability to deal with a complicated subject in an uncomplicated way . . . . I recommend it highly, especially to anyone interested in saving the '*goose that laid the golden egg*' from the chopping block of socialism." Published in a number of newspapers, including:

Citation. Karnes City, Texas (September 1, 1966);
Evening Register. Santa Ana, California (August 28, 1966) as "Anti-Capitalism Probed";
Gleaner. Northwood, North Dakota (August 25, 1966);
Highlander. Lake Wales, Florida. (August 26, 1966);
News. Lima, Ohio (August 25, 1966);
News. Pampa, Texas (August 25, 1966);
News-Observer. Crossett, Arizona (September 1, 1966);
Record. Cuero, Texas (September 9, 1966);
Times-Journal. Russell Springs, Kentucky (September 1, 1966).

Leader Herald   (Gloversville, N.Y.). "An Expert's Diagnosis." (November 13, 1956). "Dr. Ludwig von Mises is an intellectual of high attainments, so his estimate of the part played by intellectuals in current socialist activity is worthy of attention."

P.M. "Der Meinungsterror der Progressisten" [The Terror of Progressive Opinion].   *Monatsblätter für freiheitliche Wirtschaftspolitik*. 3:2 (February 1957) 119-122. This review describes in some detail the productivity of the free market and contrasts it with socialism or communism. "Freedom of the press, Mises says, is an essential characteristic of a nation of free citizens. It was the most important point in the program of old classical liberalism . . . . Freedom from censorship is the central nerve of literature. However, freedom of the press can exist only where the factors of production are in private hands. In a socialist society where publishing and printing firms belong to the state and are under government management, there can be no question of a free press." (Translated from the German)

Miller, Bradley. "Mises vs. the Green-Eyed Monster." *The Free Market Reader: Essays in the Economics of Liberty*.   Burlingame, California: Ludwig von Mises Institute, 1988. 180-184. "A truism among free-marketeers is that collectivism is flawed because it flies in the face of human nature . . . . They write about politics and economics as if they were logic or mechanics. Pull lever X for output Y. Disseminate the evidence of capitalism's success and collectivism's failures, and the capitalist paradise, in time, will come . . . . ¶Ludwig von Mises showed 31 years ago in *The Anti-Capitalistic Mentality* that reason, evidence, and humaneness have about as much impact on public policy as an Oral Roberts sermon would have on Nietzsche . . . . Mises realized that for libertarian economists to have a practical as well as scholarly impact, they must understand the non-rational factors that breed hostility to capitalism."

Mitchell, Wiley. *Christian Science Monitor*. (November 7, 1956) 17. "Dr. von Mises has not only failed to contribute to sound social criticism but has written an essay potentially harmful to the institutions it says it defends . . . . His final conclusion is that, 'What alone can prevent the civilized nations of Western Europe, America and Australia from being enslaved by the barbarism of Moscow is open and unrestricted support of laissez-faire capitalism.' . . . Does he mean, literally, that government shall never interfere between buyer and seller? . . . . Does he mean to end not only welfare payments, social security, labor mediation machinery, but also control of gambling, drugs and liquor, legal enforcement of contracts, the Federal Reserve System, government insurance of bank deposits and government monopoly of coinage?"

Monatsblätter für freiheitliche Wirtschaftspolitik.   "Die Gefahren der antikapitalistische Geisteshaltung" [The Dangers of the Anticapitalistic Mentality]. 3:1 (January 1957) 39-41. "The task of this book, Mises says in the introduction, is to analyze the anti-capitalistic bias in the United States and to reveal its roots and possible consequences. At the root are two tendencies which overlap in evaluating capitalistic business: the general improvement of living conditions, which the system of free economic activity brings with it, and resentment due to the frustrations of those who have not attained their goals through economic competition. . . . . Herein lies a widespread motive for the lack of appreciation and the defamation of the capitalistic method of production." (Translated from the German)

_____. "Die Wurzeln des Antikapitalismus" [The Roots of Anticapitalism]. 4.3 (March 1958) 185-186. A review of the 1958 German translation. "The most significant and important section of the Mises book concerns the intermediate stage, the anti-communists who attack capitalism continually: 'What these self-styled "anticommunist liberals" are fighting against is not communism as such, but a communist system in which they themselves are not at the helm'." (Translated from the German)

Mondo Econòmico. Milan, Italy. "Un' opera di von Mises sulla mentalità anti-capitalistica" [A Work by Mises on the Anti-capitalistic Mentality]. 9:52 (December 29, 1956) 29-30.

Murphy, James. "Where 'Money is King'." *The Henry George News.* New York. (May 1957). "It is not pleasant to find one's self in disagreement with an ally in the struggle for a free society, especially one as distinguished as Ludwig von Mises . . . . Professor von Mises, whether he realizes it or not, displays an anti-capitalist mentality of his own. To him the rightful basis of property is purchase, in lawful money, of whatever is for sale, be it land, slaves or voters. According to him the just distribution of wealth produced is not based on benefits received but on ability to pay in cash, however obtained."

Murray, John. *Freedom First.* London: Society for Individual Freedom,. (Summer 1957) 13-15. "The analysis of the temptations and the behaviour of the 'Cousins' [relatives and dependents of successful entrepreneurs] is a very entertaining section . . . . Some of them, perhaps most of them, will be ousted from control . . . as inefficient, while others hold their ground. Thus families and connections become divided, and the division is tinged with the suspicion and the hostility of the demoted and the dispossessed. Many of them take to anti-capitalistic agitation in various forms."

New York Sunday News. "Why They Hate Capitalism" (Editorial). (November 4, 1956). "We recommend the book as a string of brilliant comments on the American system from an unusual angle. Also, as a book carrying a moral which perhaps Dr. von Mises didn't think of; namely, that anybody who resolutely keeps conceit and jealousy out of his or her life has a far better chance of being happy, under any economic system, than one who yields to those two enemies of personal peace and contentment."

M.E.O. "Defense of Capitalism." *The Columbia Missourian.* (November 21, 1956). "The fallacy in this [anti-capitalistic] attitude is that capitalism is blamed for the abominable things and not credited for the many products which everyone approves. Men who reach the ultimate in success are not producing bad things, but rather something desired by or useful to the mass of consumers."

Ordo. Jahrbuch für die Ordnung von Wirtschaft und Gesellschaft. Dusseldorf & Munich. 10 (1958) 520. "Even those who don't agree with Mises will enjoy this book, which attributes the cause of anti-capitalism to frustrated ambition . . . . However, the reviewer reminds the reader that luck as well as effort plays a role in success or failure under capitalism." (Translated from the German)

Press. Mobile, Alabama. "Old Bias Assailed." (October 18, 1956). "The author completely discredits the world-wide campaign by intellectuals, socialists and communists to rid the world of the dynamic economic system known as capitalism . . . . It is our hope that the von Mises book receives wide distribution. Its down to earth reasoning is badly needed to offset the deluge of phony propaganda that has flowed into men's minds for generations with the result that they are about ready to go out and kill the goose that laid the golden egg."

Raico, Ralph. *Journal of Social Studies* New York: College of Liberal Arts and Sciences, City College. 13:2 (Spring 1957) 65-67. "The realistic, well-balanced person . . . adjusts his goals to what he can, as a practical matter, achieve; the neurotic romantic insists on seeing all his yearnings satisfied, and blames the social system if they are not . . . . ¶Disappointment, frustration, envy, resentment: here, the reviewer believes, von Mises has touched the nerve of the anti-capitalistic bias."

Rimanoczy, Richard Stanton. Co-author; see Clark, Fred G. (above).

Roosevelt, Edith Kermit. *The American Mercury.* 84:398 (March 1957) 153-154. "Ludwig von Mises . . . inclines to be too dogmatic. The fact remains that the United States still is not, as the author would have us believe it is, a land where all people freely compete on their merits. Some groups such as women, negroes, emigres, and persons over 40 are still denied job opportunities fully warranted by their abilities, training and education . . . . In addition, von Mises never mentions what may be the main reason for anti-capitalist thinking, namely that Americans have been indoctrinated over some 30 years by Communists strategically placed in our schools and universities, newspapers, magazines, publishing houses, the entertainment industry, government and our churches."

Rothbard, Murray N. "Why Anti-Capitalism?" *National Review.* New York. 2:25 (November 10, 1956) 21. "At the end of this profoundly stimulating work, we are left with the problem: if anti-capitalist resentment is so pervasive, how can it be overcome? Will a moral philosophy of individualism -- and a consequent moral condemnation of envy -- complement the utilitarian arguments for unhampered capitalism?"

W.S. "Ist der Kapitalismus 'ungerecht'?" [Is Capitalism Unjust?]. *Monatsblätter für freiheitliche Wirtschaftspolitik.* 3:3 (March 1957) 184-188. "Whoever considers capitalism to be an unfair system on moralistic grounds, is deceived with respect to understanding what capital is, how it originates, how it is preserved, and does not know the advantages which stem from its employment in the process of production." (Translated from the German)

Samtid och Framtid. Stockholm: Natur & Kultur. Sven Rydenfelt, ed.. Survey of opinions concerning *The Anti-Capitalistic Mentality.* One Cabinet member and three university professors "condemned the book so severely," that Trygve J. B. Hoff, editor of *Farmand,* responded; see Hoff, above, for listing of his comments in *Farmand.*

Schack, Herbert. *Schmollers Jahrbuch für Gesetzgebung, Verwaltung und Volkswirtschaft.* Berlin: Duncker & Humblot. 79:2 (1958?) 232-234 (104-106). A review of the 1958 German translation. "Is it correct to label the economic order of the west 'capitalism'? The reader will ask himself this question if the subject of the anti-capitalistic bias of intellectuals comes up. Or if the question of the anti-capitalistic attitude of the common man, of the under-developed countries, and of literature under capitalism, etc. is raised . . . . This book, the American title of which was *The Anti-Capitalistic Mentality,* is recommended especially to those studying the social market economy. For they will come to know an author who is perhaps the last champion of the classical liberal and specifically capitalistic interpretation." (Translated from the German)

Schmidt, Emerson P. "The Anti-Capitalist Mentality." *Washington Report.* Chamber of Commerce of the U.S. 5:47 (November 9, 1956) 1-2. "This book makes it clear that if the underminers of capitalism had their way and succeeded in destroying the free market economy, they would simultaneously undermine their own freedom to write and speak as they please." Excerpt of this review in *The Free Press* (Burlington, Vt.). January 18, 1957.

Schmitz, Wolfgang. "Das antikapitalistische Ressentiment" [Anti-capitalistic Resentment]. *Wirtschafts-politische Blätter.* 5:2 (April 1958) 99-100. "The renaissance of a new refined liberalism in economic-political thought would hardly be thinkable without the works of the Viennese branch of liberalism. However, it will be clear, especially after reading this latest work of Ludwig von Mises that, in spite of holding many ideas in common, even the . . . so-called neoliberal theoreticians of the social market economy will distance themselves from the 'paleoliberalism' of laissez-faire." (Translated from the German)

Teplow, Leo. *The Management Review.* American Management Association. 46:5 (May 1957) 93-94. "The main trouble with *The Anti-Capitalistic Mentality* is that it fails to identify the major threat to our profit-and-loss system. The danger resides not in a conscious, almost universal opposition to the system, as von Mises avers, but rather in the fact that a great many people do not understand it. Those who profess to believe in the competitive enterprise system but insist on demanding more and more government services may not realize that, in so doing, they are hamstringing the system itself. It is lethargy and lack of understanding, rather than outright opposition, that constitutes the greatest danger to capitalism. Dr. von Mises is at his best when he explains and defends capitalism. He is at his worst when he inveighs with more emotion than reason against those who oppose it. In mistaking the major danger to capitalism, his book renders but little service."

H. W. *Bücher für die Wirtschaft.* Deutsches Industrieinstitut. 3:7 (July 1957) 82. "For all who are economically and psychologically inclined, for all who cherish personal and economic freedom, this book, so clearly presented with graphic examples, is extremely instructive." (Translated from the German)

Watson, Phil. "Phonies Indicted." *Mercury-News.* San Jose, California. December 23, 1956. This book "is timely, needed, thought-provoking, clear and emphatic. It will be enthusiastically welcomed by those sincerely espousing libertarian doctrine, free enterprise and the capitalistic system. It will be ridiculed by the anti-anti-communists, the pseudo-anti-communists, the new concept of 'liberals,' many of the 'intellectuals' and all misfits."

Whalen, Richard. *U.S.A.* New York. (March 15, 1957) 7-8. "The backward nations, like the envious 'cousins' [relatives and dependents of successful entrepreneurs] and grumbling pseudo-intellectuals in America, need instruction in common sense economics. Moreover, many Americans enjoying the rewards of free enterprise urgently need to take a 'refresher course' in the theory of popular capitalism . . . . The best possible reading material for such a refresher course is *The Anti-Capitalist Mentality* by Dr. Ludwig von Mises."

"Die Wurzeln des Anti-Kapitalismus" [The Roots of Anti-capitalism]. No. 245 (October 21, 1958). Review of the 1958 German translation (found among Dr. von Mises' papers at Grove City College) from an unidentified, apparently West German, newspaper.

Zeitschrift für das gesamte Kreditwesen. Frankfurt am Main. "Der Anti-Kapitalismus" [Anti-capitalism]. 11:2 (January 15, 1958) 76. A review of the 1958 German translation. "Expressions of seductive precision are to be found in great numbers in the book. Otherwise, its strength stems from the fact that it was by no means written for the economically sophisticated reader only, but for the widest possible circle of citizens in all lands, just so long as they are concerned with the sociological basis of their existence." (Translated from the German)

Zentrale für Wirtschaftsdokumentation. Zurich. *Besprechungen und Hinweise* [Reviews and Comments]. 15 (1958) 1-2. The author concludes that "resentment" and "frustrated ambition" are responsible for the intellectuals' rejection of capitalism.

Bureaucracy (B-13)

American Affairs. New York: National Industrial Conference Board. "The World That Might Have Been." 7:1 (January 1945) 47-49. A joint review of *Bureaucracy* and *Omnipotent Government.* With respect to *Bureaucracy*: "It is true that bureaucrats are free to decide questions of vital importance in the individual's life; it is true that the unelected bureaucrats are no longer 'the servants of the citizenry but irresponsible and arbitrary masters'; it is true, furthermore, that 'bureaucracy is imbued with an implacable hatred of business and free enterprise.' But none of this is the fault of bureaucracy primarily. It is the outcome of 'that system of government which restricts the individual's freedom to manage his own affairs and assigns more and more tasks to the government'."

American Agriculturist. "A Critical Look at Bureaucracy." (December 3, 1949). Quotes at some length from the book. Then notes that "*Bureaucracy* is a book which could well be read and studied by every voter."

Arnold, Frazer. *American Bar Association Journal.* 49:3 (March 1963) 276. "Judged by any standard of excellence, this is a terrific little book. So brilliantly written and close-knit is the development of the thesis that a reviewer finds himself marking nearly every paragraph for possible quotation, while hoping at the same time to achieve the impossible feat of condensing the whole into a column or two of summary . . . . [M]ay conceivably be an epoch-making piece of work."

Barger, Melvin D. *Reason.* Santa Barbara, Calif. (May 1977) 42-43. A double review of Mises' *Bureaucracy* (1970 edition) and Herbert Kaufman's *Are Government Organizations Immortal?* (Brookings, 1976). "Although Mr. Kaufman supplies excellent reasons for the growth of government organizations, anybody who wants to understand the bureaucratic jungle more thoroughly would do well to consult the slender volume *Bureaucracy*, written more than 30 years ago by the late Ludwig von Mises . . . . As Mises saw it, bureaucracy has its rightful place in the scheme of things . . . . The government organization is set up to carry out certain policies and to follow detailed rules and regulations fixed by a higher body . . . . A large commercial organization also has its own policies and detailed rules and regulations, but no executive who fails to maintain profitability in his operations can escape criticism by insisting that he followed the rules . . . . Mr. Kaufman, though presenting a good analysis of the growth phenomenon, does not sound overly distressed by the prospect of bigger and bigger government. Mises, on the other hand, thought that eternal life for the bureaucracies will mean death for democracy. ¶Mises believed that a free market and personal freedom are inseparable. So far, the interventionists have only proved him right. They pay lip service to personal freedom, but under total bureaucracy real freedom just isn't in the rules!"

Book of the Month Club News. Undated quote on book jacket of *Omnipotent Government* (Yale, 4th printing): "Ludwig von Mises lifts his warning finger against permitting increased government interference with capitalism . . . . Bureaucracy is considered as a symptom of the growing movement in the direction of the socialistic state."

Boston Herald [or *Boston Traveler*]. (October 4, 1944). "Ludwig von Mises, author of *Bureaucracy*, ... [is] an authority on social and economic questions. ¶While ostensibly directed at the evils of bureaucratic government, *Bureaucracy* seems to aim chiefly at exposing the fallacies of socialism, with which it exhibits bureaucracy as inseparably linked . . . . although the arguments he uses are not new, they are none the less useful."

Branden, Nathaniel. *Book News.* Los Angeles: Academic Associates. 4 (June 1970) 8-9. Reviewed in conjunction with *Omnipotent Government* and *Theory and History*. "*Bureaucracy* is a brilliantly informative analysis of the radical difference between bureaucratic management and management for profit . . . . Professor von Mises' point is not a condemnation of bureaucracy as such; on the contrary, in the management of a government pursuing its proper functions it is useful and necessary. It becomes a disaster only when it is the method employed in areas where private enterprise ought to be free to function. That is, it becomes a disaster when government attempts to manage the economy in whole or in part."

Brookings Institution. *Bulletin.* (December 1944) 13-18. A brief "descriptive summary" of the themes in Mises' *Bureaucracy* -- profit management, bureaucratic management, bureaucracy in private enterprise, social and political implications, and psychological aspects.

Chicago Daily Law Bulletin. Undated quote on book jacket of *Bureaucracy* (Yale, 3rd printing): "A masterful critique of socialism and capitalism . . . . Truly Mises is an alchemist who transforms cold logic into warm reading."

Chicago Sun. "Contrast Between Free Enterprise and Bureaucracy." (October 23, 1944). "Dr. von Mises draws a complete and violent contrast between the conduct and organization of business and of economic affairs under the free enterprise system and under governmental intervention, control or ownership. The latter, of course, is bureaucracy . . . . Dr. von Mises believes that wealth is the only incentive for human effort; men work hard in order to get rich, and to that end only. I can't agree. I believe that men work for many ends."

Christian Century. Chicago. (October 18, 1944). "Capitalism and the profit system have not within recent years had a more clear-cut defense, or socialism a sharper attack, than this Austrian economist presents . . . . [T]he author states with dispassionate clarity the inherent difficulties of a system in which the control of production, prices and marketing is in the hands of government bureaus; it is not so certain that he faces with equal frankness the difficulties which developed under uncontrolled 'free enterprise' and in the unrestricted operation of the profit motive."

Cleaves, Freeman. *The Wall Street Journal.* Undated review quoted on book jacket of *Bureaucracy* (Yale, 3rd printing): "Considered as a thing *BUREAUCRACY* takes up little room on the bookshelf and is moderately priced. Considered as a medium of ideas it is immensely fruitful."

The Commonweal. 41:78 (November 3, 1944). Unsigned review; reviewer identified in *Conservative Book Club Bulletin* (January 1976) as J. C. Cort. "*Bureaucracy* is, in fact, one of the most amazing exhibitions seen in these parts in many years. The Professor is no dunce. He delivers a critique of socialism that is clever, penetrating, and often damaging. He is a well-read, cultivated man who knows his Plato and can quote Goethe's tribute to double-entry bookkeeping without even stopping for breath. ¶But then the Professor turns to his eulogy of pure, unregulated capitalism, and suddenly, right there before your eyes, he disintegrates completely and begins babbling the most absurd and vicious nonsense . . . . One minute you see before you the sound, cultivated scholar; the next minute a dangerous character frothing at the mouth . . . . ¶To be very calm and objective about it, the Professor's mistake is not that he thinks that [a] world of completely free, unregulated competition is the best of all possible worlds. That is a legitimate subject for day-dreaming. What is inexcusable is that an intelligent man should believe, or pretend, that such a world is possible here and now."

Fetter, Frank Albert. *American Economic Review.* 35:3 (June 1945) 445-446. "*The Road to Serfdom* by Friedrich Hayek, and *Omnipotent Government* and *Bureaucracy* by Ludwig von Mises, are essentially harmonious formulations of the present issue between freedom (political as well as economic) and the trend toward totalitarianism . . . . ¶At times even a reader in sympathy with the author's main thesis may question whether capitalism is not exalted too much by crediting it so fully with all the fruits of science, invention, and cultural progress. Yet the case for free enterprise *versus* socialism has nowhere been more ably and readably stated in brief compass . . . . Professor von Mises is a consummate general theorist in this day of specialization, and he views the problem broadly and speaks with deep conviction."

Gordon, Rosalie. "The 'Let-the-Government-Do-It' Evil." *America's Future.* New Rochelle, N.Y.   12:9 (February 27, 1970) 5-7. "It is . . . a propitious moment for the reissuance of Professor Ludwig von Mises' classic essay on *Bureaucracy*, first published 26 years ago . . . . Of most especial significance and timeliness is the author's chapter on 'The Psychological Consequences of Bureaucratization.' And don't let that mouthful of a heading throw you off. It deals with the causes and effects, in other nations, of advanced bureaucracy on wild, lawless youth movements. Though written a quarter of a century ago, it is terrifying in its relationship to today's conditions."

The Guidepost. Cincinnati. (January 1945).

J.P.H. [Jean-Pierre Hamilius]. "La Bureaucratie" [Bureaucracy]. *Letzeburger Journal.* Luxembourg. (February 25, 1959) 4. A long review of the 1946 French-language translation: "In the first part of this book the author provides a brilliant analysis of the free enterprise system, 'the profit system' characterized by social cooperation and the division of labor based on private property of the means of production. In this system, the material factors of production are the property of private persons, entrepreneurs and landowners. ¶But even if the entrepreneurs, capitalists and workers are at the helm of the ship, 'they are not free to set its course.' The commander-in-chief, the captain, is the consumer . . . . After a brief examination of bureaucracy in an authoritarian regime, von Mises criticizes bureaucracy in a democratic regime. The first quality of an administrator in an authoritarian regime is 'obedience to the rules and decrees of the "sovereign".' It must be the same in a democracy . . . . The fundamental question posed to all westerners who love liberty is: 'Should the individual relinquish more and more liberty, initiative and personal responsibility to a gigantic agency of constraint and coercion, the omnipotent State, supported by the defenders of a planned society?' To this question . . . the reader will find a wide range of interesting lucid and precise answers." (Translated from the French)

J.W.H. *San Francisco Chronicle.* (February 18, 1945). "What Dr. von Mises stands for and what he means by bureaucracy may be best understood from some of his concluding remarks: ' . . . What must be realized is only that the straitjacket of bureaucratic organization paralyzes the individual's initiative'."

Hacker, Louis M. "The Problems of Collectivism: The Conflict Between Profit and Bureaucratic Management." *New York Herald Tribune* (October 22?, 1944). "There is great merit in much of what Mr. von Mises has to say about the political and psychological dangers of state interventionism; the stultification that follows from an expansion of the governmental bureaus, the fear of innovation and the cynical contempt for the popular will -- these are real dangers against which enough warnings cannot be raised."

Hackett, Francis. *New York Times.* (September 28, 1944) 17. "The plight of the [bureaucratically-bedeviled] citizen is admitted, but what wise man has the remedy? Is it Ludwig von Mises, the Austrian economist whom the generous John Chamberlain . . . declared to be the author of 'one of the great books [*Omnipotent Government*] of our age'? . . . . Well, the profit yardstick is a good one, but it doesn't give incentive to your wife, or your priest, or the postoffice that made a good job of V-mail [a system developed during World War II, whereby letters from soldiers overseas written on special postal letter forms were censored and microfilmed, the film shipped to continental U.S. and processed, the letters then printed out (4" x 5") and distributed to the addressees], or to the Soviet Army . . . . Mr. von Mises has compressed much of a brilliant economist's hard and tight thinking into this too brief survey, but we still need a masterpiece on 'too big'. . . . The 'great society' needs a bureaucracy, but not too much of one, in order to correct the dangers of the profit system. And we want our profit system erected not on a bloodless figment, the Economic Man, but on creatures who have blood in their veins, and ethics in the offing."

Harlow, Robert M. (?) [name illegible on compilers' copy]. "Bureaucracy." *Economic & Business Review & Digest* (Summer 1945). "Although, the author points out, bureaucracy in itself is neither good nor bad, being the proper procedure for certain administrative agencies, it is bad when applied to every sphere of economic life and results in a rigidity which impairs productivity of any economic effort which comes under its domination . . . . From the argument one can gather that experience has demonstrated some great achievements of capitalism, while bureaucracy cannot yet point to such achievement and can only weakly make promises for the future . . . . Hence, on that point, it would be well for anyone concerned with this problem to read von Mises' little book, no matter what his bias."

Hazlitt, Henry. "Bureaucracy Defined." *New York Times Book Review.* (October 1, 1944) 5. "[T]he main thesis of Professor von Mises is that bureaucracy is merely a symptom of the real disease with which we have to deal. That disease is excessive State domination and control . . . . Published on the day after F. A. Hayek's *The Road to Serfdom*, Professor von Mises' *Bureaucracy* once more calls attention to the ironic fact that the most eminent and uncompromising of defenders of English liberty, and the system of free enterprise, which reached its highest development in America, should now be two Austrian exiles."

Herring, Pendleton. *The Annals of the American Academy of Political and Social Science.* 238 (March 1945) 213. "If this volume were written as a campaign document, it would merit attention at the technical level as a contrivance for obfuscating debate in accordance with the adage: 'If you can't convince them, confuse them' . . . . According to the author, the 'economists' are pitted against the 'progressives.' The latter believe in socialism, the former in a free market. Thus the author reduces the complexities of our age to a bald ideological impasse."

Hoiles, R. C. "*Bureaucracy*, a Great Book." *Santa Ana* (California) *Register* or possibly the *Colorado Springs Gazette Telegraph.* (September 28 & 29, 1944). "It is a pleasure to read a book written by a thinker . . . . If there was ever a book that shows the impossibility of making a totalitarian or a planned economy work, it is this book . . . . This book shows how impossible it is to keep books accurately when the State attempts to control production . . . . if all nations were operated as Russia, there would be absolutely no way of knowing what the consumers most wanted. There would be no way of measuring values."

Johnson, F. Ernest. *Information Service.* New York: Federal Council of the Churches of Christ in America, Department of Research and Education. 24:18 (May 5, 1945) 1-2. A triple review of *Bureaucracy*, F. A. Hayek's *The Road to Serfdom* and John T. Flynn's *As We Go Marching*. "It will be obvious that an acceptance of the views presented in these three books would invalidate most of what church bodies have been saying for many years."

Kirkus. 12:359 (August 15, 1944).

Lane, Rose Wilder. *Economic Council Review of Books.* New York: National Economic Council. 2:10 (November 1945). A triple review of Mises' *Bureaucracy* and *Omnipotent Government* together with Heinrich Hauser's *The German Talks Back.* After urging the reader to get, keep, read and reread *Omnipotent Government*, Lane adds, "And while you're about it, get Professor Mises's *Bureaucracy*, a little book which disposes of a lot of current nonsense. It explains why bureaucrats are what they are, and why it does no good to change bureaucrats in the middle of bureaucracy."

North, Gary. "Statist Bureaucracy in the Modern Economy." *The Freeman.* Irvington, N.Y. 20:1 (January 1970) 16-28. "Ludwig von Mises has offered a theory of bureaucracy that provides us with another explanation of today's inefficient firms. His discussion complements [Max] Weber's and improves upon it. Mises argues in his little book, *Bureaucracy* (1944), that there are two primary models of bureaucracy: (1) the free market structure; and (2) the statist bureaucracy. Both are necessary, he says; both perform valuable, but very different, functions. One form cannot be used to perform the tasks more suited for the other. It is an unwarranted mixing of the two categories, we can conclude, that has led to the creation of a weakened free market." (p.20)

Orton, William A. *The Yale Review*. Undated quote on book jacket of *Bureaucracy* (Yale, 3rd printing): "The present short work -- which is a pleasure to handle as well as to read -- makes a good contribution to the whole issue; it should have a wide hearing."

A. I. P. "Austrian Blasts Bureaucracy With Odd Arguments." *Hartford* (Connecticut) *Times*. (September 24, 1944). "Prof. von Mises is centering his fire upon bureaucracy, which he makes almost synonymous with socialism. However, unlike many critics, he holds that the bureaucrat blocks new ideas rather than being overgenerous in imposing them on the public . . . Perhaps it is a European point of view he expresses. To this reviewer it seems reactionary, and dangerously confusing on a vital issue."

Revere, C. T. *Cotton and Other Problems*. New York: Laird, Bissell & Meeds. October 27, 1944. "In the concluding paragraph of his notable book, *Bureaucracy*, discussing the threat to individual free enterprise imposed by government supported and directed Socialism, Professor Ludwig von Mises offered the following as the sole effective means to combat this menace: 'Against all this frenzy of agitation there is but one weapon available; reason. Just common-sense is needed to prevent man from falling prey to illusory and empty catchwords'. . . . One of the outstanding phenomena of our time has been the evidence of a growing sympathy for the principle of State-ism as opposed to the ideals expressed in the terms of individual freedom, democracy, or what have you . . . . Why this almost mysterious acceptance of over-riding power in the hands of the State so ominously manifest in the high political circles over the world, including such so-called democracies as Britain and the United States? It is not perhaps so much a case of outright endorsement as a submissive bowing to what is believed to be inevitable."

_____. Source unknown. Quoted on the book jacket of *Bureaucracy* (Yale, 3rd printing): "This little volume of only 125 pages is so compact in its treatment of the distinction between bureaucracy and capitalistic free enterprise that the reading of the entire book becomes a 'must' obligation. It is probably not going too far to pronounce it the 'Mighty Atom'."

Roberts, Mary-Carter. *Washington Star*. (October 1, 1944). Unsigned review found among Mises' papers; reviewer identified as Mary-Carter Roberts on book jacket of *Omnipotent Government* (Yale, 3rd printing). "There have been a number of books on bureaucracy lately, all good, but this one seems to the reviewer the most significant by a wide margin . . . . [The author] is a German [sic] economist of unquestionable soundness. He saw the rise of Naziism and feels that he knows the signs. We are getting it here. That is his message . . . . Nothing could be clearer or more logical than Dr. von Mises' presentation. His book is recommended."

Rubinoff. *Valley Young Republicans*. Phoenix, Arizona. (December 1977). "Quite simply, von Mises argues against the Prussian-type of bureaucrat who simply 'takes orders.' In noting the growth of bureaucracy during the New Deal, von Mises warns that profit management, infinitely preferable to bureaucratic management, is being subverted by socialists of the international (Soviet Union-type) and national (Nazi Germany-type) varieties."

Shenfield, A. A. *Economica*. New Series, 12:47 (August 1945). "His case is not new, but his arguments are fresh, his language succinct, and his mode of presentation sometimes brilliant . . . . the book has two serious weaknesses. First, Mises dismisses the socialist 'solutions' of the problem of calculation without analysis . . . . The second weakness is the worse. He dismisses Keynes with the totalitarians. Now it may be just to write off the Keynesians this way, for even the most sophisticated of them . . . are capable of totalitarian excesses . . . . Yet there remains Keynes the master economist. It will not do for Mises to declare *tout court* that in a free market there is only frictional unemployment. The greatest need of modern popular liberalism is to restate itself in a form which makes room for the Keynes approach."

The Wall Street Journal (Pacific Coast edition). (October 2, 1944). "Bureaucracy is very old. Professor von Mises mentions the bureaucratic machines of the Pharaohs of ancient Egypt and the emperors of China. These machines bred slaves and used them freely . . . . Professor von Mises defines bureaucratic management as the method applied in the conduct of administrative affairs the result of which has no cash value on the market. Carried too far, bureaucracy discounts production efficiency . . . . There are left to the entrepreneur the methods of either diplomacy or bribery."

Woods, Charles F. *Riverside* (California) *Press*. (September 27, or 28, 1944). "As becomes the product of a university press the new book on *Bureaucracy* by Ludwig von Mises does not deal in club-lounge gossip about the inconveniences, inequities or impositions of the various government bureaus but seeks to confine the argument to principles."

The Causes of the Economic Crisis (B-9) (*Die Ursachen der Wirtschaftskrise*, 1931)   See also *On the Manipulation of Money and Credit* (B-24), which includes an English translation of this monograph.

Conrad, Otto. "Der Interventionismus als Ursache der Wirtschaftskrise: eine Auseinandersetzung mit Ludwig Mises" [Interventionism as an Explanation of the Economic Crisis: A Discussion with Ludwig von Mises]. *Jahrbücher für Nationalökonomie und Statistik.* (Jena: Gustav Fischer).   137:82 (1932) 161-174. The reviewer agrees with Mises that unemployment stems from intervention with prices and wages. Mises blames the government; the reviewer, however, also blames private entrepreneurs, monopolists and cartels. According to the reviewer, Mises fails to recognize the interventionism of entrepreneurs because of his (1) vagueness in defining monopoly, (2) indefinite classification of unemployment, (3) failure to understand the effect of "rationalization" [automation] on the demand for labor, and (4) adherence to the theory that wages and prices of production stem from consumer goods prices. The reviewer concludes that unemployment is due not only to the height of wages but also to the height of prices and the tax burden. To relieve unemployment, therefore, prices and taxes must be adjusted.

Genechten, R. van. "Literatur zur Wirtschaftskrisis" [Literature on the Economic Crisis]. *Weltwirtschaftliches Archiv* (Institut für Weltwirtschaft und Seeverkehr an der Universität Kiel). (Jena: Gustav Fischer). 36:1 (July 1932) 1-18. A review of several books on the economic crisis. Comments on Mises' *Die Ursachen der Wirtschaftskrise* (B-9) appear on pp.15-18. `According to the reviewer, Mises blames the boom on artificially low interest rates which increase prices, especially those of the factors of production. The reviewer agrees with Mises that an economic crisis is due to too much credit expansion but he believes that "rationalization" [industrialization or automation] will help to maintain security prices and profits to some extent, thus counteracting the effects of an artificially lower interest rate. The reviewer also says that Mises does not explain why crises recur periodically.

Hardy, Charles O. *American Economic Review.* 22:1 (March 1932) 115-116. "This pamphlet presents with admirable clarity, but without detailed supporting argument, the essentials of the modern Austrian theory of business cycles, and an application of this theory to the special conditions of the present crisis. Professor Mises is a consistent nineteenth-century liberal who does not hesitate to follow the logic of theory to a practical conclusion. ¶Briefly, the author believes that market price offers a better guide to productive activity than does any system of authoritarian interference . . . . Attempts to cure the crisis by further governmental interference with the course of trade and prices are bound to do more harm than good."

A Critique of Interventionism. (B-8) (*Kritik des Interventionismus*, 1929; English translation, 1977).

Arlington House. *Catalog*. (Fall 1977). "When the great Austrian-school economist Ludwig von Mises penned the six essays in this never-before-translated volume, he was addressing himself to the theories and policies that animated the social and economic programs of Germany's ill-fated Weimar Republic of the 1920s. But these classic writings are as relevant today as they were half a century ago. The names and places have changed, but the same tired statist notions still hold sway. And Mises' incisive criticisms, firmly grounded in immutable economic principles, are still valid . . . . Taken together, these essays demolish the notion of the German 'Socialists of the Chair' -- and today's American 'mainstream' economists -- that there can be an interventionist middle of the road between a free social order based on private property and a totalitarian command society of government ownership or management of production and distribution. Mises leaves no doubt that the middle of the road leads to socialism, that there can be no democratic middle way between classical liberalism and communism."

Armentano, D. T. *Reason*. Santa Barbara, Calif. (May 1978) 66. "One of the little-known difficulties in the development of the contributions of the great Austrian economists has been the unavailability -- or delayed availability -- of their writings in English . . . . It is in this light that we must greet enthusiastically the recent publishing of six essays written by Ludwig von Mises in the 1920's . . . . Mises' favorite example of interventionism is price fixing, and he repeatedly describes the various consequences of price interference on the part of government. The entire scenario is summed up as follows: 'at first price control, then forced sales, then rationing, then regulation of production and distribution, and finally attempts at central planning of all production and distribution.'"

Brownfeld, Allan C. *America's Future*. New Rochelle, N.Y. 20:3 (February 10, 1978) 6-7. "Von Mises calls upon his fellow economists to look at things as they are rather than applying a Marxist or some other economic theology to economic reality. The fact is, the author declares, that socialism makes things worse for the 'proletariat' in whose name it is advocated -- not better. He notes that, 'Even the Soviets had to yield. They did not proceed with the socialization of land, but merely distributed the land to the rural population. In trade and commerce they replaced pure socialism with the "New Economic Policy." However, the ideology did not participate in this retreat . . . . The world can support teeming humanity in the manner in which it has been supported in recent decades only if men work capitalistically. Only capitalism can be expected to further raise the productivity of human labor'."

The Christian News.   New Haven, Missouri. (November 14, 1977) 15. "The publisher observes that . . . . 'Mises leaves no doubt that the middle of the road leads to socialism, that there can be no democratic middle way between classical liberalism and communism'."

Donway, Walter. "Von Mises Dissects Interventionism." *Human Events*. (October 20, 1979) 10, 14. "Von Mises identifies two major categories of intervention. ¶First, there are direct restrictions on production . . . . Von Mises directed most of his attention, however, to a second category of intervention: *price controls*. ¶If government attempts to set and enforce a price *above* that determined by the unhampered market, demand must fall . . . . ¶If, as widely advocated today, government sets and enforces a price *below* that determined by the unhampered market, demand outruns supply . . . . Unable to keep producing at the controlled price . . . marginal producers go out of business. ¶Capital and labor shift as rapidly as possible to other fields, where uncontrolled prices offer a better return . . . . ¶The case against interventionism made by von Mises (and by the 'Austrian School' of economics, to which he belonged) never received a respectable reply or rebuttal. Interventionists smeared and dismissed it as paranoid fear of 'creeping socialism'."

Ebeling, Richard M. *The Austrian Economics Newsletter.* New York: Center for Libertarian Studies. 1:3 (Fall 1978) 9-10. "When [Mises] defended theoretical analysis against the German Historicists, Mises was, in fact, defending the edifice of microeconomics -- the economics of interrelationships between individuals and sectors of the economy . . . . In perhaps the most fascinating essay in the volume, Mises discusses the phenomena [sic] of 'Anti-Marxism,' which later became German National Socialism. Writing in 1925, he prophetically argues that an attempt to unify the 'Aryan race' under a nationalist-militarist banner would have disastrous consequences: 'If Germany . . . were to assault in accordance with this principle, it would invite a coalition of all its neighbors into a world-political constellation: enemies all around. In such a situation Germany could find only one ally: Russia . . . . German Anti-Marxism and Russian Super-Marxism are not too far apart'."

_____. "Mises on Money, Intervention and Himself." *Laissez Faire Books Catalog & Review.* New York. (Spring-Summer 1978) 29-30. A triple review of *A Critique of Interventionism*, plus Mises' *Notes and Recollections* (B-23) and *On the Manipulation of Money and Credit* (B-24). With respect to *Critique . . .* the reviewer writes: "At one level, Mises had attempted to refute interventionist doctrines by showing that the policies imposed brought about conditions less desirable than the original circumstances, even when seen from the intervener's own perspective, e.g., price controls that impose prices for goods below prevailing costs of production resulting in a smaller quantity being produced than before. ¶But the most important aspect of Mises' critique of interventionism was the analysis -- developed more fully in his later works -- that interventionist measures served as a method to bestow privileges on various individuals and groups in society. The crisis of interventionism is, basically, a crisis of special interests fighting amongst themselves for better positions within a new caste system."

_____. *The Libertarian Forum.* New York. 10:11 (November 1977) 4-5. "We live in the Age of Crises. The energy 'crisis,' . . . the inflation 'crisis,' . . . the moral 'crisis,' . . . and the 'crisis' of national security . . . . But this Age of Crises is only the outer symptom of the more fundamental malady, the Crisis of Interventionism . . . . ¶Though originally published in 1929, Ludwig von Mises' *Critique of Interventionism* is one of the most relevant and important works for grasping the underlying principles causing the crises of our age."

Eshleman, Tim. *The Entrepreneur.* Grove City, Penna.: Grove City College. 3:3 (May 1978) 4. The reviewer quotes Mises: "The sole point under discussion is whether there are only two possible forms of social organization . . . that is, the public property order and the private property order, or whether there is yet a third system as assumed by interventionists, namely, a private property order that is regulated through government intervention." The reviewer then states: "Professor Mises clearly demonstrates that there can be no logical third system of interventionism . . . . Any attempt to introduce in earnest a middle system of property that is hampered, guided and regulated by government must lead to a crisis from which either socialism or capitalism alone can emerge." Reprinted in *World Research INK* (January 1979).

Evans, Medford. *American Opinion.* Belmont, Mass. (March 1978) 57-60. "Reading the essays in this little volume, and realizing that they were composed in the 1920s (von Mises' own preface to the collection is dated -- with historic irony -- June 1929, four months before the Wall Street crash that ushered in the Great Depression), one is at first tempted to express astonishment that anything so relevant to the 1970s (and 1980s) should have been written half a century ago."

Evans, M. Stanton. *National Review.* New York. (January 19, 1979) 112. Reviewed in conjunction with Mises' *Liberalism* (B-6). Concerning *Critique . . .* : "The argument of this volume is that no *via media* is possible, that once embarked on the path of intervention an economy is fated to increasing regimentation. This is so, Mises contends, because each intervention creates problems that seem to require another intervention, and so *ad infinitum.*"

Geis, Richard E. *A Personal Journal..* Portland, Oregon. (June 1978). "These are articles and commentaries written by this Holy Man of Capitalism in the 1920's, in which he demolishes the fundamentals of socialism and marxism, and shows that government intervention in the economy always results in the opposite of what is desired."

A. H. *Die Hilfe.* 10 (1930). "The book is a guide to critical thinking with respect to our economic policy and ideology." Quoted in publisher's release. (Translated from the German)

Hazlitt, Henry. "Three New Books by Ludwig von Mises." *The Freeman.* Irvington, N.Y. 28:4 (April 1978) 247-253. A triple review of *A Critique* . . . (pp.249-251), Mises' *Notes and Recollections* (B-23) and *On the Manipulation of Money and Credit* (B-24). "The main theme of this book . . . is not only the needlessness, but the immense harm done by government intervention in economic affairs . . . . In addition to interventionism properly so called, one or two of the essays in this book discuss such topics as socialism, Marxism, anti-Marxism, and the nationalization of credit. But the reasoning throughout leads to the conclusion that interventionism must disorganize production, and that in the long run there is only one alternative for economic organization: either capitalism or socialism. 'There is no third road.'"

Jarosz, Joan. *The Bulletin.* Chicago: Economic Education & Research Forum. (November 1977). "Taken together, the six essays constitute irrepressible arguments against current conventional economic thought and policies . . . . Interventionism does not work and requires ever-increasing intervention to suppress the damage of the prior interventions and to 'fix' the government programs. The middle road only leads eventually to socialism."

Magdeburgische Zeitung. (August 12, 1931). "Mises is one of the most persistent advocates of the free market economy . . . . It may be that he defends the idea of economic freedom too stridently . . . . However, at a time when coercive economic measures dominate the economy as much as they do today, it is valuable to point once more to the damage which the over-extension of such interventions bring in their wake." Quoted in publisher's release. (Translated from the German)

Mitteilungen d. Ges. für deutsche Wirtschafts- und Sozialpolitik. 1 (1930). "The policy of the 'hampered' market economy, which leads to neither socialism nor capitalism directly, is known as 'interventionism,' and it is this that Mises attacks . . . . The importance and meaningfulness of these analyses need not be pointed out again. We are already experiencing all too clearly that our present interventionist economic policy is doing more harm than good. If one looks for the reason, Mises shows that it rests on the essence of the policy itself. Anyone who wants to understand today's economic policy should read this book." Quoted in publisher's release. (Translated from the German)

Pietrusza, David A. *Human Events.* Washington, D.C. (December 31, 1977) 16 (1044). "In the opening pages of this collection of essays by the late Ludwig von Mises . . . he makes the telling point that despite the ideological firewords [sic] that the battles between socialism and capitalism set off in tone and monograph, the system winning the day is actually neither one. It is that hybrid claimed by neither of its parents -- the mixed economy, state socialism, interventionism . . . . ¶Von Mises saw the dangers of an emergent Nazi philosophy and was quick to point out that although it was anti-Marxist it was by no means anti-Socialist."

Economic Freedom and Interventionism (B-29).

Bradford, R. W. *Liberty.* Port Townsend, Wash. 4:6 (July 1991) 66-67. This "anthology of Mises' journalistic efforts, along with a few miscellaneous previously unpublished (in English, anyway) papers and addresses . . . . may not be Mises at his best, but even second-rate Mises is better than the writing of most economists or social thinkers . . . . a valuable collection of the miscellaneous Mises, of value to every serious student of Mises or Austrian economics, and . . . of interest to anyone who cares about human liberty."

Ebeling, Richard M. *Freedom Daily.* Denver, Colo. 2:9 (September 1991) 16-18. "Ludwig von Mises is quite possibly the greatest economist of the 20th century. He was one of a handful of important thinkers in our time who consistently and incessantly warned of the dangers of all forms of collectivism, and who presented an uncompromising case for the free society . . . . ¶[T]he book under review . . . . offer[s] an excellent overview of Mises' ideas on almost every economic-policy issue: inflation and monetary policy; regulation and competition; fiscal policy; international trade; wage and price controls; union power; Keynesian economics; and socialist planning . . . . ¶It is especially in the arena of the marketplace that Mises saw the greatest danger to both freedom and prosperity. Mises' method of attack was to ask a simple but important question in the process of analyzing the various policies of the interventionist state: will the policy methods chosen attain the economic and social ends desired?"

The Free Market. Auburn, Ala.: Ludwig von Mises Institute. 9:1 (January 1991) 7. "Bettina Bien Greaves has assembled 47 of Mises's shorter, popular articles into a handsome 250-page quality paperback . . . . And every article is a gem . . . . ¶If you are looking for the perfect introduction to Mises for a student or nonacademic, this is it. But the scholar should not miss this collection either. It proves once again that the powerful thought of Ludwig von Mises will long survive the trendy and fleeting ideas of his contemporaries."

Garrison, Roger W. *Review of Austrian Economics.* Auburn, Ala.: Ludwig von Mises Institute; Norwell, Mass.: Kluwer. 5:2 (1991) 119-121. "Characteristically, Mises has no patience with those who seemingly feign ignorance of economics in order to bolster their case for central control or those who flaunt their ignorance in some misdirected criticism of the business community . . . . But Mises has near-infinite patience with the layperson who is eager to understand economic principles . . . . ¶Mises emphasizes the interconnectedness of economic phenomena . . . . [He] argues that there can exist no middle way in the form of interventionism . . . . ¶Though writing decades ago, Mises incorporates into his arguments many economic theories that have emerged full-blown only in recent years. He anticipates the kernel of truth in so-called Rational Expectations Theory by criticizing Keynes for his implicit belief that inflation can deceive the public persistently; he anticipates a key aspect of Supply-side Economics and its Laffer Curve in noting that governments resort to inflation when tax rates have been pushed beyond the point of maximum returns . . . . ¶If there is a weakness that characterizes this collection of essays, it is Mises's tendency to underestimate the enduring appeal of the ideas he criticizes. For instance, he writes that 'As an economic doctrine, Keynesianism is now dead' and that with the posthumous publication of the third volume of Marx's *Das Kapital* (1894), the 'essential dogma of the Marxian philosophy, the class conflict doctrine . . . , was unmasked as a flop.' But even now, as much as then, Keynesian doctrine is still alive, and Marxist doctrine still masquerades as high theory."

McGee, Robert W. *Asian Economic Review.* Hyderabad (India). 33:1 (April 1991) 154-157. In one essay in this collection, "Mises points out that there can be morality only if there is freedom. Individuals can act morally or immorally only if they have choice. Where there is no choice, there is no freedom. Without economic freedom, there can be no personal freedom. The two go together . . . . ¶For anyone who is unfamiliar with the work of Ludwig von Mises, this volume would be a good place to start . . . . For those who are familiar with Mises, the book provides a good, brief refresher course in Misesian thought."

Peterson, William H. "Mises: The Impact of Ideas." *The Freeman.* Irvington, N.Y. 41:1 (January 1991) 35-38. "The impact of ideas is a theme that echoes and re-echoes in the works of Ludwig von Mises . . . . So, to repeat the observation of Mises, ideas direct thinking, govern lives, and forge history. Which is why *Economic Freedom and Interventionism* . . . is so vital and timely . . . . ¶Mrs. Greaves, a close friend of Mises and a faithful student in his famous graduate seminar at New York University . . . . thoughtfully collates the 47 pieces, most of them out-of-print or not easily available, into four sections: Economic Freedom, Interventionism, Mises As Critic, and Economics and Ideas. Ideas of course permeate the entire anthology -- much-needed ideas of a most constructive sort. ¶Take the Marxist idea of class conflict . . . . Mises notes how the emerging market or contractual society of some two or three centuries ago soon obliterated the class lines drawn by serfdom and slavery. ¶Yet, maintains Mises, class or status survives today only by government fiat in such dubious taxonomy and forms as subsidies . . . , discriminatory taxation . . . , affirmative action . . . , and union privileges . . . . So classes today become legal fictions and, by law, social frictions. In this sense, Marx's class struggle does persist, an undeserved triumph for the Left."

Economic Policy: Thoughts for Today and Tomorrow (B-27)

Brownfeld, Allan C. *America's Future.* New Rochelle, N.Y. 22 (November 16, 1979) 6-7.

Chamberlain, John. "Balancing the Books." *Barron's.* (April 21, 1980) 18, 20. "The lucidity of this little book is a marvelous tribute to Margit von Mises' memory of the way her husband talked to informal audiences. Some tapes were made in Buenos Aires of the von Mises lectures, but they were transcribed by a Spanish speaking secretary whose lack of facility in English led to something that might be called Spanglish. The English place name, 'Speenhamland,' which was used as shorthand for a state policy of supplementing agricultural wages, became in the transcription the 'seed in land' policy. Margit found the somewhat mangled transcription in her husband's posthumous papers. With the help of George Koether, it took a year -- and her very good Viennese actress' memory -- to prepare an authentic manuscript."

Cobb, Joe. *Journal of Economic Growth.* Wash., D.C.: National Chamber Foundation. 4:2 (Summer 1990) 33-34. "[T]here is no nation that has adopted economic policies promoting government intervention, inflation, restricted foreign investment or direct socialism in which the conditions of the masses have not deteriorated. Unfortunately, the host country for these 1958 [1959] lectures, Argentina, is a sad example supporting this claim . . . . ¶Von Mises was in every way the leading intellectual of our time. Sadly, like many great artists, he is most appreciated after his death. His greatest student, F. A. Hayek, received the Nobel Prize in Economics in 1974. Von Mises died in 1973; however, his words still reach out to us with hope and inspiration. 'Ideas and only ideas can light the darkness. These ideas must be brought to the public in such a way that they persuade people. We must convince them that these ideas are the right ideas and not the wrong ones'." (p.105)

Evans, Medford. *American Opinion.* Belmont, Mass. 23:1 (January 1980) 73-74. "This is a very simple book on economics. I wish some of our sophisticated economists would read it. I close with a characteristic quotation from von Mises: 'In socialist countries it is not the seller who has to be grateful, it is the buyer.' Think about it."

Randerson, Roger. "Ludwig von Mises -- the Master of Economics and Fearless Champion of Freedom." *Sunday Independent.* (Australia). (June 28, 1981) 14. A "precis" setting forth the principal events in Mises life, summarizing his important contributions, and announcing the scheduled reprinting in the Australian *Sunday Independent* of Mises' six Argentine lectures.

Rothbard, Murray N. "Austrian Views." *Modern Age* Bryn Mawr, Penna.: Intercollegiate Studies Institute. 25:3 (Summer 1981) 304-306. "Much of Mises' life was a lonely struggle against great odds . . . . Yet Mises continued to be of good cheer, and his brilliance and charm managed to ignite small sparks in the United States in the period following World War II . . . . In books, articles, papers, and symposia that have accumulated since the mid-1970's, there is still no suitable introduction to Austrian theory for the student or lay reader. This gap has now been partially remedied by Mises' wife, Margit, who has edited transcribed tapes of six lectures that Mises delivered at the University of Buenos Aires in 1958 [1959]."

Yamamoto, Yujiro. "A Severe Criticism of Interventionism." *Sankei Shimbun.* Japan. (January 19, 1981). A review of the Japanese translation (titled in Japanese, *Decision for Freedom*). "The significance of publishing, at this moment, Mises' lectures given 22 years ago is proved by the fact that Mises' economics of uncompromising liberalism is now in the spotlight once more . . . . Since this book is student-oriented, Mises expounds on the market economy, the quantity theory of money, and so on, in plain language. Significant remarks on the modern economy can be found on almost every page. Particularly notable is Mises' comment that the 'production of security' is the only appropriate role for government.   Also his severe criticism of interventionist policies and of indexation which, under pressure from labor unions, automatically increases wages in response to price increases." (Translation from the Japanese by Toshio Murata)

Die Entwicklung des gutsherrlich-bäuerlichen Verhältnisses in Galizien: 1772-1849. (B-1) [The Development of the Relationship between Peasant and Lord of the Manor in Galicia: 1772-1848]. No English translation available.

Wimbersky. *Zeitschrift für Volkswirtschaft, Sozialpolitik und Verwaltung.* 15 (1906) 275. "The book . . . makes copious use of documents; it is a very valuable contribution to the history of the relationships of serfs in Austria. It follows very closely the works of Grünberg on the freeing of the peasants and the dissolution of peasant-manorial relationships in Bohemia, Moravia, and Silesia, as well as Mell's work, *Die Anfänger der Bauernbefreiung in Steiermark unter Maria Theresia und Josef II* [The Commencement of the Liberation of the Peasants in Styria under Maria Theresia and Joseph II]." (Translated from the German)

Epistemological Problems of Economics (B-10)   (*Grundprobleme der Nationalökonomie*, 1933;
English translation, 1960)

Ayres, C.E. *Southern Economic Journal*. (October 1961) 199-202.

Batson, H.E. *Economica*. New Series, 2:7 (August 1935) 336-341. "Professor Mises is completely uncompromising on the general issue that a science is not a science unless it is free from philosophical prejudices, whether of an ethical, an æsthetic, or any other nature. (A proposition which is often almost incredibly confused with the proposition that a scientist is not a scientist unless he is free from philosophical prejudices.) But he is equally uncompromisingly hostile to the assertion that, because of this, it is impossible for a science to provide rules for action . . . . [This book] whets the appetite for the more comprehensive positive work to which one dares to hope it is designed as prolegomena . . . . If we escape the Dark Age which some of the more eminent and pessimistic among us foretell, this is a book which will be of great service, not only to the cause of economics, but to the whole cause of truth."

Bode, Karl. "Die Grundprobleme der Nationalökonomie: Darstellung und Kritik" [Epistemological Problems of Economics: Presentation and Critique]. *Schmollers Jahrbuch für Gesetzgebung, Verwaltung und Volkswirtschaft im Deutschen Reich*. 57:2 (1933) 571-588.

del Vecchio, Gustavo. *Giornale degli Economisti*. 75:75 (January 1935) 50. "Ludwig von Mises is beyond question a worthy and authoritative representative of the so-called Austrian school . . . . His *Epistemological Problems of Political Economy* . . . comes after a series of works dedicated to concrete problems of political economy and to general questions of theory. His broad doctrine and precise exposition have won him admirers and followers not only in his own country but also in Italy and England." (Translation from the Italian quoted on book jacket of 1981 New York University Press reprint).

Golffing, Francis. "Varieties of Conservative Thought." *Commentary*. 30:4 (October 1960) 330-334. Reviewed together with Mises' *Human Action* and Wilhelm Röpke's *A Humane Economy*. "For over three decades now Professor Ludwig von Mises has, with admirable consistency, pursued his passion for changing the world by making it stand still . . . . The essays . . . make good reading. Their tenor is polemical throughout, the diatribe chiefly directed against Sombart and other 'historicists' . . . . ¶[H]is basic objections to his liberal colleagues . . . have not changed a whit over the years. They are today exactly what they were then: liberal economics is the gravedigger of human dignity and freedom; the so-called liberals have usurped a name which properly belongs to the conservatives; the liberal (or socialist) mind lacks rigor, plays fast and loose with logic, and has not the faintest notion of those epistemological premises which determine all human action . . . . The volume . . . modernizes and refines upon the famous *Methodenstreit* [struggle over methodology] precipitated about 1890 by two economists -- Gustav von Schmoller and Carl Menger . . . . Epistemology deals traditionally with the origin and limits of human knowledge -- why we perceive what we perceive -- and not with its *modus operandi*. Yet von Mises shows an exclusive interest in the latter, while he disclaims any concern with the former . . . . ¶Von Mises is a very articulate writer, with a hard core of common sense. Even though there is no nourishing pulp around that core, one must admit that his style is forceful and full of verve." According to Golffing, Rökpe, "unlike von Mises who wants to smash the clock, . . . only wants to turn it back, gently." See below for comments by Reisman and Rothbard , who disagree with Golffing.

_____. Letter to the Editor. Responding to Reisman and Rothbard. *Commentary*. 30:6 (December 1960) 539.

Greaves, Percy L., Jr. "The Science Called Economics." *The Freeman.* Irvington, N.Y. 10:11 (November 1960) 54-57. "His careful scalpel exposes the fine points that historians and economists must first grasp before they can add to man's knowledge of their subjects. He applies the principles of his first essay to show that men cannot even think of history, much less interpret it, without first having some ideas about action and causality . . . . Several . . . essays present details of man's slowly developing knowledge of scientific economic thought. Mises cites many of the confusions that led to the popular fallacies of our day . . . . The world today is sadly in need of the knowledge that only the science of economics can provide."

Howard, Irving E. "Epistemology and Economics." *Christian Economics*. New York. 12:14 (July 12, 1960) 4. "The central thesis of this book is that economics cannot be based on an empirical appeal to sense experience, but must begin with certain *a priori* truths such as A cannot be non A, the law of non-contradiction. Dr. Mises makes a strong case for rationalism and a devastating argument against the empiricism of modern economics . . . . Likewise, statistics, the golden calf of modern economists, must be selected according to some preconceived pattern of ideas or one would be lost in a sea of data . . . . The Christian can go a long way with Ludwig von Mises and rejoice in his defense of reason against a simple appeal to sense experience . . . but when Dr. Mises states that human action is always rational, we come to a parting of the ways . . . . Nevertheless, his book makes a solid contribution in an area rarely -- if ever -- explored: the relation of epistemology to economics."

Kaufmann, Felix. *Methodology of the Social Sciences.* New York: Oxford University Press, 1944. 225. "I have nowhere found a more precise and impressive presentation of the aprioristic thesis than in L. von Mises' writings." (Quoted on the book jacket of the 1960 English translation, where Felix Kaufmann is described as an "anti-Misesian positivist.").

Löwe, Adolf. *Zeitschrift für Sozialforschung.* 3 (1934) 312-313. "These essays present a unique demonstration of the methodological critique of the social sciences without shrinking from any of the inferences to be drawn from the deductive method." (Translated from the German)

Mackenroth, Gerhard. "Neuerscheinungen zur ökonomischen Theorie" [New Releases on Economic Theory]. *Weltwirtschaftliches Archiv.* 40 (July/November 1934) 224-234. A joint review which discusses also works by Hans Peter, Horst Wagenführ and Otto v. Zwiedineck-Südenhorst.

Reisman, George. Letter to the Editor. *Commentary.* 30:6 (December 1960) 538. "As the translator of Ludwig von Mises' *Epistemological Problems of Economics,* I must express the keenest disappointment" in Golffing's review (see above).

Rothbard, Murray N. "Epistemological Problems of Economics: Comment." *Southern Economic Journal.* (April 1962) 385-387. Comments on Ayres' review (see above).

_____. Letter to the Editor. *Commentary.* 30:6 (December 1960) 538-539. "It is difficult to say which of Professor Golffing's passages [see above] is the most (unconsciously!) humorous . . . . The joke, however, is finally on Golffing: von Mises, and his Austrian forebears, have . . . broadened economics from the classical preoccupation with only tangible 'wealth' to include intangible goods and services."

Vogel, Emanuel Hugo. *Jahrbücher für Nationalökonomie und Statistik.* 141 (1935) 235. "I am in full agreement with the battle against pure, frequently blind historicism and especially against the wholly incorrect suspension of theory -- in contrast to the necessity pointed up by von Mises of underlaying all historical research with a theoretical basis. The book includes, in addition, . . . an interesting approach to a whole series of controversial questions in political economy in their relation to psychology, sociology, as well as technology, etc." (Quoted on book jacket of 1960 English translation).

The Historical Setting of the Austrian School (B-21)

Rogers, Tommy W. *The Freeman.* Irvington, N.Y. 20:1 (January 1970) 63-64. "The importance of this book is not to be measured by its size. Von Mises ranges far beyond a chronological account of the development of important men and works in the Austrian school; he goes beyond an era history -- though he provides this in revealing fashion . . . . He touches on the study and uses of philosophy, epistemology, and history as they relate to liberty and its corollary requirements of openness to free enterprise and the free flow of ideas. We have here an enlightening venture into the sociology of knowledge, or the social context in which ideas develop and do or do not take root."

Human Action (B-16)

America. (November 26, 1949). "Because of the importance of its author, many economists will refer to this work as the most up-to-date defense of an economic theory battling for its life against the pressing competition of the collectivistic and Christian socio-economic theories . . . . As propaganda it includes much over-simplification and naive evaluation."

Austria. A German-language monthly newspaper. Philadelphia & New York. Letter to the Editor. (November 25, 1949). Comments on J. E.'s review in *Aufbau* (see below): "Mises speaks with the wisdom and culture of a pioneering university professor of the old school. Through this work, Professor Mises has raised still further the reputation of Austria in America . . . . a review such as his [J.E.'s], insofar as one can call it that, would never be expected to appear in a serious newspaper." (Translated from the German)

Baker, Lisle. "Can Socialism Work? Von Mises Says 'No'." *Courier-Journal.* Louisville, Kentucky. (November 27, 1949). *Human Action* "is a scathing but logical and dispassionate attack on socialism, communism, Keynesian theories and State intervention; and will require some herculean efforts upon the adherents of those schools to refute the thesis."

Benegas Lynch, Alberto. "Una Obra Fundamental De La Ciencia Económica: *La Acción Humana: Tratado de economía.*" [A Fundamental Work of Economic Science: *Human Action: An Economic Treatise*]. *La Prensa.* Buenos Aires. (August 25, 1968. Sunday Supplement) 2a. Review of 1968 Spanish translation of the 3rd (1966) edition. "The changes introduced in this edition provide greater clarity to the general exposition and help especially to illuminate some concepts essential for an understanding of the proper interpretation of this important branch of knowledge to which Professor von Mises has contributed so much . . . . This second Spanish edition of Professor Ludwig von Mises' Human *Action* is a powerful aid for university professors and scholars in general who want to consult the highest hierarchical scientific sources to improve their understanding of the science of economics." Reprinted in *Espejo.* Mexico: Instituto de Investigaciones Económicas. 10:80 (November-December 1969) 59-63.

Bennett, Mary Jean. "Reading for Business." *The Wall Street Journal.* (August 22, 1967). Very brief note about 1966 (3rd ed.) *Human Action.*

Bernt, H. H. *Library Journal.* 74 (September 1, 1949) 1197. "Grand old man of economics develops his wide concept of economics as 'the theory of all human action' in a literally and figuratively weighty volume . . . . somewhat abstruse language . . . . Profound work, displaying an encyclopedic mind, ought to prove thought provoking for every reader, whether he disagrees (as reviewer) or not. Too difficult for general public, book is suitable for scholars only." (Quoted in *Book Review Digest.* 1949. p.644).

Bettleheim, Max G. Letter to the Editor. *Aufbau.* [Reconstruction]. A German-language paper published in the U. S. (November 11, 1949) 18. Comments on J. E.'s review (see below): "The criticism . . . of the book, *Human Action* . . . profoundly enraged and shocked me. I know that I speak for many readers of your paper if I say that it does a serious injury to the distinguished scholar. Moreover, it was published by the respectable Yale University Press, which can pick and choose its authors. No one forced it to publish this book and it would not have done so if it hadn't wanted to, if it had not considered the book worthy of publication. ¶Its reviewer need not agree with the view of the author. He has the right to express clearly and completely his contrary opinion. However that does not justify his furnishing it with such a heading ["The Most Stupid Book of the Year"]. The *Saturday Review of Literature*, for example, has certainly expressed a critical opinion of the book [see below, Harris], but in conformity with the rules of propriety and practice among critics in a free country. However, J. E.'s title, which contains a completely unjustified superlative (for no one can decide what book really is the most stupid), violates a basic law of behavior.

One should not publish such a thing. Not only the book's author, but every reasonable reader must feel concerned and hurt. ¶I am astonished that you would publish such an antagonistic headline. It did no service to your paper, and it certainly did not harm the famous author whose view one need not share. I beseech you to retract this headline." (Translated from the German)

Branden, Nathaniel. "*Human Action* by Ludwig von Mises." *The Objectivist Newsletter.* New York. 2:9 (September 1963) 34.

Brody, Alexander. *Political Science Quarterly.* 66:4 (December 1951) 606-608. "To von Mises, economic behavior involves the calculation of *all* kinds of satisfactions, moral and aesthetic, the ideal and the base. The classicists drew the boundary line between economic and non-economic behavior. Von Mises regards the economic and non-economic as two inseparable phases of human life and action. The classical economists subordinated human action to economics, whereas von Mises subordinates economics to human action generally . . . . ¶When von Mises makes economics a deductive science, he does not do justice to scientific methodology. The latter includes an examination of economic doctrines not merely from the standpoint of deductive logic, that is, demonstrable proof, but also from the standpoint of proper induction. It is not enough to show that economic theory is free from contradictions and logical fallacies, it is necessary also that the doctrine conform with observable facts. ¶Von Mises is on solid ground when he makes price a market phenomenon, and price theory the heart of economics. That value is relation, and not a substance, is a more fruitful conception than the absolute theory of value. In this respect von Mises is anti-metaphysical. But the validity of these conclusions in no way depends on his methodological preconceptions."

Brookings Bulletin. Washington, D.C.: Brookings Institution. (February 1950) 24-32. A brief summary.

Business Action. "Free Market Analyzed." (November 4, 1949) 3. Also mentions *Omnipotent Government* and *Bureaucracy.*

R. C. C. [Richard C. Cornuelle]. "A New Philosophy of Laissez Faire." *American Affairs.* New York: National Industrial Conference Board. 12:1 (January 1950) 47-51. "This is a very important book. It is a devastating refutation of the claims of socialists and interventionists. It is a powerful rationalization of *laissez faire.* ¶Dr. Mises has perfected a theory of value suggested by his Austrian predecessors. It provides the resolution of the value paradox . . . . Having found this solution of the value paradox . . . Dr. Mises goes on to develop a complete science of human action . . . . Now what Dr. Mises does is a simple thing. He raises the incomplete idea of consumer sovereignty to the plane of a philosophical concept and names it *choice.* His thesis is that choice is the entirety of life and does account for the whole of human behavior . . . . If they [men] are not free to choose they are neither whole nor real; and moreover, if they are not free, that great machine which in their freedom they built to multiply the wealth of the world will not go on working."

Chafuen, Alejandro A. *Free Marin.* Kentfield, Calif. 2:6 (August 1987) 4-5. "*Human Action* is a book that changed the life and ideas of scores of intellectuals. To my knowledge, no other economic treatise has created more admiration and phobias . . . . Anticipating the contributions of the Public-Choice School . . . . He anticipated as well some of the pitfalls of monetarist dogmas . . . . The book will also annoy all those who have a vested interest in current neo-positivist dogmas. Mises contends that 'economics can never be experimental and empirical'."

Chamberlain, John. "*Human Action* Reappraised." *The Freeman.* Irvington, N.Y. Special Memorial Issue Commemorating the 100th Anniversary of Mises' Birth. 31:9 (September 1981) 573-576. "Thirty-one years ago I was asked to review Ludwig von Mises' gigantic *Human Action* . . . . ¶I began my review with a description of the epoch of the Great Grouse . . . . Virtually everybody (I wrote) wants something out of the blue: a pension without contributing to it, a subsidy without incurring a tax, ease without prior effort, Heaven without fighting sin . . . . ¶The result was self-defeating; when everybody was getting his, nobody was better off. Indeed, everybody outside the governing bureaucracy was worse off -- there had to be a skimming to support a burgeoning state apparatus that made no contribution to primary production. With less to go around for grousers, the poverty could be shared, but hope had to be deferred for the naturally energetic individual, and progress tended to stop. ¶The foregoing was more or less my paraphrase of what Mises had set forth . . . in more classic economic language, telling of how state interventionism ran to crisis, provoking piecemeal socialism that led on to socialist centralization and eventually to tyranny or apathy or a combination of the two . . . . ¶How far have we come in thirty-one years with the truths of *Human Action?* There is much more general understanding of the Misesian system . . . . ¶But if we have reached a turn in 1981 with the timid spending cuts that leave us some thirty billion dollars short of a balanced budget, we still have a long way to travel."

_____. "On the Free Society." *The American Mercury.* 70:314 (February 1950) 239-244. "To Dr. von Mises, who is utterly uncompromising, the root of all our troubles is the abandonment of *laissez faire*. Dr. von Mises is of the school which insists that we owe practically everything we have to historic capitalism . . . . The great value of *Human Action* is that it sees economics in perspective. To Dr. von Mises, economics is part of a larger science, or study, which he chooses to call praxeology . . . . Dr. von Mises attacks the very idea of natural law, along with its corollary of natural rights. Yet his whole system of economics and praxeology would seem to depend on the ability of human beings to discover the natural law to which positive, or man-made, law must correspond if man is not continually to do violence to himself. If there is no such thing as natural law, how can the relation of means to ends be determined? . . . If Dr. von Mises' work is not actually a gigantic essay in defense of natural economic law and natural economic rights, then it is far less valuable than I take it to be. The truth of the matter would seem to be that Dr. von Mises has permitted the theological interpretation of the idea of natural law to throw him momentarily off his stride. That doesn't discredit either the idea of natural law or the great value of Dr. von Mises' book."

_____. "Smothered Without Debate." *Plain Talk.* New York. 4:4 (January 1950) 48-51. Reviewed in conjunction with John T. Flynn's *The Road Ahead*. "Twenty-five years ago no Socialist author could get a fair initial hearing in the daily or weekly 'capitalist' press. Today the shoe is on the other foot: it is the avowedly capitalistic author who can't count on a fair exposition of what he has to say. Capitalist editors may live by advertising, but when Dr. Mises writes the only valid defense of advertising that has ever been put on paper (see pages 316-319 of *Human Action*) the editors do not rush to cry his wares. Instead, they call in the Keynesians to give the intransigent Dr. Mises the bum's rush into cold outer space . . . . It matters very little when a good man is refuted or dismissed, provided his main points are first tossed into the arena for debate; what is good in him will then survive any amount of mistaken or misguided criticism. But it matters greatly when a good man is smothered without debate."

Chicago Daily News. "Case for Free Enterprise" (Editorial). (October 27, 1949). "A new arsenal of fact and logic for those at war with the Marxists and Fabians . . . . He [Mises] points out that the rich, the owners of the already operating plants, have no particular class interest in the maintenance of free competition . . . . Dr. Von Mises offers a thought for those who think that the drive for security, guaranteed by government, can continue without leading toward totalitarianism."

Chigusa, Yoshindo. "Human Action: A Treatise on Economics." *Kikan Riron Keizai* [The Economic Studies Quarterly]. Tokyo: Toyo Keizai Shimpo Sha. 2:2 (1951) 121-124. "What we should learn from this book concerns Mises' unique position as to how to deal with the relationship between economics and world views. Mises holds that the goal of every world view, except that of asceticism, is the improvement of the material conditions of human life.   Thus, in Mises' view, the subject matter of economics is to determine the best means for attaining that goal. This might be interpreted as meaning that economics was independent of world views, but that is not so, because different world views choose different means for accomplishing their respective aims. Recognizing that society is created by the will of the individuals and that it is, therefore, led by public opinion, Mises tries to identify the means for attaining the economic goal. To counteract Marxian economics and establish the advantage of modern economics, economics cannot remain aloof from the world view problem. We believe that one of the opportunities at the present time for solving this problem is to further the Misesian method . . . . ¶This book attempts to emphasize, on the basis of solid methodology, why the free market and free enterprise is the most desirable economic system for improving man's material welfare. The author opposes all works, such as Marx's *Capital* and Keynes' *General Theory,* that advocate socialization, planning, credit expansion, and government intervention." (p.121) (Translated from the Japanese by Toshio Murata).

Childs, Roy A., Jr. *Laissez Faire Books Catalog.* San Francisco. C82 (1990) 4. "Our century has properly been called the Era of Statism . . . . That's because by the turn of the century, Classical Liberalism . . . had been soundly defeated by its numerous adversaries. ¶By the eve of the first World War, scarcely a single intellectual figure survived to champion these splendid [classical liberal] ideals. It was then that one young man, working virtually alone, burst on the scene with a new vision of Classical Liberalism . . . . Mises produced many great works, but *Human Action* was his masterpiece . . . . By the end of *Human Action,* we have the broadest possible vision of economics before us, an unparalleled defense of capitalism and the unhampered market, and a sizzling critique of *the principles underlying the interventionist welfare state.* We have a commanding case for freedom, encyclopedic in scope, a true classic that remains as relevant today as the day it was written."

Cousins, Robert & S. T. Williamson. "Enterprise -- Private & Plural." *The Saturday Review of Literature.* 33 (January 28, 1950) 32-34. In a round-up of 1949 business and economic books, after criticizing the obscure gobbledygook of many writers and the left-wing bias of many reviewers, the authors write: "Candidate for this year's deepest and most important tome . . . is *Human Action* . . . by Ludwig von Mises. Heavily and profoundly are free markets upheld, government controls opposed, and the sensible contention made that people are as important as things in the study of economic forces."

Current History. 17 (August 1949) 98. "Professor von Mises (New York University) covers the whole general subject of the economics of the old world and the new, the several schools of thought -- socialist and capitalistic -- in an analysis of man's needs, aims, and methods for attainment. There is a good deal of psychology in it also." (Quoted in *Book Review Digest,* 1949. p.644).

Dalgleish, John. "The Emancipation of Laissez Faire Economics." *Train: Newsletter of Trade and Industry.* Surrey, England. 10:11 (March 17, 1950) 1-4. "[T]he two hundred years search for the 'soul' of the liberal economic system has ended successfully. Beyond doubt or argument the fundamental rectitude of the capitalist economy has been established at last. From now, in the battle of ideas, it will be the Statists who will be on the defensive . . . . ¶Just as the mental genius of Einstein has solved almost all the riddles of the physical Universe, so it has fallen to another man who sought refuge with the free peoples of the world to enunciate the new truths about economics. This man is Dr. Ludwig von Mises, an Austrian, now in New York . . . . ¶Since this book was first sent to me, five months ago, I have struggled against its remorseless logic with increasing sorrow; because, week by week, I have had to jettison more and more of my own original economic researches. Today, I have to confess that twenty years of my life's work are useless and meaningless . . . . To those of us, who like myself, have held on grimly to the belief that sovereignty of the consumer is the key to economic prosperity and human freedom, it comes as a painful shock to see that we had the key within our grasp, but could not properly recognise it. The floodgates to full understanding have been opened by Mises, with his expansion of the limited idea of consumer sovereignty into a full philosophy of Human Action, which he has called simply -- choice. ¶He has shown not only how men can be really free, but also *why* they should be free. For a man without freedom is less than human . . . . [H]e opens a new era of hope to mankind . . . . ¶For my part, I am at last free to pursue my religious convictions, believing that God granted man the reason to create the right economic machine, and having done so he left man to work out his own salvation."

Davidson, Eugene. Letter to the Editor. *New York Times*. (December 11, 1949) VII:45.   Davidson, editor of
    Yale University Press, responded to Galbraith's review: "It is an important thesis of the book, and
    therefore of the jacket copy . . . that government intervention in the market economy produced systems of
    increasing economic and political coercion that have led to totalitarianism in some countries and to near
    bankruptcy in others. This intervention in [Mises'] opinion was supported by erroneous but popular
    economic theories that have swept through Europe and made great headway in the United States . . . . The
    jacket merely attempts to condense Mr. von Mises' views." A copy of Mr. Davidson's letter (found
    among Mises' papers) contained passages omitted from the published version: "It [*Human Action*] is an
    original, creative, far-reaching inquiry, differing in scope and intention from classroom instruction . . . .
    Professor Galbraith could, with advantage, have spent more time on the book and less on the jacket,
    which is after all confined to two flaps and the author's views." Galbraith replies; see below.

J. E. "Das dümmste Buch des Jahres" [The Most Stupid Book of the Year]. *Aufbau* [Reconstruction]. A German-
    language paper published in the U. S. (October 14, 1949). "The most stupid book so far this year is the
    ponderous volume, *Human Action*, by Ludwig von Mises (Yale University Press).   This book offers the
    old Austrian school of economics a resurrection that it doesn't deserve from the grave that it does.
    Capitalism as an economic system of free competition and personal productive opportunities has many
    advantages. Here in the United States it is on its way to intelligent and serious development. Mises'
    book, however, presents a dead countenance. The book presents an inner inhumanity, mixed with a dash
    of intellectuality, such as one finds only among Jewish European reactionaries, who translate their own
    Ghetto inferiority complexes into economic theories. Mises, as well as his student Hayek, whose *Road
    to Serfdom* stems from the same psychological roots, are brothers under the skin. Only Mises' style is
    very awkward and his thought is even more barren and less fruitful than Hayek's." (Translated from the
    German) For comments on J.E.'s review, see *Austria* and Bettleheim Letters to the Editor, both above.

Ebeling, Richard M. "Forty Years of *Human Action*." *Free Market*.   Burlingame, Calif.: Ludwig von Mises
    Institute. 7:9 (September 1989) 6. "When the first edition of *Human Action* was published 40 years ago
    this month, Ludwig von Mises was already recognized as one of the leading Austrian economists thanks
    to his two masterworks [B-2 & B-4] . . . . But *Human Action* was something different. It was . . . .
    about almost *everything!* . . . ¶A work of such breadth and insight should have been hailed as a landmark
    not only in the history of economics, but in the history of science in general. Instead, Ludwig von
    Mises' *Human Action* was either ignored or condemned by most of the economists and reviewers of the
    day . . . . Why? Because in a world where most intellectuals thought socialism was the wave of the
    future, Mises showed it was not, and could not be . . . . ¶While only a few fully appreciated the
    significance of Ludwig von Mises's masterpiece in 1949, 40 years later things are very different . . . . As
    the 21st century approaches, the bright beacon pointing to the future is held by Misesians, and more and
    more economists, students, and policy makers in America and abroad recognize it."

Echigo, Kazunori (long-time Professor of Economics, Shiga University, Japan).   Comments on the 1990
    Japanese translation by Toshio Murata: "*Human Action* is not only Mises' *Magnum Opus*, but it is one
    of the greatest works in this century . . . . This translation is not only exact, but intelligible Japanese
    which reflects . . . profound knowledge . . . . [Murata] is well qualified to translate Mises' books [into
    Japanese] . . . . I am sure this will have great significance for the propagation of Misesian ideas."

The Economist. London. "Fabulous Survival." (December 31, 1949) 1464. "Professor von Mises holds among
    economists an almost legendary position; he is the limiting case, the last heir of Bastiat and Senior, the
    ne plus ultra in *laisser faire* theory . . . . Nearly 900 pages of relentless Teutonic philosophy . . . .
    Human Action is a magnificent book; intellectual power roars through it like a great wind; it has the
    impetus of first-rate polemic and the impeccable coherence of Euclid . . . . its manners often downright
    bad; but the thought thus unbecomingly clothed is crystal clear and the pursuit of its development is an
    intellectual delight . . . . ¶Having said this, one can only add that as a guide to policy; *Human Action* is
    irrelevant almost to the point of craziness . . . . It is not, of course, an intellectual crime to be in a

minority of one; but the arrogance with which Professor von Mises dismisses all contemporary economics without ever condescending to meet his adversaries on their own ground is nevertheless remarkable."

Eggleston, J. F. "A Banker on the Thesis of Professor von Mises of New York." *The Owl: A Quarterly Journal of International Thought.* London. (April 1951) 37-43. "Von Mises pays the fullest tribute and develops with the pen of a genius the social elevation which accompanies the acceptance of the great and immutable fact of the recognition of the free market. Around the CHOICE exercised by innumerable individuals revolves the whole economic world -- choice of the individual and not of the 'planner' is the keynote of liberal civilisation, and the denial of the sanctity of freely exercised choice is leading the world away from the prosperity, the tolerance and the happiness which freedom brought . . . . ¶The author reserves his magnificent range of vocabulary to flaggelate the philosophers who expatiate on the absolute as if it were a pocket watch, and he reflects that it is useless to argue with mystics and seers. As he strikes right and left, he ascribes the attraction which socialism and communism have on the intellectuals, as being motivated by envy. They envy the higher paid business man and despise him for his lack of academic knowledge . . . . ¶A theory, whether of free trade -- of free exchange -- of fixed or fluctuating prices, is either correct or incorrect. It cannot be correct for an American and incorrect for a Chinaman. A theory cannot have been correct during the last century and incorrect and harmful during this century. The trend of human logic and reasoning is almost immutable and certainly has not changed while history has been recorded. If free trade brought wealth during the last century, it cannot bring poverty to-day."

Fertig, Lawrence. *The New York World-Telegram.* (September 19, 1949). "How does the public get its ideas on economic matters? . . . . The basic idea or philosophy . . . is generally originated by some outstanding thinker who influences a group of intellectuals. These, in turn, interpret the master's ideas to the public . . . . It is about time that some truly great advocate of liberal capitalism re-stated for our time the case of the free market and the sovereignty of the consumer, as opposed to the philosophy of government intervention and the sovereignty of the bureaucrat . . . . The need for such a work has been answered by Dr. Ludwig von Mises . . . . He offers a combination of great scholarship and the rare ability to make an abstruse economic subject interesting . . . . This may be a book for scholars, but it will undoubtedly have a profound effect upon public opinion."

Free Press (Burlington, Vt.). (November 24, 1949). "When the capacities and limitations of economics are ignored or misunderstood, the result has been no less than misery and slavery for millions in an age that could have abundance with freedom and work."

Galbraith, J. K. "In Defense of Laissez-Faire." *New York Times Book Review.* (October 30, 1949) 45. "Anyone who has been yearning, if only from nostalgia, for a truly unvarnished and unconditional defense of laissez-faire should be well satisfied with this book. For nearly half a century, in Vienna, London and more recently in New York, Professor Mises has been battling socialists, planners, reformers and every other kind of sponsor, deliberate or unwitting, of government interference with economic process. As the reader will quickly discover, he has not surrendered an inch of ground . . . . ¶The implacable and omnipresent enemy of the market is government. There must be no compromise whatever with this demon . . . . He opposes regulation of banks . . . not even the prohibition of the drug traffic is permissible . . . . ¶I come now to the publisher. However much one may disagree with Professor Mises, he is a learned man and a famous teacher. The market, in spite of its virtues, does not pay for all the books that deserve publication and it is therefore both appropriate and good that a university press made this one available. But surely it should do so with some obligation to scholarly restraint. The publisher's statement on the jacket of the book says that Professor Mises' approach bears little relation to what 'is usually taught in classrooms or to the hopeful, revolutionary but bankrupt "economics" that conquered the Western World in the last decades.' It adverts to the 'malignant' political consequences of actions during the last decade at variance with Professor Mises' views. Does the Yale University Press stand on this comprehensive slur on present-day economics, including that taught in the classrooms at New Haven?" Eugene Davidson, Editor of Yale University Press, responds; see above.

_____. Letter to the Editor. *New York Times*. (December 11, 1949). Comments on Davidson's letter (see above): "I can understand why Mr. Davidson might wish that I had overlooked this jacket. But it was he who made it so fascinating."

Golffing, Francis. "Varieties of Conservative Thought." *Commentary*. 30:4 (October 1960) 330-334. Reviewed together with Mises' *Epistemological Problems of Economics* (B-10) and Wilhelm Röpke's *A Humane Economy*: "For over three decades now Professor Ludwig von Mises has, with admirable consistency, pursued his passion for changing the world by making it stand still . . . . [W]hat von Mises' theory of cognition comes down to is a pre-Kantian a-priorism, a pre-Humean belief in strict causality, a pre-Hegelian contempt for historical process . . . . Being either ignorant of dialectical operations, or merely blind to them, von Mises assumes that a body of thought can be reconstituted at will, *tel quel*, without regard for the changes wrought by time in human desires, the body politic, the particular culture . . . . [H]is science of man has turned out to be quite as insular as the economic theory it was designed to buttress, and considerably more ossified . . . . [N]ext to his impressive learning, his incorruptibility seems to me to be his greatest asset . . . . von Mises' philosophy of action . . . is well knit, eloquent, self-consistent, and eminently reasonable. It is also totally unoriginal, since it depends in all its essential features on either Hobbes or Aristotle."

Grilli, Carlo. "Contro corrente: A proposito di un recente trattato di Economica" [Against the Tide: Concerning a Recent Treatise on Economics]. *Studi Economici*. (September-December 1952) 1-8. Review in Italian of the 1949 Yale edition.

Groves, Harold M. "Prayer for the Past." *The Progressive*. (February 1950) 37-38. "Mises does a thorough and convincing job of deflating Marxian ideology . . . . much less convincing when he argues that socialism is beyond human power and would lead to inevitable chaos simply because without a free market the planners would have no means of calculation in allotting resources . . . . Mises is completely unconvincing in his oft-repeated conclusions (1) that there is no tenable middle ground between a completely free market economy and dictatorial socialism; and (2) that the free market system practically always serves the economic interests of all the people . . . . ¶The author's distrust of government is nothing short of amazing. For him the only legitimate function of government is to serve as a policeman; any notion that the government might serve human needs as a cooperative enterprise is never seriously entertained . . . . attempts to police narcotic drugs are ill-advised paternalism; neither factory legislation nor labor unions ever did or could improve the lot of the workingman; an unemployed worker could always get a job if he would only accept the right pay (Keynes thought otherwise, to be sure, but he was only one of a long line of soft-money cranks); monopoly is not a serious problem and anti-trust programs are only an obstruction to progress; public works only serve to intensify depressions."

Harris, Seymour E. "Capitalist Manifesto." *Saturday Review of Literature*. 32 (September 24, 1949) 31-32. "Forthright and courageous, Professor von Mises uses the axe, not the scalpel; and with it he strikes virtually all living economists . . . . [H]is student, Hayek, alone seems to be on the right track . . . *Human Action* . . . . is an extreme *Road to Serfdom* . . . . Here is indeed a book that would in many ways have been anachronistic in 1850 . . . On unemployment, von Mises is incredible. Any worker unemployed, he says, chooses to be so. If he wants a job, he need only accept a lower wage . . . . One could go on endlessly listing the errors, the misinterpretations, the archaic doctrines held by Professor von Mises."

Harwood, E. C. *Book Review Supplement*. Great Barrington, Mass.: American Institute for Economic Research. (September 13, 1954) 153-156. "Dr. von Mises' treatise illustrates the principal weaknesses of economics as it is written about and widely taught today. As evidence of the urgent need for reconstruction in economics, this book perhaps is without a peer . . . . In his search for knowledge, [the modern scientist] has abandoned the Greek objective, the quest for certainty . . . . Dr. von Mises denies not once but several times that his theories can ever be disproved by the facts. This point of view represents a leap backward to Platonic idealism . . . . As for von Mises' assertion that economists must rely on 'cognition and analysis of our own purposeful behavior,' this is the thoroughly discredited mode of knowing by introspection . . . . Von Mises differentiates the natural sciences from what he calls the *a priori* sciences including praxeology, which he considers the basis for his economics. This, too, is an outmoded distinction . . . . ¶Finally, we repeat that Dr. von Mises' treatise seems to us an outstanding contribution . . . . [W]e believe that Dr. von Mises may have contributed far more than he had previously realized to the needed reconstruction in economics. The first task in reconstruction always is the demolition and removal of the structure that must be replaced. That task, we believe he has facilitated." Reprinted as "Human Action, A Treatise on Economics." *Reconstruction of Economics,* E. C. Harwood, ed. (American Institute for Economic Research, 1955) 33-42.

Hazlitt, Henry. "The Case for Capitalism." *Newsweek.* (September 19, 1949) 70. "It [*Human Action*] is the consummation of half a century of experience, study, and rigorous thought. No living writer has a more thorough knowledge of the history and literature of economics than Mises, and yet no living writer has been to more pains to take no solution of any problem on faith, but to think out each solution, step by verified step, for himself. The result is a work of great originality written in a great tradition . . . . [I]t extends beyond any previous work the logical unity and precision of modern economic analysis. ¶I know of no other work . . . which conveys to the reader so clear an insight into the intimate interconnectedness of all economic phenomena . . . . Outstanding among his [Mises'] many original contributions are his 'circulation credit' theory of business cycles, which emphasizes the harm of cheap-money policies, and his demonstration that partial socialism is parasitic on capitalism and that a complete socialism would not even know how to solve the problem of economic calculation." Reprinted together with Hazlitt's (1938) review of *Socialism* (B-4) as "Two of Ludwig von Mises' Most Important Works" in the 1956 Mises Festschrift (*On Freedom and Free Enterprise.* Mary Sennholz, ed., Van Nostrand, 1956) 34-38. Reprinted also in *The Indian Libertarian* (Bombay). 5:15 (October 1, 1957) 18-19.

_____. "Mangling a Masterpiece." *National Review.* New York. 16:18 (May 5, 1964) 366-367. Hazlitt rakes Yale University Press over the coals for its excessively error-ridden 2nd (1963) edition of *Human Action.* "[T]he revised edition is . . . . full of misprints. On page 322 four lines are omitted. Page 468 is missing altogether. Page 469 is printed twice. On page 563 two paragraphs are transposed. On page 615 eight lines are wrong . . . . ¶On page after page one finds some paragraphs printed in a comparatively light type, and others in a blacker, thicker type . . . . ¶It appears that, in order to do as cheap a job as possible, the press had resorted to some mixture of photo-offset and reset never tried before. When Dr. Mises asked for page proofs, they were denied 'for mechanical reasons.' When he protested, Chester Kerr, director of the press, replied on Jan. 22, 1963: 'We are entirely willing to take responsibility for seeing that the new edition of *Human Action* is printed without error' . . . . ¶A final question. Why, in a press that has shown itself capable of producing first-rate work, did this particular book go wrong? Do the present editors of the Yale University Press (who are not those who originally accepted the book) know that this is the most important work on general economic theory that has appeared in our generation? They know it is commercially profitable; they know it sold six printings and brought in revenues from translation and quotation. But if they had any idea of its true greatness, if they even had any real respect for its author and its readers, if they had any respect for their press' own reputation, would they have permitted such a slovenly edition to go out under its imprint?"

Hicks, J. R. "Dogmatic Liberalism." *Manchester Guardian.* (December 30, 1949) 3. "[A] powerful book, which presents a real challenge, and which deserves attention even from those who will be least in sympathy with it . . . . nothing particularly original, or particularly striking . . . . [T]he majority of English economists . . . will sometimes be distressed by a certain superficiality which is noticeable whenever he comes to the really hard points . . . . Mises sets up Capitalism as a god, which it is sinful to touch. Who, since the days of the Steam Intellect Society, would have been so overpowered by the virtues of capitalism, so blind to its defects . . . . The book is presented as a counterblast to Marx; but it is impossible not to feel that Mises himself has many of Marx's characteristics. Like Marx, he knows the answer to all questions . . . . The same reasons which have prevented English Socialists from being followers of Marx must prevent English liberals from being followers of Mises."

Ichitani, Toichiro. "New Development of Austrian School of Economics." *Development of Modern Economics.* Tokyo: Kawade Shobo, 1956. 10 (Series of Economic Theory) 180. Chapter 4 summarizes the principal works of Mises and Hayek. Ichitani comments on *Human Action* as follows: "This book is a *magnum opus* in every sense of the word. It covers not only almost all fields of economics but almost all current social problems." (p.180) (Translated from the Japanese by Toshio Murata)

Lachmann, Ludwig M. "The Science of Human Action." *Economica.* 18:72 (November 1951) 412-427. "This is Professor Mises' *magnum opus* . . . . Its majestic sweep embraces almost the whole field of economics and touches at some point or other, on almost every social issue of our time . . . . Professor Mises claims *a priori* validity for the propositions of Praxeology . . . . In the field of human action we 'explain' phenomena as the outcome of the pursuit of plans . . . . [T]he plans of different individuals may be, and as a rule are, inconsistent with each other . . . . [Mises] has an answer of a kind, and we believe it, on the whole, to be a satisfactory answer . . . . the logical principle which coordinates the plans of different individuals is the division of labour . . . . Professor Mises' real answer to the dilemma lies in his conception of entrepreneurship and the function of entrepreneurial profits . . . . Among the members of the governing class of present-day Western society [Mises] is not a popular figure. Politicians and bureaucrats dislike him; the intellectuals who produce the ideologies to sustain their rule abhor him. The Fabians worship other idols . . . . The outlook for the praxeological sciences is not exactly bright . . . . Yet, in the long run, society ignores the praxeological sciences at its peril." Reprinted (pp. 94-111) in Lachmann anthology, *Capital, Expectations, and the Market Process.* Walter E. Grinder, ed. Kansas City: Sheed Andrews and McMeel, 1977.

Lalley, J. M. "Book Events." *Human Events.* Washington, D.C. 6:39 (September 28, 1949) issue 296. "[M]ore a work of philosophy than a technical treatise on economics . . . . [O]ur professor employs the word 'liberal' in the traditional or 'bourgeois' sense, and with none of the connotations attached to it by the political Left . . . . Liberalism means the voluntary and progressive division of labor and the adjustment of prices and wages by the open market. And yet . . . the ostensible aim of liberalism and collectivism is the same; that is, the improvement of the material condition of the generality of mankind; his thesis, however, is that possibility of achieving this purpose under the liberal organization of Society has been demonstrated; and it has been further demonstrated, he insists, that collectivism and economic *autarky* lead only to strife, impoverishment and barbarism."

Lane, Rose Wilder. *Economic Council Review of Books.* New York: National Economic Council. 6:10 (October 1949) 1-3. "I think that *Human Action* is unquestionably the most powerful product of the human mind in our time, and I believe it will change human life for the better during the coming centuries as profoundly as Marxism has changed all our lives for the worse in this century. ¶Human action makes the human world what it is . . . . Readers of this Review have seen my feeble yipping that nobody knows the principles of human relationships . . . . Unquestionably, all expedient, efficient, rewarding human action on this earth must conform to what men can only call the will of God. Human beings do not make the principles operating in this world; men must *discover* them. Men could not make a telephone until they began to discover the principles of electronics, nor kerosene -- much less gasoline -- until they began to discover the principles of chemistry, nor a wheel until they discovered the simplest principle of mechanics. How then (I asked) can men make a human world that will work to the ends they desire, until they begin to discover the principles of human relationships? -- those surely existing but not known *principles* of morality . . . . ¶Everyone knows the transformation that increasing knowledge of the principles of the so-called 'natural sciences' has made in the conditions of living. With such scientific knowledge of the principles operating in the relationships of persons to each other -- think of it. *Human Action* describes the method of this new science . . . . ¶I find only one brief passage that seems to me irrational . . . . [G]lancing at the political field of action, Professor Mises seems to say that action controlled by the acting individual is impossible. 'The alternatives to the liberal and democratic principle of *majority rule* are the militarist principle of armed conflict and dictatorial oppression' .... If the alternative to a dictator's directing my action is its being directed by a majority of other persons, how can my own choice direct my action? .... ¶I think that this book begins and will stand for a new epoch in human thought, therefore in human action and world history."

Linhardt, H. "Mensch und Wirtschaft [Man and Economy]: *Human Action.*" *Betriebswirtschaftliche Forschung und Praxis.* 3:3(1951) 151-162. An overview with frequent references to source pages in *Human Action.* "Such a comprehensive work (889 pp.) cannot be satisfactorily evaluated in a general review. The title would lead one to expect something different; however, one hardly comes forth poorer or duller from reading the work of von Mises. The field of investigation lies in the theme *Human Action* which derides every kind of scientific inquiry, even this fundamentally new kind. Interpersonal transactions are not entirely accessible by scientific method .... The distinction between economic theory and economic history is explained logically and exemplarily; the old *Methodenstreit* [struggle over methodology] between the Austrian school and the historical school is clarified anew as the dead spirits awake to struggle once more audibly and openly. Even more evident and more important for many people, however, is the difference between quantitative and qualitative inquiry." (Translated from the German)

The Listener. (January 12, 1950) 77-78. "Professor von Mises writes his Q.E.D. with all the confidence of a medieval schoolman demonstrating a theological refinement from an unquestionable dogma. To follow his beautifully expounded (if often repellently expressed) argument is to enjoy an intellectual treat, though a strenuous one .... ¶One can cordially agree with Professor von Mises that such and such a policy is self-contradictory, destructive and generally idiotic .... One certainly need not agree that all collectively pursued policies must inevitably be such .... So to agree would be to despair of the human race; for it would be to see the only escape from destruction not merely in philosophers becoming kings, but in every man's becoming a philosopher."

The Magazine of Wall Street. (December 31, 1949)."Professor von Mises' approach bears little relation to what is usually taught in classrooms or to the hopeful, revolutionary but bankrupt 'economics' that conquered the Western world in the last decades. It is a closely reasoned statement of scientific principles, of stirring generalizations about man and his wants and how, with certain ends in view, they may be fulfilled."

The Management Review. (August 1950).

Manchester Guardian. (January 12, 1950).

Mercado (Mexico). 1:2 (October - December, 1989).

Modern Industry [New York City]. "Capitalist counter to *Das Kapital.*" (December 15, 1949). "This book, touted by its publisher as the definitive philosophical treatise on capitalism, has only one fault. So academic is the vein in which it is written that it is as hard to read as its opposite number -- Marx's *Das Kapital* .... He [Mises] cautions against ignoring the lessons of economics .... If you can take heavy thinking don't hesitate to get hold of this."

Murata, Toshio [translator into Japanese of *Human Action*].   "Fascinated by Mises for Thirty-five Years. " *Shunju* (Shunju-Sha). 330 (July 1991) 1-4. "Mises' *Human Action* is filled with his precious wisdom, written in a very concise style, extending into many spheres. It is a treasury of thoughts and ideas, any one of which may be explored further and developed into a new thesis or a new book." (p.4) (Translated from the Japanese by Toshio Murata).

NAM [National Association of Manufacturers] *News.* (October 8, 1949) 15. "Seldom, if ever, has a more comprehensive and detailed book been written under a title which is as simple and as appropriate."

Nelson, Godfrey N. "Progressive Tax, Business Menace." *The New York Times.* (October 2, 1949) [Section] 3, 1. Quotes from *Human Action* in news article format: "'But today,' says Professor von Mises, 'taxes often absorb the greater part of the newcomer's "excessive" profits. He cannot accumulate capital; he cannot expand his own business . . . . In this sense progressive taxation checks economic progress and makes for rigidity'."

The New Haven Register. (September 15, 1949).

New York Herald Tribune. (July 18, 1949). "A weighty treatise on human nature and economics . . . . a refutation of Marxist economics, stating that if economic theory is based on a sound understanding of human nature, it will be true for all nations and peoples at all times."

Pellizzi, Camillo. "*L'azione umana* di Ludwig von Mises" [Ludwig von Mises' *Human Action*]. *Il Borghese* (Milan). 1:11 (August 15, 1950) 332-333.

Philbrook. Clarence E. *The National Book Foundation*. (December 1, 1960) 1-4. A double review of *Human Action* and Eugen von Böhm-Bawerk's *Capital and Interest.* "[A] fundamental treatise in the 'Austrian' tradition of economics; . . . the *magnum opus* of a man who possessed prodigious scholarship, who formed a storm-center of intellectual controversy, who exercised a rarely matched degree of influence upon the thinkers of his time, and who stood foremost among those who have kept alive the conception of freedom under free enterprise as an alternative to the seemingly inexorable trend to socialism . . . . ¶Friend or foe must regard the book [*Human Action*] as a stupendous work having no true substitute in all literature, a product of amazing scholarship always tightly guided by integrative purpose in a mind of rare subtlety and power."

Rothbard, Murray N. "Praxeology." *Analysis.* New York. 6:7 (May 1950) 4. "Every once in a while the human race pauses in the job of botching its affairs and redeems itself by producing a noble work of the intellect . . . . ¶Among [Mises'] contributions are: the integration of the theory of money into the general framework of individualist 'utility' economics; the demonstration that free banking leads to 'hard' money rather than 'cheap' money; a complete portrayal of the evils of inflationism and credit expansion; the superb analysis of the causes of the business cycle (the result of credit expansion); the demonstration that world socialism is economically unfeasible; the demonstration that interest is an eternal category of human action and not the wicked device of usurers; a demonstration of the possibilities of capital consumption and of forced saving; and a thoroughgoing portrayal of the vicious effects of every type of governmental intervention in economic life . . . . ¶Mises is the first to work out economics on a firm foundation on the principle of *individual* action . . . . To state that *Human Action* is a 'must' book is a great understatement. This is the economic Bible for the civilized man."

_____. "Mises' *Human Action:* Comment." *American Economic Review.* 41:1 (March 1951) 181-185. Critiques George J. Schuller's review of *Human Action* (*American Economic Review*, June 1950; see below). Discusses one by one each of Schuller's criticisms. See also Schuller's second rejoinder (March 1951; below) and Rothbard's second reply (December 1951).

_____. "Praxeology: Reply to Mr. Schuller." *American Economic Review.* 41:5 (December 1951) 943-946. Rothbard replies to Schuller's (June 1950) and (March 1951) rejoinders: "The fundamental praxeological axiom is that individual human beings *act* . . . . This axiom of action is indisputably an important truth, and must form the basis of social theory." Rothbard lists the categories of praxeology.

_____. *Faith and Freedom* (Spiritual Mobilization, Los Angeles). 2:1 (September 1950) 14-15. "Throughout the history of mankind, a handful of individuals have significantly enriched human thought. Pioneers in carving out new paths in the eternal search for truth, they have integrated the truths they have found into great edifices of thought. It is no exaggeration to assert that *Human Action* is such an edifice; it is a work of monumental grandeur . . . . ¶[F]or the first time in history the reader is presented with a complete structure of economic science, a science which Mises demonstrates . . . is firmly grounded in *praxeology*, the general principles of individual action. Not only is this book free from all the fallacies that plague other tomes in economics, but amazingly vast portions of this structure are the original contributions of the author himself."

Royster, Vermont. "The Paradox of Planning: Groping in the Dark, Planned Economies Can Plan Only Chaos." *The Wall Street Journal.* (October 28, 1949). "Unfortunately Dr. von Mises' case rests upon logic, a cold logic without emotional appeal. It cannot be popularized with catchy labels, and therefore it is not likely to offer much opposition to demagogues who talk of planning and welfare and security." Excerpt of this review in Spanish translation: "Un libro fundamental" [A Basic Book]. *Ideas Sobre la Libertad*. Buenos Aires: Centro de Estudios Sobre la Libertad. 14:41 (April 1982) 1.

Rukeyser, M. S. "On von Mises' *Human Action.*"*New York Journal American.* (November 21, 1949). "In the give and take of foreign exchange the United States, which has been greatly exploited in recent years, received an offsetting benefit when a quiet, little known personality, Ludwig von Mises . . . migrated to New York. ¶Mises, who is a monumental scholar in the realm of economic understanding, has summed up his life work in the controversies which are besetting the contemporary world in a new volume entitled *Human Action* . . . . In the spirit of objective realism, he is neither an optimist nor a pessimist."

Ryan, Gabriel G. *America.* (September 24, 1949). "The present volume is a full-scale philosophy of individualism, an analysis of the implications of human choice ('praxeology') as applied to the market economy ('catallactics'). It is the author's oft-repeated thesis that the unhampered market price system is the only conceivable arrangement under which freedom may be retained in an interdependent society; all who disagree are either fools or fellow-travellers, since all shades of 'interventionism' lead to totalitarian slavery . . . . The economic thought which Professor von Mises represents [the 'marginal utility approach] . . . . has provided helpful 'tools' for economists who recognize the limitations of its assumptions. Failure to recognize these limitations accounts for much of the sterility of classical economics. The present work, in the subjectivist tradition, likewise over-reaches itself."

H.L.S. "All God's Children Want Shoes." *Taxes: The Tax Magazine.* (January 1950) 83-84. "The theme of this book and the theme of capitalism can be summed up in a statement that appears innocently enough on page 670. Here the author says: 'The fact that my fellow man wants to acquire shoes, as I do, does not make it harder for me to get shoes, but easier.'" The reviewer says that Mises asserts that Roman Catholicism would substitute socialism or interventionism "for the manifestly unfair capitalistic mode of production." The reviewer disagrees: "[The] *Quadragesimo Anno* of Pope Pius XI . . . . does not advocate socialism and certainly . . . it cannot be said that the Catholic Church advocates communism . . . . The Encyclical is addressed to the misuses of the capitalistic system . . . . Professor von Mises' book is outstanding in defining in a scholarly manner the rules that are now necessary in this fractional division of labor in order that man, in the collective, may earn his bread."

_____. *Labor Law Journal.* (December 1949) 251-253.

Saal, John J., Jr. "Mises' *Human Action* Considered in the Light of the Social Teaching of the Church." M.A. thesis, Fordham University, 1951. Concludes that the views expressed in *Human Action* are sharply contrary to the social principles taught by the Catholic Church.

Schriftgiesser, Karl. "The Literary Summing-Up." *The Saturday Review of Literature.* (December 31, 1949) 5-7. In a lengthy year-end summary of the important books of 1949, Schriftgiesser writes: "it may well turn out that Ludwig von Mises is the prophet of our time and his *Human Action* the *Das Kapital* of the New Era of Free Enterprise! But I doubt it."

Schuller, George J. *American Economic Review.* 40:3 (June 1950) 418-422. "*Human Action* advances beyond previous orthodox treatises in several important respects. (1) It is a system in the grand manner not merely of Marshall or J. B. Clark but of Marx or Oppenheimer . . . . (2) Whereas the early orthodox theorists concerned themselves with the market economy as a transmutation from a controlled economy and their successors took the permanence of the market economy for granted, Mises' book is perhaps the first general treatise which is centrally concerned with the preservation of the market economy against a developing controlled economy. (3) Mises makes numerous original contributions, economic and extra-economic, throughout the book . . . . [H]is theories of money, business cycles, and socialism are well known from his other writings. In addition, he offers the best defense the reviewer has seen of apriorism in economic methodology and some important modifications of marginalist theory in relation to quantitative and temporal analysis. ¶The book has, however, serious shortcomings. (1) The author provides no clear test of incorrect versus 'correct praxeological reasoning' . . . . (2) The author's attitude toward his principles is one of uncompromising dogmatism . . . . (3) He frequently neglects to distinguish his praxeological from his historical observations and often applies his dogmatism to what seems to be the latter as well as to the former . . . . (4) Mises creates a dualism between *a priori*   praxeology and *a posteriori*   history which he is unable to bridge . . . . (5) The arbitrariness of Mises' catallactic principles in application to historical reality . . . . (6) The apparent contradiction between economic rationality and political irrationality Mises attempts to remove by his insistence that intelligent choice of means requires calculability . . . . (7) The choice which Mises gives us is as foreign to rational human action . . . as that offered by the extreme Marxist . . . between . . . market economy . . . and socialism . . . (8) The opposition which Mises finds . . . between intervention and economic law is as spurious as that between airplanes and gravitation . . . . ¶The book is unnecessarily long and repetitious." See Rothbard's March 1951 rejoinder (above).

_____. *American Economic Review.* 41:1 (March 1951) 185-190. A rejoinder to Rothbard's comment in this same issue (see above). "In Mises' uncritical usage introspection becomes not a scientific method but the basis of a creed . . . . Mises' use of logic as a scientific instrument falls short of perfect rigor . . . . After telling us that 'it is nonsensical to reckon national income or wealth' or other aggregates, . . . he insists that the free market 'raised the average standard of living to an unprecedented height'." See Rothbard's December 1951 rejoinder (above).

Sherrard, Alfred. "The Free Man's Straightjacket." *New Republic.* 122 (January 9, 1950) 18-19. "In the most literal sense, as technical economics, *Human Action* is not acceptable. It is a polemic, and must be so judged. For all its ponderosity, it is frivolous -- and must seem so especially to those who would welcome a serious conservative work on the subject . . . .Yet this book is not likely to convert anyone who is not already at one with its author, and even those who agree may be embarrassed . . . . The book is a holocaust of straw men."

Solterer, Josef. *Review of Social Economy.* 8 (1950) 123-133.

Sovren, Peter. *New Statesman & Nation.* London. 38 (December 10, 1949) 702. "The arguments which were expressed with ice-cold logic in the essay on economic calculation [Article 20.6] are now set out in *Human Action* as bombastic propaganda . . . . This use of economic theory to express personal prejudice can only bring discredit on a science which does in fact achieve a truly 'scientific' standard of objective consistency when it is practised by less passionate economists than Professor von Mises. ¶It may be that Professor von Mises is writing more loudly and insistently because he has nothing new to say."

Spitaler, Armin. *Weltwirtschaftliches Archiv.* Institut für Weltwirtschaft, Universität Kiel. 65:1 (1950) 14-16. The reviewer cites three fundamental principles on which Mises' economic theory is based: (1) his anti-historical school, anti-institutionalist methodology which holds that "there can be no constant relations in the field of interpersonal transactions and that therefore there is no unit of 'measurement' in economics"; (2) "all economic accounting and calculations are carried on with money prices"; and (3) "the concept of equilibrium is completely untenable in economics . . . . ¶The author's ideas, at times bold but always stimulating, are in most cases the very opposite of what has been published in Anglo-Saxon literature in recent years . . . . The success of this work is remarkable for already, only three months after its appearance in September 1949, the publisher must proceed with a new edition." (Translated from the German)

Stafford, John J. *Hartford* (Conn.) *Courant.* (October 27, 1949). Reviewed jointly with Marshall E. Dimock's *Business and Government. Human Action* is "diffuse, protracted, frequently testy, often belligerent . . . . Mises set out to rehabilitate classical economics, the economics of laissez-faire . . . . [H]e attempts to give it a sounder basis by developing a more modern theory of human action which he terms praxeology . . . . A conscientious person attempting to build or rebuild a system of thought and analysis usually feels bound to give evidence that he has understood his opponents. Not so von Mises . . . . The [Westbrook] Pegler approach might be acceptable in journalism, but it hardly aids the conservative cause when used by academic economists."

The Times Literary Supplement. London. "Economics and Human Action." (March 31, 1950). "In as blatantly irrational an age as ours, with its flags lowered and its standards down, to be ruthlessly rationalistic -- above all, in economic affairs -- is to fly in the face of the People as well as Providence. Yet Professor von Mises . . . was ever bold to the point of brashness . . . . and Professor von Mises has already had to suffer from their unthinking ministrations in no less than four countries. In this big book . . . he returns to his charge, unabashed, invigorated, indignant rather than choleric. And he shivers many a lance on many a helm. It reminds one of the unimaginative, unreasoning English nobleman in *Saint Joan* who, when told of Copernicus' perihelial theory, burst out 'Couldn't the fool use his eyes?' Professor von Mises, like a Copernicus, is confronted with millions who say 'Economic values are not ultimates' or 'Waste may be more worthwhile to the majority than economicalness,' or -- to use the current jargon -- 'Costs must include social costs'."

Trends in Church, Education and Industry Cooperation. National Association of Manufacturers. (November 1949) 28. "[A] meticulous study of people all over the world and their search for the economic necessities of life . . . . [The author] clearly points out why only free enterprise in a free market can produce the necessary outpouring of goods and services."

U. S. Quarterly. (December 1950?). "Although Professor von Mises holds that economics is a science concerned only with means and not with ends, the animus of many of his remarks will raise doubts in some minds about the objectivity of his approach. The rigidity of his reasoning, the emphasis on deduction unalloyed by observation, and the use of sharp dichotomies are, however, sufficient to account for the author's extreme views."

Western Economics Encyclopedia. Review by the Economic Research Department, Bank of Taiwan in 1971.

Wright, David McCord. *Annals of the American Academy of Political and Social Science.* 268 (March 1950) 229-230. "In this massive volume Dr. von Mises says a great deal that is sound, interesting, and valuable, and it is a pity that his many worth-while and often acute observations should be presented in a manner and context which will probably greatly reduce their influence and efficacy. The book is almost two books . . . . both a philosophical treatise and an economics text. The reviewer is obliged to admit that he found the philosophical portions the more interesting. The economics of the volume is narrowly and dogmatically 'Austrian.' There is something a little inconsistent in von Mises' simultaneous attacks upon 'panphysicalism' and 'mechanism' and his very mechanical, unilateral approach to the business cycle . . . . ¶Perhaps the basic defect of the book is indicated by its fundamental terminology. If 'praxeology' is too broad, 'catallactics' is too narrow . . . . His narrowly monetary theory of the cycle prevents him from fully diagnosing the unstable factors inevitably involved in growth."

Liberalism   (*Liberalismus*, 1927; first English translation 1962: *The Free and Prosperous Commonwealth* ; later
   editions 1978 & 1985, *Liberalism*) (B-6)

Augusta Chronicle-Herald.   "Tired of booms and abuses, never ending inflation, labor strife and racial antagonisms?
   Looking for world peace, a prosperous economy, and the opportunity to pursue happiness? Then perhaps
   we should turn away from the medicine men . . . whose 'cure all' schemes have resulted in high taxes,
   cruel inflation, chronic unemployment and a lagging economy. Perhaps instead we should examine the
   words of one of the world's greatest economists, Ludwig von Mises, in this book." (Quoted on book
   jacket of 1978 Sheed Andrews & McMeel edition)

Browne, Harry. A syndicated review. American Way Features, Release #344. (Week of June 27, 1967).   "With
   political solutions by the hundreds being offered for economic problems, one is hard-pressed to keep up
   with all of the panaceas suggested for poverty, farm problems, international trade, etc. ¶And yet, one
   solution never seems to get a hearing. That answer is *economic freedom*: let each man alone to work out
   his economic problems in voluntary cooperation with others. ¶The eminent economist Ludwig von Mises
   has laid out an outline of a society based upon the principle of economic freedom." Published in:
   > *Citation* (Karnes City, Texas). (July 6, 1967)
   > *Chronicle* (Jacksonville, Florida). (June 30, 1967)
   > *Gazette-Telegraph* (Colorado Springs). (July 1, 1967)
   > *Highlander* (Lake Wales, Florida). (July 3, 1967)
   > *News* (Lima, Ohio). (June 27, 1967)
   > *News* (Pampa, Texas). (June 29, 1967)
   > *Record* (Cuero, Texas). (June 30, 1967)
   > *Telegraph-Forum* (Bucyrus,Ohio). (July 12, 1967)
   > *Times* (Fulton, Mississippi). (June 29, 1967)
   > *Times* (Russell, Kentucky). (July 6, 1967)
   > *Times-Post* (Houston, Mississippi). (July 6, 1967)

City Press. London (England). Editorial. (September 13, 1963) 10. Quotes from *The Freeman* review of the 1962
   English translation: "'How can we stem the present tide of pseudo liberalism? How can we start a surge
   towards real liberalism?' asks Dr. von Mises. ¶He gives the answer:-- 'There is nothing in the world more
   powerful than ideologies and ideologists and only with ideas can one fight against ideas . . . . ¶'In a battle
   between force and an idea, the latter always prevails. The minority that deserves [desires] to see its ideas
   triumph must strive by intellectual means to become the majority'."

Dorfman, Joseph. "Crowns and Pounds and Rubles." *Saturday Review of Literature.* (December 29, 1962) 34-35.
   Reviewed in conjunction with Jan Tinbergen's *Shaping the World Economy.* The reviewer credits Mises'
   contribution to the economic calculation debate with "having raised the level of discussion of the
   economic theory of Socialism . . . . Professor von Mises believes that so delicately adjusted are the
   manifold parts of the economic system, through the working of the law of supply and demand embodied in
   the mechanism of the free market, that interference at any point must result in an accumulation of
   disturbances which would require interference at all points . . . . For this overzealous belief in the
   accomplishments and possibilities of planning [implied by the second book under review], Professor von
   Mises's monograph is a healthy corrective."

Ebeling, Richard M. *In Pursuit of Liberty.* New York: Center for Libertarian Studies. 4:1 (Spring 1979) 11. Mises
   "argues that the liberal position is grounded upon philosophical utilitarianism originating in the works of
   Bentham and others and that, therefore, the rationale for a liberal society is that it maximizes social utility
   and harmony . . . . But Mises' own utilitarian premises can easily be shown to throw doubt on his
   conclusion that only an *extreme* laissez-faire economy is socially desirable. Since all utility decisions are

made at the margin, it is conceivable that some (or many) individuals would be quite willing to forgo a marginal amount of economic liberty in exchange for an additional amount of government-imposed restrictions on certain forms of ethical or economic behavior that was considered 'undesirable' .... ¶But regardless of these criticisms, the volume is superb, for it offers the reader a glimpse of all the strengths and weaknesses of the classical liberal *Weltanschauung* [world view] by one of the leading economic and social thinkers of the century."

_____. *Laissez Faire Books Catalog.* New York. (Spring-Summer 1979) 9. "But the inestimable value of the *classical* liberal order is realized in his [Mises'] penultimate chapter on 'Liberal Foreign Policy.' A broad vista is opened in which national borders become nothing more than night watchmen administrative demarcations; people, ideas and goods freely move from one part of the globe to another, prosperity grows and the right of secession and self-determination assures that no individual or community need ever again feel threatened by the dead hand of statism. ¶Professor Mises offers the vision of a *truly* Great Society and a liberal order that should serve as a banner for all freedom-loving peoples."

Erkelenz, Anton. *Die Hilfe* (1928?). "We welcome this book and thank the publisher for his effort. It is essential that the grand idea of liberalism once more be better known and experienced . . .Thus, we hope this book has many readers." (Quoted from publisher's promotion; translated from the German)

Evans, M. Stanton. "Dark Horses." *National Review.* New York. (January 19, 1979) 112. "While acknowledging that the word 'liberal' has undergone considerable change of meaning since the last century, Mises clearly establishes title to it for his free market, limited-government view: first, because the premises of his discussion are entirely secular and scientific, and therefore very different from what we are accustomed to think of as conservative discourse on such subjects; and second, because he places such pervasive emphasis on personal freedom .... ¶The essence of Mises' argument is that only by protecting private property, permitting maximum freedom to the individual, and eliminating official barriers to trade can efficient utilization of resources and general prosperity be assured."

Fowler, Elizabeth M. "Business Book Shelf." *The New York Times.* (April 15, 1963) 96. A survey of several economics books. "What is a liberal? This book [*The Free and Prosperous Commonwealth*] . . . has an answer that may startle quite a few readers who think they are liberals . . . . By traditional definition, today's businessman probably can be called a 'liberal.' The book helps show the confusion that can arise by those two tags -- liberal and conservative."

The Freeman. Irvington, N.Y.: Foundation for Economic Education. 35:11 (November 1985) 667-682. A symposium of articles commenting on the newly published 3rd English language edition:
Boaz, David. "Liberalism and Change." 680-682. "By freeing people from ancient bonds, it [liberalism] showed them that progress was possible . . . . And with the coming of liberalism came an end to settled society. Change became the only constant."
Greaves, Bettina Bien. "The Meaning of Liberalism." 668. "In *Liberalism* Mises . . . presents, more explicitly than in any of his other books, his views on government and its very limited but essential role in preserving social cooperation under which the free market can function."
Kirzner, Israel M. "Liberalism and Limited Government." 678-680. "Preservation of this fundamental framework of individual rights calls for government that protects these rights against potential enemies; the concern that such protection emphatically refrain from itself invading those very rights is not the expression of any kind of compromise -- it is merely the other side of the very same coin, the essentiality to liberalism of a protected, inviolate sphere of individual rights."
Opitz, Edmund A. "Liberalism and Religion." 676-678. "It was the great achievement of classical liberalism, with its roots in the post-Reformation era and mood, to desacralize the political order, thus stripping the State of its religious and moral pretensions . . . . The State's

ability to punish evil should not create any expectation that the State can enforce good."

Raico, Ralph. "The Place of Mises' Liberalism." 669-671. "In clean, clear lines it sets out what it meant to be a liberal when liberalism was the spectre haunting Europe and, indeed, much of the rest of the world."

Sennholz, Hans F. "Liberalism and Capitalism." 671-673. "For Ludwig von Mises, the private-property order, commonly called capitalism, was the only practical social and economic order."

Wortham, Anne. "Liberalism and Individualism." 673-675. "One finds Mises' utilitarian individualism at work throughout his discussion of the connection between liberalism's advocacy of private ownership of the means of production and its demand for limited functions of government, and in his analysis of the relation of the state to the individual."

Greaves, Percy L., Jr. *The Freeman.* Irvington, N.Y. 13:8 (August 1963) 62-64. "Back in 1927 he [Mises] pictured the pitfalls ahead for nations whose governments grant privileges to the political groups that keep them in power. More than a generation ago, he foresaw that the existence of such privileges would disrupt world trade and lead to political persecutions, wars between the western powers and bloodshed in Asia and Africa, while Russia continued to act 'like a robber who lies in wait for the moment he can pounce on his victim and plunder him of his possessions' ¶ . . . . Under real liberalism, the function of government is to maintain that peace by protecting the lives and property of all who come to rely on the market for their supplies of necessities, as well as the luxuries that become the necessities of the next generation . . . . ¶Unlike some of the other fundamental books of Mises, this volume is exceedingly easy to read. Those who shudder at heavy tomes will find it written in simple style and delightfully clear."

Manas. Los Angeles. "An Honest Partisan." 39:12 (March 19, 1986) 6-7. "The contention of this book is that capitalism is by far the best system for satisfying the needs of a mass society of consumers . . . . ¶What seems entirely missing in the liberal school of thought . . . is recognition that there is a way of thinking about economics which grows out of ethical ideas. This is the Gandhian view . . . . As E. F. Schumacher put it . . . 'The materialist's idea of progress is an idea of *progress without limit* . . . . Material things are of real importance -- for a person, a family, or a nation -- only "up to a point"' . . . . ¶Who will decide when the point of sufficiency has been reached? There can be only one authority on this -- the individual human being . . . . Mises teaches the importance of freedom, but not the necessity of self-restraint in economic enterprise . . . . We suggest a reading of Schumacher to enthusiasts of von Mises."

Michels, Robert. *Schmollers Jahrbuch für Gesetzgebung, Verwaltung und Volkswirtschaft.* 52 (1928). "Ever since Frédéric Bastiat's immortal works, it has been the style and the method of the best champions of liberalism to present their opinions in aphorisms with bold, refreshing, courage and pride. This characteristic may be found in Mises' work with regard to its contents . . . . In many points one cannot subscribe to what he says . . . . On the other hand we certainly do not want to deny that Mises' remarks, as the counterweight to the pervasive overgrown materialism of economic thought, seem like a fresh invigorating wind . . . . ¶Mises' work enriches our world view literature, especially as it rises above the old master Bastiat from the vantage point of three-quarters of a century of experience." (Quoted in publisher's release; translated from the German)

Neue Zürcher Zeitung. (1928?). "The book in itself is a valuable achievement at a time when antiliberal theories are being broadcast in an almost morbid manner and any unbiased judgment of economic affairs becomes difficult." (Quoted from publisher's promotion; translated from the German)

Peterjohn, Karl. *World Research INK.* San Diego, Calif. 3:3 (March 1979) 2. "Well Ludwig von Mises is one author who does not need to be rediscovered by supporters of free enterprise . . . . But even among Mises aficionados there is one work which has generally been overlooked which is definitely a classic . . . . ¶While Mises attacked socialism, and Marx capitalism, Marx never took the next step to outline how a socialist society would operate. Mises did. The result is *Liberalism*, a thought provoking book on political economy which is quickly becoming a classic."

Posse, Ernst. *Kölnische Zeitung.* (January 16, 1928). "Mises distinguishes himself from many competent scholars in that he offers the reader no stylistic enigmas. He says what he has to say with knife-sharp logical reasoning, in clear sentences, with carefully chosen words. In this way he leads the reader to follow effortlessly. Thus this book is actually a manual . . . . What Mises give us is firmly grounded on the specific, economically-directed, challenges of liberalism. (Quoted from publisher's promotion; translated from the German)

Richman, Sheldon L. "Mises's Blueprint for the Free Society." *Free Market.* Burlingame, Calif.: Ludwig von Mises Institute. 7:8 (August 1989) 6-7. "The Chinese students . . . . were calling for freedom of speech and assembly and an end to official corruption. These are laudable objectives, but . . . they cannot be guaranteed without more fundamental changes in China's communist system . . . . ¶The best place to explore the foundations of classical liberalism is in Ludwig von Mises's classic work *Liberalism*. This is Mises's succinct statement of the meaning of the political philosophy that liberated mankind from the old order of feudalism and mercantilism and raised man's standard of living such that the noblemen of old would envy the position of today's poor . . . . ¶Mises identifies seven tenets that form the foundation of classical liberalism: **Private Property; Freedom; Peace; Equality; Limited Government; Tolerance** and **Democracy** . . . . ¶The passionate young people of China and those who struggle for freedom all over the world can learn from Mises and his integrated philosophy of liberalism."

Sennholz, Hans F. "There IS Human Action." *The Individualist.* Philadelphia, Penna.: Intercollegiate Society of Individualists. 2:3-4 (November/December 1963) 4-5. Reviewed with *The Ultimate Foundation* . . . (B-22). "Von Mises wrote this book in 1926, shortly after the disastrous experiences of World War I and a few years before the world began to gird anew for even more barbarous manifestations of Western decline . . . . von Mises' words of warning have even more meaning today in the age of nuclear weapons than in the 1920's . . . . ¶With masterful lucidity von Mises elaborates the problems created by the rise of collectivism . . . . In short, the genuine liberalism as it was understood by its eminent disciples during the eighteenth and nineteenth centuries provides the only sound basis for civilization."

Sulzbach, Walter. *Archiv für Sozialwissenschaft und Politik.* 59:2 (1928). "This work takes up courageously and relentlessly a discussion ignored for decades by the official, i.e. the socialist-oriented economy . . . . Whoever appreciates this . . . will be grateful to Mises for presenting in a new form the old unfashionable theme of 'liberalism'." (Quoted in publisher's release; translated from the German)

Summers, Brian. *The Freeman.* 29:2 (February 1979) 126-128. Reviewed with Mises' *The Ultimate Foundation* . . . (B-22). "*Liberalism* is an excellent introduction to Mises' thought . . . . ¶Mises bases his case for the free market on the enormous productivity of the division of labor . . . . ¶In these times of political turmoil, terrorism, and war, one insight of Mises is especially pertinent: without government regulations, trade barriers, special privileges, public services, oppressive taxation, and other restrictions on the free movement of men and goods, it would matter little which government one lived under or what party happened to be in office. Roll back the state, and politically inspired conflicts will tend to disappear."

Zimbler. *Juristische Blätter.* 4 (1928). "This book is written in the service of a great idea and a fascinating ideal. Neither the author nor his work is unworthy of this idea and ideal . . . . His wide knowledge equips Mises, the important economist and sociologist, to deal with the subject of liberalism . . . . Certainly no other liberal will agree completely with all that Mises says. Still anyone who wants to take a position on the problems with which Mises deals -- and today that must include everyone with an interest in his own fate and that of western man -- must read this work." (Quoted in publisher's release; translated from the German)

Monetary Stabilization and Cyclical Policy (B-7) (*Geldwertstabilisierung und Konjunkturpolitik*, 1928). English translation in *On Monetary Stabilization and Cyclical Policy* (B-24).

Altschul, Eugen. *Magazin der Wirtschaft*. 47 (1928). "It is his [Mises'] merit to have vigorously pointed out the uncertainty of the foundations of the economic theory of monetary cyclical policy. His accomplishments are full of good ideas and, even though they may provoke opposition, they offer opponents much stimulation. Certainly they will not fail to influence the discussion of cyclical theory and policy in the future. (Translated from the German)

Balogh, Thomas. *American Economic Review*. 19:2 (June 1929) 315-316. "Criticizing the well-known propositions of Professor Fisher and Mr. Keynes . . . the author maintains that the great advantage of the gold standard . . . lies in the impossibility of governmental influence. An index number system would cause harm, because it would introduce political and other alien influences. ¶His further criticism of Professor Fisher's plan is not convincing. Mises holds that the concept of a general price level is but a fiction to facilitate the analysis of price movements, and that it is impossible to use it for such purposes as Fisher proposes . . . . ¶In the second part of his book Mises gives his well-known theory of business cycles . . . . ¶The fear of authoritative influences upon the monetary and credit system which obviously underlies Mises' deductions, leads him into exaggerations. Some of his distrust may be justified by the history of banking practice; but he is certainly going too far in suspecting that banks or governments will inflate at every opportunity. ¶Although Mises' criticism of inflationist tendencies is clear and excellent, his practical conclusions may be questioned."

Der deutsche Oekonomist. 35 (1928). "The volume gives a clear outline of the problem . . . . In his careful investigation, the author comes to the conclusion that there is only one theory of monetary value today, the Quantity Theory. And only one theory of business cycles and crises, namely the Circulation Credit Theory which evolved from the Currency Theory." (Translated from the German)

Eisler, Robert. "Zur Kritik der 'Kompensierten Goldwährung' nach Fisher-Keynes" [A Critique of the Fisher-Keynes "Compensatory Gold Standard"]. *Wiener Börsen-Kurier*. 37 (September 11, 1933) 2-4; 39 (September 25, 1933) 5. A lengthy 2-part review. The side-heads reveal the subjects covered: 1. The Value of Money and Monetary Policy; 2. What Does "Stabilization" of the Currency Mean? 3. The Problem of Index Numbers. "The effects of the causes of price movements on the commodity side would be neutralized and the changes on the money side compensated for only if the index encompassed a great number of commodity prices (for example not around 45, as does the French wholesale price index, but hundreds and thousands of prices) and only if the numerous price fluctuations were very small and independent of one another, i.e. entirely by accident." According to the reviewer, "central banks, with their eyes on the relation between notes in circulation and metallic reserves, respond inadequately and too slowly, often months even years too late, to the demand to expand or contract credit. (Translated from the German)

_____. "Die Gegenbewegung von Gold und Ware und die Goldproduktion unter einem Irving Fisher'schen Währungssystem" [The Reaction of Gold and Commodities and Gold Production under an Irving Fisher Monetary System]. *Wiener Börsen-Kurier*. 40 (October 2, 1933) 3-4; 42 (October 16, 1933). A two-part article which refers to Mises' book. "It is simply not true that the banks, by creating credit and reducing the interest rate, enable new (profit-making, round-about) enterprises to be started, for the completion of which 'there is not enough means of subsistence to maintain the workers during the entire period of the expanded process of production' and that 'sooner or later this must become evident.'" (Translated from the German)

Neisser, Hans. "Notenbankfreiheit?" [Freedom of the Banks of Issue?]. *Weltwirtschaftliches Archiv.* Institut für Weltwirtschaft und Seeverkehr, Universität Kiel. 32:2 (October 1930) 446-461. The reviewer is critical of Mises' free banking theory. "Only a central bank of issue *not* based on private enterprise principles will use its discount policy properly to restrict the cash in circulation during the boom and thus the superstructure of checkbook money. This does not exclude, but rather fosters, that the same central bank of issue will avoid the danger of a complete collapse of the credit system in a real crisis of trust by the compensatory creation of credit and cash. Or is Mises of the opinion that the breakdown of such an 'insolvent' banking system, which is of advantage only for the banker, will be of no concern to the other members of the economy?" (Translated from the German)

Strigl, R. *Mitteilungen des Verbandes österreichischen Banken und Bankiers.* 10:7/8 (1928). The book "deals with proposals for the artificial stabilization of monetary value, which have found eloquent champions especially in English literature. The usefulness and expedience of the gold standard is defended in response to the advocates of monetary manipulation by control of purchasing power. Mises is concerned with the idea of eliminating cyclical fluctuations that follow the artificial stabilization of the purchasing power. In opposition to vast projects, a sound cyclical policy is staked out . . . . Happily Mises' statement, presented here with lively spirit, can supplement the more detailed treatment of profound theoretical questions by referring to the author's major work, *Theory of Money and Credit* (B-2). So this volume offers not only a desirable recapitulation to the specialist, but also a useful introduction to those unacquainted with theory. It is to be hoped that this volume will win new friends for modern monetary theory, that it will serve to enlighten wider circles, and finally that it will also contribute to seeing that proposals for dangerous experiments meet with the needed criticism." (Translated from the German)

Money, Method, and the Market Process (B-28)

Childs, Roy A., Jr. *Laissez Faire Books Catalog.* San Francisco. C84 (1990) 9. "Mises was always much more than a mere critic of socialism. He was the greatest advocate of laissez faire capitalism of his time, an untiring visionary whose hammer blows against statism in all its forms and whose eloquent defenses of individualism, private property, the free market and international free trade are legendary. There can be no greater tribute to him than to point out the true monument to his life and work: the death of communism in Eastern Europe, and the prospective rebirth of the free market out of the ashes of totalitarianism . . . . *Money, Method, and the Market Process* is a great collection. Richard Ebeling has written a superb introduction to it, placing Mises's work in the context of twentieth century thought."

The Free Market   Burlingame, Calif.: Ludwig von Mises Institute. 8:8 (August 1990) 4. "A Misesian milestone! This new collection of essays by Ludwig von Mises, many of them published here for the first time, fully displays his intellectual power."

Hoppe, Hans-Hermann. *Austrian Economics Newsletter.*   Auburn, Ala.: Ludwig von Mises Institute. 13:2 (Spring 1992) 8-10. "Throughout his life, Mises relied exclusively on the power of his words -- and his unwavering conviction that even the most rampant forms of statism, and the most relentless statist propaganda of a steadily growing class of 'public educators' in schools and universities, could not stamp out the human desire for independent thinking, logic, and truth . . . . ¶*Money, Method, and the Market Process,* . . . edited and with a knowledgeable introduction by Richard Ebeling, contains 21 articles written by Mises between 1930 and 1969 . . . . [and is] organized under five headings [Method, Money, Trade, Comparative Economics Systems, and Ideas] . . . . ¶In the final section on "Ideas" Mises restates the Humean insight, which has only recently received another dramatic confirmation with the sudden collapse of the seemingly impregnable power of the communist rulers of the Soviet Union, that no government can last without majority support, be it active or passive. Once this support is gone, even the most ruthless tyrant will be toppled. In the last resort, then, the course of history and the outcome of man's ceaseless struggle for liberty will be decided in the realm of ideas."

Peterson, William H. "Communism's failure foretold." *Washington Times.* (August 9, 1990). "As early as 1920, Ludwig von Mises virtually alone saw the inner contradictions of Soviet communism and predicted its breakdown . . . . ¶The extraordinary events of the last 12 months in Eastern Europe testify to the insight of von Mises. ¶In *Money, Method, and the Market Process: Essays by Ludwig von Mises,* Margit von Mises has collected out-of-print articles and previously unpublished papers of her husband, who died in 1973 -- a year before his student F. A. Hayek won the Nobel Prize in economics. The book, which has a long and incisive introduction by economist Richard Ebeling of Hillsdale College, provides another opportunity to review the life of a brilliant mind confronting the upheavals of the 20th century . . . . In the last essay in this book, he sees the history of civilization as the record of a ceaseless struggle for individual freedom. He maintains that social cooperation under division of labor is the ultimate and sole source of man's success in his struggle for survival and well-being. ¶But social cooperation still requires suppression of those disturbing the peace. So von Mises says society cannot do without a social apparatus of coercion and compulsion -- that is, a government, a state. ¶But therein is the great dilemma and challenge of all civilizations, past and present: Who guards the guardians?"

Nation, State, and Economy (B-3) (*Nation, Staat und Wirtschaft*, 1919; English translation, 1983)

Greaves, Bettina Bien. *The Freeman.* Irvington, N.Y. 34:3 (March 1984) 187-190. "Mises deals with the concepts of 'nation,' 'state,' and 'economy'. . . . To appreciate the situation in post World War I Europe, with its countless intermingled minorities, many with different languages, dialects, cultures, religions and special interests, an understanding of these concepts is essential . . . . ¶Nineteenth-century Europe had been trending toward the freedom ideas of classical liberalism. To understand the origins of German nationalism which led to World War I, therefore, it must be explained how liberalism, always pacifist and anti-militaristic, was overthrown. '[T]he last trace of the liberal spirit had first to disappear from Germany and liberalism had to become regarded as a kind of dishonorable ideology before the people of poets and thinkers could become a weak-willed tool of the [imperialist] war party' . . . . Mises explains that the path to lasting peace depends on adopting the freedom philosophy of classical liberalism . . . . This book . . . offers important insights to us today for understanding current problems . . . . Mises himself realized its importance, for he referred to it . . . in his 1940 recollections: 'It was a scientific book with political design. It was an attempt at alienating the affections of the German and Austrian public from National-Socialist [Nazi] ideas . . . . My book remained unnoticed and was seldom read. But I know that it will be read in the future'." *Notes and Recollections* (p.66)

Hazlitt, Henry. "Mises and Keynes: A 20th-Century Puzzle." *Reason.* Santa Barbara, Calif. 15: 8 (December 1983) 38-41. Compares *Nation, State, and Economy* with Keynes' *The Economic Consequences of the Peace*, both published shortly after World War I. "Most present-day readers, having in mind the subsequent work of the two authors, might be surprised by a comparison of the two books. Instead of the sharp contrast that they may expect, they will find striking similarities. This is because the Keynes who wrote *The Economic Consequences* in 1919 was quite different from the Keynes who produced the *General Theory* in 1936 . . . . In *The Economic Consequences* he wrote one of the most eloquent denunciations of inflation that has ever been penned . . . . There is one further important point of agreement between the Mises and Keynes books of 1919. Keynes thought that the reparations demanded by the Allies from the Central Powers were vindictive and far too burdensome. And so did Mises . . . . Yet these areas of agreement between Keynes and Mises were not to last long . . . . ¶Mises's *Nation, State, and Economy* is a wide-ranging book . . . . [W]hen he [Mises] writes on a subject that he has discussed elsewhere, he seldom merely repeats himself. He nearly always manages to throw some additional light on it . . . . A substantial section of the book . . . is devoted to a discussion of socialism . . . . Of private ownership, he remarks that it 'fulfills its social function by converting the means of production into the hands of those who best understand how to use them'. . . . ¶In his final chapter Mises deals with such ultimate questions as the goals of human life . . . . ¶The irony is that the unstable and mercurial Keynes was widely hailed in his own lifetime as the greatest living economist, while Ludwig von Mises, who really deserved the title, labored for most of his life in comparative obscurity. Even now a true recognition of his contributions is confined to a small 'Austrian' coterie. But it will grow."

Tucker, Jeffrey A. "Mises' *Nation, State, and Economy*" *The Free Market.* Auburn, Ala.: Ludwig von Mises Institute. (March 1987) 6, 3. "In 1919, the World War had just ended, and Germany and Austria were devastated. Mises applied sound economics and political analysis to explain why the war began, how to repair the damage, and how to avoid war in the future. . . . ¶There is a persistent myth that war stimulates the economy by providing jobs and boosting manufacturing. Mises knew better: 'War prosperity is like the prosperity that an earthquake or a plague brings. The earthquake means good business for construction workers, and cholera improves the business of physicians, pharmacists, and undertakers; but no one has for that reason yet sought to celebrate earthquakes and cholera as stimulaters of the productive forces in the general interest'. . . . ¶His [Mises] advice was not followed in 1919. But because the principles of free markets and liberty are universally applicable, almost seven decades later we still know, as Ludwig von Mises said, that 'whoever wishes peace among peoples must fight statism'."

Nationalökonomie   (B-11)   (German-language predecessor to *Human Action*,   B-16; no English translation available)

Graber, Karl. *Die Presse.*   Vienna. (November 23, 1981) 7. After a short discussion of labor policy, union policy, and unemployment, the reviewer quotes from "the most recently published major work [*Nationalökonomie*, 1980] of an old, long-since deceased Austrian economist . . . . 'If commodities find no customers or workers no work, there can be only one cause: The prices and wages asked are too high'. . . . Our author's name is Ludwig von Mises . . . . Ludwig von Mises' 100th birthday was celebrated on September 22 of this year in Vienna, characteristically behind closed doors and out of the sight of the scientific world." (Translated from the German)

Hayek, F. A. *The Economic Journal.* (April 1941) 124-127. "The reader who knows Professor Mises' earlier works on money, socialism, and the methods of the social sciences will find much that is already familiar if not accepted doctrine . . . . Much of it sounds now far less revolutionary than it did twenty or thirty years ago -- indeed, nothing is more instructive than a glance at the reviews which the earlier works of the author received . . . or proves better how much of his views which then were hotly attacked or even ridiculed has since become common property . . . . But it must be admitted that he seems to have been little affected by the general evolution of our subject during the period over which his work extends. What growth there is appears to be decidedly autonomous, and one even feels that the author, having been so often attacked for what later proved to be correct views, has developed a certain contempt for contemporary economics which has prevented him from deriving much advantage from it . . . . ¶The most original and at the same time probably the most controversial developments in Professor Mises' views will, however, be found in the opening parts of the book, in which he gives the outlines of a general theory of human action of which economic theory is a special part . . . . Although the reviewer would put many things differently, he must confess . . . . that on the main point Professor Mises' lone voice seems to him considerably nearer the truth than the commonly accepted views . . . . [T]here appears to be a width of view and an intellectual spaciousness about the whole book which are much more like that of an eighteenth-century philosopher than that of a modern specialist . . . . To the many who will disagree with most of it, this will no doubt prove a profoundly irritating book, but not one which they can afford to disregard."

Honegger, Hans. "Die 'Nationalökonomie' von L. v. Mises." (1941 ?). Unidentified copy of this review found among Mises' papers at Grove City College. "The thoroughness, originality, and logical consistency of his treatment contrasts advantageously with most systems of economics offered us in recent decades; one must certainly go back to Adam Smith's *Wealth of Nations* to find a counterpart to this theory of economics with regard to its grasp of problems and its unity. ¶This economic theory meets half way both the wishes of the scientist and at the same time those of the practical person . . . . It even goes farther toward an attempt to present a thorough explanation of the great and at times unusual political and economic problems of the present and recent past. In support of this remark, I should like to cite the five sections of the last chapter of Part 6. The chapter is titled 'War Economy' and the separate sections are 'War and the Market Economy,' 'A War of Armies and Total War,' 'Total Mobilization,' 'Economic War Autarky,' and 'The Problem of the Most Recent War,' -- and he does not mean the First but the Second World War, the War that began in 1939. ¶These statements are offered because the introductory parts of the work seem to me exceedingly erudite and somewhat awkward so that the superficial reader might easily be inclined to put the work down in the beginning as too 'philosophical' or 'abstract.' . . . ¶The work is an unlimited avowal of economic liberalism, in the sense that basically and in the long run only freedom-oriented measures, not force or coercion, will help the European economy to its feet again and thus enable our continent, like other lands, to save itself from final destruction." (Translated from the German)

Knight, F. H. "Professor Mises and the Theory of Capital." *Economica.* New Series. 8:32 (November 1941) 409-427. A fairly lengthy review article. "I agree with Professor Mises' view that depression, or the 'cycle,' is fundamentally a phenomenon of credit expansion and contraction. But much of his analysis seems to me inconsistent and contrary to facts. However, I also find it obscure, and concede that my impression might be modified by more intensive study. He seems opposed to government having any monetary policy -- which is surely carrying his well-known anti-interventionist attitude to extremes . . . . [W]here I agree with Professor Mises' conclusions, I often find him right for wrong reasons -- and reciprocally, right premises being used to support 'error'." The remainder of the review discusses Mises' and Böhm-Bawerk's capital and interest theories.

K.R.L. *Die Industrie.* (January 23, 1981). "This major work of Ludwig von Mises, one of this century's great social philosophers and economists, now issued in a second edition, has remained practically unknown in German circles since its original publication date (1940 in Geneva). However, the English version of this important work [*Human Action*, (B-16)], which appeared in 1949, has been exceptionally successful for a scientific book. Praxeology is the theory of the means for attaining goals, not one of the choice of proper goals." (Translated from the German)

Orientierungen. (September 9, 1981). "Among the important liberal works issued recently by the Philosophia Verlag is Ludwig von Mises' 'magnum opus,' *Nationalökonomie.* (Translated from the German)

K.R. *Die Kammer.* IHK [Industrie Handels Kammer]. No. 7 (July 14, 1981). The library of the Chamber of Industry and Trade calls attention to *Nationalökonomie* with a few brief comments similar to those in K.R.L.'s review quoted above.

Seuss, Wilhelm. "Mises -- neu aufgelegt" [Mises, newly published]. *Frankfurter Allgemeine Zeitung.* (December 9, 1980). "It is welcome news that the German version [of Mises' *Human Action*] is at last once more available. The vigor of the thoughts and the German scientific tradition from which Mises stems, also the beauty of the argumentation, may be better preserved in the mother-tongue of the author than would be possible in the English edition or in a translation back into German . . . . ¶The original idea of developing economics as the understanding of the theory of coordination of the autonomous adjustments of men, is the most beautiful gift that Mises has bequeathed the reader." (Translated from the German)

Sulzbach, Walter. *Journal of Social Philosophy and Jurisprudence.* 7 (October 1941) 74-77. "According to Mises, economics is a part of the science of human action . . . . ¶Starting from the facts that men seek happiness and wish to avoid pain and privation, that goods are scarce and labor disagreeable, we are able to grasp the axiomatic truth of doctrines such as that of marginal value and of increasing and decreasing returns of industry . . . . ¶Proceeding step by step from his original utilitarian premises, always keeping within the confines of 'praxeology,' Mises develops a comprehensive system of economic theory . . . . ¶Mises has written a remarkable book . . . . It is the work of a man who combines an immense knowledge of economic history, economic theories and present-day facts with a thoroughly logical mind . . . . For while he starts with premises almost axiomatic which are contested by practically nobody, he ends up with the theisis that fundamentally it is one and the same thing to be an economist (a real, not a political or sentimental one) and to be a 'liberal' in the sense of a believer in *laissez faire* . . . . It would be highly desirable if an American publisher would sponsor an English translation of *Nationalökonomie.*"

Terakawa, Suejiro. "Methodology of Sociology and Economics." *Shodai Ronshu.* Kobe University of Commerce, Economic Institute. 2 (February 1950) 42-51. The reviewer criticizes Mises' use of aprioristic logic especially and his criticism of Max Weber's "ideal types." "Only a few scholars in history have firmly asserted that sociology and [theoretical] economics are not empirical. Throughout more than 200 years in the history of economic thought, no one has ever consistently held to aprioristic logic. Only Senior and Cairnes did so partially . . . . and Senior was careful, it is said, not to make economic theory a fruitless excercise in logic. It is difficult to find similar caution in Mises." (pp.2-3) The reviewer holds that Mises was influenced by the philosophical scholars of his age. He sees some similarity between Mises' work and phenomenology. "We must reject excessive logical speculation," he writes. "No one is bold enough to reject completely all empirical evidence." (p.9) The reviewer continues for several pages to criticize Mises' apriorism and his "excessive" use of the deductive method. (Annotation based on translation from the Japanese by Toshio Murata)

Tribune de Genève. Switzerland. June 16/17 1940. "Nationalökonomie." A brief announcement. "The scholarly economic theorist, Ludwig von Mises, devotes this huge work of 756 pages to a profound study of the theory of commerce and economics; it makes a valuable contribution to our understanding of the national economy . . . . In his conclusion, the author examines the science with respect to life, politics and the future." (Translated from the French).

Tuchtfeldt, E. "Nationalökonomie -- Theorie des Handelns und des Wirtschaftens: Zur Neuauflage des Hauptwerkes von Ludwig von Mises: Ein ungewöhnliches Leben" [*Economics: Theory of Action and Exchange:* On the Publication of Ludwig von Mises' Major Work: An Extraordinary Life]. *Neue Zürcher Zeitung.* 207 (September 8, 1981) 18. "Even during his lifetime, he [Mises] could see the beginning of a development which is known today as the 'Mises Renaissance'. . . . ¶Ludwig von Mises was just as clear a thinker as he was an unconventional one. His basic position rests on the subjective value theory, characterized by a consistent individualism. He proceeds from a general theory of human action, praxeology, which he contrasts with history . . . . ¶Mises' *Nationalökonomie* is certainly not a textbook which presents the current state of economic research . . . . It wasn't even that at the time of the book's first appearance in 1940, at a time when Keynesianism was beginning to conquer the world economy. Never throughout his long life, did Mises make the slightest concession to the many streams of fashion which have dominated 20th century economic thought and which have increasingly led to a deterioration in the relationship of science to practice. ¶What Ludwig von Mises offers in *Nationalökonomie* is no more and no less than a fully elaborated theory of the free market economy. Whoever cannot grasp the economic and political aspects of American Reaganomics, which has followed in the wake of the interventionist bias, will find here the theoretical explanation. Moreover, it is written in a clear and flowing style." (Translated from the German)

Unsere Wirtschaft. IHK. Dusseldorf: Industrie Handels Kammer. "Ein moderner Nationalökonom" [A modern economist]. (August 1981). "The central theme of this new, unrevised, edition of the major work, *Nationalökonomie,* now available once more to the German reader, is the comprehensive presentation of a free market and social order . . . . Of special interest are the semi-unconventional thoughts on monetary stability and the business cycle, which could give a new impetus to present day politico-economic discussions. Of fundamental significance also is the critique of interventionist economic policy." (Translated from the German)

Notes and Recollections (B-23)

Austrian Information. 31:5 (1978) 8. "Although written under the influence of the bloody war in Europe and Austria's demise as an independent state, these recollections are not totally pessimistic . . . . ¶This book is an essential part of Mises' legacy. It is preceded by a short foreword by Margit von Mises, the author's widow, and followed by a Postscript of thirty pages, describing Mises' later years and works, by one of his friends and students, Professor Hans F. Sennholz."

Blaich, Fritz. *Vierteljahrschrift für Sozial- und Wirtschaftsgeschichte.* Wiesbaden: Franz Steiner Verlag. 67:2 (1980) 267-268. "Originally intended as autobiography, these notes give a complete and clear picture of the development of the author as scientist and academic teacher." (Translated from the German)

The Chalcedon Report. Vallecito, Calif. 153 (May 1978). Reviewed jointly with *On the Manipulation of Money and Credit.* Concerning *Notes and Recollections*, the reviewer writes: "The foreword by Mrs. Mises and the postscript by Dr. Hans Sennholz . . . are. . . important. Mises' *Notes and Recollections* manifest a grim pessimism or realism with respect to the world's future. He saw virtually no hope . . . . The failure of the intellectuals to comprehend the problem left Mises with a 'hopeless pessimism'. . . . But Mises lacked the perspective of Christian theism. At the root of our political and economic crises is a moral failure, the triumph of envy, theft, and fraud. The beginning of a change must be a moral renewal, and the tools then will be the use of Mises' economic research."

Ebeling, Richard M. *The Austrian Economics Newsletter.* New York: Center for Libertarian Studies. 1:3 (Fall 1978) 9-10. "He [Mises] speaks frankly about the personalities and ideologies of Austria and Germany in the period between the World Wars. Written in 1940, the volume carries in it the despair of the forced exile recently arrived in America. Indeed, throughout the book the air hangs heavy with the intellectual isolation and political pessimism of one who cared deeply about the pursuit of knowledge and the preservation and advancement of human liberty . . . . Mises explains his reluctant decision to enter the discussions over methodology in the social sciences and how he came to his views about the *a priori* character of economic theory."

_____. "Mises on Money, Intervention and Himself." *Laissez Faire Books Catalog & Review.* (Spring-Summer 1978) 29-30. Reviewed jointly with *A Critique of Interventionism* (B-8) and *On the Manipulation of Money and Credit* (B-24). Concerning *Notes and Recollections*: "[A]t an early point in his writing career Mises decided that his goal was not to address particular problems in economic theory, but, rather, to build the necessary foundation for a new 'world-view' in the social sciences -- a general theory of human action. Insisting that 'economics necessarily must be a complete and united whole . . . . To deal with a part one must do so on the foundation of a theory that comprises all the problems'."

Evans, Medford. *American Opinion.* 21:2 (February 1978) 57-67. "The greatness of Ludwig von Mises is seen when we realize that he spent the whole of his long life (1881-1973) in societies where the nominal intellectual leadership was fatuously devoted to socialism or 'interventionism,' rejecting the Free Market. Yet he never was deceived by false argument or intimidated by social or financial pressure into accepting or pretending to accept either the socialist or the interventionist illusion . . . . There are any number of fascinating angles to this slender book by Ludwig von Mises, to which Hans Sennholz has added so much. My process of evaluation puts the whole thing in the top rank."

Hazlitt, Henry. "The Evolution -- and Ordeal -- of an Economist." *The Wall Street Journal.* (February 9, 1978). "If the sadness of this book is not hard to explain, neither is the bitterness. Living through one world war, on the side of the defeated, frustrated by the intellectual decline in Austria after the war, Mises lived to see the rise of Hitler. Driven from Vienna by the threat of a Nazi takeover, he spent six comparatively happy years as a professor at the Graduate Institute of International Studies at Geneva. But the outbreak of World War II in Europe made it seem to him advisable to emigrate with his wife to the United States in August 1940. In the three months that he then devoted to writing this book, he had no idea of the future he would have in his new country. ¶That future too was to prove full of early anxiety and difficulty. With the help of his American friends, he was finally, in 1945, appointed Visiting Professor at the Graduate School of Business Administration of New York University. But even then his salary did not come from the university, but had to be entirely provided from the outside -- by friends and foundations. ¶This book is an essential part of Mises' legacy."

_____. "Three New Books by Ludwig von Mises." *The Freeman.* Irvington, N.Y. 28:4 (April 1978) 247-253. Reviewed jointly with *A Critique of Interventionism* (B-8) and *On the Manipulation of Money and Credit* (B-24). Concerning *Notes and Recollections* (pp.247-249), Hazlitt writes: "The great intellectual influences in Mises' own development were, of course, the founders of the 'Austrian school,' Carl Menger and Eugen von Boehm-Bawerk . . . . As Mises matured intellectually, he came to recognize that Austrian thought and culture were already in decline. Menger and Boehm-Bawerk were still alive; but they were being succeeded by mediocrities who failed to grasp their revolutionary insights . . . . Some of us may regret that Mises' great personal reticence kept him from telling more about his early childhood and his emotional life, but we can still count ourselves fortunate to have this important addition to his legacy."

Kershner, Howard E. *Answers to Economic Problems.* Cedar Hill, Texas: Northwood Institute. 4:10 (October 1978) 4. "Although sure of the correctness of his economic views, and confident that if his philosophy could be followed, freedom and economic prosperity would prevail, he [Mises] was nevertheless saddened by the fact that he was witnessing the decline of freedom and economic well-being."

K.R.L. *Die Industrie.* 49 (n.d.) 34. Review of German (1978) translation: "Although Ludwig von Mises must certainly be counted among the most significant thinkers of our time in the field of economic science and social philosophy, in a certain sense he remained until his death in 1973, at least in the German-speaking world, the great outsider of economists . . . . These reminiscences of Ludwig von Mises contain his political principles and convictions and describe his struggle against interventionism and socialism and for the free market." (Translated from the German)

Peterson, William H. "Mises and His Legacies." *Modern Age.*   Bryn Mawr, Penna.: Intercollegiate Studies Institute. 22:3 (Summer 1978) 315-317. "His [Mises'] conversion from statism centers around Christmas of 1903 when he read Carl Menger's *Principles of Economics.* Mises confesses: 'It was the reading of this book that made an "economist" of me.' In addition, Mises' 'Austrianism' was reinforced by his attendance at the seminars of another great leader of the Austrian School, Eugen von Boehm-Bawerk, a man who all but destroyed Marx intellectually . . . . Mises returned to teaching in a way by starting what he called 'The younger Austrian School'. . . . All who have survived Mises attest to his enormous integrity, to his unbending, almost slavish adherence to principle . . . . Mises was, above all, a rationalist, a towering monument to consistency."

Rothbard, Murray N. "The Mises We Never Knew." *Libertarian Review.* San Francisco. (April 1978) 37-38. "This is the sort of autobiography we would expect from a private person of great courtesy and Old World reserve. It is an *intellectual* autobiography, explaining his ideological struggles and how he arrived at his ideas. There is no Instant Intimacy here, nor is there any fodder for emotional *voyeurs* . . . . a fascinating companion volume to his widow Margit's lovely valentine to their life together, *My Years with Ludwig von Mises* . . . . There is no more fitting way to end this review than to pay tribute to the remarkable integrity and fighting spirit of Ludwig von Mises. In the 1910s and 1920s, as today, there were small-minded men who criticized Mises' consistency and candor. If only he had been willing to bend principle a bit! Mises charmingly refers to such criticisms: '. . . . As I look back today at my activity with the Chamber I regret only my willingness to compromise, not my intransigence'."

Omnipotent Government (B-12)

American Affairs. New York: National Industrial Conference Board. "The World That Might Have Been." 7:1 (January 1945) 47-49. Reviewed jointly with *Bureaucracy.* Concerning *Omnipotent Government*: "There is in man the very principle of frustration. Once, and perhaps for the first time, he did find the right way. Beginning with the optimistic social philosophy of eighteenth century liberalism he discovered the solutions of the free market, free competition, free private enterprise -- that is to say, capitalism -- and how at the same time to put government in its place . . . . But the government, which he had put in its place, began to overtake him, offering to do him good and to help him on his way . . . . Offering only to help him on his way to a new free world of unlimited well-being it was really all the time hostile to anything he was doing for himself . . . . But the tragedy was that when the government's intervention in the modern case had gone rather far man embraced it, and there arose in the world the great cult of what von Mises calls etatism, a word he prefers over *statism* . . . . Such is the theme of *Omnipotent Government.* Since the eclipse of the classical economists no writer has more powerfully or with fewer misgivings defended free private capitalism, not only as the system that works and contains within itself the mechanisms of self-correction, but as a social philosophy . . . . ¶So one may come to the end of the book, or to almost the end, with a sense of nostalgia for the optimism of the eighteenth century liberals and a certain hopefulness. If it was once there it must be there still -- the right way to a free world of relative peace and yet greater well-being. But, alas! his conclusion is that the old liberals were after all wrong. Their economic theories were right, almost too right, but they believed in the perfectibility of man; they believed mankind 'was on the eve of lasting prosperity and eternal peace' and that reason would henceforth be supreme. Therein they were tragically wrong. They left out of consideration the principle of frustration."

Basch, Antonin. *The American Economic Review.* 34:4 (December 1944) 899-903. "The author had a good case for analyzing the dangers to national welfare and freedom which bureaucratic handling of economic problems generates. This reviewer, however, is afraid that Professor von Mises has weakened his case by his absolutely uncompromising opposition to what he calls étatism or 'statolatry' and by his unrelenting consistency in presenting '*laissez faire* capitalism' in its orthodox and theoretical form as the only acceptable economic system . . . . ¶To assert that 'modern monopoly is the result of government policies aiming at a reform of the market economy and would collapse with a regime of free trade' is to do away with the whole theory of imperfect competition and not to see the problems of big industrial combines due primarily to their technological strength . . . . ¶It seems to me that the author sometimes tries to embrace too many topics without taking the time to check on all pertinent data . . . . ¶Antisemitism is discussed at some length and the author concludes with the certainly interesting assertion that the present war would never have originated but for antisemitism . . . . ¶Von Mises raises the question so often posed by various writers, namely, why the nazi régime has not in time met with a vigorous opposition in other parts of the world. His explanation is rather simple. 'The fundamental tenets of the Nazi ideology do not differ from the generally accepted social and economic ideologies' . . . . This is another example of von Mises's oversimplifications . . . . ¶In his conclusions the author reveals once more his Cato-like, uncompromising belief in a complete *laissez-faire* capitalism. Durable peace is possible only under perfect capitalism . . . . In a world of perfect capitalism, entirely free trade and free migration, no international conflicts could arise. There would be no economic causes of war . . . . ¶Though this reviewer cannot agree with Professor von Mises on a number of important subjects, he certainly recommends the reading of his book. It is highly stimulating and, in these times of indiscriminate advocacy of government intervention and of popular belief in the wisdom and power of bureaucracy, this book might have a sobering effect, inducing the reader to consider more critically the role of the government in economic life."

Baster, A. S. *Economica*. New Series. 12:45 (February 1945) 39-40. "Broadly stated, the main argument of this book is that State intervention in the free market is bound to be undertaken on behalf of members of a particular national group and is therefore bound to produce friction in the international sphere, leading ultimately to the danger of war . . . . [T]he present book may perhaps be regarded as an elaboration of the chapters in *Die Gemeinwirtschaft* [*Socialism*, B-4] on the Foreign Relations of a Socialist Community . . . . ¶The case seems to the present reviewer to belong to the large, and unhappily growing class of economic truths which people neglect at their peril . . . . Those who hope that a new and better world will emerge out of the plans of highly nationalistic governments to improve the economic position of (their own) national groups, may be in for some serious disappointments. The effect of the war . . . has been to exacerbate nationalism and to strengthen and elaborate the economic controls of the belligerent national Governments . . . . ¶Those who swim against the strong intellectual tides now running have a heavy task indeed. They must defend their own beliefs in the current idiom of their opponents, and they must restate received truths acceptably to a generation grown sceptical of them . . . . His [Mises'] book shows tellingly that the present trend towards economic interventionalism is liable to lead to disastrous international conflict. This is only half the task. He ought now to tell us precisely what a 'free market economy' means, what sort of government action is necessary to sustain it and enable it to meet the shocks which theory and practice alike show to be inevitable; and what are the practical stages by which it can be finally reached in a world which, for the last thirty years, has been moving ever faster in the opposite direction."

Bernt, H. H. *Library Journal*. 69 (April 1, 1944) 303. "Exaggeration often diminishes value of otherwise interesting work. Recommended for university and larger public libraries." (Quoted from *Book Review Digest*, 1944. p.530)

Branden, Nathaniel. *Book News.* Los Angeles: Academic Associates. No.4 (June 1970) 8-9. Reviewed in conjunction with *Bureaucracy* (B-13) and *Theory and History* (B-20). "In *Omnipotent Government*, Professor von Mises provides an explanation of the international conflicts that caused both world wars, and of the ideological issues behind those conflicts. He shows very clearly and persuasively the relationship between governmental intervention into the economy and the consequent growth of belligerent nationalism. He also shows the relationship between free trade and free enterprise, on the one hand, and world peace, on the other . . . . Speaking personally, I have never found economics a particularly exciting subject. But Professor von Mises' books were among the very first that I read, when I initially became interested in problems of political economy -- and to this day I find myself returning to them, again and again, for the pleasure and instruction of observing a brilliant mind bring clarity and sanity to a field in which clarity and sanity tend to be so conspicuously absent."

Chamber of Commerce of the U. S. *Business Action*. "Add to your list of great books: *OMNIPOTENT GOVERNMENT* -- a book described by the *New York Times* as one of the great books of our age. It is a penetrating analysis of the rise of the total state leading to total war. It describes in flowing language and with great depth the true inward meaning of policy-making by economic pressure groups and the state." Quoted on book jacket of the first edition of *Bureaucracy* (B-13).

Chamberlain, John. *New York Times*. (May 27, 1944) 13. "In 1913 the world was on the threshold of a golden age . . . . ¶Yes, even as the world moved toward the Golden Age the storm clouds blew up. The great experiment in a global division of labor ended in a frightful war, a stultifying peace and a reversion to the cut-throat economics of eighteenth-century mercantilism . . . . ¶How did such madness come about? To Ludwig von Mises, exiled Viennese economist, the only explanation is that human beings are idiots . . . . Von Mises' explanation of what ails the world is to be found in *Omnipotent Government*: *The Rise of the Total State and Total War*, which is one of the great books of our age. ¶Von Mises is absolutely uncompromising in his criticism of what he calls 'etatism' . . . . He fails in realism when he seeks to

136

exonerate business men from leading the push toward etatism; after all, the first great interventionists were the tariff-seeking manufacturers, the railroad builders who cried out for Government subsidies, the oil and steel men who sought to corrupt Legislatures in the hope of getting politically supported advantages . . . . ¶When a nation of continental proportions and endowments, such as Russia or the United States, goes in for interventionism or autarchy, it does not necessarily make that nation bellicose. But it is the cause of belligerence in less favored nations . . . . But no matter where the ultimate blame should lie, the facts of recent history remain what they are: the intervention of 'have' nations has been accompanied by the bellicosity of the 'have-nots' . . . . ¶An uncompromising anti-Nazi, von Mises insists that Hitlerism must be eradicated root and branch. But he hasn't much hope that the defeat of Hitlerism will lead the nations back to economic sanity. Like his Viennese colleague, F. A. Hayek, who is also an exile from nazified Austria, von Mises thinks the nations of the West are committed to the heresies of Government intervention in the economic process . . . . To von Mises the answer is obvious: a world war every generation."

Cleaves, Freeman. *The Wall Street Journal.* (May 9, 1944). "Keynote to *Omnipotent Government* is the chaotic result of government intervention in the business and enterprise of its private citizens. This analysis of the rise of economic nationalism in Europe is admirably detailed, and is faithful to fact rather than legend, although this is a field where legends abound."

Coker, F. W. *American Political Science Review.* 38 (October 1944) 1003. "The author, here as in his earlier analysis of socialism (first published in 1922), displays considerable dialectical skill. Readers cannot well deny the effectiveness of some of his challenges of the whole complex of recent socialist and liberal-collectivist ideas. Yet (the reviewer believes) Professor von Mises has not considered, broadly and dispassionately, either the moral implications or the practical economic consequences of his own extreme doctrine." (Quoted from *Book Review Digest,* 1944. p.529).

Deuel, Wallace R. "For a Free Capitalism." *New York Herald Tribune, Weekly Book Review.* (August 20, 1944) 8. Professor von Mises "is, above all, uncompromising in both the style and the substance of what he has to say. He is dogmatic, not to say pedantic . . . . His spirit and address are in the too frequent manner of the classroom -- intransigent, testy, dry, often acidulous and not infrequently sententious . . . . ¶In principle, the author opposes interferences of all kinds and from all quarters in the functioning of free capitalism. In fact, by far the greater number of interferences he dwells upon and denounces are interferences by politicians and by and for labor . . . . Malefactors of great wealth hardly figure in the world of Professor von Mises . . . . ¶It is enormously heartening, moreover, to find some one asserting, for a change, that 'the Treaty of Versailles was not unfair to Germany and did not plunge the German people into misery . . . . The mischief was not that the treaty was bad as far as Germany was concerned, but that the victorious powers permitted Germany to defy some of its most important clauses' . . . . ¶Professor von Mises' whole political and economic philosophy is reminiscent of that of a good many academic economists of the era which ended in 1929. That seems a long time ago."

Fetter, Frank Albert. *American Economic Review.* 35:3. (June 1945) 445-446. Fetter links*Omnipotent Government* with Hayek's The *Road to Serfdom* and Mises' *Bureaucracy* (B-13) as "essentially harmonious formulations of the present issue between freedom (political as well as economic) and the trend toward totalitarianism."

Foreign Affairs. 23 (April 1945) 332.

Frederick, J. T. *Book Week.* (September 10, 1944) 2.

J.W.H. *San Francisco Chronicle.* (July 23, 1944). "While getting in many telling blows against the idea of planned societies as the solution of our dilemma, he goes to the other extreme by placing his faith in free enterprise to such an extent that he does not seem to have much hope for civilization since he is realistic enough to concede that really free enterprise is beyond hope of restoration. ¶Most of the book is a study of the development of the German state . . . . ¶As a solution for the problems of Eastern Europe he proposes a federation of all the nations between Germany and Russia, from the Baltic to the Mediterranean, a sort of customs or free labor exchange union and amorphous state in which there is to be no public education and the state and the official language would be English . . . . ¶Whatever objections the 'liberal' planners may propose, this is nevertheless a thought-provoking book reflecting wide scholarship and an abiding faith in freedom."

S.H. "If Only . . ." *The Nation Magazine.* (August 28, 1944). "Whether one is a Socialist, a New Dealer, or even a Hoover Republican, one is likely to find the reading of *Omnipotent Government* by Ludwig von Mises an exhilarating experience. It is so extreme, angry, and perversely doctrinaire that one can enjoy it without believing a word of it . . . . Only a difference of degree and consistency separates the economic philosophy of Coolidge and Hoover from that of Norman Thomas, Stalin, and Hitler . . . . [T]his volume is so full of abuse and passionate misstatement that it cannot be taken as anything more than a succession of despairing cries by one who feels the world is irrevocably headed for a 'statist' hell . . . . ¶One curious turn: the whole mess of Nazism and war could have been avoided if only the Germans had chosen free trade at any time during the last sixty years. Why didn't they? 'It is impossible to explain why'."

Hessen, Robert. *The Objectivist.* New York. (August 1970) 11-16.

Hexner, Ervin. *Social Forces.* 23 (May 1945) 466. "The author of this volume is one of the outstanding economists of the world who has to be credited with rearing a generation of excellent scholars. He is also a brilliant writer and fighter of his cause. The reader, wherever he stands, will enjoy the thought-provoking propositions of von Mises, presented with unsurpassed intellectual courage. Moderate liberals will regret that the argument of von Mises is not based on available alternatives. Even these 'moderates' will read this volume with profit and delight." (Quoted from *Book Review Digest,* 1945. p.496).

Hillbrook, Roy. *Current History.* 7 (December 1944) 497. "He is forthright in his opinions and presents a strong case for free enterprise and capitalism." Quoted on book jacket of 1944 edition of *Bureaucracy.*

Kirkus. 12 (March 15, 1944) 131. "Controversial -- dogmatic -- tough reading." (Quoted from *Book Review Digest,* 1944. p.530)

Kohn, Hans. *American Historical Review.* 50 (April 1945) 531. "This extremely readable and stimulating book presents two aspects of unequal value. The one is a restatement of the belief, current a century ago, that in a world of perfect and unhampered capitalism, of free trade and democracy, there would be no incentives for war and conquest. This faith is as utopian as the presently widely accepted myth that in a world of unhampered socialism and of the common man there would be no incentives for war . . . . By far more important, and in many ways brilliant, is the interpretation of recent German history in Part III of the book."

_____. "Cause and Cure of Totalitarianism." *Saturday Review of Literature.* 27 (September 9, 1944) 21-22: "Professor von Mises has written one of the most thoughtful and challenging books published for a long time. It deals primarily with the cause and cure of the menace which Germany offers to the contemporary world. Many sharp and surprisingly well formulated observations and penetrating judgments will be accepted even by those who, like the present reviewer, regard the author's explanations as rather onesided . . . . ¶But even if he rejects the author's purely economic interpretation of history, or disagrees with his all-out emphasis on economic liberty, the reader will find the book most clear-sighted and interesting on the present world crisis, written with an incisive clarity which makes the reading of it a pleasure . . . . ¶It is impossible in a brief review to give an adequate picture of the wealth of fertile suggestions and interpretations in the book. Though there are many fine points, some of them fundamental, in which this reviewer entirely disagrees with the author, he has found even those arguments which he thought wrong challenging and thought-provoking. To the critical reader this book should be highly recommended."

Lane, Rose Wilder. *Economic Council Review of Books.* New York: National Economic Council. 2:10 (November 1945). Reviewed in conjunction with Mises' *Bureaucracy* (B-13) and Heinrich Hauser's *The German Talks Back:* "This book explains the economic fallacy that leads men to create the total State, total war, and total disaster to the State and to themselves. A sensible child can understand Professor Mises's explanation of the reason why the economic tyranny now called 'administrative law' destroys a productive economy and, of course, the State that a productive economy supports . . . . ¶Unfortunately, Professor Mises himself is a victim of the confusion into which this declaration threw European political thinking. In economics he is absolutely sound, but in politics he is bewildered . . . . ¶For the whole crux of the matter is the structure of the State -- the means and methods of restricting the police power of men in public office in a manner that will permit the energy of other men to work in producing and distributing wealth . . . . ¶He implies vaguely that the antithesis of hereditary absolutism is democracy, without defining the word 'democracy.' The definition, of course, is majority absolutism . . . . ¶These political fallacies, running through this book side by side with rational economic thinking and an accurate report of events in Europe, add to the book's value for the discriminating American reader . . . . ¶I urge you, therefore, to get this book and keep it; read it and reread it. It is essential to an American's education today."

Library Journal. "Former professor of Vienna and Geneva attempts explanation of Nazism. Deals extensively with Germany's social and economic development of last hundred years. An outspoken adherent of economic liberalism he traces most of the evils of our times, such as wars, unemployment, inflation, anti-semitism and Nazism back to 'etatism' either in the form of (state) interventionism or socialism." (Quoted from *Book Review Digest,* 1944. p.529).

Merriam, C. E. *Yale Review.* 34 (Autumn 1944).

Parkes, Henry Bamford. *Baltimore Sun.* (May 27, 1944). "Admirably concrete and specific. Repeating the defense of economic liberalism which he has already formulated in earlier writings, he argues in this book that the growth of government planning must lead to totalitarianism, either of the Communist or Nazi variety."

Peardon, T. P. *Political Science Quarterly.* 60 (March 1945) 130. "This book is narrow and rigid in its whole conception. It dictates a prescription for our present discontents that even its author apparently does not expect to see applied. Translated from the realm of theory to the realities of politics it is essentially reactionary in its implications. Yet it is a major work, full of learning, powerful in construction, trenchant in style." (Quoted from *Book Review Digest,* 1945. p.496)

Reinhold, H. A. *Commonweal.* 40 (July 21, 1944) 329.

Rothbard, Murray N. *Libertarian Review.* Washington, D.C. 4:6 (June 1975) 1. Reviewed with Theory *and* History (B-20). "Ludwig von Mises' *Omnipotent Government* (B-12) and Theory *and* History (B-20) are the great laissez-faire economist's most neglected books . . . . ¶*Omnipotent Government* was published during World War War II and was one of Mises' first books written in English . . . . Mises was one of the first analysts . . . to show that nazism and fascism were totalitarian collectivist systems which had far more in common with communism than with free-market capitalism. And, what is more, they were the logical outcome of the galloping statism and militarism of the pre-fascist societies. Mises' linkage of fascism with Marxian socialism was a shocker in the Marx-laden intellectual world of the 1940s . . . . But his linkage of the totalitarian countries as common examples of aggravated statism remains, of course, perfectly sound, as does his insight that the only viable alternative to the interventionist-collectivist path is laissez-faire capitalism, the free-market economy and free society."

Schuman, Frederick L. "The Dry Bones of Laissez-Faire." *The New York Times Book Review.* (May 21, 1944) 22. "To develop a new formula whereby all virtue and vice can be neatly connected with a fresh set of simple causes is no small achievement. Such is the latest accomplishment of Ludwig von Mises, the Austrian economist who has long out-Manchestered the Manchester School in his impassioned devotion to laissez faire. The new devil is something called 'etatism' or 'statolatry,' by which is meant that form of alleged dementia which drives its victims to belief in governmental regulation of (or, *horribile dictu*, even ownership of) business enterprise. From this insanity, says Mr. von Mises, comes bureaucracy, despotism, Marxism, fascism, imperialism, militarism, nationalism and war . . . . ¶On almost every page straw men are set up and knocked down with brilliance and abandon . . . . ¶In the end the author wants a Federal union of the western democracies, based on free trade and the social gospel of Herbert Spencer -- and an East European federation capable of defending its seventeen language groups against Russia, Germany or Italy . . . . ¶The prospects would indeed be black if the thinking of Ludwig von Mises represented the best that economists or business leaders had to offer . . . . ¶*Omnipotent Government* is less an indictment of tyranny than an epitaph, from the pen of the most dismal practitioner of the dismal science of an age long dead and forever past recapture."

Seligman, Ben B. "Lost Economic Horizons." *The New Leader.* (July 29, 1944). "Von Mises' portrayal of the world of laissez faire is an awkward amalgam of faith, hope and historical distortion. In the world of laissez faire, says the author, those who were penniless had a free hand to develop new industries, provided they had the ingenuity to do so . . . . What von Mises ignores is the obvious fact that some voters have more pennies than others . . . . ¶[L]aissez-faire theory, carried to its logical and cruel conclusion, would insist that labor be dealt with as the merchant deals with corn. People were bound to protest against a system of economics that converted them into inanimate adjuncts of the loom and the steam engine . . . . Capitalists, too, discovered that the extensive technical apparatus necessitated by modern mass production could not be operated in accordance with free market principles . . . . ¶The author claims for himself a dispassionate and scholarly approach that is nowhere apparent. To describe the evils of state intervention, he invents the ugly word 'Etatism' . . . . ¶The book really strikes bottom with the author's dissertation on what's wrong with labor . . . . Labor unions, furthermore, employ coercion and intimidation and they are supported in their base practices by public opinion . . . . ¶After the first ten pages, one naturally expects a broadside attack on economic planning. The reader is not disappointed. In keeping with the general tone of his discourse, von Mises presents an excited oration on the sins of the planned economy. He implies that planners are neurotic. They are afflicted with megalomania and want to install dictatorships. His only rational argument is based on the disappearance of the free market . . . . Yet this seemingly powerful argument was refuted long ago by such writers as Lange, Taylor, Dickinson and Landauer."

Simons, Henry C. *The Annals of the American Academy of Political and Social Science.* 236 (November 1944) 192-193. "Professor Mises, patriarch of the modern Austrian school, is the greatest living teacher of economics . . . . He is also the toughest old liberal or Manchesterite of his time. Arch enemy of nazism, communism, socialism, syndicalism, protectionism, and all governmental interventionism, he is also perhaps the worst enemy of his own libertarian cause . . . . ¶Distrusting government as concentration of power, he refuses to accept it as means for the dispersion of power; and he seems to reject all political processes or instrumentalities for moving toward his good society. Etatism, it seems, must be undone, if at all, without international co-operation or organization, and merely by the rational, separate decisions of majorities in each nation . . . . ¶It is as German history that this book most merits attention . . . . His own historical theses, though doctrinaire, stress considerations which recent discussion seriously neglects

. . . . ¶It is hardly possible to discuss fairly a book which, without good organization, touches upon almost everything. If some misrepresentation of the author's position is involved in this review, the same is probably true of the book itself."

Solper, Toni. *Book of the Month Club News.* (May 1944). "Von Mises, an expert economist and an original thinker with a background of pre and post 1914 Austria and between-the-wars Geneva, takes a psychologically strong position. He has held a consistent view through manifold experiences, and moreover a view in vigorous opposition to the prevalent trends of thought. With strict logic he formulates his accusations against his pet culprit *etatism* . . . . Expounding this thesis in many aspects of our troubled life, Mises has innumerable intelligent witty, clarifying things to say."

Southern California Business. "Peace and 'Socialists of the Chair'." (September 4, 1944). "*Omnipotent Government* is a notable book for many reasons. It gives the most powerful arguments for economic liberty as opposed to state domination that have been advanced in this country for a long time. It portrays the historical background of the rise of fascism with a clarity never before pictured to Americans. It debunks a whole host of popular fallacies . . . . ¶Rich in the economics of free enterprise and 'etatism,' the book is even richer in historical lore so necessary to an understanding of the tragedy of Europe. Perhaps the most significant reaction to the revelation of the background of fascism is the feeling that no American should form any ideas on peace treaties or punishments until he has the facts that von Mises can give him. Until those facts are in hand, and dealt with, the hope for world peace and economic democracy will be chimerical."

Squires, J. Duane. "Capitalism or Chaos." *Christian Century.* 62 (January 24, 1945) 112. "*Omnipotent Government* has been praised as one of the great books of our generation and dismissed as a 'dreary morass of monopoly capitalism apologetics.' It is neither. Rather it is a keen and penetrating analysis of the socio-economic conditions of our time, occasionally a little one-sided and even dogmatic in its leaning toward economic individualism . . . . Even those who will not agree fully with von Mises -- and the reviewer is one -- must be impressed by the vigor of his argument and the wealth of logic and history in it . . . . ¶Because he denies absolutely the possibility of any permanent 'middle way' between capitalism as the classical economists envisioned it and totalitarianism, his book is essentially gloomy. Admitting that the way to destruction is broad and that many have found it, the reviewer still feels that we can and must find the means of adjustment and synthesis between older economic ideas and modern needs. To locate this straight and narrow gate leading to a sensible 'mixed economy' is the task of socially minded Christianity in the days that lie ahead."

Tead, Ordway. *Survey Graphic.* 34 (March 1945) 104. "One gathers that the world is going inexorably to the dogs. ¶The influences which are rampant are all in the wrong direction -- namely toward a more conscious social control of economic forces . . . . ¶Essentially the book is the product of a mind that turns with nostalgia to the formulas of the past, that puts a low value on the capacities of the human self, that sees the complexities of the future with foreboding and with panic at the challenge presented to men's constructive imagination by the creative tasks ahead . . . . ¶Because these problems have not been solved by any methods thus far brought forward, it is better to approach their solutions in terms of old approaches than even to admit the possibility that men may be able to create better for themselves."

Thompson, Maxine. *Chicago Daily Law Bulletin.* (May 9, 1944). "It is a book of towering importance by a foremost economist whose accurate and early anticipations of German inflation and later of the 1929 business collapse confounded the world. His analyses, his dialectics in this book lack not one whit of his former acumen . . . . The book is a superb example of the clear exposition of an economist's thought; it is closely written and elegant in the mathematician's sense; its diction is a thing of beauty."

Time. "Gloomy Debate." 43 (June 19, 1944) 99. Reviewed with Harold J. Laski's *Faith, Reason and Civilization.* "In their most recent books, Harold Laski and Ludwig von Mises write about the same world crisis. But a Zulu savage, should he be miraculously endowed with the ability to comprehend fairly complicated English, would hardly recognize it as the same. To Laski, the British socialist, the breakdown has been caused by a century of unbridled economic individualism and the cure is the traditional Marxist specific: let government take over the means of production. To Mises, the Austrian free-trade economist now exiled in the U.S., the evil that afflicts the world has one origin everywhere: too much government intervention in men's livelihoods. To Mises, Laski's way of thinking is mumbo jumbo, utterly divorced from reality. To Laski, Mises' ideas are about as useful as a stone hatchet."

Valley Young Republicans. Phoenix, Arizona. (February 1978). "Mises is in tune with present historiography in writing that, 'The present war (WWII) would never have originated but for anti-Semitism.' Here again, he was way ahead of his time not only in denouncing big government, bureaucracy, and socialism, but in blasting the myth of racism as well."

The Wall Street Journal (Pacific Coast edition). San Francisco. (October 2, 1944).

Washington (D.C.) *Star.* (September 17, 1944). Reviewed jointly with Hayek's *The Road to Serfdom*. "The authors of these two books are both Germans [sic], both economists, both expatriates by reason of dislike of Naziism. They have written, moreover, on the identical theme . . . . the imminent destruction of human freedom by collectivist mechanisms, the wiping out of the rights of man by an oncoming regime of socialism . . . .¶Prof. Von Mises treats more directly of the rise of socialism in Germany, a phenomenon, which he says began in the 1860s and made not only Naziism but imperialism and militarism inevitable . . . . ¶Neither author disputes the need of protective legislation in matters of health, unemployment relief and the rights of labor. Their objections are aimed at the system which proposes to achieve such ends by wrecking the system of market economy."

Weller, George. "Foreign Scholar Challenges America's Economic Policies. " *Chicago News.* (August 16, 1944). Mises "is not only anti-Nazi, anti-Marxist and a foe of the creeping collectivism he discerns in American government, but he uncompromisingly leads off by declaring that 'while fighting the German aggressors Great Britain and the United States are step by step adopting the German pattern of socialism'. . . . Education, not dismemberment like that proposed by Sumner Welles, is the answer to Germany."

Yoder, F. R. *American Sociology Review.* 10 (April 1945) 326.

On the Manipulation of Money and Credit (B-24). Includes English translations of *Die geldtheoretische Seite des Stabilisierungsproblems* [Stabilization of the Monetary Unit from the Theoretical Viewpoint], 1923 (B-5); *Geldwertstabilisierung und Konjunkturpolitik* [Monetary Stabilization and Cyclical Policy], 1928 (B-7); and *Die Ursachen der Wirtschaftskrise* [The Causes of the Economic Crisis], 1931 (B-9).

Browne, Harry. *New Profits from the Monetary Crisis.* New York: William Morrow & Co., 1978. 451. "*On the Manipulation of Money and Credit* . . . . is much easier reading than *Human Action*, but deals only with the monetary cycles. Although some of the essays were written in the early part of the century, the material is quite relevant to today's problems."

The Chalcedon Report. Vallecito, Calif. 153 (May 1978). Reviewed together with Mises' *Notes and Recollections* (B-23). *On the Manipulation of Money and Credit* "is important, not only for Mises' studies, but for Greaves' own introductory essays and epilogue. Among other things, Greaves is noteworthy for his care with terminology. Thus he makes clear that the idea of subjective values in economics does not mean that objective values do not exist but that economic values are the personal values of individuals as they vary from time to time and operate on the marketplace."

Chronicles of Culture. Rockford, Ill: Rockford College Institute. "Von Mises Redivivus." 2:2 (March/April 1978) 21. "The sore point is that so many are unaware of it [von Mises' influence], as von Mises, a gentle scholar and unbending anti-Marxist, was sentenced to oblivion long ago by the liberal media. That his thought and his writings are almost inaccessible to anyone without a degree in economics does not help either. But for anyone who sees money as something more than a mysterious element of happiness or despair, located in wallets, checkbooks and cash registers, the title above may be of enormous interest."

Ebeling, Richard M. *The Austrian Economics Newsletter.* New York: Center for Libertarian Studies. 1:3 (Fall 1978) 8-9. "The subjectivist revolution, with its emphasis on methodological individualism, opened new vistas for developing a sound microfoundation for the early attempts of Cantillon and Cairnes to explain changes in relative prices that followed in the wake of monetary disturbances. ¶A valuable contribution towards this goal was made by Ludwig von Mises. The focal point in Mises' theory is the transmission mechanism and the necessarily non-neutral manner in which expansions and contractions influence not merely the *general scale* but also the *relative structure* of prices . . . . ¶The most valuable work in the volume is his [Mises'] 1928 monograph, *Monetary Stabilization and Cyclical Policy* . . . . ¶Mises was critical of Irving Fisher's proposal for stabilizing the 'price level' with the use of index numbers. Estimating the purchasing power of money by computing the value of a 'basket' of goods tends to totally submerge the monetary influence upon relative prices. It, therefore, could create the impression of stability when, in fact, significant disturbances were occurring . . . . ¶Anticipating some aspects of the 'rational expectations' literature, Mises pointed out, in a 1933 essay, that a lowering of the money rate of interest will stimulate investment activity only if the new rate of interest is expected to prevail for some time into the future . . . . Five years before the publication of Keynes' *The General Theory*, in a 1931 lecture on *The Causes of the Economic Crisis*, Mises analyzed a 'new idea' that was gaining popularity: the concept of 'money illusion.' He criticized the belief that trade unions would passively accept a fall in real wages by allowing money wages to remain constant in the face of rising prices. 'Labor unions,' Mises said, 'no longer contend over the height of *money* wages, but over the height of *real* wages'." The reviewer comments negatively on Percy Greaves' introduction.

_____. *Libertarian Review.* San Francisco, Calif. 7:5 (June 1978) 38-39, 41. At the height of the great German inflation in 1923, "Mises explained that 'In some situations it is considered more advantageous to cover government expenditures by issuing new notes, than by increasing the burden of taxes or borrowing money . . . .' ¶Unwilling and afraid to admit that programs and privileges that benefit some must be paid for by 'others,' the government brings about the redistribution of income through the indirect method of inflation . . . . ¶The method Mises used for analyzing what he called the 'social consequences' of inflation was the 'step-by-step' approach . . . . A refined exposition of this method is presented in the longest essay in the volume, Mises' 1928 monograph, 'Monetary Stabilization and Cyclical Policy '. . . . ¶At the end of his 1931 essay analyzing 'The Causes of the Economic Crisis,' Mises hoped that 'it is . . . not too optimistic to assume that those governments and parties whose policies have led to this crisis will some day disappear from the stage and make way for men whose economic program leads, not to destruction and chaos, but to economic development and progress.' ¶We can only have the same hope today."

_____. "Mises on Money, Intervention and Himself." *Laissez Faire Books Catalog & Review.* New York. (Spring-Summer 1978). Reviewed together with Mises' *Notes and Recollections* (B-23) and *A Critique of Interventionism* (B-8). Concerning *On the Manipulation of Money and Credit:* "Continuing the arguments first presented in *The Theory of Money and Credit* (B-2), Mises offers a systematic analysis of the social consequences that follow from monetary expansion and contraction. He demonstrates that the older quantity theory of money that had assumed that prices were proportionally and simultaneously affected by increases or decreases in the quantity of money was fundamentally incorrect . . . . In an analysis of attempts to measure the 'price level,' Mises very forcefully shows the impossibility of successfully indexing prices to compensate for inflation."

Evans, Medford. *American Opinion.* Belmont, Mass. 22:2 (February 1979) 57-59. Reviewed in conjunction with Percy L. Greaves, Jr.'s *Mises Made Easier: A Glossary for Ludwig von Mises' HUMAN ACTION.* "Treatment of the manipulation of money and credit is about as topical -- or 'relevant,' if you like -- as a subject can well be in 1979. It is instructive to learn that Mises' work herewith welcomed was done in the 1920s. It should have been easier to understand then than now, there has been so much Samuelsonian obfuscation since." After favorably reviewing the books, the reviewer concluded with his own views on the conspiracy theory of money.

Hazlitt, Henry. "Three New Books by Ludwig von Mises." *The Freeman.* Irvington, N.Y. 28:4 (April 1978) 247-253. Also reviewed here are *Notes and Recollections* (B-23) and *A Critique of Interventionism* (B-8). "Readers sufficiently acquainted with the work of Mises that has hitherto been available in English will already be familiar with the general outline of his business cycle theory . . . . ¶Mises elaborated his trade cycle theory both in subsequent editions of *The Theory of Money and Credit* (B-2, 1953 ed.) and in *Human Action* (B-16). He also presented elsewhere much of the substance of the other papers translated in this volume. Nevertheless, Mises never repeated himself mechanically or by rote . . . . As a result each exposition threw its own special illumination on the problem, or supplied some connecting link that his other expositions may have omitted to make quite so explicit or clear. This the present trade cycle essay notably does." Segment on *On the Manipulation of Money and Credit* (pp.251-253) reprinted in *The Individualist* (South Africa). 5:3 (1980) 11-12.

Journal of Economic Literature. 16:2 (June 1978) 647. "Includes five newly translated papers by Mises (1881-1973) and five previously published articles (in Epilogue), by P. L. Greaves, Jr."

Kirzner, Israel M. *Reason.* Santa Barbara, Calif. 10:12 (April 1979) 45-46. "The volume is a monument to their [the editor's and translator's] meticulous and scholarly attention to the slightest detail -- whether relating to terminological precision, to the accuracy of citations, or to capturing nuances of meaning in translation. The translator appears to have successfully overcome all the obvious obstacles confronting a would-be translator of so profound a writer as Mises. The editor has provided us with all the background and footnote material necessary for the proper understanding of Mises. This includes copious references to Mises's earlier and later works, clarification of allusions, as well as elucidation of difficult passages.The result is a volume that should in many ways serve as a model for similar efforts."

Nippon Hyoron-Sha. *Economic Seminar.* No. 280 (May 1978) 50. Japanese language review.

North, Gary. *Remnant Review.* Durham, N.C. 5:16 (August 18, 1978) 96. Regarding Kondratieff's theory of cycles, "Ludwig von Mises, the great Austrian economist, stated that he didn't think Kondratieff had proven his case; he said so in 1928: *On the Manipulation of Money and Credit* . . . . p. 132n. Mises' student, Dr. Murray Rothbard, subjected the Kondratieff theory to a devastating critique in the June 14, 1978 issue of the *Inflation Survival Letter* . . . . But the Kondratieff theorists roll on, undaunted."

_____. *Remnant Review.* 6:9 (May 4, 1979) 53. "Back in 1837, Britain's Lord Overstone wrote an essay on the boom-bust cycle which Ludwig von Mises quoted favorably in his 1928 essay, '*Monetary Stabilization and Cyclical Policy*'. . . . Here is Overstone's description [quoted in *On the Manipulation of Money and Credit*] of the psychology of the cycle:

> We find it [the 'state of trade'] subject to various conditions which are periodically returning; it revolves apparently in an established cycle. First we find a state of quiescence -- next improvement, -- growing confidence, -- prosperity, -- excitement, -- overtrading, convulsion, -- pressure, -- stagnation, -- distress, -- ending again in quiescence. (p.134)

Mises comments that this description is 'unrivaled for its brevity and clarity.' I would have to agree."

Pathfinder. Center for Education and Research in Free Enterprise, Texas A & M University. 2:3 (January/February 1980) 6. "The most important conclusion to be drawn from this analysis is that government intervention, and not the free market, is the primary cause of inflation and unemployment."

Summers, Brian. "Stagflation: No Puzzle To Mises' Followers." *Barron's.* (February 13, 1978). "Any business cycle theory must explain two recurring phenomena: why do large numbers of businesses with excellent track records suddenly suffer heavy losses, and why does the recession hit hardest in the capital goods industries? ¶Mises explained both phenomena by showing how credit expansion misleads businessmen into questionable (from the standpoint of later profitability) projects, setting off a boom in the capital goods industries. But the boom lays the seeds of recession because, as Mises showed, credit expansion cannot be maintained indefinitely. Continued credit expansion eventually leads to hyperinflation, while a tightening of credit brings on a recession in the overextended capital goods industries. ¶But how does Mises explain stagflation -- an inflationary recession? . . . With rising costs, an uncertain regulatory climate and monetary policy dependent on the vagaries of Washington politics, stagflation came as no surprise to Mises and those familiar with his writings."

Wolfe, Charles Hull. "Ludwig von Mises: His Insight and Foresight on Money." *The Intercollegiate Review.* Bryn Mawr, Penna.: Intercollegiate Studies Institute. 16:1 (Fall/Winter 1980) 53-56. "[C]ontains new translations of several studies, not previously available in English . . . . The first of these . . . (1923) was sent to press in January of that year and it describes 'runaway inflation' as Germany was to experience it in the following months. The second . . . (1928) analyzes schemes similar to those which have been discussed recently to 'stabilize' the purchasing power of money by 'indexation' as a means to forestall economic depression. The third, *The Causes of the Economic Crisis* (1931), explodes the 'full employment' recommendations Keynes was to make five years later in his *General Theory* (1936) . . . . ¶Mises' analysis leads him to advocate free banking and the avoidance of all attempts to manipulate interest rates and the quantity of money and credit . . . . ¶When Mises wrote, he realized that even the relatively simple goal, of rejecting a banking policy aimed at reducing interest rates below market rates, was not then politically feasible. Nor is it any more so now. Public opinion must change first. People must reject the philosophy of big government spending that so many of them still want and believe they can afford. At the close of each of the translations in this anthology -- in 1923, 1928, and again in 1931 -- Mises reiterated that the first step toward monetary reform *must* be a shift in the climate of opinion away from reliance on government toward the freedom philosophy."

Planned Chaos (B-14) Incorporated as the Epilogue in the 1951 and later editions of *Socialism* (B-4).

Analysis (Frank Chodorov, ed.). New York. "Rule by the 'Inner Voice'." 3:9 (July 1947) 4. "I have never met a planner who did not reveal by his enthusiasm a deep conviction that in the cherished scheme of things he would be qualified to do a bit of the planning . . . . In 96 pages of close reasoning, and lucid writing, Ludwig von Mises has again shown up this weakness (and strength) of the planned mentality . . . . ¶The only thing I can find against this excellent booklet is its price. Sixty-five cents presents a problem in buying by mail. But, if you make out a check or money order, you might as well buy two copies, one for yourself and one for the fellow you have been trying to convince of his error. You will not succeed, even with the help of von Mises, because one possessed of the 'inner voice' is beyond redemption. But you will at least sadistically enjoy his squirming."

P.B. "Un Livre à lire: Le Chaos du Planisme" [A book to read: *Planned Chaos*]. Luxembourg. Unidentified review found among Mises' papers. "But no economist has ever dared to say that interventionism can have any other outcome than disaster and chaos. The defenders of interventionism -- among them members of the Prussian Historical School and the American institutionalists -- were not economists. On the contrary, to realize their plans they ignored the existence of economic laws. ¶Do we not also encounter this same denial of economic laws regularly here at home? Is it not at the basis of certain decisions, certain government and parliamentary interventions, the consequences of which are only foreseeable? . . . ¶We highly recommend the reading of Ludwig von Mises book to all near and far who are interested in economic life and public affairs . . . . In addition to its general value, Ludwig von Mises' work has special interest for us. Published in English in New York, it has been translated into French by Professor of Economic Science, Jean-Pierre Hamilius of Esch-sur-Alzette [Luxembourg]." (Translated from the French)

Branden, Barbara. *The Objectivist Newsletter* (Ayn Rand & Nathaniel Branden, eds. & pubs.) New York: NBL Book Service. 1:1 (January 1962) 2.

Chamberlin, William Henry. "The Executive's Bookshelf: A Tract for Our Time." *The Wall Street Journal*. (September 24, 1947). Professor Ludwig von Mises "has now summed up the case for the free and against the planned economy in a hard-hitting pamphlet, written in simple, non-technical language and containing the gist of theories which he has outlined in more learned and elaborate books . . . . ¶Certainly in this age, when the case for intervention and controls is stated so frequently, it is refreshing and beneficial to hear from a man who believes passionately in classical liberal capitalism and who refuses to trim his sails to prevailing winds of opinion in the slightest degree. He makes the flat statement that democracy cannot exist where there is planning . . . . ¶The author believes that what we are living through is a crisis not of capitalism, but of interventionism . . . . [H]e pours the full vials of his scorn on those interventionists who honestly believe that their methods will strengthen capitalism. He thinks the capitalist system can get along best without such 'friends' . . . . ¶Von Mises in this pamphlet shows himself anything but the dry-as-dust professor. His language is clear and incisive and he is capable of dry humor, as when he offers the following comment on the Stalin-Trotsky controversy: 'In their feud both were right. Stalin was right in maintaining that his regime was the embodiment of communist principles. Trotsky was right in asserting that Stalin's regime had made Russia a hell'."

The Commercial & Financial Chronicle. "Businessmen, Not Bureaucrats, Responsible for America's High Living Standard." 166:4614 (July 24, 1947) 47. "The increase in American standards of living in the last quarter of a century was accomplished because businessmen enlarged their factories and built new ones . . . . Dr. Mises shows how the development of interventionism, or the planned interference by government with the operation of a capitalistic market, produces a state of affairs which even from the viewpoint of its advocates is worse than the previous state it was designed to alter . . . . ¶Dr. Mises believes that socialist propaganda never encountered any decided opposition, and that the devastating critique by which economists have exploded the futility and impracticability of socialist schemes did not reach the molders of public opinion . . . . The masses favor socialism only because they trust the socialist propaganda of the intellectuals, and it is those intellectual leaders who have produced and propagated the fallacies which are on the point of destroying liberty and western civilization. What is needed to stop the trend toward socialism and despotism, Dr. Mises concludes, is common sense and moral courage."

The Executive.   New York: Executive Book Club. "Planned Chaos." (September 1947). "Having watched the congealing of the Soviet, German and Italian social and economic systems, he [Mises] issues in *Planned Chaos* a grim warning for Americans to consider how interventionism -- and by this he means government interference with market economy -- under the guise of various shibboleths, is setting the stage for an overthrow of voluntary society, market economy and constitutional government . . . . ¶Dr. Mises re-analyzes for our time the age-old issue between liberty and authority . . . . Torchbearers of socialism and communism, both of whom pursue political and economic philosophies rested more in concept than in experience, will find a storehouse of evidence here to demolish completely their arguments."

Hayes, H. Gordon. *The American Economic Review.* 38:3 (June 1948) 415-416. "Professor Mises' pamphlet is an attack upon 'interventionism' which 'is setting the stage for the final overthrow of the voluntary society, the market economy and constitutional government' . . . . Mises backs away a little from the pure anarchy into which he leads us. The 'prevention and suppression of antisocial activities benefit the whole society.' But having made this concession to those who support regulation of public utilities and minimum wage legislation, he plunges forward again in sweeping denunciation . . . . ¶This is the 'all if anything' fallacy in its most blatant form. As well might a boy refuse to comply with a request that he take off his hat in the house by insisting that if he lets his elders begin to undress him, there would be no stopping place short of nakedness . . . . ¶The severest strictures against this pamphlet concern the quotations from Laski and the Webbs. With flagrant misrepresentation he has them support his thesis that democracy and planning are incompatible . . . . What colossal calumny! ¶This pamphlet is a travesty on scholarship. It is published by a body with the name of (God save the words) The Foundation for Economic Education, among whose officers and directors are listed the well-known economists, Leo Wolman, Fred R. Fairchild and W. A. Paton. Never in the history of modern economics, one may guess, has a work of such low quality come from presumptively respectable sources."

d'Letzeburger Land.   Luxembourg. 23 (1956) 11. "Planwirtschaftliches Chaos" [Economically-planned chaos]. Brief unsigned, announcement of the 1956 French translation by "our countryman, J. P. Hamilius, Jr., Professor in Esch, who is as confirmed and as uncompromising a liberal as the author [Mises] himself . . . . He [the translator] has produced a translation from the English of notable clarity and precision. The little book *Le Chaos du Planisme* offers a light, absorbing and challenging reading. We wish for it wide distribution in the French-speaking world as well as here [in Luxembourg]." (Translated from the German)

N.M., "Le professeur Mises contre l'interventionisme" [Professor Mises against interventionism]. *Luxemburger Wort: Die Warte - Perspectives*. (n.d.). First installment of a 2-part review of the French-language translation by J. P. Hamilius. "What liberalism has to offer civilization already exists and we would no longer have need of it if its historical abuses had not provoked such an extreme reaction as Marxism . . . . ¶Professor L. von Mises' work consists of several chapters devoted to the defense of liberty against various forms of intervention, all equally disastrous in his view even if unequally aggressive." This translation is "intelligent and adequate, occasionally assisted by brief commentaries in the notes . . . . ¶The economic laws, in real life, are not at all as rigid and certain as the author implies . . . . The control of economic and social life is just as necessary as penal legislation and the police." (Translated from the French)

————. "Encore la planification du chaos" [Planning for chaos again]. *Luxemburger Wort: Die Warte, Perspectives* 9:24/357 (June 13, 1956). Second installment of 2-part review: "It is certainly easier to refute the various Marxist theories than it is to define the role of the state and of the free society . . . . There is one Marxist theme that has practically been abandoned by the communists themselves. This is the inevitability of the communist revolution which must arise out of mature capitalism and its fatal collapse . . . . ¶The little book of Professor Mises, translated by our fellow countryman, J. P. Hamilius, contains several chapters consisting of historical analyses of various systems, the prospects for their realization, and for their final defeat; it would be difficult not to approve his judgments here . . . . ¶One can also agree when the liberal theoretician undertakes to explain that the supposed social laws are far from having the rigor of natural laws, understood to be laws derived from the natural sciences which may be examined in the laboratory. But it seems to me, the same reasoning applies here too, as it does to the laws called economic. Here too the 'facts' are not the result of a single factor experimentally controlled or controllable. Here too, the complexity of everything that happens on earth in the wake of human activity plays a role, influencing and being influenced by all the various elements . . . . ¶Read "Chaos du planisme." It will not be time lost. Whoever you may be, you will not accept every thesis of the author. But you will read the book with pleasure and profit. You will be convinced especially by his last chapter in which he shows clearly that socialism (or communism, which is the same thing) is not inevitable." (Translated from the French)

McDowell, Edwin. "Professor Punctures Propaganda Balloons of All Types of Socialists." *The Arizona Republic.* (March 7, 1963) 26. "The dogma that government is the embodiment of all that is good and beneficial and that individuals are wretched underlings, exclusively intent upon inflicting harm upon one another and badly in need of a guardian, is almost unchallenged, von Mises says. It is taboo to question it in the slightest way. ¶Taboo or not, that dogma is subjected to rigid scrutiny and questioning by von Mises, the foremost contemporary spokesman for the Austrian school of economics . . . . ¶In his eloquent peroration, the author says it is just not true that the masses are vehemently asking for socialism and that there is no means to resist them. The masses, he points out, favor Socialist policies because they trust the Socialist propaganda of its spokesmen. ¶It is these spokesmen, in and out of the academy, who have themselves generated the Socialist ideas and indoctrinated the masses with them. And it is they who are responsible for the many crimes which have been perpetrated in the name of socialism."

NEMA News. National Electric Manufacturers Association. 14:10 (July 10, 1947). "Dr. Ludwig von Mises, the notable author of *Omnipotent Government*, discusses the 'easy, bloodless and non-violent transition to socialism' through the gradual growth of governmental 'interventionism'. . . . He tells why the popularity of this policy is not a safe test of its soundness; why it fails in its avowed purposes; and what it does to nations which pursue it."

Wirtschaftspolitische Mitteilungen. "Geplantes Chaos" [Planned Chaos]. (Zurich). 3:7 (October 6, 1947) 6-9. "What the defenders of 'planning' intend is not the substitution of a formal plan for planless confusion, but the suppression of the plans of various individuals for the benefit of their own plan. ¶An economic planner is nothing but a potential dictator, for he aims simply and only toward the absolute domination of his own plan." (Translated from the German)

Planning for Freedom (B-18) Includes *Profit and Loss,* 1951 (B-17)

Abdala, Raúl Oscar. "De un ilustre pensador de nuestro tiempo" [From an illustrious thinker of our time]. *La Prensa* . Buenos Aires. (September 7, 1986). "In the title essay, Mises presents a lively refutation of the middle-of-the-road position of Keynes, Beveridge and their predecessor, Bismarck, the position between total public planning, i.e. communism, and the market economy . . . . ¶Even though a revival of regimes inspired by the great theme of liberalism is becoming apparent, the statist ideologies have certainly not struck their colors. This can be corroborated without going very far afield in our own country, the government of which appears determined to maintain the destructive system started 40 years ago by Peronist populism. ¶So long as this lamentable intention to submerge us ever deeper in depression persists, books like this are destined to fulfill an indispensable mission of enlightenment. Only with the aid of minds illuminated by the light of truth, will Argentina be able to return once more to enjoy its lost grandeur." (Translated from the Spanish)

Alexander, Ruth. *Sunday Mirror.* New York. (November 30, 1952). "Lord Keynes, the father of New Deal fiscal policy, is reported to have remarked cynically, 'In the long run we are all dead.' ¶That is the best explanation of deficit financing I have ever heard. But it takes no account of our children and their children, who must carry on despite the grievous moral wrong we committed against them by our wild spending . . . . ¶A book has been published that tells the story in language the average man and woman can understand . . . . ¶I suggest this book as the answer to the nation's prayer for guidance in the 'dismal' science of Economics which must serve as an intelligent superintendent of statesmanship if we are not to betray our trust for future generations."

American Institute for Economic Research. *Weekly Bulletin.* Great Barrington, Mass. (November 3, 1952) 176. Reviews *Profit and Loss* (B-17). "Our only criticism of this small volume is that discussion of the accounting 'profits' of special privilege is inadequate. However, the wealth of good sense concentrated in a few pages overbalances this deficiency."

American Way Features, Inc. "Planning for Freedom." *Between the Bookends.* 196 (August 25, 1964). "Von Mises contends that the planners have made great headway in politically controlling our economy by claiming that they are 'planning for freedom' rather than planning for socialism. His book is an excellent refutation of the idea that freedom can be planned for."

Baudin, Louis. *Revue d'Économie Politique.* 6 (November-December 1956) 1006-1007.

The Book Exchange. London. (June 1953). "He [Mises] subjects Marx, Veblen and Keynes, and still more their disciples, to rigorous censure. Even more in America than here, and even more in economics than in other disciplines, it is forgotten that there are two sides to every question. Professor Mises is not afraid to tilt at popular beliefs."

Branden, Nathaniel. *The Objectivist Newsletter.* (Ayn Rand & Nathaniel Branden, eds. & pubs.). New York: NBL Book Service. 1:9 (September 1962) 38.

Chamber of Commerce of the U.S.A., Economic Research Department. "Well Worth Reading." *Economic Intelligence.* 42 (January 1952) 4. Reviews *Profit and Loss* (B-17). "Antiprofit arguments are the outcome of an erroneous interpretation of the operation of the free market economy and the role of the entrepreneur. ¶'Tycoons are too powerful, too rich and too big; they abuse their power; bigness of an enterprise is in itself an evil; there is no reason why some men should have millions while others are poor; the wealth of a few is the cause of the poverty of the masses' -- all of these passionate denunciations are false. ¶This booklet is a clear statement of the functions of the entrepreneur and of the profit and loss system."

Crane, Burton. *The New York Times.* (November 24, 1952). "Now and again one is reminded that it was Karl Marx who perfected the technique of vituperation to support economic views. Using prose that rolls its r's heavily, Ludwig von Mises has borrowed his polemic methods from both Marx and Senator McCarthy. Anybody who disagrees with him is certainly a psuedo-economist and probably a Communist as well. ¶There is a lot of meat in *Planning for Freedom*. It is a vigorous statement of what Bentham and Ricardo and Say might decide about our present economic system if they could look at it without changing their nineteenth century minds . . . . ¶But Professor von Mises has not contented himself with the moderate and provable statement. Consider this one: 'It is impossible to understand the mentality and the policy of the Progressives if one does not take into account the fact that the Communist Manifesto is for them both manual and holy writ'."

R.F.D. *Social Order.* (October 1953) 373. "The author rejects all controls on wages, prices and credit . . . . With these highly debatable premises von Mises indulges in some over-simplifications which border on the fantastic. ¶Social theorists will accept this book as a clear and frank statement of a position which simply cannot be sustained in the light of modern economic and sociological realities."

Economic Digest. London (England): Economic Research Council. 6:2 (February 1953) 93. "It is doubtless good for everybody, bearing in mind the leftish trend of the age, to have this uncompromising and unrepentant liberal thundering away on the right. At least this particular thunderer knows his job as an economist and he has no inhibitions whatever as a propagandist."

Economist. 4 (1953) 331.

Faith and Freedom. Los Angeles: Spiritual Mobilization. 3:7 (March 1952) 16. Reviews separate pamphlet version of "Middle-of-the-Road Policy Leads to Socialism" (Article 50.4), included in *Planning for Freedom*. "Without ever having really explored the economic problems involved, far too many [clergymen] still hope, however, that we can establish a half-way house in our country between free enterprise and socialism . . . . ¶In this pamphlet Dr. Mises has demonstrated, . . . that this is a gross illusion. The so-called 'middle-way' is plainly and simply nothing but a method for the transformation of capitalism into dreaded socialism on a piecemeal basis."

_____. 4:6 (February 1953) 14-15. "Having been worsted in intellectual encounter, opponents of the market economy abandoned the effort to defend the Socialist dogmas for a strategy of giving power to politicians at the expense of other elements in society. The bellwether of this new tack, J. M. Keynes, proved so useful to the politicians that they made him a lord . . . . Unless people are protected against the excesses of freedom, say the planners, they will fall victim to the Socialists or even to the Communists. Keynes with his government intervention in the market place will save us from both Adam Smith and Karl Marx! ¶This is not a philosophical position so much as a technique for getting and holding power . . . . ¶He [the libertarian] must demonstrate, as von Mises does, that intervention, or planning, or the so-called mixed economy, leads to socialism . . . . ¶Von Mises doesn't stop here but goes on to elucidate the meaning of a market economy, pointing out that it means the utmost liberty for each person to plan and act free from arbitrary interference on the part of other people or government."

Fertig, Lawrence. "Censorship of Ideas?" *New York World-Telegram and Sun.* (December 22, 1952) 25, 27. "Dr. von Mises has a way of brushing away dust from dark corners and exposing the true nature of modern economic ideas. His book is concerned with freedom and his basic premise is that 'political freedom is the corollary of economic freedom.' He ends on a note of optimism. 'Trends can change' says Dr. von

Mises, after surveying the history of ideas for several hundred years. There is still a chance that people will swing back to true liberalism and away from statism."

Free Enterprise. Chicago. (October 12, 1953) 4. "If you wish to effectively combat the economic quackery that has been practiced in these United States in recent years, and that is unfortunately taught in many of our schools and colleges, you will find this of inestimable help."

_____. 17:6 (December 1964) 77. "It is a sad fact that in most of the American universities the students are today indoctrinated with the counterfeit philosophy that has ruined Europe. Very old fallacies, a hundred times refuted, are flamboyantly advertised under the deceptive label 'new economics'. . . . ¶From the very beginnings of his work as an economist Dr. Mises vigorously opposed those tenets and creeds whose application was bound to destroy Europe's civilization and prosperity . . . . And he fights today in America the ascendancy of the same mentality of all-round regimentation."

H.G. *Revue de Droit International.* Geneva (Switzerland). (May 12, 1967). "This work is an outline, a commentary on the burning questions and great ideological conflicts of our time. ¶Even though the author is pessimistic with respect to the future, in the last part he tries to show that there are no substantial reasons for this somber outlook." (Translated from the French)

R.G. "Freedom Can't Live According To Plan." *The Charlotte Observer.* (December 7, 1952) 22-C. "The conspiracy of silence that greets the works of those thinkers who are trying to conserve the sound values of our social, political, and economic systems has never been better illustrated than by the treatment of the books of Ludwig von Mises. ¶When his monumental work, *Human Action,* was published in 1949, you could look in vain in any of the so-called literary journals and supplements for a review that even began to do it justice . . . . ¶The current volume by von Mises has a sarcastic title, *Planning for Freedom.* It shows with the author's usual cold logic that planning for freedom is a contradiction of terms; that planning is a synonym for socialism and interventionism; and that intervention by government in the operation of the economy is the road to dictatorship, not to freedom . . . . ¶One of the most devastating parts of this book is the attack on the leftist conspiracy. Von Mises, himself a university professor, shows by marshaling plain facts that it is not the so-called liberal professor who is persecuted, but the conservative teacher . . . . ¶Dr. von Mises' books are not easy reading. *Human Action* in particular is to be recommended only for advanced students of economics. *Planning for Freedom* is less prolix and will give the general reader a wealth of information about the fundamentals of economics if he will give it serious study."

Greaves, Percy L. Jr. "Nuggets of Wisdom." *Christian Economics.* New York. 5:1 (January 13, 1953) 1, 3. "We need wise men in every field . . . . We need men who will brave the scorn of professors and politicians who peddle popular panaceas . . . . Such a man is Ludwig von Mises. If the world had listened to him, there would have been no 1929 depression or World War II. If it listens now, it can put an end to wars and depressions forevermore. ¶But modern men seldom listen to savants who advocate sanity, service and saving for self and society . . . . ¶If you want to know the problems of our age along with the answers, get a copy of this little book. Dr. Mises closes with an optimistic essay that tells us that trends can change."

Hess, Fritz. "Planning for Freedom." *Schweizer Monatshefte.* 34:7 (October 1954) 476-477. "A collection of addresses, newspaper and magazine articles that the author has given or written on various occasions . . . . Such pieces are usually forgotten all too soon and all too easily. Therefore it is fortunate that, before such a fate befell them, Ludwig von Mises has preserved in the collection at hand his contributions to the conflict of ideas concerning planning and market economy . . . . ¶In all his comments, the author reveals his unwavering belief in the beneficial power of a free market as well as the pungency of his arguments with which he answers opponents and exposes their weaknesses." (Translated from the German)

Lonigan, Edna. "Middle of the Road." *Economic Council Review of Books.* New York: National Economic Council. 9:11 (November 1952) 1. "Professor von Mises does not see Socialism as a vague form approaching from a distance, as so many Americans do. He has met it face to face, felt its hot breath . . . . ¶In *Planning for Freedom,* Dr. von Mises takes apart that darling of the intellectuals, 'a little planning,' planning to 'strengthen' freedom, or to 'help' private enterprise, or to reduce a little its evils for the poor or the weak. This doctrine of the 'middle of the road' is the favorite American illusion . . . . ¶The principal rival of the civil servants on the propagation of Socialist reforms has in every country been the universities. And wherever any one tried by logic to refute their claims, he met the same intolerance. The few economists who objected, said Dr. von Mises, 'were very soon silenced and barred from access to the universities, the press, the leadership of political parties, and public office'."

La Nación. Buenos Aires. (October 26, 1986). "One interesting chapter is 'Laissez Faire or Dictatorship.' The author revives the theory developed in the second half of the 18th century by Quesnay, Turgot, Gournay and Mirabeau, whose goal was the establishment of a free economy. Von Mises presents not only the evolution of the theory but also the position of its detractors, concluding that 'Laissez faire means: let the individual citizen, the much talked-about common man, choose and act and do not force him to yield to a dictator'." (Translated from the Spanish)

Noel, Martin Alberto. "Tarea tan útil como necesaria" [A Task as Useful as It is Necessary]. *La Nación.* Buenos Aires. (November 2, 1986). "Step by step, from the point of view of his central [free market] theme, von Mises gives the reasons why he considers doctrines based on inflation and credit expansion erroneous; they are the originators of an inevitable final collapse. He tries to prove that cyclical depressions are not inherent in capitalism but consequences of government interferences in the operation of the market. And he offers an analysis of the negative influences on the market of ideologies such as socialism and other types of central planning leading to controls of doubtful effectiveness . . . . ¶The pages commented on here have value as an introduction to the more difficult works of the Austrian maestro . . . . [T]he most important doctrines of today's important controversies are referred to." (Translated from the Spanish)

Overdruk Economist. #4 (1953) 331. Dutch-language review under the heading of "Books received."

Ranganathan, A. *The Indian Libertarian.* Bombay. 5:22 (February 1, 1958) 27. Review of *Economic Planning,* pamphlet containing "Planning for Freedom" (Article 45.2) and Rufus S. Tucker's "The Return to Enlightened Despotism." Concerning Mises' essay: "After a brilliant analysis . . . he states that there is no alternative to totalitarianism than freedom, without which full employment, rising real wage rates and a high standard of living are not possible."

Schweizer Monatshefte. (September 1952) 400-401. Review of *Profit and Loss* (B-17). Cited by Fritz Hess in his review of *Planning for Freedom* (see above).

Soule, George. *The Journal of Political Economy.* 62:1 (February 1954) 71-72. "Ludwig von Mises' well-known theses are argued with all the verve of a convinced polemicist in this short collection of papers addressed mainly to economic laymen. Some of his opinions ought to be popular among laymen and economists alike as long as there is danger of inflationary price increases . . . . Certain other of von Mises' assumptions, however, will arouse more doubt . . . . ¶Free markets assuredly have their uses; it would be nice if we could have a few more of them. But valuable though von Mises may be in emphasizing the often ignored virtues of a free market, he exhibits in marked degree the faults with which he charges his opponents. They are, he says again and again, ignorant of or unable to understand the reasoning on which he rests his faith. But he evinces not the slightest sign of being able to understand other doctrines. Least of all is he aware of the scholarly conventions that scientific assurance cannot be attained merely by the elaboration of a series of logically consistent propositions and that no hypothesis is ultimately reputable which cannot be tested in the real world."

Summers, Brian. "Von Mises' *Planning for Freedom.*" *Human Events*. Washington, D.C. (September 12, 1981) 10. "He [Mises] was the first economist to integrate the theory of money and credit into general economics. He was the first to fully explain the cause of economic recessions. He was the first to demonstrate the inherent inefficiency of socialism. And, as a crowning achievement, he laid the foundation on which he transformed economics from an *ad hoc* discipline into a coherent science of human action .... As so often happens, Mises' death in 1973 brought renewed interest in his work .... Now 17 of Mises' essays and addresses have been brought together in *Planning for Freedom*. Here, for the intelligent layman, is Mises in bite-size chapters ranging over such topics as inflation, Keynesianism, price controls, profits, capital, unemployment and government intervention."

Tucker, Jeffrey A. "Review of Planning for Freedom." *The Free Market*. Burlingame, Calif.: Ludwig von Mises Institute. 6:1 (January 1988) 7. "When Mises wrote these essays, he was surrounded by cries for more State planning. Socialism was the most popular system. It was alleged to be superior to all others. Under such a system, the State would own all the means of production, direct all investments, tax profits, control prices, and provide welfare. And the whole program was to be enforced by police power. This was the 'progressive' program, imposed through the threat of violence, and the one necessary to save us from the evils of capitalism. ¶These progressive socialists, and their interventionist counterparts, rarely attempted a refutation of free-market arguments. As Mises shows, they smeared their opponents, engaged in *ad hominem* attacks, and stuck erroneous labels on all those who disagreed with them .... ¶Mises's principle of 'no-compromise' led him to admonish his students when they failed to understand the true character of intervention. Thus the reader discovers Mises's strong disagreements with F. A. Hayek's position on the welfare state. ["Liberty and its Antithesis" (Article 60.2) included in the 4th enlarged 1980 edition of *Planning for Freedom*] Mises notes that in *The Constitution of Liberty*, Hayek makes a distinction between the tendency to welfarism, which is 'compatible' with liberty, and the different tendency toward all-out socialism. But, following the logic of interventionism, Mises says 'the Welfare State is merely a method for transforming the market economy step by step into socialism.'"

Socialism (B-4) (*Die Gemeinwirtschaft,* 1922, 1932; first English translation, 1936) N.B. 1951 and later English-language editions include *Planned Chaos* (B-14) as the epilogue.

The climate of opinion in post-World War I Europe was predominantly socialist. Socialism appeared to be the wave of the future, its arrival considered not only desirable but inevitable. Mises' detailed critique of all aspects and forms of socialism struck the German-speaking world like a thunderbolt. F. A. Hayek, one of Mises' leading students, said of *Socialism*:

> "It was a work on political economy in the tradition of the great moral philosophers, a Montesquieu or Adam Smith, containing both acute knowledge and profound wisdom. I have little doubt that it will retain the position it has achieved in the history of political ideas. But there can be no doubt whatever about the effect on us who have been in our most impressible age. To none of us young men who read the book when it appeared (1922) was the world ever the same again . . . . Not that we at once swallowed it all. For that it was much too strong a medicine and too bitter a pill. But to arouse contradiction, to force others to think out for themselves the ideas which have led him, is the main function of the innovator. And though we might try to resist, even strive hard to get the disquieting considerations out of our system, we did not succeed. The logic of the argument was inexorable." (Tribute to Mises, New York, March 7, 1956. Reprinted in Margit von Mises' *My Years with Ludwig von Mises*, 1976, 1984)

Bayern Rundblik. February 3, 1982. "Neuentdeckung eines Klassikers der Nationalökonomie" [Rediscovery of an Economic Classic]. "The most astonishing thing about this ponderous 500-page book is the fact that Mises, one of the leading representatives of the Viennese School of Economics, recognized the error in socialism long before Milton Friedman and other modern exponents of the market economy. Thus he is esteemed as the rediscoverer of the 19th century classical ideal of freedom . . . . ¶In his work, *Gemeinwirtschaft* [*Socialism*], which should be compulsory reading at German universities, Mises resolves the ideological confusion surrounding socialism. He characterizes market and command as the two fundamental principles behind all known economic orders. The market order can result, therefore, from either the market orientation on the part of the interested economic subjects (market economy) or by orders from above which are binding on all parties concerned, i.e. orders issued by a bureaucratic central office . . . . ¶State capitalism, economic planning and state socialism deviate only in secondary matters from the classical ideal of egalitarian socialism; as Mises recognized in 1932, they agree in all essentials." (Translated from the German)

Blundell, J. E. "Criticism." *Daily Worker.* London. (October 10, 1936). "To one who tries to meet the orthodox economist on his own ground, Comrade Jackson's review [*Daily Worker,* October 7, 1936, see below] does untold injury. It is only necessary for the orthodox economist to cut out this review and say, 'now that is the level which Marxists achieve,' and the prospect of placing Marxian economics in the position it deserves is doomed. The review is sectarian in the highest degree. ¶Comrade Jackson writes as though Austrian subjectivism is a thing of the past: 'A voice from the tomb.' ¶Unfortunately, this is the exact reverse of the truth, since 'consumer economics' still occupies the centre of the scene. The one thing most urgently required in the fight of economic theory is a renewal of the attack upon subjectivism, carried out in such a way that no detail is left unchallenged. We must rid ourselves of sheer scornful derision. Our economic analysis lags far behind our political analysis."

Carsow, M. *Le Journal des Économistes.* (March-April 1938). "Mr. von Mises' work destroys the prejudices that socialist propaganda pours out to the public to prevent them from gaining access to impartial knowledge concerning their problems. And this is not the least of its merits. The task of refuting the socialists is made the more difficult by that fact that one must persuade impassioned, mystical devotees of socialism of 'the absurdity and folly of their idea' without having recourse to the methods of the adversary, the demagogue, or to the tactics favored by the Marxists. ¶The majority of men look to socialism because it promises a social organization that will improve their welfare: 'It is not because socialism really conforms to their interests that the masses want socialism, it is because they believe that it does.'" (Quoted in publisher's catalog; translated from the French)

Childs, Roy A., Jr. *Laissez Faire Books*. San Francisco. C80 (July 1990) 9. "It was just after the end of the devastating First World War. Europe lay in ruins, and both intellectuals and political parties everywhere had finally succeeded in stamping out the last vestiges of nineteenth century liberalism and laissez faire capitalism. They turned instead to the new God, Socialism, which was to guide their paths for decades to come. It was during those dark and lonely years of Socialism's near-complete triumph that one single figure rose up to deal the Socialist ideology a blow that was to prove devastating: Ludwig von Mises. It was he who began the reconstruction of the liberal-libertarian, pro-capitalist ideology that had everywhere been discarded . . . [A]lthough it was written in 1922, there is a reason it has become a classic . . . . That's because by addressing the great issues of our time, in terms of principles, and with a passion for truth that rings through the decades, Mises's *Socialism* speaks perhaps even more tellingly, with greater relevance and urgency, to our generation than to any that has come before us."

Cole, G. D. H. "Two Views of Socialism." *New Statesman and Nation.* London. (November 14, 1936). A double review of Mises' *Socialism* and John Strachey's *The Theory and Practice of Socialism*. "Mr. Strachey writes well . . . . He is never dull . . . . For it is always very plain in his books that he is still learning . . . . ¶In his new book, he presents, with his accustomed attractiveness of style, a purely Communist interpretation of Socialism . . . . He opens with a sharp contrast between Capitalism and Socialism as economic systems, drawing fruitfully on the positive experience of Socialism in the U.S.S.R. . . . . ¶Professor von Mises' *Socialism* makes a singular contrast to it. For, whereas Mr. Strachey makes many of his most telling points by describing . . . the actual achievements of the Soviet Union, the Austrian professor uses up more than 500 pages in proving to his own satisfaction that these achievements cannot possibly exist . . . . Singularly, though the book was published in 1922, the author, revising it in 1932, appears to have felt no need to modify his judgment in view of the actual experiences of Russia. He continues . . . to rely on a purely *a priori* judgment. His book was perhaps worth translating as a supreme example of academic absurdity; but it is difficult to imagine any other reason for its appearance. It has all the complacent arrogance of those who, having described a purely imaginary perfect Capitalism in which everything works out *ex hypothesi* for the best, blandly assume the actual existence of this imaginary regime, and then deny the possibility that anything different from this ensample [sic., i.e. example or pattern] of perfection can exist at all."

La Cote des Frais (?). August 19, 1938. "By showing that a socialist economy, far from being inevitable, is unrealizable, L. von Mises overthrows the central claim of socialism that, by replacing the pursuit of capitalist profit with the satisfaction of needs, it would lead to a more moral and just society . . . . A planned economy depends on the arbitrary decrees of a totalitarian state, while the liberal economy rests on the daily plebiscites, i.e., the prices, of a democracy of consumers." (Translated from the French)

Daniels, G. W. *The Manchester School.* 8:1 (1937) 85-87. "For making the work thus available to English readers the publishers -- and especially the translator -- are deserving of thanks in which, it may be assumed, even those who find their own views vigorously controverted in the volume will be ready to join. The ground of this assumption is that, if a case can be made against views earnestly held, it is well that it should be as thorough and powerful as can be, and the case here presented certainly complies with that condition . . . . ¶Part II, of the volume which is headed 'The Economics of a Socialist Community,' . . . will be generally recognized as containing the kernel of the indictment . . . . As stated by the author, the subject of his volume is the theoretical 'problem of choice between alternative uses of the limited resources by means of which we satisfy our economics needs' (i.e., the problem of economic calculation) in a socialist economy. While the author is not prepared to accept the views of von Mises and others of the same school, he recognises that the problem is not easy of solution . . . . ¶The second part of the volume is concerned with the large question of the organisation and methods required for the successful working out of the socialist solution . . . . All that can be said here is that it does not appear that, at bottom, these methods would be very different from those which must necessarily operate in a less obtrusive way in the existing economic system . . . . Even though everyone might not agree that it contains the last word in that discussion, everyone might well agree that it will serve an extremely useful purpose in its emphasis on the fact that there exists such a problem for discussion."

Deschamps, Fernand. "Une réfutation magistrale du socialisme" [A Masterly Refutation of Socialism]. *La Libre Belgique.* (May 13, 1938). "I believe I am rendering a service in calling attention . . . to the appearance in French of one of the most decisive refutations of socialism that has been published . . . . Ludwig von Mises' great work, celebrated worldwide in its German edition . . . . has been attacked by the socialists. But it has not been refuted because it is irrefutable. ¶This critique of socialism is not complete. It deliberately omits all philosophical and religious aspects of Marxism . . . . It extends only to the economic and sociological doctrines. But in this area, it digs deep down to the roots of the Marxist utopia. It defines socialism as the transfer of the means of production from private property owners to the society organized by the State . . . . ¶The argument of von Mises, concerning which I can do no more than indicate its orientation, appears to me economically irrefutable . . . . I do not espouse all the social ideas of von Mises, far from it. I place human values above economic values and among the human values I venerate above all morality and religion. ¶But there is one economic technique that the Popes would be well advised to have never dreamed of condemning. It is not their business. The socialists never cared about this technique, the Marxists even less than the St. Simoniens. That is why they have failed wherever they have tried to introduce their utopias . . . . It is not enough to sing hymns to production. One must produce with profit and for that one must reduce production costs, force Statism to shrink and alleviate the fiscal burden." (Translated from the French)

Dominique, Pierre. "Les Nations et Les Hommes: Le Socialisme" [Nations and Men: Socialism]. *Les Nouvelles Litteraires.* (April 9, 1938). "Professor Ludwig von Mises is one of the luminaries of the University of Vienna . . . . known, esteemed or admired by social scientists . . . . although unfortunately ignored by the general public . . . . ¶The professor opposes not only Marxist communism, but all brands of socialism, including what he calls the military-statist spirit which leads States into war and at the same time impels them toward State Socialism. ¶According to Mr. Ludwig von Mises, it matters little whether the management of State Socialism is conducted by a caste of country squires, an army, a group of industrialists, or technicians, a Marxist party or an anti-Marxist party, whether it is blessed by the Church or not, whether it be implemented by State Capitalism, the last of the forms of socialism; it always results in deterioration of character and a drop in production . . . . ¶How to extricate ourselves [from Communism and National Socialism]? It is not enough, says the author, to defend liberalism; the majority of the intellectuals must be brought over to the cause . . . . [T]he instinct of property, creation, and economy is firmly enough anchored in the hearts of men to give them the power to sweep away socialism in the struggle, the rewards for which are civilization and culture." (Translated from the French)

_____. "Le libéralisme a pour lui l'avenir" [The Future Belongs to Liberalism]. *La Republique.* (July 3, 1938) 1, 3. "Our contemporaries need not be wrong. The time of Karl Marx is past. I am speaking here of Karl Marx as the father of two infants: Collectivism #1 and Collectivism #2; the first better known as 'Sovietism' and the second as 'Hitlerism.' For Hitlerism is nothing but Marxism which refuses to acknowledge its father. ¶To be sure, the time of Karl Marx is past. The liberal doctrine is once more beginning to assert itself. Its strongest supporters are those who want to save civilization and culture at any price and who as a result abhor war. Its prophets are -- and pray remember their names -- Walter Lippmann, Ludwig von Mises and Louis Rougier. Walter Lippmann is American and his excellent book, *La Cité Libre* [The Good Society] (Librairie de Médicis) has just been translated. Ludwig von Mises is Austrian and his *Le Socialisme* has been translated by the same publisher. Finally Louis Rougier is

French . . . . ¶We need not wait for Marxist errors to produce their full effect; their effects have developed since 1914. The men of today are beginning to understand that the State should carry out its duties as supervisor and judge, that political and economic liberalism are synonymous with peace, and that human beings can attain their highest potential only in a climate of peace. They are beginning to understand especially that collectivism is not inevitable and that humanity may become something other than a vast ant hill. The notions of liberty and of hierarchy -- for they go together -- are more and more defended and exalted; if France learns to identify herself with the liberal doctrine, a great century will open up for our country." (Translated from the French)

Eckardt, Hans v. *Das demokratische Deutschland* [Democratic Germany]. 17 (1923). "It is well nigh time to review the entire field of scientific as well as practical socialism, to appraise and re-examine, without prejudice and timidity, its usefulness and spiritual meaning. This task, which Prof. Mises has attempted, needed to be undertaken unconditionally -- further half truths and obvious errors should not be permitted out of sheer laziness . . . . This book was needed, yearned for, by all who are concerned with socialism intellectually and politically. Mises dares to reveal the destructive meaning of unprincipled socialism; he shows the deep lack of spiritual understanding among the supporters of the materialistic interpretation of history; he proves the disintegrating, destructive idea of this monstrous political power, which has learned how to blow up its one-sidedness and lack of clarity into a new world order. Mises says all this, not superficially and demagogically, but he investigates, proves, thinks through the problem of property and economic order, the situation of the family and the economy . . . . The book is no polemic, no pamphlet; it is proof of a scientific lack of prejudice." (Quoted from publisher's announcement; translated from the German)

The Economist. London. "An Attack on Socialism." (November 14, 1936). "Ordinary English readers, Socialist or otherwise, will be astonished by the manner of Professor Mises' book. For his argument is of an extreme and uncompromising character seldom encountered in English controversy. Everything that could possibly be represented as Socialism is to Professor Mises wholly and unconditionally bad; every departure from Socialism is wholly and unconditionally good. Professor Mises condemns absolutely not only nationalisation, 'planning,' and State control of industry, but redistributive taxation, health insurance, unemployment insurance, trade unions and labour legislation. Indeed, he is even prepared to argue that health insurance creates disease; that capitalist monopolies are on balance good because they restrict production of exhaustible raw materials; and that the functions of a post office might very well be better performed by private enterprise . . . . It [*Socialism*] was worth translating, however, if only to demonstrate how different is the Teutonic mind's approach to social problems from that of the compromising English. One may, perhaps, hope that Professor Mises' pupils will sometimes read Marshall and Mill."

_____. (May 19, 1951) 1161. "Professor Ludwig von Mises's *Socialism* is one of those books -- like *Das Kapital* itself -- on which numbers of people hold decided opinions without ever having read the actual text; a common fate of classics. Here is at once the purest, intellectually most powerful and most uncompromising statement of the extreme anti-collectivist case . . . . Up-to-date, however, is not an epithet to be applied to it. Its defense of the most complete *laisser-faire* ignores, where it does not beg, the whole question of any possible inherent instability in the dynamic price economy; no whiff of the welfare controversy penetrates its pages; an unbelievable complacency concerning the cash nexus and the social sufficiency of the acquisitive instinct betrays total ignorance of the findings, over the last thirty years, of sociological research. Professor von Mises punctures fallacies, deflates claims, confronts contradictions, attacks sheer intellectual muddle with the ruthlessness of a fire consuming rubbish; but he proves so much too much as to spoil his case."

García-Beraza, Felipe & Gonzalo Piedras S. "El Pro y el Contra de un Libro" [For and Against a Book]. *Novedades.* Mexico. (July 30, 1961). Review of Spanish (1961) translation: "With the same passion as that which divided and bloodied the world during the religious struggles of the 16th century, today's prevailing social order is violently defended and attacked. The goals of communism and capitalism now arouse the spirits just as did Protestantism and Catholicism four centuries ago. And just as Protestantism and Catholicism both claimed to offer the only way to attain heavenly bliss, so do both capitalism and communism argue today, each on its own behalf, that it offers the only means, not to celestial, but to an earthly life of abundance . . . . ¶Fortunately Luis Montes de Oca, Secretary of the Treasury under three presidents of Mexico, known for his extreme urbanity and his intellectual righteousness and integrity, completed this translation, the first in our language, before his death . . . . Gustavo R. Velasco says, in his excellent Foreword, that don Luis intended to add an explanation of the contradictions of the interventionists and the socialists, the most important thesis of the work, and of the reasons 'why economic freedom and civil and political liberty are inseparable and why freedom fosters human well-being and progress.' ¶Von Mises knows the theme of his book thoroughly and treats it passionately. There is vigor in the book's 600 pages which does not conceal the intricacy or complexity of the problems . . . . ¶Mises' study is exhaustive; it treats and analyzes all social, judicial and economic aspects of a socialist community in the light of economic and sociological theory. On some pages, the book [written four decades ago] shows its age. For example, no socialist would defend free love today, as Russia decreed some time ago that the family is the basis of the social order. ¶His [Mises'] most lucid chapters are those which deal with economics; also his epilogue . . . . ¶The work invites the thoughtful reader to reflect and analyze, to reject or to form judgments on the basic problems of our time. In Mexico nowadays, as previously elsewhere, the fate which destiny has presented our generation must be resolved: either we must preserve a free society, improving it and perfecting it: or we must adopt the collectivist order, which as the author shows will be totalitarian. To make an informed and intelligent choice, the directors of our society -- not only government officials but all who presume to direct and shape public opinion -- should study this work. ¶The careful and fluent translation deserves congratulations." (Translated from the Spanish)   For "Contra," see Piedras (below).

Grunau, Joachim. "Rationalprinzip, Wirtschaftsrechnung und Wirtschaftssystem" [The Rationality Principle, Economic Calculation and the Economic System]. *Weltwirtschaftliches Archiv.* 64 (1950) 254-294. Review of 1932 Jena edition.

J. P. H. [Jean-Pierre Hamilius]. "Le Socialisme." *Letzeburger Journal.* Luxembourg. (1957?). The reviewer reports on each of the book's three parts. "It is impossible to sum up this important work which one may consult with profit on every aspect of socialism. In studying this book, the reader will become acquainted with one of the most lucid and most penetrating spirits of this century. No one else has ever examined the different aspects of modern socialism with such clarity and precision . . . . ¶To understand liberalism as a doctrine which defends the interests of men of wealth, is to misunderstand it. 'Liberalism calls for private property, not in the interest of men of property, but in the general interest; it starts from the idea that the preservation of the capitalist order is consistent . . . with the interest of society' . . . . ¶For von Mises, the defense of property and private initiative as well as the struggle against socialist, planning and interventionist tendencies on the ground of principles has nothing to do with the defense of the particular interests of some or all entrepreneurs." (Translated from the French)

Hayes, H. G. *The American Economic Review.* 27:3 (September 1937) 625. "The position taken is one of strong opposition to socialism. The method followed is wholly deductive. The present-day widespread conduct of enterprise by governments is discussed, or rather alluded to, without any use of statistical data . . . . And there is no discussion of the operation of the economy of the Soviet Union, although there are a few references to it. The book not only suggests that the writing was done in an ivory tower but in the pre-war period. ¶The central theme is that socialism is impracticable . . . . The author states that Russia would long ago have collapsed if not supported by finance from capitalist countries . . . . ¶There is grave need today for careful consideration of the problem which von Mises considers. Government regulation and government ownership and operation are being extended rapidly in all capitalist countries, and socialism is a going concern in Russia. Critical and thorough analysis of the problems involved and of the results achieved is needed. Panegyrics concerning capitalism and *a priori* diatribes against socialism do not help. It is even doubtful if much help is to be found in the voluminous writings of the nineteenth century socialists, a review of which is by far the best part of the book under consideration."

Hazlitt, Henry "A Revised Attack on Socialism." *The New York Times Book Review.* (January 9, 1938) 20. This book "examines socialism from almost every possible aspect -- its doctrine of violence as well as that of the collective ownership of the means of production; its ideal of equality; its relation to problems of sex and the family; its proposed solution for the problem of production as well as of distribution; its probable operation under both static and dynamic conditions; its national and international consequences . . . . [It] must rank as the most devastating analysis of socialism yet penned. Doubtless even some anti-Socialist readers will feel that he occasionally overstates his case. On the other hand, even confirmed socialists will not be able to withhold admiration from the masterly fashion in which he conducts his argument. He has written an economic classic in our time."

> Mentioned in Henry Hazlitt's review of A. C. Pigou's *Socialism vs. Capitalism, The New York Times Book Review.* (January 16, 1938) 19.
> Reprinted in *On Freedom and Free Enterprise: Essays in Honor of Ludwig von Mises.* Mary Sennholz, ed. Princeton, N.J.: Van Nostrand, 1956. 34-37.
> Spanish translation: *Espejo.* Mexico. 2:19 (September 15, 1961) 21-24.

_____. "The Pros and Cons of Socialism." *Human Events.* Washington, D.C. (January 6, 1973). A joint review of Mises' *Socialism* and Michael Harrington's *Socialism.* Most of the review is devoted to Harrington's "baffling" book. "What is baffling first of all is how such a book -- so piously reflecting the century-old and long-discredited Marxian ideology, vocabulary and prophecies -- can come to be written in this day and country . . . . ¶The book is well-written, at moments even eloquent . . . . ¶Capitalism is represented as the sum of all evil. Socialism on the other hand, may not bring an earthly paradise . . . but whatever evil remains after it has been achieved will hardly be worth talking about . . . . Harrington plumps without reservation for the Marxian theory that 'labor' is everywhere 'exploited' by the 'capitalist'." The reviewer cites "a bundle" of economic fallacies and "numerous factual errors." For Harrington, "words seem to have lost their dictionary meanings . . . . ¶What is amazing is how, with all his knowing allusions to scores of authors, Harrington has managed to insulate himself so completely from any knowledge of real economics or of even the most famous refutations of Marxist socialism." Then, with respect to Mises' book Hazlitt writes: "No open-minded reader can fail to be impressed by the closeness of Dr. Mises' reasoning, the rigor of his logic, the power and penetration of his thoughts . . . . ¶Mises' *Socialism* is an economic classic written in our time. "

> Reprinted in *The Freeman.* Irvington, N.Y. 23:3 (March 1973) 148-154.
> Portion on Mises' *Socialism* in *Books for Libertarians.* Washington, D.C. (February 1973).

Heimann, Eduard. *Annals of the American Academy of Political Economy.* n.d.

Herkner (Professor). "Sozialpolitische Wandlungen in der wissenschaftlichen Nationalökonomie" [Sociopolitical Changes in Economic Science]. *Der Arbeitgeber.* February 1, 1923. N.B. This paper sparked a discussion of "The Crisis in Social Policy" in *Sozialen Praxis* (1923): "The most meaningful performance by far in this direction appears in the brilliantly written, thoughtful work of the Viennese economist L. Mises, *Die Gemeinwirtschaft* [Socialism]. With full knowledge of modern scientific advances, the author presents a direct and crushing critique, proceeding in part from a completely new viewpoint, of every kind of socialism and of everything he considers to be socialism. As he points out, socialism is entirely out of the question, even for satisfying the most modest claims with regard to the economy of production, because it eliminates the principles of self-responsibility, self-interest and monetary calculation. Without the last, rational economic transactions are completely unthinkable." (Quoted in publisher's announcement; translated from the German)

Hobson, J. A. "An Able Attack on Socialism." *Manchester Guardian.* England. (October 2, 1936). "The confident claim that social evolution makes for Socialism is disposed of by an array of philosophic and historical learning which tears it to shreds and tatters . . . . But the brunt of the attack is directed against the economic practicability of Socialism as a substitute for Capitalism . . . . The disappearance of a price calculus applicable to units of capital and labour in a full Socialism will make it impossible for public planning to give a right direction to the productive resources of the community . . . . In the existing capitalist system the 'democracy of consumers' by their demands direct all the productive processes into their most useful channels . . . . ¶This, of course, is Adam Smith's doctrine of 'the invisible hand', though von Mises does not truckle to any such 'mysticism' as this expression might imply. His reasoning throughout is conducted upon a rationalist utilitarian basis, and his indictment of Socialism is that it must greatly reduce the economic product . . . . ¶Thus the rejection of Socialism is partly due to its inherent defects, partly to the excellent operation of capitalism . . . . ¶The writer denounces all factory and other 'humanitarian' legislation of health and unemployment insurance, all trade union activities, political or other, as detrimental to the general productivity of labour, while the inflationism practised or threatened everywhere is the final act of a 'Destructionism' which he sees threatening our civilisation . . . . ¶I think it is incumbent upon thinkers 'of the Left' to face and confront, if they can, the central positions here taken by von Mises in what is perhaps the most thorough attack upon their accepted principles that has ever been presented."

Hulet, Craig B. *The Brief.* Missoula, Montana. (September 15, 1985). "You can bet that von Mises' works are not a great part of the curriculum of most institutions. The answer is obvious. To introduce just this one text would obliterate the course that is taught by many a professor. The professor is quite often a socialist . . . . *Socialism* (the book) tears each version of socialism into very tidy, thin, shreds . . . . ¶[W]hile written originally in 1922 . . . *Socialism* . . . still stands today as the single most devastating critique of every form of socialist theory, utopian social theories, to today's absurd attempts at profit sharing."

Jackson, T. A. "As Dead as the Dodo." *Daily Worker.* London. (October 7, 1936). Reprinted here in full: "Young students of Socialism who would like to experience some of the thrills the pioneers of their grandfathers' generation went through on the propaganda platform, might (if the effort did not exhaust them) get something of the kind from reading this all-too-learned and academical work. ¶Its standpoint is partly and unequivocally the standpoint of Bentham and Malkus [i.e. Malthus]. Its economics are those of the once-lauded Austrian 'subjectivist' school; its author quotes with the accents proper to sacred names those of Böhm-Bawerk and Stanley Jevons. ¶In a word -- although its author, like the fabled Uncle John, 'still persists in living on' -- it is a voice from the tomb. ¶There is not an idea in it that is not as dead as the Dodo. ¶Its practical worth is found in the fact that to maintain his thesis (that Socialism is 'impossible') the author has not only to lump together as 'all alike Socialist,' Nazi-ism, Utopianism and Marxism, but also to include modern British Liberalism which is, according to von Mises, only another sort of Socialism. ¶The really-truly-fine standpoint, he says, is that of classic Manchester school utilitarianism -- as it was before John Stuart Mill surrendered to the Socialists. ¶It would be a crying shame to argue with such a doting old darling. But what must be the state of mind of the people who have gone to the trouble of translating and producing (and very well, too) a work which would have been out of date in 1860? ¶Let it rest." See "Criticism" of this Jackson review by J. E. Blundell (above).

Jay, Douglas. "A Critic of Socialism." *The Spectator.* London. (October 23, 1936). This book "is certainly a remarkable work. 'My book,' Professor Mises tells us in the preface, is a 'scientific inquiry, not a political polemic.' Yet later on we read that 'Socialism is the expression of the principle of violence crying from the workers' soul, just as Imperialism is the principle of violence speaking from the soul of the official and the soldier'; and that the 'Socialist idea is nothing but a grandiose rationalisation of petty resentments' . . . . Professor Mises finally reaches his zenith of hilarious unreality when he tells us that because 'being ill is not a phenomenon independent of conscious will', such institutions as health insurance 'promote accidents and illness, and hinder recovery.' 'By weakening or completely destroying the will to be well and able to work, social insurance creates illness . . . . In short it is an institution which tends to encourage disease, not to say accidents . . . .' It would be uncharitable not to admit that these portions of Professor Mises' work are not extremely entertaining. ¶Hidden away beneath pages of turgid extravagance, however, there are items of serious criticism which English Socialists ought not to ignore . . . . Professor Mises' important contribution to the debate is his contention that economic calculation is impossible in a socialist community . . . . ¶The other subjects discussed by Professor Mises are commonplaces of controversy in this country, and he adds little to them . . . . ¶Nevertheless, at the end of Professor Mises' 500 pages, one can scarce forbear to cheer. It is indeed wonderful that so much subtlety, so much learning, so much intellectual vigour and ruthlessness, can give birth to so much unreason."

Jèze, Gaston. "Méthodes périmées" [Out-of-date Methods]. *Journal des Finances.* (April 22, 1938). "The two weak points in the present financial situation are: (1) the budget deficit; (2) the crisis of economic production. ¶If these two problems were resolved in a satisfactory manner; monetary stability and the revival of public credit would also ensue. ¶The budget deficit and the crisis of economic production have a common cause: the excessive demagogy which has battered France for two years, less violent forms of which have been manifest since the end of the war [World War I] . . . . ¶Demagogy is inseparable from Marxism. The development of Marxism in France since the end of the war has led to demagogy. ¶As has been demonstrated in a magnificent scientific study of *Socialism* by Professor Ludwig von Mises: 'the socialist scribblers may keep on writing books about the end of capitalism and the coming of the socialist millennium; they may portray the evils of capitalism in the most violent colors and offer in opposition all the seductions of socialist benefits; they may win with their works great success among unthinking persons; but that will change nothing with respect to the destiny of the socialist idea. The attempt to organize the world along socialist lines will be able to bring about the annihilation of civilization, but never the erection of a socialist society' . . . . ¶As Professor François Perroux, of the Paris Law Faculty, says in his masterly preface to von Mises' book, one must combat without mercy 'the barren socialism of the politicians and babblers' . . . . ¶A tax is a process for dividing equitably among individuals the costs of public services. Thus it is legitimate. To pay the tax is a civil duty. ¶But in socialist doctrine and practice, the tax is transformed into an instrument of plunder . . . . ¶The same distortion takes place with respect to budgetary methods . . . . ¶These two fundamental principles have been completely disfigured by the demagogues of the political assemblies imbued more and more with socialism. They vote large expenditures for the exclusive gain of a certain social class and enact taxes which will be paid by another social class. ¶The result is not only an inequitable social regime but budgetary disequilibrium." (Translated from the French)

Knight, Frank H. *The Journal of Political Economy* 46 (April 1938) 267-269. In view of Professor Knight's importance as a leading spokesman for the "Chicago School," his review is reprinted in full:

"English-speaking readers interested in any way in socialism -- as who can fail to be under present conditions? -- will be grateful to the translator and publishers for the chance to read in clear and excellent English this book, which is perhaps the most discussed work attacking the socialist position on the ground of 'sound' economic theory in the post-war generation. It is true that Professor Mises' general position has been made fairly familiar to economists of the English-speaking world through the discussion which it has aroused in journals, and especially the publication in English of the original article of 1920, out of which the book has grown; this article was the pivotal item in Professor Hayek's *Collectivist Economic Planning* (London, 1935). It is not so pleasant to have to add that many who can read German find it difficult to 'skim' a bulky work in that language, and that this is the appropriate treatment of Professor Mises' tome. Not long ago Dr. Oskar Lange suggested in an excellent article ["On the Economic Theory of Socialism," *Review of Economic Studies,* October 1936] that a statue of Professor Mises might well be placed in the position of honor in the capital of the socialist state, since it is due to his denial of the possibility of rational economic management apart from private property that socialists themselves have been forced to give the subject serious consideration.

"It seems to this reviewer that the whole discussion is largely sound and fury. It is truistical [sic] to observe that unless the whole technical basis of economic life is to be completely transformed under socialism, which is not proposed, it will be in general form about what it has been under 'capitalism'; this means that the managers of various technical units in production -- farms, factories, railways, stores, etc.-- would carry on in essentially the same way, which in turn means that socialism is 'essentially' a proposed method for selecting, motivating, and remunerating such functionaries, displacing the property owners who are now formally the ultimate authority in control. The reality of control, of course, inheres primarily in consumers and workers, in so far as effective competition prevails, and would do so under socialism also, if it really preserved freedom of choice in consumption and freedom of choice of occupation. Socialism is a political problem, to be discussed in terms of social and political psychology, and economic theory has relatively little to say about it.

"On the central issue, Professor Mises shows a certain tendency to shift his ground. In this English edition of his book he has added a section of five pages (137-42) on the 'artificial market,' to meet some of the recent criticism of his original position. In this, his argument is really based on political probability. The reviewer fully agrees that a socialistic government would not try intelligently to function in accord with economic principles in securing maximum satisfaction of the economic needs of the masses. It probably wouldn't try at all but, instead, would lead the masses on some romantic adventure, some 'crusade.' But such political prediction or prophecy is one thing, and reasoning in terms of economic principles is another.

"There would be no justification to taking the space to comment on this book in detail, or in any proportion to its own length. The essential fact is that, on any of the main issues which call for discussion, it is disappointing. We find assertion at great length but little penetrating criticism of the property system; and on the deeper ethical questions regarding economic individualism, beyond the unanalyzed notion of efficiency, there is practically nothing. Part IV of the book (pp.395-453) is devoted to socialism as a moral imperative but contains little excepting the usual dogmas on incentive, and philosophical disquisitions on justice, of a 'puritanical' cast. Professor Mises is at his best in criticism and shows wide reading in social theory, particularly the literature of and on Marxism. Yet his Part III (pp.361-421) on the alleged inevitability of socialism is an amazing tissue of question-begging assertion and mere quibble. Practically the only discussion of monopoly is given incidentally in this connection and reduces to the unsupported assertion that 'most cartels and trusts would never have been set up had not governments created the necessary conditions by protectionist measures .... monopolies owe their origin not to a tendency immanent in capitalistic economy but to governmental interventionist policy directed against free trade and laisser-faire' (pp.390-391). The topic is dismissed with the statement that 'we can discover nothing which could justify the assertion that growing monopolization makes the capitalist system intolerable' (p.392). The last division of the book (Part V) is entitled 'Destructionism' and is hardly more than a diatribe against labor legislation, social insurance, public ownership, and practically every species of modern reformism. Economic analysis of these movements, or even recognition of the economic issues involved, is conspicuously absent."

Laski, Harold J. "Two Views of Socialism." *Sunday Times.* London. (September 27, 1936). Laski (1893-1950), a prominent member of the British Labour Party, visited Mises' economics seminar in Vienna in 1925. "Professor Mises has long been known as one of the leading members of that school of economic thought of which, perhaps, Professors Gregory and Robbins are the most distinguished exponents in this country. They are opposed to Government in general and to Socialism . . . in particular . . . . ¶Professor Mises does not suffer from any doubts . . . . ¶So that Professor Mises can show the futility of Socialism in all its shapes and forms, whether it be that of Marx or that of Christian social reformers, it is all one long error . . . . By means of private ownership in a world of free contract, Professor Mises writes, the goods are put 'into the hands of those who know best how to use them, into the hands, that is, of the most expert managers' . . . . We have only to enlarge the realm of free contract to increase productivity and so enlarge our share . . . . ¶What, of course, Professor Mises has done is to construct for himself an abstract capitalism the postulates of which logically require all the premises and conclusions which he produces so triumphantly. He then proceeds to transfer this abstraction to the world we know and to assume their identity . . . . ¶That there is an important case to be made against Socialism, that, further, its problems of economic organization are profound, no one acquainted with the issues is likely for a moment to doubt seriously. But only a fanatic will find any real comfort in this extravagant and often ignorant diatribe. A good deal of what Professor Mises discusses he frankly does not understand at all; a notable instance of this is the Marxian theory of the 'withering away' of the State, which, on the premises of Marx, is a necessary logical conclusion. He has not grasped the materialistic interpretation of history. He has no sense of the historic causes which led to the rise of capitalist industry, or the significance which attaches to the 'frictions' which have led to the wholesale perversions of the pure pattern he seems to imagine as actually existent in the real world . . . . ¶He lives in a private world into which the experience of ordinary people cannot penetrate. Nothing disturbs his conviction that his private world is unmistakably the actual universe outside . . . . But the programme that would result from the acceptance by any statesman of Professor Mises' hypothesis would produce a violent revolution in any normal community in a fortnight. That would not, it is true, lead Professor Mises to regard his approach as wrong. He would merely assume that the failures of society were wreaking their vengeance upon the fundamental constitution of the universe. His book is an interesting illustration of the fact that neither logical capacity nor wide reading is a substitute for the saving grace of common sense. I know no book of recent years which does so much to explain the disrepute into which economists have fallen in our generation." (See Meinl response, which follows.)

Meinl, Julius. "To the Editor of the *Sunday Times*." *Sunday Times*. London. (October 11, 1936). "Professor H. J. Laski, in his review of Professor Mises' book, *Socialism*, in your issue of September 27, brings charges that seem to reflect on himself. Mises, says Professor Laski, has not grasped the materialistic interpretation of history. There is no evidence to show that Professor Laski has done so himself. ¶The evidence of the post-war years, had Professor Laski eyes to see it, is an incrimination of State interference, and not of capitalism. The catastrophes which have heaped up in Europe during the last few years, when State interference, whether masquerading as Socialism or as some form of totalitarianism, has reached unprecedented heights, prove the worthlessness not of capitalism, but of any system of State Socialism that has yet been tried. One suspects that Professor Laski's picture of the Russian economic system is as remote from reality as he alleges Professor Mises' picture of capitalism to be."

Mercure de France. (October 1938). "Finally! Here is a book on socialism that exhausts the subject . . . . I do not know another work in the contemporary literature on the social sciences that is more complete, more conscientious and more scholarly. Its 626 pages do not omit a single aspect of the numerous problems which the word socialism evokes; to persuade the reader it will suffice to reproduce the chapter titles . . . . ¶No one has proven more irrefutably than this author that socialism was an absolute error. Those who will take the trouble to read the book will certainly be persuaded." (Quoted in publisher's catalog; translated from the French)

Meyer, Gerhard. *Zeitschrift für Sozialforschung*. No. 45 in a collective article on "economic planning." 1 (1932) 399.

Murry, J. Middleton. *Criterion*. England. (January 1937) 336-341. "Ludwig von Mises' book ends with these sentences: 'Neither God nor a mystical "Natural Force" created society; it was created by mankind. Whether society shall continue to evolve or whether it shall decay lies -- in the sense in which causal determination of all events permits us to speak of freewill -- in the hand of man. Whether society is good or bad may be a matter of individual judgment; but whoever prefers life to death, happiness to suffering, well-being to misery, must accept society. And whoever desires that society should exist and develop must also accept, without limitation or reserve, private ownership in the means of production.' ¶A more direct and advised challenge to the fundamental Socialist position could hardly be imagined; certainly none has come my way. And von Mises' book is by far the most interesting book on Socialism that I have read since I first read *Das Kapital*. . . . ¶Von Mises' challenge to Socialism is primarily directed to it on the level of its own 'scientific' professions . . . . ¶Radical economic criticism of this kind Socialism seldom, if ever, receives in this country. Today, it will be met with the naive reply that the problem of economic calculation has been solved in Russia: whereas, in fact, this problem has not been solved. The world has yet to learn whether, in fact, such an economy as the Russian, can supply goods and services as abundantly as the capitalist system has done. With the majority of Socialists today the belief that it does so is a matter of blind faith. ¶But what von Mises does not admit as resolutely as he pushes home his criticism of Socialism, is that the capitalist system, in his sense of free capitalism, does not exist, never has existed, and is much further from existence today than it was three-quarters of a century ago . . . . It is axiomatic with the pure and abstract Liberalism, which von Mises professes, that where wealth accumulates, men cannot decay. ¶With such a position argument is scarcely possible. Not that it is a stupid position, exactly; because its stupidity lies in its excessive reasonableness. This Liberalism is, in respect to any actual condition achieved by the world, as Utopian as the Socialism it combats. It demands . . . universal peace. Von Mises does not deny this. His picture of the nineteenth century is that the world almost on the brink of a pure and universal *laisser-faire,* suddenly went mad. To the crucial question: *Why* did it go mad? his answer is so incredibly naïve that he dares not really formulate it. The world went mad because there were not enough reasonable people in it: reasonable people being those who are as deeply convinced as von Mises himself of the perfect harmony which an œcumenical Liberalism would achieve . . . . ¶This pure Liberalism is, in reality, a nightmare -- a nightmare even worse than the world-chaos in which we live today. Such, inevitably, is the concrete outcome of any theory which begins by abstracting society from the individual person . . . . Compared with von Mises' Liberalism, Marxism is a living creed . . . . Mankind may be either good or bad, but it will never be reasonable, in the Liberal sense. . . . ¶In the last analysis -- in spite of all its façade of 'scientific inevitability' -- Marxist Socialism is an appeal to the individual man to take conscious responsibility for the workings of society. Von Mises' Liberalism consists in the affirmation that a sense of responsibility is not merely unnecessary, but positively pernicious . . . . There is no place for such an instinct [the human instinct for social justice] in von Mises' psychology. The economic man is, for him, the total man . . . . He can explain history up to the arrival of capitalist society, not unjustly, as the continual effort of man in society towards the abolition of legal privilege. But the history of capitalist society itself becomes incomprehensible, except as a collective madness -- an inexplicable impulse in man to escape from Paradise, so soon as he had entered it."

Piatier(?), André. "Le Socialisme." *Politique Étrangère.* 3 (December 6, 1938) 634-635.

Piedras S., Gonzalo, and Felipe García-Beraza. "El Pro y el Contra de un Libro: *El Socialismo*" [For and Against a Book: *Socialism*]. *Novedades.* Mexico. (July 30, 1961). A review of the Spanish (1961) translation: "Recently a voluminous work on socialism (from 1922) by the German sociologist and economist Ludwig von Mises has been put into circulation." The author [Mises] denies that he intends to "demolish" Marxism; Marxism is already dead, he says. And editor Gustavo R. Velasco declares that "Thanks to Boehm-Bawerk, it is dead as an economic doctrine." Yet, according to the reviewer: "the greater the reports of Marxism's demise, . . . the more it grows . . . . ¶It is worthwhile to point out that Professor Mises uses an old intellectual trick -- let us say -- 'to kill a corpse.' He [Mises] quotes Marx as saying something he didn't say -- and then refutes it brilliantly." The reviewer cites three examples, each of which in turn he presumes to refute: (1) Mises says that Marxism denies the scientific character of logic and holds that an idea "is a function of the thinker's social class;" (2) Mises writes: "The dialectical process leads inevitably to socialism. The object and end of history is the socialization of the means of production."; and (3) Mises says that the Marxists failed to concern themselves with plans for organizing the socialist regime. According to the reviewer, Mises did not understand Marx. Communism was not a system that needs to be "established." "Nor is it an ideal to which reality will have to accommodate itself. It is the real movement which will supersede actual conditions . . . . [It] will arise out of prevailing conditions. Thus, the future of the historic process cannot be precisely predicted." (Translated from the Spanish) For "Pro" see García-Beraza (above).

Plener, E. *Zeitschrift für Volkswirtschaft und Sozialpolitik.* New Series. 2:10/12. "A great performance, because it investigates critically the entire realm of socialism, within broad but legitimate boundaries, and presents in great detail the author's strong conviction of the superiority of the liberal economic theory over socialistic doctrine." (Quoted from publisher's announcement; translated from the German)

Pribram, K[arl]. *Schmollers Jahrbuch für Gesetzgebung, Verwaltung und Volkswirtschaft.* 49:1 (1925). "Of the literature in the social sciences in recent years, Mises' work is an astonishingly unique event; it is the only systematic and basic attempt to attack and to refute socialism as a world view and as a program for a new economic order, proceeding to be sure from the doctrine of liberalism . . . . Replete with profound conviction, the book is an outstanding witness to the [author's] critical acuteness of mind, exceptional economic knowledge and complete mastery of economic problems . . . . ¶Out of respect for the many deep problems it treats and the many-faceted points of view under which they are examined, it merits serious study and far reaching consideration." (Quoted from publisher's announcement; translated from the German)

Rageot, Gaston. "La Mode intellectuelle: A Qui la Faute?" [The Intellectual Fashion: Whose Fault Is It?]. *Le Temps.* (May 1, 1938) 3. "Ludwig von Mises, Professor at the International Institute of Graduate Studies, has dedicated many years to the study of the spread of socialist ideas in the world, and he does not hesitate to attribute the doctrine's success to the intellectuals. ¶Every time the world or the people hesitate they turn to the intellectuals as a source . . . . ¶Personally, I do not consider writers, scholars, or artists particularly qualified to direct their country's policy, to govern or to counsel their government; by the same token, I am convinced that the influence which they can exercise on policy through their personality, their ideas and their writings goes far beyond what they themselves can imagine. ¶It is this indirect responsibility that Professor Ludwig von Mises has in mind when he attributes to the intellectuals the present social disarray and devotes his effort to demonstrating their error." To illustrate Mises' thesis the reviewer cites Lucien Herr who, in a library setting through conversation with students and his friendship with Leon Blum, had substantial pro-socialist influence. "The originality of von Mises is in having tried to show scientifically that socialism is not justifiable. To socialize the means of production, in effect, is to wipe out the grounds for production, and the grounds cannot be replaced, as experience has shown, except by coercion of the State. Thus, socialism should be condemned not as a political doctrine -- that it denies it is -- but as scientific economics -- which it presumes to be." (Translated from the French)

Rougier, Louis. "Parmi les Livres" [Among the Books]. *Revue de Paris.* n.d. (1938 ?) 710-713. A double review of Mises' *Socialism* and Walter Lippmann's *La Cité Libre* [The Good Society].   "The modern world is not merely the final struggle between capitalism and socialism; it is the conflict between liberalism, which rests on individual initiative, and state planning . . . . ¶The originality of von Mises' work is in having attacked for the first time the scientific study of Marxist predictions and postulates . . . . It is not a matter of discussing whether socialism is desirable, but of examining whether or not it is feasible. What renders socialist management unrealizable is not the low level of the bourgeois morality: it is a purely intellectual matter. The notion of economic policy involves economic calculation, i. e. the possibility of calculating the optimal combination of the means of production so as to permit the greatest satisfaction of the needs and desires of consumers according to their urgency and precedence, as indicated by the pricing referendum . . . . ¶The liberal order is not an economic order aimed at enriching capitalists, but at satisfying consumers. True, it is a democracy in which the majority right to vote reigns. But the ability to dispose of a great number of votes cannot be acquired and maintained except by satisfying the needs of consumers in the most appropriate way. 'Every child who prefers one toy to another,' writes Mises, 'puts his ballot in the ballot box, out of which will emerge eventually the elected *captain of industry*.' ¶Only this democracy is compatible with liberal democracy, the rights of man and of the citizen, individual initiative, respect for merit and selection of the elite . . . . ¶If the book of Mises is the most pertinent critique of socialism, that of Walter Lippmann is the most enthusiastic rehabilitation of liberalism . . . . ¶These two masterworks belong in the library of all who are concerned with defending civilization and culture against barbarism and the apocalyptic war that threatens." (Translated from the French)

C.S. "*Socialism* Denounced." *New Leader.* London. (November 27, 1936). "*Socialism* . . . contains more nonsense in 500 pages than any other I have recently read."

Schuyler, G[eorge]. S. *Pittsburgh Courier*. (n.d.). "Running to 600 pages, this remarkable work explores every facet of the socialism-versus-capitalism controversy with brilliant insight and sparkling logic. Every claim for socialism is demolished and the arguments against capitalism are exposed and exploded." As quoted on the book jacket of Mises' *Theory and History* (B-20).

Schwiedland, E. *Preussische Jahrbücher.* (October 1923). "In the book at hand the courage and the independence with which the author opposes everyday opinions are delightful. Delightful also . . . is the fact that he discusses them not as a philosopher but with common sense . . . . It is noteworthy that this work was begun before the war [World War I] and has been published during the [post-World War I] turmoil. It is not surprising that its appearance has evoked copious insults from the Marxists. That, however, can do the work no further harm." (Quoted in publisher's announcement; translated from the German)

Sosa Ferreyro, A. "El Socialismo: Las Armas de la Verdad" [Socialism: The Weapons of Truth]. *Libertad.* Caracas (Venezuela): Instituto para la Defensa Activa de la Libertad. 2:14 (October 1972) 19pp. Surveys Mises' accomplishments, pays tribute to the prominent Mexican businessman, Luis Montes de Oca, who translated *Socialism* into Spanish, and to his nephew, lawyer Gustavo R. Velasco, who saw the project through to completion after Montes de Oca's death. Discusses the contents of the book and explains that socialism and communism are the same. "Western civilization, freedom, and democracy, must be defended," the reviewer writes. "The aggression and subversion come from the Kremlin . . . . ¶Behind a pacifist facade, the Soviet imperialists try to paralyze the free world so as to facilitate the conquest of their red agents and to impose Marxist dictatorship with its system of slavery, hunger, terror and death . . . . ¶What to do, then? Fight, oppose, employ all energy, ability, human and material resources to stop the Marxist imperialist conquest! We have the weapons of truth and reason on our side, and the testimony of discontent in the 'socialized' countries which translates into determined escapes, and walls to prevent the slaves from fleeing their communist prison." The reviewer closes by quoting Mises: "The course of human events is not determined by mythical material productive forces, but by truth and ideas. What is needed to prevent the trend toward socialism and despotism is the support of public opinion and moral fortitude." (Translated from the Spanish)

Stamp, J. C. *Economica.* New Series. 4:14 (May 1937) 223-225. "Although in one sense he [Mises] writes *sub specie æternitatis,* yet it cannot be denied that time has staled his infinite variety, and that, with certain exceptions, the work seems inevitably dated . . . . For extensive treatment is given to writers and their notions that have passed into the limbo -- over generous space given for museum pieces . . . . ¶[W]e go a long way back into history, deep down into law, philosophy and ethics, wide afield for everything that savours of check upon pure competition and can be related to a socialistic concept, in this massive, erudite, encyclopædic work. Although it has been my companion for leisure moments for over a month, I have never felt lost, or bored, or wanting a sense of direction . . . . ¶The economic student . . . turns to the chapters on economic calculation as the contribution of vital importance. Indeed, Professor von Mises himself must stand or fall by this part of his work . . . . If he is wrong, and there actually *is* a substitute for price in practical socialism, or totalitarianism of any kind, then not merely this section, but most of the rest, must be reargued to justify the conclusions . . . . [O]ne short paragraph on Russia simply states that she has not had to face the problem squarely because she moves in a world of pricing economic systems and her own values are referable thereto . . . Russia looks over the shoulder of the writer at the next desk and sneaks his results . . . . ¶This great work, judged by British standards, is over-elaborated in parts and much of it has already entered the museum stage. Readers with little leisure may think it tiresome in parts. It can be recommended to the harassed student rather as an encyclopœdic work of reference (with its remarkably complete index) than as a model textbook for study. But it has a permanent place in the history of the development of thought; it is a full and photographic picture of the ideas of a particular time, and it has done yeoman service in giving a true measure of Marxism and influencing continental opinion saturated with Marxist ideas, for it lifted the ban, so skilfully laid by Marx, upon the examination of his scheme by the tests of scientific economic analysis."

Steiner, Fritz Georg. *Mitteilungen des Verbandes österreichischer Banken.* (December 12, 1922). "The key point of Mises' critique lies in the evidence given of the impossibility of socialistic economic calculation . . . . It is most suitable that Mises considers the distribution problem under socialism . . . . A careful examination of the socialist economy in isolation permits Mises to pursue the problem of carrying out transactions in the socialist commonwealth. All known forms of socialism are described, their possibilities examined and their special influence on the socialistic economy considered. At the conclusion, Mises analyzes the ethical side of socialism. With a clarity not previously attempted he explains the weaknesses in the argument which advances an ethical ideal that is unattainable in this world as it is and condemns the capitalistic economic order as being immoral because it does not correspond to its ideal. This is the most courageous part of a work that follows new and untrod paths throughout. After the flood of utopian economic literature which has too long confused the spirit, we now have a critique of socialism so profound that a thorough justification of the predominant capitalistic economic system results." (Quoted in publisher's announcement; translated from the German)

The Times Literary Supplement. London. "A Liberal Critic of Socialism: Orthodoxy Challenges the Modern Outlook." (January 9, 1937). "This is an important book, well worth the exceptionally competent translation which it has now received. No reasonably critical mind will deny the effectiveness of its challenge to the whole complex of ideas summed up in the word Socialism. But its defects are at least as apparent as its qualities . . . .¶For him [Mises] there can be no possibility of sinfulness in a pride which has complete rational justification . . . . ¶The average modern opponent of Socialism condemns its flower; but Dr. von Mises attacks its roots. The bent of his mind is always towards first principles . . . . ¶Coming to the theoretical basis of the Socialist argument, Dr. von Mises at once cuts the ground from under his opponents' feet by admitting that ownership ultimately originates in violence. But this fact does not prove that its abolition is morally justified, still less that it is economically desirable. On the contrary, economic action demands stable conditions, and the longer the chain of production the greater the need of maintaining stability. Probing this matter further, Dr. von Mises contends that not only the stability which makes an economic order possible, but the leisure which is the foundation of a civilized life, result from the division of labour. This and nothing else is what has made man a social animal. Society is his creation, and he has created it because he has found it advantageous. On this theory the alleged discrepancy between individual and public interest ceases to exist . . . . ¶In the whole body of Socialist doctrine nothing shocks him so much as the assertion that thought is conditioned by economic status. Thought, he insists, is conditioned by reason, and reason rises superior to circumstances and pursues universal truth. To have realized this is the achievement and justification of Liberalism; and it is because Dr. von Mises has apprehended the essential nobility of his faith -- for faith it is, though he would probably shudder at the word -- that he is led, unfortunately so often and so willingly, to pass beyond a critical standpoint into excesses of dogmatism and intolerance."

Unser Bremen. (November 1982). "Economic order can come about either by direction of the interested economic participants or through instruction from above which is made binding on all concerned, that is by order of a central bureaucracy." (Translated from the German)

Unsere Wirtschaft. (March 1982). "In the socialist view, market distribution is rejected because it does not provide for just distribution according to need. Further, the abolition of private property, presumably the source of 'exploitation,' is demanded. In this new edition of this almost classical work, Ludwig von Mises, one of the most important liberal economists and social theoreticians of our time, analyzes the fundamental problems of the socialist economy." (Translated from the German)

van Sickle, John. *La Revue d'Économie Politique.* Paris. 37 (1923). In this review, van Sickle says, he recommended Mises' *Socialism,* though with some reservations. See p.394 in John van Sickle's "What Mises Did for Me," *Toward Liberty: Essays in Honor of Ludwig von Mises.* Menlo Park, Calif.: Institute for Humane Studies, 1971. Vol.2, 392-397.

_____. *The American Economic Review.* 13:3 (September 1923) 533-536. *Socialism* "deserves careful reading by friend and foe of the movement. It is a reëxamination of the theory of socialism and a clear, vigorous, and convincing restatement of the case for individualism, much in the tone of a Manchester Liberal of the '60s . . . . ¶Whoever accepts the Austrian theory of value even in part . . . can hardly refuse to follow the reasoning of Professor Mises as to the impossibility of complete socialism. More open to criticism, however, is his conclusion that complete laissez-faire is the solution. All compromise he regards as merely the result of a breathing pause in the struggle of conflicting principles. Accordingly, he condemns as destructive forces all legal limitations on the hours and conditions of labor, public insurance, unemployment relief, trade unionism, labor representation in the councils of industry, public ownership, heavy taxation, and natural inflation . . . . If Professor Mises believes in the ultimate success of the appeal to reason, he need not fear the trade unions, or the presence of laborers in the councils of industry. Trade unionism has proved an educational force as well as at times a destructive one. Industrial democracy will prove as great an education in the intricate problems of production as political democracy has proved in that of citizenship'."

Wang, Fuchow. *Western Economics Encyclopedia.* (1971). Compiled by the Economic Research Department, Bank of Taiwan.

Wilkinson, Ellen. *Time and Tide.* London. (December 12, 1936). "In quiet and scholarly fashion, with great care and many footnotes showing great erudition, the author sets out to prove that socialism cannot exist and if it does it didn't ought to. But there are pearls scattered through Dr. von Mises' five-hundred and twenty-one closely printed pages."

Wirtschaftswoche. (May 14, 1982). "The unstable inter-war period, with economic crises in the West and socialist experiments in the East, saw debates in economic theory that have lasted until the present . . . . Concerning the widespread skepticism during that time of the market economy he [Mises] pointed out that without the market no real prices can be fashioned and without them allocation criteria for efficient production are lacking . . . . Ludwig von Mises' work, written more than 50 years ago, has lost none of its relevance today [1982]." (Translated from the German)

Yorkshire Post. Leeds (England). (December 21, 1936). "Many books have been written on the fallacies of Socialism; but nothing yet produced has equalled in completeness and painstaking scholarship this work of Professor Mises. He pulls down the structure brick by brick . . . . But in his enthusiasm for the self-adjusting nature of capitalism, Professor Mises extends his attack towards all forms of 'interventionism,' whether labour legislation or health or unemployment insurance . . . . Whatever their abstract validity, such arguments have little relevance to-day."

Theory and History (B-20)

Bien [Greaves], Bettina. *The Freeman.* Irvington, N.Y. 7:11 (November 1957) 59-62. "Since men first started to record events, they have sought to understand why things happened as they did. It has been suggested variously that all actions of man were predestined according to some superior over-all design; that they were merely the consequences of physiological phenomena; or that they arose solely from environmental conditions or characteristics of society or race. Such explanations, however, as Ludwig von Mises shows in his new book, are inconsistent with real life on this earth as we know it . . . . ¶The major part of the book is devoted to analyzing various interpretations of history and to comparing each in turn with the philosophy of utilitarianism which Mises calls 'a philosophy of individualism,' because it 'rejects universalism, collectivism, and totalitarianism'. . . . ¶Perhaps the most startling idea brought to light by Dr. Mises in this book concerns the role historians have played in promoting various types of collectivism."

_____. *Wall Street Journal.* (February 6, 1958). Comment on Peterson review (see below). "Mr. Peterson has written a very good review (Jan. 27) of a most important book. However, one quotation was inadvertently taken out of context . . . . The point Mr. Peterson was trying to make of the 'individuality' of history is well taken . . . . This, however, is very different from saying that there is no regularity in the sphere of human action. As a matter of fact, as Mises has explained in his writings, the subject of economics *is* the 'regularity in the concatenation and sequence of phenomena in the sphere of human action.' It is this regularity which makes it possible for men to understand economic laws and to make certain qualitative, although not quantitative, predictions in this field."

Branden, Nathaniel. *Book News.* Los Angeles: Academic Associates. 4 (June 1970) 8-9. Reviewed together with *Bureaucracy* (B-13) and *Omnipotent Government* (B-12). "*Theory and History* is a . . . philosophical work . . . and, I regret to say, contains a good deal of material with which I cannot agree -- for example, Professor von Mises' subjectivist theory of values. The book is concerned with theoretical interpretations of history, and contains a magnificent critique of dialectical materialism (to me, the most valuable chapter in the book); it also contains excellent critical commentaries on positivism, behaviorism and historicism."

Deutsche Zeitung. "Die Täuschung der allwissenden Wahrsager" [The Disappointment of an All-knowing Seer]. 48 (February 25-26, 1961) 20. Unfortunately bibliographers' photocopy of this review is incomplete; reviewer's name is missing. "Ludwig von Mises had taught economics for two decades at the University of Vienna, before he went to Geneva in 1934 and then later to America. He is among those professors whose migration has been considered an especially serious loss. It is only natural that not all of the best returned after the war. Men like Mises soon found recognition and a field of operation abroad that held them. Even at an advanced age, he has published a whole list of valuable books in America, the last, *Theory and History,* a work that allows us to recognize clearly the personality of this clear-thinking author. ¶The loss of valuable men who were driven to emigrate from Germany in 1933 and Austria in 1938, has been much deplored. There would be less concern at the loss of these men if their works at least were repatriated by translation into German. One such work that should be repatriated is the one discussed here. ¶*Theory and History* is an analysis of the relationship between human knowledge and human action. It offers a brilliant analysis of different modern philosophical schools and a devastating critique of Karl Marx and the so-called dialectical materialism . . . . ¶The most important chapter of the book deals with history and the philosophy of history." (Translated from the German)

The Economist. London. "Decline and Fall." (April 19, 1958) 204-205. "As a guide he [Mises] might be inadequate; his refusal to take cognisance of any modern development, whether welfare economics or the theory of imperfect competition (to say nothing of the abhorred heresies of Keynes) and his weakness for imputing discreditable motives to adversaries increasingly disqualified him for serious influence. But as a landmark, immovable and majestic, he was superb. Of this curious *olla-podrida* [hodgepodge] of a book it must be said, regretfully, that the landmark has crumbled . . . . ¶There are, certainly, good things in *Theory and History* . . . and at its worst it is better than the lamentable *Anti-Capitalistic Mentality* published last year. Abuse is not slung around quite so irresponsibly; assertion is more often backed by argument; attacks on an opponent are sometimes preceded by a recognisable statement of that opponent's case; and there is less sheer silliness, though some pearls may be discovered . . . . ¶Finally, to bad logic and historical travesty, Professor von Mises adds a capacity for ignoring current facts more remarkable than either. Had no experiments in collectivism ever been carried out by democratically-minded peoples, were it only possible to argue about them in a vacuum, it would already be hard to accept his Buttered-Slide-to-Serfdom argument against the slightest tampering with market forces. In the face of British, Scandinavian and Antipodean experience, to cite no other, his picture of blood-boltered tyranny, mass liquidation of heretics, and general Stalinism as the inevitable outcome of such tampering would be funny if it were not, all things considered, rather pitiable."

Eller, Cornelius A. *America.* New York. (March 22, 1958) 731-732. "No economist educated in American colleges and universities could have written this book . . . . the European commonly links economics with philosophy, theology and history, as Austrian-trained von Mises does so deftly in this book . . . . ¶His exposition and critique of dialectical materialism are perhaps the best this reviewer has ever seen. Anyone who is searching for a clear explanation and criticism of Marxism need look no farther. The same comment applies to the author's treatment of historicism . . . . ¶Very few readers will accept every position the author takes, but everyone who is interested in the social sciences will find his latest book full of provocative thought."

Entre Nous: Bulletin. Overseas Rotary Fellowship of New York. 17:2 (February 1958) 4. "Our best good wishes go to Member MISES for this great work which adds another laurel to his credit."

Fitzsimons, M. A. *Natural Law Forum.* Notre Dame Law School. 1:1 (1958) 384ff. "Ludwig von Mises has the reputation of being an obsessed defender of economic liberalism . . . . He knows only one thing, and for him the one thing is all-important. His limitation, however, is the ground of his strength -- for everything is acutely scrutinized in relation to economic liberalism . . . . ¶The tone is eighteenth century, and not by accident . . . . The waxed body of Jeremy Bentham, seated on a chair in the Senior Common Room of University College, London, has the fate of all philosophers -- Bentham now has a disciple who is more Benthamite than the master. ¶There are echoes here of Adam Smith's invisible hand and Hegel's 'craftiness of reason,' although von Mises does not explicitly recognize them . . . . ¶In his eyes the natural law tradition yields only a bewildering diversity of doctrines. This is just enough as an historical judgment. But the sequel is astonishing . . . . To the credit of natural law is its rejection of legal positivism. But, perniciously, the doctrine abstracted and supplanted the teachings of liberal social philosophy. For example, it preached the biological equality of all men. In so outraging nature the tradition of natural law finally caused wars, nationalism, and racism. ¶Here, it is finally necessary to interject the single word -- nonsense. This reviewer has severely held himself to the task of clarifying the thought of a writer with whom he rarely agrees, and never wholeheartedly. Von Mises' knowledge of history is strangely old-fashioned, as might be expected from his Benthamism. He adds little to the subject of his book, *Theory and History*, apart from the recognition that history is not a science but an inquiry which must proceed in the examination of evidence by means of logic, with a knowledge of psychology, not the science of the physiologists and behaviorists but of the human spirit. The historian must, also, know the universally valid laws of economics. To fail to do so is to compound human error and to yield to historicism. Where Acton was a hanging judge of historical actions in the name of morality, von Mises is a hanging judge in the name of liberal economics. The book is a lesson in the primacy of that discipline, and a warning to historians to respect it . . . . ¶He is merciless with historicists, positivists, and believers in historical cycles. He scores on philosophers of the history of civilization who glibly contemplate the universals of civilization, when, as yet, no one has been able to define and comprehend what a civilization is, or, as a matter of history, describe the life course of a civilization. He rightly criticizes all those who would imprison man's future in the dungeons of their speculative patterns. This is no small service, when history and the philosophy of history face the terrible temptation of intruding upon philosophy and theology to usurp the functions which the latter in their parlous condition so poorly discharge."

Greaves, Percy L. Jr. "Ideas and History." *Christian Economics.*   New York. 9:23 (December 24, 1957) 1, 3. Part 1 of a 2-part review. "Most Americans are now worried about the Soviet Union. They are scared of its sputniks, its nuclear power and its intercontinental missiles . . . . But should we really fear the temporary material trappings of dictatorships? . . . . ¶In his latest book, *Theory and History,* Professor Ludwig von Mises analyzes many widely held ideas and exposes the fallacies inherent in a number of them . . . . ¶The tyranny that we should fear most is the tyranny of an uninformed majority that does not listen to sound ideas, but acts instead on the basis of unsound ideas -- ideas that produce results contrary to those sought . . . . ¶Today we often hear that only the strong can be free. This places the cart before the horse. A true saying would be that only a society of free and moral men can be strong. Men who are not free can take no steps to protect themselves or improve their situation . . . . ¶This great book is for scholars seriously interested in understanding the genesis and solutions of the problems of our day. Those who take the trouble to read and digest it will have a better understanding of the ideas that can save our civilization . . . . ¶Popularly held ideas are far more important than guns, bombs, material wealth or temporary political power in determining the shape of things to come."

_____. "Faith and Reason." *Christian Economics.* New York. 10:1 (January 7, 1958) 1, 3. Part 2 of a 2-part review. "In every man's life there is a place for faith and a place for reason. No man can live by faith alone, nor can any man live by reason alone. Faith supplies man with his goals in life. Reason supplies him with the means he uses in his attempts to reach these goals . . . . ¶Christ left man to choose between those actions which are in conformity with loving 'thy neighbor as thyself,' and those which are not . . . . Sound human reasoning must always precede the selection of proper actions for attaining any human goal. ¶No one knows this better than Ludwig von Mises, the great world renowned economist. As an economist, he resorts to reason . . . . But Mises is more than an economist. He is also a great scholar of history and human nature. As such, he knows well man's need for faith and religion. This is quite evident in many passages of his latest book, *Theory and History*. . . . ¶The Enlightenment came when man started to use his reasoning powers for purposes other than conquest by force or fraud. Some of the wiser then began to reason that voluntary social cooperation -- the free market -- could provide everyone with more satisfaction and happiness. Despite the quite evident harmony of this thought with Christian teachings, the organized churches remained for decades on the side of privilege and the status quo . . . . ¶One reason for this antipathy of some religious men for right reason has been the survival of the old dogma that condemns self-interest and exalts indifference to material riches . . . . ¶There is nothing wrong with satisfying men's material wants, although as Mises writes: 'It is justifiable if ethics and religion tell people that they ought to make better use of the well-being that capitalism brings them; if they try to induce the faithful to substitute better ways of spending for the objectionable habits of feasting, drinking, and gambling; if they condemn lying and cheating and praise the moral values implied in purity of family relations and in charity to those in need. But it is irresponsible to condemn one social system and to recommend its replacement by another system without having fully investigated the economic consequences of each . . . . ¶It must be reiterated that no reasoning founded on the principles of philosophical ethics or of the Christian creed can reject as fundamentally unjust an economic system that succeeds in improving the material conditions of all people, and assign the epithet "just" to a system that tends to spread poverty and starvation'."

Hacker, Louis. "A Testament of Faith in Man and in His Capacity for Growth." *The New York Times Book Review.* (December 29, 1957) 6, 13. "Ludwig von Mises, who, in a long lifetime, has again and again raised his voice in defense of liberty -- his *Human Action, Omnipotent Government, Bureaucracy* and *Socialism* are all richly figured variations on the same large theme -- now at the age of 76 takes up the many philosophical problems involved in the study and uses of history, once more as they relate to freedom. Mr. Mises is a committed man and his refusal to compromise is understandable, even if, here and there, the reader will refuse to follow him all the way . . . . ¶Capitalism's accomplishments are visible everywhere. Thus, in the face of all contemporary talk of planning, stabilization and intervention, Mr. Mises proclaims his bold defiance. He believes in man's capacity to think and to apply to his problems the methods of reason."

Hazlitt, Henry. "Our Moral Disarmament." *Newsweek.* (December 9, 1957). Mr. Hazlitt discusses the "serious" collaboration with Communist jailers, the "brainwashing" of U. S. prisoners during the war in Korea. "We face in the world today a supreme irony. Millions of people are fanatically devoted to the slave system called Communism and are willing to die for it. Yet few of us are zealously devoted to its opposite, the system of capitalism, or willing to die for it by that name . . . . [F]ew of us are willing to make sacrifices to preserve this system even when it bears a true name, such as free enterprise . . . . ¶This paradox is discussed in the course of a brilliant new philosophical work by Ludwig von Mises, *Theory and History.* Mises points out that the slavery and debasement under Russian Communism, or any system of complete Socialism, are not accidental . . . . ¶Yet leading writers and scientists of the West are contemptuous of economic freedom, the basis of all freedom, and speak with admiration of a system that eclipses all tyrannies of the past in pitiless persecution of dissenters."

Hessen, Robert A. "Mises Contra Marxism." *The Rampart.* New York: Queens College. 19 (February 18, 1958) 5, 7. In this book, Mises "exposes the countless contradictions, confusions, evasions and deliberate falsifications of the Marxists which entirely negate their conclusions and [he] tears away the thin veneer of intellectual respectability which covers them. That Marx was a vile polemicist without any original contribution to economic or social thought is discernible to any alert student of the history of economic doctrines, but less well-known are the inherent absurdities within these eclectically-derived doctrines."

Meyer, Frank S. "Philosophy of History." *The National Book Foundation.* Burlingame, Calif. [February 1958]. Reviewed in conjunction with Karl A. Wittfogel's *Oriental Despotism* and Eric Voegelin's *Order and History: Volume I, Israel and Revelation*. "These three books represent three different facets of a movement in thought which may well turn out to be the most significant intellectual development of the mid-twentieth century: a fundamental transformation in the way of looking at history that has prevailed for more than one hundred years. Each of them in its own sphere contributes to the restoration of a concept of the freedom of men in history all but forgotten beneath the weight of long-dominant theories of historical determinism."

[Nymeyer, Frederick]. "Ludwig von Mises's New Book: *Theory and History.*" *Progressive Calvinism.* South Holland, Ill. 3:11 (November 1957) 348-352. "Mises's new book, *Theory and History*, is a book in the field of epistemology. It is a study of what can be known and what cannot be known; it is also a study of the basic difference between the natural sciences and the sciences of human action; it is further a study of defective methodologies and erroneous ideas in the field of the sciences of human action. Mises considers in his book the 'limits of what can be known,' and he makes his own original and penetrating analysis, starting with his special field, economics . . . . ¶For Mises a statement is not necessarily right *because* somebody declared he was a spokesman for God; for Mises something is necessarily right if it is logically and pragmatically right. He is, therefore, basically an unqualified *utilitarian* in the best sense . . . . We believe that it would be impossible for genuine reason and genuine revelation to disagree. We see no conflict. Where Mises has one leg to stand upon, namely reason, we have two, namely reason and revelation . . . . ¶Mises's thinking is anti-socialist and in favor of freedom. His book is full of strictures regarding the fallacies and absurdities of socialism."

Peterson, William H. "History and the Haze of Theory." *The Wall Street Journal.* 151:18 (January 27, 1958) 10. "The inevitable correlation of theory and the interpretation of history is a problem that involves other walks of life besides historians. Statesmen, businessmen, stock investors, generals, doctors, newspaper-writers, lawyers -- all, like the historian, must analyze the past to understand the present or anticipate the future. The wrong theory, and errors, are highly likely. The historian may lose perspective and draw wrong conclusions -- the investor may lose on his investment, the doctor may lose his patient, the general a war. ¶Theory, then, is critical in unlocking the elusive secrets of history . . . . ¶Can theory be derived from history? . . . History is too complex, too variable, too much of a kaleidoscope to yield 'laws of history,' which von Mises says is a contradiction in terms. Declares the author: 'There is no regularity in the concatenation and sequence of phenomena in the sphere of human action.'" (See Bien (above) for comments.)

Raebeck, Albert J. *The Ethical Outlook.* New York: American Ethical Union. 42:4 (July/August 1958) 138-139. "The method of economics is logical reasoning, and the results are correct or erroneous, not good or bad. But because people in general agree about certain ends -- e.g., improved material well-being -- the statement of the consequences of human action can readily be interpreted by people to govern their choice of policies. ¶These points will probably be accepted by most readers. But Mises contrasts his position almost exclusively with Marxism, against which he rails intemperately . . . . ¶[H]istory should be accepted . . . without reading into it any grand design or inexorable laws. Here, too, Marxian dialectical materialism is the major illustration he uses of erroneous views. There is no basis in history for the assumed inevitability of socialism -- socialism will result only if men bring it about voluntarily."

Reischer, Otto R. *The American Scholar.* 27:2 (Spring 1958) 240-242. "This important book deals with the epistemology of the social sciences, which have as ultimate data the value judgments of individuals and the ideas that engender those value judgments. The knowledge we have about this is not 'theoretical,' like the knowledge the natural sciences provide about natural events, but 'historical,' serving mainly to elucidate past events . . . . ¶Economics studies the choice among means to attain selected ends in the social sphere and shows that social co-operation is the great means for the attainment of all ends. And no unanimity with regard to value judgments is required to make social co-operation work. ¶This proposition is denied by dialectical materialism and related egalitarian philosophies, all tending toward totalitarianism. Von Mises therefore devotes a major portion of his book to a brilliant refutation of dialectical materialism and presents a stout defense of capitalist economics. Unfortunately he imputes to business an intrinsic goodness not always discernible in the real world."

Rothbard, Murray N. "Theory and History." *Austrian Economics Newsletter*. Auburn, Ala.: Ludwig von Mises Institute. 5:2 (Fall 1984) 1-3. An excerpt from Rothbard's Preface to the 1985 edition: "Mises' fourth and last great work, *Theory and History* (1957), has made remarkably little impact, and has rarely been cited even by the young economists of the recent Austrian revival. It remains by far the most neglected masterwork of Mises. And yet it provides the philosophical backstop and elaboration of the philosophy underlying *Human Action*. It is Mises' great methodological work, explaining the basis of his approach to economics, and providing scintillating critiques of such fallacious alternatives as historicism, scientism, and Marxian dialectical materialism." Excerpts also in *The Free Market*. Burlingame, Calif.: Ludwig von Mises Institute. 7:10 (October 1989) 4.

_____. *Libertarian Review.*   Washington, D.C. 4:6 (June 1975) 1.   Reviewed together with *Omnipotent Government* (B-12). "*Theory and History* is more than useful; it is one of Mises' greatest works, and indeed one of the great works in this century on the philosophy and methodology of the social sciences. Its neglect is no less than an intellectual tragedy . . . . Implicitly refuting all of modern determinist (including mathematical) economics and other social sciences, Mises shows that each event resulting from the action of individual human beings is necessarily unique . . . . Adherents of the Austrian school of economics have been accused of being antiempirical, mystical a priorists, divorced from economic reality. But a thorough reading of *Theory and History* reveals quite the opposite; it is the Misesians -- the Austrians -- who have the proper respect for the unique, empirical events of human history, whereas it is the pretentious quantitative 'economic scientists' who necessarily abuse and distort the rich empirical facts of history in order to arrive at their allegedly 'scientific' quantitative 'laws' and (invariably wrong) forecasts of the future . . . . The only weak part of the book is Mises' defense of subjectivist ethics, a position stemming from his utilitarian approach to ethics. But this is the only weak spot in a glorious and highly significant work."

Times Literary Supplement. London. "*Theory and History* is a defense of individualism in the social sciences . . . an excellent book. It is original, interesting, and lucid." Quoted in *Conservative Book Club Bulletin* (January 1976).

Western Economics Encyclopedia. (1971) Compiled by the Economic Research Department, Bank of Taiwan.

The Theory of Money and Credit (B-2)   (*Theorie des Geldes und der Umlaufsmittel*, 1912, 1924; English translation, 1934, enlarged with a new essay, 1953, 1971, 1980)

When this book was published (1912), Georg Friedrich Knapp's *Staatliche Theorie des Geldes* (Leipzig, 1905) was the rage in European academia. Knapp's book was translated into English (*The State Theory of Money*, 1924) and the theoretical portions have been reprinted by Augustus M. Kelley (1973). Knapp's thesis, that money was whatever the State said it was, was widely accepted. Thus the academic world was ill-prepared to comprehend Mises' radically different approach and his argument that money was a market phenomenon, the value of which was determined by the ideas and subjective values of market participants.

In 1928, Mises commented on the reception given his 1912 book: "Sixteen years ago when I presented the Circulation Credit Theory of the crisis in the first German edition of my book on *The Theory of Money and Credit*, I encountered ignorance and stubborn rejection everywhere, especially in Germany. The reviewer for Schmoller's Yearbook [Somary] declared: 'The conclusions of the entire work [are] simply not discussable.' The reviewer for Conrad's Yearbook [Lotz] stated: 'Hypothetically, the author's arguments should not be described as completely wrong; they are at least coherent.' But his [Lotz's] final judgment was 'to reject it anyhow.' Anyone who follows current developments in economic literature closely, however, knows that things have changed basically since then. The doctrine which was ridiculed once is widely accepted today [1928]. LvM" These comments appeared in Mises' *Monetary Stabilization and Cyclical Policy* (B-7), now translated and included in *On the Manipulation of Money and Credit* (B-24); see p.60 n.6.

Professor Mises once told this compiler [B.B.G.] that he would like very much to see the reviews of the first edition of his book on money translated into English and published. Therefore, we are reproducing those early reviews here in full. They reveal the incredulous response of the academic world of 1912 to Mises' radical monetary theory.

T.S.A. *Manchester Guardian.* England. "The Theory of Money." (January 21, 1935). "Austrian ideas are increasingly affecting economic thought at London and elsewhere; and many of the conceptions round which controversy rages to-day (and will rage tomorrow) derive from Mises. Both in the treatise itself and in the introduction written for this English edition the author sets down his views boldly. He holds that one of the worst fates that can befall a community is that its money should become the plaything of politics. Hence he is for gold against paper, for the currency school against the banking school, for the restrictionists against the expansionists. And he sees in the extension of fiduciary media by the banks a danger only less menacing than the inflationary tendencies of Governments."

Banker. England. (February, 1935). "Recent developments are covered by a Preface to the English edition. In this Professor von Mises discloses quite an unusual degree of dogmatism. He accuses Great Britain of suspending the gold standard 'instead of employing the customary and never-failing remedy of raising the bank rate'. . . . It would be unfair, however, to condemn the book for its preface. It is doubtless a standard work in monetary literature, and its translation was a welcome undertaking."

Bien [Greaves], Bettina. *The Freeman.* New York. 4:15 (April 19, 1954) 535. "Dr. Mises starts with the fundamental thesis that 'the function of money is to facilitate the business of the market by acting as a common medium of exchange,' and he continues by demonstrating the importance to modern economics of the subjective (marginal utility) theory of value for the development of a complete and satisfactory theory of money and credit in our changing world."

Braun, Martha Stephanie. "Zwei wichtige Beiträge zur Geldtheorie unserer Tage" [Two important studies on the monetary theory of our time]. *Zeitschrift für Volkswirtschaft und Sozialpolitik.* New Series:5 (1925-26) 160-164. Reviewed together with Fritz Machlup's *Die Goldkernwährung* [The Gold Exchange Standard].

Burchardt, Fritz. "Entwicklungsgeschichte der monetären Konjunkturtheorie" [The Historical Development of the Monetary Theory of the Trade Cycle]. *Weltwirtschaftliches Archiv.* 28:1 (July 1928) 77-143. A review of books by several authors including Wicksell, Hahn, Hawtrey, Fisher and Mises. Paraphrasing reviewer's remarks on the 1924 edition of Mises book (pp.123-125): The unique characteristic of Mises' theory lies in the attempt to explain the monetary business cycle on the basis of the Austrian marginal utility theory. It starts from the position that equilibrium between the supply and demand for subsistence depends on the interest rate. A reduction of the bank interest rate below the "natural" rate is possible when the interest rate is forced down and banks are relieved of the responsibility of redeeming their notes. Mises' theory consists of three points: (1) periodic interference with interest policy leads to the cycle and explains the general tendency to higher prices; (2) it also leads to more roundabout means of production; (3) the adjustments explain prices, production and the cyclical bust. The last two factors are non-monetary, and yet they are the cause of cyclical fluctuations.

Chase, Harvey S. "Bank Deposits versus Money." Paper prepared for the Annual Meeting of the American Economic Association, N.Y., Session on Banking, December 27, 1935. Printed privately. 8pp. Not included in the AEA's *Papers and Proceedings* of that meeting. Chase, a CPA, describes the process of credit expansion and then refers to the English edition of *The Theory of Money and Credit* which "provides American students and economists with a work whose logical unity and power of economic analysis has never been surpassed . . . . The logic of his presentation is clear as well as profound." In a "Sequel," Chase writes: "In continental circles Prof. von Mises' phenomenal work has long been regarded as the standard text book on money and credit. Professor Lionel Robbins of the London School of Economics says of it, 'I know few works which convey a more profound impression of the logical unity and the power of modern economic analysis'." Chase quotes extensively from the book.

Chronicle. Augusta, Georgia. November 13, 1934. "Recognized in Europe as a standard and important treatise on the fundamental questions of banking and finance."

del Vecchio, Gustavo. "Questioni fondamentali sul valore della moneta" [Fundamental Questions of the value of money]. *Giornale degli Economisti e Rivista di Statistica.* 55:3 (September 1917) 117-174. According to the article's "Summary," Section III discusses Mises and Wicksell.

Dick, Ernst. "Die Zwiespältigkeit der Zinstheorie" [The Dichotomy of Interest Theory]. *Jahrbücher für Nationalökonomie und Statistik* (Conrads Jahrbuch). 131 (July/December 1929). III:76; II:65-89.

The Economist. London. "Money and Credit." (January 5, 1935) 16-17. "It is right that an English version should be available; Professor Robbins should be warmly encouraged in his laudable work of promoting and editing these translations. And if he tends a little to overstate their merits in his introductory notes, the weighty cadences of which are beginning to ring familiarly in the ears of economists, it would be most ungenerous to cavil or to grudge him these paeans . . . . ¶The section that will best repay the attention of the reader interested in modern problems, both on account of its inherent interest and because its doctrines have recently been revived in a challenging way by members of the Austrian school, occurs in a chapter towards the end of the book (part III, chapter V) . . . . ¶He discusses the reduction by the banks of the market rate of interest below the equilibrium rate . . . . ¶It cannot be said that Professor von Mises' theory in this section is convincing. But it is immensely to his credit that he made an attempt to tackle this particular problem in a fundamental way at a time when no such treatment was to be found in English economic literature."

_____. (October 17, 1953) 173. "This massive classic . . . is now re-published with a postscript on 'Monetary Reconstruction' inspired by the events of the intervening decades. Those events have not altered Professor von Mises's views; unchangeably, magnificently, he remains the limiting case, some would say the *reductio ad absurdum* of liberal economic opinion . . . . His debating style, packed with innuendo, imputation of motive, arrogance and plain misrepresentation, recalls that of the Marxists themselves; and he never explicitly faces the political necessities -- the outlawing of trade unionism, the total razing of the welfare state, the extirpation of every form of group solidarity -- implicit in his proposals for economic salvation."

Eucken, Walter. *Schmollers Jahrbuch für Gesetzgebung, Verwaltung und Volkswirtschaft im Deutschen Reich.* 50:2 (1926) 153-157. Eucken criticizes Mises on several counts. "An entire line of scholars, who generally consider themselves of the marginal utility school, have turned away from using marginal utility theory in monetary theory. Mises believes, however, that he has overcome the recognized difficulty. He goes back to the point at which the objective exchange value of money 'ceases to be monetary value, and is commodity value only' . . . . ¶This theory of Mises has already been contradicted a number of times. It has been objected that it is impossible to mix a logical analysis with a chronological regressum (Anderson, *Value of Money*, 1922, p.104). Or else it is rejoined that theory is helped very little by pre-history (von Bortkiewicz, "Der subjective Geldwert" [The Subjective Value of Money]. *Schmoller's Jahrbuch*, 1920. 44:178/179) On this point one must agree with the critics . . . . ¶Also the division of money substitutes into money certificates and fiduciary media seems to me unfortunate. Then too bank notes and giro money, if not fully covered or not covered at all by money in the Mises sense, are assigned in part to money certificates and in part to fiduciary media; thus creating unnecessary complications . . . . ¶Still the work of Mises provokes discussion on other basic questions which offer a framework for further discourse. In spite of all objections, it must be emphasized once again that the work merits a prominent place in the newer German literature on monetary theory." (Translated from the German)

The Gold Standard News: *Bulletin #50.* Latrobe, Penna.: Gold Standard League, (n.d.) 3. Reviewing the enlarged (1953) edition: "Readers of von Mises' *Socialism* and *Human Action* will not be surprised to find again a merciless exposure of the sham of managed currencies . . . . ¶The author gives a detailed plan for his proposed procedure for restoring the gold standard in the United States. He doesn't make a convincing argument for the abolishment of five and ten dollar bills, and completely fails to substantiate his thesis against the $35 parity standard . . . . ¶In other respects the volume is as sound a book as exists on the theory of money and credit."

Gross, William J. *News-Sentinel.* Fort Wayne, Indiana. (July 20, 1935). "Of course, kings and republics have repeatedly refused to recognize the fact that in an economic system based on private ownership of the means of production, no governmental regulation can alter the 'terms of exchange' except by altering the facts that determine them. But as Dr. von Mises points out, '. . . . they could have achieved their aim only in a socialist state with a centralized organization of production and distribution'". . . . ¶The commodity dollar is attacked with reference to the considerable dubiety attaching to the scientific correctness of 'index numbers' and to the practicability of turning them to satisfactory account in eliminating those unintended modifications of long-term contracts that arise from variations in the value of money as referred to various commodities."

Guillebaud, C. W. "Money and Credit." *Cambridge Review.* England. (February 5, 1935). "It was largely in reaction against the [statist] teachings of Knapp and his school that Professor Mises brought out the first edition of the present work in 1912, and, coming when it did it undoubtedly represented a very considerable achievement . . . . ¶The chief merits of Professor Mises book when it appeared in 1912 were, firstly, the restatement of the classical doctrines in regard to the value of money, a restatement which was characterised by much subtle and acute reasoning; and secondly, the fresh presentation of

Wicksell's now famous distinction between the natural and money rates of interest . . . . But two questions present themselves -- firstly, whether the orthodoxy of the nineteenth century in fact represents the last word that even then could have been said on the subject of monetary theory; secondly, whether the circumstances of the present time may not be so far removed from those which prevailed when the classical economists formulated their doctrines, that the conclusions of the nineteenth century are no longer applicable in their entirety to-day."

Hahn, Albert. *Archiv für Sozialwissenschaft und Sozialpolitik.* 53 (1924-25) 509-516.

Handbuch der Finanzwissenschaft in Verbindung mit zahlreichen Fachmännern des In- und Auslandes [Financial Handbook, in Cooperation with Domestic and Foreign Specialists]. Wilhelm Gerloff & Franz Meisel, eds. Tübingen: J.C.B. Mohr [Paul Siebeck], 1925. 7:149. 800. Discusses 2nd edition (1924) as well as the work of other monetary theorists. (pp.57-85)

Hawtrey, R. G. *The Economic Journal.* (September 1935) 509-518. "It is not necessary now to add anything to the very judicious appraisement of the general merits of the work made by Mr. Keynes, the reviewer of 1914. [*Economic Journal*, September 1914; see below] . . . . ¶In what follows I propose rather to offer some detailed criticisms of the economic reasoning contained in the book . . . . ¶He [Mises] has a special antipathy to the 'nominalist' theory of money, typified in the school of Knapp. He detests Etatism, and holds that it is usage, not law, that establishes anything as a medium of exchange, and that legal tender laws, which appear to prescribe the form of money, are usually in reality no more than a recognition of this usage." Hawtrey then criticizes Mises' description of the consequences for the market of different kinds of money (commodity, fiat, and credit), and characterizes as "far-fetched" Mises' theory that the value of money is explained by tracing it "back and back to the time when the material of which the commodity money is composed was valued merely as a commodity." Hawtrey also severely criticizes Mises' analysis of the consequences when banks reduce the rate of interest they charge: "The idea that expansion [of credit] will be brought to an end by the exhaustion of the 'subsistence fund' is quite baseless . . . . ¶If our lapse from the gold standard was (as it seems) 'an attempt to carry out an economic reform from the monetary side,' does he [Mises] condemn it as necessarily leading to the sequence of excessive expansion, crisis and depression? According to his doctrine the danger is that, if the banks, which have in the past, as he says, invariably of themselves put a limit to such an expansion, fail to do so, the country will be faced eventually with an exhaustion of the 'subsistence fund,' which will no longer be sufficient to sustain the excessive investment activity which will be in progress! Surely there will be time enough to think of the 'subsistence fund' when the investment activity has begun. And meanwhile the depreciation of the pound seems to be the most logical and natural correction of the disproportion between prices and costs."

Hazlitt, Henry. "The Return to Gold." *Newsweek* (Business Tides Column). (July 6, 1953). "No two economists seem to agree in every detail regarding the monetary policies that should now be adopted and the order in which particular steps should be taken, but Mises' discussion seems to me on the whole the soundest, most thorough, and most illuminating that has so far appeared. ¶No one, for example, has explained better than Mises the detailed process of inflation and the exact nature of the evils it entails . . . . ¶Today, unfortunately, only a minority of economists agree that it is both possible and desirable to return eventually to a gold standard. When it comes to such questions as *when? under what conditions? how?* and *at what rate?* even this minority of gold-standard advocates is split 40 different ways . . . . ¶But though there will be dissent from some of his detailed conclusions, Mises' answer cannot be neglected by any serious student of the problem of returning to a gold standard. And that return is imperative if the world is not to drift even deeper into monetary chaos."

_____. *The National Book Foundation.* Burlingame, Calif. (May 1959) 1-4. A triple review of Mises' book on money plus Benjamin M. Anderson's *Economics and the Public Welfare* (1949) and Costantino Bresciani-

Turroni's *The Economics of Inflation* (1937). "These three books are all authoritative contributions to the subjects of money, credit, and inflation . . . . The volume by von Mises is exclusively theoretical, though it is full of concrete historical illustrations . . . . ¶The postscript to the Mises volume, written in 1952, applies the major principles of sound money and credit policy to the current scene."

Hellwig, Hans. "Die Vorzüge der Bankfreiheit: Marktgeld ist besser als Staatsgeld" [The Advantages of Free Banking: Market Money is Better than State Money]. *Deutsche Zeitung*. Stuttgart. 12:100 (December 14, 1957) 23. Hellwig compares recently enacted West German legislation -- the law against limiting competition (July 27, 1957) and the Deutsche Bundesbank Law (July 26, 1957) -- with proposals made by John Maynard Keynes and concludes that the first will no more protect competition than the second will safeguard the currency. "Only if governments are removed from having any influence on the determination of money supply, be it with the help of the gold standard or by some other means, need a dangerous inflation no longer be feared. Objections to the Quantity Theory of Money rest largely on ignorance of this theory . . . . ¶Ludwig von Mises, who recommends 100% cover of credit money with cash, considers this proposal only a stepping stone. He leaves no doubt that he stands firmly for the view that free banking, with no intervention of the state at all in money and banking affairs, is the best solution to the monetary problem . . . . Formulae for minimum reserves, even up to 100%, are only a hindrance, a means to accustom the public to state regulation of money, without accomplishing what is expected . . . . ¶The advantages of full free banking, encompassing notes and deposits, as opposed to free banking limited only to deposits, are not economic, but politico-psychological in nature. Unhampered free banking, tied to the circulation of gold coins, makes government-inflation impossible once and for all." (Translated from the German)

Hilferding, Rudolf. *Die Neue Zeit*. Stuttgart: German Social Democratic Party. 30:2 (1912) 1024-1027. Rudolf Hilferding (1877-1941) served as German Finance Minister during the German hyper-inflation (August-October 1923) and again in 1928-1929. Page references are to the first German (1912) edition of Mises' book. Hilferding's review is translated and printed here in full:
"The leaders of the marginal utility theory have a very lofty opinion of their doctrine. In spite of the fact that this arrogance involves a psychological process which actually works in opposition to the methodology the school professes, they transmit it to their followers. It is inspired by a truly religious faith, which even an almost 40 year voyage through the wilderness of fruitless speculation has done nothing to diminish. This doctrine actually appears to be undying, to enjoy a kind of super-immortality. ¶The school lives, so to speak, by suicide. Every marginal utility theoretician inevitably begins by referring resolutely to the very serious errors perpetrated by his predecessors. And, says the reader thankfully, may they rest in peace. But this positive exposition is followed by a negative portion. This second part furnishes material to be similarly demolished in turn by successors of the cheerful executioner. And so, round and round on the Merry-go-round. In pious Austria, monuments are erected in memory of every such intellectual disaster. University lecturers and professors blaze the holy trail the school has trod since Carl Menger, freely emulating Gossen who invented it, sat with Böhm-Bawerk in judgment on university appointments. For the marginal utility school is not only a partisan of monopoly in theory -- it knows also how to put monopoly power into practice. This is probably the school's one and only bond that actually links it with reality. ¶Among the school's unsolved problems -- and all its problems are unsolved -- the monetary problem naturally occupies a place of prime importance. It is the real cross its theoreticians bear. Under its weight, so far, they have all collapsed. If it hadn't been for this calamity, salvation for the erring human race might have been found. The question to be answered is: How, according to subjective value theory, is the exchange ratio between money and commodities determined? The 'value' of a commodity is fixed by its marginal utility, i.e. by the utility ascribed to the last unit of its supply. Thus, to use the famous example which reflects so faithfully the daily events on the world market: If I have a bag of grain which is absolutely necessary to sustain my life, I shall on that account attribute to it a high value. On the other hand, if I own five bags, then I shall value much less the fifth bag, which is useful only for feeding parakeets, as my other needs for

grain have already been satisfied by the first four bags. This evaluation of the fifth bag, the last unit of supply, is the marginal utility and this determines for the lucky owner the value of the grain. What then is the situation with respect to the marginal utility of money? The utility of money consists of nothing but the utility of the goods which may be received for the money. Or, as Professor Wieser expresses it: 'The exchange value of money is the anticipated value in use of the things to be acquired for the money.' How many commodities I receive, however, depends again on the value of the money and thus on its use. It is a never-ending circle. ¶The contribution of von Mises lies in pointing out in the first (positive) portion of his work how prior attempts of the 'psychological' school to measure value went awry. Then he describes the dilemma in which subjective value theoreticians have found themselves as follows: 'Consideration of the subjective value of money without discussion of its objective exchange-value is impossible. In contrast to commodities, money would never be used unless it had an objective exchange-value or purchasing power. The subjective value of money always depends on the subjective value of the other economic goods that can be obtained in exchange for it. Its subjective value is in fact a derived concept. If we wish to estimate the significance that a given sum of money has, in view of the known dependence upon it of a certain satisfaction, we can do this only on the assumption that the money possesses a given objective exchange-value . . . . Whenever money is valued by anybody it is because he supposes it to have a certain purchasing power.' (p.95) ¶The bankruptcy of the subjective theory of value, its inability to explain the basic problem of economics, could not be more clearly stated. But if theory retches at the task, history rides to the rescue. We hear a fable of long, long ago: 'It follows that a valuation of money is possible only on the assumption that the money has a certain objective exchange-value. Such a foundation (!) is necessary before the bridge (!) between satisfaction and "useless" money can be crossed.' (The wealth of metaphors only betrays the vagueness of the ideas. If the exchange value of the money is given, then no room remains for subjective evaluation. In place of a 'foundation' we would then have a positive assertion and also a stable monetary value. This, however, as we shall see, Mises cannot accept.) 'Since money, as such, does not have a direct connection with any human want, individuals can conceive of its utility and consequently of its value, only because it has a definite purchasing power. But it is easy to see that this supposition cannot be anything but an expression of the exchange ratio between money and commodities existing momentarily on the market. ¶'Once an exchange-ratio between money and commodities has been established on the market, it continues to exercise an influence beyond the period during which it is maintained; it provides the basis for the further valuation of money. Thus, the past objective exchange-value of money has a certain significance for its present and future valuation. The money prices of today are linked with those of yesterday and before, and with those of tomorrow and after. ¶'But this alone will not suffice to explain the problem of the historical continuity in the value of money; it only postpones the explanation.' (Very true!) ¶And now it comes: ¶'The earliest value of money historically was clearly the value which the goods used as money possessed -- thanks to their suitability for satisfying human wants in other ways -- at the moment when they were first used as common media of exchange. When an individual first (!) acquired an object for use as a medium of exchange rather than for consumption he valued it according to the objective exchange-value it already had on the market (!) by reason of its "industrial" usefulness plus, for the first time, an additional consideration (but please be a little more specific. How much more? That would be very important to know!) on account of the possibility of using it as a medium of exchange. The earliest value of money traces back to the commodity value of the monetary material.' (p.108ff) ¶What an appealing idea! ¶If we buy a 10¢ roll of bread at a neighborhood delicatessen, we are bound to the past in a way which was hitherto mysteriously secret, but has now been at long last illuminated. This link with history is not something called to mind by the dryness of the bread; nor is it the despicable value in use; it is the objective exchange value that joins us directly with the time when, for the first time, one of our barbaric ancestors took a gold ring from his chest in order to buy with it a crust of bread. But perhaps we should go back still further? Isn't there a 'recurring relationship,' as Knapp would say, between cowry shells, or cattle, money and gold money? The school's interpretation of history obviously derives from the loftiness of its psychological point of view. ¶Mises unfortunately tarries no longer to explain his notion of holding the psychological attitude of the far distant past responsible for the manifestation of economic evaluation by living individuals in the present-day economy. He hastens to abandon his 'foundation' and to leap on the bridge to the present. To be sure he recognizes that there is a difference in principle between the formation of the exchange value of money and that of other economic goods (p.111); that in actuality a fundamental contradiction exists between his 'historical' derivation of the value of money and the psychological basis of the theory, the cohesiveness of which is punctured if exchange relations are determined not by the evaluations of the living but to some extent (the question is how much?) by persons long since dead and gone. This 'objective' value of money, however, resurrected as it is from the grave, generally has no significance for the future. For the 'historically transmitted value is transformed by the market without regard to its historically produced content' (p.119). This happens in this way: The available money supply changes -- let us say it increases. This 'always means an increase in the cash holdings, i.e. an increase in the wealth, of specific individuals in the economy. These may be either the issuers of the fiat or credit money or the producers of the substance of which commodity money is made. For these persons, the ratio between the demand for money and the stock of it is altered; they have a relative superfluity of money and a relative shortage of other economic goods. The immediate consequence of both circumstances is that the marginal utility to them of the monetary unit diminishes as compared with that of the economic goods concerned. This necessarily influences their behavior in the market. They are better able to trade; they are in a stronger position as buyers. They will now express more intensively than before their demand on the market for the objects they desire; they can offer more money for the commodities they wish to acquire. The obvious results of this will be that the prices of the goods concerned will rise and that the objective exchange-value of money will fall in comparison.' (p.151) ¶But we have only just learned that: 'Since money, as such, does not have a direct connection with any human want, individuals can conceive of its utility and consequently of its value only because it has a definite purchasing power.' A change in the supply, it now appears, alters the marginal utility directly. The circle of logic, which Mises broke open with his historical allusion, is now theoretically and fortunately closed once again. ¶Moreover, the entire construction is completely arbitrary. "A" who earlier had 100 Marks, now has 200. He is aware of the historical exchange ratio but he doesn't consider that as grounds for changing his opinion about them. However, should my supply of suits increase from one to two, the marginal utility of one suit decreases. The situation is different with money. The marginal utility of money is exactly equal to the marginal utility of what it can purchase. The marginal utility of a suit is not changed in any way by the fact that my supply of money has doubled. If 100 Marks were the equivalent of one suit, 200 Marks are now the same as two suits. Nothing makes me give more for the suit than before, for there has been no change in the marginal utility of the seller of the suit; he will hand the suit over to me at the old 'historical exchange ratio.' Mises rescues himself from the dilemma in which he finds himself when he seeks simply to explain in this way the relationship between supply and demand. He merely says that with increasing wealth more things are in demand -- but this is a foregone conclusion. Also it is not unknown that temporary price increases can occur as a result of a rise in demand. Production then usually expands, other things being equal, up to the point at which the old level is re-established. Thus a sustained shift in the exchange ratio is not explained in this way. ¶As the relationship between supply and demand is at the core of marginal utility theory, Mises returns to it once more, for the clarification of economic events, by a long round-about detour. He lapses completely into the old quantity theory, the inferences of which he not only accepts but its errors also, which he even exaggerates. It is unnecessary here to follow him into specifics. Indeed, it appears merely funny that Mises, for example, scolds the capitalists because they do not take into consideration in their business affairs the continual changes in the value of money. It becomes even more ridiculous since Mises himself cannot say how they should do this. It could even happen, if Mises' conclusions were ever accepted, that steel magnate Thyssen, as well as financial tycoon Gwinner, might be denounced in order to make business conform with marginal utility theory. Incidentally it should be noted that Mises -- as a consistent quantity theoretician -- champions the view that banks can expand credit arbitrarily without limit. Since he shares the opinion of Böhm that interest is dependent on the size of the national subsistence fund, it is impossible for him to find the specific causes determining the height of the rate of interest. As a result he arrives at an absurdity; the banks, by reducing the interest rate for transactions, can increase to a considerable extent the demands of their customers and also by expanding the emission of fiduciary media they can satisfy these demands. This, according to Mises, is a serious threat to capitalism. The modern system of the division of labor 'carries within it the germ of its own destruction. The development of fiduciary media must necessarily lead to its breakdown.' (p.472) And thus, this most recent harbinger of catastrophe dismisses us with the very comforting prospect that here 'lie problems which may lead beyond the individualistic organization of production and distribution to new, perhaps collectivist, organizational forms of society.' (p.476) On this account, therefore, no hard feelings! ¶It is a shame about Mr. von Mises. He is a well-informed author; he proved that in his treatise -- in part so excellent -- on "The Problem of the Legal Resumption of Gold Payments in Austria-Hungary.' [Articles 9.1 & 10.2] There are many interesting discussions in the book under review also. Precisely on that account the book's complete futility is most effective proof of the utter fruitlessness of the marginal utility theory. Because Mises develops with logical consistency, although to be sure with indifference as to any agreement with reality, all the deductions to be derived from his assertions, the result condemns the fallacious starting point, the subjective theory of value." (Translated from the German)

Hoiles, R. C. *Colorado Springs Gazette Telegraph.* (January 22 & 25, 1960).

Investors' Chronicle and Money Market Review. London. "Money a Medium of Exchange." (December 8, 1934). "Professor von Mises expresses the belief [in the preface to the English edition] that all proposals that aim to do away with the consequences of perverse economic and financial policy merely by reforming the monetary and banking system are fundamentally misconceived . . . . His investigations have led him to the conclusion that expansion of credit cannot form a substitute for capital."

R. J. *Education Outlook.* England. (Spring 1935). "There are many books on money, or on money and credit . . . . But there is no general, comprehensive, authoritative work on the whole subject of Money and Credit by any English economical or financial student. ¶It seems to be claiming much for this volume to say that it fills so large a gap; but that is a fair description of it."

Keynes, John Maynard. *The Economic Journal.* (September 1914) 417-419.   Reviewed jointly with Friedrich Bendixen's *Geld und Kapital* [Money and Capital].   According to Keynes, Bendixen was "evidently a devoted disciple and admirer" of G. F. Knapp. The popularity of Knapp's book, *Die staatliche Theorie des Geldes* [The State Theory of Money] and the widespread acceptance of his thesis, namely that money is what the State says it is, were among the reasons Mises decided to write on money.   "Dr. von Mises' treatise is the work of an acute and cultivated mind. But it is critical rather than constructive, dialectical and not original. The author avoids all the usual pitfalls, but he avoids them by pointing them out and turning back rather than by surmounting them. Dr. Mises strikes an outside reader as being the very highly educated pupil of a school, once of great eminence, but now losing its vitality. There is no 'lift' in his book; but, on the other hand, an easy or tired acquiescence in the veils which obscure the light rather than a rending away of them. One closes the book, therefore, with a feeling of disappointment that an author so intelligent, so candid, and so widely read should, after all, help one so little to a clear and constructive understanding of the fundamentals of his subject. ¶When this much has been said, the book is not to be denied considerable merits. Its lucid common sense has the quality, to be found so much more often in Austrian than in German authors, of the best French writing. ¶The field covered is wide. The first Book deals with the meaning, place, and function of money; the second with the value of money, the problem of measuring it, and the social consequences of variations in it; and the third with the relation of bank-money, of notes, and of discount policy to the theory of money. With the exception of the section on the value of money, where Dr. von Mises is too easily satisfied with mere criticism of imperfect theories, there is a great deal on every one of these topics very well worth reading. Perhaps the third Book is, on the whole, the best. The treatment throughout is primarily theoretical, and quite without striving after *actualité*. The book is 'enlightened' in the highest degree possible. ¶The second of the two books under review [Bendixen's *Money and Capital*] is a collection of brief essays . . . . The first seven essays deal with the theory of money, and are chiefly intended to popularise the ideas of G. F. Knapp . . . . ¶Dr. Bendixen trounces . . . with the vigour of a convert [the 'superstitious' metallist view of money]. Money is the creation of the State; it is not true to say that gold is international currency, for international contracts are never made in terms of gold, but always in terms of some national monetary unit; there is no essential or important distinction between notes and metallic money; money is the measure of value, but to regard it as having value itself is a relic of the view that the value of money is regulated by the value of the substance of which it is made, and is like confusing a theatre ticket with the performance. With the exception of the last, the only true interpretation of which is purely dialectical, these ideas are undoubtedly of the right complexion . . . . ¶I have described Dr. von Mises' book as 'enlightened.' If a corresponding epithet is to be applied to Dr. von Bendixen's book, I should describe it as 'emancipated' -- which, within the sphere of what is liberal and intelligent, is at the opposite pole. Dr. von Bendixen is without the cultivated subtlety of Dr. von Mises, but his practical wisdom is of a high order. Hamburg's mind is not so clever as Vienna's, but more comes of it."

   In the light of this review by Keynes of the 1912 German-language edition of Mises' book, see Keynes' comments in "Books and Articles About Mises: 1930."

Leffler, Ray V. *American Economic Review.* 25:2 (June 1935) 353-355. "Subjective use-value is emphasized as fundamental throughout the book . . . . ¶Senior, Menger, Jevons, Carver, Fisher, Kinley, Kemmerer, Laughlin, Wieser, and others are criticized for missing the fundamental point in explaining the value of money. Wicksell seems to have done better . . . . [I]n the opinion of von Mises, changes in the amount of money do not necessarily lead to proportionate changes in the price level . . . . It is difficult to disagree with von Mises' observations on these matters . . . . Von Mises accepts Wicksell's distinction between the Natural Rate of Interest and the Money Rate of Interest, but he disagrees with the idea that the two always tend toward equilibrium through banking operations . . . . His final conclusion is that a credit policy aiming at stability of the objective exchange-value of money (price level) is possible only when political forces are not antagonistic to private property in the means of production."

Lotz, W. *Jahrbücher für Nationalökonomie und Statistik.* Jena. Series III. 102:47 (1914) 86-93. Lotz's review is translated and printed here in full. Page references are to the 1912 edition:
"The author is a follower of Carl Menger, von Wieser and von Böhm-Bawerk. From them he derives his monetary theory. However, he also analyzes other authors who take a different view. Against the widely held position taken in Knapp's work that money is only that which fulfills the four functions, as a general medium of exchange, a store of value, a measure of value and a legal tender medium of account, while all other forms must be considered money substitutes, Mises argues that it is a 'very naive idea' to believe that the meaning of money can be fully appreciated only by considering its other functions. (p.10) For him [Mises] the function of the generally used medium of exchange in an economic order of free exchange of goods is the essential thing. All other functions may be traced back to this basic function. So the function of money is first of all as an intermediary in the exchange of capital, i.e. in the exchange of present goods against future goods. Thus also its function as a store of value and as a medium of account is not a function of its principal role as a general medium of exchange. Mises, together with Menger, rejects the function of money as a general measure of value. In accord with the marginal utility principle, the subjective use value of goods decreases with an increase in the supply, but the corresponding measurement here is not possible. One can certainly calculate objective exchange value in money, because any commodity can be related on the market to money and money can be converted into any commodity. If one wants to speak of measuring prices in this sense as one function of money, one can do so. However, it is not correct; one should also not designate astronomical orientation as a function of the stars (p.30). ¶Mises distinguishes three categories that derive from the function of the general medium of exchange: (1) 'Commodity Money,' that is at the same time a commodity on the market, i.e. gold and silver, (2) 'Token money' -- arising out of special legally qualified pieces that show no technological distinction, (3) 'Credit Money,' which 'possesses' a right of demand against some

physical or legal person. (p.45) Whether or not Token Money as he defines it has ever actually existed in history, the author does not doubt that it may be possible in theory. As to Credit Money, he holds that the basic claim should not be redeemable upon demand and secure, for if it were there would be no difference between the value of the claim and the sum of money represented. Claims which are redeemable upon demand and are secure will surely be used as media of exchange; however, they are not money; nor are they Credit Money in Mises' sense; rather they are money substitutes about which, in a uniform concept of money, the author has some thoughts. There are two elements in the appraisal of the right to a claim: first the evaluation of the commodity to which the claim vouchsafes title; then the greater or lesser likelihood of actually achieving, by means of the claim, the power of disposal over the good in question. Distinguishing these claims from the concept of money as special money substitutes, which appears unavoidable to all those who emphasize the function of money as a measure of value, seems to von Mises to be only a matter of expediency. (p.36) Beginning here the author considers the small coin and the German Taler until October 1, 1907. The small coin is a draft on money; but it is not money; von Mises seems to consider it as a money substitute, even though the small coin does not legally represent a claim to money in the meaning of the legal order. It depends upon whether the administration actually takes care of the redemption of small coins; the case of the Taler is similar. If the actual exchange of small coins into money is discontinued and its circulation is not limited, then the small coin is transformed into credit money of a special valuation as opposed to commodity money. (p.41) ¶It is obvious that the author's terminology differs not only from traditional terminology, but it also differs substantially from that of Knapp. More meaningful than this terminological difference, however, is the material difference between the other statements of the author and those of Knapp. In Chapter 4, 'Money and the State,' von Mises stresses the fact that money is a general medium of account because it is a medium of exchange. Only trade, not the state, can raise a commodity to the status of a generally used medium of exchange. A major argument of the author is that credit money has never entered directly into trade without having circulated previously in trade as a money substitute. (p.69) Further something other than the medium of account prescribed by the state may be stipulated by private agreement, the protection of which the state cannot completely neglect. (p.60) Mises rejects Knapp's standpoint especially by means of the following reasoning. The crux of the problem rests on the development of the laws that determine the exchange relationship between money and other economic goods. (p.33) According to von Mises, the nominalistic monetary theory is 'characterized by a total inability to say anything about the major problem of monetary theory, one could even call it the *only* monetary problem, namely to explain the exchange relationship between money and other economic goods; it cannot even say anything that could be interpreted as a weak attempt to approach this problem.' (p.50) If the nominalists look at the problem of the evaluation of the German Taler since the discontinuance of the coinage of the Taler, and the evaluation of the Austrian silver Florin since 1879, they are, according to von Mises, erecting an ingenious system of fallacies in order to prove that the state, the law, the legal order determine the value of the money. ¶How then does von Mises stand with respect to what he designates the essential problem of the ratio of the value of money and other commodities and especially also to the single question which, according to Knapp, plays such an important role, namely the valuation of the Austrian currency since 1879? ¶Mises, together with Menger and Wieser, deal with the 'objective exchange value of money.' Adherents of the subjective theory of use value succeed in constructing the 'objective exchange value of money' in the following manner. Money is valued by individuals subjectively as an exchange commodity according to the subjective evaluation of the other economic goods which may be obtained in exchange for the money. Mises cites Wieser: 'The exchange value of the money is the anticipated use value of the things which are procurable with the money.' Naturally this so-called objective exchange value is not a property of the commodities themselves, but just as in the case of use value it is traced back in the last analysis through individuals to the subjective evaluation of the particular commodities. (p.97) It has already been shown, as the author argued in an earlier section, that the function of money as a measure of value would not proceed from this idea. Once the idea is established, two expressions, again stemming from Menger, are encountered: (1) 'the inner exchange value of money,' so far as the grounds for determining the formation of prices on the side of money influence the exchange ratio of the money to goods on the market, (2) 'outer exchange value' to refer to the problem of changes in place and time that affect the objective exchange value of the money. (p.132) ¶Here the author finds in the Quantity Theory something useful, namely 'that there exists a connection between changes in the value of money on the one hand and changes in the relationship between the supply of, and the demand for, money on the other hand.' (p.140) But the author does not want to follow this to the conclusion that an increase in the supply of money must finally lead to a proportionate increase in the prices of all economic goods. (p.152) First of all, it is easy to prove by the consistent application of the marginal utility idea that a doubling of the money supply available to an individual does not mean a 50% drop in the evaluation of the monetary unit. Secondly, profits and losses, which every enterprise experiences as a result of a price change proceeding from changes in the value of money, must be traced as they progress from one class to another. This examination of the social effects of changes in the value of money, which von Mises undertakes in recognition of inflationary and bimetallist movements, is in my opinion the most valuable part of the work. Less original and less instructive than these considerations are the sections on the problem of measuring the objective exchange value of money. Also on the supposed local differences in the exchange value of money. ¶One specific question which is investigated in connection with von Mises' theory of monetary value, is the source of the value of the Austrian Gulden since the cessation of silver coinage. As is well known, Knapp has dealt exhaustively with this problem. His interpretation is rejected by von Mises, as well as by the avowed metallist [J. Laurence] Laughlin who has regarded as essential for the momentary evaluation of the Austrian paper Gulden since the cessation of the silver coinage the prospect for its future redemption in gold -- a view with which at first I could not agree, until Laughlin had related to me the facts, which certainly render his opinion very acceptable. Against Laughlin (p.136), Mises raises the following objection: In 1884 the exchange rate on the Viennese Exchange of the Austrian 5% interest notes was quoted on the average at 4.19% below par. Holders of the 5% interest notes take into consideration the same situation as was obvious also to the holders of the claim contained in the state notes, without considering constitutional fineness. How could it be that the state bonds are valued less than non-interest bearing state notes? It is not possible that this could be due to the fact that hope prevails that the state notes would be redeemed in gold sooner than the interest would be repaid. The fact that the state notes are generally accepted media of exchange is much more decisive. As such, in addition to the value which they represented as claims on the state, they would also have value as money. Otherwise, a claim to a certain sum whose date of maturity lies at an uncertain date in the future, would be assessed at considerably less than its face value. Laughlin's theory gives no answer to these questions; only by taking into consideration the fact that the monetary function also creates value can a satisfactory explanation be found. (p.137) In my view, it is a matter of opinion whether one wants to accept these arguments of von Mises; I do not find them impressive. In justification of Laughlin however, I should like to remark at this point that in the 1880s, he was informed by the leading house of high finance in Vienna, one relies on it, that at some time or other the paper Gulden would be redeemed in gold at a practicable rate of exchange. It is also important that the circulation of the paper Gulden and silver Gulden was quantitatively substantial and that these means of payment from the public treasury were accepted at face value: nevertheless the expectations that the leading house of Viennese high finance has a motive to provide for the future can in no way be unimportant for the international evaluation of the Austrian paper Gulden. So, in spite of von Mises, it would appear justifiable to give some weight to this information concerning Laughlin's interpretation. ¶Concerning the statements of the author in the third Book of his work one point is to be discussed more thoroughly. He devotes considerable attention to the question: Aside from commodity money, what is the significance of redeemable banknotes, bills of exchange and checks? Here much is neither original nor appropriate, leaving grounds for criticism. We will not discuss what can only be deduced by the follower of Böhm-Bawerk's interest theory concerning the relationship between the value of money and the height of interest, nor what convinces no one who asks at least for one clear example, inductive evidence, of such difficult problems. The author also discusses the questions of the bank of issue, to be sure in a somewhat doubtful way because of the rather questionable methodology. Concerning the controversy between the Currency School and the proponents of bank reserves, the author instructs us with great assurance, which is astonishing, that one of the most disastrous errors of Fullarton and his followers was that they overlooked the fact that redeemable banknotes also remain perennially in circulation and can produce an oversupply of currency in circulation. (p.408) The demand for credit is not fixed; it grows when the interest rate falls and falls when it rises. 'If we expand the quantity of commodity bills offered at a discount at certain times, and at other times cause it to decline, then we cannot conclude prematurely that these fluctuations may be explained by changes in the demand for money on the part of individual enterprises. The only permissible conclusion is that, given the conditions established at the time by the banks no greater number of credit applications are presented . . . . The cause of the fluctuations in the demand on the credit banks for circulation credit is to be sought only in the credit policy they follow.' (p.359) Hitherto it had been assumed that a bank of issue that paid out cash, which limited itself to discounting bills, would be safeguarded from the danger of overemission, as it only exchanges readily acceptable existing credit instruments, bona fide commercial paper, for other acceptable means of payment, banknotes. To this von Mises responds most dogmatically. Surely there was a time when commercial bills passed from hand to hand in Lancashire as a means of payment in business transactions, as well as being used for obtaining credit. This assertion is now obsolete. And it is also not correct to say that the bank of issue is an intermediary between the lender and those into whose hands the notes actually go. 'This assertion in no way corresponds to the actual situation. Whoever receives and possesses notes does not grant credit; he does not receive a present good in exchange for a future good. The note of a solvent bank that is redeemable upon demand is available as circulation credit in lieu of money, and it makes no difference to anyone whether he has in his vault money or notes. The note is just as much of a present good as is the money.' (p.311) The author generally mistrusts in principle the operation of the discounting bank of issue. 'The basic error of the Banking School lies in the failure to recognize the nature of the issue of fiduciary media. If the bank discounts a bill of exchange or otherwise grants a loan, it receives a future good in exchange for a present good. In view of the emissions role, the present goods that the bank gives out, the fiduciary media, are created, so to speak, out of nothing; one can speak of a natural limit to their supply only if the supply of the future goods that reaches the loan market in exchange for present goods is strictly limited. That, however, is by no means the case. To be sure, the supply of future goods is limited by outside circumstances; but this is not the case with respect to the supply of future goods which are offered on the market in the form of money. The issuers of circulation credit are in a position to increase the demand for fiduciary media, by reducing the interest rate asked by them below the natural interest rate, that is below the rate of interest which would be established by supply and demand if real capital were loaned *in natura* without the intercession of money. On the other hand, this must stop immediately if the bank interest rate should be raised above the natural capital interest rate.' (p.353) Mises also rejects the assumption that a superfluity of notes in circulation must be corrected by the payment in full in notes of the discounted bills of exchange. 'If the loans which are granted by the banks by the issue of fiduciary media fall due for repayment, a corresponding sum of fiduciary media flows back to the banks; then to be sure, the supply in circulation is reduced. At the same time, however, new loans are granted by the bank and new fiduciary media stream out into circulation. To be sure, the adherent of the commodities bill theory will object: Only if new commodity bills are in existence and presented for discount, can a further issue of circulation credit take root. That is correct. However, whether new commodity bills exist, depends precisely on the credit policy of the banks.' (p.358) Accordingly the author even denies the elastic nature of the banknote. For the interest rate policy of the banks influences the supply of the applications for discount and, thus, in their execution the circulation of notes. 'It is within the power of the banks give out fiduciary media by issuing currency; it is within their control to increase without limit the total supply of money and money substitutes in circulation. By the issue of currency, they can increase the money supply in the broader sense in such a way that a rise in the demand for money, which otherwise must lead to a rise of the inner objective exchange value of money, is frustrated by its effect on the formation of monetary value.' (pp.359/360) According to von Mises, the view that convertible banknotes, issued according to need, would not remain permanently in circulation, is one of the most serious errors. 'If what Fullarton emphasized also is true, that the banknotes which are given out as loans flow back again automatically to the bank after the expiration of the period of the loan, then nothing further need be said about it, whether or not the bank can, through continual prolongation of the loan, keep them in circulation longer. The statement that forms the central point of the Banking theoreticians' position is untenable -- namely that more notes than correspond to the demand of the public could never be put out and kept continually in circulation. For the demand for credit is not a fixed amount; it grows with a falling, and falls with a rising, rate of interest.' (pp.408-409). With a radical pessimism which proceeds from the trivial observation that no bank of issue could redeem all notes at any one time if all of them were presented simultaneously, the author proceeds still further to deny the value of short-term cover for notes. 'In the event of a general "run," it is immaterial whether the assets of a bank of issue exist in bills of exchange with short-term maturity or mortgage loans. If the bank needs large quantities of money immediately, it can provide these only by the sale of its assets. If the aroused people are besieging its counters and presenting notes for redemption or demanding to have their demand deposits back, it can no more wait for the maturity of a bill of exchange which still has 30 days to run, than it can for that of a mortgage claim, which is not redeemable for so many years.' (p.389) Thus to the work's conclusion, a 'Look into the Future of Money and Credit,' in which the author phantasizes about a worldwide bank of issue or a world-wide cartel of banks of issue and instructs us that the development of fiduciary media necessarily must lead to a collapse of the modern organization of exchange intercourse. 'As soon as an agreement is struck between the various banks of issue as to the general principle for credit policy, or as soon as the plurality of the banks of issue is replaced by a single world bank, every barrier to the issue of credit disappears. First of all, the expansion of credit can continue so long as the objective exchange value of the money is held down to the level given by the further employment of the money commodity,' and so on. (p.472) ¶So far characteristic expressions of the author have been reproduced without comment -- when possible in his own words. From the standpoint of a thoughtful critique it might be added that hypothetically the statements of the author should not be described as completely wrong; they are at least coherent, insofar as a bank of issue which offers to redeem its notes may actually adopt a management policy of depressing the discount rate artificially and handing out its notes to discount bills of exchange which do not originate from the purchase of commodities but from speculation, or even from payable drafts, and may even -- according to the statement of the author -- renew these bills willingly upon the maturity of the bill of exchange. Also if a bank of issue makes loans too cheaply against security, the possibilities of which von Mises speaks are not entirely precluded. However, to expect men, who in theory and practice advocate the principle of adequate bank cover, to view as appropriate and normal such a rotten method of operation on the part of a check-issuing institution, or such a credit policy, reveals at least extraordinary ignorance of the world. If the author had considered the pains taken by the German Reichsbank's administration since 1908, to exclude from its portfolio all bills of exchange which were not entirely liquid, and even to follow a high discount rate policy when necessary, often in opposition to the interested parties, if the author had then investigated further the causal connections, through specific studies of situations wherein banks of issue maintained a non-liquid cover and thus came into difficulties, he might also have demonstrated inductively in individual cases the changes in the nature of the commodity bills in recent times since the introduction of bank acceptances. He would then have delayed finishing his work. He would also most likely have spoken less apodictically. But he would have produced a book more useful for science. Upon reading this book, one is led to ponder how a predominantly deductive handling of problems of an experimental science leads to wrong conclusions, even if the author is widely read and not of limited intelligence. Although the work contains many very useful and ingenious insights, it must unfortunately be characterized as immature and lacking in important respects. Whether the work lives up to earlier works as a textbook on monetary affairs, it may be pointed out that in any case the sections on banking should be rejected." (Translated from the German)

Lutz, H. L. *The American Economic Review.* 3:1 (March 1913) 144-146. Lutz became a noted economics professor (Oberlin, Stanford, and Princeton) and served on governmental advisory commissions, especially concerning finances and taxation. His review is reproduced here in full:

"The work under review apparently represents an effort to develop a theory of money which will be in accord with the utility theory of value in its most extreme subjective applications. The process has been chiefly one of excision, in which much of current monetary principle and practice has been pruned away. The failure to recognize the general limitations upon the utility theory detracts from the merit of the work, while the thoroughgoing application of this theory in all of its detail leads to mainly negative results. ¶The starting point is, of course, the general theory of value. Here the author presents and elaborates all of the refinements of objective exchange-value, subjective exchange-value, and subjective use-value. (pp.99-100) While exchange-value is more prominent in modern economic organization, yet from the social point of view, objective exchange-value leads back to a subjective use-value as the real origin of the condition or fact of value. In the case of money, however, such reference to a subjective use-value is not made, and the only form which is manifested by the medium of exchange is that of objective exchange-value. The task of the theory of money is to formulate the laws of the objective exchange-value of money, that is, of its purchasing power. (pp.106-107) The most important attempt at the formulation of such a law has been in the so-called 'quantity theory of money.' While this theory contains a germ of truth in the proposition that the demand for and the supply of money are conditions which affect its value, it does not afford an adequate explanation of the value of money. It explains changes in the value of money, but does not account for this value itself. Further, even the quantity of money in a community is determined by subjective forces. Each individual will require a stock of money which will be conditioned by the organization of the whole social productive and exchange apparatus. This apparatus can only motivate the individual, however, and cannot affect directly the concrete level of the money demand, which is dependent upon the subjective considerations of the individual. Two communities, under exactly similar objective environments, may maintain different stocks of money, owing to the differing subjective estimates which prevail as to the advantages or disadvantages of a large supply. The mechanical conception of the relation of the quantity of money to its value is combatted, and the contention advanced that the extent to which a change in the money supply will affect its value will depend solely upon the subjective value (*Wertskala*) of the individual. (p.155) That is to say, an increase in the quantity of money can affect its value only by affecting the marginal utility (*Grenznutzen*) of money to the individuals who comprise the community. (p.151) ¶The problem of measuring changes in the value of money presents difficulties also, which to the author are well-nigh insurmountable. All of the factors which enter into the determination of price operate only through the subjective valuations of the individual, and these factors cannot be measured. The index number may be of some use in ascertaining objective use-value, although this is of relatively little significance, compared with the subjective significance of a given money quantity. (p.221) As an agency for historical and statistical investigations into prices, the index number may render a useful service; but it is of no significance for the development of the value of money. (p.217) A proposal recently made to use the budgets of a number of individuals for the construction of an index number based upon the real incomes of these persons, is given greater approval than the index number based upon price quotations, though the practical difficulties in the way of a proper application of the principle are recognized. (p.219) ¶So much for the point of view in this book. The attempt at a psychological basis for economic theory may be pleasing to some, but to the reviewer it appears to be relatively futile. Granted that in a certain sense the roots of these theories run down into the unknown strata of self, an overemphasis of these vague unknowable origins negatives all theorizing. Behind the phenomena of price may lie certain real but intangible subjective considerations which are indeterminable, and hence unmeasurable. But there are certain external objective phenomena of price which may be known, recorded, and studied; and on the basis of these objective manifestations safe conclusions may be drawn regarding the course of prices and its relation to human welfare. What further object is there to be attained? The elaborate refinements of the extreme devotee of the psychological school appear to confuse rather than to clarify useful thinking in the field of economics proper."

Luzzetti, Carlos. "Nota Bibliográfica: Reconstrucción Monetaria" [Bibliographical Note: Monetary Reconstruction]. *Espejo*. Mexico: Instituto de Investigaciones Sociales y Económicas. 3:25 (March 15, 1962) 54-55. A review of the Spanish (1961) translation of *Monetary Reconstruction*, the 1953 epilogue to B-2.

Machlup, Fritz. *Econometrica*. (July 1954) 401-402. "The first German edition [1912] failed to make much of an impression on English monetary discussion . . . . The reception of Mises' work by German economists was different in that they had no language difficulties but, trained in the historical school, had difficulties with theoretical reasoning . . . . I wonder whether at present a young student of economics having done his assigned readings on economic analysis, monetary theory, interest, employment, and cycle and growth theory of recent vintage, would appreciate just what it was that Mises contributed to the development of that knowledge. Would such a student have to read first some of the books of pre-1912 vintage, so that he could judge by comparison? Would he have to be told that no writer before Mises had succeeded in explaining the demand for cash balances with marginalist principles, or that hardly anyone before Mises had recognized what significance Wicksell's theory of cumulative expansion and contraction had for the joint explanation of monetary and cyclical phenomena? . . . ¶The new material on Monetary Reconstruction shows Mises as an unreconstructed sound-currency advocate . . . . But Mises has no illusions: 'There cannot be any question of the gold standard' until there comes 'a radical change in economic philosophies'."

Neurath, Otto. *Zeitschrift für die Gesamte Staatswissenschaft*. (1912) 776-781. According to Mises, Otto Neurath was a leading organizer of a group of "logical positivists" and in 1919 served "as the head of the socialization bureau of the short-lived Soviet republic of Munich." (*Human Action*, 1966, p.703n.) His review is translated and printed here in full:

"The author is concerned in a very commendable way with supporting his keen economic discussions with principle. However, lacking is a point of view which would enable him to judge the meaning of money for the satisfaction of needs independently of criteria provided through the monetary order. Without a thorough investigation into the insufficient profitability of an enterprise, it cannot be said that 'economic goods, which could serve for the satisfaction of more important needs are used for the satisfaction of less important needs.' (p.433) Unfortunately we do not live in a social order in which one always increases national wealth by fostering the greatest possible profitability. Connected with this also is the thoroughly unsatisfactory management of crises which, according to the author, must also appear periodically, even in every natural (barter) economy. He is not at a loss for an explanation of the reason for this opinion. Crises are obviously connected with the drive for profitability. It is not comprehensible, therefore, why periodical declines in wealth should appear even in a non-socialistically oriented natural (barter) economy, an economy which provides for the exchange of goods through a natural clearing bank. Even the most irrational distribution of the labor force could lead at the very most to unsatisfactory consumption, not however to a shrinking of the production of the most necessary articles, such as we are experiencing today in this time of crisis with labor dismissals and bankruptcies. Mises even recognizes no discrepancy between the phenomena of the money market and of the world of real goods; for him 'a surplus or scarcity of money and a surplus or scarcity of capital' are identical. (p.402) ¶Under these circumstances it is conceivable that Mises generally ignores the influence of money on production, one of the most critical points of every complete theory of money. The description of the gradual increase in prices following from a monetary increase is very vivid. It culminates in the contention that the increase in prices can only have an illusory effect on welfare, because the business promoters, for example, may profit from the increase in prices, while others, to whom the higher prices come later, suffer; the farmer pays more dearly for industrial products, before the increased prices for agricultural products provide him with any compensation. Mises overlooks completely a second possibility: Until now, a state has obtained a certain quantity of iron annually from the iron cartel. Now it needs double the amount for which it intends to pay with paper money. The cartel will probably be able to deliver double the amount of iron at less than double the quantity of money; in this case the greater quantity of money would have stimulated production without an increase in prices. Yet this result [more production without higher prices] is frequently attributed only to increased production sparked by the emission of paper money. However, even if the iron cartel demands double the sum of money for the entire quantity of iron, it can fulfill delivery only by expanding production. Unemployed workers can then be employed; semi-employed workers would be permanently employed; higher qualified workers who had not been fully utilized would find suitable occupations. Thus wages need not rise on that account. If agriculture knows that a growing demand for foodstuffs is imminent, it can perhaps expand production immediately. ¶The unpopularity of paper money rests, to be sure, in part on the fact that it is generally issued in times of need, when it is not able to stimulate productive forces and, thus, it has the effect primarily of raising prices. However, it can be issued also in developing lands, when it should enrich everybody, as it has in the United States. We possess reserves of productive powers, which Mises always ignores. So if Mises is correct, that during the time of paper money in America real wages fell somewhat, that alone proves nothing. We must know how large the totality of real wages was before and after the emission of paper money. It is possible that the number of unemployed went down, that six family members are now employed while only five found work before. We should not forget that the unemployed usually become burdens on the employed. It frequently happens also that those who continue to work are often promoted during such an upswing. It may be that the real wages of a class in which wages are rising relatively are actually rising in real terms; thus with real wages falling in some occupations, the real wages of others may rise. As neither the situation described here, nor that projected by Mises, comes about in precisely this way, he should not have limited himself to one model only, a model which, moreover, he represents as the only one. ¶When the influence of changes in purchasing power on international trade is discussed, production is not given satisfactory consideration, i.e., pp.212, 254, 260. According to Mises, if imports become more expensive, the result is only that more goods than before must be exported in order to keep up. That this increase in the prices of imports may have consequences for the production of these commodities in certain countries is overlooked. However, when an increase in production for export follows, this can be advantageous for the productive forces. Again, as in the case of the emission of paper money, that depends on whether or not the land is capable of being developed. Protective tariffs are certainly more effective than changes in purchasing power. But Mises does not consider that the former foster international arrangements, while the latter, at least up to now, can proceed entirely freely. ¶Given the universal disregard of production, the theory of circulation is in no way adequately outlined. Mises always contrasts direct and indirect exchange in the traditional way (p.5), which he considers beneficial; he completely ignores direct exchange among more than two persons. For him there exists only one patriarchal or socialistic natural (barter) economy; a private economy without a medium of exchange or without units of account seems to him impossible. An exhaustive discussion of these fundamental questions would have been much more important than the digressions on value theory. Therefore also, the computation of the value of a sum of goods by totalling the succeeding marginal utilities in line with 'Schumpeter's formula' (pp.24, 27) has not been examined for some time, for example not since this was advocated by Jevons and Oskar Kraus. If Schumpeter does not cite his forerunners, he is covered by his introduction in which he gives the motive for omitting the citation -- he does not always follow them strictly. ¶Mises draws exaggerated conclusions from the indisputable fact that the present monetary order is connected in every respect with the past. He rigorously defends the assertion that a State can create no money which is not connected with money of the past; moreover it can only make an already useful medium of exchange into money (pp.58, 110); token money can exist only if it is redeemable in objects that are already acceptable in trade. It is doubtless unnecessary to create money which is completely separated from the past, but in principle it is entirely possible. One could conceive of all outstanding claims being liquidated or abolished -- remember the *novae tabulae* [new tablets] of the Ancients. The State could then introduce a monetary unit and simultaneously proclaim a head tax, establish railroad fares, etc., in terms of this monetary unit. Anyone who is not in direct contact with the State could use the new unit if he had anything to do with those who had to make payments to the State. Mises admits only as an aside that the State can influence the money as tax collector and as employer. The State could also bring the new monetary unit into trade if it were to publish controls on prices for some time and introduce controls on production for all industries, such as already exist today in many lands for mining. Price controls are by no means always an ineffective means as Mises says, on the basis of erroneous generalizations concerning historical facts, they are. However, he emphasizes repeatedly that in a purely individualistic economy no command could change exchange relationships unless one at the same time were to change the circumstances. From this point of view, it must be repeated that an individualistic economic order has never existed and especially that no such economic order exists today. Still, it is permissible to write about a monetary theory for the purely individualistic economy, but anyone who aims at a complete theory of money, especially a theory which could be put into use currently, must consider all possible kinds of economic order. What has been said also disproves the statement that every medium of exchange given must in the final analysis be traced back to commodity money, especially also that purchasing power can only be fully explained in that manner. In view of what has been said, it is understandable that Knapp's theory is severely attacked by Mises. In any case Mises is definitely mistaken when he says that the only reason standard money is not used domestically in payment according to weight is because it does not vouchsafe for small sums of money. (p.55) One would attempt to do this only if one needed the money for payments abroad. It is certain that only what commerce acknowledges as such can be the medium of exchange. This acknowledgment can be accomplished, however, by state coercion. The metallic provision in credit contracts mentioned by Mises is not always permissible. A certain method of payment can also actually be imposed by force. ¶Why Mises absolutely refuses to treat money as a bill of exchange need not be examined. Strictly speaking, he only shows that it is a quite inappropriately contrived bill of exchange. This is not a question of terminology. Whoever perceives of money as a bill of exchange adopts a point of view which makes it possible to characterize the function of money in the society, something the author manages so poorly. A comparable investigation could show, for example, that the money of our time, which represents a bill of exchange of indefinite qualities and fluctuating quantities is less suitable for satisfying the needs of society than other types of bills of exchange. The scornful tone which the author employs against everything which assails the monetary order as such must be rejected. On the whole it is regrettable that the author joins in the tradition, unfortunately so widespread in German scholarly circles, of disparaging as much as possible all unsympathetic theories, and announcing, for example, that they find approval only among laymen, the semi-educated, and others who show a similar friendliness. ¶Those who strive for a monetary order liberated from the contingency of the production of the precious metals come off especially poorly. Wherever the goods character of the modern commodity money comes into question, Mises is somewhat vague. He really should not say that the subjective use value of money always agrees with its subjective exchange value. His discussions concerning the disassociation of the reserve of precious metals from the supply of money and raw materials are also faulty. He treats very thoroughly the fact that little attention is given to changes in the purchasing power of money; references in this connection, which are to be found occasionally in contracts in the form of sliding scales tying wages to the price of foodstuffs, for example, and the prices of manufactured goods to the prices of raw materials, are not discussed. He also does not deal with the question of how another organization than ours would manage these problems. So long as relations remain settled, a money that retains a constant purchasing power is obviously not adequate for general demands because, with a universal increase in production, the fixed wage earners, pensioners and debtors would receive no share of the general increase in wealth. It appears that one could get by most easily with the rudiments of our order if the purchasing power of a wage earner on a fixed monetary income were to change, for example, so that his position with respect to the rest of the population remained unchanged on the whole. When the prices of foodstuffs change sharply while incomes remain relatively steady, the State has often intervened, whether through price controls or by appearing on the market as a powerful seller. Mises devotes some interesting sections to the principal difficulties which stand in the way of the effort to make possible a satisfactory distribution by changing the supply of circulation credit. Still research into the entire economic mechanism is also lacking here. Exaggerations are frequent; thus the author says (p.359) that the cause of the fluctuations of the currency banks' fiduciary media is to be sought only in the credit policy they follow. The contrast between absolute liquidity and being prepared to transact business is suitably characterized. The critique of the attempts to measure the objective exchange value of money is helpful, as is also the discussion of the problems connected with the employment of index numbers. ¶In his eagerness to combat the aims of neo-mercantilism and nominalism, which often go hand in hand, the author sees an achievement of the Classicists in the sentence: 'No economy need ever fear having less money than it needs to satisfy its demand for money.' Thus Mises takes no position concerning the fact that out of an upheaval in German trade, stagnation of industrial development for example, it may arise that England needs large quantities of gold for a war in the far east. In the course of his presentation, Mises returns again to his polemic against Federn. Without introducing new material, he repeats his assertion that the Austro-Hungarian Bank gives up gold or gold notes at any time to anyone under the upper gold point, even though in the meantime the difference in the yield of foreign exchange was officially acknowledged. ¶In some closing paragraphs that do not have any direct connection with the book itself, there is described the possibility of realizing in the not too distant future world-wide counterpoised unions of consumers and producers, such as Wilhelm Neurath has investigated. In doing so, however, Mises remains superficial. He fails to see that such an upheaval would change the entire formation of prices. For example, a greater supply of goods could then never yield a lesser return than would a smaller supply of goods, as so often now occurs. The author also does not consider the fact that the cartelization of producers and consumers would always, through firm payment obligations, place evermore of the share of the burden in accordance with the currently existing burden. These trains of thought are also regularly ignored by the author. The major problem of modern banking theory, as he sees it, concerns the ability or inability of credit to pay, while the most meaningful suggestions in this field aim at much less, namely to make credit interest free -- through the payment of profits as Rodbertus wanted for example, or by suppressing a portion of the burden, because it is precisely the obligation of having to repay the sum loaned out that burdens vast circles the worst. According to Mises, the cartelization of production and consumption would mean that the producers' cartel, as the stronger, would extort higher prices, to which the consumers would readily consent, because they could compensate themselves as members of other producers unions. The author doesn't know anything more to say about the circumstance of circulation credit in such a world, than that it could be increased without limit by a world bank, with the result of further price increases. ¶The book claims to expound a comprehensive theory. Still one misses a leading basic idea which, by taking hold of the critical endeavors, would create a totality. Nevertheless, one can recommend the book most warmly as a very interesting collection of observations on money and circulation credit. For even when one is provoked to sharpest disagreement, it proves quite stimulating." (Translated from the German)

New Statesman and Nation. London. (April 20, 1935). "Dr. Ludwig von Mises' *Theory of Money and Credit* has, from the point of view of the English reader, suffered somewhat from the long delay between its original publication and its translation by Mr. Batson. True, it bears no mark, in its purely theoretical portions, of having been written over twenty years ago; indeed, it is the measure of Dr. von Mises' analytical acumen and almost prophetic grasp of essentials that his book links up so aptly and smoothly with the controversies of the thirties. But it is a pity that he should lose in this country the credit to which he is entitled as an innovator . . . . It has all the qualities of classical economics at its best: the logical completeness, the single-minded concentration, the scrupulous accuracy of language. It has corresponding defects, such as extreme abstraction, an undeniably heavy style, and an intellectual arrogance sometimes amounting to sheer bad manners. The serious student is used to these things; but only the bravest of laymen or beginners are likely to tackle this book."

New York Herald Tribune. New York. (June 9, 1935). "[T]here are relatively few good books showing where and how finance fits into the general framework of society. The publication of this twenty-year-old work in English gives us exactly such a book. ¶In the light of contemporary events the author will probably be regarded as a 'high Tory' because his entire economic psychology revolves around the notion of laissez-faire . . . . [H]e is also opposed to the idea of the Federal Reserve system . . . . The Austrian school of economics recently acquired a considerable following among professional economists in America, and [it] is therefore quite appropriate to have one of its standard texts appear in English."

Röpke, Wilhelm. "Der Kampf gegen den Inflationismus" [The Fight Against Inflation]. *Zeitschrift für das gesamte Kreditwesen.* 7:3 (February 1, 1954) 94-95. "Whoever, like the author of these lines, belonged to the generation of economists who lived through the post World War I inflations, especially the most destructive one of all, the German inflation, and who experienced the shattering collapse of monetary policy at the same time, will remember with undying gratitude, a single book which was a veritable beacon to us thirty years ago. In spite of the author's ideas in other fields, even in social philosophy in general, which may have separated us, we will never forget this book and the service it rendered, and still renders us . . . . ¶[This] standard work of our friend, now an American, has recently appeared in English enriched with timely additions. Once again we review his logical chain of clear and transparent thought . . . characteristically spiced with irony and anger over the errors and wrong paths which have caused so much misery . . . . the courage and cutting sharpness with which he wages the battle with weapons taken both from the classical and modern money theories. Once again we are led through the classic chapters from the 'Functions of Money' to 'Problems of Credit' and once more we wish that many others would entrust themselves to his guidance. We remember what the then path-breaking investigation of credit creation, the role of interest, forced savings, and the causes of fluctuation meant to us. Once more we recommend them to others . . . . ¶Seldom is a book still fresh enough half a century after its first appearance to be truly worthy of a new edition. This one is." (Translated from the German; another translation by Elizabeth Henderson included in Röpke's *Against the Tide* (Chicago: Henry Regnery, 1969).

The Scotsman. Edinburgh. "An Austrian Classic." (February 4, 1935). A review of four books -- by Mises, Irving Fisher, Arthur D. Gayer, and Edgar Milhaud. The major part is devoted to Mises: "The book . . . is indeed twenty years old, and has for most of that time been an acknowledged classic . . . . Of late years, however, a translation . . . has rapidly been becoming a necessity, since references to Mises have been multiplying in the serious economic literature of recent times. Mises, in short, is . . . pre-eminently a 'seminal' writer . . . . ¶Looking at the book in its English dress, certain features are noteworthy. The first point is perhaps the extraordinarily comprehensive sweep of the treatise . . . . Then, secondly, it is difficult to avoid being impressed by the sanity and the balance of the writer . . . . And, thirdly, despite its profundity, this book is pre-eminently readable, a tribute both to the original German and to the work of the translator."

Sennholz, Hans F. *The Freeman.* Irvington, N.Y. 22:4 (April 1971) 253-256. "Few books have contributed more to the advancement of monetary theory . . . . And yet, few serious books have had such little impact on contemporary thought and policy as this treatise. The world continues to ignore or reject it while it is clinging to antiquated notions and practices . . . . ¶Nearly all contemporary economists adhere to holistic theories that are utterly futile and sterile for an understanding of monetary phenomena . . . . ¶Von Mises' subjective theory makes individual choice and action the center of his investigation . . . . ¶This Mises theory has explained numerous economic booms and busts ever since 1912 when the first edition of *The Theory of Money and Credit* appeared in print. And it continues to provide the only explanation of the rapid succession of booms and recessions that continue to plague our system. ¶The subjective theory of Professor Mises also points up the desirability of money that is not managed by government . . . . ¶For nearly 60 years of worldwide inflation and credit expansion, depreciations and devaluations, feverish booms and violent busts, Ludwig von Mises' *Theory of Money and Credit* has given light in the growing darkness of monetary thought and policy. The world should be grateful that the light is maintained through a new printing of this remarkable analysis."

Somary, Felix. *Schmollers Jahrbuch für Gesetzgebung, Verwaltung und Volkswirtschaft im deutschen Reich.* 37:1 (1913) 445-449. Prior to writing this review, Somary, born 1881 in Vienna and thus a contemporary of Mises, served as assistant to Carl Menger and E. V. Philippovich in their capacities as bank directors. Later in Switzerland he became a banker himself. His review is translated and printed here in full:
"Marginal utility theory has so far failed to solve the problem of the value of money. Since the

appearance of Knapp's book, the gaps in the theory have become even more perceptible than before. Mises now attempts to formulate a monetary theory from the standpoint of the Austrian school. Carl Menger outlined the most important problems and Wieser has more recently made valuable contributions to the discussion. However, the Austrian school has been far from having a complete monetary theory. ¶Mises sets as the task of monetary theory the elaboration of the laws which determine the relationship between money and other economic goods. Up to now the fact that the value of commodities, by which the marginal utility of money might be measured, is itself created by the exchange value of money, was raised as an objection to applying marginal utility theory to the value of money. To get around this obstacle, Mises tries to follow in Wieser's footsteps. He harks back to the time when the value of money was determined by its use as a commodity: 'the earliest value of money links up with the commodity value of the monetary material . . . . The theory of the value of money as such can trace back to the objective exchange-value of money only to that point where it ceases to be the value of money and becomes merely the value of a commodity.' ¶This, Mises continues, does not lead to an explanation of the development of the objective exchange value of money. Rather it clarifies the laws that determine the changes in a given exchange ratio between money and other commodities. The basis of this explanation must proceed from the relationship between the demand for and supply of money. The quantity theory correctly established a connection between changes in the value of money and the demand for money. It erred, as did hitherto prevailing theory concerning the demand for money, in starting with the entire economy instead of with the individual's demand for money. Thus the track connecting the money supply with the subjective evaluation of individuals was blocked. One must start with the demand for money by the acting individual, for the need of the entire economy is the sum of that of all individuals. ¶After establishing the demand of the acting individual, Mises assumes that 'every better household' generally has at its disposal a normal cash balance; whoever has on hand more idle cash than he thinks he needs buys, indicating by his conduct on the market that the valuation of one unit of the money supply has decreased. An increase in the money supply of the economy means an increase in the money owned by individuals and a reduction of the marginal utility of the monetary unit. The individual members of the economy who receive the new money supply first are in a better position to trade; the goods they buy go up in price; as a result the incomes of the sellers of these commodities are raised; and in this way price increases continue until all commodities are affected -- although in varying degrees. Proportional price increases, such as the old quantity theory often assumed, do not appear since the money prices of commodities are no longer in the same relation to one another. ¶This, briefly, is the monetary theory set forth in the book. It is hardly possible to criticize the theory of monetary value alone. If one accepts the idea of a continuous connection through all periods of history, then one will agree with Mises' monetary theory, which simply says that the investigation of money's subjective value is the task of ancient history not of political economy. Mises comments profusely on his modified quantity theory. His conclusions, however, are open to objections. One cannot speak of a 'normal' cash balance for the majority of industrial enterprises; above all because an increase in the cash balance is not identical with a rise in real income, as the author appears to assume. ¶In order to defend his quantity theory, Mises criticizes the objections raised by the Banking Theory. He disposes a little too hastily of the first -- Fullarton's theory with respect to hoards. As is well known, in criticism of the quantity theory, Fullarton had protested that money in a depression flows out of circulation into reserves. In opposition to this, Mises emphasizes that money never lies idle: 'the hoarded sums of money do not lie idle . . . . They serve to satisfy a demand for money just as much as any other money does.' That is no answer to Fullarton. Let us assume that the coverage for notes at the Reichsbank is 50% on December 31, while on the following February 15, it amounts to 90%; in the interval a third of the metallic money and banknotes have flowed back to the Reichsbank; nevertheless, as frequently happens, the bank of issue has not reduced the interest rate. For the economy, although not for the bank, the situation is just the same as if gold had flowed out of the country. According to Mises' theory, a decline in prices must take place then also little by little, because the money which returned to the issuing bank does not lower the marginal utility of the monetary unit at the bank, at least not so as to affect the market. Mises' objection that this money must correspond also to a need for providing for a future contingency is untenable. If in February or May money streams back to the bank of issue in large quantities, its 'need for money' -- if one uses that term for the bank's reserve requirements -- can be considerably surpassed; quite a number of such instances occurred between 1875 and 1895, also during the last two decades; that is the regular course of events during the less severe months of a depression. ¶In the third volume of his book, Mises concerns himself with his second objection to the quantity theory, namely that it relates only to economic conditions in which metallic money and notes are used as payment and not to an economy with credit money. Due to one fundamental error, this section on fiduciary media proves a complete failure. Mises defines uncovered notes and credit money. However, since he sees only their outwardly similar operation, he overlooks the fact that credit money, even though not based on metallic money or notes, is still not without cover. 'Those banks that issue notes or open current accounts . . . . have a fund from which to grant loans over and above their own resources and those resources of other people that are at their disposal.' 'Fiduciary media are the indefinitely augmentable products of the arbitrary issuing activity of the banks.' This fundamental thesis of the author is untenable. Except for banks of issue and the central offices of the London banks of deposit, banks open regular credit accounts to the extent that they obtain deposits or negotiate acceptances. It is not true, as the author assumes, that savings deposits are not taken into consideration for monetary transactions. They combine to form the basis for credit transactions. If credit institutions could conjure money up out of nothing, they would not need to compensate for interest on deposits nor draw up acceptances. It should be the task of marginal utility theory to determine on what factors private and banking rates depend -- and that Mises has in no way attempted. ¶From false premises, there ensues an untenable interest theory. Following Wicksell, Mises proceeds from the concept of the 'natural' rate of interest, that is the rate which would prevail if loans were made in the form of real capital goods without the intercession of money. The issuance of fiduciary media could, he continues, increase the demand for credit on the one hand by lowering the interest rate below the 'natural' rate; on the other hand, the demand must cease as soon as the bank rate is raised above the 'natural' rate. When the interest rate asked by the banks approaches the natural rate, the demands made on them for credit diminish in volume; when they reduce the interest rate decidedly below the 'natural' rate, then the demands increase. The cause of fluctuations in the use of circulation credit is to be sought in the credit policy of the banks only. ¶To this we might add the following: The credit banks transform available funds into credit; with few exceptions, the duration of their loans coincides, as a matter of principle, with the length of time capital is entrusted to them. If, in the natural economy, there were organizations to arrange exchanges of real capital, then the 'natural' rate of interest on such loans would be the same as the 'private rate.' It is true that a margin remains at the banks of issue for managerial discretion; if Mises' contentions with respect to uncovered notes only are logically thought through, however, then scarcely a single conclusion can be maintained. Mises would have been correct only if the banks of issue depressed the rate of interest to an 'unnatural' minimum, using Mises' terminology, by numerous emissions of uncovered notes during a depression and, as a result, called forth an increase in demands. However, the issuing banks are in a worse situation in time of depression because their discount rate is usually considerably higher than the private, the 'natural,' rate of interest. Mises will certainly not say that the 247 million uncovered Marks issued by the Reichsbank in the depression year of 1902, together with the accounts opened without cash deposits, gave rise to the boom of the following year. ¶From Mises' thesis it would follow that credit would be more used when the interest rate was low and less when the rate was high. In his opinion, the banks are in a position to reduce interest to their cost of doing business; and they would follow this practice if each bank didn't have to take care to maintain surplus cash on hand. Competition among the banks slows down the reduction in interest; a world cartel of credit banks, however, could expand credit without limit and drive down the rate of interest. Therefore, Mises proposes restraint on the additional issue of credit, the reaffirmation of the fundamental principle of Peel's Banking Act to include credit. ¶I read the chapter on banking with growing astonishment. It is inexplicable why banks are interested in lower interest rates, why they should form cartels for the reduction of interest; up to now cartels have followed a different course. ¶The assumption that credit banks can fabricate money in unlimited quantities out of nothing suffices to give the author grounds for a whole chain of deductions which carry him ever farther from all experience. In view of the false premises, the conclusions of this section of the book are simply impossible to discuss. Add to this the fact that the author has acquired only sketchy information concerning the questions considered; otherwise he would have omitted the abortive objections to the Banking Theory from the standpoint of the banks as well as the curious interpretation of the proportional quarterly increase at the Reichsbank. One cannot avoid reproaching Mises for not seeming to be fully aware of the great responsibility which goes along with advancing extreme propositions in an important area of economics; he should either have brought forward proof of his arguments or still better have omitted the entire third book. His failure to do this, in the interest of the book's success, is to be regretted. ¶It is worthwhile to investigate essential economic problems on the basis of serious theoretical studies. The book's first two sections on monetary matters set forth many interesting observations. Mises' book provides future monetary theory with a few successful statements of principles, but the anxiously awaited economic theory of money is still lacking." (Translated from the German)

The Times Literary Supplement. London. "Money and Credit." (June 6, 1935). "For many years, . . . it has been regarded as a standard text-book in Continental countries, but the ideas it contains have been very slow to percolate to the English-speaking world. Its translation into English five years ago would have been a considerable event in the history of economics. But now, after its ideas have been propagated by Professor Hayek in this country for several years, its interest is partly historical and only partly scientific . . . . ¶It is a remarkable achievement, as Professor Robbins points out, to have related monetary theory satisfactorily to the general theory of economic value, and to have written in 1912 'of forced saving, of disparities between the equilibrium and the money and natural rate of interest and of the cycle of fluctuations in the relations between the prices of producers' goods and consumers' goods which is the result of the instability of credit' . . . . ¶But there are some remarkable blind spots in his mind . . . . ¶Nowhere is the blind side of his mind so plainly apparent as when he is forced by his own sense of logic to consider the possibility that the banks may keep the rate of interest too high as well as too low; that is to say, that they may start deflations as well as inflations . . . . The possibility which is regarded by perhaps the majority of economists as the chief originating and protracting cause of the present depression is dismissed in five lines of casual and obscure language."

Tucker, Jeffrey A. *The Free Market.* Auburn, Ala.: Ludwig von Mises Institute. 5:9 (September 1987) 8, 7. "Monetary theory attracts more quacks, cranks, and crackpots than any other area of economics. And, as it has been since 1912, the best answer to their nonsense remains Ludwig von Mises's *The Theory of Money and Credit* . . . . ¶Professor Mises was 31 years old when this, his first book, was published . . . . ¶The Austrian school teaches that all economic value ultimately resides in the mind of the individual. Thus, the subjective theory of value. Nothing has an 'intrinsic' economic value . . . . Money has no intrinsic value whatsoever, but is given value only by acting individuals . . . . ¶The value of money relies on its 'objective exchange value' or purchasing power, but not just for one period of time. As Mises says, 'the money prices of today are linked with those of yesterday and before, and with those of tomorrow and after' . . . . ¶Mises's amazing 31-year-old mind developed the answer: the objective exchange value, the purchasing power, of money originates with the value it held for use as a commodity the moment before it became a medium of indirect exchange . . . . ¶This insight on the origin of the value of money, later called the regression theorem, has powerful policy implications: it defines the boundaries of reform toward sound money."

Western Economics Encyclopedia. (1971). Compiled by the Economic Research Department, Bank of Taiwan.

Wicksell, Knut. *Zeitschrift für Volkswirtschaft, Sozialpolitik und Verwaltung.* 23:1 & 2 (1914) 144-149. Through Wicksell's work Mises' attention was called to the significance of a deviation between the "natural rate" of interest and the market interest rate. Wicksell's review of Mises' book is translated and printed here in full. Page references are to the first (1912) edition:

"This is a very studiously written, serious book. Mises successfully avoids the immature know-everything attitude which, in my opinion, mars so many works of otherwise gifted authors nowadays. He is constantly concerned with evaluating correctly the ideas of his predecessors. And he conscientiously bases his own work in the field on their ideas in order to press onward along the path they blazed. This method is certainly the earmark of any truly promising study. ¶Characteristic of this method, however, is the decided tendency for an author to vacillate back and forth and to endorse conflicting doctrines. Unfortunately Mises has not always been able to avoid this pitfall. As a result, his book contains a number of vague statements which have not been fully thought through, and even some outright contradictions. For example, on pages 170-174 he mentions the view recently expounded by Wagner, concerning the permanent predominance of the supply side of money over the demand side in the formation of prices. Mises 'definitely denies that it can be deduced from this that there is a tendency toward generally higher prices.' (p.173) However, on pages 180-184, he seems to have entirely adopted the view that there *is* such a tendency. He even tries to refute the obvious objection that increased prices would necessitate correspondingly expanded cash holdings which cannot perhaps be satisfied by the available supply of money. He writes 'that the very force exercised on individual enterprises by price increases [could lead] them to avoid excessive expenditures . . . . and even to reduce their supplies of cash.' (p.184) Somehow this seems rather fantastic to me. ¶In the same way he levels more or less valid arguments against Wieser's assertion, to me completely paradoxical, that the increase in commodity prices is caused by the development of the money economy. But he promptly adds that 'with these remarks [Wieser may have] revealed significant relationships between the market and the formation of prices,' etc. (p.176) Judging from other parts of his book, however, the author knows full well that the situation must be quite the opposite. Prices have increased in our time not on account of the expanding money economy, but in spite of it. During this same period gold production has increased and credit operations have improved still more rapidly than the spread in the use of money. On page 314 -- in contradiction to the position I have taken -- Mises stresses the legal difference between time-bills and notes. It is 'not correct to say' -- as, incidentally, I didn't -- 'that if a bank discounts time-bills it does no more than substitute convenient notes as currency for inconvenient bills.' Yet on page 326, he points out that in the past 'the circulation of notes [was] outwardly similar to that of fiduciary media,' etc. ¶On pages 425-433, which I shall discuss in further detail later, the author seems to multiply contradictions to such an extent that it is practically impossible to grasp his meaning correctly. To be sure the subject matter dealt with on these pages belongs to the most difficult areas of monetary theory. ¶Two parts of his work -- unfortunately not the best -- seem especially to require more careful discussion: First, his treatment of the quantity theory, and secondly the question of the influence that the interest policy of the banks has on commodity prices. In the section on the quantity theory, side by side with many sound observations, there unfortunately emerges a very confused statement of problem and method. The author very carefully establishes, in what seems to me a completely convincing manner, the premises supporting the validity of that theory. Only he seems not to have been convinced by them himself. Among other things, he reproaches the quantity theoreticians for having dealt only with the causes of a shift in the state of price equilibrium, instead of having first explored in a truly scientific manner the fundamental nature of the state of equilibrium itself. This, according to Mises, could be done only on the basis of the 'subjective theory of value.' Exactly what he means by this remains obscure, in spite of his wordy explanations. ¶As I see it, the entire matter is simple enough. Assuming a money economy, it is obviously the amount of cash needed which determines the demand for money. And thus, the amount of cash needed determines indirectly the level of commodity prices. Carl Menger, whom the author cites, seems to me not to be very logical on this point. He states that the supply of money and its velocity of circulation are not sufficient to explain the height of prices. Rather, one must also take into consideration the function of money as a store of value, whereby certain amounts always remain idle for longer or shorter periods. However, such inevitable periods of rest on the part of money are only the reverse side of its velocity of circulation. If they are known or if we may assume that they remain the same on the average under like conditions, then the height of the monetary value or of commodity prices is explained. It is immaterial that some monetary units may remain idle in strong boxes years on end; they could very well have been exchanged at any time for other more rapidly circulating coins. Thus each and every piece of money maintains in fact the average velocity of the entire supply. ¶This brings us to the question of the state of equilibrium itself. There is, in my opinion, no precise state of price equilibrium at all in a developed credit economy. Furthermore, if we imagine an economic system where each and every payment takes place simply by a transfer on the bank's books, so that the only measure of value is the unit in which these accounts are kept, then we can readily visualize an equilibrium of prices at any height. Thus the problem which Mises wants to solve 'first' doesn't exist at all; the question becomes merely one of trying to explain the cause of relative price shifts in an otherwise entirely normal configuration of prices. In other words, 'the state of price equilibrium' may be compared with the so-called neutral equilibrium in mechanics; it does not change automatically, but forces are gradually set in motion by various changes which necessarily tend once more to restore the previously existing balance. ¶And now I come to the part of the work (pp.401ff.) which interested me especially. For here the author follows very closely my views regarding the relationship between interest and commodity prices. Later in the book he appears to have adopted these views as his own. According to Mises, the principal cause which stimulates a demand for credit derives from, and is relatively limited by, the difference between the 'natural rate of interest,' or more simply stated what one can, or believes he can, earn with money on hand, and the interest actually asked by the banking institution. Also under present conditions, according to Mises, this difference is one of the main reasons for shifts in the value of money.[1] If we actually had such an ideal banking setup -- which of course could appear only upon the discontinuance of free gold coinage -- the difference between the 'natural' and market interest rates *would* be the only regulator of commodity prices. But certainly under present circumstances the banks are not free to set interest policy; a too-low discount would soon drive prices up so that the bank reserves would be endangered by the increased demand for metallic money. ¶Mises then says that it would be 'impossible' for the banks 'to lower the interest rate on loans at will within these [very often] broadly fixed limits.' However, his supporting argument, which fills more than eight pages (pp.425-433), is very difficult to understand. The idea which seems uppermost in his mind is that the production period would be continually lengthened on account of the reduction in the interest rate. According to Böhm-Bawerk's theory, this would lead also to a lowering of the natural rate of interest on capital, so that the previously existing difference between the two interest rates would soon disappear. If this were to happen, the upward movement of prices would necessarily cease. And this interruption of price rises would not be prevented by a new reduction in the interest rate on loans by the banks in the attempt to drive prices up still further. However, even this statement may not be correct. Mises forgets that under conditions of economic equilibrium the length of the actual periods of production must always yield the greatest possible gain on his capital to the individual entrepreneur. If he can borrow money at a considerably lower rate, he need not lengthen the production period on that account but can very quietly pocket the difference as an extra gain. On the other hand, if he is led to expand his enterprise, wages are driven up by the competition of other entrepreneurs and, if commodity prices were to remain the same, this would certainly compel them

---

[1] In my *Geldzins und Guterprise* [1898; English translation, *Interest and Prices*, 1934] I referred to this as the only cause of price fluctuations. I stated that an increased production of gold would influence prices exclusively through the bank rate of interest. As I saw it, if gold shipments were principally entrusted to the central banks directly, they could not help but lower the interest rate on money below that previously existing. This, then, would be the direct cause of an increase in prices. However, I later abandoned this view as too one-sided. An increase in gold production obviously increases the demand for commodities in gold-producing countries. The influence this exercises to increase commodity prices is consequently a direct one. Under certain circumstances it may be so significant that the resulting price increases appear even before the crates of gold reach Europe in payment for the commodities and, in that case, no general surplus of gold would be evident. In the soon to be published second volume of my 'Lectures' I have attempted to examine this interesting but difficult point more closely.

to lengthen the periods of production concerned. However, real capital and consequently the supply of commodities have not been increased. They have rather been diminished with the lower rate of interest on loans and the resulting reduction in savings and increased consumption by would-be savers. Consequently, increased loans must necessarily call forth a corresponding increase in commodity prices. As a result, in spite of the increased money loans, the entrepreneurs find themselves no better off than before. ¶Surprisingly, however, at the close of these rambling and, unfortunately, not very clear remarks, Mises comes astonishingly to exactly the same conclusion as I. He says: 'The banks must eventually reach a point beyond which they cannot go, when no further expansion in the supply of fiduciary media in circulation is possible. This limit may be reached because of the use of commodity money, for the purchasing power of the fiduciary media and of the monetary unit cannot sink below that of the commodity money without forcing the bank to discontinue redemption of its notes. Perhaps this point may be reached because the reduction in loan interest has reached the limits fixed by the technical costs of bank management. Or the point beyond which the banks cannot expand may be reached because the rising avalanche of fiduciary media in circulation[2] results in an incalculable depreciation of the objective exchange value of the unit of money and credit. But whatever the cause, when that point is reached, the bank must cease from any further attempt to underbid the natural rate of interest.' (pp.431ff.) ¶That, to be sure, is precisely the position I have taken. In my opinion, however, a substantial reduction in the interest rate could, if only continued long enough, well increase prices acutely. Why then do we argue? The quotation just cited is quite a remarkable statement of the precise hypothesis which was to be established. ¶The conclusion is not justified, however, that all or even the greater part of Mises' work evidences as much confusion and as many contradictions as in the particular sections criticized in this review. On the contrary, as soon as he abandons the giddy heights of abstract theory to discuss the area of practical monetary matters, his analysis gains meaningfully in sharpness and calm assurance. For example, what he writes about the Banking School, Peel's Act, the Gold-premium Policy, etc., belongs in my opinion to the best that one can read on these and similar matters. As a matter of fact, a single additional editing of the entire work would probably have sufficed to bring the purely theoretical part up to the same standard of clarity and coherence as prevails in the more practical arguments. Unfortunately, however, this book's premature appearance by a matter of months, not to mention years, testifies to pious hopes which may be traced to contemporary impatience and literary impetuosity." (Translated from the German)

---

[2] This point has been stressed in my writings.

The Ultimate Foundation of Economic Science (B-22)

Diamond, Arthur M., Jr. *Reason.* Santa Barbara, Calif. 11:5 (September 1979) 45-46. A double review of Mises' book plus *New Directions in Austrian Economics* (Louis Spadaro, ed., 1978). "Neo-Austrians these days are quick to observe 'an expanding influence of Austrian thought in economic debate'. . . . But the publication of the[se two] books seems to reflect, not so much the increased influence of neo-Austrian economics among intellectuals, as it does the increased generosity of those who underwrite such Austrian work. Whatever the reason for publication, the books make readily available some evidence that should be useful to the libertarian trying to make an informed choice between the neo-Austrian and the Chicago approaches . . . . ¶Two major claims separate von Mises's neo-Austrian method from the method of the rest of the profession. They are that all of economics can be deduced from the axiom that 'man acts' and that empiricism in economics is worthless. ¶That all of economics can be derived from the axiom 'man acts' sounds no less miraculous than the claim that Jesus fed a large crowd with a couple of fish and a loaf of bread. The question is . . . . How can an admittedly tautological proposition yield other propositions that have explanatory power? ¶Von Mises . . . . claims that those who criticize the tautological character of the action axiom are confusing economics with geometry. It is as if Jesus, when asked how he had multiplied the loaves, had responded: 'Beware not to confuse loaves with rocks!' One might heed the warning, yet still remain puzzled . . . . ¶The praise of deduction in von Mises's methodology is surpassed in passion only by the disdain for empiricism."

Ebeling, Richard M. *Laissez Faire Books Catalog & Review.* New York. (Fall-Winter 1978-79) 36. "It may seem trite to point out that all that exists in our world that is not a gift of nature has been brought into being through the actions of human beings and that if we want to understand the meaning and functions of these man-made objects and entities we must relate them back to the purposes of the individuals who created them. Yet, this is exactly what many social scientists who have embraced positivism seem to have forgotten . . . . ¶The 'Austrians,' on the other hand, have insisted that without including data about the subjective meanings of individual actions, complete understanding of social and market phenomena is impossible. The recently reprinted 1962 work by Ludwig von Mises on *The Ultimate Foundation of Economic Science* focuses directly on this fundamental question . . . . ¶After laying the theoretical foundation, Professor Mises discusses the role of forecasting in economics, the place of statistics in applied economics, problems with the general approach of macroeconomics (including a critical discussion of national income analysis) and the use of different methodological approaches and their implications for policy conclusions."

Greaves, Percy L., Jr. *The Freeman.* Irvington, N.Y. 12:11 (November 1962) 63-64. "The science of economics has been erected, step by step, on a foundation of such simple, but fundamental, premises as the following: 'The characteristic feature of man is action . . . purposive action . . . conscious behavior . . . . Actions are directed by ideas, and ideas are products of the human mind'. . . . ¶The above quotations are from the new book by Ludwig von Mises, world renowned author of *Human Action* and a dozen other books no economist should ignore. His latest volume not only probes the basic roots of all human action, but also exposes the ill-founded basis of some key fallacies that now stand in the way of human progress . . . . ¶Among the other myths that Mises smashes is the anarchists' dream of a peaceful society without any government. He points out that 'man alone among all living beings consciously aims at substituting social cooperation . . . for the law of the jungle. However, in order to preserve peace, it is, as human beings are, indispensable to be ready to repel by violence any aggression, be it on the part of domestic gangsters or on the part of external foes' . . . . ¶Mises also explodes once more the still popular myth that 'one man's gain is necessarily another man's loss'. . . . ¶This little book deserves to be read and inwardly digested by all who seek enlightenment on the economic and political problems of our times."

Hazlitt, Henry. "The Basis of Economics." *Newsweek* (Business Tides column). 60:12 (September 17, 1962) 94. "The new book by Prof. Ludwig von Mises . . . is . . . a basic investigation not only of the methods appropriate to economics but of how we can discover and prove its fundamental truths and propositions. ¶His theme might be stated negatively. He tries to show that the present fashionable idea that all sciences, including economics, must imitate the methods of physics, that they must be empirical, experimental, statistical, and quantitative, is not itself a scientific idea, but an arbitrary assumption. He rejects materialism, panphysicalism, and logical positivism, in fact, as 'metaphysical' ideas that have perverted and set back rather than advanced economics and have led toward a philosophy of collectivism and totalitarianism."

Krogdahl, Matthew. *The Austrian Economics Newsletter.* New York: Center for Libertarian Studies. 2:1 (Spring 1979) 12. "The subject of this small but weighty volume is the epistemological nature of the sciences of human action, particularly economics (praxeology). Mises shows how the theorems of economics . . . are deduced from *a priori* mental categories enjoined on all human thought by the 'logical structure of the human mind.' Theorems deduced from these categories are neither established nor verified by experience . . . . ¶The epistemological doctrine known as positivism, however, 'does not acknowledge any other ways of proving a proposition than those practiced by the experimental sciences and qualifies as . . . nonsensical all other methods of rational discourse'. . . . It is on this empiricist prejudice that Mises has trained his formidable intellectual artillery in this book . . . . ¶It is most appropriate that this new edition of Mises' final book includes a Foreword by his distinguished student, Professor Israel Kirzner. Kirzner notes the 'passion' which animates the book. Mises' ardor and tenacity in championing the cause of classical liberalism has seemed paradoxical to some in view of his insistence on *Wertfreiheit* in scientific inquiry. But, as Kirzner shows, Mises understood that liberal goals -- peace and prosperity -- could be served only by taking account of truths established by scientific inquiry untainted by value judgments. ¶Kirzner observes that 'since the first publication of this book . . . the pendulum of philosophical fashion has . . . swung decisively in Mises' direction.' He is optimistic that 'this work cannot fail to leave its impression in this present more hospitable intellectual atmosphere.' We hope he is right."

Peterson, William H. "Economist, His Pupil, Press Freedom's Case." *The Wall Street Journal.* (July 31, 1962). Reviewed in conjunction with Murray N. Rothbard's *Man, Economy, and State* (1962). "The theme of two new works on economics, one by Ludwig von Mises and the other by his former student, Murray N. Rothbard, is individualism; throughout the two works the authors urge the cause of freedom versus coercion . . . . ¶In the von Mises-Rothbard view the consumer is anything but passive, wooden, susceptible to the commands and wiles of hidden persuaders and wastemakers. In this view, the consumer is the director of production, deciding what shall be made and who shall make it, designating which corporations shall survive and which shall perish . . . . ¶Professor von Mises, in *The Ultimate Foundation of Economic Science*, deplores the empirical method with its unavoidable inference that there is no permanence in economic theory, no laws that could explain both the inflation in Rome from 45 to 62 A.D. and the inflation in the U.S. from 1945 to 1962 A.D. . . . ¶The von Mises and Rothbard books are important contributions to the literature of the dismal science. But whether our times will be influenced by these books and rediscover the conventional wisdom remains to be seen."

Sennholz, Hans F. "There IS Human Action." *The Individualist.* Phila., Penna.: Intercollegiate Society of Individualists. 2:3-4 (November/December 1963) 4-5. Reviewed in conjunction with *The Free and Prosperous Commonwealth* [*Liberalism*] (B-6). Concerning *The Ultimate Foundation of Economic Science*: "the only theme of this book is the fallaciousness of the fundamental thesis of positivism and to depict its disastrous consequences. ¶According to the author, the ultimate foundation of economics is the self-evident truth that man acts, i.e., consciously aims at ends chosen and resorts to the means that he considers appropriate to attain these ends . . . . By denying any cognitive significance to the *a priori* propositions of economics, positivism ignores precisely what makes man specifically human and different from all other animals and treats him exclusively from the zoological point of view . . . . ¶In the course of his analysis, the author also brings under critical scrutiny the logical contradictions involved in all forms of materialism."

Summers, Brian. *The Freeman.* Irvington, N.Y. 29:2 (February 1979) 126-128. Reviewed in conjunction with Mises' *Liberalism* (B-6). *"The Ultimate Foundation of Economic Science* is a critique of positivism, which has dominated economics for several decades. The positivist paradigm may be summarized as follows . . . ¶1. The positivist observes data . . . . 2. He constructs a theorem to explain the data . . . . 3. He 'tests' the theorem by further empirical observations . . . . ¶This paradigm is vitiated by the fact that the data used in steps 1 and 3 cannot derive from controlled experiments . . . . ¶In contrast with positivism, Mises' methodology does not need controlled experiments because he treats economics as a praxeological science -- a science of human action. Mises' paradigm may be summarized as follows: ¶1. The praxeologist postulates that all conscious human action is directed toward goals . . . . 2. From the actions of men, the praxeologist deduces their goals . . . . 3. Assuming a given set of actors' goals, the praxeologist constructs a theory based on the human actions that necessarily follow from the set of goals . . . . ¶In these difficult days, with mainstream economics in disarray, and freedom under constant attack, we welcome the reappearance of these two books by Ludwig von Mises, and hope that this time their lessons will be heeded."

Western Economics Encyclopedia (1971). Compiled by the Economic Research Department, Bank of Taiwan.

BOOKS AND ARTICLES ABOUT MISES

These books, articles, dissertations and other materials that refer to Mises
are arranged chronologically by year and then, within the year,
alphabetically by author.

Mises has been listed in several biographical dictionaries. The following list includes
all such entries the compilers have located; the list could undoubtedly be expanded.

American Men and Women of Science. New York: R. R. Bowker Co. 10th ed., 1962;
 11th ed., 1968. Also listed in the 12th edition.

The Austrian Presence in the United States. New York: Austrian Information Service,
 1976.

Contemporary Authors. Detroit: Gale Research Company, 1974.

Dictionary of International Biography. 10th edition. Cambridge, UK: International
 Biographical Centre, 1973.

Encyclopedia of World Biography. New York: McGraw-Hill.

Der grosse Brockhaus. 16th, fully revised, edition. Brief mention of Mises in Volume
 VIII (1955), p.46.

Das grosse Buch der Österreicher: 4500 Personen-darstellungen in Wort und Bild [The
 Great Book of Austrians: 4500 Presentations in Word and Picture]. Vienna:
 Kremayr & Scheriau, 1987. p. 349.

International Encyclopedia of the Social Sciences. New York: Macmillan, 1968. Article
 by Murray N. Rothbard.

The International Who's Who. 15th edition. London: Europa Publications Ltd., 1951.
 p.661.

The New York Times Obituaries Index 1969-1978. Volume II. New York: The New
 York Times, 1980. p.122. Alphabetized under "von."

Obituaries On File. Volume II. New York: Facts On File, 1979. Alphabetized under
 "von."

Österreich Lexikon [Austrian Encyclopedia]. *Volume II.* Dr. Richard Bamberger & Dr.
 Franz Maier-Bruck, eds. Vienna & Munich: Österreichischer Bundesverlag für
 Unterricht, Wissenschaft und Kunst. p.770.

Webster's Biographical Dictionary. Springfield, Mass.: G & C Merriam, 1976.
 p.1029.

Wer Is Wer [Who is Who]. Vienna, 1937.

Werdegang und Schriften der Mitglieder [Development and Writings of Members].
 Cologne: Kölner Verlags-Anstalt und Druckerei, 1929.

Who's Who in America. 37th edition. Chicago: Marquis, 1973.

Who's Who in Austria. 1959/1960.

Who's Who in the East. 7th edition. Chicago: Marquis, 1959.

Who's Who in Europe. Brussels: Editions de Feniks, 1963.

Who's Who in the World. Chicago: Marquis, 1973. Also in the first edition (1971-
 1972). Alphabetized under "von."

Who Was Who in America. Vol. VI, 1974-1976. Chicago: Marquis Who's Who, 1977?)
 p.418. Alphabetized under "von."

World Biography. New York: Institute for Research Biography, 1948.

1909

Federn, Walther. "Nochmals die Aufnahme der Barzahlungen" [Again the Resumption of Gold Payments]. *Der Oesterreichische Volkswirt.* 1:44 (July 31, 1909) 5-6. Federn credits Mises with having presented a good description of Austria-Hungary's currency reform in Article 09.1 on the problem of the legal resumption of gold payments in Austria-Hungary. However, Federn disagrees with Mises' position that the Austro-Hungarian Bank could instigate legal cash redemption simply by raising interest rates and refusing to issue foreign exchange below the gold points. Federn claims that Mises underestimates the effect that the Bank's refusal to satisfy the demand for foreign exchange would have on the market. Unlike the Bank of England, which redeems its money in gold, the policy of the Austro-Hungarian Bank is to satisfy the demand for foreign exchange; it follows an active foreign exchange policy.

_____. "Das Problem gesetzlicher Aufnahme der Barzahlungen in Österreich Ungarn" [The Problem of the Legal Resumption of Gold Payments in Austria-Hungary]. *Schmollers Jahrbuch für Gesetzgebung, Verwaltung und Volkswirtschaft.* Leipzig: Duncker & Humblot. (1909) 151-172. "In his presentation, Mr. von Mises argues that the Austro-Hungarian Bank has long been, actually if not legally, a bank of redemption and that this explains the stable value of its currency . . . . ¶If this were the case, then there would be no other problem than to repeal the paragraphs in the banking legislation suspending redemption and one could not then understand why also . . . many theoreticians and practitioners who are concerned with the question reject redemption as disadvantageous. However, Mr. von Mises is mistaken in this decisive point. The Austro-Hungarian Bank works in many respects like a redemption bank . . . . but its monetary policy shows important differences as opposed to the actual redemption banks . . . . ¶With the assertion that the bank has never refused to give out foreign exchange under the upper gold points, yet always thinks of refusing, Mr. von Mises stands in opposition not only to my position in the aforementioned article, but also to the facts. The opposite is true and this can be confirmed by the statements of all practicing Austro-Hungarian bank officials who deal with the business of foreign exchange." (Translated from the German) See Mises' 1910 response, Article 10.2.

Spann, Othmar. *Die Haupttheorien der Volkschaftslehre* [Leading Economic Theories]. 1912. For listing of English translation of the 19th revised edition (1929) of this book published as *Types of Economic Theory;* see "Books and Articles About Mises: 1930."

1914

Günther, Dr. "Erkenntnistheorie und Statistik" [Theory of Knowledge and Statistics]. *Deutsches Statistisches Zentralblatt.* 6:5 (May 1914) 145-150. Comments on Mises' Article 13.1 on the rise in the cost of living.

1917

Anderson, Benjamin M. Jr. *The Value of Money.* New York: Macmillan, 1917; 1936. "Austrian writers on the value of money, as Wieser and von Mises, have recognized more clearly than anyone in America or England, the essential dependence of the theory of the value of money on the general theory of value (p. 49) . . . . In von Mises there seem to me to be very noteworthy clarity and power. His *Theorie des Geldes und der Umlaufsmittel* [B-2] is an exceptionally excellent book." (p.100) This book introduced economic journalist Henry Hazlitt to Mises' work.

Bukharin, Nikolai. *The Economic Theory of the Leisure Class.* Completed in 1914, published in Russian in 1917; English translation issued by International Publishers, 1927; reprinted by Monthly Review Press, N. Y. and London, 1972. In the Preface to the Russian (1917) edition, Bukharin writes that he "went to Vienna after succeeding in making [his] escape from Siberia; [he] there attended the lectures of Böhm-Bawerk . . . . In the library of the University of Vienna, [he] went through the literature of the Austrian theorists." (p.7) "One of the latest advocates of the Austrian School, a specialist in the theory of money, Ludwig von Mises, admits, in his book, *Theorie des Geldes und der Umlaufsmittel* [B-2], that the Austrian money theory is not satisfactory." In a footnote to his study on "The Theory of Value," Bukharin quotes the same passage from Mises that Hilferding does in his 1912 review (see above, p.180, lines 10-17). Bukharin then continues: "Mises attempts to eliminate this circulus *vitiosus* [vicious circle] historically, somewhat after the same fashion as Böhm-Bawerk does in the section on substitution value, and of course with the same success. On this point *cf.* Rudolf Hilferding, *op. cit.*" (p.198, n.100)

1918

Rosenbaum, Siegfried. "Zur Währungsfrage" [On the Currency Question]. *Mitteilungen des Verbandes österreichischer Banken und Bankiers.* 1:5/6 (1918) 1-2. Rosenbaum asks several questions raised by the Quantity Theory: "Should the measures which follow from the Quantity Theory be carried out partially now and partially after the end of the war? And which measures should be effected immediately? . . . Do new vigorous issues of notes really help the state's finances?"

Mitteilungen des Verbandes österreichischer Banken und Bankiers. 1:5/6 (1918) 4-5. An unnamed bank president comments on Mises' Article 18.2 on the Quantity Theory which appeared in the previous issue of this same journal: "I do not believe, as Prof. Mises does, that the Quantity Theory already shows the way 'back to ordered currency relationships.' Unfortunately he does not say how 'to raise the gold exchange rate of the Austrian Crown to its August 2, 1892 position'. . . . ¶For 50 years we have been seeing two events occur at the same time and we are naturally inclined to connect them . . . . Just as we consider smoke the result of fire, so do we attribute higher prices to inflation. ¶Commodity prices could, however, never be explained from the money side, always from the goods side only . . . . ¶For four years, we have been consuming from our stocks; do we need any more serious explanation of the fantastic prices of the scanty stocks of remaining goods . . . . ¶If I may cite a great thinker, even if he was not a financial expert, F. M. Dostojewski: 'To return to sound finances in a state, after that state's finances have gone through convulsions, one must think not so much of present needs, no matter how urgent they may be; one must consider first of all the recovery of the roots and the finances will then improve themselves . . . .' ¶And these roots are the same as before: savings and increased production." (Passages quoted translated from the German)

Mises replies to both commentators in this same issue of *Mitteilungen* . . . ; see Article 18.3.

1920

Cohn, A. W. *Kann das Geld abgeschaft werden?* [Can Money Be Abolished?]. Jena: Gustav Fischer, 1920. Discusses Mises' Article 20.6 on the socialist calculation debate. Cohn claims the calculation problem has already been solved by A. Schäffle's "social tax." (*Bau und Leben des sozialen Körpers* [Construction and Life of the Social Entity] vol. 3, Tübingen, 1878). In Article 23.6, Mises comments on Cohn's claim concerning Schäffle: "Schäffle's proposal is unfortunately completely useless; it rests on a misunderstanding of our problem. Schäffle would have his taxes established by official decree . . . . Schäffle's serious error rests on the fact that he believes there is a 'socialistic,' a 'direct social measure of value,' i.e. its yield which exists 'in each aliquot [fractional] portion of the entire quantity of socially (socialized) labor time actually performed'." (Translated from the German) NOTE: This discussion of Cohn and Schäffle not included in the excerpt from Article 23.6 reproduced as the "Appendix" to the 2nd (1924) and later editions of *Socialism*, B-4.

1921

Schwarz, Felix. *Stabilisierung.* Vienna: Peter Floyd. #95/96 (May 3/4, 1921). "In his most worthy *Theory of Money and Credit* (B-2), Professor Ludwig von Mises pointed out in a very clever way under what circumstances interest in the regulation of foreign exchange revived toward the end of the 1880s in Austria-Hungary. So long as the exchange rate 'crept' upward, so long as industry enjoyed export premiums and agriculture enjoyed rising prices for grain, there was little interest in foreign exchange. When things began to improve and the British pound became cheaper, the wish arose everywhere for 'orderly' foreign exchange relations . . . . With stabilization, should the [Austrian] Crown be prevented only from rising above a certain rate in Zurich? Or should it also be prevented from dropping below a certain rate?" (Translated from the German)

1922

Heimann, E. *Mehrwert und Gemeinwirtschaft* [Surplus Value and the Socialist Commonwealth]. Berlin: Hans Robert Engelmann, 1922. Mises comments on this book in Article 23.6: Heimann is "a believer in an ethical or religious Socialism . . . . [who] tries to prove that one could calculate in a socialist economy." See the "Appendix" to the 2nd (1924) and later editions of *Socialism* (B-4) where portions of Article 23.6 are reproduced.

Kautsky, Karl. *Die proletarische Revolution und ihr Programm* [The Proletarian Revolution and Its Program]. Berlin: Dietz Nachfolger, 1922. Kautsky rejected the labor theory of value as the basis for socialist economic calculation and advocated using historical market prices, adjusted somehow -- he did not say how. In Article 23.6, Mises quoted Kautsky: "Instead of attempting the hopeless task of measuring flowing water with a sieve -- and that is what determining value is like -- the proletarian regime in distributing commodities should cling to what it can grasp, i. e. historically-established prices. These are measured in gold today; they do not abolish, but only mask and distort the most extreme inflation." This, Kautsky says, "is far more easily undertaken from case to case than by reckoning the labor value of all commodities for the introduction of a labor money. Naturally one cannot proceed with this arbitrarily." Mises then criticized Kautsky: "regrettably Kautsky fails to show how this could happen other than arbitrarily. And although he recommends retaining the capitalistic monetary system, he hints that he does not want a monetary theory at all." (Translated from the German) This portion of Article 23.6 not reprinted in the "Appendix" to the 2nd (1924) and later editions of *Socialism* (B-4).

Weber, Max. *Wirtschaft und Gesellschaft* [Economy and Society]. Tübingen: Grundriss der Sozialökonomik, 1922. For annotated listing of English translation of Vol. I, Part 1, published as *The Theory of Social and Economic Organization* (London: Oxford University Press, 1947), see "Books and Articles About Mises: 1947."

1923

Braun, Martha Stephanie. *Die Doppelnote: Währungs-politische Projekte der Nachkriegszeit (1918-1922)* [The Double Standard: Post War Project for Financial Policy]. *Schriften des Vereines für Sozialpolitik.* Duncker & Humblot, 1923. pp.107-165. Braun cites Mises' book on money (B-2) as her authority for saying that "if two kinds of money were recognized as legal tender and their value in relation to one another was fixed -- that is if a double standard were created -- all the consequences of Gresham's law would appear in their most extreme form." (p.134) (Translated from the German)

Leichter, O. *Die Wirtschaftsrechnung in der sozialistischen Gesellschaft* [Economic Calculation in the Socialist Society]. Vienna: Wiener Volksbuchhandlung, 1923. Leichter's position in the economic calculation debate is that prices under socialism should be determined by using the labor theory of value. Mises comments in Article 23.6: "Leichter's assertion that all these problems are solved daily every day of the week during which the wages for every kind of labor are formed is entirely mistaken. The wage rate is formed through market transactions on the basis of subjective value judgments; and the problem exists already in the investigation of whether it would be possible also in an exchange-less society to trace the different qualities of labor back to a uniform expression. Leichter sees in this objection nothing but 'market fetishism,' (an expression of which he is immensely proud of having coined) . . . . The source of Leichter's error is to be found in the inadequacy and in the lack of clarity of his understanding of the nature of the market and of the formation of market prices." (Translated from the German) This portion of Article 23.6 not included in the "Appendix" to the 2nd (1924) and later editions of *Socialism* (B-4).

Marschak, J. "Wirtschaftsrechnung und Gemeinwirtschaft: Zur Misesschen These von der Unmöglichkeit sozialistischer Wirtschaftsrechnung" [Economic Calculation and the Socialist Commonwealth: the Misesian Thesis of the Impossibility of Socialist Economic Calculation]. *Archiv für Sozialwissenschaft und Sozialpolitik.* 51 (1923/4) 501-520. By arguing that rational economic calculation wasn't possible under capitalism either, Marschak attempts to refute Mises' position, as expressed in Article 20.6, that economic calculation was not possible under socialism. Mises responded in Article 28.3: Marschak "simply follows the example given by all socialist authors: speaking as little as possible of socialism and as much as possible of the inadequacy of the capitalist economic order. Marschak seeks to prove that economic calculation is possible also under syndicalism. That has never been disputed, least of all not by me [Mises]. But the scientific problem under discussion is economic calculation in the socialist society, not in a syndicalistic society." (Translated from the German)

Polanyi, Karl. "Sozialistische Rechnungslegung" [Socialistic Accounting]. *Archiv für Sozialwissenschaft und Sozialpolitik.* 49 (1923) 377-420. Polanyi concurs with Mises that the problem of economic calculation is insoluble in a centrally administered economy. However, he proposes to solve the problem by means of "a functionally organized socialist transition-economy." Mises' criticism of Polanyi in Article 23.6 translated and reprinted in the "Appendix" to the 2nd (1924) and later editions of *Socialism* (B-4).

1924

de Bordes, J. van Walré. *The Austrian Crown: Its Depreciation and Stabilization.* London: P. S. King & Son, 1924. Discusses the Austro-Hungarian Bank's foreign exchange policy. Cites Mises' Article 09.2 (p.220n).

Haberler, Gottfried. "Kritische Bemerkungen zu Schumpeters Geldtheorie: Zur Lehre vom 'objektiven' Tauschwert des Geldes" [Critical Comments on Schumpeter's Monetary Theory: On the Objective Exchange Value of Money]. *Zeitschrift für Volkswirtschaft und Sozialpolitik.* New Series. 4:10-12 (1924/25) 647-668. Includes a discussion of the ongoing terminological debate between Mises and Haberler concerning the "inner" and "outer" (market) exchange value of money. Mises' comments on this controversy on p.29n in *Geldwertstabilisierung* . . . (B-7); on p.86n of the English translation in *On the Manipulation* . . . (B-24).

Polanyi, Karl. "Die funktionelle Theorie der Gesellschaft und das Problem der sozialistischen Rechnungslegung" [The Functional Theory of Society and the Problem of Socialist Accounting]. *Archiv für Sozialwissenschaft und Sozialpolitik.* 52 (1924).

1925

Bukharin, Nikolai. "O novoi ekonomicheskoi politike i nashikh zadachakh" [Concerning the New Economic Policy and Our Tasks]. *Bolshevik.* 8-9/10 (April 30, June 1, 1925). Translated from the Russian and published (pp.183-208) in *Selected Writings on the State and the Transition to Socialism.* Translated, edited, and introduced by Richard B. Day. Armonk, N.Y.: M. E. Sharpe, 1982. Bukharin wrote: "One of the most learned critics of communism, the Austrian Professor Mises, presented the following propositions in a book on socialism written in 1921-22. In agreement with Marxist socialists he declared that one must brush aside all sentimental nonsense and accept the fact that the best economic system is the one that develops productive forces most successfully. But the so-called 'destructive' socialism of the communists leads to the collapse of productive forces rather than their development . . . . mainly because the communists forget the enormous role of private, individualistic incentives and private initiative . . . . So long as the communists attempted to arrange production by commands, with a stick, their policy would lead, and already was leading, to an inevitable collapse. ¶There is no doubt that the system of War Communism . . . somewhat resembled this [Mises'] caricature of socialism . . . . Thus when we began to reject this system and shift to a rational economic policy, the bourgeois ideologists began to cry: Now they are retreating from communist ideas . . . and are returning to time-honored capitalism . . . . ¶When we crossed over to the NEP we began to overcome in practice the above-outlined bourgeois case against socialism . . . . [B]y using the economic initiative of the peasants, of the small producers, and even of the bourgeoisie, and by allowing private accumulation, we also placed these people objectively in the service of socialist state industry and of the economy as a whole . . . . [W]e encouraged these strata to work in such a way that their *private* interests would promote an upsurge of social production." (pp.188-189)

Cassau. Contribution to *Festgabe für Lujo Brentano zum 80. Geburtstag* [Festschrift commemorating Lujo Brentano's 80th birthday]. Munich: Duncker & Humblot, 1925.   According to Mises' Article 28.3, Cassau is sympathetic to socialism and "the experiences of recent decades had passed him over without influencing his ideology at all." (Translated from the German)

Neurath, O. *Wirtschaftsplan und Naturalrechnung* [Economic Plan and Natural (Barter) Accounting]. Berlin: E. Laub, 1925. Mises discussed Neurath's book in Article 28.3: "It is certainly true that without having recourse to money one may, as Neurath says, compare two concrete portions of different goods and designate one portion more valuable, the other less valuable. That is not disputed. However, that has nothing at all to do with the question of how one can arrive at a recapitulation and a comparison in accounting terms of supplies of various kinds of goods and services." (Translated from the German)

Röpke, Wilhelm. "Sozialisierung" [Socialization]. *Handwörterbuch der Staatswissenschaften.* 4th ed. L. Elster, Ad. Weber, Fr. Wieser, eds. Jena: Gustav Fischer, 1925. pp.567-578. Cites Mises (p.569n) in support of the thesis that there can be no middle ground between centralized socialism and syndicalism. Refers also (p.575n) to Mises' comments in *Socialism* (B-4) on the international division of labor.

Spitzmüller, Alexander von.   "Volkswirtschaft, Finanzwirtschaft und Geld" [Economy, Finance, and Money]. *Handbuch der Finanzwissenschaft.* 7:149 (1925) 57-85. Mises is mentioned briefly (p.59) in part 1 on "The Nature and Meaning of Money in General."

1926   Mises Founds the Austrian Institute for Business Cycle Research

Angell, James W. *Theory of International Prices: History, Criticism and Restatement.*   Cambridge: Harvard University Press, 1926. In Chapter XIII, "German and Austrian Thought since 1860," Angell distinguishes among several theories concerning the effect of money on prices and international trade: "Finally, and especially in Austria, a number of theories have been advanced which are derived from a *subjective* doctrine of value . . . . They assert the entire lack of any necessary proportionality between the amount of money and its value, and tend to stress the 'commodity' side of the complex of factors which alter that value. Of the writers in this school, it is sufficient to name Menger, Wieser, Philippovich, and Mises. Wieser and Mises give, too, what has at another point been called the 'direct' chain of effects produced by an increase in the quantity of money. That is, they begin with the augmented purchasing power of those who first receive the new increment of money, and show how this purchasing power, gradually diffused throughout the given society, leads to an irregular rise in general prices." (pp.326-327) Angell also discusses Mises' views on foreign trade under depreciated currencies, foreign exchange and inter-local price equalization.

Herzfeld, Marianne. "Die Geschichte als Funktion der Geldbewegung: Zum Problem der inflationistischen Geschichtstheorie" [History as a Function of the Movement of Money: The Problem of the Inflationist Theory of History]. *Archiv für Sozialwissenschaft und Sozialpolitik.* 56:3 (1926) 654-686. Herzfeld quotes from Mises' book on money (B-2) in opposition to the pro-inflationist views of Paul Barth, Brooks Adams, and others, including Werner Sombart who thought it was only "the opening of rich silver mines and gold fields in America" that made the success of the modern state and the transformation of the social organization possible. (Translated from the German)

1928

Brutzkus, Boris. *Die Lehren des Marxismus im Lichte der russischen Revolution* [Marxist Theory in the Light of the Russian Revolution]. Berlin: H. Sack, 1928. This work, first published in 1922 in Russian, led to its author's imprisonment and then banishment. Brutzkus agrees with Mises that economic calculation is impossible if only labor is used as a yardstick; land, labor and capital, all three, are needed. Mises considered Brutzkus the first to deal in a scientific way with post-revolutionary Soviet Union. Mises commented in Article 28.3: "Brutzkus' work, now in German, analyzes the unfortunate attempts of Tschajanow, Strumilin and Varga, who, right after the publication of my [Mises] 'Economic Calculation in the Socialistic Commonwealth' [Article 20.6], attempted to find a system of socialistic accounting. This discussion, amplified by Brutzkus, led to recognition that without value calculation rational economic conduct in the traditional economic system would be completely impossible . . . . The work of Brutzkus is the first and so far the only scientific publication which deals with the fundamental problems of the Soviet state."   (Translated from the German)

Burchardt, Fritz. "Entwicklungsgeschichte der monetaren Konjunkturtheorie" [The History of the Development of the Monetary Theory of the Trade Cycle]. *Weltwirtschafiliches Archiv.*   28:1 (July 1928) 77-143. Discusses Mises' theory on pp.123-125.

Eaton, Howard Ormsby. "The Austrian Philosophy of Value." Ph.D. dissertation, University of Wisconsin, 1928. See also "Books and Articles About Mises: 1930," Eaton.

Horn, Erich. *Die ökonomischen Grenzen der Gemeinwirtschaft: Eine wirtschaftstheoretische Untersuchung über die Durchführbarkeit des Sozialismus* [The Economic Limits to the Socialist Society: A Theoretical Economic Investigation into the Feasibility of Socialism]. Halberstadt: H. Meyers, 1928. Mises comments on Horn in Article 28.3. Contrary to Neurath (1925), Mises says, Horn concludes: "If a socialistically-oriented economic order values economic conduct, it must turn to capitalistic calculation with a generally-accepted money to determine an enterprise's wealth, profit and income. In spite of upheavals and socializations, capitalism is understood as unalterable and unchanging because it is the prototype of economy." (Translated from the German)

Strigl, Richard. "Aenderungen in den Daten der Wirtschaft: Untersuchungen über die Anwendbarkeit der ökonomischen Theorie" [Changes in Economic Data: Investigations into the Applicability of Economic Theory]. *Jahrbücher für Nationalökonomie und Statistik.* Jena: Gustav Fischer, 1928. 128 (3:73) 641-662. Thinking of "need," in the physiological sense only, may lead to misunderstandings. Strigl writes: "Since religion and national pride participate just as does a boundless craving for pleasure, they play fundamentally the same role as does the need for food and housing." (p.651) In referring to such "needs" that stem from so-called "non-economic goals," Strigl footnotes Mises' Article 28.2 on subjective value theory. (Translated from the German)

_____. "Wirtschaftstheorie im Dienste der Wirtschaftspolitik" [Economic Theory in the Service of Economic Policy]. *Archiv für Sozialwissenschaft und Sozialpolitik.* 60:2 (October 1928) 353-367. Strigl refers to Mises' thesis that the international division of labor was "one of the most magnificent concepts" in classical theory (p.355). He also cites Mises in support of the position that interventionist measures based on historical economics, rather than theory, produce not only direct results but also unintended and undesired consequences. (pp.360-361)

Weber, Adolf. *Allgemeine Volkswirtschaftslehre: Eine Einführung* [Basic Economic Theory: An Introduction]. Munich: Duncker & Humblot. [1928 ?]. Mises summarizes Weber's position in Article 28.3: If the socialist economy is to follow rational principles to attain its goal, it cannot ignore competition among consumers; only with market prices and free and open competition can decisions be made to expand or contract production. Monetary calculation is necessary also to determine the profitability of the various enterprises, to arrange cooperation among them, and to use specialized labor rationally. Prices must be established not only for finished products but also for all intermediary stages, especially for the scarce elements of production labor and capital.

1929

Bundsmann, Ernst. *Das Geld als Einkommensquelle: Eine wirtschaftstheoretische Untersuchung über Kapital und Kapitalzins* [Money as a Source of Income: A Theoretical Economic Investigation of Capital and Interest]. Innsbruck: Universitäts-Verlag Wagner, 1929. Bundsmann refers in his book, on the pages indicated in brackets, to *The Theory of Money and Credit* (B-2): "Mises sees a sharp distinction between capital and money. In the modern economy -- Mises informs us -- the demand for real factors of production, the demand for capital, appears in the form of a demand for money . . . . The supply of capital is apparently a supply of money. What one usually calls a surplus or a scarcity of money is really a surplus or scarcity of capital [p.6] . . . . ¶So Mises, who would like to construct a distinction between money and capital, has also failed to find a plausible difference between money-interest and capital-interest . . . . ¶If Mises wanted to say that all demand for money seeks to establish the relation to commodities, one could agree with his view . . . . However, if Mises in association with Wicksell distinguishes between the natural rate of interest, i.e. the rate of interest which would be established by supply and demand if real capital were loaned *in natura* without the intercession of money, and the money rate of interest, i.e. the rate of interest which is asked for and which is given for loans existing in money or money substitutes, then I reject this distinction; I cannot imagine the determination of the natural rate of interest." [pp.70-71] (Translated from the German)

Engel-Jánosi, Friedrich. "Zur Geschichte der Finanzwirtschaft Wiens" [On the History of the Financial Economy of Vienna]. *Zeitschrift für Nationalökonomie.* Vienna: Julius Springer. (1929) 461-466. A review of Otto Brunner's *Die Finanzen der Stadt Wien von den Anfangen bis ins 16. Jahrhundert* [The Finances of the City of Vienna from the Beginning to the 16th Century]. *Studien aus dem Archiv der Stadt Wien.* 1/2 (1929) 462. Credits Brunner with having made good use of his source materials and for not having discounted the importance of theory in interpreting historical events. In support of this thesis, the reviewer cites Mises' "Sociology and History." (Article 29.2)

Heydel, Adam. "Gospodarcze Granice Liberalizmu I Etatyzmu" [The Economic Limits of Liberalism and Etatism]. *Towarzystwa Ekonomicznego W Krakowie.* 35 (Kracow, 1929). 29pp. According to Polish translator's summary, the author is a proponent of less government control over the economy. Reduced government involvement will increase productivity and will benefit the entire society. All business activities should be privately owned. Cites Mises' positions on drugs, coffee and tobacco, on luxury which is relative (what is a luxury today is a necessity tomorrow) and on government which should be forced to stay uninvolved in the economy. Reprinted in *The Lost Twenty Years, 1918-1939: Polish Capitalism in the Claws of Statism.* Wroclaw [Breslau], Poland, 1987 (?).

_____. "Ludwik Mises o Liberalism" [Ludwig Mises on Liberalism]. Poznan: Ruch Prawniczy i Ekonomiczny. #3, 1929. A recent correspondent in Poland, writes that this article presents the principal ideas of Ludwig von Mises and defends them against Polish statist economists. Our Polish correspondent says that Heydel was killed during World War II at Auschwitz. Reprinted in *The Lost Twenty Years, 1918-1939: Polish Capitalism in the Claws of Statism.* Wroclaw [Breslau], Poland, 1987 (?).

Lipiner, Josef Alex. "Nationalökonomie und ärztliche Standespolitik" [Economics and Policy Respecting the Status of the Medical Profession]. *Mitteilungen der Wirtschaftlichen Organisation der Ärzte Wiens."* Nos. 9 & 10 (1929). Reprinted separately (Vienna and Leipzig: Moritz Perles) 27pp. Discusses Mises' *Critique of Interventionism* (B-8) with special attention to chapters 1, "Interventionism," and 5, "Theory of Price Controls." Applies Mises' "Critique" to medical profession policy: "Only through the laws of the unhampered labor market is freedom over our means of production and self-determination of the prices for our product regulated . . . . A renunciation of the present system of continuing 'interventionist policy,' which has been criticized here, would undoubtedly bring about the qualified material and indirect cultural improvement of the Austrian medical profession (the natural selection of qualitatively better doctors would be a further effect); in the final analysis it would also improve the health of the people and the welfare of the entire population. ¶Only such a radical renunciation of the methods up to now in force can really bring relief from existing grievances. Anything else must inevitably remain only patchwork. A return to any other apparently cheaper, coercive form of medical care (with or without individual compensation) or with a doctoral system of fixed payments would lead in a short time to absurdity." (pp.23-24) (Translated from the German)

Machlup, Fritz. "Geldtheorie und Konjunkturtheorie" [Monetary Theory and Cyclical Policy]. *Mitteilungen des Verbandes österreichischer Banken und Bankiers.* 11:5/6 (August 8, 1929) 166-174. Discusses the works of several authors, including Mises, on monetary theory and cyclical policy.

Tismer, Alfred. *Die Stabilisierung des Geldwertes als Ziel der Währungspolitik* [The Stabilization of the Value of Money as a Goal of Monetary Policy]. Berlin-Charlottenburg: Hoffmann, 1929. On pp.42-49, Tismer discusses and footnotes Mises' *Geldwertstabilisierung* . . . (B-7; English translation in *On the Manipulation* . . . B-24). "Mises proclaims the victory of the 'Monetary Theory of the Trade Cycle' over the obsolete view of the Banking School and considers it the further development of the Currency School's perception . . . . ¶The Currency Theory [according to Mises] is a monetary theory of the trade cycle since it is 'the theory which traces the cause of changes in business conditions to the phenomenon of circulation credit.' In contrast, the Banking Theory with its view of the inability of the banks to force notes into circulation overlooked completely the fact that the banks, by reducing their interest rate, could expand the turnover of notes at will. ¶A critique of the 'Monetary Theory of the Trade Cycle' on this interpretation of the dispute between the Banking and Currency Schools cannot be neglected . . . . ¶It is incomprehensible how Mises can reproach the Banking School for its inattention to the interest problem. The Banking Theory not only recognized the meaning and the workings of the bank interest rate in the course of the cycle; in discussing the inability to impose the bank notes by force, it also emphasized the independence of the entrepreneurial point of view . . . . ¶The foundation for Mises' interpretation is to be found in the Banking, not the Currency School. Tooke's criticism of the discount policy which the Bank of England followed in its more rigid application of the principles of Peel's Act during the years preceding the crises of 1848 and 1857 rest, so far as they have historical justification, on authorized 'monetary' perceptions with which Mises should agree instead of reproaching the Banking Theory for its inadequacy in such harsh words . . . . ¶For Mises, the proposal for full gold cover for all notes and demand deposits (except for the currently uncovered supply as a contingency), which he recommends as the most important and only 'cyclical policy for avoiding the crisis,' stands incomprehensibly in opposition to the facts . . . . ¶The assertion that Mises really builds on the Banking Theory is corroborated once one determines that he relies on the Banking Theory in his advocacy of free banking principles also. If he had inquired a little more carefully into this contradiction, he would perhaps have found that the inconsistency lies not with the Banking School but with him. It was Adolph Wagner who never tired of deploring how the centralization of the issue of banknotes, the suspension of freedom in the issue of notes, creates the tendency toward the creation of excessive credit that Mises wants to make responsible as the starting point of cyclical movements. ¶Still another point on which Mises' banking theory expresses the Banking School viewpoint: as in English banking law, he does not ask for absolute full gold cover for all note- and deposit-balances, but would leave the present uncovered supply standing as a contingency. This contingency then allows an opportunity for the emission of money by the banks. ¶Mises considers the theory he advocates as the further development of a theory which cannot be traced back any farther; he ties its monetary policy goal to the complete adjustment of notes in circulation to the gold in existence. Therefore, he does not draw the same conclusion for monetary policy which Hahn draws from an understanding of money. This is an example of historically false interpretations of doctrines having a bewildering influence on the determination of practical goals for the present." (Translated from the German)

1930

Eaton, Howard O. *The Austrian Philosophy of Value.* Norman, Oklahoma: University of Oklahoma Press, 1930. See also Eaton's Ph.D. dissertation, 1928.

Harris, S. E. *The Assignats.* Cambridge: Harvard University Press, 1930. Cites Mises' *Die geldtheoretische Seite* . . . (B-5; English translation in *On the Manipulation* . . . B-24). Commenting on the "thesis that changes in the value of money are caused in large part by changing political fortunes," Harris notes that "Mises observes that military success was accompanied by final depreciation during both the French and American revolutions." (p.203) Harris also remarks on Mises' "extreme position" with respect to the effect of inflation on foreign exchange rates. (p.235n)

Keynes, John Maynard. *A Treatise on Money.* 2 vols. New York: Harcourt Brace, 1930. Keynes' interventionist, pro-inflationist treatment of money differed radically from that of Mises. In this 1930 Treatise, however, he referred in a footnote to Mises' contributions: "The notion of the distinction which I have made between Savings and Investment has been gradually creeping into economic literature in quite recent years. The first author to introduce it was, according to the German authorities,* Ludwig Mises in his *Theorie des Geldes und der Umlaufsmittel* (1st edition, pp. 227 ff. and 411 ff.) published in 1912. [B-2] Later on the idea was adopted in a more explicit form by Schumpeter, and 'Forced Saving' (*i.e.* the difference between Savings and Value of Investment as defined by me, though without there being attached to the idea -- so far as I am aware -- anything closely corresponding to the analysis of chapters 10 and 11 above) has become almost a familiar feature of the very newest German writings on Money." (Vol.I, p.171n)

> *In a footnote to this footnote, Keynes refers to Hahn, "Kredit," *Handwörterbuch der Staatswissenschaften* (4th ed.) vol. v. p. 951; Schumpeter, *Theorie der wirtschaftlichen Entwicklung* (2nd ed., 1926), p. 156; and Mises, *Geldwertstabilisierung* . . . (B-7; English translation in *On the Manipulation* . . . B-24).

Farther on in the *Treatise* (p.199), Keynes refers to "a school of thought . . . developing in Germany and Austria" with such economists as Ludwig Mises, Hans Neisser, and Friedrich Hayek. Then in a footnote he confesses, "I should have made more references to the work of these writers if their books, which have only come into my hands as these pages are being passed through the press, had appeared when my own thought was at an earlier stage of development, and if my knowledge of the German language was not so poor (in German I can only clearly understand what I know already! -- so that *new* ideas are apt to be veiled from me by the difficulties of language)." (p.199n)

Linpinsel, Elsbet. "Zur Theorie und Kritik des philosophischen und ökonomischen Anarchismus" [On the Theory and Critique of Philosophical and Economic Anarchy]. *Zeitschrift für Politik.* Berlin: Carl Heymanns Verlag, 1930. 19: 386-405. Cites Mises several times and footnotes his works as indicated: "There is by no means agreement on the criterion for socialism. All that can be said with certainty is that socialism strives for an organized standardized, communal life for the people, regulated in a certain way and above all, authoritarian . . . . The socialist economy is nothing more nor less than a new social 'organization' like State and Church; 'like State and Church, this socialist state rests on the principle of violence.' [*Socialism* (B-4)] . . . . ¶The scarcity of products available cannot, as the anarchists believe, be distributed at will. If the allocation may be influenced somewhat by the exercise of force, even this exercise of force is restrained within limits. The allocation is directed finally according to the value acknowledged to the recipient for his performance in the production process, the value of which is influenced on his side by the scarcity of his contribution. Moreover the inequality in the distribution of goods is the dynamic force in economic life. [*Liberalism* (B-6)] ¶We are dealing here with the old conflict; does the economic organization conform to laws, or does it depend only on the caprice of certain groups? The anarchists maintain the optimistic view that only 'historical-legal' categories are decisive. They overlook the fact 'that Nature grants no rights at all, and just because she dispenses only the scantiest means of subsistence . . . man is forced to take economic action.' [*Socialism* (B-4)] . . . ¶The role of liberalism in economic life is characterized by an understanding of relatively unlimited private ownership. 'Private property creates for the individual a sphere in which he is free of the state' [*Liberalism* (B-6)] and as a result it becomes the basis for the development of spiritual (intellectual) powers . . . . ¶Liberalism generally permits, therefore, the greatest amount of wide-ranging freedom for the individual, without rejecting organization completely." (pp.395, 404-405) (Translated from the German)

Neisser, Hans "Notenbankfreiheit?" [Freedom for Banks of Issue?]. *Weltwirtschaftliches Archiv.* 32:2 (October 1930) 447-461. A critique of free banking as presented by Mises in *Geldwertstabilisierung* . . . . (B-7; English translation in *On the Manipulation* . . . B-24). Neisser holds that the controversy between government central banking and private banking with freedom to issue notes was settled in 1869 by Adolph Wagner in his *System der Zettelbankpolitik* [System of Central Bank Policy]. Neisser quotes his own 1928 book, *Tauschwert des Geldes* [The Exchange Value of Money], in opposition to Mises' thesis. The page numbers in parentheses refer to pages in Neisser's article. "Only in an economically oriented non-private bank can one expect to find concern for cyclical changes and the indispensable policy of maintaining reserves." (p.447) Neisser then criticizes Mises' position that competition would limit the excesses of a system of free banking: "To be sure Mises does not believe that cyclical fluctuations would be fully eliminated or even that stabilization of the price level is attainable; however he believes that freedom in the issue of banknotes will bring about a far reaching reduction in cyclical waves (p.448) . . . . ¶Mises, formerly the sharpest enemy of the Banking Theory, obviously believes that one can handle the problem under discussion entirely outside the Banking-Currency struggle. Thus it is possible for him to be unfaithful in one respect to the Currency doctrine and his system of unrestricted liberalism and still continue to his radical end, i..e. the elimination of all state intervention from economic life. The following investigation will show on the contrary that all arguments for bank freedom and also for Mises' special view of a competitive system resting on an extensive automatic mechanism of restriction are based on Banking School principles, and that one cannot accept freedom for the issue of banknotes and at the same time throw out the theory of the automatic flow-back of notes to the banks of issue. (p.449) . . . . ¶A single bank which out of cautious business practices, leans in this direction [promising redemption on demand in the legal media of exchange, eventually gold] would adjust very little, even if there were other possibilities to expand their credit business by the issue of notes for the sake of high profit; then in the event of a sudden strong demand for credit and cash money the prudent bank would have no fewer demands made on it than the incautious bank; and since no cash reserves yield 100%, if the emission business continues to be economically profitable privately, the cautious bank would have to suffer to about the same extent the consequences of its competitors' lack of caution, while the advantages of higher interest returns to the banking business had not been similarly advantageous to it. ¶Mises is of the opposite opinion. It would not be the prudent bank that would be drawn into the whirlpool of the incautious, but rather the other way around; the incautious would not be able to hold out along side the cautious. (pp.449-450) . . . ¶Will things work out as Mises says . . . . ? (p.451) ¶Now, we can clearly recognize also the last cause of Mises' fallacy: it rests on equating notes and checking accounts (demand deposits, as he calls them), the circulation of which is in fact very different. Banknotes can be unlimited in quantity, their distribution throughout the entire populace, even if the issuing offices are private banks, while the circulation of checks is much narrower; sooner or later the time comes when a circulating check is converted into cash money in order to be able to retain its function as money. Hence an increase to a bank's checking deposits, as it is effected through credit expansion, leads to a stronger claim to its cash reserves, which necessarily limits the creation of credit, while a similar shrinking in the issue of notes may not be perceptible if the public is accustomed to using the bank's notes in trade as a means of payment and if considerable stocks of cash are still maintained outside the banks (p.454-455) . . . . ¶It seems to me that Mises overrates the meaning of state intervention: First of all historically: the ability of the American treasury to come to the aid of the national banking system before and during the [1907] crisis was limited legally and also economically; in fact government intervention knew how to prevent neither the breakdown of all the banks nor serious losses to the banks that did not collapse (p.456) . . . . ¶Excessive emission of notes through individual banks would be possible only as an effect of the capitalistic principle of profitability, also as a result of the absence of any 'ideology of low interest rates.' Only a central bank of issue not oriented toward private economically-based principles will properly limit the extent of checkbook money in the cyclical boom." (p.461) (Translated from the German)

Robbins, Lionel. "The Economic Works of Phillip Wicksteed." *Economica.* (November 1930) 245-258. In the course of this rather laudatory account of Wicksteed's works, Robbins writes: "[A] small group of economists -- Wicksteed and Knight in English-speaking countries, Schumpeter and Mises in Central Europe -- have raised the whole discussion of equilibrium analysis on to an entirely new plane -- a plane on which Economics is seen to be a discussion not of the nature of certain *kinds* of behaviour arbitrarily separated off from all others, but of a certain *aspect* of behaviour viewed as a whole." (p.257) This article based on a chapter written by Robbins for inclusion in C. H. Herford's *Philip Henry Wicksteed, His Life and Work* (1931).

Röpke, Wilhelm. "Liberale Handelspolitik" [Liberal Trade Policy]. *Archiv für Rechts- und Wirtschaftsphilosophie.* 24:3 [1930?] 345-365. Röpke discusses the confusion over the definition of the term "liberal." "In no area of economic policy is the meaning and sense of the word 'liberal' so clear and unambiguous as it is in the field of foreign trade policy. The truly liberal attitude in the field of social policy, farm policy or industrial policy seems to be so uncertain that meanings diverge widely; the social policy or farm policy that one person calls 'liberal,' another will call the opposite." However, Röpke disapproves of the tone of Mises' critique of governmental intervention in "Sozialliberalismus" (Article 26.4): "[B]order-line cases are conceivable in which Liberalism as method -- the method of state non-intervention -- could endanger Liberalism itself as end and value; a discussion of the possibility of such a danger can at least be held without having to stigmatize the enemies of the liberal method as disloyal. In the light of such a view it seems wrong to dismiss 'social liberalism' -- as Mises does -- as a degeneration and a heresy against pure liberal theory." Röpke discusses protective tariffs, tariffs for revenue, various interventions in domestic affairs, one-way free trade, migration barriers, etc. His theme throughout is that, in spite of the "triumph" of protectionism throughout the world, the liberal idea of free trade has lost none of its strength as a "principle." (Translated from the German)

Spann, Othmar. *Types of Economic Theory* (1st ed., 1909). Translated from the revised 19th German edition (1929) by Eden & Cedar Paul. London: George Allen & Unwin, 1930. "Midway between the metallist view [that the essence of money is in its metallic commodity nature] and the chartalist [that money has lost its metallic commodity quality] is the outlook of Friedrich von Wieser, who ascribes only a historical role to the material or substantial nature of money, but considers that paper money owes its entity to 'mass custom' (and not, therefore, to the juridical order) -- an idea which likewise found earlier expression in the writings of Adolf Wagner. The same opinion is voiced by Mises." (pp.287-288) Spann groups Mises with the "more recent economists" who have espoused the quantity theory of money. (p.289)

1931

Hayek, F. A. *Prices and Production.*   First published September 1931; reprinted, January 1932; New York: Macmillan, 1932; 2nd, revised and enlarged edition, London: George Routledge, 1935.   In his Foreword (June 1931), Lionel Robbins writes: "Misled by a preoccupation with the value of money, they [the early economists] failed completely to produce a theory which explains those changes in the 'real' structure of production which are the most characteristic feature of trade fluctuation as we know it . . . . ¶The School of Vienna, which in recent years, under the leadership of Professor Mayer and Professor Mises, has experienced such a marvelous renaissance, has laid the scientific world under yet another lasting obligation. Working on the basis of the Böhm-Bawerkian theory of capital and the Wicksellian theory of divergences between money and equilibrium rates of interest, Professor Mises and Dr. Hayek have advanced theories which . . . . explain the effects of fluctuations in the supply of money not so much in terms of fluctuations of the general price level as in terms of fluctuations of relative prices and the consequent effects on what may be called the 'time-structure' of production." (pp.viii-ix). Hayek points out in the text: "Mises has improved the Wicksellian theory [of forced saving] by an analysis of the different influences which a money rate of interest different from the equilibrium rate exercises on the prices of consumers' goods on the one hand, and the prices of producers' goods on the other." (1st ed., p.22; 2nd ed., p.25) Hayek also cites Mises' book on money (B-2) in footnotes. In Hayek's "Preface to the Second [1935] Edition" (dated August 1954), he writes: "so far as the general theory of money (as distinguished from the pure theory of capital) is concerned, it is the work of Professor Mises much more than that of Knut Wicksell which provides the framework inside which I have tried to elaborate a special point." (p.xiii) Robbins' 1931 Preface not included in the 1935 edition.

Hellman, Julius "Probleme des Zinses in Theorie und Wirtschaft: Eine Gegenüberstellung von Geldzins und Kapitalzins" [The Problems of Interest in Theory and Economics: A Comparison of Interest on Money and Interest on Capital]. *Zeitschrift für Betriebswirtschaft.* 4 (1931) 1-19. Hellman quotes Mises: "The demand for money and money substitutes which appears on the loan market is in the final analysis a demand for capital goods or . . . for consumers goods. Whoever seeks to borrow 'money' needs it, in the final analysis, for the production of other economic goods." With reference to a bank's ability to increase the demand for loans and fiduciary media by reducing artificially the interest rate, Hellman refers to Mises' books on money (B-2) and monetary stabilization (B-7; English translation included in *On the Manipulation of Money and Credit,* B-24). (Translated from the German)

Kuznets, Simon. "German Business Cycle Theory." *The Quarterly Journal of Economics.* (1931). Criticizes the Austrians.

Machlup, Fritz. *Börsenkredit, Industriekredit und Kapitalbildung*   [Stock Market, Credit and Capital Formation]. Vienna: Austrian Institute for Trade Cycle Research. (1931).   See "Books and Articles About Mises: 1940" for annotated listing of English translation.

Roper, Willet Crosby Jr. *The Problem of Pricing in a Socialist State.* Cambridge, Mass.: Harvard Univ. Press, 1931.

Schmidt, Carl Theodore. "The Austrian Institute for Business Cycle Research." *The Journal of Political Economy.* 39:1 (February 1931) 101-103. "The Institute, maintained as a private research organization, is supported by its founders and, to some extent, by subscribers to its services . . . . It is under the chairmanship of the president of the National Bank, Professor Dr. Richard Reisch. Assistant chairmen are former Vice-Chancellor Walter Breisky, now president of the Federal Statistical Office, and Professor Dr. Ludwig Mises, secretary of the Vienna Chamber of Commerce. The latter is a well-known contributor to monetary theory . . . . As is evident, the Institute has intimate relationships with the government and with the more important public and private business organizations. It thus has immediate access to most of the significant statistical data relating to Austrian economic life . . . . ¶As is true of most of the cycle-research agencies in Europe, the Austrian Institute has made extensive use of the experience of American research organizations . . . . ¶The Institute, then, has avoided commitment to any more-or-less rigid formula for business forecasting -- it makes no pretense of offering a definite basis for a prognosis of cyclical fluctuations . . . . ¶The Institute devotes a large part of its activity to special studies."

Sulzbach, Walther. "Gegenwart und Zukunft des wirtschaftlichen Liberalismus" [The Present and Future of Economic Liberalism]. *Wirtschaftsdients: Weltwirtschaftliche Nachrichten.* Hamburg. 16:20 (May 15, 1931) 840-844. Sulzbach portrays true classical liberalism, i.e. capitalism, as the system most consistent with "economic harmony," a term which he attributes to Bastiat. Popular government interventions -- tariffs, minimum wage laws, subsidies, etc. -- will in time hurt the very groups or classes they were designed to help. However, there is hope. "It so happens that now once more some young theoreticians are basically liberal and the theories of Ludwig Mises [Sulzbach cites Mises' *Liberalism* (B-6), *Socialism* (B-4), and *Critique of Interventionism* (B-8)] are no longer considered as extreme as they have been for years. From the point of view of history, to be sure, the myth is proving victorious in the short run; the recent success of National Socialism in Germany shows that. However, in the long run man is still *homo sapiens*. The majority will suffer only harm from the economic interventions in their various fields . . . . The assertion that a system that takes the sentient, acting individual as its starting point, will no longer be considered absurd, but rather 'more natural' than a system based on the fiction of the economic collective or the 'class.' Then one may not only hope, but also believe, that liberal economic ideas will become generally accepted in the not too distant future." (Translated from the German)

Vleugels, Wilhelm. "Theorie der gebundenen Preisbildung" [The Theory of the Formation of Controlled Prices]. *Die Wirtschaftstheorie der Gegenwart.* Vienna: Julius Springer, 1931. pp.135-146. A 4-volume Festschrift to Friedrich von Wieser, published 1927-1932. Vleugels says opposition to price controls is either unnecessary (if the fixed prices coincide with market prices) or harmful (if they are above or below market prices); this is consistent with the teachings of the classical economists who rejected government intervention in general. During World War I the question of free or controlled prices was discussed at length. One argument for controls was to oppose monopoly. Vleugels refers to Schmoller who believes that prices may be fixed at historic levels without disastrous long-range consequences and Schäffle who maintains that supply and demand might conceivably be harmonized and market processes coordinated at some undetermined time in the future by government-controlled prices. The task of price control theory, Vleugels says, is to examine these ideas on "the suppression through social controls of market price formation." Vleugels criticizes government price controls, cites Mises' Article 23.5, and concludes that, even though a thorough system of controls is conceivable as an economic goal, in practice it would be a step toward socialism. Mises also contributed to this Wieser Festschrift; see Article 32.1.

Wagner, Karl. "Brechung der Zinsknechtschaft?" [Abolishing Interest Slavery]. *Jahrbücher für Nationalökonomie und Statistik.* Jena: Gustav Fischer. 3:79 (1931) 790ff. Criticizes the unattainable proposal by Gottfried Feder, originator of the German Nazi Labor Party's economic program, for the abolition of interest rates. From Mises' book on money (B-2), Wagner quotes Mises' "very clear" statement on the determination of money's purchasing power. Wagner also cites Mises' *Socialism* (B-4) on wages and labor legislation.

Zeisl, Hans. "Marxismus und Subjektive Theorie" [Marxism and Subjective Value Theory]. *Schriften des Vereins für Sozialpolitik.* (undated; post-1930) 179-200. In analyzing the subjective value theory, Zeisl cites Mises several times. After discussing the Marxian labor theory of value, he concludes: "After Marx's death, economics has gone other ways. Recent times appear to be preparing the way, however, for a renaissance of Marxian methodology. We do not want to recommend reactionary universalism. Rather we refer to those movements which join with the natural sciences and seek to organize economics into a unified science of social events. Signs are visible in philosophy which are preparing the way for such a development: Positivism sees it as one of its foremost tasks to prove that the construction of a unified general science is possible and the limitation of individual sciences is really a matter of necessity." Here Zeisl footnotes philosopher Rudolf Carnap. (Quotes translated from the German)

1932

Conrad, Otto. "Der Interventionismus als Ursache der Wirtschaftskrise: Eine Auseinandersetzung mit Ludwig Mises" [Interventionism as the Cause of the Economic Crisis: An Exchange with Ludwig Mises]. *Jahrbücher für Nationalökonomie und Statistik.* Jena: Gustav Fischer. 3:82 (1932) 161-174. Conrad criticizes Mises' 1931 monograph on the causes of the economic crisis (B-9; English translation included in *On the Manipulation of Money and Credit,* B-24). Conrad's critique centers on Mises' "imprecise and incomplete" position on monopoly, his "lack of clarity" in classifying unemployed workers, his "imprecision" in describing the effects on the demand for labor of "rationalization" (i.e. industrialization or automation), and the wage problem.

Greidanus, Tjardus. *The Value of Money: A Discussion of Various Monetary Theories, and an Exposition of the Yield Theory of the Value of Money.* London: P. S. King, 1932. Chapter IX, "An Application of the Theory of the Marginal Utility to the Doctrine of the Value of Money" (pp.107-113), is devoted to Mises: "Prof. von Mises tries to show that money is neither production good nor consumption good . . . . [He] adopts the classification of Knies, who distinguishes consumption goods, production goods, and media of exchange . . . . ¶Prof. von Mises' less felicitous definition of money has had an injurious influence on his theory of the value of money . . . . ¶The value theory of money [according to Mises] must trace the objective value in exchange of money back to the moment when the commodity, operating as money, did not yet act as money, hence to the moment when it had value only for another reason . . . . Then there came a moment when this commodity was also used as a medium of exchange. Starting from this moment it was valued first of all because it was useful in the usual sense, and, in addition, because it could also be used as a medium of exchange . . . . ¶The fundamental principle according to which the subjective valuations are also value-determining factors for money is what confers its great significance on Prof. von Mises' theory." Greidanus maintains that Mises' critique of Helfferich to the effect that he "regards the marginal utility of money from the standpoint of the whole community, and not from that of the individual . . . . has not refuted the essential point of Prof. Helfferich's criticism." Greidanus then quotes Mises: "The subjective money value always leads back to the subjective value of the other commodities obtainable in exchange for money; it is a derived conception." "Through this statement" Greidanus writes, "Prof. von Mises himself adopts, indeed, the standpoint of the followers of the *Anrecht* [legal title] theory, such as Bendixen. And from this point of view there is no independent marginal utility of money." According to Greidanus, "it is owing to this influence of the *Anrecht* theory that Prof. von Mises has not been able to attain the end in view with the theory of marginal utility."

Haberler, Gottfried von, "Money and the Business Cycle," pp.43-47 in *Gold and Monetary Stabilization,* Quincy Wright, ed. Chicago: University of Chicago Press, 1932. A brief introduction to the Misesian analysis of the business cycle. Reprinted by the Center for Libertarian Studies in *The Austrian Theory of the Trade Cycle and Other Essays,* Occasional Paper Series #8 (New York, 1978), by the Ludwig von Mises Institute (Auburn, Ala., 1983), and included in *Austrian Economics, II.* Stephen Littlechild, ed. (Aldershot, Hants, England; Brookfield, Vt.: Edward Elgar, 1990) pp.297-310.

Hansen, Alvin Harvey. *Economic Stabilization in an Unbalanced World.* New York: Harcourt, Brace, 1932. "The *credit-cycle theory* holds that the business cycle is due to the divergence of the market rate of interest from the natural rate . . . . It follows from this theory that price stabilization is not a sufficient basis for the stabilization of the business cycle. What is needed, according to this theory, is to maintain the proper balance between investment and true saving, and this could be achieved, it is argued, by adjusting the market rate of interest to the natural rate." (p.306) This analysis is credited in a footnote to the first (1912) German-language edition of Mises' book on money (B-2). In discussing economic calculation under socialism, Hansen writes: "There has been much discussion, especially during the last decade, of the possibility of a genuine *Wirtschaftsrechnung* (economic accounting) in a socialistic society. [Footnote reference to Article 23.6]   This is a question of very great importance, for without genuine economic accounting a rational utilization of the productive resources of the community is not possible. ¶Let us note at the outset that a socialistic economy need not adopt a rationing method of distributing goods . . . . ¶Nor is there any reason why the price system should not also reach back to the agents of production . . . . ¶Dr. Mises has, however, advanced the thesis that while the price system might indeed under socialism operate effectively with respect to consumer goods, such could not be the case with respect to producer goods. And the reason is that while consumer goods would be bought and sold in a free market, producer goods would have no market, since there would be no private ownership of capital . . . . In a capitalistic society, however, with a free securities market in which capital goods are evaluated, a basis for judging efficiency is provided, Professor Mises argues. This is true of a *competitive* society, but not of a *monopolistic* capitalism. In fact the distinction which Mises has in mind is not, as I see it, between socialism and capitalism, but rather between competition and monopoly . . . . Mises's argument is valid only to the extent that socialism almost of necessity tends to be more monopolistic than capitalism." (pp.329-334)

Kerschagl, Richard. "Die Möglichkeit einer Wirtschaftsrechnung in der sozialistischen Planwirtschaft" [The Possibility of Economic Accounting in the Planned Socialist Economy]. *Ständisches Leben.* 2:4 (1932) 203-210. From a preliminary version of a larger study, *Wirtschaftlichkeit und Sozialismus* [Economy and Socialism]. Part I, "Calculation of Profitability;" Part II, "Calculation of Wages and Yield on Capital." These subjects have been dealt with, Kerschagl says, from the point of view of universalism by Othmar Spann (1929), from the point of view of liberalism by Ludwig Mises (1922, *Socialism,* B-4) and from the point of view of modern price theory by Adolf Weber (1932).

Passow, Richard. "Freie und gebundene Wirtschaft" [Free vs. Hampered Economy]. Hanover: Deutschen Handwerks und Gewerbekammertag, 1932. Lecture at German Chamber of Trade and Industry meeting, Dresden, April 6, 1932.Discusses the basic difference between the free and the controlled economic systems, which Passow attributes to the difference in the way factors of production are owned. It is not difficult, he says, to transfer the ownership of private property from private individuals to the collective; "the difficulties begin once one tries to create a single collective economy from the multiplicity of individual competitive economic units." (p.5) Passow footnotes the recent literature on the subject, including Mises' *Socialism* (B-4) and works of Carl Landauer and Eduard Heimann. On price controls (pp.18-19) he quotes at some length from Mises' *A Critique of Interventionism* (B-8). (Quoted passage translated from the German)

Robbins, Lionel. "Consumption and the Trade Cycle." *Economica.* (November 1932) 413-430. In this paper Robbins "examines critically" the theories of Major C. H. Douglas and J. A. Hobson, "which attribute trade depression to a deficiency of consumption."   Robbins then "indicates very briefly and very tentatively what seems to [him] to be a more correct view of the relationship between consumption and the downward turn of trade." He has "simply tried," he writes, "to adapt to the subject . . . views which, if not yet universally accepted, today command the adherence of economists of standing in many different parts of the world . . . . Besides the well-known works of Professors Mises and Hayek," he cites Haberler, Bresciani-Turroni, Hicks, and Strigl. (p.413, 413n)

_____. *An Essay on the Nature & Significance of Economic Science.* London: Macmillan, 1932; 2nd ed., 1935. In his Preface to the first edition, Robbins acknowledges "especial indebtedness to the works of Professor Ludwig von Mises and to the *Common Sense of Political Economy* of the late Philip Wicksteed." Miscellaneous Mises citations throughout re human action, methodology and monetary theory. For comments on Robbins' views and the second, revised (1935) edition, see "Books and Articles About Mises: 1935."

Röpke, Wilhelm. *Krise und Konjunktur* [Crisis and Cycle]. Leipzig: Quelle & Meyer, 1932. "The origin of the monetary theory of the trade cycle may betraced back to the English monetary and credit theoreticians (the Currency theoreticians) of the first half of the 19th century." (p.82n) Röpke lists L. Mises, L. Hahn, and R. G. Hawtrey as more recent advocates. In other footnotes he cites several Mises works on money and cyclical policy. (This is a preliminary version of the English translation, *Crises and Cycles,* 1936.)

Tisch, Kläre. *Wirtschaftsrechnung und Verteilung im zentralistisch organisierten sozialistischen Gemeinwesen* [Economic Calculation and Distribution in the Centrally Planned Socialist Society]. Doctoral dissertation submitted to the Faculty of Jurisprudence and Political Science of Friedrich-Wilhelms-Universität, Bonn, 1932. Tisch presents her theory of economic calculation as well as those of others, including Neurath, Tschajanoff, Mises, Halm, Weber, Heimann, Owen, Polanyi, Marx, Kautsky and Leichter. She discusses Mises at length, also Marschak's critique of Mises. Tisch quotes from Mises' *Socialism* (B-4): "Socialism is the transfer (*Überführung*) of the means of production from private ownership into the ownership of organized society, the state." Socialism is not a "transfer," says Tisch, but a "condition" or "state of affairs." She also criticizes Mises for not saying who would have the right of disposal. She maintains that, since consumer goods will exchange for money under socialism, the exchanges that take place in the socialist economy will be sufficient to establish exchange ratios.

van Rhijn, A. A. "De Economische Calculatie in het Socialism" [Economic Calculation under Socialism]. *De Economist.* (s'Gravenhage [The Hague], 1932).

1933

Dickinson, Henry Douglas. "Price Formation in a Socialist Community." *Economic Journal.* 43 (June 1933) 237-251. According to Karen I. Vaughn, Dickinson's economic theory of socialism "set the outline for many socialist models to follow. In direct response to Mises' challenge, Dickinson constructed a model of a socialist economy with the following characteristics: personal goods were private property, there was common (that is, state) ownership of natural resources and the means of production, and most importantly, there was a large sector of individualized consumption for which cost calculation would have to be carried out using prices . . . . Essentially Dickinson proposed the construction of a mathematical model of the economy much like some computer simulation models." Annotation quoted from Vaughn's "Introduction" to Trygve Hoff. *Economic Calculation in the Socialist Society* (1938/1949). Indianapolis: Liberty Fund, 1981. (p.xiii)

Hansen, Alvin H. & Herbert Tout. "Annual Survey of Business Cycle Theory: Investment and Saving in Business Cycle Theory." *Econometrica.* 1:2 (April 1933) 119-147. A critique, primarily of Hayek, introduced as follows: "The problem of the business cycle has been attacked from many angles . . . . ¶Foremost among the champions of the investment and savings approach are the economists of Vienna, led by Mises, but more recently represented by F. A. Hayek. In the English-speaking world the outstanding proponent of this particular method of analysis is John Maynard Keynes, who has arrived at his conclusions for the most part independently and without close knowledge of the works of the continental economists. It is in these contributions, and in the controversies which they have engendered, that we find the most signal recent developments of business cycle and of monetary theory. ¶The use made by Keynes and Hayek of the method above suggested is strikingly different, and the results which they achieve stand out in sharp contrast."

Hayek, F. A. *Monetary Theory and the Trade Cycle.* Translated from the German by N. Kaldor and H. M. Croome. London: Jonathan Cape, 1933. Although Hayek bases his theory of the trade cycle largely on Mises, whom he cites frequently, he disagrees on some points. For instance: "A theory [of the trade cycle] which has to call upon the *deus ex machina* of a false step by bankers, in order to reach its conclusions is, perhaps, inevitably suspect. Yet Professor Mises himself -- who is certainly to be regarded as the most respected and consistent exponent of the monetary theory of the Trade Cycle in Germany -- has, in his latest work, afforded ample justification for this view of his theory by attributing the periodic recurrence of the Trade Cycle to the general tendency of Central Banks to depress the money rate of interest below the natural rate.* Both the protagonists and the opponents of the Monetary Theory of the Trade Cycle thus agree in regarding these explanations as falling ultimately within the exogenous and not the endogenous group . . . . By disregarding those divergencies between the natural and money rate of interest which arise automatically in the course of economic development, and by emphasizing those caused by an artificial lowering of the money rate, the Monetary Theory of the Trade Cycle deprives itself of one of its strongest arguments; namely the fact that the process which it describes *must* always recur under the existing credit organization, and that it thus represents a tendency inherent in the economic system, and is in the fullest sense of the word an *endogenous* theory." (pp.145-147)

> "*While it seems to me that in the analysis of the effects of a money rate of interest diverging from the natural rate Professor Mises has made considerable progress as compared with the position adopted by Wicksell, the latter succeeded better than Mises did in explaining the origin of this divergence." (p.145n)

Mahr, Alexander. "Neutrales oder wertstabiles Geld?" [Neutral Money or Money of Stable Value?]. *Weltwirtschaftliches Archiv.* 38:1 (July 1933) 16ff. According to Mahr, the Anglo-Saxons advocate the stabilization of purchasing power while the Germans favor "neutral money" with unchanging exchange value on the side of money.   When it comes to defining the value of money as the sum total of the influences on prices from the side of money, Mahr associates Mises with Helfferich; they both say that the demand for, and the supply of, money determine prices. According to Mahr, however, higher or lower price levels are caused entirely by the supply and demand for *goods*; it is not true that the demand for, and supply of *money* determine prices exclusively. The views of Mises, Hayek, Röpke, Weiss, Helfferich, and others are discussed.

Piotrowski, Roman. *Cartels and Trusts: Their Origin and Historical Development from the Economic and Legal Aspects.* London: George Allen & Unwin, 1933. One book by the German Wolfers, which the author discusses at some length, was "backed by a serious editorial committee . . . of the *Verein für Sozialpolitik.* The reputation of this association and the patronage of the editorial committee, on which such names as Ludwig Mises are conspicuous, and to some extent also the scientific standing of the author, may mean that in the eyes of some persons Wolfers's book is a signpost in the German science on cartels and a foundation for further studies." (pp.27-28)

Richter, Robert. *Kollektivwirtschaft oder freie Unternehmer?* [Collectivism or Free Entrepreneur?]. *Österreichs Wirtschaft* [Austria's Economy]. A presentation of February 17, 1933, before the Nieder-Österreicher Gewerbeverein [Lower Austrian Business Association]. Reprinted separately, 31pp. From the Foreword: "Since the end of the World War [World War I], the open conflict between collectivism and individualism is not only pursued more intensely politically; it also dominates the literature and forces itself ever more into the thinking of economic circles. This phenomenon cannot take us unawares, as the reorganization of the world depends on this struggle and its outcome; perhaps the most important questions of our time, a time which is teeming with problems, are under discussion here . . . . It is hoped that this reprint can contribute to an explanation of why free enterprise not hindered at all by government interference is preferable to any kind of coercive management." Richter refers to the Austrian School of Economics that has attained "world recognition." In contrast to the socialist doctrine, according to which the value of a good is determined by the labor expended, Richter says the Austrian School "with its value theory has created the foundation for recognizing the individual as the central point of every economic action . . . . the economic value of a good is that which the individual attributes to it." In the course of his address, Richter cites Mises' on equality (*Liberalism,*   B-6) and on economic calculation under socialism (*Socialism,* B-4 and *Critique of Interventionism,* B-8). (Quoted passages translated from the German)

Robbins, Lionel. "Introduction" (October 1932) to Philip H. Wicksteed's *The Common Sense of Political Economy.* London: Routledge & Kegan Paul, 1933. "[I]t may be contended . . . that those [inquiries] which have been based on the subjective theory of value have thrown the whole corpus of economic science into an entirely new light -- a light in which Economics is seen to be a discussion not of the nature of certain *kinds* of behaviour arbitrarily separated off from all others, but of a certain *aspect* of behaviour viewed as a whole." (p.xxii) Robbins footnotes this passage to Mises' Articles 29.2 and 31.2.

Roll, Erich. *Spotlight on Germany: A Survey of Her Economic and Political Problems.* London: Faber & Faber, 1933. "[T]he most striking development, since the war, has been the extraordinary revival of liberal economics. The overwhelming majority of all the eminent economists in German Universities, who before the war were strongly inclined towards a mild form of socialism, are now again returning to the economics of Nassau-Senior, and Böhm-Bawerk; to the philosophy of Bentham . . . . [B]ut, in the matter of policy, social reform -- *Kathedersozialismus* -- has always been of great importance. Now this discrepancy between theory and policy is disappearing, the latter being adapted to the former. There is a general revulsion from interventionism, and most of the suggested remedies of the crisis consist in the abolition of measures which restrict the free play of economic forces. The full restoration of the free market would be considered as the ideal to aim at by most of the leading economists. The chief exponent of this revival is Professor Mises of Vienna, who claims that economic theory proves the impossibility of socialism. In the field of applied theory, he and his disciples trace the causes of crises to monetary phenomena: the changes in the structure of production which excessive bank-credit and low interest rates will bring about. ¶The prevailing liberalism was particularly well illustrated by . . . a conference . . . . [which] was overwhelmingly Liberal in temper. Free trade, free capital movements, complete abolition of restrictive measures, a withdrawal of intervention by the State, these were the measures generally advocated. But side by side with this strengthening of the theoretical case of liberalism its influence in contemporary politics has practically disappeared. Economic theory seems to have no connexion whatever with the contemporary struggle over policy. There is now no important political party in Germany which is not committed to a more or less drastic policy of intervention; no party which could, in any way, be taken to represent Liberal theory. The struggle which is going on now centres round the precise nature, but not round the principle of State interference." (pp.210-213)

1934   Mises leaves Austria to accept position with the Graduate Institute for International Studies in Geneva, Switzerland.

Bopp, Karl R. *The American Economic Review.* 24:3 (September 1934) 487-488. A review of *Probleme der Wertlehre II* . Munich: Duncker& Humblot, 1933, in which Mises' Article 33.4 (The Controversy over the Theory of Value) appeared. "Interestingly enough, they [the contributors to this volume] do not concern value theory *per se,* nor even what the problems of value theory really are. A common mode of attack is the accusation that the opponent has passed in review age-old arguments which have long since been disproved. Mises (Vienna) makes such an accusation (p.116); Weiss (Prague) accuses Mises of the same fault. A common mode of *defense* is the accusation that the opponents have a caricatured or antiquated notion of the theory -- that they have ignored the 'great advances' of a generation. Again Mises leads the defense. He accuses those who attack the *modern* subjective value theory (p.6). Yet, Spiethoff (Bonn) accuses Mises on the same score concerning the historical school (pp.57-58); and Lederer (Berlin) accuses Mises concerning socialism -- even of the Marxian variety. Likewise Rosenstein-Rodan (Vienna) accuses Engländer (Prague) concerning the Austrian school (p.102)."

Eisler, Robert. "Stabilisierung der Kaufkraft des Geldes" [Stabilization of the Purchasing Power of Money]. *Die Welt Wirtschafts Woche.* Vienna. (May 2, 1934) 10-11.

Ellis, Howard S. *German Monetary Theory, 1905-1933.* Cambridge, Mass.: Harvard University Press, 1934. Chapter V, "The Marginal Utility Theory," Section I, "Ludwig Mises": "In his zeal to controvert some of the worst casuistry in Knapp's *State Theory*, Mises seems to incline toward too rigorous individualism . . . . No doubt Knapp envisages the state as something very nearly omnipotent; Mises in turn makes of the 'laws of the market' something very nearly immutable and sacrosanct." (pp.77-78) Chapter XIX, "The Mises-Hayek Analysis of Cycles": "With the publication of his special monograph on cycles in 1928 [B-7, English translation included in *On the Manipulation of Money and Credit*, B-24], Mises comes definitely to the position that aside from economic disturbances caused by war, natural events, and adaptation to new economic data such as new wants and technique, the ebb and flow of business activity turns upon the development of credit. It is the artificial depression of their rates on the part of banks which initiates conjunctural [cyclical] movements. But why do banks launch into inflation when they know from experience its disastrous consequences? . . . This it does in response to popular sentiment for cheap money. The final cause of crises is ideological: since the state always yields to this pressure, the whole banking community relies upon outside relief in extremity and proceeds to drive a lucrative business on low discount rates . . . . ¶Mises' position has aroused adverse comment even from members of the monetary group because it lays the whole responsibility upon the activity of banks." (pp.335-338)

Hayek, F. A. Introduction (English-language) to 1934 London School of Economics reprint (German-language) of Menger's *Grundsätze der Volkswirtschaftslehre* [Principles of Economics]. "Until the work of Professor Mises twenty years later, the direct continuation of Menger's work, this article [Menger's article on money in the *Handwörterbuch der Staatswissenschaften, III* (1892)] remained the main contribution of the 'Austrian School' to the theory of money . . . . The main Austrian achievement in this field is the consistent application to the theory of money of the peculiar subjective or individualistic approach which, indeed, underlies the marginal utility analysis, but which has a much wider and more universal significance. Such an achievement springs directly from Menger." Reprinted: *Economica* (November 1934); also as "Hayek on Menger," pp.526-533 in *The Development of Economic Thought.* H. W. Spiegel, ed. New York: John Wiley & Sons, 1952. pp.526-553. Passage above quoted from Spiegel, p.547.

Morgenstern, Oskar. *Die Grenzen der Wirtschaftspolitik* [The Limits of Economic Policy]. Vienna: Julius Springer, 1934. When Morgenstern wrote this book, he was working with Mises at the Austrian Institute for Business Cycle Research, which published this study. Among other references cited are Mises' *Liberalism* (B-6), *Critique of Interventionism* (B-8), and *Epistemological Problems . . .* (B-10).

Robbins, Lionel. *The Great Depression.* London: Macmillan, 1934. Explains "the great depression" as the consequence of monetary expansion, over-investment in capital goods industries most affected by the rate of interest, and failure to take the proper steps to restore confidence. Robbins' critique of "economic planning," he says (p.148n), "owes much to the work of Professor Ludwig von Mises. See especially his *Gemeinwirtschaft* [*Socialism*, B-4] . . . . shortly to appear in English."

Roll, Erich. *About Money.* London: Faber & Faber, 1934. Roll cites Mises *Grundprobleme . . .* (B-10) with respect to money's "standard of value function": "Professor Mises has pointed out . . . that 'monetary calculation is as little a function of money as astronomy is a function of the stars'." (p.33n) ¶Roll refers to Mises' book on money (B-2) several times with reference to the classification of money (p.40), the distinction between commodity credit and circulation credit (p.45), the definition of "capital" (p.75), the distortion of exchange ratios "through the mere fact that money is used" (p.121), the impossibility of "a general purchasing power of money, or a general price level which is applicable to the whole of an economic system." But, Roll continues, "however much theoretical righteousness may impel us to abandon the concept of a general price level, we are constantly making reference to it, and finding it very useful for expressing the results of everyday observations." (pp.127-128) ¶Roll considers it "perhaps, advisable at this stage . . . to attempt to trace out the effects of an increase of money (*mutatis mutandis* this will apply to a decrease too) stage by stage. This procedure will make our results more correct if less definite." (p.149) He cites Mises on the banks' creation of credit "beyond the savings of the public entrusted to them" and then discusses two theories suggested as explanations for the boom-bust "cycle": alternating waves of entrepreneurial optimism and pessimism, and fluctuations in the demand for capital instruments (p.158) "[B]y introducing a monetary explanation of the causes of the 'real' movements," Roll writes, "a combination between the two theories was made possible. This combination which goes back to earlier writers (the old Austrian school, particularly Böhm-Bawerk, then, Wicksell and Mises) was developed by a large number of economists in different countries; but its most recent advances are due to the works of a number of English and Austrian economists." (pp.168-169) Roll says that Mises, "one of the foremost advocates of economic liberalism and of sound money, claims [in nearly all his works, particularly in his book on money (B-2)] that there is a constant pressure by the banks, acting under an inflationary ideology, to lower the rate of interest below its equilibrium level and thus to set up forced saving." (p.238) ¶Roll refers briefly to Mises' argument (B-4) that "Socialism is . . . impossible . . . because it is wasteful, because it cannot fulfil that which it promises." (p.245)

Sommer, Louise. "Geldwährung und Goldtheorien" [Monetary Standard and Gold Theories]. *Die Welt Wirtschafts Woche.* Vienna. (April 25, 1934).

Sweezy, Alan R. "The Austrian School and the Interpretation of Subjective Value Theory," Ph.D. dissertation. Harvard University. (1934).

_____. "The Interpretation of Subjective Value Theory in the Writings of the Austrian Economists." *Review of Economic Studies.* (June 1934) 176-185. "Sweezy devotes a good part of the article to a criticism of Mises as the leading exponent of the demonstrated preference approach," according to Murray N. Rothbard, "Toward a Reconstruction of Utility and Welfare Economics" in *On Freedom and Free Enterprise: Essays in Honor of Ludwig von Mises*, Mary Sennholz, ed. Princeton: Van Nostrand, 1956). p.225n.

1935

Hayek, F. A. (ed.). *Collectivist Economic Planning.* London: Routledge & Kegan Paul, 1935. Reprinted (1975)
by Augustus M. Kelley (Clifton, N. J.). Long a classic work on the possibility of economic calculation
in a socialist society, a field pioneered by Mises in 1920, this volume represented the capitalist position
that rational economic calculation was *not* possible under socialism. The socialists vigorously attacked.
This collection includes Mises' original Article 20.6 (pp.87-130) plus:

Barone, Enrico. "The Ministry of Production in the Collectivist State" (1908). (pp.245-290).
According to Hayek this article "is of considerable interest as an example of how it was
thought that the tools of mathematical analysis of economic problems might be utilized to
solve the tasks of the central planning authority." (p.29)

Halm, Georg. "Further Considerations on the Possibility of Adequate Calculation in a Socialist
Community." (pp.131-200). Translated by H. E. Batson. Reviews the German literature on
the subject. "Mises rightly observes that all partial socialization is only made possible by
'the actions of the undertakings in question being so far supported by the uncontrolled
commercial organism that surrounds them that the essential characteristics of the socialist
economy cannot appear in them at all'." (p.190)

Hayek, F. A. "The Nature and History of the Problem" (pp.1-40). Reprinted as "Socialist
Calculation I: The Nature and History of the Problem." F. A. Hayek. *Individualism and
Economic Order.* University of Chicago Press, 1948. pp.119-147. See 1948 for
publication history.

_____. "The Present State of the Debate" (pp.201-243). Reprinted as "Socialist Calculation II: The
State of the Debate." F .A. Hayek, *Individualism and Economic Order.* University of
Chicago Press, 1948. pp.148-180. See 1948 for publication history.

Pierson, N. G. "The Problem of Value in the Socialist Society." (pp.41-85). Translated from the
Dutch by G. Gardiner. First published as "Het waardeprobleem in een socialistische
Maatschappij." *De Economist.* 41 (s'Gravenhage [The Hague], 1902) 423-456; reprinted in
N. G. Pierson, *Verspreide Economische Geschriften.* C. A. Verrijn Stuart, ed. Haarlem,
1910. vol. I, 333-377. According to Hayek, a lecture by Karl Kautsky, a leading Marxian
theoretician who appeared unaware of the impracticability of socialism, "gave Pierson the
opportunity to demonstrate in detail . . . that a socialist state would have its problems of
value just as any other economic system and that the task socialists had to solve was to
show how in the absence of a pricing system the value of different goods was to be
determined." (p.27)

Lerner, Abba. "Economic Theory and Socialist Economy." *Review of Economic Studies.* 2 (February 1935) 51-61.
According to Karen I. Vaughn, "Lerner, a former student of Friedrich Hayek . . . was also favorably
disposed toward socialism, yet perhaps because of Hayek's influence he recognized the analytic importance
of Mises' claim that without prices, economic calculation is impossible. He therefore argued that
[Maurice] Dobb's criticism that consumer preferences should not necessarily guide the planning board's
decisions was beside the point. Regardless of whose preferences were going to be satisfied, those of the
consumer or the central planners, prices are still needed to determine whether resources are being used
most efficiently to achieve the goals the planners set for themselves and society." Annotation quoted from
Vaughn's "Introduction." Trygve Hoff. *Economic Calculation in the Socialist Society* (1938/1949).
Indianapolis: Liberty*Press,* 1981. (p.xv).

Machlup, Fritz. "The Consumption of Capital in Austria." *The Review of Economic Statistics.* (January 15, 1935)
13-19. "Professor Ludwig v. Mises was the first, so far as I know to point to the phenomenon of the
consumption of capital. As a member of a committee appointed by the Austrian Government . . . he also
emphasized comprehensive factual information." (p.13n.)

E.P. "American Notes," *New English Weekly.* (London). (February 7, 1935). A "tongue-in-cheek" column: "Frankie Roosevelt, 'the beloved' . . . . is undoubtedly the grrrreates' amurkn invention since the days of the wooden nut-meg. . . . ¶An Austrian named von Mises is preaching the commodity theory of money in Geneva. So did Calvin centuries ago. These cases of intellectual sadism recur . . . . ¶A correspondent writes that school-children in Portland, Oregon, are being taught economics. Good, so they ought to be. We can only kneel in prayer and wonder what economics."

Robbins, Lionel. *An Essay on the Nature & Significance of Economic Science.* 2nd ed., revised and extended. London: Macmillan, 1935. (1st ed., 1932). In Preface to this edition (1935) Robbins writes that he had "not found it necessary to change the main trend of the argument" although he considered it "much more incumbent" to revise Chapters IV and V on "economic generalizations." For discussions of Robbins, see:

Hollis, Martin & Edward J. Nell. *Rational Economic Man: A Philosophical Critique of Neo-Classical Economics.* Cambridge University Press, 1975. Compares the two editions of *An Essay on the Nature and Significance of Economic Science [ENSES].* According to Hollis and Nell, Robbins in 1932 emphasized "the spirit of von Mises' remark that 'in the concept of money all the theorems of monetary theory are already implied'. . . . ¶Between 1932 and 1935 Logical Positivism gained its ascendancy. Robbins remained unrepentant but [in 1935] did give more weight to his other [more Positivist] answer." (p.201)

Kirzner, Israel M. *The Economic Point of View: An Essay in the History of Economic Thought.* ©Institute for Humane Studies. Princeton: Van Nostrand, 1960; Kansas City [Mission, Kansas]: Sheed & Ward, 1976. "Writers have tended to group Mises and Robbins together as continuators of Weber in their stress on the ends-means dichotomy and its importance for economic activity. But the two views place economic science in two quite distinct positions. ¶Economizing consists in the allocation of scarce resources among competing ends. Acting, in the praxeological sense, consists in selecting a pattern of behavior designed to further the actor's purposes . . . . [T]he concept of action is wider and at the same time more fundamental than that of economizing." For Robbins, economics was "economizing"; for Mises it was "acting." (p.161)

O'Brien, D. P. *Lionel Robbins.* New York: St. Martin's Press, 1988: "A better idea of Robbins's sources can be obtained from the first edition of *An Essay on the Nature and Significance of Economic Science [ENSES]* rather than from the more widely available second edition. In particular, seven of the Mises references in the first edition are missing from the second edition." (p.184 n.13)

Stonier, A. W. *Der logische Charakter der Wirtschaftswissenschaft* [The Logical Character of Economics]. Heidelberg: C. Winter, 1935. Stonier was "among the first" to react "critically to Mises's praxeology," according to Stephan Boehm (*Method, Process, and Austrian Economics,* Israel M. Kirzner, ed. Lexington, Mass.: D. C. Heath, 1982) p.49,n4.

1936

Bernadelli, H. "What Has Philosophy to Contribute to the Social Sciences, and to Economics in Particular?" *Economica* (November 1936). Comments on Mises' apriorism. (p.449)

Kaufmann, Felix. *Methodenlehre der Sozialwissenschaften* [Methodology of the Social Sciences]. Vienna: J. Springer, 1936. Kaufmann was a regular participant in Mises' private seminar in Vienna. Yet, according to Stephan Boehm (*Method, Process and Austrian Economics*. Israel M. Kirzner, ed. Lexington, Mass.: D. C. Heath, 1982. p.49,n.4), Kaufmann was among the early critics of Mises' praxeology.

Keynes, John Maynard. *The General Theory of Employment, Interest and Money.* New York: Harcourt Brace, 1936. "A peculiar theory of the rate of interest has been propounded by Professor von Mises and adopted from him by Professor Hayek and also, I think, by Professor Robbins; namely, that changes in the rate of interest can be identified with changes in the relative price levels of consumption-goods and capital-goods . . . . By a somewhat drastic simplification the marginal efficiency of capital is taken as measured by the ratio of the supply price of new consumers' goods to the supply price of new producers' goods. This is then identified with the rate of interest. The fact is called to notice that a fall in the rate of interest is favourable to investment. *Ergo*, a fall in the ratio of the price of consumers' goods to the price of producers' goods is favourable to investment." (p.192)

Knight, Frank H. "The Place of Marginalist Economics in a Collectivist System." *American Economic Review: Supplement.* 26:1 (March 1936) 255-266. "[T]he absence of any difficult or peculiar economic problem (such as has been asserted by some opponents of collectivism, notably von Mises) is only a part of the case from the collectivist's standpoint." (p.263) For comments, see Orton, below.

Lange, Oskar. "On the Economic Theory of Socialism." *Review of Economic Studies.* 4:1 (October 1936) 53-71; 4:2 (February 1937) 123-142. This two-part article (reprinted, pp.55-143, in *On the Economic Theory of Socialism.* Benjamin E. Lippincott, ed. University of Minnesota, 1938), was the most thorough elaboration of the socialist position up to 1937, and was intended to be a complete refutation of the Misesian-Hayekian position. Lange pointed to some of Hayek's comments, claiming that the capitalist position in the economic calculation debate was in retreat. About Mises, Lange wrote: "Socialists have certainly good reason to be grateful to Professor Mises, the great *advocatus diaboli* of their cause. For it was his powerful challenge that forced the socialists to recognize the importance of an adequate system of economic accounting to guide the allocation of resources in a socialist economy. Even more, it was chiefly due to Professor Mises' challenge that many socialists became aware of the very existence of such a problem. And although Professor Mises was not the first to raise it, and although not all socialists were as completely unaware of the problem as is frequently held, it is true, nevertheless, that, particularly on the European Continent (outside of Italy), the merit of having caused the socialists to approach this problem systematically belongs entirely to Professor Mises. Both as an expression of recognition for the great service rendered by him and as a memento of the prime importance of sound economic accounting, a statue of Professor Mises ought to occupy an honorable place in the great hall of the Ministry of Socialization or of the Central Planning Board of the socialist state. I am afraid, however, that Professor Mises would scarcely enjoy what seems the only adequate way to repay the debt of recognition incurred by the socialists, and it is difficult to blame him for not doing so. First, he might have to share his place with the great leaders of the socialist movement, and this company might not suit him. And then, to complete the misfortune, a socialist teacher might invite his students in a class on dialectical materialism to go and look at the statue, in order to exemplify the Hegelian *List der Vernunft* [The Craftiness of Reason] which made even the stanchest of bourgeois economists unwittingly serve the proletarian cause." (pp.57-58 of the Lippincott edited book)

Orton, William. *American Economic Review: Supplement.* 26:1 (March 1936) 285-288. Comments on Knight, above: The "nightmarish quality" of "the situation envisaged by Halm, von Hayek, and von Mises . . . . rests on the contention that without free economic activity no workable price, value or costing system can obtain . . . . Nothing is more dangerous for economics, or for economists, than to confuse their private ideals with public realities; the history of both the classical and the Marxian schools shows us that . . . . In the current Austrian doctrine there is, I fear, some such confusion; that is why von Hayek is so pessimistic." (p.286)

Roll, Erich. "Menger on Money." *Economica.* (November 1936) 455-460. "Economists everywhere have, it is true, been familiar with the summary of his [Menger's] views on money contained in the *Grundsätze* [Principles of Economics, 1871; English translation, 1950], but it is in Austria more than anywhere else that his work (with that of Wieser) has been successfully developed. Professor Mises' treatise is based on it; and Vienna's recent work on fluctuations can be directly traced to the ideas of the older Austrians (p.455) . . . . Thus, Menger can be seen as the forerunner both of the neutral money theorists (*e.g.,* Mises, Hayek, Koopmans) as well as of those who are now developing monetary theory by linking it up with the theory of anticipation." (p.458)

Röpke, Wilhelm. *Crises and Cycles.* London: William Hodge, 1936. Röpke's *Krise und Konjunktur* (1932) translated and enlarged. Discusses the Misesian/Hayekian monetary theory of the trade cycle, especially at pages 109-119: "In spite of the keenness and acuteness with which it has been added to and refined in the last few years, this exposition of the monetary theory of the trade cycle still remains full of unsolved or not entirely satisfactorily solved problems. To these belongs first and foremost the question as to what causes the banks to embark again and again on a credit expansion: is it a matter, as Mises thinks, of the effect of a certain ideology, or, as Hayek believes, of a process into which the banks are forcibly drawn? The probability is that the latter of these two contentions is right, but this does not mean that no effective limitation of credit expansion and therewith of over-investment is possible." (pp.116-117)

Smith, Vera C. *The Rationale of Central Banking.* London: P. S. King, 1936. Based on Smith's 1935 Ph.D. thesis written under F. A. Hayek's supervision, University of London School of Economics. Reprinted 1990, repaged, with a new Preface by Leland B. Yeager. Indianapolis: Liberty Fund, 1990. Smith analyzes central banking systems country by country. She refers to Mises' work several times, primarily to his 1928 monograph on monetary stabilization and cyclical policy (B-7). Smith lists in a two-by-two matrix, the chief disputants in the Free Banking v. Central Banking controversy, cross-grouped with their position on the Banking and Currency controversy. She classifies Mises with Cernuschi, Hübner and Michaelis as adherents of the Free Banking/Currency school position. The other three quadrants in the matrix list adherents of: (1) Free Banking/Banking School, (2) Central Banking/Banking School, and (3) Central Banking/Currency School positions. (1936 ed., p.127; 1990 ed., pp.144-145)

Thomas, Brinley. *Monetary Policy and Crises: A Study of Swedish Experience.* Preface by Hugh Dalton. London: George Routledge, 1936. "[O]nly the accident of language . . . has prevented Swedish economic thought from exercising a greater influence on other countries. In the last few years economic analysis in England has been enriched by the absorption of ideas from another small country -- Austria . . . . ¶The foundations of the Swedish and Austrian schools have much in common. Some of the ideas worked out in their fullness by Böhm-Bawerk are to be found in Davidson's first book published in 1878; and Wicksell's contribution to capital theory consists in a refinement of the work of Böhm-Bawerk. But the edifice which Professors Lindahl and Myrdal . . . are building on these foundations is of rather a different style from the structure of which the architects are Professors Mises and Hayek." (p.xix) "Professors Mises and Hayek, though deeply distrusting the idea of an average price level, have made the concept of the 'average period of production' the corner-stone of their theory of fluctuations. It is very doubtful whether the movements of this arbitrarily defined average correspond to anything in the real world. There is not even the prospect that more abundant statistics will one day fill this empty box. The idea is important in the static theory of capital; but it has serious limitations in dynamic analysis." (pp.101-102)

Wien-Claudi, Franz. *Austrian Theories of Capital, Interest and the Trade Cycle.* London: Stanley Nott, 1936. Compares and contrasts the views of Mises, other Austrians, and non-Austrians, on capital, interest and trade cycle theories. "The question of the length of this process of adjustment can easily be decided with regard to the other contents of v. Mises' theory. It will depend on the former credit policy of the Central Banks. If the banks have kept the issue of loans as much as possible within the proportion of the discounted increase of the fund of subsistence, the period of adjustment will be small and vice versa. It is, therefore, in the power of the banking system to mitigate the unwholesome results of the upward movement. v. Mises, however, does not clearly state how the credit-supply of the banking system could be adjusted in proportion to the increase in the fund of subsistence. An attempt to measure this increase in the fund of subsistence in terms of money was made by Hayek. Hayek in this sense has further advanced v. Mises' theory." (p.135)

Wiener Taglatt. "Sir Josiah Stamp über Oesterreich" [Sir Josiah Stamp on Austria]. (March 10, 1936) 14. For Stamp, "who is not only a practitioner but also an economic theoretician, Austria and especially Vienna have always had a special power of attraction as the home of the Viennese school of economics which is highly regarded today as it has been for three decades. Sir Josiah referred to those Austrians, who like Professor Dr. v. Mises and Professor Dr. Hayek enjoy esteem and recognition in the Anglo-Saxon countries also, as today's successors to the high scientific tradition." (Translated from the German)

1937

Basler Nachrichten. Basel, Switzerland. "Die Autarkiepolitik und die europäischen Industriestaaten" [Autarky and the Industrial States of Europe]. 26 (January 27, 1937). Mises gave at least two talks in Basel on autarky, illustrating his lecture with examples showing the absurdity of such a policy if carried to extremes. His talk was reported also in *National Zeitung* (Basel), January 27, 1937, and an account appeared in Vienna in *Der Wiener Tag,* February 4, 1937, headlined "Der Wahnsinn der Autarkiepolitik" [The Madness of Autarky].

Bresciani-Turroni, Costantino. *The Economics of Inflation: A Study of Currency Depreciation in Post-War Germany, 1914-1923.* Italian edition: Universita Bocconi, 1931; English translation by Millicent E. Sayers. London: George Allen & Unwin, 1937; New York: Barnes & Noble, n.d.. Mises' 1923 monograph on inflation (B-5; English translation included in *On the Manipulation of Money and Credit,* B-24) is cited: "[I]t should be mentioned that some German writers expressed moderate judgment on the influence of reparations on foreign exchanges -- as, e.g., Professor Hirsch . . . . Also Professor Mises wrote: 'The progressive depreciation of the mark could not be the effect of reparations payments; it is simply the result of the Government's financing itself by issuing additional notes'." (p.93n.)

Einzig, Paul. *The Theory of Forward Exchange.* London: Macmillan, 1937. Einzig discusses the debate between Mises and Federn concerning the Austro-Hungarian Bank's forward rate policies of 1906-7, a debate "practically unknown to the English-speaking public." (See Mises' Articles 09.1 and 10.2, and "Books and Articles About Mises: 1909," Federn.) The issue was whether the overvaluation of the forward krone and the depreciation of the spot krone were really the result of deliberate policy or merely stemmed from the higher bank rates in London and Berlin and from speculative forward buying of kronen, stimulated by the fact that the spot krone was at the gold export point. (p.335) Federn said that official policy was the cause; Mises disagreed. Einzig supports Federn's position (pp.330ff.) and accuses Mises of being "a very bad loser indeed." (p.340n.) This accusation removed from 1961 revision: *A Dynamic Theory of Forward Exchange.* London: Macmillan; New York: St. Martin's Press, 1961. pp.410-419.

_____. *World Finance: 1935-1937.* New York: Macmillan, 1937. "The London School of Economics and Political Science has always been the spearhead in the academic field of the movement in favour of an orthodox monetary policy . . . . It will be remembered that soon after the war [World War I] Professor Cannan went so far in his deflationary zeal as to start a legal action against the Treasury for profiteering on the ground that it was selling for ten shillings or a pound bits of printed paper worth a fraction of a farthing. It is in accordance with the traditions of that School that it should provide the theoretical ammunition for the fight in favour of immediate stabilisation. Professor Hayek, inspired by a dislike for any departure from orthodoxy that originated during the disastrous inflationary period in Austria, has infused fresh blood into the School. With Professors Gregory and Robbins, he has constituted a trio which is a factor of importance in the controversy. Between them they set up a cult of the Austrian economist, Professor Ludwig von Mises, with his fanatic belief in cutting down prices, and especially wages, as a remedy for all evil." (p.201)

Gregory, T. E. "Money." *Encyclopedia of the Social Sciences.* New York: Macmillan, 1937; first published 1933. Vol. 10: 601-613. Discusses various theories of money including those of Mises and Knapp, a major target of Mises in his early years: "Ludwig von Mises has suggested that one great dividing line between such theories lies in the compatibility of the view which each takes of the nature of money with the facts of an exchange economy; he thus classifies theories of money as 'catallactic' and 'acatallactic,' that is, those which can and those which cannot be fitted into a theory of exchange . . . . But it seems better to start from a somewhat different point of view. Even purely 'symbolistic' theories of money point to one important characteristic of money -- that it acts as a unit of account . . . . Thus the theories of the nature of money can be divided into those which stress the primacy of the medium of exchange function and those which stress the unit of account function . . . . The state theory of money should be regarded as a third variant of the unit of account theories. To Knapp and his followers money is simply an instrumentality created by the state with which to settle debts; it has no value as such but is merely the symbol or unit by which value (or debts) is expressed." (pp.603-604) Gregory also discusses Mises' "principle of historical regression" and his theory as to why the purchasing power of money changes. (p.609)

Haberler, Gottfried. *Prosperity and Depression.* Geneva: League of Nations, 1937. A survey of business cycle theories. On his opening pages, Haberler writes: "Money and credit occupy such a central position in our economic system that it is almost certain that they play an important role in bringing about the business cycle, either as an impelling force or as a conditioning factor . . . . But, in any case, the analysis of a theory which puts the monetary factor at the centre of its scheme of causation will almost certainly reveal important features of the business cycle which no adequate synthesis can afford to neglect." (pp.14-15) He classifies Mises as an overinvestment, rather than as a malinvestment, theorist. (See Chapter 3, "The Over-Investment Theories," especially pp. 31-33 in 3rd. ed. New York: United Nations, 1952). He discusses at some length the Keynesian proposals, the multiplier effect, economic rigidities, public spending as the means for recovering from depression, and the complexities and difficulties involved. In concluding, he assures the reader that "what has been said should not be interpreted as a plea for *laissez faire,* for a policy of inaction relying entirely on price and wage flexibility and perfect competition for the cure of slump conditions." (p.501)

Hall, R. L. *The Economic System in a Socialist State.* New York: Russell & Russell, 1937. Hall discusses the contributions to the economic calculation debate made by Mises, Halm and Hayek; see pages 68-79.

Hayek, F. A. "Economics and Knowledge." *Economica.* 4 (February 1937) 33-54. Presidential address before London Economic Club, November 10, 1936. "Clearly there is here a problem of the *division of knowledge* [Hayek footnotes Mises' *Socialism* (B-4)] which is quite analogous to, and at least as important as, the problem of the division of labor. But, while the latter has been one of the main subjects of investigation ever since the beginning of our science, the former has been as completely neglected, although it seems to me to be the really central problem of economics as a social science. The problem which we pretend to solve is how the spontaneous interaction of a number of people, each possessing only bits of knowledge, brings about a state of affairs in which prices correspond to costs, etc., and which could be brought about by deliberate direction only by somebody who possessed the combined knowledge of all those individuals."

    Reprinted in *Individualism and Economic Order.* London: Routledge and Kegan Paul, 1949, from which this quotation was taken (pp.50-51); reprinted also in *L.S.E. Essays on Cost.* J. M. Buchanan & G. F. Thirlby, eds. New York: New York University Press, 1981.

Lippmann, Walter. *An Inquiry into the Principles of THE GOOD SOCIETY.* 1st ed., 1937; 2nd ed. Boston: Little, Brown, 1943. Refers to Mises' query in *Socialism* concerning Marx's theory of history: "What reason is there for thinking that until socialism 'a history has existed' but that after socialism 'none exists any longer'?" (pp.69-70) "The original discoverer of the idea that a planned economy in peace is incapable of 'economic calculation' appears to have been the Austrian economist, Professor Ludwig von Mises . . . . Others, notably the German sociologist Max Weber and the Russian economist Boris Brutzkus, seem to have reached the same conclusions independently and concurrently." (p.94n)

Meyers, Albert L. *Elements of Modern Economics.* New York: Prentice-Hall, 1937. According to the author, his Chapter XVIII, "Money," "is based primarily on Mises, Ludwig von, *Theory of Money and Credit,* Harcourt, Brace & Co., Inc., New York, 1935, and Hayek, F. A. von, *Prices and Production,* George Routledge & Sons, Ltd., London, 1931." (p.278n.)

Phillips, C. A., T. F. McManus and R. W. Nelson. *Banking and the Business Cycle: A Study of the Great Depression in the United States.* New York: MacMillan, 1937. Footnotes p.20 of Mises' *The Theory of Money and Credit* (B-2), in support of the following statement: "It is clear, then, that neither scarcity of gold on an absolute scale, nor deficiency in the rate of increase in the monetary gold stocks of the world, nor excessive demand for gold in relation to its supply, nor the inherent nature of the gold standard as such can be charged with primary responsibility for throwing the economic machine into reverse gear." (pp.54-55) The authors discuss Hayek's critique of Mises: "Hayek criticizes Mises' explanation of the origin of the new credits as emanating from this 'inflationistic ideology' of the central banking system -- see his *Monetary Theory and the Trade Cycle*, especially pp. 145 and 150. But Hayek's claims for his 'perfectly endogenous' theory are unconvincing to the writers for the very simple reason that his explanation of how the banking system creates credit (perfectly valid except for this one point) when a 'certain amount of cash is newly deposited' never satisfactorily explains where the newly deposited cash comes from!" (p.139n.)

Röpke, Wilhelm. *Die Lehre von der Wirtschaft* [The Theory of the Economy]. Vienna: Julius Springer, 1937; 9th German edition: Erlenbach-Zurich: Eugen-Rentsch, 1961. See "Books and Articles About Mises: 1963" for annotation of English translation: *Economics of the Free Society* (1963).

The Times. London. (October 2, 1937). "The Economics of Socialism: Inequality and Redistribution." In a review of Dougla]
s Jay's *The Socialist Case*: "Mr. Jay visualizes Socialism as coming in three instalments." (1) A determined attack on inequality of distribution; (2) A moderate interference with the price system; and (3) The nationalization of the banks and direct control of investment and public works. "[I]n regard to the second stage his [Jay's] enthusiasm is tempered by caution, as he realizes the force of the case made by Professor von Mises against 'tampering with the price system'."

_____. (October 23, 1937). A review of Maurice Dobb's *Political Economy and Capitalism* (Routledge). This book " contains a very able statement of the Marxian criticism of current economic orthodoxy . . . . Mr. Dobb argues that 'in a socialist society . . . there would be no reason for the emergence of interest as a category of income at all.' But he now encounters opposition from another formidable and influential school of economists, led by Professor von Mises, who declare that the same economic laws must rule in a socialist economy as rule in a capitalist economy, and that socialism is *a priori* impossible owing to the absence of the valuation-system of the individualist market. To this attack on socialist economics an elaborate if not wholly convincing reply is made in the concluding chapter of the book."

Whittlesey, Charles R. *International Monetary Issues.* New York & London: McGraw-Hill, 1937. Discusses the profitability of banks dealing in foreign exchange. Cites (p.191n) Mises' Article 09.2 on the Austro-Hungarian Bank.

1938 Anschluss (Germany's annexation of Austria).   Margit   (née Herzfeld) Sereny Flees
     Vienna. Ludwig von Mises and Margit Sereny Wed in Geneva, Switzerland, July 6.

Gazetta di Venezia. "Conferenza del Prof. von Mises a Ca' Foscari" [Conference by Professor Mises at Foscari's]. 16
     (March 10, 1938) 4.   A newspaper account of Mises' talk on March 9.

Hazlitt, Henry. "Economic Programs." *The New York Times Book Review.* (January 16, 1938) 19. A review of A.
     C. Pigou's *Socialism vs. Capitalism,* which outlines a path of gradualism as a means for adopting
     socialism. Hazlitt writes: "Professor Pigou's little volume cannot be compared with the brilliant work
     on 'Socialism' by Ludwig von Mises of the University of Vienna that has just been translated. In scope,
     in range of knowledge, in the acuteness, rigor and power of its reasoning, the Austrian work stands
     unrivaled among contemporary volumes on its subject."

Hoff, Trygve J. B. *Økonomisk kalkulasjon i socialistiske samfund.* Oslo: H. Ashekovg, 1938. English translation,
     Economic Calculation in the Socialist Society (1949); see annotated entry under "Books and Articles
     About Mises: 1949."

Hutchison, T. W. *The Significance and Basic Postulates of Economic Theory.* London: Macmillan, 1938. According
     to Stephan Boehm (*Method, Process and Austrian Economics.* Israel M. Kirzner, ed. Lexington, Mass.:
     Lexington Books, 1982, p.49 n4), Mises was the principal target of this book.

Lippincott, Benjamin E. (editor). *On the Economic Theory of Socialism.* Minneapolis: University of Minnesota
     Press, 1938/1948; London: Geoffrey Cumberlege, Oxford University Press; New York: McGraw-Hill,
     1964. Volume II in a series on "Government Control of the Economic Order." According to the Preface,
     Volume I pointed out that "the political scientist cannot hope to deal intelligently with the problem of
     control . . . unless he first acquaints himself with the nature of what is to be controlled." Volume II is
     concerned with control of a socialist economy and consists of the following papers:
     Lippincott, Benjamin E. "Introduction" (pp.3-38): "Oskar Lange, in this volume, shows that Mises is able
          to deny the existence of prices in the capital goods industries of a socialist state by confusing the
          nature of prices." (p.11)
     Taylor, Fred M. "The Guidance of Production in a Socialist State" (pp.41-54). Reprinted from *American
          Economic Review.* 19:1 (March 1929) 1-8. Presidential address at 41st Annual Meeting of the
          American Economic Association, Chicago (December 27, 1928). Taylor outlines a scheme which
          he believes would permit the authorities in a socialist state to determine without difficulty just
          what commodities should be produced from the available economic resources.
     Lange, Oskar. "On the Economic Theory of Socialism" (pp.57-143). Reprinted from *Review of Economic
          Studies,* (October 1936; February 1937) Section headings as follows: "The Present State of the
          Debate," "The Determination of Equilibrium on a Competitive Market," "The Trial and Error
          Procedure in a Socialist Economy," "The General Applicability of the Trial and Error Method,"
          "The Economist's Case for Socialism," and "On the Policy of Transition." See annotated entry
          under "Books and Articles About Mises: 1936."
     This Lippincott anthology reviewed by Henry Hazlitt, *The New York Times Book Review.* June 5,
          1938.

Marget, Arthur W. *The Theory of Prices: A Re-Examination of the Central Problems of Monetary Theory. I.*   New
     York: Prentice Hall, 1938. Criticizes Keynes' monetary theory. Considers Mises' dynamic monetary
     theory better than static theory. Discusses Mises' view of Fisher's theory. Referring to the difference
     between the natural and market rates of interest which affect the profitability of borrowing, Marget

writes: "The use of the term 'price-premium' in a sense which is relevant to the present discussion is principally due, so far as I am aware, to Mises." (p.276,n.22) Here Marget cites *Geldwertstabilisierung*. . . (B-7; English translation in *On the Manipulation of Money and Credit,* B-24). He also mentions Mises' views on the "velocity" of money, the cash balance approach and subjective value. Volume II published 1942.

The New York Times (May 29,1938)."Behind Autarchy." Editorial, probably written by Henry Hazlitt, then on the *The New York Times* editorial staff and acquainted with Mises' work.

"Secretary Hull did not exaggerate last week when he described the dangers of autarchy, or absolute sovereignty and national self-sufficiency. As he pointed out, the development of order under law and the growth of international commerce have been two of the principal forces in shaping the growth of Western civilization, and the revitalization of these forces is 'an urgent and outstanding task.' In the long run, as he continued, excessive efforts toward autarchy will undermine and breakdown the domestic economic structure of the country persisting upon such a course, yet 'too many nations in the world are today steering straight in the direction of such an economic, political and social Niagara.'

"The same point has been made powerfully by Ludwig von Mises, the Austrian economist, in a recent pamphlet on 'The Disintegration of the International Division of Labor.' [Article 38.5] As Mises shows, the new, like the old, arguments for protectionism and autarchy are primarily not economic but political and military. He examines all the 'modern' arguments in turn -- the argument of national prestige, the war argument in neutral countries, the wages argument, the overpopulation argument, the monetary or foreign exchange argument -- and shows that each is partly or wholly fallacious, and that protectionism, exchange control and autarchy time and again defeat their purpose and often bring about the very opposite of the results they are designed to achieve."

Pepe, Mario. "All'insegna della pace liberale" [Concerning the Characteristic of Liberal Peace]. *Rivista del Lavora.* (Bologna). 10 (1938) 26-33.

Ridgeway, George L. *Merchants of Peace: Twenty Years of Business Diplomacy through the International Chamber of Commerce, 1919-1938.* New York: Columbia University Press, 1938. Mises' Articles 36.3 and 36.4 on exchange stabilization listed among ICC publications (p.382); listings deleted in later editions.

Robbins, Lionel. "Live and Dead Issues in the Methodology of Economics." *Economica.* 5 N.S.:19 (August 1938) 342-352. Discusses Mises and apriorism.

Roll, Eric. *A History of Economic Thought.* Englewood Cliffs: Prentice-Hall, 1938, plus later editions. Cites Mises' claim (Article 32.1) that John Law was the first to relate the subjective value theory to money. (p.117) Also on p.460n: "The most comprehensive work of the non-interventionist school is Mises, L., *Die Gemeinwirtschaft* (1932) [Socialism, B-4]."

Rougier, Louis. *Les Mystiques Économiques: Comment L'on Passe Des Démocraties Libérales Aux États Totalitaires* [Economic Doctrines: How Liberal Democracies are Transformed into Totalitarian States]. Paris: Librairie de Médicis, 1938. Cites Mises' *Le socialisme* (1938, French translation of B-4) and his "Faux arguments en faveur du protectionnisme et de l'autarcie" [False Arguments in Favor of Protectionism and Autarky] (1938), apparently "Les Illusions du Protectionnisme et de l'Autarcie" (Article 38.5).

Le Temps. "Le Parodoxe de l'Autarcie" [The Paradox of Autarky]. 78:28122 (September 10, 1938). A newspaper story commenting on Hitler's protectionist and autarkic goal for Germany. "Autarky is absolutely impossible. Not even large countries like the United States or Russia could become autarkic without facing privation . . . . ¶First of all, a nation that follows this policy risks having mediocre quality military equipment, and as a consequence risks being less well armed than her adversaries. Moreover, the price increases that result mean that it will take more labor and capital to obtain the same production." Quotes Mises (Article 38.5; see *The World Crisis*, p.256): "It is the paradox of self-sufficiency as economic preparation for war that it weakens the military potential of the nation by rendering its arms less efficient." (Translated from the French)

Westerfield, Ray B. *Money, Credit and Banking*. New York: The Ronald Press, 1938. Refers (p.420) to the regression theorem, as presented in Mises' book on money (B-2). This reference not included in later editions.

Williams, John Burr. *The Theory of Investment Value*. Amsterdam: North-Holland Publishing Co., 1938. "While von Mises argues [B-2] that the banks, by the liberal emission of credit, cannot depress interest rates permanently, and will only bring on a crisis if they try to do so, he does not go on to say, as we do, that the long-term rate is the result of the successive short-term rates that the banks see fit to set. In other words, while von Mises distinguishes between the actual or money rate (*Geldzins*) and the equilibrium or natural rate *(natürliche Kapitalzins)*, as we do, he does not distinguish between the short- and the long-term rate, nor show how these latter are related mathematically. Von Mises insists that the *Geldzins* should be made to equal the *Kapitalzins*, whereas the present book maintains that the chain of short-term rates (and thus the long-term rate) should be made to equal the *Kapitalzins*, if inflation or deflation is to be avoided." (p.366n.)

Ellis, Howard S. "Exchange Control in Austria and Hungary." *Quarterly Journal of Economics.* 54:1 (November 1939) 1-186. "Writing for the International Chamber of Commerce, Professor Mises maintained that 'Countries which do not resort to inflation . . . do not put themselves in a position where it might appear advisable to have recourse to those measures comprised under the term 'Foreign Exchange Control'.* Ostensibly this opposes inflation and does not actually recommend deflation. But when world prices are falling, mere passivity spells relative inflation: a country experiencing capital withdrawals must deflate absolutely, and indeed to a greater degree than foreign countries." (p.9)

    *"Ludwig von Mises, 'The Return to a Free Foreign Exchange Market,' mimeographed report to the Vienna Congress of the International Chamber of Commerce, May 30, 1932. (Paris, 1932) p.2."

Hayek, F. A. *Profits, Interest & Investment.* London: Routledge & Kegan Paul, 1939. A collection of previously published essays. Mises is mentioned briefly in several. Hayek quotes Mises' *Geldwertstabilisierung* . . . (B-7, English translation included in B-24) in response to the allegation "that the 'Austrians' were unaware of the fact that the effect of an expansion of credit will be different according as there are unemployed resources available or not." (p.42n) "The 'Paradox' of Saving" (1929) criticizes the pre-Keynes Keynesian theme of William Trufant Foster and Waddill Catchings that the savings of some people deprive consumers of needed purchasing power. Foster and Catchings are "victims of that uncritical fear of any kind of fall in prices . . . a fashion which is all the more regrettable since many of the best economists . . . [Hayek lists Marshall, Pierson, Lexis, Edgeworth, Taussig, Mises, Haberler, Pigou, and Robertson] have repeatedly emphasized the misconception underlying it." (p.253-254).

Heilperin, Michael A. *International Monetary Economics.* London: Longmans, Green and Co., 1939; Philadelphia: Porcupine Press, 1978. Heilperin remarks that it had been "a privilege . . . to work for three years in almost daily contact with Professor Ludwig von Mises." (pp.xi-xii) In the book, Heilperin comments: "We find the word 'price level' used in the English translation of Professor von Mises's book where the word 'Preisgestaltung' [configuration of prices] is used in the German text (*Theorie des Geldes und der Umlaufsmittel*, 2nd edition, Munich and Leipzig, 1924, p. 235 [B-2]). I note this in passing because (1) Professor von Mises criticizes elsewhere the statistical notion of a 'price level' and (2) because it is not necessary to introduce that notion in order to propound the present theory of exchanges. The situation is different for the purchasing power *parity* theory." (p.115,n.3) Heilperin discusses Mises' views on exchange rates and finds it "impossible to agree with the advocates of the purchasing power of money theory of foreign exchanges when they say, in Professor von Mises's phrase, that 'it is . . . the purchases and sales induced by the price-margins that determine the balance of payments'." (p.118)

Nussbaum, Arthur. *Money in the Law* (Columbia Council for Research in the Social Sciences). Chicago: The Foundation Press, 1939. "In so far as the legal definition turns on the economic uses of money, its central use should be chosen for that purpose . . . . There is a remarkable uniformity of judicial opinion, strongly supported by notable writers,* to the effect that the function of being the common medium of exchange, is the basic one, and permits an unambiguous characterization of 'money'." (p.3)

    *Nussbaum footnotes Menger, Mises and Cassel, plus English and American writers, Jevons, Walker and Kemmerer who "put the medium of exchange function first."

Wu, Chi-Yuen. *An Outline of International Price Theories.* London: George Routledge, 1939. Wu's 1939 Ph.D. dissertation (University of London under Lionel Robbins) was on price theory. Includes several references to Mises' monetary theories, including forced savings, international exchange ratios, the Bank of England's structure, and the Currency School. "The classical doctrine of the international comparison of the values of moneys is expounded with great clarity by Mises. Like Ricardo, Mises declares that the money metal is distributed among different trading countries 'according to the extent and intensity of the demand of each for money'." (p.233)

1940   Mises Migrates to the United States

Chandler, Lester V. *An Introduction to Monetary Theory.* New York: Harper & Brothers, 1940. In his section on "Changes in the Money Supply and Their Effects on Prices," Chandler says (p.81n) that he "leans heavily upon L.von Mises, *The Theory of Money and Credit.*" (B-2)

Eucken, Walter. *Die Grundlagen der Nationalökonomie* (1940). English translation: *The Foundations of Economics: History and Theory in the Analysis of Economic Reality;* see annotated entry under "Books and Articles About Mises: 1951."

Hayek, F. A. "Socialist Calculation: The Competitive 'Solution'." *Economica.* N.S. 7:26 (May 1940) 125-149. Primarily a critique of two major critics of the Mises' thesis -- Oskar Lange (1936/7) and H. D. Dickinson (1939). "N. G. Pierson, L. v. Mises, and others pointed out that if the socialist community wanted to act rationally its calculation would have to be guided by the same *formal* laws which applied to a capitalist society . . . . [T]he question raised by Professor Mises and others was not whether they ought to apply but whether they could in practice be applied in the absence of a market." (pp.126-127) Hayek makes a concession to the socialists: "There is, of course, no *logical impossibility* of conceiving a directing organ of the collective economy which is not only 'omnipresent and omniscient'. . . but also omnipotent, and which therefore would be in a position to change without delay every price by just the amount that is required . . . . ¶With given and constant data such a state of equilibrium could indeed be approached by the method of trial and error." (p.131) This position differs from Mises' thesis that in a socialist society, without private property and competitive bidding, there would be no prices, no market, no economy, and hence calculation would not be possible.

Reprinted (Chapter IX, pp.181-208) in Hayek. *Individualism and Economic Order.* University of Chicago Press, 1948; Routledge & Kegan Paul, 1949; paperback, Chicago: Henry Regnery, 1972. Included (pp.77-97) in Bornstein, Morris. *Comparative Economics Systems.* Richard D. Irwin, 1965. Also in Stephen Littlechild, ed. *Austrian Economics III.* (Aldershot, Hants, England; Brookfield, Vermont: Edward Elgar, 1990) pp.295-319.

C. L. *Die Neue Zürcher Zeitung.* "Das Gold in den Vereinigten Staaten."   #787 (May 29, 1940). Mises not mentioned by name, but the author comments on the gold standard chapter of Mises' *Nationalökonomie* (B-11) reprinted in *Die Neue Zürcher Zeitung* (May 26, 1940): "One comes to the conclusion that the only solution for the American gold [inflow] problem rests on a great worldwide reconstruction of monetary, economic and trade policy . . . . In an address to students at Yale, [Adolph Berle] said: 'The proposal to give away a part of our supply of gold after the war for the reconstruction of international currencies and to help other nations rebuild and reconstruct normal trade, may seem fantastic today. However, in a few years that will not seem as fantastic as it does today'." (Translated from the German)

Machlup, Fritz. *The Stock Market, Credit and Capital Formation.* Translated from the German by Vera C. Smith. London: William Hodge, 1940. First edition: *Börsenkredit, Industriekredit und Kapitalbildung.* Vienna, 1931. When Machlup wrote this book, he was attending Mises' private seminar.   Mises is cited frequently. For instance: "Mises' emphasis on the interest rate policy of the banks as the primary cause of the cycle was attacked by both bankers and theorists . . . . Hayek was able, without abandoning the main lines of the theory of credit cycles, to show that the money rate of interest may be below the equilibrium rate not because of positive action on the part of the banks but because there is a rise in the natural rate of interest unaccompanied by any rise in the money rate . . . . In this case the expansion of bank credit is not the result of active inflationism, as Mises considered it, but of passive inflationism." (pp.247-248)

Rist, Charles. *History of Monetary and Credit Theory: From John Law to the Present Day.* Translated from the French by Jane Degras. New York: Macmillan, 1940. First edition: *Histoire des Doctrines relatives au Crédit et à la Monnaie.* Paris, 1938. Rist discusses Tooke's view that distinguishes paper currency, *money,* from convertible bank notes, *credit instruments.* Rist apparently agrees with Tooke, and adds a footnote to the effect that Mises "does not recognize the difference between the two instruments." (p.197n). Rist associates Mises with Wicksell as maintaining "the distinction between metallic currency serving as the standard, and means of circulation." (p.322n.)

Whittaker, Edmund. *A History of Economic Ideas.* New York: Longmans, Green, 1940. "The Austrian economist, Ludwig von Mises . . . . in *Die Gemeinwirtschaft* [B-4] . . . has asserted that economic individualism is desirable because neither socialism nor the so-called *planning* has anything to offer by way of an alternative means of ensuring the economic utilization of productive resources. It is probably true to say that, on the economic side, Mises's work has furnished the most potent criticism of socialist tendencies in recent years . . . . Robbins's writings have been in a similar vein and, undoubtedly, have gained both inspiration and support from Mises." (pp.172-173) Whittaker quotes Mises and discusses his position on economic calculation under socialism: "Mises has argued that competition is necessary for the scientific distribution of productive resources . . . . ¶There is no doubt whatever that the government of a collectivist State could decide how the factors of production are to be disposed of and what commodities are to be produced. What Mises questioned is whether, in the absence of a free market that reflects the relative scarcities of the productive factors and the intensities of demands for the various products, economic considerations can receive proper attention . . . . Those who have given their allegiance to socialism or authoritarianism on other grounds do not appear to be perturbed by the thesis of Mises that, under collectivism, probably productive resources would be used wastefully." (pp.484-485) Whittaker also says that the Austrians, including Mises, "endeavored to apply their general value theory to the value of money." (p. 669).

Wilson, T. "Capital Theory and the Trade Cycle." *Review of Economic Studies.* 7 (June 1940).

1941

Hayek, Friedrich A. *The Pure Theory of Capital.* London: Routledge & Kegan Paul, 1941. According to the book jacket, this is "the first systematic restatement of the theory of capital which has grown up on the foundations laid by Jevons, Böhm-Bawerk and Wicksell." Two brief mentions of Mises: "[A]lthough his [Mises'] published work deals mainly with the more complex problems that only arise beyond the point at which this study ends, he has suggested some of the angles from which the more abstract problem [the productivity of capital] is approached in this book." (p.45)   "[T]o mention only the leading representative of a school that is often accused of overlooking" the effect on employment of available capital, Professor Mises "clearly" recognized it. (p.439n) In this connection Hayek cites *Geldwertstabilisierung* . . . p.49 (B-7); see p.125 of English translation in *On the Manipulation of Money and Credit,* B-24).

1942

Marget, Arthur W. *The Theory of Prices: A Re-Examination of the Central Problems of Monetary Theory. II.* New York: Prentice Hall, 1942. (Annotated entry for Volume I under "Books and Articles About Mises: 1938") A critique of Keynesian price and monetary theory. "In the case of the 'Austrian' school, the degree of concern with this problem [of analyzing the forces determining the value of money] evidenced by Wieser, among the members of the older generation, and by Mises, among the members of the 'middle' generation, was so articulate that the relevant writings of both were seized upon for intensive discussion, if not always for enthusiastic comment, by other writers concerned with the relation between the two bodies of theory." (p.79) Refers repeatedly to Mises' views on monetary theory, especially as set forth in his early book on money (B-2).

Mexico. *Excelsior.* (February 14, 1942); *Novedades.* (February 21, 1942) 5. Newspaper accounts of Mises' lectures sponsored by the Asociación de Banqueros de México and the Universidad Nacional Autónoma. According to *Novedades,* "His words are always accurate and appropriate and his expressions reveal a suitable attitude of observation and study." (Translated from the Spanish)

Schumpeter, Joseph A. *Capitalism, Socialism, and Democracy.* 3rd ed. New York: Harper, 1950. 1st ed., 1942. In Chapter 16, "The Socialist Blueprint" (pp.172-186), Schumpeter recognizes Mises' central role in the economic calculation debate. However, Schumpeter concludes that a socialist central planning board *would* be able to calculate: "There is nothing wrong with the pure logic of socialism. And this is so obvious that it would not have occurred to me to insist on it were it not for the fact that it has been denied and the still more curious fact that orthodox socialists . . . failed to produce an answer that would meet scientific requirements. ¶The only authority standing for denial that we need to mention is Professor L. von Mises (p.172) . . . . ¶[If] we jettison our 'markets,' . . . . [t]here would have to be an authority to do the evaluating, i.e., to determine the indices of significance for all consumers' goods. Given its system of values . . . . the rest of the planning process could then run its course . . . . ¶In any normal situation it [a socialist central planning board] would command information sufficient to enable it to come at first throw fairly close to the correct quantities of output in the major lines of production, and the rest would be a matter of adjustments by informed trial and error . . . . ¶[S]olution of the problems confronting the socialist management would be not only just as possible as is the practical solution of the problems confronting commercial managements: it would be easier . . . . The managements of socialized industries and plans would be in a position to know exactly what the other fellows propose to do and nothing would prevent them from getting together for concerted action. The central board could . . . act as a clearing house of information and as a coordinator of decisions; . . . . This would immensely reduce the amount of work to be done in the workshops of managerial brains and much less intelligence would be necessary to run such a system than is required to steer a concern of any importance through the waves and breakers of the capitalist sea." (pp.184-186)

Stolper, Gustav. *This Age of Fable: The Political and Economic World We Live In.* New York: Reynal & Hitchcock, 1942. "Hardly ever do the advocates of free capitalism realize how utterly their ideal was frustrated at the moment the state assumed control of the monetary system. There is today only one prominent liberal theorist consistent enough to advocate free, uncontrolled competition among banks in the creation of money. [Stolper cites Mises' early book on money (B-2).] Mises, whose intellectual influence on modern neo-liberalism was very strong, has made hardly one proselyte for that extreme conclusion. Yet without it the ideal of the state-free economy collapses. A 'free' capitalism with governmental responsibility for money and credit has lost its innocence. From that point on it is no longer a matter of principle but one of expediency how far one wishes or permits governmental interference to go. Money control is the supreme and most comprehensive of all governmental controls short of expropriation." (p.59)

1943

Lauterbach, Albert T. *Economics in Uniform: Military Economy and Social Structure.* Princeton University Press, 1943. "An orthodox supporter of *laissez faire* in our time, Ludwig von Mises, summarizes the economic philosophy underlying this concept as follows: 'The development of an international division of labor took place with the expectation that wars would henceforth be avoided. For the liberal ideology this appeared to be self-evident. In its eyes, human history was progress from militarism to industrialism . . . . The superseding of dynastic absolutism by democracy and the right to national self-determination was supposed, therefore, to secure peace forever'." (p.167) Mises' quote as in Lauterbach, translated from the German, p.723, *Nationalökonomie* (B-11).

Machlup, Fritz. "Capitalism and Its Future Appraised by Two Liberal Economists." *American Economic Review.* 33:2 (June 1943) 301-320. According to Machlup, Schumpeter, in *Capitalism, Socialism and Democracy* (1942), "proves to his own satisfaction that socialism (1) is *possible* as an economic system, that is, as a system with rational cost calculation (which had been denied by Professor Mises); that it is *practicable,* if the necessary bureaucracy is existent (which had been denied by Professor Robbins and Hayek); (3) that it may be *superior in efficiency* to the capitalist system (which is denied probably by the majority of economists) . . . . that [it] (4) is *compatible with democracy* (which economists and political scientists are inclined to deny); and . . . that [it] (5) is *inevitable* (which, again, is rather controversial)." Schumpeter's Socialist Blueprint is for "an automatic economy, which allocates productive resources . . . through prices resulting from competitive bidding on the part of the independent managements of firms and industries." Machlup notes that Schumpeter and Lange used this construct "to prove the possibility of an economic system of socialism," while Mises used the same construct "to show its impossibility; for to Mises, the competitive-bidding pattern constituted capitalism." (p.318)

McConnell, John W. *Basic Teachings of the GREAT ECONOMISTS* (Everyday Handbook Series). New York: Doubleday, 1943. In Chapter IX, "Business Cycles," Frederick [sic] A. von Hayek, Ludwig von Mises, and Knut Wicksell are listed as "representatives" of the "monetary explanation of over-investment." (p.273).

1944

Boddy, Manchester. *Daily News.* Los Angeles, Calif. (October 25, 1944) 32. Report on Mises' October 20, 1944 lecture before Los Angeles Chamber of Commerce directors. "In the beginning, the governments of Europe did not anticipate a socialistic economy any more than does the government of the United States. The governments of Europe were confronted from time to time with specific ailments that called for specific prescriptions. Each remedy -- in itself -- seemed relatively innocent and certainly not sufficient to bring about a drastic economic change. Taken as a whole, however, they formed a dynamic nucleus that created more and more changes. And the changes, in toto, actually accomplished a result that was not originally intended. ¶Dr. von Mises sees a similar history now being unfolded in the United States."

Braunthal, Alfred. "Von Mises on [Adolf Sturmthal's] *The Tragedy of European Labor*: Comment." *American Economic Review.* 34:1, Part I (March 1944) 121-123. Comments on Mises' Article 43.10. "Ludwig von Mises . . . has based his criticism on assumptions which cannot remain unchallenged. Mises claims that all European countries, except Russia, are comparatively overpopulated, lacking in favorable natural conditions for production, and hampered economically by the protectionism of the countries with excess production of foodstuffs and raw materials. From these assumptions Mises infers -- although only by implication -- that there is only one alternative left for European countries: conquest of 'Lebensraum' or genuine free trade on an international scale. ¶This view, though not so intended, amounts to a vindication of European fascism . . . . ¶Mises's remarks about the economic policy of what he calls the European 'Marxians' cannot remain unchallenged, either. He maintains that the European labor or socialist parties - - which for a long time have ceased to be 'Marxian' in the classical meaning of this word -- were prevented by their economic prejudices from rebutting the economic content of the nationalist tenets . . . . It is an incontestable fact that, while the impact of the national socialist movement on nearly all other parties was terrific, the socialist parties in all free elections withstood like a rock the onslaught of national socialism and did not succumb but to naked terror."

Hutt, W. H. *Plan for Reconstruction: A Project for Victory in War and Peace.* New York: Oxford University Press, 1944. "Since the crude conceptions of Socialist planning were fruitfully challenged two decades ago in a now famous contribution from Professor L. von Mises [see B-4, *Socialism*], there has been evidence of serious misgivings in certain Socialist quarters. The force of Mises' criticisms gradually had an effect, mainly through the influence of intermediary economists.*" (p.311)

> "*The most important of the 'intermediary' contributions are F. A. Hayek (Editor), *Collectivist Economic Planning*, L. Robbins, *Economic Planning and International Order*, and *The Economic Basis of Class Conflict*." (p.311n)

Kaufmann, Felix. *Methodology of the Social Sciences.* New York: Oxford University Press, 1944. Reprinted: Humanities Press (New Jersey), 1958 & 1978; Harvester Press (Sussex, UK). Although apparent in "some of the basic works of the marginal utility school . . . I have nowhere found a more precise and impressive presentation of the aprioristic thesis than in L. von Mises' writings . . . . It should be noted that von Mises gives the term 'action' the meaning of 'rational action' and treats 'rational action' and 'economic action' as synonyms." (1978 ed., p.225) Kaufmann quotes, in English translation, from pp.22-25 of Mises' *Grundprobleme* . . . (B-10) and then continues: "It should be clear from the analysis throughout this book [referring to Kaufmann's book] that we cannot accept von Mises' argument. To derive the concepts 'value,' 'good,' 'exchange,' etc. from the basic category 'action' and to establish necessary relations among these concepts is to operate with analytic propositions. It is impossible to arrive at any synthetic proposition (whether categorical or hypothetical) about economic reality through these operations. Hence it is inappropriate on the one hand to claim *a priori* validity for the laws and on the other to declare that certain conditions are required for their validity. The logical analysis of concepts is not relative to any conditions." (pp.226-227)

1945   Mises Appointed Visiting Professor, New York University, Graduate School of
Business Administration.

Hayek, Friedrich A. "The Use of Knowledge in Society." *American Economic Review.* 35:4 (September 1945)
519-530. "The thesis that without the price system we could not preserve a society based on such
extensive division of labor as ours was greeted with a howl of derision when it was first advanced by von
Mises twenty-five years ago. Today the difficulties which some still find in accepting it are no longer
mainly political . . . . When we find Leon Trotsky arguing that 'economic accounting is unthinkable
without market relations'; when Professor Oscar Lange promises Professor von Mises a statue in the
marble halls of the future Central Planning Board; and when Professor Abba P. Lerner rediscovers Adam
Smith and emphasizes that the essential utility of the price system consists in inducing the individual,
while seeking his own interest, to do what is in the general interest, the differences can indeed no longer
be ascribed to political prejudice." (pp.329-330) Reprinted (pp.77-91) in *Individualism and Economic
Order* (Chicago University Press, 1948; Routledge & Kegan Paul, 1949; Henry Regnery/Gateway, 1972).
Also in: *Comparative Economic Systems.* (Homewood, Illinois: Richard D. Irwin, Inc., 1969. pp.21-32);
The Essence of Hayek. Chiaki Nishiyama & Kurt R. Leube, eds. (Stanford, Calif.: Hoover Institution,
1984, pp.211-224); and *Austrian Economics III.* Stephen Littlechild, ed. (Aldershot, Hants, England;
Brookfield, Vt.: Edward Elgar, 1990) pp.320-331. Excerpt in *The Freeman.* 11:5 (May 1961) pp.44-53.

Heimann, Eduard. *History of Economic Doctrines: An Introduction to Economic Theory.* New York: Oxford
University Press, 1945. Heimann refers to Mises as a present-day representative of the Manchester school
(p.19) and as having revived the question of local price differences (p.43). Concerning the economic
calculation debate: "Ludwig von Mises, the pupil of Böhm-Bawerk and Wieser, launched what was the
keenest and most radical defense of capitalism to be made in recent times. He lumps together as
'destructionism' everything that tends to interfere with the normal formation of exchange values under
capitalism, such as social reform, socialism, inflation, Christianity, and war; they all diminish economic
welfare. As to socialism, it is most obviously utopian, since the values needed for an exact cost
calculation cannot be ascertained by a salaried bureaucrat, but only by private businessmen whose profits
depend on the correctness of their calculation. Where there is no free market for cost factors, for instance,
the use of capital, prices do not provide an infallible guide for production. The extraordinary vigor of this
attack on socialism led to a renewed discussion, which has confirmed once more the fact that the difference
between the two systems is in social arrangements and psychological incentives rather than in purely
economic issues." (pp.208-209) According to Heimann, Mises "made really significant progress" in
cyclical theory. (p.223) Yet: "The explanatory value of theories like those of Mises and Hayek is, of
course, limited because of the fact that the disturbing element to which they trace the cycle is regarded as
illegitimate, i.e. outside the activities necessary for the carrying on of the economic process. Hence, the
importance of these theories in the development of economic thinking is considerably surpassed by Joseph
A. Schumpeter's achievement in at last providing a theoretical understanding of the cycle as a
phenomenon quite legitimate and even indispensable in capitalism." (p.225)

Lerner, Abba P. "A Socialist's Estimate: Hayek's 'Vagueness' on Good, Bad Planning Called Aid to Reactionaries."
Minneapolis Tribune. (February 25, 1945). A review of Friedrich A. Hayek's *The Road to Serfdom* by
Lerner, described by the *Tribune* as "a leading Socialist who opposes Hayek's basic thesis." From the
review: "[The book] is a warning against planning . . . .[It] is in direct line of succession to von Mises'
Socialism which also made a stir in America when translated several years ago. It can be considered the
anti-socialists' rejoinder in the political field to their defeat in the economic field. ¶Von Mises' attempt to
show that socialism is impossible because there can be no guide to the efficient use of resources without a
price mechanism was thoroughly demolished by the development of a theory of pricing in a socialist
society. This led to the withdrawal of the more intelligent anti-socialists to the political fields where they
could argue against socialism in terms of its alleged incompatibility with individual liberty."

R. H. M.   "Toward a Spiritual Solution." *Christian Science Monitor*. (August 28, 1945). Comments on *Approaches to National Unity* (Harper) which included Mises' Article 45.3. The reviewer quotes Mises: "From the point of view of true liberalism, all the supporters of the conflict doctrine [government privileged groups] form one homogeneous party."

Philadelphia, Pennsylvania (March 30, 1945). Three-way symposium sponsored by American Academy of Political and Social Science. Speakers: Alvin H. Hansen (Professor of Political Economy, Harvard University), Rufus S. Tucker (Chief Economist, General Motors), and Ludwig von Mises. Topic: "Are the Democracies Becoming Totalitarian?" Mises' talk later published as "Planning for Freedom" (Article 45.2). The symposium received considerable press coverage:

Evening Journal. (April 25, 1945) 14. "Not Freedom but Slavery" Comments on F. A, Hayek's *The Road to Serfdom* (1944) and Ludwig von Mises' remarks: "The two of them [Hayek and Mises] are agreed that -- ¶1. 'Planned economy' operated by government at the expense of 'individual initiative within a framework of private enterprise,' LEADS INEVITABLY INTO COMMUNISM OR HITLERISM. ¶2. Capitalism, and not any form of Socialism, provides the ONLY economic system in which there may be a progressive and sustained advancement of wages and of standards of living. ¶3. All 'ideologies' of governmental planning, from Bismarck to Sir William Beveridge and his American disciples, have the same fatal effects and can produce only SIMILAR FORMS OF SOCIAL AND ECONOMIC TYRANNY .... ¶The most recent expression of these thoughts was given by Professor von Mises [March 30, 1945]: . . . . 'All that good government can do to improve the material well-being of the masses is to establish and to preserve an institutional setting in which there are NO OBSTACLES to the progressive accumulation of new capital and its utilization for the improvement of technical methods of production.'"

Journal of Commerce. (March 31, 1945). "The only known means to increase a nation's welfare, Professor von Mises told the meeting, is to increase and to improve the output of products."

New York World-Telegram. "The Function of Capital" (Editorial). (March 31, 1945) 10: "The framework in which this country achieved its envied prosperity gave capital a place and function not only respectable but essential. Nor was profit, without which capital can be neither attracted nor increased, treated as something inherently dishonest and depraved."

Philadelphia Evening Bulletin. (March 31, 1945). Mises is quoted extensively. Symposium participant Hansen took issue with Mises. According to Tucker: "planned economy, as outlined by its leading advocates, is merely a modification of totalitarianism, phrased in language not so shocking to the ears of free men as the language of Communism and Fascism."

Philadelphia Inquirer. (March 31, 1945). "Safeguard Urged in State Planning." Same article also published under a different headline: "Economist Urges State Planning." Mises: "There are no means by which the general standard of living can be raised other than accelerating the increase of capital as compared with population . . . . All that good government can do to improve the material well-being of the masses is to establish an institutional setting in which there are no obstacles to the progressive accumulation of new capital and its utilization for the improvement of technical methods of production." According to Tucker: the U. S. Constitution was written "to prevent our government from repeating the mistakes of the colonial planning policy of King George III."

Philadelphia Record. (March 31, 1945) 3. "Calls U.S. Aid Key To Jobs For All: Professor Asserts Federal Action Alone Can Solve Unemployment." Harvard professor Hansen is quoted as follows: "Forty percent of our children are growing up in areas with seriously deficient educational opportunities . . . . The deficiencies in our public health facilities have again been laid bare by the draft . . . . We have 7,000,000 slum houses. These are things for which we need to plan." Mises responds: "The only known means to increase a nation's welfare is to increase and improve the output of products." Rufus S. Tucker, General Motors economist: "[E]ven. when competently and honestly carried out, [planning] is the antithesis of democracy."

1946   Mises Becomes Naturalized U. S. Citizen.   Joins Staff of the Foundation for Economic Education as Part-time Adviser.

Hazlitt, Henry. *Economics in One Lesson.* New York: Harper & Brothers, 1946; revised 1962; several editions. In his Preface, Hazlitt recognizes his intellectual debt to Frédéric Bastiat, Philip Wicksteed, and Ludwig von Mises. He also thanks Professor Mises "for reading the manuscript and for helpful suggestions." In this book, Hazlitt discusses government programs and projects that are "seen," and analyzes their "unseen" economic consequences. His thesis is pro-Mises and anti-Keynes.

Mexico. *El Porvenir.* "La Inflación en México, el Reflejo de la Economía de los E. Unidos" [Inflation in Mexico the Reflection of the U. S. Economy]. (August 20, 1946); *El Norte,* "Ludwig von Mises Condenó al Estado Intervencionista" [Ludwig von Mises Condemned the Interventionist State]. (August 21, 1946). Newspaper accounts of Mises' lectures in Monterrey, where he spoke upon the invitation of the Consejo del Crédito Industrial de Monterrey. Quoting from *El Porvenir*: "All the refined courtesy of 1914 Europe, the depth of thought of Old World scientists, the awe that has excited thousands of philosophers, mathematicians, sculptors, surgeons and wise men of science, the vigor of America, North and South, which has given them refuge after the barbarous war that almost destroyed Europe, are revealed . . . in the gentle smile of the eminent economist Ludwig von Mises, in his broad thoughtful countenance, and in his lively clear blue eyes that peer out through his eyeglasses at his audience." (Translated from the Spanish)

1947

Bye, Raymond T. & William W. Hewett. *Applied Economics: The Application of Economic Principles to the Problems of Economic Control.* New York: Appleton, Century, Crofts, 1947. "Socialists reject the system of capitalism because of the wastes of competitive industry, the occurrence of business depressions and unemployment, the inequality of incomes, the immorality and ugliness which it engenders, and its lack of a definite plan . . . . ¶Socialists believe that collectively owned and operated industry will correct the wastes of competitive production, and that the abolition of property incomes will reduce the evils of inequality . . . . It is important to encourage the orderly evolution of our economy, while watching attentively the British experiment with socialism . . . . ¶Critical attacks on the socialistic proposal are offered by Ludwig von Mises in his *Socialism* [B-4]. . . and his *Bureaucracy* [B-13]. . . . A. C. Pigou presents a more thoughtful weighing of the issues in *Socialism versus Capitalism* (1937)." (pp.658-659)

Hartmann, Heinz. "On Rational and Irrational Action." *Psychoanalysis and the Social Sciences.* 1 (1947) 359ff. "It has been suggested, that the concept of irrational action be dropped completely [Hartmann cites Mises' Article 44.2]. The argument runs as follows: since psychoanalysis has shown, that the behavior of neurotics, and even of psychotics, is meaningful, can be understood, and that mentally ill people no less than the normal basically strive toward satisfaction (though by using other means), what previously was thought to be irrational action is proved to be not irrational at all, and the term, therefore, is misleading. However, for us, neither the statement that pathological as well as normal action strive toward satisfaction, nor that both can be understood and explained by analysis, does imply that they are, or in how far they are, rational. We refer to rational and irrational as to empirical psychological characteristics of action that may be present or absent. In this sense the terms are meaningful and useful." (p.365n.)

Weber, Max. *The Theory of Social and Economic Organization.* Translated from the German by A. M. Henderson and Talcott Parsons. New York: Oxford University Press, 1947. (German edition, *Wirtschaft und Gesellschaft,* 1922). "The formulation of monetary theory, which has been most acceptable to the author, is that of von Mises." (p.176) Weber pondered the problem of economic calculation. "[I]f calculation were in kind, the situation described [the need to make arbitrary assumptions as to the means of production which have no market price] . . . would be universal . . . . ¶Everywhere it has been money which has been the means in terms of which calculation has been developed. This explains the fact that calculation in kind has remained on an even lower technical level than the actual nature of its problems might have necessitated." Weber footnotes this passage: "While the above was in press, the essay of Ludwig von Mises [Article 20.6], dealing with these problems, appeared. Unfortunately it was impossible to comment upon it." (pp.209-211) Republished as *Economy and Society: An Outline of Interpretive Sociology* Bedminster: Totowa, N.J., 1968; Berkeley: University of California Press, 1978.

Westerfield, Ray B. *Money, Credit and Banking.* New York: Ronald Press, 1947. "Before World War I the quantity theory had gained quite general adoption, in the English-speaking world at least. Neither Marshall's cash-holding theory nor von Wieser's money income theory -- both attempts at applying the marginal analysis -- were able to displace it. But with the revival of monetary controversy after 1913, the cash-balance or [cash]-holding theories (of Marshall, Cannan, von Mises, Pigou) and the income theories (of von Wieser, Hawtrey, Aftalion, Keynes) gained great attention and respect." (p.422) N.B. This reference not located in earlier (1938) edition; see above.

1948

Bergson, Abram. "Socialist Economics" in *A Survey of Contemporary Economics.* H. S. Ellis, ed. Published for the American Economic Association.   Homewood, Ill.: Richard D. Irwin,   1948. pp.412-448.   A comprehensive survey of the economic calculation debate, with special reference to Oskar Lange's "market socialism." Bergson writes: "Among the studies to be considered, of course, are the recent contributions to the debate, provoked originally by the famous article of Mises [Article 20.6], as to whether socialism can work at all, and how well. By now it seems generally agreed that the argument on these questions advanced by Mises himself, at least according to one interpretation, is without much force . . . . ¶In view of the special circumstances in which the Russian Revolution has unfolded, the experience of that country perhaps is not so conclusive on the question of planning and freedom as is sometimes supposed. It must be conceded too that the emphasis that critics of socialism have lately placed on this issue sometimes has the appearance of a tactical maneuver, to bolster a cause which Mises' theories have been found inadequate to sustain." (pp.412-413) "¶To come finally to Mises, there are two questions to ask: What does he say and what does he mean? ¶On the first question, let Mises speak for himself . . . . ¶As to what Mises means, there appear to be two views. According to that which seems to have gained the wider currency, Mises' contention is that without private ownership of, or (what comes to the same thing for Mises) a free market for, the means of production, the rational evaluation of these goods for the purposes of calculating costs is ruled out conceptually. With it goes any rational economic calculation. To put the matter somewhat more sharply than is customary, let us imagine a Board of Supermen, with unlimited logical faculties, with a complete scale of values for the different consumers' goods and present and future consumption, and detailed knowledge of production techniques. Even such a Board would be unable to evaluate rationally the means of production. In the absence of a free market for these goods, decisions on resource allocation in Mises' view necessarily would be on a haphazard basis . . . . ¶According to the other interpretation of Mises, which has the authority of Hayek, the contention is not that rational calculation is logically inconceivable under socialism but that there is no practicable way of realizing it." (pp.445-446)

Samuelson, Paul A. *Economics: An Introductory Analysis.* New York: McGraw-Hill, 1948 + many later editions. This widely used college text describes Mises as an advocate of the "overinvestment theory" of the business cycle theory (1st ed., 1948, p.401n; 2nd ed., 1951, p.385n.; 3rd ed., 1955, p.327n; 4th ed., p.257n). Concerning the economic calculation debate, Samuelson writes in essentially the same words in several editions: "Around 1900 Pareto showed that an ideal socialism would have to solve the same equations as competitive capitalism. Around 1920, Ludwig von Mises, perhaps unaware of Pareto's proof, set forth the challenging view that rational economic organization was *logically* impossible in the absence of free markets. Fred Taylor of Michigan, A. P. Lerner of England and N.Y.U., and Oscar Lange of Poland answered Mises with the view that socialism could conceptually solve the problems of economic organization by a decentralized process of bureaucratic trial and error -- 'playing the game of competition' and 'deliberately planning not to plan'." (7th ed., 1967, p.617n.; 8th ed., 1970, p.617n.; 10th ed., 1976, p.642)

1949

Beckwith, Burnham P. *The Economic Theory of a Socialist Economy.* Stanford University Press, 1949; 2nd enlarged ed., *Liberal Socialism: the Pure Welfare Economics of a Liberal Socialist Economy.* Jericho, N. Y.: Exposition Press, 1974. "The first and most persistent advocate of this extremist thesis [that economic calculation is impossible under socialism] was Ludwig von Mises . . . . Von Mises apparently believed that . . . markets are highly competitive and therefore establish relatively ideal prices, and that factor prices cannot be properly determined by socialist managers. Both beliefs are mistaken. The subsequent theories of monopolistic and imperfect competition have made it clearer than ever that capitalist factor prices are not ideal. And the new theory of marginal-cost pricing has made it clear that ideal pricing is possible only in a socialist economy. ¶Von Mises arrived at his radical conclusion because he was eager to develop a new and effective argument against the socialists. The problem of economic calculation in a socialist economy is obviously important, but von Mises made no serious or prolonged effort to solve it. He even ignored the efforts of other outstanding capitalist economists to solve it. He merely asserted dogmatically and hopefully that the problem he had not tried to solve was unsolvable." (2nd ed., p.19)

Cortney, Philip. *The Economic Munich: The I.T.O. Charter; Inflation or Liberty; The 1929 Lesson.* New York: Philosophical Library, 1949. Cortney, President of Coty Inc. and Coty International, studied economics and wrote this book when his business was slow during World War II. He quotes from Mises' Article 45.2 (p.102) and Article 48.3 (p.140).

Haney, Lewis H. *History of Economic Thought: A Critical Account of the Origin and Development of the Economic Theories of the Leading Thinkers in the Leading Nations.* 4th and enlarged ed. New York: Macmillan Co., 1949. This book (1st ed., 1911) was widely used as a college text and went through many editions and printings. Chapter 31, "The Austrian School," discusses Menger, Wieser, and Böhm-Bawerk. There are only brief mentions of Mises. A new chapter in the 4th edition, No.34, "The Development of Business Cycle Theory," includes a section on "Overinvestment Theories of Overproduction, Monetary." Here Haney writes: "Ludwig Mises (b.1881) made his theory of cycles a part of the Austrian School's general theory.* . . . . Mises treats cycles as the result of a continuous tendency among politicians and businessmen to favor inflation of bank credit -- the 'inflation ideology' of central banking authorities . . . . ¶On this base, Mises's pupil, Frederick [sic] A. Hayek (b.1899) has erected a more elaborate and complete theory of cycles which may be taken as representing a full development of the so-called overinvestment theory." (pp.680-681)

> "*Mises is a strong defender of competition and critic of socialism. He presents a notable attempt to explain the value of money in terms of marginal utility. His general system is set forth in *Nationalökonomie*, Geneva, 1940 [B-11]. (Revised and enlarged edition in English, 1949 under title of *Human Action* [B-16])."

Concerning value theory, Haney writes: "On the whole, it may be said that the straight marginal-utility theory had few adherents, among whom the Austrians, Sax, Zuckerkandl, Philippovich, Mises, and Hayek, deserve especial mention aside from the original Austrian leaders. The marginal idea seems to have served merely to develop a neglected point, leaving the refined Classical theory, so modified as to include developments on the utility side, in the ascendant . . . . ¶Most of the members of this [subjective] school stand for deduction and more or less criticism of the Historical School. Needless to say, the members of the Austrian School are included, and not only Philippovich, Mises, and H. Mayer, but also Wieser and Böhm-Bawerk, continued to do notable work in the first quarter of the twentieth century." (pp.817-819)

Hoff, Trygve J. B. *Economic Calculation in the Socialist Society*. (Norwegian edition: *Økonomisk kalkulasjon i socialistiske samfund*. Oslo: H. Ashekovg, 1938). English translation by M. A. Michael. London: William Hodge, 1949; Indianapolis: Liberty Fund, 1981. Hoff writes: "The economist who has done more than any other to bring the problem up for discussion is Professor Ludwig von Mises . . . . That the question of economic calculation has not been more ventilated is due to the fact that but few have been aware of the existence of such a problem." (pp.1, 3, 1949 ed.) This book discusses in detail the possibility of economic calculation under socialism; it contains a large bibliography listing books, treatises and papers concerned exclusively or mainly with economic calculation in the socialist society. According to one reviewer, H. D. Dickinson: "The author has produced a critical review, at a very high level of theoretical competence of practically everything that has been written on the subject in German and English. (*Economic Journal*. 50 (June-September 1940) 270-274)." Dickinson quote from Karen I. Vaughn's "Introduction" to 1981 reprint of Trygve Hoff's book. (p.ix)

Mayer, Hans. editor. *Hundert Jahre Österreichischer Wirtschaftsentwicklung, 1848-1948* [100 Years of Austrian Economic Development: 1848-1948]. Vienna: Springer Verlag, 1949.
   Gratz, Alois. "Die österreichische Finanzpolitik von 1848 bis 1948" [Austrian Financial Policy from 1848 to 1948]. pp.222-310. "The Austrian economist and subsequent Executive Secretary of the Chamber, Ludwig von Mises, played a decisive role in preparing Chamber opinions and in the later deliberations with the Finance Minister." (p.307n.70) "The instigator and leader in the process [of establishing the Chamber's tax policy in the late 1920s] was Ludwig von Mises, who then held the position as Executive Secretary in the Viennese Chamber of Trade and Industry and who, as has already been pointed out, played a decisive role in the Chamber's tax policy in 1908-1913." (p.309 n123) (Translated from the German)
   Weber, Wilhelm, in cooperation with Ernst John. "Wirtschaftswissenschaft und Wirtschaftspolitik in Österreich 1848 bis 1948" [Economics and Economic Policy in Austria, 1848-1948]. pp.674-678. "Between Böhm-Bawerk and Wieser, whose students they are, and the younger generation of economists stand Hans Mayer, Wieser's successor at the University of Vienna, and Ludwig von Mises, who, according to the noted English economist, L. Robbins, achieved 'a remarkable revival of the Viennese School'." (pp.642-643). Weber lists Mises major writings. Then: "In the final analysis, all the more recent and latest publications of 'Neo-liberals' such as Hayek, Röpke and others are based on these works of Mises." (p.644) (Translated from the German)

Sweezy, P. M. *Socialism*. New York: McGraw-Hill, 1949. See Chapter 11, "Can Socialism Utilize Resources Rationally?" pp.221-239. Discusses the economic calculation debate and the "refutation" of Mises' position. Mises comments on this book in Article 52.3: "Its author, Paul M. Sweezy, opens his preface with the declaration that the book 'is written from the standpoint of a Socialist.' The editor of the series, Professor Seymour E. Harris, in his introduction goes a step further in stating that the author's 'viewpoint is nearer that of the group which determines Soviet policy than the one which now [1949] holds the reins of government in Britain.' This is a mild description of the fact that the volume is from the first to the last page an uncritical eulogy of the Soviet system."

1950

Fortune. "The Economists." 42:6 (December 1950) 109-113, 126-138. "Western economists of the classical tradition, like Frank Knight, have posed an equally remote ideal of a competitive society. (Knight is by no means the most extreme; he might be regarded as a weak sister by, for example, Ludwig von Mises)." (p. 111)

Haberler, Gottfried von. "Joseph Alois Schumpeter: 1883-1950." *The Quarterly Journal of Economics.* 64:3 (August 1950) 333-384. "When Böhm-Bawerk resigned as Minister of Finance in 1904, he returned to academic life as professor in the University of Vienna, and conducted in 1905 and 1906 a famous seminar, in which Schumpeter was an active participant. Other prominent members were Ludwig v. Mises and Felix Somary, his lifelong friend. It was made lively and at times stormy by the participation of a group of young Marxists who later became theoretical and political leaders in the Austrian and German Social Democratic parties. There was Otto Bauer, the brilliant theorist, dialectician, and intellectual leader of the Austrian socialists after 1918, who seems to have been mainly responsible for Schumpeter's appointment as Minister of Finance of the Austrian Republic in 1919. There was Rudolf Hilferding, the author of the famous book *Das Finanzkapital* and twice Minister of Finance of the German Republic. Another member was Emil Lederer, later Professor in Heidelberg and Berlin, who in 1934 became Alvin Johnson's main collaborator in the foundation of the Graduate Faculty at the New School for Social Research in New York." (p.337) Reprinted in abbreviated form as "Haberler on Schumpeter" in *The Development of Economic Thought: Great Economists in Perspective.* Henry William Spiegel, ed. (New York: John Wiley, 1952) 734-762.

1951 Mises Turns 70 on September 29

Austria. "Univ. - Prof. Dr. Ludwig Mises." (September 1951). Announcement of Mises' 70th birthday.

City Press. City of London. "Laissez-faire Rebounds." 6339 (February 16, 1951) 4. Announces *The Owl*, a new quarterly journal of international thought, which "contains a study of the philosophy of *laissez-faire* based on the recent work, *Human Action*, by Professor von Mises, of New York."

Eucken, Walter. *The Foundations of Economics: History and Theory in the Analysis of Economic Reality.* First edition: *Die Grundlagen der Nationalökonomie* (1940). English translation by T. W. Hutchison from the 6th German edition. Chicago: University of Chicago Press, 1951. "On the problems of the direction of a centrally administered economy see *Collectivist Economic Planning*, edited by Hayek, London, 1935, and L. Mises: *Socialism* [B-4]. The attempts of recent decades to solve these problems practically in many industrialised countries has brought them to a new stage . . . . In Germany, after 1936, various methods were used for overcoming the problem. But it was found impossible to construct a satisfactory machinery for economic calculation in the centrally administered economy, in so far as this type of economy was realised." Eucken discusses the German attempts to overcome this problem with special attention to Barone's 1908 study (included in *Collectivist Economic Planning*, F. A. Hayek, ed.; see above, "Books and Articles About Mises: 1935"). Barone sought "to prove that the Ministry of Production in a collectivist state must and can act as thought perfect competition existed." This thesis, Eucken says, "can neither be proved nor maintained." (p.333 n.32)

Halm, Georg N. *Economic Systems: A Comparative Analysis.* New York: Holt, Rinehart & Winston, 1951, 1960, 1968. Quotes Mises extensively, especially with reference to the attempts of Oskar Lange, D. H. Dickinson, Maurice Dobb, et al, to respond to the economic calculation challenge. "Mises' exaggerations are not worse than the Marxist claim that the private enterprise system is anarchic. Mises did not mean to deny that some form of bureaucratic coordination of production was possible; he only wanted to point out that the centrally planned economy would have to forego the great advantage of economical factor allocation and accordingly be far less productive than it otherwise could be." (3rd ed., p.256)

Hayek, F. A. "Die Uberlieferung der Ideale der Wirtschaftsfreiheit" [The Transmission of the Ideals of Economic Freedom]. *Schweizer Monatshefte.* 31:6 (September 1951) 3-8. A tribute to Mises on his seventieth birthday. "Mises' work as a whole covers far more than economics in the narrower sense. His penetrating studies of the philosophical foundations of the social sciences and his remarkable historical knowledge place his work much closer to that of the great eighteenth-century moral philosophers than to the writings of contemporary economists. Mises was strongly attacked from the very beginning because of his relentlessly uncompromising attitude; he made enemies and, above all, did not find academic recognition until late . . . . Even some of Mises's own pupils were often inclined to consider as 'exaggerated' that unfaltering tenacity with which he pursued his reasoning to its utmost conclusions; but the apparent pessimism which he habitually displayed in his judgment of the consequences of the economic policies of his time has proved right over and over again, and eventually an ever-widening circle came to appreciate the fundamental importance of his writings which ran counter to the main stream of contemporary thought in nearly in nearly every respect . . . . He . . . has given us a comprehensive treatment ranging over the whole economic and social field. We may or may not agree with him on details, but there is hardly an important question in these fields about which his readers would fail to find real instruction and stimulation." English translation by Elizabeth Henderson: "The Ideals of Economic Freedom: A Liberal Inheritance" in *The Owl* (London). (December 1951) 7-12. Slightly revised version: "A Rebirth of Liberalism" in *The Freeman.* 2:22 (July 28, 1952) 729-731. Reprinted as Chapter 13 (pp.195-200) in F. A. Hayek, *Studies in Philosophy, Politics and Economics.* (Chicago: University of Chicago Press, 1967) Passage quoted from Hayek's *Studies . . .* , pp.197-198.

Korner, Emil. *The Law of Freedom as the Remedy for War and Poverty.* London: Williams & Norgate, 1951. 2
vols. "This work, translated from the original German, contains much that seems to me confused and
crotchety, but also much that is illuminating," according to Henry Hazlitt.   Hazlitt's commentary on
Korner continues by quoting Theo Surányi-Unger (*The American Review*): "Korner offers stimulating
viewpoints to those who adhere to L. Mises', F. A. Hayek's and L. Robbins' doctrines of economic
freedom or to H. C. Simons' *Positive Program of Laissez-faire* and reject Marxism as well as
Keynesian economics." Comments on Korner quoted from Hazlitt's *The Free Man's Library,* pp.102-103;
see "Books and Articles About Mises: 1956."

Kuffner, Raoul. *Planomania: Capitalism Makes Sense.* New York: Richard R. Smith, 1951. The author, born in
Hungary, inherited a thriving business but was forced to part with it in 1938 as Hitler rose to power.
Willard E. Atkins and A. Anton Friedrich write in their "Introduction": "Here is a story of the rise and fall
of an economy reflected in the day-to-day experiences of a business enterprise . . . . What is particularly
impressive is both the kinship and the contrast of this book with such works as Hayek's *Road to
Serfdom* and von Mises' *Omnipotent Government.* The kinship lies in the fact that the conclusions
reached are somewhat similar; the contrast is in the rich flavor of personal experience and reflective
interpretation of personal experience which Baron Kuffner's book contains. In a very real sense, this book
applies the everyday facts which in the end must either fail or succeed in justifying such theses as are laid
down by von Hayek and von Mises." (pp.iii-iv)

Mayer, Hans. "Professor Ludwig Mises." *Die Presse..* Vienna. 896 (September 30, 1951) 9. After reviewing
Mises' contributions, Mayer writes: "To illustrate Mises' personality as teacher and human being, the
main features of his character should be stressed: Consistency in the pursuit of his scientific goals,
unyielding rejection of any compromise, courage in the advocacy of his convictions and -- what must
have been a source of special pride to him: he is one of the few Austrian emigré economists to the
United States (where he has been Visiting Professor at the University of New York since 1945), who did
not simply adapt passively to the new scientific milieu. Professor Mises has been active and has sought
successfully to spread the ideas of the Austrian School, to work for its further development and for its
utilization in solving actual economic problems. It is the wish of his colleagues in his native land and
at the University of Vienna where he served so many years as a prominent lecturer that he may be
permitted to do this for many more years." (Translated from the German) Reprinted as "Zu Professor
Ludwig Mises' 70. Geburtstag" [To Professor Ludwig Mises' 70th Birthday]. *Zeitschrift für
Nationalökonomie.* Hans Mayer, ed. 13 (Vienna: Springer-Verlag, 1952) 513-516.

Moley, Raymond. "The Real RFC Lesson." *Newsweek.* (March 26, 1951) 108. Describes Mises' *Human Action*
as "the finest economic treatise of this generation."

Mötteli, Carlo. "The Regeneration of Liberalism." *Neue Zürcher Zeitung.* 1:8 (November 1951). Writes of four
leading "strongholds of liberal thought" -- (1) the London School of Economics, (2) a group influenced by
Ludwig von Mises, (3) the "Chicago group" and (4) a group influenced by Walter Eucken and Wilhelm
Röpke. Mötteli also mentions the Mont Pèlerin Society, founded 1947. Reprinted in *The Mont Pèlerin
Quarterly.* 3:3 (October 1961) 29-30.

N. Y. Staats-Zeitung und Herold.   "Einen Augenblick, bitte! [Just a minute, please!]. (October 24, 1951) 8.
Announces Mises' 70th birthday.

Oesterreichischer Volkswirtschaftler. "Personalia aus der Wirtschaft: Ludwig von Mises" [Economic Celebrities:
Ludwig von Mises]. (September 28, 1951). A brief review of Mises' activities and contributions.
"Tomorrow Ludwig von Mises will be 70 years old. For more than 40 of those years he has devoted
himself to the critique of socialism and its counterparts. As a result, he has proved to be the great liberal

scourge of socialism. Yet for every one of its heads that he thought he had knocked down, he has obviously been unable to prevent countless others from springing up." (Translated from the German)

Polanyi, Michael. *The Logic of Liberty: Reflections and Rejoinders.* Chicago: University of Chicago Press, 1951, 1980. Chapter 8, "The Span of Central Direction" (pp.111-137): "Before the Russian Revolution the question [of the feasibility of central economic planning] had not been examined systematically, but as early as 1920 Professor Ludwig v. Mises started a critique of Socialism on the grounds that in the absence of a market for factors of production these could not be rationally allocated to industrial plants and that, in consequence, a centrally directed economy could not function. His book *Die Gemeinwirtschaft* [*Socialism,* B-4] . . . elaborated this criticism in detail . . . . ¶It seems to me that in response to this new phase in Russia, both the opponents and adherents of Socialism somewhat changed their grounds. An eminent critic of Socialism, Professor F. H. Knight, joined issue with v. Mises (*American Economic Review*, 1936, Supplement, p.259) by pointing out that economic theory did not contradict the possibility of a centrally directed economy. It only required that such an economy should be administered according to marginal principles . . . . ¶To me it seems that these varied, shifting and obscure ideas concerning economic planning, all reflect the same essential deficiency. They lack throughout the clear recognition of the fact that a centrally directed industrial system is administratively impossible -- impossible in the same sense in which it is impossible for a cat to swim the Atlantic." (pp.122-126)

Saal, John J., Jr., "Mises' *Human Action* Considered in the Light of the Social Teaching of the Church." M.A. thesis, Fordham University, 1951. See "Book Reviews: *Human Action.* "

1952

Barron's. "By Their Own Petard: The Universities' Troubles Are Partly of Their Making." (December 1, 1952). Universities teach the wrong kind of economics and social science; they need more teachers like Mises and Hayek.

Lachmann, L. M. *Capital and Its Structure.* London School of Economics and Political Science: G. Bell & Sons, 1952. Changes in capital structure reflect price changes, expectations, interest rates, and the drive for complementarity. Discusses disequilibria and various trade cycle theories, including the Mises/Hayek "Austrian theory of Industrial Fluctuations."

Machlup, Fritz. *The Political Economy of Monopoly.* Baltimore: Johns Hopkins Press, 1952. Machlup quotes Mises' position that monopoly is the result of government intervention rather than an outgrowth of the market economy. (pp.236-237)

Markhof, Manfred Mautner & Franz Nemschak. "Zum 25 Jährigen Bestand des Österreichisches Institutes für Wirtschaftsforschung" [On the 25th Anniversary of the Founding of the Austrian Institute for Economic Research]. Vienna: Österreichisches Institut für Wirtschaftsforschung, 1952. Institute President Markhof reviews the Institute's first 25 years. Mises founded it in the 1920s. Although like Austria itself, it has gone through three different periods since World War I and has changed its name several times, it has retained its identity and continuity. From December 1926 until March 1938, when Austria lost its independence, it was called the Österreichisches Institut für Konjunkturforschung [Austrian Institute for Business Cycle Research]. From March 1938 until April 1945, it was known as the Wiener Institut für Wirtschaftsforschung [Viennese Institute for Economic Research]. Since then, it has been called the Österreichisches Institut für Wirtschaftsforschung [Austrian Institute for Economic Research].

Masai, Keiji. "Theory of Interest by Mises." *Banking.* Tokyo: Sangyo Keizai Sha.   49 (April 1952) 42-51. This book summarizes Mises' theory of interest and includes short comments on *Human Action* (B-16). Mises is "diametrically opposed to Keynes' *General Theory:* he advances the philosophy of the pure market economy."

Paton, William A. *Shirtsleeve Economics: A Commonsense Survey.* New York: Appleton-Century-Crofts, 1952. "The central proposition of this book," says the author, "is very simple: *We can't consume any more than we produce and only through increased production is a higher standard of living possible.* " (p.v) Paton quotes from Mises' *Planned Chaos* (B-14) on the effects of price controls (p.209), from "Planning for Freedom," Article 45.2 (p.290-291), and from "The Alleged Injustice of Capitalism," Article 50.5 (p.431)

Schuman, Frederick L. *The Commonwealth of Man: An Inquiry into Power Politics and World Government.* New York: Alfred A. Knopf, 1952. "With the slow demise of competitive free enterprise or *laissez-faire* capitalism, and the progressive breakdown and disappearance of the 'automatic' mechanisms of the free market for the most efficient utilization of productive resources, the Great Society has long since entered upon an era of 'economic planning' . . . . ¶This is not the place to expound the mythology, eschatology, nonsense, and wisdom of 'planning,' nor to consider the question of whether 'planning' means the end of 'freedom' (*à la* Hayek, Mises, Henry Hazlitt, and the *Chicago Tribune*) or signifies the dawn of 'liberty' (*à la* Lenin, Clement Attlee, Mao Tse-tung, the first New Dealers, and the Technocrats)." (pp.305-306)

Soule, George. *Ideas of the Great Economists.* New York: Viking Press, 1952. "The drift toward the choice of goals for a national economy as a whole . . . has been bitterly attacked by a few theoretical economists who still adhere strongly to the tradition of classical economics. Prominent among these are two who carry on the ideas of the Austrian school of marginal analysis -- Ludwig von Mises and Friedrich Hayek . . . . ¶Governmental activities of the present magnitude must be planned. If Messrs. Hayek and von Mises can show us the way to pure laissez faire it is their privilege to do so, but merely to contend that it would be better than the existing scheme of things does not seem to get us anywhere." (New American Library paperback, pp.153-154)

Thirlby, G. F. "The Economist's Description of Business Behavior." *Economica* (May 1952). Reprinted in *L.S.E. Essays on Cost*. J. M. Buchanan & G. F. Thirlby, eds. London School of Economics and Political Science, 1973; New York University Press, 1981. Concerning equilibrium: "The businessman does not make a decision about a situation with which he is already 'in equilibrium': while out of equilibrium with the situation, he makes a decision to bring himself into equilibrium with it," Thirlby footnotes this passage (p.206, LSE ed.) to *Human Action*. Thirlby also footnotes *Human Action* with respect to "rationality" (p.216 LSE ed.).

Watts, Vervon Orval. *Away from Freedom: The Revolt of the College Economists*. Los Angeles: Foundation for Social Research, 1952. A critique of the Keynesian "new economics" taught in the colleges. Mises' "scholarly but readable little books, *Bureaucracy* and *Planned Chaos*" show "perhaps better than any other modern author why government interference with the free market leads to crisis, totalitarianism, and war." (p.72)

1953

Alemann, Roberto T. *Sistemas económicos.* (Argentina, 1953). Alemann "devotes ten pages out of 252 to a summarization of Mises' thinking . . . . and in addition refers to Mises on eighteen other occasions," according to William S. Stokes (p.188), "State Interventionism and Democracy in Latin America," pp.179-198 in *Central Planning and Neomercantilism.* Helmut Schoeck & James W. Wiggins, eds. Princeton, N.J.: Van Nostrand, 1964.

Frankel, S. Herbert. *The Economic Impact on Under-Developed Societies: Essays on International Investment and Social Change.* Cambridge, Mass.: Harvard University Press, 1953. "Moreover, the use of these 'income' aggregates *as if* they were automatic and trustworthy criteria of development and investment policy overlooks the fact that these aggregates are only statistical estimates of events which lie wholly in the past: they are abstractions which cannot serve as a guide to future action. They are therefore not adequate criteria of *calculation* . . . . ¶As Professor Mises has so well expressed the matter [*Human Action,* B-16, 1949 ed., p.56]: 'The impracticability of measurement is not due to the lack of technical methods for the establishment of measure. It is due to the absence of constant relations . . . . [T]he main fact is that there are no constant relations. Economics . . . . is not quantitative and does not measure because there are no constants." (pp.60-61)

Kirk, Russell. *The Conservative Mind: From Burke to Santayana.* Chicago: Henry Regnery, 1953. "Professor Ludwig von Mises, as the inheritor of Ricardo and Cobden, cannot accurately be described as a conservative, though often he takes common ground." (p.421n.)

_____. "The New Humanism of Political Economy." *The South Atlantic Quarterly.* 52:2 (April 1953) 180-196. "Its publishers claim that *Human Action* is a counterweight to Marx's *Capital* and Keynes's *General Theory.* Certainly this book of nine hundred closely printed pages is the work of a wise man much read in history and literature . . . . ¶How much effect will *Human Action* or a dozen books like it have upon popular opinion? This bold economist seems wilfully oblivious of the historical truth that men respect property, private rights, and order in society out of deference to the force exerted by the 'myths' von Mises tries to dissipate, the 'myths' of divine social intent, of tradition, and of natural rights. Capitalism has been imperiled directly in proportion to the decay of these principles in society. Hardly anyone but Ludwig von Mises and his intellectual ancestors of Manchester ever pursued beneficent social conduct upon the ground of reason and utility . . . . ¶Von Mises has another yawning chink in his armor. 'Capitalism' (in which term he usually includes 'industrialism') is an absolute good, he says; it has enabled increasing populations to live better than they possibly could otherwise. Why then are men dissatisfied? Because they are deluded by false prophets. He admits no genuine cause for dissatisfaction; he does not mention the ugliness, the monotony, the ennui of modern industrial existence . . . . ¶In Professor von Mises, then, we see a thinker steeped in liberal doctrines who is trying to maintain a conservative position . . . . But for all that, *Human Action* is an important book." (pp.184-187)

Korner, Emil. "Grenznutzentheorie und Preisbestimmung" [Marginal Utility Theory and the Determination of Prices]. *Schmollers Jahrbuch für Gesetzgebung,Verwaltung und Volkswirtschaft.* 77:1 (Berlin: Duncker und Humblot, 1953?) 1-46. Korner refers to Mises' argument that "It was precisely the 'Copernican revolution' that enabled marginal utility theoreticians to overcome 'the difficulties presented by the apparent antinomy of the phenomenon of value'." Korner criticizes as 'dogmatic' Mises' position that "Whoever rejects the basics of subjective [marginal utility] theory of value also rejects each and every economic theory." (*Epistemological Problems,* B-10) Previously, Korner says "only [religious] dissenters have been treated to such outlawry and excommunication . . . . ¶At this point, it is important to show only that the precise opposite of that [Mises'] anathema is true, namely: that it is only those who accept the fundamentals of subjectivist value theory who *reject* the basis of economic theory." (pp.3-4) Korner continues: "The goal of this essay is to prove the extent of the postulate that 'one should not only set forth the truth but also the cause of the error' (Aristotle) and at the same time show that the revolution of economic science and of tax policy caused by the marginal utility theory way of thinking means upsetting directly the substance of the 'Copernican [marginal utility] change in the social sciences.' 'The step which leads from the Classical to the Modern' did not add to knowledge. Rather, it was directed backwards; it was no 'step' forward, but rather a plunge into the night and fog which leads, not to understanding and knowledge, but to conviction where one trusts feelings instead of evidence. With a single blow, the 'Copernican [marginal utility] revolution in social science' set us back in the development of opinion and truth from which the much despised 'earlier theory' once rescued us." (p.46) Korner also rejects (p.39) the Regression Theorem, the explanation for the origin of the value of money, as presented in Mises' book on money (B-2). (Translated from the German)

Roy, Ralph Lord. *Apostles of Discord: A Study of Organized Bigotry and Disruption on the Fringes of Protestantism.* Boston: Beacon Press, 1953. "Some ramifications of the economic theory underlying both Spiritual Mobilization and the Christian Freedom Foundation are hatched on the banks of the Hudson River by the Foundation for Economic Education, Inc., the self-styled 'intellectual arsenal' for this anarchistic crusade . . . . ¶Besides their own essays, the staff circulates standard texts of economic 'laissez-faireism' . . . speeches and tracts . . . and the writings of . . . [among others] Ludwig von Mises, visiting professor of economics from Austria." (p.299)

Wiseman, Jack. "Uncertainty, Costs, and Collectivist Economic Planning." *Economica.* (May 1953) 118-128. Discusses the Mises-Lange debate on economic calculation under socialism. Raises some questions not usually discussed -- re uncertainty, opportunity costs, the authority of the central planners to overrule the investment decisions of managers, etc. "The most effective general rule for managers of enterprises in a liberal collectivist economy would seem to be one similar in nature to the profit maximisation 'rule' of the market economy." He concludes that it might be worth considering "whether a competitive market economy might not function more efficiently even while accepting . . . impairment of the force of the profit motive . . . from policies of income redistribution."

1954

Menger, Karl. "The Logic of the Laws of Return: A Study in Meta-Economics." *Economic Activity Analysis.*
    Oskar Morgenstern, ed. New York: John Wiley; London: Chapman & Hall, 1954. pp.419-482. Karl
    Menger, son of Austrian School "founder" Carl Menger, writes that this paper was "stimulated by a
    conversation with Mises." (p.419n.) He discusses (pp.457-459) Mises' proof of the law of diminishing
    returns on land, as outlined (pp.145-146) in German 1933 edition of *Epistemological Problems* (B-10).

Morgenstern, Oskar. "Experiment and Large Scale Computation in Economics." *Economic Activity Analysis.*
    Oskar Morgenstern, ed. New York: John Wiley; London: Chapman & Hall, 1954. pp.483-549.
    Mentions contributions by Mises and Barone to the economic calculation debate (pp.494-495).

Rothschild, Kurt. "The Wastes of Competition." *Monopoly and Competition and Their Regulation.* E. H.
    Chamberlin, ed. London: Macmillan, 1954. pp.301-314. "Thus the strange thing happened that in the
    'thirties conservative and a certain school of socialist economists were at one in their aims. While after
    the First World War the discussion raged between liberal and conservative defenders of free competition and
    socialist planners who had no high opinion of the competitive solution, in these later days one could see
    Hayek and Mises, and Lange and Dickinson united in their admiration of the competitive ideal and only
    divided about the question whether socialism leads away from this target or is the only way of reaching
    it." (p.302)

Santa Ana Register (California). "Writers to Remember." (January 17, 1954). A brief overview of Mises and his
    work. "The course of history has been changed by quiet men working out abstract problems in their quiet
    studies. No one can argue for a free society and for free men today without echoing the ideas and
    conclusions of Ludwig von Mises. He stands on a lonely pinnacle of integrity in a time when even the
    forces and parties of freedom are infiltrated and swayed by the proponents of ever-increasing state
    intervention in the lives of men. Ludwig von Mises is one of the most vigorous and important thinkers
    in the world today."

Schumpeter, Joseph A. *History of Economic Analysis.* Edited from manuscript by Elizabeth Boody Schumpeter.
    New York: Oxford University Press, 1954. A vast survey of economic thought and economists
    throughout the ages. Mises' works are footnoted several times, especially in Chapter 8, "Money, Credit,
    and Cycles." Schumpeter calls Mises "the foremost critic of the price-level concept. He [Mises] denied
    that there is sense in holding that an increase in money will *ever* increase the price level proportionately.
    All he averred (*Human Action,* 2nd ed., p.111) was that there is 'a relation' between changes in the value
    of money and changes in the proportion of demand for to supply of money. This he called the useful
    element in the quantity theory . . . . I think we had better . . . pigeonhole him with the opponents of the
    quantity theory in the historical sense, i.e. the quantity theory opponents meant to combat." (p.1099n.)

Tompkins, E. F. "Housewives' Role: An Economist's View." *New York Journal American.* (January 21, 1954).
    Quotes from Mises' "The Political Chances of Genuine Liberalism" (Article 51.3) concerning "the
    growing housewives' revolt against household taxes and high prices caused by governmental controls."

Van Sickle, John V. & Benjamin A. Rogge. *Introduction to Economics.* New York: D. Van Nostrand, 1954.
    Compares governments that abandon the principle of proportionality in taxation to ships that try to steer
    without a rudder: "The possibility that the captain might have to exercise tyrannical powers to keep order
    was not seriously considered until after Professor Mises's attack on socialism in the early 1920s." (p.606).
    Later the authors discuss "The Mises Indictment" of socialism. (pp.654-655)

Vito, F. "Monopoly and Competition in Italy." *Monopoly and Competition and Their Regulation.* Edward H. Chamberlin, ed. London: Macmillan, 1954. pp.43-60. "When F. Knight speaks of an Ethics of Competition or L. v. Mises reduces all human actions to exchange relationships, they denounce, however the result of their effort may be evaluated, the need for a more profound demonstration of the desirability of competition." (p.58)

Wandruszka. Adam. "Österreichs politische Struktur: die Entwicklung der Parteien und politischen Bewegungen" [Austria's Political Structure: The Development of Parties and Political Movements]. *Geschichte der Republik Österreich.* Heinrich Benedikt, ed. Vienna: Verlag für Geschichte und Politik, 1954. "Liberal tendencies, which may be traced back not only to the adoption of national liberal elements, certainly won out in the Austrian Volks [Peoples] Party. In Austria, as everywhere in Europe, the opposition to totalitarianism created favorable conditions for the revival of liberal thought. Neo-liberalism, among whose founders and most outstanding advocates quite a few are operating abroad such as Mises, Hayek and Haberler, is represented in the anticlerical press, especially in the nonpartisan papers *(Die Presse, Salzburger Nachrichten,* etc.). Neo-liberalism is interested in the rejection of economic planning and in carrying out the economic stabilization policy of Finance Minister Dr. Reinhard Kamitz." (p.357) (Translated from the German)

Wingfield, Alvin, Jr. "The General Economic Outlook" (Special Essay Series). Irvington, N.Y.: Foundation for Economic Education, [1954]. 28pp. Discusses the prospects for inflation, deflation, and depression. Quotes Mises' ridicule of the idea that deflation is a cure for inflation, and vice versa: "There are those who say that the cure for inflation is deflation. That is like saying that if a man is run over by an automobile from North to South, the cure is to run over him again from South to North." Wingfield talks about the Federal Reserve's built-in bias toward inflation, its violations of sound money principles, and recommends Mises' *Human Action* (B-16) and Mises' book on money (B-2) to anyone interested in studying the free economy. Wingfield then quotes from Mises 1923 book which anticipated the German runaway inflation: "Once the practice has been firmly established of covering the deficit in the public household by new issues of notes, then the day must inevitably come, sooner or later, when the financial system of the State which chose this course completely collapses. The purchasing power of the money sinks lower and lower and finally disappears completely." *Stabilization of the Monetary Unit -- from the Viewpoint of Theory* (B-5). (Passage translated from the German by Wingfield)

Yeager, Leland B. "The Methodology of Henry George and Carl Menger." *American Journal of Economics and Sociology* (April 1954) 233-238.

1955

Eastman, Max. *Reflections on the Failure of Socialism.* New York: Devin-Adair, 1955. Eastman, for many years editor of the socialist journal, *Masses,* explains his rejection of revolutionary socialism for the ideas of Mises, Hayek and Röpke, who "have shown that the competitive market and the price system are the basis of whatever real political freedom exists." (p.30) In a review of this book (*The New Leader*, May 2, 1955), Upton Sinclair described Eastman's intellectual transformation epigrammatically: "From *Masses* to Mises."

Gilbert, J. C. "Professor Hayek's Contribution to Trade Cycle Theory." *Dundee Economic Essays.* J. K. Eastham, ed. Dundee, Scotland, 1955.

H. H. "Der Boom ist am Zügel" [The Boom Is Under Control]. *Wirtschafts Zeitung.* 10:78 (October 1, 1955). "Ludwig von Mises, the important Austrian economist (who witnessed the first World War as an officer, the second as an alert and watchful observer emigré in the U.S.A.) has explained relentlessly in his major work, *Human Action,* the dangers of the idea that the skimming off of profits seems more important than the production of weapons." (Translated from the German)

Kalamazoo Gazette. Michigan. "The Dilemma of the Have-Nots." Editorial. (November 18, 1955). Discusses the idea expressed in Mises' Article 55.3 that "People who are beset by poverty are inclined to blame their plight on the people who are better off . . . . ¶[A] tremendous forward stride can be made wherever hostility toward wealth can be erased and faith in the usefulness of capital established."

Machlup, Fritz. "Problem of Verification in Economics." *Southern Economic Journal.* 22:1 (July 1955) 57-77.. Distinguishes two schools of thought, the "apriorist" and the "ultra-empiricist." "[T]he ultra-empiricist is so distrustful of deductive systems of thought that he is not satisfied with the indirect verification of hypotheses . . . instead, he insists on the independent verification of all assumptions, hypothetical as well as factual." Machlup calls Mises an "apriorist;" he cites T. W. Hutchison as an "Ultra-Empiricist." For Machlup, the "apriorists" are a broad group epistemologically, ranging from J. S. Mill to Mises.

Pettengill, Samuel B. "Marx and von Mises." Letter to the Editor. *Wall Street Journal.* (August 17, 1955). Ludwig von Mises "demonstrated that without the 'indicator' of free market prices, a socialist state operates in the dark . . . . The 'master minds' are being tried -- in Russia -- and found wanting -- by Russians."

Sennholz, Hans F. *How Can Europe Survive?* New York & Toronto: Van Nostrand, 1955. Originally his Ph.D. dissertation under Mises, New York University Graduate School of Business Administration. Sennholz analyzes various proposals made over the years for the unification of Europe; maintains that cooperation based on liberty and free enterprise is the only arrangement freedom-loving peoples can recommend.

Spadaro, Louis M. "Salvation Through Credit Reform: An Examination of the Doctrines of Proudhon, Solvay, and C. H. Douglas." Ph.D. dissertation under Ludwig von Mises, New York University Graduate School of Business Administration, 1955. In his analysis of credit reform, Spadaro relies heavily on monetary theory as presented by Mises in his book on money (B-2). See Chapter 4, "The Credit Reform Proposals, Monetary Theory, and the 'Real-Bills' Doctrine." Spadaro's thesis is "that the ultimate refuge of the reformers examined [Proudhon, Solvay, and Douglas] (and probably of most others) lies in the 'banking principle' (or 'real-bills' doctrine) and that the failure to settle the century-old dispute in banking theory has blocked the way to effective criticism of their proposals (p.3) . . . . ¶The three schemes examined share the view that what hinders consumption is a shortage of money. Inasmuch as the rate of interest appears to them to be a purely monetary phenomenon . . . they propose to bring down the rate of interest by some form of expansion of credit." (p.51)

1956   Fiftieth Anniversary of Mises' Doctorate at the University of Vienna

Hall, Everett W. *Modern Science and Human Values: A Study in the History of Ideas*. Princeton, N. J.: Van Nostrand, 1956. When the depression starting in 1929 turned attention to "the evils of the current capitalist system . . . . Economists increasingly asked whether it was not possible to base an economic system on the motive of welfare rather than private profits. Thus, a somewhat desultory controversy between some of the later marginalists -- for example, Ludwig von Mises and Friedrich von Hayek, and some of the disciples of Pareto, such as Barone and the socialist economists influenced by him -- took on new significance. This controversy was over the question: Is it possible in a state-owned or at least state-controlled economy to come to any rational decision as to quantities of various products to be produced? Von Mises in a most vehement condemnation of all forms of socialism claimed no rational decision could be made, whereas completely free enterprise did decide the matter -- by the democratic 'vote' involved in the consumer's dollar." (pp.261-262)

Hayek, F. A. "Tribute to Ludwig von Mises Given at a Party in Honor of Mises, New York, March 7, 1956." Included in Margit von Mises' *My Years With Ludwig von Mises*. New Rochelle, N. Y.: Arlington House, 1976. Appendix Two, pp.187-191; 2nd enlarged ed., Cedar Falls, Iowa: Center for Futures Education, Inc., 1984. Appendix Three, pp.217-223. "I believe it is true of all of Professor Mises' works that they were written in constant doubt whether the civilization which made them possible would last long enough to allow their appearance. Yet, in spite of this sense of urgency in which they were written, they have a classic perfection, a rounded comprehensiveness in scope and form which might suggest a leisurely composition . . . . ¶I cannot help smiling when I hear Professor Mises described as a conservative . . . . There couldn't have been anything more revolutionary, more radical, than his appeal for reliance on freedom. To me Professor Mises is and remains above all, a great radical, an intelligent and rational radical but, nonetheless, a radical on the right lines."

Hazlitt, Henry. *The Free Man's Library: A Descriptive and Critical Bibliography*. Princeton, N. J.: D. Van Nostrand, 1956. A bibliography of "works on the philosophy of individualism." Hazlitt hopes it "will help to clarify as well as to mobilize the case for individualism and true liberalism." (p.15) Includes brief descriptions of Mises' works then in English -- *Human Action* (B-16), *Socialism* (B-4), *The Theory of Money and Credit* (B-2), *Omnipotent Government* (B-12), *Bureaucracy* (B-13), *Planning for Freedom* (B-18) -- and two Mises books which were not translated from the German until after 1956 -- *Liberalism* (B-6) and *Critique of Interventionism* (B-8).

Hoiles, R. C. "Better Jobs: War on Business." *Colorado Springs Gazette Telegraph*. (October 25, 1956) 34. Hoiles paid Mises' expenses to Santa Ana in 1944 (see Article 44.4) and considered himself fully repaid by Mises' comment on the economic situation: "It would have been much better to let the banks that overexpanded credit go broke one at a time and let the stock holders and depositors suffer than to have the government step in and try to save the banks that had overexpanded credit . . . [as a result] the dollar will become worth less and less and finally go out the ceiling by inflation." The article quotes at length from the excerpt of *The Anti-Capitalistic Mentality* (B-19), *U. S. News & World Report* (October 19, 1956).

Hutchison, T. W. "Professor Machlup on Verification in Economics." *Southern Economic Journal*. (April 1956) 476-483. Hutchison responds to Machlup (1955), denying that he is an "ultra-empiricist" who "refuse[s] to recognise the legitimacy of employing at any level of analysis propositions not independently verifiable." Hutchison also rejects Machlup's position that "wholesale political conclusions" are "logically deducible" from the fact that "people act rationally" as Machlup and Mises, "whom Professor Machlup seems so concerned to defend." seem to maintain. Hutchison then quotes Mises' *Critique . . .* (B-8) and *Liberalism* (B-6). (pp.482-483)

Knight, Frank H. *On the History and Method of Economics.* Chicago: University of Chicago Press, 1956. In Chapter 7: "Professor von Mises would hardly be generally accepted as 'the leader of contemporary Economic Liberalism,' unless this means the academic opponent of socialism most conspicuous for the extremism of his position." (p.170n)

Machlup, Fritz. "Rejoinder to a Reluctant Ultra-Empiricist." *Southern Economic Journal.* (April 1956) 483-493. Machlup writes, "Professor Hutchison asks whether my category of apriorism in economics is 'so stretched to include all the middle ground up to the frontier line of "ultra-Empiricism".' . . . The answer is that I know very few 'extreme apriorists' (e.g., Professor von Mises). The middle ground between the extreme positions is very large indeed." (p.485)

One Man's Opinion. Belmont, Mass. 1:1 (February 1956). "This Month We Salute Ludwig von Mises. . . . [T]his gentle man, profound scholar, and steadfast crusader for sound principles appears to grow in stature the better we come to know him. We salute one of America's most highly-regarded and most justly honored adopted citizens."

Sennholz, Mary (ed.) *On Freedom and Free Enterprise: Essays in Honor of Ludwig von Mises.* Princeton, N. J.: D. Van Nostrand, 1956. Commemorating the 50th anniversary of Mises' doctorate. Essays arranged topically under the following headings: "Grato Animo Beneficiique Memores" [In Memory of a Dear Friend and his Contributions]; "On the Nature of Man and Government;" "On Scientific Method;" "The Economics of Free Enterprise;" "The Hampered Market Economy;" and "On Socialism."

Antoni, Carlo. "Some Considerations on Economic Laws." Translated from the Italian by Micheline Mitrani. pp.135-139. "[I]t had become the fashion after World War I to proclaim that the war had demonstrated the spuriousness of all economic laws. In reality the war provided an almost experimental confirmation of their validity. The alleged spuriousness simply consisted in the fact that the war provided politicians with an opportunity to commit a multiplicity of blunders, the inevitable effects of which were then ascribed to the war . . . . Socialism claims to repress that very economic factor in the economic world itself, rejecting or even censuring the formidable vital force . . . . And yet, since not even the merciless dictator can deprive the human soul of that vital motive, economic laws reappear also in collectivist societies, alive and petulant, in the form of guilt and crime, sabotage and reason, or less vividly as black markets." (pp.135, 138-139)

Ballvé, Faustino. "On Methodology in Economics." Translated from the Spanish by O. L. Ballvé. pp.128-134. "L. von Mises advances a number of rules of understanding for the interpretation of past events. We believe that economists should also endeavor to find interpreting rules that serve as guides for the solution of practical cases and the discovery of the major premise, even if such guides are not exact or infallible. Indeed, it is deplorable to err in the interpretation of past historical cases as, for example, in the interpretation of the last depression. But it is fatal to err in actions affecting the future, especially if they concern not only an individual, but also a collective body." (p.133)

Baudin, Louis. "French Socialism." Translated from the French by Stephen DiBari. pp.311-319. Baudin is "at a loss for a proper definition of French socialism . . . . [S]ocialism is nothing more than a label affixed to a flask whose contents vary according to the whim of the shopkeeper . . . . [I]ts greatest strength is its vagueness . . . . ¶Oscar Lange suggested that socialists erect a statue to Ludwig von Mises in gratitude for having made them elaborate their doctrine . . . . The proper inscription [at] the base of the monument should announce the destruction of socialism rather than its perfection, for this alleged elaboration of doctrine is nothing more than its substitution by vague planning." (pp.314, 318)

de Jouvenel, Bertrand. "Order vs. Organization." pp.41-51. "Practically all men enjoy the orderliness of a military parade, but they are dangerously prone to mistake this enjoyment for the recognition of a supreme form of organization . . . . A parade is costly; equally costly is the parade spirit with which we approach the operations of men in general." (p.50)

Greaves, Percy L. Jr., "Is Further Intervention a Cure for Prior Intervention?" pp.285-307. Cites the "right-to-work" laws to illustrate Mises' position that government attempts to fix problems lead to still further interventions. "Every legislative proposal should be weighed on the scales of economic understanding. Does it tip the balance toward a free economy or toward a socialist dictatorship with the politicians in control of the means of production? The so-called 'right-to-work' laws are definitely a step in the direction toward Socialism. They limit the right of free men to negotiate contracts for morally acceptable purposes and attempt to substitute the decisions of politicians for those that consumers would like to express in the market place." (p.307) Separate reprint by the Foundation for Economic Education (Irvington, N. Y., n.d.)

Harper, F. A. "The Greatest Economic Charity." pp.94-107. "Professor Mises' main renown is as an economist. Yet to me he is a charitable person even more than an economist. His charity is not of the fashionable kind . . . . His is not even primarily of the material sort at all but is, instead, in the form of his inspiring mind and spirit. In my opinion there can be no greater charity than this, for it endures beyond any material form of benevolence." (p.94) Separate reprint by Ingersoll Milling Machine Co., Rockford, Ill., n.d. Reprinted also in *The Writings of F. A. Harper, II.* Menlo Park, Calif.: Institute for Humane Studies, 1979. pp.564-578.

Hayek, F. A. "Progressive Taxation Reconsidered." pp.265-284. Raises several aspects of progressive taxation not often discussed. For instance: "The whole attitude which regards large gains as unnecessary and socially undesirable springs from the psychology of people who are used to sell their time for a fixed salary or fixed wages . . . . ¶It must appear somewhat doubtful, however, whether in a society which will recognize no other rewards than what to its majority appears a very ample income and do not admit the acquisition of a fortune in a comparatively short time as a legitimate form of remuneration for certain kinds of services, it is possible in the long run to preserve a system of private enterprise." (pp.278-279)

Hazlitt, Henry. "The Road to Totalitarianism." pp.81-93. "One of the great contributions of Ludwig von Mises has been to show . . . how government intervention in the market economy always finally results in a worse situation than would otherwise have existed." Rather than discussing the economic consequences of intervention, Hazlitt chose to write on "the *political* consequences and accompaniments of government intervention in the economic sphere." (p.83)

_____. "Two of Ludwig von Mises' Most Important Works." pp.34-38. Hazlitt's reviews of *Socialism* (*The New York Times*, January 9, 1938) and *Human Action* (*Newsweek*, September 19, 1949), both annotated above under "Book Reviews."

Hutt, W. H. "The Yield from Money Held." pp.196-216. Money has long been categorized as barren, sterile, unproductive. Yet, Hutt claims, it is "as productive as all other assets, and *productive in exactly the same sense.* . . . ¶The prospective yield from investment in money assets consists . . . (a) of a prospective *pecuniary yield*, in which case the money assets are producers' goods; or (b) of a prospective *non-pecuniary yield* in personal convenience, in which case the money assets are consumers' capital goods; or (c) of a prospective 'real,' i.e., *non-pecuniary*, speculative yield, in which case the assets are producers' goods, whether held privately or in the course of business." (pp.197-198) Mises comes close to this interpretation, Hutt says, when he "stresses their 'services.' And in a most lucid passage he describes the nature of their *productiveness* (although without using this word)." (p.211) Reprinted in *Individual Freedom: Selected Works of William H. Hutt*. Svetozar Pejovich & David Klingaman, eds. Westport, Conn.: Greenwood Press,1975. pp.207-229.

Lachmann, Ludwig M. "The Market Economy and the Distribution of Wealth." pp.175-187. The distribution of wealth, "far from being an 'independent variable' of the market process . . . is, on the contrary, continuously subject to modification by the market forces . . . . ¶The market process is thus seen to be a leveling process. In a market economy a process of redistribution of wealth is taking place all the time before which those outwardly similar processes which modern politicians are in the habit of instituting, pale into comparative insignificance, if for no other reason than that the market gives wealth to those who can hold it, while politicians give it to their constituents who, as a rule, cannot . . . .¶Why, then, do so many economists continue to regard the distribution of wealth as a 'datum'. . .'? We submit that the reason has to be sought in an excessive preoccupation with equilibrium problems . . . . [and] the inability of economists preoccupied with equilibria to cope at all with the forces of disequilibrium." (pp.177, 179, 184-185)

Machlup, Fritz. "The Inferiority Complex of the Social Sciences." pp.161-172. Social scientists who urge some mechanical approach on others as "the only truly 'scientific' [method] . . . are apparently ashamed of the one thing that really distinguishes social sciences from natural sciences, namely, the fact that *the student of human action is himself an acting human being* and therefore has at his command a source of knowledge unavailable to the student of the phenomena of nature . . . . [G]ood historical and institutional studies, interesting holistic hypotheses and behavioristic research . . . improved quantitative-empirical research . . . better training in mathematics -- all these are highly desirable things in the social sciences. What is harmful is the attitude of snubbing, disparaging, excommunicating, or prohibiting the working habits of others and of preaching a methodology that implies that they are inferior in scientific workmanship. ¶Good 'scientific method' must not proscribe any technique of inquiry deemed useful by an honest and experienced scholar." (pp.170, 172)

Peterson, William H. "The Accelerator and Say's Law." pp.217-223. Peterson argues that the refutation of the accelerator doctrine was contained in Say's Law. He concludes: "One, the accelerator is groundless as a tool of economic analysis. Two, Say's Law has yet to meet an effective refutation. Three, acceptance of the acceleration doctrine leads to false conclusions in other areas of economics. And four, accelerationists must look elsewhere for an answer to the business cycle." (p.223)

Rappard, William E. "On Reading von Mises." pp.17-33. Quotes at length from *Human Action* to show Mises' insistence, on the one hand, on "the purely scientific character and functions of economics" and, on the other, his advocacy of "complete *laissez-faire* in an unhampered market economy." Rappard points to his country, Switzerland, as an apparent contradiction of Mises thesis that people tend to vote for their material advantage. "My country, in which farmers represent less than 20 per cent of the population, has in the course of the last generations repeatedly favored this small and dwindling minority by protectionist measures on corn, dairy products, and wine . . . . A more agricultural Switzerland, though poorer, such is the dominant wish of the Swiss people today." (pp.17-18, 33)

Read, Leonard E. "Unearned Riches." pp.188-195. "Are the riches received in a free society unearned? Only in the sense that all producers reap fantastically more than they could earn in isolation. The benefits flowing from our division of labor are available to all of us in willing exchange if freedom prevails." (p.195) Reprinted in *The Freeman*. 6:12 (December 1956) 23-30.

Röpke, Wilhelm. "The Place of Economics Among the Sciences." Originally published in *Studium Generale*. Berlin, Göttingen, Heidelberg: Springer. (July 1953). Translated from the German by George D. Huncke. pp.111-127. "[E]conomics is in the main, a science which is rooted in our market economy. It is, to speak with Ludwig von Mises, pre-eminently catallactics. That is the field where its actual scientific discoveries have been made . . . . Indubitably economics demands a kind of thinking which, if not difficult, is certainly peculiar to itself and which must be the product of training as well as of intensive practice. Such must inevitably be the case since its subject, economic activity, is so prodigiously varied and complex that it eludes our best efforts to grasp it by the methods customary in scientific study generally." (pp.115-116)

Rothbard, Murray N. "Toward a Reconstruction of Utility and Welfare Economics." pp.224-262. "[W]hile the formerly revolutionary and later orthodox theories of utility and welfare deserve an even speedier burial than they have been receiving, they need not be followed by a theoretical vacuum. The tool of Demonstrated Preference, in which economics deals only with preferences as demonstrated by real action, combined with a strict Unanimity Rule for assertions of social utility, can serve to effect a thoroughgoing reconstruction of utility and welfare economics." (p.261) Reprinted as Occasional Paper Series #3 (Center for Libertarian Studies, N. Y., 1977) and in *Austrian Economics: III.* Stephen Littlechild, ed. (Aldershot, Hants, England; Brookfield, Vt: Edward Elgar, 1990) pp.361-399.

Rueff, Jacques. "The Intransigence of Ludwig von Mises." Translated from the French, "Le refus de Ludwig von Mises" by George D. Huncke. pp.13-16. "If we compare the guile of economic irrationality with the imperturbable intransigence of his lucid thinking, Ludwig von Mises has safeguarded the foundations of a rational economic science . . . . By his teachings he has sown the seeds of a regeneration which will bear fruit as soon as men once more begin to prefer theories that are true to theories that are pleasing." (p.16)

Sennholz, Hans F. "On Democracy." pp.52-80. "'Democracy' is the ambiguous catchword with a multiplicity of connotations harboring conflicting political and economic ideas and practices." (p.52) Sennholz discusses the "People's Democracies" of the communist nations as well as the "Western Democracies." "To defend democracy, we must defend capitalism. For it is in the soil of capitalism that democracy has grown and without which it must vanish." (p.80)

Spadaro, Louis M. "Averages and Aggregates in Economics." pp.140-160. "To the extent that economic action is ultimately dependent for explanation on individual differences, the employment of averages puts us out of reach of such explanation simply by understating these differences." (p.145) Spadaro explains how averages and other aggregates "tend to suppress individual differences and actual typicalness . . . . [T]he current resort to aggregates of all kinds is a facet of our hastening approach to central control as an ideal in economic affairs . . . . The aggregative approach in economics suits this program very well." (pp.159-160) Spanish translation: "Promedios y Agregados en Economía." *Libertas* (Buenos Aires: Escuela Superior de Economía y Administración de Empresas). 3:4 (May 1986) 215-239.

N.B. This Festschrift anthology reviewed by:

Bagiotti, Tullio. *Rivista Internazionale di Scienze Economiche e Commerciali.* (July-August 1956) 796ff.

Bien, Bettina. "A Festschrift for Doctor Mises." *The Freeman.* 6:4 (April 1956) 29-32.

Burns, Arthur E. *The Scientific Monthly.* (April 1957) 216. "Mises is noted above all for his uncompromising opposition to socialism and to all forms of government intervention that distort the operation of the price system . . . . [Socialism's] rejection of the free-market mechanism denied it the means of calculating cost and return essential to a rational allocation of economic resources. Events have largely vindicated his economic and sociologic analysis of socialism . . . . Yet Mises is not popular. His intransigeance repels many who incline toward a more moderate version of his position. And those of a different persuasion have large investments of emotional and intellectual capital in the cause of interventionism."

Crane, Burton. "Business Bookshelf." *The New York Times.* (August 13, 1956)

Jaquemet, Gaston. "Lob der Wirtschaftsfreiheit" [Praise of Economic Freedom]. *Schweizer Monatshefte.* Zürich. 36:5 (August 1956) 411-412.

McKenna, Joseph P. *Social Order.* Institute of Social Order, St. Louis. (February 1957)

Oliver, Henry M. Jr. *The American Economic Review.* 46:5 (December 1956) 983-984 "The volume does not rank among the neotraditional liberals' more serious efforts. Much of the content is eulogy and reiteration without benefit of substantial argument."

Opitz, Edmund A. "In Honor of Ludwig von Mises." *Christian Economics.* 8:11 (May 29, 1956) 4.

Sommer, Louise. *Economia Internazionale.* Genoa. 10:2 (May 1957) 3-22. The review is in English.

Other reviews include:

Deutsche Zeitung und Wirtschafts Zeitung. "Ludwig von Mises." 78 (September 29, 1956) 8. "One essay deals with Mises' 'intransigence'. . . . which has earned him some enemies but also many friends, who give him credit for profound and ample explanations." (Translated from the German)

The Economist. (September 22, 1956). "Ultra Ultra."
The Journal of Political Economy. (February 1957)
National Review. "Von Mises." (March 28, 1956) 7.

Soviet Survey. London. #10 issue. (No copy available to compilers). In a letter to Mises from Walter Laqueur (November 20, 1956): "Since your work has been the object of comment in the Soviet Union I thought you would be interested in having the current issue of 'Soviet Survey' in which some details are given."

Tompkins, E. F. "The Looming Danger: A Trend to Fascism." *New York Journal American.* (February 3, 1956). "Dr. Ludwig von Mises is an economist of international stature . . . . His name comes up for two reasons -- (1) addressing a learned society some years ago, Dr. von Mises dissected the anatomy of Socialism; and (2) current events prove that we are unwittingly treading one of the 'party lines' which he warned us not to follow! . . . ¶Peacetime price controls are a phase of Fascism -- political control of economic activities without confiscation of property . . . . ¶Obviously, we are in much greater danger of getting Fascism by trick and device -- under the pseudonym of Liberalism -- than we are of getting Communism 'by force and violence'."

1957

Baltimore (Maryland) *Sun.* "Prices in Poland." (November 6, 1957). Dr. Oskar Lange, who tried in 1938 to refute von Mises' thesis, later returned to his native Poland and "soon rose to high place in the new Red Polish bureaucracy, . . . chairman of a top-level economic advisory council . . . . ¶And what is Dr. Lange's council advising the Polish Communist Government to do these days? Why nothing less than to move the Polish economy somewhat nearer to a workable price system. 'A selective number and variety of Polish industries are to receive more autonomy than they have ever enjoyed [under communism] . . . . They will control their own investment programs and will no longer be under the heavy control of central authority'. . . . ¶What mountains of materials and what oceans of blood have been expended by the Socialists in relearning what was already clear to Professor von Mises in 1920!"

Burgerrecht (Amsterdam). "Ludwig von Mises: De Mens en de Strijder" [The Man and the Fighter]. 12:515 (August 31, 1957) 1. Includes Dutch translations of passages from *Human Action*. Also an announcement of Mises' scheduled lecture, September 16, 1957, "Het Staatsingrijpen en zijn gevolgen." (Article 57.5)

Kauder, Emil. "Intellectual and Political Roots of the Older Austrian School." *Zeitschrift für Nationalökonomie.* 17:4 (December 1957) 411-425. A survey of the three "pioneers" of the Austrian school -- Menger, Böhm-Bawerk and Wieser. "Today only von Mises, the most faithful student of the three pioneers, maintains the ontological character of economic laws. His theory of human action (in his words praxeology) is a 'reflection about the essence of action'. . . . ¶The three economists tried to compromise between British and Austrian tradition, between free competition and paternalistic bureaucracy. Consistent with their theoretical assumptions, Menger, Wieser, and Böhm-Bawerk should be defenders of free competition. They hesitate to draw this conclusion. At variance with the second generation, with Mises and Hayek, they rather condemn laissez-faire with faint praises and strong criticism." (pp.15, 19) Reprinted in *Austrian Economics: I.* Stephen Littlechild, ed. (Aldershots, Hants, England; Brookfield, Vt: Edward Elgar, 1990) pp.9-23.

Myrdal, Gunnar. *Economic Theory and Under-Developed Regions.* London: Gerald Duckworth, 1957. "From the beginning of the 'twenties there was a lively discussion in our learned journals about the possibility of any rationality in a planned economy. It was started off by Professor Ludwig von Mises who declared that economic planning must fail, because the absence of a free market, and of a cost and profit system untampered with by the state, would preclude the application of any economic criteria to determine in an objective way what should or should not be done. ¶This thought, that there are such things as 'objective' criteria for determining how the social process should evolve, and that the market itself provides these objective criteria while planning is necessarily 'arbitrary,' contains in a nutshell all the inherited irrational predilections holding back economic theory . . . . ¶The ironical fact is that this very type of economic planning, the rationality of which has so recently been shown to be an impossibility on logical grounds, is now proceeding in almost all under-developed countries -- often with the competent guidance of economists, many of whom, in another compartment of their thinking, harbour whole learned structures of fallacious arguments in the old tradition to which von Mises did no more than give a particularly unqualified, and therefore crude, expression.*

> *"Many Socialist writers have fallen in line with the main assumptions of von Mises' argument but taken the opposite stand and insisted that it is quite possible for economic planning to be rational by maximising 'welfare'."

Passage quoted from the U. S. edition of this book, titled *Rich Lands and Poor.* Harper & Row, 1957/8; reprinted (pp. 417-434) in *History of Economic Thought: A Book of Readings*, 2nd ed. K. William Kapp & Lore L. Kapp, eds. New York: Barnes & Noble, 1963 (?).

[Nymeyer, Frederick].   "Mises on: 'Righteousness As The Ultimate Standard Of The Individual's Actions'."
    Progressive Calvinism. 3:10 (October 1957) 302-320. Many religious spokesmen "declare that they are
    for a just and righteous economic system," as does *Progressive Calvinism.*   What do these different
    spokesmen mean?   Author quotes Mises' critique of proposals to make moral "righteousness," rather
    than the drive for profit, the goal of economic activities (*Human Action,* pp.719-725, 1949 ed.; pp.724-
    730, 1963 and 1966 eds.). Mises shows that "the new principle of righteousness, which is proposed as a
    substitute for the market . . . . must be some *coercive* system applied by the government . . . .
    [E]conomic freedom underlies all freedom." Thus, according to *Progressive Calvinism,* Mises has "cut
    the ground out from under the fiction of a certain kind of righteousness . . . . This righteousness which
    Mises has analyzed turns out to be spurious and pseudo righteousness," not the "righteousness" of
    economic freedom advocated by Mises and *Progressive Calvinism.*

Petro, Sylvester. *The Labor Policy of the Free Society.* New York: Ronald Press, 1957. An analysis of labor,
    employment, trade unions, collective bargaining, etc., from the point of view of private property, freedom
    of contract and the free society. Petro has been greatly influenced by "the great social scientist Mises"
    (p.33) and often quotes him. The "labor policy for a free society" that Petro describes calls for repeal of
    the Norris-LaGuardia Act, abolition of the National Labor Relations Board, and the settlement of labor
    disputes through the regular courts, subject to review by the Supreme Court. (p.282)

Rothbard, Murray N. "In Defense of 'Extreme Apriorism'." *Southern Economic Journal.* 23:3 (January 1957) 314-
    320. A defense of Mises against articles by T. W. Hutchison and Fritz Machlup (*Southern Economic
    Journal*, April 1956). "Whether we consider the Action Axiom 'a priori' or 'empirical' depends on our
    ultimate philosophical position. Professor Mises, in the neo-Kantian tradition, considers this axiom a
    law of thought and therefore a categorical truth *a priori* to all experience. My own epistemological
    position rests on Aristotle and St. Thomas rather than Kant, and hence . . . I would consider the axiom a
    law of reality rather than a law of thought, and hence 'empirical' rather than 'a priori'. . . . ¶Dean
    [William E.] Rappard [see his contribution to the Mises Festschrift, *On Freedom and Free Enterprise.*
    M. Sennholz, ed., 1956] has posed the question: how can Mises be at the same time a champion of
    Wertfreiheit [freedom from value judgments] in economics and of *laissez-faire* liberalism . . . . ¶Economic
    science . . . establishes existential laws, of the type: if A, then B. Mises demonstrates that this science
    asserts that *laissez-faire* policy leads to peace and higher standards of living for all, while statism leads to
    conflict and lower living standards. Then, Mises as a citizen chooses *laissez-faire* liberalism because he is
    interested in achieving these ends." (pp.317, 319) Reprinted in *Invictus.* (September 1972) 23-29. Also
    included in *Austrian Economics I.* Stephen Littlechild, ed. Aldershot, Hants, England; Brookfield, Vt:
    Edward Elgar, 1990. pp.445-451.

Yeager, Leland B. "Measurement as Scientific Method in Economics." *The American Journal of Economics and
    Sociology.* 16:4 (July 1957) 337-346. The point "has been much emphasized by Ludwig von Mises"
    that: "In economics, no numerical constants occur." (p.341) "This paper," the author says, "does not
    attack measurement in economics. It simply attacks naive exhortations to concentrate on gathering
    numbers . . . . It shows how the essential function of measurement in the natural sciences is largely
    replaced in economics by direct empirical knowledge of the most generally applicable principles and
    concepts." (p.345)

1958

Friedman, Milton. "Capitalism and Freedom." *Essays on Individuality.* Felix Morley, ed. Philadelphia: University of Pennsylvania Press, 1958; Indianapolis: Liberty Fund, 1977. "The relation between economic freedom and political freedom is complex and by no means unilateral. In the early nineteenth century England, the philosophical radicals and their allies regarded political reform as primarily a means toward economic freedom . . . . Political reform would give the power to the people and the people would naturally legislate in their own interest, which is to say, would legislate *laissez faire*. ¶From the end of the nineteenth century to the present, the leading liberal writers -- men like Dicey, Mises, Hayek and Simons, to mention only a few -- emphasized the reverse relation: that economic freedom is a means toward political freedom." (pp.169-170, 1958 ed.)

Galbraith, John Kenneth. *The Affluent Society.* Boston: Houghton Mifflin, 1958. Galbraith quotes from *The Anti-Capitalistic Mentality* (B-19) and then comments: "Professor Mises, it should be observed in fairness, would be regarded by most businessmen as rather extreme." (p.185 n.3)

Hellwig, Hans. *Kreditschöpfung und Kreditvermittlung* [Creation and Granting of Credit]. Stuttgart: Curt E. Schwab, 1958. Relies heavily on Mises' theories of money, credit and stabilization policy, and quotes Mises frequently.

Howard, Irving E. "Christ and the Libertarians." *Christianity Today.* 2:12 (March 17, 1958) 8-10. "Three libertarian organizations that have had the most to do with the religious community have been the Foundation for Economic Education, Irvington-on-Hudson, New York; Spiritual Mobilization, Los Angeles; and the Christian Freedom Foundation, New York City . . . . All three are indebted for much of their economic thought to the Austrian school of economics mediated by Professor Ludwig von Mises and Professor Friedrich Hayek and their disciples. Beyond that, these three organizations have followed different paths."

Kirk, Russell. "Cultural Debris: Two Conferences and the Future of Our Civilization." *Modern Age.* Chicago: Foundation for Foreign Affairs. 2:2 (Spring 1958) 164-169. Kirk comments on two recent meetings: the Tenth Anniversary of the Mont Pèlerin Society (St. Moritz, Switzerland) and the Conference on North Atlantic Community (Bruges, Belgium). "The common bond among the members of the Mont Pèlerin Society is a belief in the enduring relevance of the 'classical' political economy; . . . the fundamental doctrines of the champions of a free economy . . . . ¶A considerable diversity of view exists, nevertheless: Professor Wilhelm Röpke of Geneva, for instance, is what Walter Bagehot would have called a 'liberal conservative,' a believing Christian, an opponent of the 'cult of the colossal'; while Professor Ludwig von Mises is the complete disciple of Jeremy Bentham, contemptuous of religious belief and social tradition, dedicated to pure efficiency -- what he called himself at this meeting (though with a degree of irony), [was] an 'entrepreneurial Marxist'. . . . ¶Near the end of the week's conference, . . . Hayek went counter to the trend of much of the meeting . . . . [I]n a paper called 'Why I am not a conservative,' [he] called upon all faithful liberals to reject alliances with conservatives."

_____. "The Drug of Ideology." *The Catholic World.* 186:1116 (March 1958) 440-446. In commenting on Raymond Aron's *Opium of the Intellectuals* (1957), Kirk asks: "How have the intellectuals become slaves to deterministic theories of history and to secular messiahs? . . . . ¶One explanation -- and far too simple an hypothesis -- is put forward by Professor Ludwig von Mises in his recent book *The Anti-Capitalistic Mentality* [B-19]. The intellectuals (particularly in America) suffer from frustrated ambition, he thinks, and consequent resentment . . . . ¶So far as this theory goes, it has much truth in it; but it does not go very far . . . . ¶M. Aron, however, knows that the impulse behind the radicalism of the intellectual is not merely economic or egoistic. The intellectual has lost religious faith; and he is seeking a substitute for religion."

V. M. [Volkmar Muthesius]. "Der gespaltene Liberalismus" [Divided Liberalism]. *Monatsblätter für freiheitliche Wirtschaftspolitik.* 4:4 (April 1958) 195-196. Defends classical liberalism and Mises' *The Anti-capitalistic Mentality* (B-19), which had recently been published in German translation, against charges made in the *Neue Zürcher Zeitung* (see below): "Mises, who stems from the Viennese school and is now living and teaching in New York, is guardian of the heritage, which for us means he is the guardian of classical liberalism. His works, especially his critique of socialism and etatism . . . . are the foundation of the renewal of liberal thought in our century. Without Mises this renaissance would have been unthinkable . . . . ¶The true liberals have at all times advocated that the state should not interfere in the economic affairs of the citizens. But in doing this, they were not, and they are not, recommending a weak state. On the contrary they have supported a strong state, but a state that devotes its strength to the task that is its only legitimate obligation, namely the actual protection of the legal order, that is the protection of property and the protection especially of the private affairs of individuals." (Translated from the German)

Mexico. *La Prensa* and *ATISBOS* (September 23, 1958). Newspaper reports of the visit by Mont Pèlerin Society members, including Mises, to Mexico.

Meyer, Frank S. "Principles and Heresies: Ferment Among Historians." *National Review.* 6:3 (July 5, 1958) 65. Discusses Mises' *Theory and History.* "Professor von Mises, although he is without doubt the world's greatest living economist, has always shown a utilitarian bias on philosophical and historical questions, which carried to its logical conclusions could only lead to relativism. The power of his grasp of reality, however, which has enabled him to avoid relativist futility in his analysis of the laws of the economy, seems now to have affected his outlook on history . . . . [T]he utilitarian bias is still strongly apparent in his formulations, but the judgments that he makes on critical problems of history break beyond the bounds of those formulations and show an astonishing affinity to the [ultimate spiritual freedom] line of historical thought I have been discussing." Excerpt included in Meyer's *The Conservative Mainstream* (New Rochelle, N.Y.: Arlington House, 1969) pp.398-400.

Monatsblätter für freiheitliche Wirtschaftspolitik. "Ludwig von Mises über Lohnpolitik, Inflation und Kapitalbildung" [Ludwig von Mises on Wage Policy, Inflation and Capital Formation]. 4:5 (May 1958) 286-287. By way of commenting on the British Cohen Report on prices, productivity, and income, includes a translation of a substantial portion of Mises' Article 58.2, "Wages, Unemployment and Inflation."

Neue Zürcher Zeitung. 72 (March 14, 1958). According to V. M. (*Monatsblätter für freiheitliche Wirtschaftspolitik.* April 1958; see above), the *Neue Zürcher Zeitung* considers Mises' statement in *The Anti-capitalistic Mentality* (B-19), that the only safeguard against "the barbarism of Moscow" is laissez-faire capitalism, to be an "anachronistic antithesis." V. M. says this article argues that capitalism "cannot be directed by an economic order which 'heightens social contrasts until they are unbearable,' which makes competition a caricature 'as a result of the concentration of power and denial of the private market' and which looks upon 'the nightwatchman state' as laissez-faire capitalism." (Translated from the German)

Velasco, Gustavo R. *Libertad y Abundancia* [Liberty and Abundance]. Mexico: Editorial Porrua, 1958. Mises wrote the prologue (Article 58.4) to this book. Mises is also cited several times in the book by Velasco.

1959

Beveridge (Lord). *A Defence of Free Learning.* London: Oxford University Press, 1959. "Twenty-five years ago, on an evening at the end of March 1933, I was enjoying myself with friends at a café in Vienna; the friends included the Austrian economist Ludwig von Mises and Lionel Robbins of the London School of Economics and his wife. As we talked of things in general, an evening paper was brought in giving the names of a dozen leading professors in German universities who were being dismissed by the new Nazi régime on racial or political grounds. As Mises read out the names to our growing indignation, Robbins and I decided that we would take action in the London School of Economics to help scholars in our subjects who should come under Hitler's ban. I posted the newspaper cutting at once to the Secretary of the School, now my wife, so that she might prepare for what was afoot." (p.1)

Buckley, William F., Jr. *Up from Liberalism.* New York: McDowell, Obolensky, 1959. "I believe firmly . . . that most professors are to some extent indoctrinators . . . . ¶The relevant question is not so much, 'how many indoctrinators are there in the big name American colleges,' but 1) what is it they are inculcating; and 2) what techniques do they, as indoctrinators, use? ¶As to the first question, they certainly inculcate Liberalism . . . . Specifically: the typical economics department makes little or no use of the dissenting works of Hayek, von Mises, Robbins, Hazlitt, Knight, Watts, Roepke, *et al.* The economic generalization of Lord Keynes [is] established doctrine." (pp.56-57)

Chamberlain, John. *The Roots of Capitalism.* Princeton, N.J.: Van Nostrand, 1959; Indianapolis: Liberty Fund, 1976. A primer in economic theory, highlighted by incidents from economic history and references to the development of economic thought. Chapter 10 discusses Mises' concept of the "'consumers' plebiscite,' . . . the vote being counted in whatever money unit is the handiest. With his votes the consumer directs production, forcing or luring energy, brains and capital to obey his will." Concerning the consequences of adopting the inflationist proposal presented in Keynes' *General Theory* [1936]: "the plausibility of the book seems more and more limited to the short run. Ludwig von Mises has dismissed it with magisterial scorn by calling it 'the Santa Claus fable raised . . . to the dignity of an economic doctrine.' And there is little doubt that von Mises is right -- for the long run." (1959 ed., p.199; 1976 ed., p.263)

Fortune. "Socialism's Debt to von Mises." 60:2 (August 1959) 74. Discusses economics professor Nathan Reich's lecture at Hunter College, N. Y., concerning Oskar Lange's tribute to Mises for bringing up the subject of calculation under socialism.

Grote, Adolf. "Ludwig von Mises." *Monatsblätter für freiheitliche Wirtschaftspolitik.* 5:5 (May 1959) 275-279. A brief survey of Mises' writings. In the world of Sombart, Knapp, and Adolf Wagner, Mises' book on money (B-2) shone forth like a "lighthouse beacon;" his *Socialism* (B-4) described socialism as the product of "wishful imagination;" his *Epistemological Problems* (B-10), *Nationalökonomie* (B-11) and *Human Action* (B-16) expanded economics from a study of "need-satisfaction" to that of "rational human action." (Translated from the German)

Hazlitt, Henry. *The Failure of the "New Economics: An Analysis of the Keynesian Fallacies."* Princeton: Van Nostrand, 1959. A chapter-by-chapter critique from the Austrian perspective of Keynes' *The General Theory of Employment, Interest and Money* (1936). Hazlitt cites Mises on money, interest, and mathematical economics. He pays tribute to Mises' prescience in having criticized, in *The Theory of Money and Credit* (B-2), Keynes' theory of interest, even before Keynes' book on the subject was published. (pp.194-195)

McGraw-Edison Co. "A Tribute." *Book Review Supplement.* New York: Committee for Public Affairs. (December 1959) [4-6]. An outline of Mises life plus summaries of his major books.

Niksa, Vladimir. "The Role of Quantitative Thinking in Modern Economic Theory." *Review of Social Economy.* 17:2 (September 1959) 151-173. After presenting the views of leading mathematical economists, the author writes: "According to Mises, all known economic quantities are data of economic history, derived from certain geographical areas and definite historical periods . . . . ¶In Mises' opinion, the mathematical method must be rejected not only because of its barrenness and sterility, but more on account of starting from false assumptions which lead to fallacious inferences; the mathematical method diverts from the study of real problems and distorts the relations between various phenomena (pp.159-160) . . . . ¶There is no existing problem of economics which could be expressed in terms of mathematics, but not in ordinary language . . . . ¶The fecundity of mathematics in natural science could serve as an incentive, but not as a proof that the same must be applied in social science . . . . ¶It is disputable whether a fragmentary reformulation of stagnating economic theory into a difficult language really means an advancement of economic science. Why must economics only be the guinea pig of applied mathematics?" (pp.171, 173)

Petro, Sylvester. *Power Unlimited -- The Corruption of Union Leadership.* New York: Ronald Press, 1959. A report on the U. S. Senate's McClellan Committee hearings which investigated labor union corruption. Petro quotes Mises attribution of the average American worker's high standard of living to the "capital invested per head of the employees," not to the labor unions (p.266). "The truth about the big unions is that they have done great social harm in the past and that they constitute at present a threat to our survival as a good and strong nation (p.266) . . . . The real problem, the real fault, lies in a theory of government which insures an awful paradox: a virtual anarchy within a plethora of laws. We have thousands upon thousands of rules and statutes, millions upon millions of government employees. Yet we have no *law.*" (p.304)

La Prensa. Buenos Aires. *Seis Conferencias en Buenos Aires: Crónicas publicadas por el diario "La Prensa" de Buenos Aires* [Six lectures in Buenos Aires: accounts published in the daily, *La Prensa*]. Buenos Aires: Centro de Difusión de la Economía Libre, 1959. Newspaper reports (June 3, 5, 9, 11, 13, 14, and 16, 1959), each summarizing briefly Mises' remarks of the evening before. These English-language lectures transcribed and published posthumously as *Economic Policy: Thoughts for Today and Tomorrow* (B-27).

Reisman, George. "The Classical Economists and the Austrians on Value and Costs." M.B.A. thesis, prepared under Ludwig von Mises. New York University Graduate School of Business Administration, 1959. 86 pages.

Seldon, Arthur. "Free Trade and Free Society." *The Free Trader.* London. 303 (February 1959) 6-10. Quotes from Mises' "Planning for Freedom" (Article 45.2), *Human Action* (B-16), and comments on William Rappard's thesis in the Mises Festschrift, *On Freedom and Free Enterprise* (1956), that "[q]uite deliberately and expressly, [Swiss] political parties have sacrificed the immediate material welfare of their members in order to prevent, or at least somewhat retard, the complete industrialization of the country. A more agricultural Switzerland, though poorer, such is the dominant wish of the Swiss people today." Seldon comments: "Von Mises will have none of the subtleties employed by those who argue for 'non-material values.' For him, all these are the wrappings which enclose the very material interests of producers' pressure-groups." If "a nation collectively . . . . desires something as a community which it is not getting as individuals through the free market . . . . the way to get it is not by impairing the market process but by supplementing it through general assistance or general reliefs granted in democratic assembly."

Hayek, F. A. *The Constitution of Liberty.*   Chicago: University of Chicago Press, 1960. In his
    "Acknowledgments," Hayek writes: "[I]f I had decided to express not my aim but my indebtedness in the
    dedication of this book, it would have been most appropriate to dedicate it to the members of the Mont
    Pèlerin Society and in particular to their two intellectual leaders, Ludwig von Mises and Frank H.
    Knight." (p.416) Hayek cites Mises frequently. In a review of this book (Article 60.2), Mises wrote in
    part as follows: "In the first two parts of this book the author provides a brilliant exposition of the
    meaning of liberty and the creative powers of a free civilization. Endorsing the famous definition that
    describes liberty as the rule of laws and not of men, he analyzes the constitutional and legal foundations
    of a commonwealth of free citizens . . . . ¶Unfortunately, the third part . . . is rather disappointing. Here
    the author tries to distinguish between socialism and the Welfare State. Socialism, he alleges, is on the
    decline; the Welfare State is supplanting it. And he thinks the Welfare State is, under certain conditions,
    compatible with liberty."

Hoff, Trygve J. B. "Soviet Economists Part Company with Marx: I & II." *Farmand*   (February & March 1960).
    Translated from the Norwegian, condensed and reprinted in *The Freeman.* 10:9 (September 1960) 29-34.
    According to Hoff, L. A. Leontiev broke with Marxian doctrine when he pointed out (1943) that "the law
    of value is valid in a socialist system, too. Perhaps the most sensational feature of the article is its
    contention that this economic law relates to *the universal factors: scarcity and utility*, and that these
    factors have essentially the same content in socialist as in capitalist societies . . . . The point is that if
    utility is introduced, the labor theory of value must be abandoned . . . . ¶As early as 1854 the originator
    of the marginal utility theory, the German economist, H. H. Gossen, declared that only through private
    enterprise would it be possible to produce a yardstick by which to determine how much might rationally
    be produced with existing resources. ¶Other economists who have given the problem their attention
    include the Dutchman, N. G. Pierson, the French Professor Bourguin, Max Weber . . . . and Professor
    Boris Brutzkus. The one who merits the greatest praise, however, is Professor Ludwig von Mises."

Kirzner, Israel M. *The Economic Point of View: An Essay in the History of Economic Thought.* Princeton: Van
    Nostrand, 1960; 2nd ed. Kansas City [Mission, Kansas]: Sheed & Ward, 1976. According to Murray N.
    Rothbard, "Israel Kirzner was one of Ludwig Mises' best and most productive students. [B]ased on his
    doctoral dissertation under Ludwig Mises . . . . the work is a lively, clear and important book; it suffers
    from none of the usual turgidity that generally afflicts doctoral theses . . . . ¶[T]he book is a history of
    the methodology of economics, specifically, on the history of the definition and the scope of economics .
    . . . Kirzner shows how the classical economists of the nineteenth century wrongly identified economics
    as the 'science of wealth,' and then shows how the scope of economics was gradually broadened by later
    economists, first as a science of exchange, then as an analysis of money. Finally Kirzner shows how
    economics developed into the currently orthodox view of Lionel Robbins (who was heavily influenced by
    Mises) as the formal science of means-ends relationships and the maximization of ends; and then finally
    reached its culmination in the work of Ludwig von Mises as 'praxeology,' the formal science of purposive
    human action, of 'acting man,' in contrast to Robbins' static analysis of 'economizing man'." Quoting
    from Rothbard's review of the 1976 reissue of this book. (*Laissez Faire Books Catalog*, Spring 1976)

Rothbard, Murray N. "The Mantle of Science." *Scientism and Values.* Helmut Schoeck & James W. Wiggins, eds.
    Princeton, N. J.: Van Nostrand, 1960. pp.159-180. "Scientism is the profoundly unscientific attempt to
    transfer uncritically the methodology of the physical sciences to the study of human action." (p.159)
    Rothbard then proceeds to criticize scientism's various false "mechanical" and "organismic" analogies:
    "The fundamental axiom, then, for the study of man is the existence of individual consciousness, and we
    have seen the numerous ways in which scientism tries to reject or avoid this axiom. Not being

omniscient, a man must learn; he must ever adopt ideas and act upon them, choosing ends and the means to attain these ends. Upon this fundamental axiom a vast deductive edifice can be constructed. Professor von Mises has already done this for economics . . . . Mises has shown that the entire structure of economic thought can be deduced from this axiom (with the help of a very few subsidiary axioms)." (p.170) Reprinted together with Rothbard's "Praxeology as the Method of the Social Sciences" (1973) in *Individualism and the Philosophy of the Social Sciences* (CATO Paper No. 4). San Francisco: CATO Institute, 1979.

Scott, K. J. "Methodological and Epistemological Individualism." *The British Journal for the Philosophy of Science.* 2 (1960/1961).

Veritas Foundation Staff. *Keynes at Harvard: Economic Deception as a Political Credo.* New York: Veritas Foundation, 1960. Basically a critique of Keynes, Fabian Socialism in England, Keynesianism in the U. S. and socialism. "'Veritas' feels that without doubt the following study will prove that the Keynesian 'system' -- if it can be called a system -- is the primary economics system being taught in Harvard. 'Veritas' also feels that 'Keynesian economics' is a misnomer. It is not economics. It is a left-wing political theory (p.2) . . . . It remained for Ludwig von Mises, an economist advocating private enterprise, to goad the left-wing into taking public notice of the incredible lack of socialist economic theory." (p.27)

Ward, Benjamin N. "Kantorovich on Economic Calculation." *Journal of Political Economy.* 68 (1960) 545-556.

1961

Drewnowski, Jan. "The Economic Theory of Socialism: A Suggestion for Reconsideration." *Journal of Political Economy.* 69:4 (August 1961) 341-354. "When Pareto and, later, Barone discussed the working of the socialist state, no such state existed. They solved a theoretical problem and that was all they could do. Mises, as everybody agrees now, was wrong in his main contention that economic calculation under socialism is theoretically impossible, but he may be forgiven for not taking into account the realities of socialist economics, as he certainly could not have possessed sufficient data at that time [1920] about the actual economic problems of the Soviet Union and how they were being solved in practice. ¶But strangely enough when the discussion of the problem was resumed in the thirties it continued along the same lines." Reprinted in *Comparative Economic Systems*, revised. Morris Bornstein, ed. Homewood, Ill.: Richard D. Irwin, Inc., 1969. pp.110-127.

Einzig, Paul. *A Dynamic Theory of Forward Exchange.* London: Macmillan, 1961. Einzig continues his discussion of the Mises-Federn controversy; see "Books and Articles About Mises: 1937." See also Mises Articles 09.1, 10.2, and Federn's responses in "Books and Articles About Mises: 1909." "There can be no doubt that the reason why money rates in Austria remained low was that, as a result of the Central Bank's tactics, the transfer of short-term funds to London or Berlin, whether through covered or uncovered arbitrage, was checked . . . . Federn staked his whole reputation on his assertion in his various articles that official policy was the cause. On the other hand, his formidable antagonist, Mises, was equally emphatic in denying that any special devices had been applied by the Austro-Hungarian Bank, in 1907 or at any other time, for the purpose of discouraging the outflow of funds . . . . Being in close contact with the market as the leading financial Editor of his day he [Federn] was in an excellent position to ascertain the facts, and his facts were never called in question by anyone apart from Mises. ¶Although Mises had a well-deserved international reputation as a theoretical economist, he had no first-hand contact with the market, nor even, it seems, an adequate knowledge of its essential technical details." (pp.411-412)

Fertig, Lawrence. *Prosperity Through Freedom.* Chicago: Henry Regnery Company, 1961. An edited collection of *New York World-Telegram and Sun* newspaper columns. Fertig credits Mises with warning against "excessive wage costs" which create unemployment (p.113) and against inflation "[a]s early as 1911 [sic], when most economists said there could never be another big national inflation such as occurred in France after the Revolution." (p.189)

Frankfurter Allgemeine Zeitung. #226 (September 29, 1961). "Der List der Vernunft" [The Craftiness of Reason]. "Mises might not appreciate having a statue to him erected, as Oskar Lange suggested, along with those of the Marxist leaders. An instructor might then tell his students that even the bourgeoisie's own economist exemplified the Hegelian 'craftiness of reason.' It is doubtful if Lange would scoff so much now that he himself has developed a partially useful price system. Moreover, Hegelian 'craftiness of reason' has not succeeded in squaring the circle, and cannot because of the inherent nature of the system. Götz Briefs has quoted a social planner as saying: 'Upon the conclusion of the world revolution, a tamed capitalistic land will remain, from which we will be able to obtain a measuring stick for prices.' Briefs points out that this is consistent with Mises' thesis. Thus, rather than representing Hegelian 'craftiness of reason,' Mises' statue will stand for 'the power of reason' to understand things ideologues do not dream of." (Translated from the German)

Keus, Ir. H. I. "Professor Dr. Ludwig von Mises: Meester op de Klassieke Wapenen" [Master of Classical Weapons]. *Burgerrecht: Nationaal Weekblad, Officieel Orgaan van het Comite Burgerrecht.* 16:716 (September 30, 1961) 3.

Mallén, Rubén Salazar. "El cálculo económico según L. von Mises" [Economic calculation according to L. von Mises]. *Espejo* (Mexico). 2:22 (December 15, 1961) 50-52. Refers to Mises' *Socialism* (B-4) as "one of the works which has contributed the most to demolishing the fallacies on which socialism is based." Reprinted from *El Universal* (Mexico). (Passage cited translated from the Spanish)

Muthesius, Volkmar. *Geld und Geist: Kulturhistorische und Wirtschaftspolitische Aufsätze* [Money and Soul: Essays on Culture, History, Economics and Politics]. Frankfurt am Main: Fritz Knapp Verlag, 1961. In an address, "Die Unternehmerische Vermögensbildung" [The Entrepreneurial Creation of Wealth] (October 16, 1959, Heidelberg), the author refers to Mises when discussing the fact that wealth does not grow of itself. (pp.136-137) In "Dichtung und Wahrheit über den Bankier" [Poetry and Truth about the Banker], first published in *Zeitschrift für das gesamte Kreditwesen,* Muthesius quotes (p.156) from Mises' *Socialism* to show that as far as monetary calculation is possible, there is no room for arbitrariness.

Valadés, José C. "Karl Marx, von Mises y [and] Montes de Oca." *Espejo* (Mexico). 2:16 (June 15, 1961) 3-7. Marx and Mises need no identification; Montes de Oca was a prominent Mexican professional and businessman, a friend of Mises, and Spanish translator of *Socialism* (B-4). Reprinted from *Excélsior* (Mexico).

Mises Turns 80 on September 29, 1961.

Chamberlin, William Henry. "Von Mises at 80: Venerable Conservative Economist Still Hasn't Quit Jousting With the Statists." *The Wall Street Journal.* (October 20, 1961).

Frankfurter Allgemeine Zeitung. "Ludwig von Mises." #226 (September 29, 1961). Birthday announcement.

_____. "Ludwig von Mises." #227 (September 30, 1961). Quotes from *Mont Pèlerin Quarterly* tributes (see below).

J.P.H. [Jean-Pierre Hamilius]. "Ideen bestimmen die Weltgeschichte [Ideas Determine World History]: Renaissance des Liberalismus. Ludwig von Mises: Ein Achtzigjährige im Dienst des Liberalismus und der Nationalökonomie [Renaissance of Liberalism: An Eighty-year Old in the Service of Liberalism and Economics]." *Letzeburger Journal* (Luxembourg). 283 (December 9, 1961) 3-4. Includes a survey of Mises' life, plus quotes from his major books in French and German.

Die Krone. "Ludwig von Mises 80 Jahre." 9:19 (October 1, 1961) 1. Photo of the "grand old man," von Mises, with Dr. Otto Habsburg at a recent Mont Pèlerin Meeting.

Röpke, W. "Bij de tachtigste veraardag van Ludwig von Mises" [On the 80th Birthday of Ludwig von Mises]. *Burgerrecht.* 16:717 (October 7, 1961) 7.

Wirtschaftspolitische Blätter. "Ludwig Mises--80 Jahre" [Ludwig Mises -- 80 years]. 8:4/5 (November 1961) 316.

The Mont Pèlerin Quarterly. 3:3 (October 1961). Devoted almost entirely to Ludwig von Mises:

Fertig, Lawrence. "The Significant Role of Ludwig von Mises," pp.11-15. Reprinted in *The Freeman*.11:10 (October 1961) 33-38.   Also in *Essays on Liberty: X.*   Irvington, N.Y.: Foundation for Economic Education. (1962). pp.93-102.

_____. "Reply to Dr. Hunold," pp.32-33. Concerning Hunold's critique of Fertig's criticism of the doctrine that a person must "ponder not only his own self-interest but the public interest as well." (p.13)

Haberler, Gottfried. "Mises' Private Seminar," pp.20-21. Reprinted in Mises' *Planning for Freedom* (B-18), 3rd and later editions. An expanded version published in 1981 Festschrift issue of *Wirtschaftspolitische Blätter* in honor of Mises' 100th birthday. 28:4 (1981) 121-126.

Hazlitt, Henry. "In Honor of Ludwig von Mises," pp.8-10. Tribute delivered October 17, 1961, at Mises' 80th birthday party (New York University Club, N. Y.). (382 people attended.

Hunold, Albert. "Editorial," p.3.

_____. "How Mises Changed My Mind," pp.16-17. Reprinted in Mises' *Planning for Freedom* (B-18), 3rd and later editions.

Kaufmann, Felix. "Diskussion Mises-Mayer" [Mises-Mayer Discussion], pp.22-26. Kaufmann, a philosopher, was a regular participant in Mises' private seminar. He composed the words to this song, and others, for the fun and amusement of the participants.

Mötteli, Carlo. "The Regeneration of Liberalism," pp.29-30. Reprinted from *Neue Zürcher Zeitung*. 1:8 (November 1951). See "Books and Articles About Mises: 1951."

Röpke, Wilhelm. "Homage to a Master and a Friend," pp.5-7.

1962

Benson, Ezra Taft. *The Red Carpet*. Salt Lake City, Utah: Bookcraft, 1962. Benson, Secretary of Agriculture under President Eisenhower, "not only sounds the warning that socialism in America is today the 'red carpet' providing a 'royal welcome' to communism, but he firmly faces the issues and calls for the necessary plans of action to meet them effectively." (Quoted from the book jacket) In the book, Benson quotes from Mises' *Socialism* (B-4) in support of the thesis that "a definite source of socialistic danger in America is the college campus." (p.186)

Branden, Nathaniel. "Depressions." *The Objectivist Newsletter*. New York: Ayn Rand & Nathaniel Branden, eds. & pubs. (August 1962). Refers to Mises' analysis, in *Human Action,* of monetary manipulation by government. Reprinted in Ayn Rand's *Capitalism: The Unknown Ideal*   (New York: New American Library, 1966) pp.70-76.

Campbell, William F. "Theory and History: The Methodology of Ludwig von Mises." M.A. thesis. University of Minnesota, 1962.

Chicago Sunday Tribune. Editorial. (September 30, 1962). Part 1:16. "From a recent discourse on the competitive market economy: 'It is well to remind ourselves from time to time of the benefits we derive from the maintenance of a free market system. [plus more in the same vein] . . .' ¶All very true. All very well phrased. A von Mises, a Hayek, or a Hazlitt could hardly define the function of the market better . . . . ¶So it is with great pleasure, and some incredulity, that we give you the author -- President John F. Kennedy."

Colm, Gerhard. "Central Planning in Poland." *Looking Ahead*. Washington, D. C.: National Planning Ass'n. 10:6 (September 1962) 7. In his review of John Michael Montias' book of this title, Colm mentions Mises' position that "rational prices could be determined only through the competitive process."

Fertig, Lawrence. "Soviet Weakness -- Capitalist Strength." *New York World-Telegram and Sun*. (October 22, 1962). "The Communists are having trouble -- economic trouble -- from one end of their empire to the other . . . . ¶What is the basic weakness of Communist society? It is the simple fact that they have no meaningful price system . . . . ¶This basic weakness of communism was first pointed out in 1920 by Dr. Ludwig von Mises."

Hessen, Robert. "Child Labor and the Industrial Revolution" and "Women in the Industrial Revolution." *The Objectivist Newsletter*. (April and November 1962). Draws heavily on Mises' explanation of the Industrial Revolution, Chapter XXI, *Human Action* (B-16). Reprinted in Ayn Rand's *Capitalism: The Unknown Ideal*. New York: New American Library, 1966. pp.104-111.

New York University, School of Commerce, Washington Square College. *Square Journal*. (October 25, 1962). "Prof Cited By Austria." Dr. Ludwig von Mises "received [Saturday, October 20] the Austrian Medal of Honor for Science and the Arts (Oesterreichisches Ehrenzeichen fuer Wissenschaft und Kunst)." Award also announced in *The New York University Alumni News*, November 1962.

Rothbard, Murray N. "The Case for a 100 Per Cent Gold Dollar." *In Search of a Monetary Constitution*. Leland B. Yeager, ed. Cambridge: Harvard University Press, 1962. pp.94-136. Lecture presented in the fall of 1960 at the Thomas Jefferson Center for Studies in Political Economy, University of Virginia. Rothbard generally favors Mises' contributions to monetary theory, his "regression theorem" (p.103), his formulation of Gresham's Law (pp.106-107), etc.. However, he takes issue with Mises on free banking. Rothbard would prohibit fractional-reserve banking by law "as part of the general legal prohibition of force and fraud." (p.119) He advocates "a 100 per cent gold standard." (p.128) He also disagrees with Mises' "suggestion for returning to the gold standard by first establishing a 'free market' in gold by cutting the dollar completely loose from gold, and then seeing, after several years, what gold price the market would establish." (pp.134-135) Reprinted November 1974 by Libertarian Review Press (Washington, D. C.), and 1991 by The Ludwig von Mises Institute (Auburn, Ala.).

_____. *Man, Economy, and State: A Treatise on Economic Principles*. 2 volumes. Princeton: Van Nostrand, 1962; Los Angeles: Nash, 1971; New York University Press, 1979. According to Henry Hazlitt, Rothbard "treats economics as a coherent edifice . . . . ¶This was the method of the 'Austrian' economists. It is the method of Ludwig von Mises. In fact, Rothbard, a former student of Mises, frankly takes off from *Human Action*." (*National Review*, September 25, 1962). Mises himself reviewed this work in part as follows: "[I]t is a comprehensive and methodical analysis of all activities commonly called economic. It looks upon these activities as human action . . . . In a few brilliant lines he demolishes the main device of mathematical economics . . . . ¶In every chapter of his treatise, Dr. Rothbard, adopting the best of the teachings of his predecessors, and adding to them highly important observations, not only develops the correct theory but is no less anxious to refute all objections ever raised against these doctrines . . . . ¶Less successful than his investigations in the fields of general praxeology and economics are the author's occasional observations concerning the philosophy of law and some problems of the penal code. But disagreement with his opinions concerning these matters cannot prevent me from qualifying Rothbard's work as an epochal contribution to the general science of human action, praxeology, and its practically most important and up-to-now best elaborated part, economics." (Article 62.3; *New Individualist Review*, Autumn 1962)

Schlag, Wilhelm. "The Great Exodus." *Österreich und die angelsächsische Welt* [Austria and the Anglo-Saxon World]. Otto Hietsch, ed. Vienna: Wilhelm Braumüller Universitätsbuchhandlung. Lists economist Ludwig von Mises as one among many artists, musicians, philosophers and scientists who left Austria and migrated to the U. S. because of Hitler's rise to power in Germany and the Anschluss. "These refugees . . . . were among the most gifted individuals Austria has ever produced . . . . The alleged provincialism of Vienna today is explained by some with the loss of this element . . . In many respects they were the most Austrian of all emigrants from that country. They represented that Vienna which is the epitome of Austrian culture." Reprinted in *Austrian Information*. New York: Austrian-Information Service. (March 17, 1962) 4-5.

Seligman, Ben B. *Main Currents in Modern Economics: Economic Thought Since 1870*. New York: Free Press of Glencoe, Macmillan, 1962. Outlines the Mises-Hayek attack on socialist calculation and the Lange-Taylor response. (pp. 104-119) From the section titled "Ludwig von Mises: Libertarianism 'in Extremis'" (pp.328-342): "The most extreme form of the individualism implicit in the Austrian tradition was exemplified by the work of Ludwig von Mises . . . . Inflexible and thoroughly opinionated, he has defended the last vestiges of laissez faire with an intransigence as admirable as it was wrong-headed. He has conducted polemics with all sorts of opponents, mainly historicists, socialists, and institutionalists, and has defended staunchly the *a priori* approach to economics, which he defined as a system of logic stemming from universal principles incapable of empirical verification. His writing has been filled with an exasperating arrogance and a dogmatism that would have been laughed out of court had it come from anyone else." (p.328)

Time. "Recipe for Victory." (March 16, 1962). Economist Ludwig von Mises, 80, one of several speakers at a Young Americans for Freedom (Y.A.F.) rally which "packed the 3,200-seat Manhattan Center and turned several thousand away," was quoted as saying: "Until a few years ago, I thought freedom was dead on the American campus; now I see that you young men will make us free." See Article 62.1.

1963

Branden, Nathaniel. "The Role of Labor Unions." *The Objectivist Newsletter.* (November 1963). Quotes from Mises' "Profit and Loss" (B-17) and "Wages, Unemployment and Inflation" (Article 58.2), concerning the role of capital investment in raising living standards. Reprinted in Ayn Rand's *Capitalism: The Unknown Ideal.* New York: New American Library, 1966. pp.76-81.

Hoff, Trygve. "The Achilles Heel of Socialism." *Farmand* (Oslo, Norway). 34 (August 24, 1963); "Money and Psychology." *Farmand.* 51-52 (December 21, 1963). These two articles deal with economic calculation under socialism. Mises explained, Hoff says, that "prices presuppose markets and that markets presuppose private ownership." As Socialism lacks both private property and markets, it cannot calculate. Socialist economists all agree that Mises is completely wrong, Hoff says, but they disagree among themselves and reject the arguments of *other* Socialists. In the second article Hoff reviews Norman O. Brown's *Life Against Death*, a psychological treatise that "refers to Ludwig von Mises as a great economist who has tried to refute Socialism . . . . ¶If Mises is right, claims Brown, he (Mises) has discovered, *not* a reason for refuting socialism but a psychoanalytical justification of socialism." Brown has not read Mises writings, Hoff says, but quotes him on the basis of a book by a socialist.

Hutt, W. H. *Keynesianism -- Retrospect and Prospect.* Chicago: Henry Regnery, 1963. Hutt acknowledges his "special indebtedness to the courageous and independent work (in vastly different fields and forms) of Marget, Mises and the late H. C. Simons." (p.x) He refers several times to Mises. This book, was revised substantially and published, with the addition of Hutt's contribution in the Mises' 1971 Festschrift *(Toward Liberty),* as *The Keynesian Episode* (Indianapolis: Liberty Fund, 1979).

Kemp, Arthur. "The Monetary Basis of a Free Society." *The Necessary Conditions for A Free Society.* Felix Morley, ed. Princeton: Van Nostrand, 1963. pp.39-54 "Some proponents of a free society . . . . would, if they could, formulate a system akin to what they think individuals would voluntarily choose in the absence of governmental intervention. But, as Professor F. A. Hayek has pointed out so clearly, it is already too late to go back; the spontaneous developments in the monetary processes that might have taken place in the absence of governmental direction cannot now be called into being.* (p.46)

"*F. A. Hayek, *The Constitution of Liberty* . . . pp.324-326. On this point, too, it is interesting to compare Professor Mises' position in *Human Action* . . . pp.429- 445, with that of Professor Hayek and that of Professor Friedman, *A Program for Monetary Stability* . . . pp.4-9." (p.54n.5)

Kirzner, Israel M. *Market Theory and the Price System.* Princeton, N.J.: Van Nostrand, 1963. Mises' *Human Action* (B-16) is included among "Suggested Readings" for most chapters and cited in a couple of footnotes.

National Review. (June 18, 1963) 482. Announces Mises' N.Y.U. honorary doctorate.

The New York Times. "Colleges and Universities Confer Honors and Degrees." (June 6, 1963). Announces the honorary doctorate awarded Mises by New York University.

New York University Bulletin. 63:27 (July 8, 1963). Mises awarded honorary Doctor of Laws at New York University's 131st commencement, June 1963. The citation, signed by NYU Vice President and Secretary Thomas C. Pollock, read: "Author of literally hundreds of books and articles, his major works are recognized as classics of economic thought. He has brought one of the most powerful minds of the age to bear on his subject, and has clarified it with a philosophic conscience and a scientific integrity of a rare order. His writing unites the best of many traditions, combining the thoroughness and epistemological depth of the German with the lucidity and common sense of the English. He is an elegant scholar, a scholar's scholar, and the force of his ideas has been multiplied many fold by the able economists he has trained and influenced. For his great scholarship, his masterly exposition of the philosophy of the free market, and his advocacy of a free society, he is here presented for our doctorate of Laws."

Reisman, George. "The Theory of Aggregate Profit and the Average Rate of Profit." Ph.D. thesis. Mises was one of Reisman's advisors. New York University, Graduate School of Business Administration, 1963. 265pp.

Röpke, Wilhelm. *Economics of the Free Society.* (First edition: *Die Lehre von der Wirtschaft.* Vienna: Julius Springer, 1937). English translation by Patrick M. Boarman from the 9th German edition. Chicago: Henry Regnery, 1963. Mises is cited -- in the text: "Finally, money's function as a medium of exchange renders it an appropriate means of *capital saving* and *capital movement.* Or to express this idea somewhat differently, money becomes a vehicle of value through time and space (von Mises). (p.85) -- and in footnotes: "There is also increasing recognition of the fact that money is indissolubly linked to all economic phenomena." (p.11n.1). In footnotes, the author lists additional readings and discusses the historical development of the economic theories presented. Re the elasticity of supply on demand: "see L. von Mises, *Human Action* . . . a book which takes a decided and, we may add, justified stand on the issues in question and simultaneously warns of the misuses of mathematical methods in economics." (p.176n.2). Mises is cited also with reference to marginal utility, money, interest theory, bank credit, and economic calculation in a collectivist state.

Rothbard, Murray N. *America's Great Depression.* Princeton: Van Nostrand, 1963; Los Angeles: Nash, 1972; Kansas City: Sheed & Ward, 1975; Oakland, Calif.: Liberty Tree Press, 1983. A theoretical analysis of the boom/bust cycle and an historical study to 1933. Mises is cited heavily. According to Percy L. Greaves, Jr., "Dr. Rothbard presents [Part I] the positive Mises theory quite simply . . . . He very aptly puts his finger on the fractional reserve defect in 'the banking principle'. . . . ¶In Part II, Dr. Rothbard reveals how the upward political manipulation of the supply of money-substitutes, not free enterprise, created the inflationary boom of the twenties and made the depression inevitable . . . . ¶Part III is entitled, 'The Great Depression: 1929-1933.' Here, Dr. Rothbard is at his best. He presents a masterly account of the development of the depression policies of the Hoover Administration . . . . ¶While this reviewer . . . learned much from this book and recommends it highly, he cannot agree with all its premises. Perhaps the most serious objection is to Dr. Rothbard's predilection for deflation as an antidote for prior politically created inflation . . . . ¶There are other minor flaws, but it is a great book." (*The Freeman*, November 1963)

Tanaka, Michitaro. "Criticism of Modern Historicism." *Theory of History and Philosophy of History.* Michitaro Tanaka, ed. Tokyo: Jinbun Shoin, 1963. pp.402-403. Tanaka, a leading philosopher in Japan, has been a critic of militarism and fascism since before World War II. "According to Mises, 'history' should certainly reject any 'historicism' which aims at 'the formulation of historical laws, i.e., laws of historical change' and, therefore, at making predictions. In other words, 'historicism' is the very opposite of what Mises had in mind. And ever since the Historical School, Mises' use of the term 'history' conforms with commonsense usage and is correct; on the other hand, we must say that Popper's usage shows a lack of commonsense." (p.402) (Translated from the Japanese by Toshio Murata)

The Wall Street Journal. "An Honor for a Philosopher." Editorial. (June 17, 1963). Describes as "particularly noteworthy" the honorary Doctorate of Law bestowed on Mises by New York University. "[I]t was given specifically with reference to von Mises' philosophy. For one of his greatest contributions is his demonstration that socialism, or the planned economy by any other name, cannot provide a rational substitute for the functions of the free market. More than that; the free market and the free society are indissoluble. ¶In this sense von Mises is the champion not merely of an economic philosophy but of the potential of Man." Reprinted in 4th (1980) edition of *Planning for Freedom.* (B-18)

1964

Bishop, Robert L. "The Impact on General Theory." *The American Economic Review*. 54:3 (May 1964) 33-43. An analysis of Mises, Hayek, Hicks, Friedman and Stigler, all critics of E. H. Chamberlin's and Joan Robinson's doctrines of monopolistic and imperfect competition. Concerning Mises: "[T]he central ideological resistance to a due acknowledgement of the widespread relevance of monopolistic competition comes from those theorists who have a strong emotional stake in an absolute and uncompromising defense of the optimality of unregulated markets . . . . To Mises, imperfect or monopolistic competition is 'mythology'. . . . [H]e concedes the existence of all of the basic phenomena with which the theory of monopolistic competition is concerned . . . . [E]ven more curiously, he also argues that it does not follow by any means that monopolists necessarily, or even presumptively, charge monopoly prices. Now it should not be thought that Mises is talking about the *curiosum* of a 'monopolist' who faces a perfectly elastic demand; for he is ludicrously confused about this."

Blau, Peter M. *Exchange and Power in Social Life.* New York: John Wiley, 1964. Blau excludes from the concept of "social exchange" (1) the coerced transfer of money as at the point of a gun in a holdup and (2) an individual's gift of money in response to "conscience demands," to help support the underprivileged, without expecting anything in return. "Ludwig von Mises refers to this type as autistic exchange." Blau then quotes from *Human Action* (B-16): "The donor acquires the satisfaction which the better condition of the receiver gives to him. The receiver gets the present as a God-sent gift. But if presents are given in order to influence some people's conduct, they are no longer one-sided, but a variety of interpersonal exchange between the donor and the man whose conduct they are designed to influence." (p.91n)

Forster, Arnold & Benjamin R. Epstein. *Danger on the Right.* New York: Random House, 1964. "Written as part of ADL's [Anti-Defamation League of B'nai B'rith's] total public service program" (p.vii), this book discusses the Radical Right, which is considered "a fringe political activity," and the Extreme Conservatives, which "unlike the Radical Right . . . generally do not tend to ascribe the alleged socialism and softness to any sinister plot in high places, but rather to blindness, stupidity, and bungling on the part of four Presidents and their liberal advisers." (p.xvi) The book is not intended to cover racists and anti-Semites. According to the authors, Mises is associated with Ayn Rand, the Young Americans for Freedom (YAF), the Intercollegiate Society of Individualists (ISI, later the Interscholastic Studies Institute), and the William Volker Fund.

Hamilius, Jean-Pierre. "La Nouvelle École: Contributions á la Nouvelle Pensée Économique [The New School: Contributions to Recent Economic Thought]. 20:1, *Les Essais: Cahiers Trimestriels, 1964-1965.* Paris: L'Imprimerie du Delta, 1964. pp.3-20. Discusses the defense of liberalism by Mises, Röpke and Hayek.

Hazlitt, Henry. *The Foundations of Morality.* Princeton: Van Nostrand, 1964; Los Angeles: Nash Publishing, 1972. Hazlitt writes that he was "originally led to write the present book by the conviction that modern economics had worked out answers to the problems of individual and social value of which most contemporary moral philosophers still seem quite unaware." As he thought and read more about the problems of ethics, he "became increasingly impressed with the enormous amount . . . that ethical theory had to learn from what had already been discovered in jurisprudence . . . . The legal point of view leads, among other things, to explicit recognition of the immense importance of acting in strict accordance with established *general rules* . . . . ¶[He] was increasingly struck by the falsity of the *antithesis* so commonly drawn by moral philosophers between the interests of the individual and the interests of society. When the rightly understood interests of the individual are considered in the long run, they are found to be in harmony with and to coincide (almost if not quite to the point of identity) with the long-run interests of society. And to recognize this leads us to recognize conduciveness to *social cooperation* as the great criterion of the rightness of actions . . . . ¶In a field that has been furrowed as often as ethics, one's intellectual indebtedness to previous writers must be so extensive as to make specific acknowledgement seem haphazard and arbitrary. But the older writers from whom [he] learned most are the British Utilitarians . . . . ¶[His] greatest indebtedness to a living writer . . . (as . . . will be evident from . . . specific quotations from his works) is to Ludwig von Mises -- whose ethical observations, unfortunately, have not been developed at length but appear as brief incidental passages in his great contributions to economics and 'praxeology'." (pp.vii-ix)

Machlup, Fritz. *International Payments, Debts, and Gold.*   New York: Charles Scribner's Sons, 1964; 2nd ed., New York University Press, 1976. Machlup discusses the question of whether capital movements lead trade balances or whether trade balances direct capital movements. He classifies Mises as being in the classical group that believes capital movements are the cause and trade balances the effect. He lists Taussig, Wicksell, Cassel, Angell, Ohlin, Iversen and (with some qualification) Haberler as other proponents of this view. (p.451 in both editions)

Martin, Anne. "Empirical and A Priori in Economics." *The British Journal for the Philosophy of Science.* 15 (1964) 123-136. Martin rejects Mises' position on *a priori* methodology. "The most extreme, persistent and able of the exponents of the view that the whole of Economics is essentially a priori is probably Professor von Mises. He refers often to a special kind of knowledge which he calls 'apodictic certainty.' (p.128) . . . . ¶What I want briefly to show is that, in so far as I can understand von Mises' position, it is not, in fact, Kantian. He seems to be sheltering in the wrong trench, and once his position is exposed, and left to stand on its own logical legs, its tenability seems highly doubtful (p. 129) . . . . ¶If von Mises's fundamental propositions cannot rightly lay claim to the grandeur of Kant's 'synthetic a priori' statements, is there anything to which they can lay claim? (p.134) . . . . ¶I hope I may have succeeded in weakening the extreme *laisser-faire* position by depriving it of its twin claims to rest on irrefutable logic *and* to be about the real world." (p.136)

McDowell, Edwin. *Barry Goldwater: Portrait of an Arizonan.* Chicago: Henry Regnery, 1964. Goldwater was the Republican Party's candidate for U. S. President in 1964. According to McDowell, individuals have been converted to conservatism by following many different paths; Goldwater, Hayek, Mises, Rand and Kirk have been among the most influential in gaining converts. (p.108) McDowell also comments on "New Jersey Sen. Clifford Case's non sequitur to the effect that nobody reads Ludwig von Mises anymore, therefore his economic theories are passé." (p.159)

Rothbard, Murray N. *What Has Government Done to Our Money?* Colorado Springs, Colo.: Freedom School, 1963; Santa Ana, Calif.: Rampart College, 1964; 2nd ed., 1974; reprinted 1985; Auburn, Ala.: Praxeology Press, Ludwig von Mises Institute, 1990. A short, fairly easy-to-read study from the free market viewpoint of money, banking, inflation, and the gold standard, with special reference to the U. S. situation. Includes several footnote references to Mises' works.

Samuelson, Paul. *Economics.* 6th ed. New York: McGraw-Hill, 1964. "In connection with the exaggerated claims that used to be made in economics for the power of deduction and *a priori* reasoning -- by classical writers, by Carl Menger, by the 1932 Lionel Robbins (first edition of *The Nature and Significance of Economic Science*), by disciples of Frank Knight, by Ludwig von Mises -- I tremble for the reputation of my subject. Fortunately we have left that behind us." (p.736). This Samuelson quotation taken from T. W. Hutchison (p.201) in *Method and Appraisal in Economics,* Spiro J. Latsis, ed. (1976), not verified by compilers. For other Mises references in Samuelson, see "Books and Articles About Mises: 1948."

Schoeck, Helmut and Wiggins, James W. (eds.). *Central Planning and Neomercantilism.* Princeton, N. J.: Van Nostrand, 1964. This anthology includes several essays that refer to Mises. For instance:

Peterson, William H. "Steel Price Administration: Myth and Reality," pp.155-178."[S]cholars have already abundantly demonstrated the weak underpinnings of [Gardiner C.] Means' conceptualization of administered prices. His conceptualization of competition in concentrated industries, however, is another matter. Scholars have not displayed much unanimity in their views of competition -- a spectrum which ranges from the monopolistic, oligopolistic, imperfect competition school of [E. H..] Chamberlin and [Joan] Robinson to the laissez-faire competition school of von Mises and Rothbard." (p.166)

Rothbard, Murray N. "Money, the State, and Modern Mercantilism," pp.138-154. "On the free market, then, money arises as another -- and highly important -- use for a commodity on the market; in the civilized era, these chosen commodities have been gold and silver.* (p.139)

"*Professor Mises has demonstrated that money can originate *only* in this way -- as a commodity on the free market -- and that it cannot originate by government fiat." (p.153n.)

Stokes, William S. "State Interventionism and Democracy in Latin America," pp.179-198: "Ludwig von Mises, in a series of profound analyses beginning in 1920, sought to prove that the socialist theoreticians proposed to abolish the price system and the competitive market without being able to devise a rational substitute that was economic. If there is a logical refutation of Dr. Mises' position, his critics, such as D. H. Dickinson, Maurice Dobb, Oskar Lange, Abba P. Lerner, and Fred M. Taylor, have not, in the author's opinion, provided it. Mises can be said to have killed socialism in an intellectual sense. However, a sample of some hundreds of sources on Latin American economics and economic thinking reveals very few serious mentions of Mises." (p.188)

Tanarda, J. "Von Mises e la Prasseologia," [Von Mises and Praxeology]. *L'Idea Liberale.* Centro Studi dell'idea Liberale. 5:5 (March/April 1964) 11-19. Italian-language paper comments favorably on Mises' position on praxeology, his view of liberalism and his critique of socialism.

Velasco, Gustavo R. *Bibliographía de la Libertad* [Bibliography of Freedom]. Mexico: Editorial Humanidades, 1964. Velasco, a prominent lawyer and businessman, translated several works of Mises into Spanish and was responsible for the publication of the Spanish translation of Mises' *Socialism* (B-4). Velasco's criterion for including a book on this bibliography was whether or not it "represented a contribution of some importance for the understanding of the political and social philosophy of freedom." Only Spanish-language works, including all those of Mises then available in Spanish translation, are listed here.

Veritas Foundation Staff. *The Great Deceit: Social Pseudo-Sciences.* West Sayville, N.Y.: Veritas Foundation, 1964. A study of "the greatest danger to the Free World today . . . creeping socialism." (p.1) Quotes (p.278) Mises' description of a "social engineer" from *Theory and History* (B-20).

1965

Branden, Nathaniel. "Alienation" (3 parts). *Objectivist Newsletter.* New York: Ayn Rand & Nathaniel Branden, eds.
& pubs. (July, August, September 1965). Quotes from Mises' *Socialism* (B-4) on the unpopularity of
capitalism. Reprinted in Ayn Rand's *Capitalism: the Unknown Ideal.* New York: New American
Library, 1966. pp.259-285; paperback, 1967. pp.270-296.

Clark, Wilson, Jr. "Best System: Laissez-Faire." *The Daily Tar Heel.* Chapel Hill, N.C.: University of North
Carolina. (December 9, 1965). Counters Norman Thomas' charges of "great misery" during the
Industrial Revolution and "inhuman" capitalism's "conception of the economic man and the supremacy of
a pure and undiluted profit motive" by quoting from Mises' *Human Action* (B-16) and *The Anti-
capitalistic Mentality* (B-19). For response, see Fowler (below).

_____. "Capitalism Belongs in World Today." *The Daily Tar Heel.* Chapel Hill, N.C.: University of North
Carolina. (December 15, 1965). Discusses Mises' decimation of the argument that "capitalism was fine
for a simple, agrarian society, but surely one must recognize the necessity for strong governmental
planning in today's complex world." Cites *Bureaucracy* (B-13). Announces a lecture that evening by
Ludwig von Mises under the sponsorship of the Carolina Conservative Club.

Fowler, Terry. "Capitalism and Problems." *The Daily Tar Heel.* Chapel Hill, N.C.: University of North Carolina.
(December 16, 1965). A reply to Clark's articles about Ludwig von Mises; see above. Fowler bases his
comments on Mises' *Bureaucracy* (B-13): "The first [pro-capitalist argument] concerns capitalism's
efficiency. Since competition's ultimate goal is to eliminate competitors, and since it is often successful
in this goal, the result is monopoly. Monopoly is under no compulsion to produce the cheapest product
efficiently . . . . ¶Second, he [Mises] has not shown that something akin to the profit motive operates in
a bureaucracy, which was created to deal with the wants and needs of different interests in society . . . . ¶If
the agency does not satisfy its clientele . . . , complaints can be made to Congress, to the President, to
the courts . . . . ¶Capitalism . . . created monopolies and poverty and could not deal adequately with them
. . . . The Invisible Hand proved to be all thumbs."

Kauder, Emil. *A History of Marginal Utility Theory.* Princeton, N.J.: Princeton University Press, 1965. Kauder
announces that he is "interested in the marginal utility doctrine, especially in its Austrian formulation."
This book, "written in the late twilight period of the marginalist schools," sought "to describe the
development, the ninety years of domination, and the final decline of this theory." (pp.xvi-xix) "Mises is
against [the] philosophies of his forerunners, Menger, Boehm-Bawerk, Jevons, who relegate the sacrifices
of life, health, or wealth for the attainment of 'higher' goods -- for instance religious, political, and
philosophical convictions -- into the realm of the irrational. The striving for higher goals is as much a
matter of choice as the selection of food and shelter. Therefore it is arbitrary, Mises concludes, to consider
the satisfaction of bodily needs alone as rational and everything else as artificial and therefore irrational. It
is easy to rest the case here and to capitulate before Ludwig von Mises' elegant logic. But, I believe, it
would be a capitulation and not a conviction." (p.118) Kauder attributes the decline of marginal utility
theory to the rise of equilibrium theory, the influence of Keynes and of statisticians. (pp.221-227)
"Today only small circles around Mises fight back vigorously . . . . theorists are no longer as interested
in the value theory in general as they were thirty years ago. The measuring controversy attracts greatest
attention." (p.225)

Kirzner, Israel. "What Economists Do." *Southern Economic Journal..* 31:3 (January 1965) 257-261. Comments
on James Buchanan's 1964 address, "What Should Economists Do?" Kirzner cites Mises' *Human Action*
(B-16) in support of the position that economists should stress "that markets become competitive; that it
is the task of price theory to analyze the course of this process; that the degree of competitiveness is

something to be explained, not something to be taken as data." Reprinted in *Austrian Economics I.* Stephen Littlechild, ed. (Aldershot, Hants, England; Brookfield, Vt.: Edward Elgar, 1990) pp.308-312.

Machlup, Fritz. *Involuntary Foreign Lending.* Stockholm: Almqvist & Wiksell, 1965. Machlup speaks of his "indebtedness to Knut Wicksell. His *Geldzins und Güterpreise* was among the required readings my teacher Ludwig von Mises assigned to us for careful study." (p.7)

Melman, Richard. "Von Mises on Economics: Current Thinking Is Faulty." *Phoenix.* New York: Queens College. (January 12, 1965) 5. In addressing the Students for a Free Society on "epistemological problems in economics," Mises "identified two major faults in current economic thinking." The first is describing economic events historically, rather than theoretically. The second is the "positivistic approach," the attempt to make economics. "This positivistic approach," Mises said, "would rule out *a priori* assumptions and 'eliminate human action from theories dealing with human action' . . . . ¶Not only does the positivistic approach ignore a subject of much interest, but, according to von Mises, its scientific validity is in doubt."

Moss, Laurence S. *Phoenix.* New York: Queens College. (January 5, 1965). Describes an appearance by Mises at Queens College. After reading an account of "an upcoming meeting of the International Monetary Fund . . . to discuss the perennial balance of payments problem . . . . Mises asked if someone would be kind enough to suggest an answer [to the problem]. No one volunteered . . . . Suddenly he spoke, 'Please do not be afraid to make a mistake, the greatest mistakes in economics have been made already'." (Quoted by Moss in *The Economics of Ludwig von Mises.* Kansas City: Sheed & Ward, 1976. pp.6-7)

Moszkowska, N. "Methodologischer Subjectivismus in der Nationalökonomie" [Methodological Subjectivism in Economics]. *Schmollers Jahrbuch für Gesetzgebung, Verwaltung und Volkswirtschaft.* 85 (1965) 513-524. Views marginal utility theory as nothing more than psychology.

Rothbard, Murray N. "Left and Right: The Prospects for Liberty." *Left and Right: A Journal of Libertarian Thought.* New York. 1 (Spring 1965) 4-22. "One would think that free-market economists would hail the confirmation and increasing relevance of the notable insight of Professor Ludwig von Mises a half-century ago: that socialist States, being necessarily devoid of a genuine price system, could not calculate economically and, therefore, could not plan their economy with any success. Indeed, one follower of Mises, in effect, predicted this process of de-socialization in a novel some years ago. [Henry Hazlitt's *The Great Idea*, 1951; later editions titled *Time Will Run Back*] Yet neither this author nor other free-market economists have given the slightest indication of even recognizing, let alone saluting this process in the Communist countries -- perhaps because their almost hysterical view of the alleged threat of Communism prevents them from acknowledging any dissolution in the supposed monolith of menace." (p.19) Rothbard's essay reprinted (CATO Paper #1 with a Foreword by Arthur Ekirch): San Francisco: CATO Institute, 1979. Quote on pp.27-28 of CATO reprint.

Sennholz, Hans F. "Von Mises." *American Opinion.* (Belmont, Mass.) 8:9 (October 1965) 107-113. "[T]o the reader of these pages Ludwig von Mises means more than a great economist with a keen analytical mind. He is the staunchest, most undaunted, and most uncompromising champion of economic liberty. For more than half a century he has been the rallying point for the forces of freedom, never wavering or compromising, imperturbable and unyielding, unaffected by the scorn and ridicule of his adversaries or by the temptations of this world." Sennholz then comments briefly on Mises' major works. Concerning Mises' proposals for monetary reform ("Essay on Monetary Reconstruction in 1953 and later editions of B-2): "It is obvious that Dr. Mises' proposals have received no serious official consideration by American monetary authorities. But it is also obvious that the U. S. dollar has lost more than fifty percent value during the last twenty-five years, and that it continues to depreciate at an accelerating rate, facing devaluation and gold payment suspension, and international embarrassment."

1966

Chambers, Raymond J. *Accounting, Evaluation and Economic Behavior.* Englewood Cliffs: Prentice-Hall, 1966. A theoretical approach to accounting. "There are few basic works in the literature of accounting that undertake a thoroughly theoretical approach . . . . ¶This [theoretical] foundation is built of propositions that are ' . . . admitted only because their premises are believed to be acceptable or demonstrable and because they comprise a consistent system' (p.10). The propositions are drawn from the theory of signs and language, measurements, logic, social structures, communication, etc. The belief in their acceptability is based on copious references to authorities in these fields. (The economist quoted most often is von Mises.)" Quoted from a review by George J. Benston in *The American Economic Review* (March 1967) 297-299.

Fusfeld, Daniel R. *The Age of the Economist.* Glenview, Ill.: Scott, Foresman, 1968. "While the Soviet Union was forging a practical system of planning based largely on political goals, economists in other countries debated whether or not planning as a purely economic system could be efficient . . . . ¶One of the leaders in the attack on planning was Ludwig von Mises, an Austrian neoclassical economist who argued that socialism and planning could not provide a rational basis for economic decision-making . . . . ¶Interestingly enough, von Mises' argument had been refuted some years before by an Italian economist, Enrico Barone, who had maintained that accounting prices established by planners could substitute for prices set in competitive markets, at least in theory. However, followers of von Mises continued the attack, dismissing Barone's theoretical solution as impractical because it would require literally millions of decisions based on a vast amount of information about consumer preferences which plainly was not available to any planning board . . . . ¶The second answer was published in 1936-1937 by the socialist Oscar Lange, a Polish economist who was to become an important participant in that country's planned economy after World War II . . . . ¶Critics, too, have shifted ground. Taking their cue from the European dictatorships of the 1930's, they now argue that planning may be workable in an economic sense, but only at the expense of personal and political freedom. The foremost statement of this position was made by Friedrich von Hayek, another Austrian economist, in *The Road to Serfdom* (1944)." (pp.115-117)

Grant, Richard W. *The Incredible Bread Machine: A Study of Capitalism, Freedom -- and the State.* Privately published, 1966. Based on Grant's 1964 poem, "Tom Smith and His Incredible Bread Machine." A breezy explanation of the "incredible bread machine," i.e., the free enterprise system, to which we owe the production of wealth. Pages 23-27 deal with "The Boom-and-Bust Business Cycle" and "The von Mises Theory." (Revised 1974; see "Books and Articles About Mises: 1974," Brown).

Hazlitt, Henry. "A reply to Frank Knight." *Ethics.* 77:1 (October 1966) 57-61. See below for Knight's review of Hazlitt's *The Foundations of Morality* (*Ethics*, April 1966), to which Hazlitt was responding. "To say that he [Knight] misrepresents my views is putting it mildly . . . . Knight constantly accuses me of believing what I do not believe and of saying what I did not say." In one instance, Hazlitt writes (p.59), Knight attributed to Hazlitt a sentence from Mises that Hazlitt had quoted: "Society is nothing but the combination of individuals for cooperative effort." Knight considered this "an oversimplification." This was not an "oversimplification," Hazlitt wrote; it was "merely intended to emphasize . . . that 'the antithesis so often drawn between the "individual" and "society" is false'." Hazlitt concludes by asking, "Is he [Knight] merely attacking my conclusions, and those of Clark, Hayek, and Mises, or is he also repudiating the views that he himself formerly espoused?"

Kirzner, Israel M. *An Essay on Capital.* New York: Augustus M. Kelley, 1966. "The understanding of the nature of capital, and of the economic process in a capital-using market economy . . . . sees economic theory as the extensively worked out *logic of acts of individual choice* . . . . ¶While it may be submitted that the theory of the market as traditionally developed, does (at least implicitly) follow this approach, it will be argued . . . . that capital theorists have on the whole, and with unfortunate results, abandoned it." (p.2) For Kirzner, the market "consists in the systematic chain of events that ensue from the interaction in the market of the decisions of numerous participants . . . . This pattern of adjustment constitutes the market process." (p.4) "Our approach, as always in micro-economic theory, is to trace back economic events to the decisions out of which they sprang." (p.75) Chapter 4, "Measuring Capital," deals with the problems inherent in economic aggregates and in attempts to "measure" capital. "Now insofar as the individual capital owner is concerned, it is quite true that the market value of his capital goods expresses the immediate consumption that he rejects in order to ensure for himself the future output flow to be derived from his capital stock . . . . But it is difficult to see how this provides the basis for an aggregate measure of capital." (p.138) Kirzner cites Mises with respect to exchange, time, waiting, etc.

Knight, Frank H. *Ethics.* (April 1966). A review of Henry Hazlitt's *The Foundations of Morality* (1964). This review was an expansion of Knight's brief reference to Hazlitt's book near the end of a paper ("Liberal Movements in Socialist Countries," unpublished, delivered 1965, before the Mont Pèlerin Society, in Stresa, Italy). In that paper, Knight had said: "Unhappily, my critique cannot adopt the polite course of excepting present company fellow members of the Mont Pèlerin Society. For many of their writings, while not strictly positivistic, are essentially anarchistic, or individualistic, another position that is untenable, on different grounds . . . . The matter is not mentioned by the latest and worst, to my knowledge -- Henry Hazlitt, in his book of last year, *The Foundations of Morality*. But he quotes Hayek or von Mises on a large proportion of his fantastic oversimplifications." Knight writes in the *Ethics* review that Mr. Hazlitt's "position is in large part sound, if it were not so over-simplified and over-worked . . . . ¶Values cannot be entirely reduced to desires; and it cannot be held, as do Hazlitt (and Hayek and Mises, whom he constantly quotes) that a society can rely entirely on rules -- or patterns -- that will be produced automatically by mores historically determined and agreed upon, needing only enforcement by a "state," of some unspecified kind." See above for Hazlitt's reply (*Ethics,* October 1966).

Lachmann, Ludwig M. "Die geistesgeschichtliche Bedeutung der oesterreichischen Schule in der Volkswirtschaftslehre" [The Significance of the Austrian School of Economics in the History of Ideas]. *Zeitschrift für Nationalökonomie.* 26 (1966) 152-167. Translated by Robert F. Ambacher and Walter E. Grinder. Included (pp.45-64) in Lachmann anthology, *Capital, Expectations, and the Market Process* (Sheed, Andrews & McMeel, 1977). Lachmann maintains "that there is a characteristic and demonstrable 'intellectual style' of the Austrian school . . . geared to the interpretation of cultural facts . . . . [and] that the ideas and aims of the representatives of the Austrian school, perhaps unconsciously, were always directed not only toward the discovery of quantitative relations among economic phenomena but also toward an understanding of the meaning of economic actions. (p.46) . . . ¶The significance of the Austrian school in the history of ideas perhaps finds its most pregnant expression in the statement that here man as an actor stands at the center of economic events (p.51) . . . . ¶It is to Mises that we owe the clear formulation of the logic of choice. (p.57). . . . ¶Thus Mises was correct when he asserted that only logic, and not experience, can warrant the validity of economic theories." (p.58)

Rand, Ayn. *Capitalism: the Unknown Ideal.* New York: New American Library, 1966; paperback, 1967. Reprints articles mentioning Mises by Nathaniel Branden (1962, 1963 & 1965) and Robert Hessen (1965). Its "Recommended Bibliography" lists Mises' major books.

Wright, Malcolm L., compiler. *Quotes for Conservatives: Over 900 Conservative and Libertarian Quotations from Ancient Times to the Present.* New Rochelle, N.Y.: Arlington House, [1966 ?]. Includes three pages of quotes from Mises' *The Anti-Capitalistic Mentality* (B-19).

1967

Dallas Times Herald. "Economist Claims LBJ Wastes Money." (September 27, 1967) p.4. Mises, in Dallas to speak at the University of Plano, was interviewed: "Foreign spending did not make people more friendly to America. It was in many cases simply wasted on projects which did not benefit the country's economy."

Dutch, O. O. "Seeds of a Noble Inheritance." *The Jews of Austria: Essays on their Life, History and Destruction.* Josef Fraenkel, ed. London: Vallentine, Mitchell, 1967. pp.177-193. "It is more than a coincidence that most of the former members of the Austrian 'Konjunkturforschungsinstitut' (Institute for the Studies of Economic Trends) found refuge in the States and in England. Professor Ludwig von Mises, the well-known founder of the Institute, continued his teaching in the States; Fritz Machlup, head of the Institute, works in statistics and economic trends in a leading position in New York; Dr. [Franz] Pick, the expert in currency reform and 'black market' exchanges, has a world-wide organisation with headquarters in New York." (p.190)

Entre Nous. Bulletin of the Fellowship of Former Overseas Rotarians. 26:1 (January-February 1967) Announces "Distinguished Service Award" bestowed on Mises "in Recognition of his invaluable services as dedicated Professor teaching economics . . . . His keen perception of what constitutes 'The Ultimate Foundation of Economic Science' as reflected in a shelf full of books he has authored; His theory of how to avoid economic disaster; His persevering Advocacy of the maximum of freedom for all men; and His undaunted devotion to the Rotarian ideal of service above self."

Institut Universitaire de Hautes Études Internationales, Genève: 1927-1967. 40th anniversary. A brief history of the Graduate Institute of International Studies, in French, by Jacques Freymond. Discusses briefly the Institute's founder and Rector, William Rappard, and its learned professors, including Mises who taught there 1934-1940. In 1939, Guglielmo Ferrero proposed to Rappard that its professors give their views on how to deal with Europe's post-World War II problems. Mises contributed the outline of a study plan for "Monetary Reconstruction." (p.58)

Kirzner, Israel M. "Divergent Approaches In Libertarian Economic Thought." *The Intercollegiate Review.* Philadelphia, Penna.: Intercollegiate Studies Institute. 3:3 (January/February 1967) 101-108. The dissenting economists who have argued against "the powerful currents that sweep the modern world toward centralized authority, interventionism, and statism . . . . defend the efficiency of the unhampered market economy . . . . ¶On the one hand there is an academic [free market] tradition strongly associated with the University of Chicago" which Kirzner calls neo-classical and Marshallian. "On the other hand there has since the 1940's been felt in this country an expanding, well-articulated influence that clearly traces back to the Austrian subjectivist school. This influence is almost synonymous with the work of Ludwig von Mises." Kirzner contrasts the views of these two "schools" with respect to equilibrium, empirical investigation and monopoly.

Valiente, Wilfredo Santiago. "La Interpretación Económica Praxeológica de Ludwig von Mises en el Contexto Análisis Contemporaneo del Desarrollo Económico" [The Praxeological Economic Interpretation of Ludwig von Mises in the Context of a Contemporary Analysis of Economic Development]. M.A. thesis, Universidad de Puerto Rico, December 1967.

1968

Bailey, Norman A. "Toward a Praxeological Theory of Conflict." *Orbis.* (Winter 1968) 1081-1112. Discusses praxeology, Polish logician and praxeologist Tadeusz Kotarbinski, and Talcott Parsons. Advocates a study of "a praxeological theory of conflict." (p.1095) To Mises, who according to Bailey "has perhaps done more than any other person to give currency to the term 'praxeology' . . . . [c]onflict is seen as arising from interferences with the market mechanism . . . . There is no recognition of conflict as a means to the attainment of human ends. For Mises, conflict is as aberrational and pathological as for the psychologists or for Parsons." (p.1098) Bailey suggests "that praxeology, when expanded much more fully into the study of conflict, may hold the key to the development of a political science in every way comparable to pure economic theory, that is, deductive and aprioristic in method, objective and indifferent as to ends, prescriptive as to means, and both operational and instrumental." (p.1109)

Halm, Georg N. "Mises, Lange, Liberman: Allocation and Motivation in the Socialist Economy." *Weltwirtschaftliches Archiv.* Hamburg: Hoffman & Camp 100:1 (1968) 19-40. An English-language article with resumés in French, German, Italian & Spanish. "The authoritarian socialists ignored Mises and criticized the liberal socialists who, in trying to answer Mises, had sacrificed the advantages of central planning for a mere imitation of the capitalist economy . . . . ¶This attitude of authoritarian socialists is now changing. Of course, they still reject Mises' argument as absurd in the light of the successes of the Soviet economy, but their new concern with the disproportionate development of the different branches of the economy, inconsistent resource allocation, and the faulty incentive system shows clearly that they are becoming aware of the very weaknesses which Mises predicted." (pp.21-22) Halm describes the Liberman and Kosygin reforms being discussed in the USSR. Neither, he says, would solve the problems due to wrong cost prices and capital values. Halm concludes: "Liberman's and Kosygin's reform proposals have reminded some Western observers of the 'Keynesian Revolution,' that major change in Western economic thinking which taught the governments of the private enterprise economies how to maintain high employment levels . . . . [T]he 'Keynesian Revolution' in the West . . . helped create the necessary climate for a successful functioning of the private enterprise system. It achieved this through application of *indirect* monetary and fiscal controls which did not interfere with the price mechanism. On the contrary, they created the conditions for its proper functioning . . . . ¶But central planning and managerial freedom on the basis of consistent pricing are today as incompatible as they appeared to Mises half a century ago."

Spanish translation: "Mises, Lange, Liberman: Asignación de Recursos y Motivación en la Economía Socialista." *Orientación Económica.* Caracas. 29 (November 1968) 5-17.

Hayek, Friedrich A. von. "Economic Thought: The Austrian School." *The International Encyclopedia of the Social Sciences.* David L. Sills, ed. New York: Macmillan & Free Press, 1968. 4:458-462. Deals primarily with the School's first and second generations, mentioning Mises only as a leading member of the third generation, "who continued the tradition of Böhm-Bawerk." Reprinted in *Austrian Economics: I.* Stephen Littlechild, ed. (Aldershot, Hants, England; Brookfield, Vt: Edward Elgar, 1990) pp.4-8.

Levy, David. "Marxism and Alienation." *New Individualist Review.* 5:1 (Winter 1968) 34-41. "Not too many years ago there was no Marxist challenge to the rationale for a market system which deserved to be taken seriously; Mises and friends did their work so well that advanced Western socialists adopted the market as their own, and even communists learned the glories of directing resource allocation by an Invisible Hand. Much has changed; a streamlined form of Marxism has returned to present the market with a most formidable challenge. The thesis, which we shall call the alienation argument, that the market's operation systematically forces workers to participate in a psychologically damaging method of production is widely pressed by a number of well known social thinkers."

Marcuse, Herbert. *Negations*. Boston: Beacon Press, 1968. pp.9-10. According to Murray N. Rothbard, Marcuse attempts in this book to smear classical liberalism "by wrenching a passage of *Liberalism* (B-6) out of context in attempting to make Mises seem to be pro-fascist." Rothbard quote from *The Journal of Libertarian Studies*. (Summer 1981) p.251n.3.

North, Gary. *Marx's Religion of Revolution: The Doctrine of Creative Destruction*. Nutley, N.J.: Craig Press, 1968. North dedicated this book to "two profound scholars," Cornelius Van Til and Ludwig von Mises. North's "chief motivation" for this study, he writes, was the "desire to subject Marx to an evaluation based upon the perspective of that contemporary Calvinist system known as 'presuppositionalism'." (p.16) The first part of the book discusses the Marxian position on history, revolution, classes, alienation, etc.; the second half offers an Austrian critique of Marx's economics. Mises is often cited, especially in the Appendix on "Socialist Economic Calculation." Spanish translation with an updated preface: Tyler, Texas: Institute for Christian Economics, 1990.

Rothbard, Murray N. "Von Mises, Ludwig." *International Encyclopedia of the Social Sciences*. David L. Sills, ed. New York: Macmillan & Free Press, 1968. 16:379-382. Very brief outline of Mises' life plus discussion of his major contributions to (1) monetary theory, (2) business cycle theory, (3) critique of socialism and interventionism, and (4) scientific methodology. Includes a list of works by Mises and a short "Supplementary Bibliography."

1969   Mises Retires as Visiting Professor at New York University

American Economic Review. "Ludwig von Mises, Distinguished Fellow, 1969." 59:4/1 (September 1969) frontispiece. Reprinted in 3rd (1974) and 4th (1980) editions of *Planning for Freedom* (B-18).

Armentano, Dominick T. "Resource Allocation Problems under Socialism." *Theory of Economic Systems: Capitalism, Socialism, and Corporatism.* William P. Snavely, ed. Columbus: Charles E. Merrill, 1969. pp.127-139. Discusses economic calculation under socialism from an Austrian, especially Misesian, perspective.

Buchanan, James M. *Cost and Choice: An Inquiry in Economic Theory.* Chicago: Markham Publishing, [1969]; University of Chicago Press, 1978. In Chapter 2, "The Origins and Development of a London Tradition": "[T]he concept of opportunity cost . . . was independently developed by later Austrians and notably by Ludwig von Mises. In his monumental, polemic, and much neglected treatise, *Human Action*, Mises advances a theory of opportunity cost that is, indeed, almost equivalent to the full-blown LSE [London School of Economics] conception . . . . [T]he German treatise that provides the basis for the English-language work was not published until 1940. For the period in question, therefore, Mises' earlier writings must be examined." (pp.20-21) Further: "There seems no doubt that subjectivist economics was explicitly introduced at LSE by Hayek . . . . ¶*Subjectivist economics*, for Hayek and Mises, amounts to an explicit denial of the *objectivity* of the data that informs economic choice." (pp.24-25)

_____. "Is Economics the Science of Choice?" *Roads to Freedom: Essays in Honor of Friedrich A. von Hayek.* Erich Streissler, ed. London: Routledge & Kegan Paul, 1969. pp.47-64. "The acting unit responds to environmental stimuli in predictably unique fashion; there is no question as to the 'should' of behavior . . . . Failure to note this basic difference between the pure logic of choice and the pure science of behavior provides, I think, an explanation of the claim, advanced especially by Mises, that economic theory is a general theory of human action. The logical theory is indeed general but empty; the scientific theory is nongeneral but operational." (p.52) Reprinted in Buchanan's anthology: *What Should Economists Do?* (Indianapolis: Liberty Fund, 1979) pp.39-63.

_____. "Professor Alchian on Economic Method." A paper "developed for a seminar presentation at the University of California, Los Angeles, in November 1969." Included in *What Should Economists Do?* Indianapolis: Liberty Fund, 1979. pp.65-79: "What we get [from a logic of economic choice] is a *general* theory of human action, or choice, as von Mises argues, but because it is general it must remain nonoperational and empirically empty (p.65) . . . . It is as much of a sin for von Mises or his followers to decry government failure on the basis of their empirically empty model as it is for Bator to neglect governmental failure in his extremely restricted model." (p.77)

Chamberlin, William Henry. "Conservative Books Over the Last Quarter Century." *Human Events.* Washington, D.C. (April 12, 1969) 49-51 (273-275). Describes Mises, author of *Human Action* (B-16), as one of "the redoubtable battlers for the economic and moral values of economic freedom."

Duke, Winston. "The Man Who Should Have Received The Nobel Prize in Economics." *The Harbus News.* 32:13 (December 4, 1969) 6, 8. "Harvard Business School stands undaunted in its blatant prejudice against the whole class of legitimate capitalistic thought and teaching: The 'Austrian School'. . . . ¶[I]f a world-renowned prize is to be given to any economist since Adam Smith, it is Ludwig von Mises that deserves the nod." (p.6)

Gersch, Alexander. *On the Theory of Exchange Value*. Würzburg, Germany: Universitätsdruckerei H. Stürtz, AG, 1969. "In economics of all topics value is the most disputed . . . . [B]eing of essential importance to economics and a problem which was not solved, it invites adventurous minds to attempt its solution . . . . More than 250 monographs and textbooks dealing with said subject were carefully studied ere I [Gersch] decided to select those theories which merit the attention of economists." He then lists von Mises as one of the authors he dismisses for "lack of originality." (Preface).

Hazlitt, Henry. *Thinking as a Science*. Los Angeles: Nash Publishing, 1969. A reprint of Hazlitt's first book published by E. P. Dutton in 1916, when Hazlitt was only 21 years old. In a new Epilogue, Hazlitt presents some of his more mature thoughts. Among the books he recommends there are Mises' *Planning for Freedom* (B-18) and *Human Action* (B-16) which, Hazlitt says, "extends the logical unity and precision of economics beyond any other work." (p.151)

North, Gary. "The Crisis in Soviet Economic Planning." *Modern Age*. Chicago: Foundation for Foreign Affairs. 14:1 (Winter 1969-1970) 49-56. "It was in 1920 that Ludwig von Mises first presented his critique of socialist economic planning. Without the private ownership of property, and without a free market in which consumption goods and especially production goods can be exchanged, it is impossible to achieve rational economic calculation of costs." By quoting Sovietologists, North shows that: "The crisis has grown steadily more critical. 'The authorities that hand down plans,' writes Alec Nove, 'are often unaware of the tasks already given that enterprise by other authorities'. . . . ¶[T]oo many blind cooks are spoiling the soup." Discussion of the problem is based, North says, on the "presupposition that the choices of the planners, if only they could be coordinated, would be rational. That assumption in itself is highly suspect." Directives keep on proliferating. "In one case . . . a staggering (literally) total of 430 pounds of documents was generated. In another instance, an 'autonomous' Republic, the Tatar ASSR had its investment plan changed almost five hundred times in 1961." Enterprise managers survive politically only thanks to *blat* (the black market) and the *tolkatchi* (the pushers). "In the final analysis, the theory of Mises, Hayek, and other free market advocates appears to be justified, or at least hardly disproved, by Soviet economic practice." Portions of this essay in Appendix I of North's *Marx's Religion of Revolution* (see "Books and Articles About Mises: 1968"); entire essay reprinted in North anthology, *An Introduction to Christian Economics*, pp. 258-268 (see "Books and Articles About Mises: 1973").

Österreichisches Institut für Wirtschaftsforschung. *Zur Eröffnung des eigenen Hauses* [On the Opening of its Own Offices]. Vienna. (October 13, 1969) 22-29. Celebrates the move of the Austrian Institute for Economic Research to new quarters. Hayek reminisces about the founding and early years of the Austrian Institute for Economic Research which Mises founded. Mises helped make it possible for Hayek to spend fifteen months studying in the United States. Upon Hayek's return to Vienna in 1924, he and Mises began to discuss whether or not something similar to W. C. Mitchell's National Bureau of Economic Research should be established in Austria. The idea of making it a part of the Austrian Chamber of Commerce, for which Mises was financial adviser, was rejected lest the new institution be subject to Chamber influence. To maintain its independence from government and other business and labor organizations, the new Institute was set up as an entirely separate organization. It commenced operation at the start of 1927 in two rooms on the fourth floor of the Austrian Chamber of Commerce building.

Rothbard, Murray N. *Economic Depressions: Their Cause and Cure* (National Issues Series of Politics). Lansing, Mich.: Constitutional Alliance. 4:8 (March 5, 1969). A 30-page minibook. A brief explanation of the business cycle; points out, as Mises does, that it is due to bank credit expansion. Reprinted (pp.21-34) in *The Austrian Theory of the Trade Cycle and Other Essays* (Occasional Paper No. 8). New York: Center for Libertarian Studies, 1978; Auburn, Ala.: Ludwig von Mises Institute, 1983.

Sennholz, Hans F. *Inflation or Gold Standard?* National Issues Series of Politics. 4:20 (May 28, 1969) Lansing, Mich.: Constitutional Alliance, 1969. A 29-page minibook; expanded (1973) to a 64-page minibook. Footnotes several statements to Mises. After a brief discussion of the way the gold standard evolved over centuries, Sennholz writes: "Ludwig von Mises, the great dean of monetary theory, would establish the gold standard without this circuitousness [the path previously followed to the gold standard via bimetallism]. He would, once the market price of gold has been found, adopt this price as the legal parity of the U. S. dollar and secure its unconditional convertibility at this parity."

Tamedly, Elisabeth L. *Socialism and International Economic Order.* Caldwell, Idaho: Caxton Printers, 1969. "The objective of this investigation is to study the effect of socialism on the framework of international economic cooperation." (p.x) In Chapter 6, Tamedly gives a good overview of the socialist calculation debate which Mises started in 1920, and even relates it, as few economists have, to underdeveloped countries: "Thus, Mises' theory on the impossibility of rational resource allocation in a centrally planned economy holds good also for a developing country. Only, it is here even more relevant because all factors of production -- usually with the exception of labor -- are extremely scarce and the price to be paid for faulty investment falls as a correspondingly heavy burden on an already poor population." (p.205) Tamedly concludes: "What can be affirmed with certainty is that every measure decreed by the state that represents a direct interference with the forces of supply and demand -- such as price stops, import quotas, exchange control, and prohibitive tariffs -- constitutes one step away not only from a free enterprise economy, but also from an integrated international economic order." (p.283)

1970

Bien [Greaves], Bettina. *The Works of Ludwig von Mises.* Irvington, N. Y.: Foundation for Economic Education, 1970. 60pp. This bibliography, originally presented to Mises at his 80th anniversary dinner (1961), was updated as of 1969. However, after Mises' death it was found to be incomplete as more articles were located among his papers. The present volume includes these previously missing articles.

Duke, Winston L. "Libertarian Philosophy: Capitalism's 'Raison d'être.'" *Careers and the MBA 70.* Boston, Mass.: Harvard Business School, 1970. pp.29-35. Profiles primarily Rand, Mises and Hazlitt.

Henry, Bill. "Ludwig von Mises on Money." *The Torch.* Grove City, Penna.: Conservative Club, Grove City College. 3:2-3 (December 7, 1970) 2-3. Resumé of Mises' speech at the college, November 17, 1970.

H. [Hoff]. "En klarseer" [a seer, or prophet]. *Farmand.* Oslo, Norway. 75:3 (January 17, 1970) 25, 27. Discusses Mises' 1969 citation by the American Economic Association as a Distinguished Fellow.

North, Gary. "Statist Bureaucracy in the Modern Economy." *The Freeman.* Irvington, N.Y. 20:1 (January 1970) 16-28. Mises offers "a theory of bureaucracy that provides us with another explanation of today's inefficient firms. His discussion complements Weber's and improves upon it. Mises argues in his little book, *Bureaucracy* (1944) [B-13], that there are two primary models of bureaucracy: (1) the free market structure; and (2) the statist bureaucracy. Both are necessary, he says; both perform valuable, but very different, functions. One form cannot be used to perform the tasks more suited for the other. It is an unwarranted mixing of the two categories . . . that has led to the creation of a weakened free market." (p.20)

Opitz, Edmund A. *Religion and Capitalism: Allies, Not Enemies.* New Rochelle, N.Y.: Arlington House, 1970. Opitz quotes Mises to the effect that economics is "a value-free . . . science of means, not one of ends." (p.5) For this widely-read scholar, a Congregationalist minister, religion and capitalism deal with different aspects of life but are compatible: "Christianity is a total philosophy of life . . . . Capitalism, by contrast . . . . is a way of organizing economic life for the efficient meeting of our creaturely and material needs." (p.7). Opitz stresses the importance of limiting government, both for the sake of production and of religious freedom. The entrepreneur, he says, contributes to production by "supplying the creative mind" and he quotes Mises: "Production is a spiritual, intellectual, and ideological phenomenon." (p.75) There is "a realm of life outside the realm of economic calculation, on which the market depends," i.e. the world of moral goods, "goods of the first order" which, Mises says, we can value directly. (p.106).

Sennholz, Hans F. "Ludwig von Mises: Dean of Rational Economics." *The Freeman.* Irvington, N.Y. 20:7 (July 1970) 439-444. "When in future centuries, historians search for the reasons for the phenomenal decline of Western civilization, few contemporary sources will be of any use . . . . [T]heir explanations are usually infested with the very bacillus that is destroying our magnificent order. Future historians will be bewildered about our blindness and madness, our moral lethargy and decay . . . . ¶We hope for their sake that they will discover the works of Ludwig von Mises who, since the beginning of this century has been warning his contemporaries . . . . about the growing popularity of ideologies of conflict and war, the rise of collectivism, and the sway of tyranny in the Western world."

Taylor, Thomas Cullom, Jr. *Accounting Theory in the Light of Austrian Economic Analysis.* Ph.D. dissertation. Louisiana State University and Agricultural and Mechanical College, 1970. "Austrian theory places heavy emphasis upon the subjectivity of value." (p.302) Subjective values affect pricing, economic calculation, the determination of profits and losses, resource pricing, saving and investment. Taylor quotes Mises frequently on the significance for accounting of the insight derived from subjective value theory.

1971

Colorado Springs Gazette Telegraph. "Human Action." Editorial. (November 21, 1971) 10C. Editor reminisces on his introduction to the works of Ludwig von Mises.

Gutierrez, C. "The Extraordinary Claim of Praxeology." *Theory and Decision.* 1 (1971) 327-336. Deals with the modern controversy over praxeology. Cited by Stephan Boehm in *Method, Process and Austrian Economics.* Israel Kirzner, ed. (Lexington, Mass.: D.C.Heath, 1982). p.49n.

Ives, C. P. "Gomulka's First Economist." *The Baltimore Sun.* (January 1, 1971) A14. Wladyslaw Gomulka, "blown into power" in Poland by the food shortages of 1956, "was blown out of power in 1970 by an explosion of fury at food shortages." In 1938, his economist, Oskar Lange, had rebutted Mises' 1920 thesis that economic calculation under socialism was not possible. Now, however, the question Gomulka should be "asking himself is not whether Lange was right, but whether even Lange would any longer think of Ludwig von Mises as being wrong."

C. M. "Simplifizierung des Liberalismus" [Simplification of Liberalism]. *Neue Zürcher Zeitung.* 256:152 (June 6, 1971) 17. Speaking in Munich, John Kenneth Galbraith referred to "a noted quartette of Austrian and German philosophers and economists -- F. A. von Hayek, L. von Mises, Wilhelm Röpke and Ludwig Erhard -- who have sung the praises of the idea that 'it is good if the individual spends but bad if he hands over something to the government'." C. M. calls this an "oversimplification." The views of these four men are not homogeneous, yet none of the four opposes government financing of infrastructure. What Galbraith overlooks, says C. M., is that the question is whether the state should distribute income or whether the individuals themselves should be allowed to retain the means to fulfill their own obligations. (Translated from the German)

Robbins, Lionel (Lord). *Autobiography of an Economist.* London: Macmillan, 1971. In concluding "that both personal liberty and economic efficiency were likely to be less prevalent under the centralized ownership and controls of collectivism than under the dispersed initiatives of a system of markets and private property," Robbins says he "was considerably influenced by the examination by von Mises of the possibilities of economic calculation under total collectivism . . . . [T]here are doubtless many who believe that his position has been completely refuted. But that I would venture to question . . . . I think it was a pity that he stated his denials in terms which were liable to suggest that productive activity of any kind was impossible (*unmöglich*) in a totalitarian system -- which is obviously not true." (p.106) "In classical economics and later there are to be found speculations which attribute the causation of economic crises to the excessive conversion of circulating capital into fixed . . . . But it [this theory] had recently been given much greater coherence by the work of the so-called second Viennese School, conspicuously von Mises and Hayek, in which the coming into existence of this 'real' disproportionality was explained in terms of a failure of money rates of interest to reflect adequately the relation between the disposition to save and the disposition to invest. Presented in this way, the explanation acquired much greater appearance of completeness and logical force; and . . . it affected my thought powerfully. ¶Now I still think that there is much in this theory as an explanation of a *possible* generation of boom and crisis . . . . But, as an explanation of what was going on in the early thirties, I now think it was misleading . . . . I shall always regard this aspect of my dispute with Keynes as the greatest mistake of my professional career, and the book, *The Great Depression* [see "Books and Articles About Mises: 1938"], which I subsequently wrote, partly in justification of this attitude, as something which I would willingly see forgotten." (pp.154-155)

Roberts, Paul Craig. *Journal of Political Economy* (November/December 1971) 1426-1431. A review of Howard J. Sherman's *The Soviet Economy* (1969). "The intention of Marxian socialism was to replace a system of market relations with a system of socialist planning. Whatever Mises's familiarity with the intellectual foundations of Marxian socialism, he was faced with a declared program of action that was fantastic in its lack of foundation . . . . Mises correctly emphasized that value categories are necessary if there is to be economic organization. The efficiency of the economic organization will flow from the degree to which the value categories reflect relative productivities and utilities. To illustrate the point, Mises examined the problem of the allocation of investment in the absence of a capital market." (pp.1428-1429)

Rothbard, Murray N. "Ludwig von Mises and the Paradigm of Our Age." *Modern Age.* Chicago: Foundation for Foreign Affairs. 15:4 (Fall 1971) 370-379. "Thomas S. Kuhn . . . . states that scientists, in any given area, come to adopt a fundamental vision or matrix of an explanatory theory, . . . a 'paradigm'. . . . [O]nce adopted the paradigm governs all the scientists in the field *without* being any longer checked or questioned'. . . . ¶If the Kuhn thesis is correct about the physical sciences, . . . how much more must it be true in philosophy and the social sciences, where no such laboratory tests are possible!" Believing that "the fundamental paradigms of modern twentieth century philosophy and the social sciences . . . including the aping of the physical sciences" are basically flawed, Rothbard turns to the "Austrian School" and Ludwig von Mises who "offers us nothing less than the complete and developed *correct paradigm* of a science that has gone tragically astray over the last half-century . . . . Many students *feel* that there is something very wrong with contemporary economics, . . . but they are ignorant of any theoretical alternative . . . . [I]n the vernacular, 'You can't beat something with nothing,' and 'nothing' is all that many present-day critics of economic science can offer. But the work of Ludwig von Mises furnishes that 'something'; it furnishes an economics grounded . . . on the very nature of man and of individual choice." Reprinted in Murray N. Rothbard, *Egalitarianism as a Revolt Against Nature.* (Washington, D.C.: Libertarian Review Press, 1974) pp.134-146.

_____. "Milton Friedman Unraveled." *Individualist.* Silver Spring, Md. 3:2 (February 1971) 3-7. Rothbard criticizes Friedman for his positions on egalitarianism, welfare, money, stable prices, taxation, etc. "But it is in the 'macro' sphere, unwisely hived off from the micro by economists who remain after sixty years ignorant of Ludwig von Mises' achievement in integrating them, it is here that Friedman's influence has been at its most baleful."

Rousselot, John H. "Inflation -- Cause and Effect." *Congressional Record: Extension of Remarks.* 117:170 (November 10, 1971) E12058.

Sennholz, Hans. "Chicago Monetary Tradition in the Light of Austrian Theory." *Reason.* Santa Barbara, Calif. 3:7 (October 1971) 24-30. Reprint of Sennholz's contribution to the 1971 Mises Festschrift, *Toward Liberty* (1971, below).

Wang, Fuchow. "Ludwig von Mises and His Works." *The Eastern Miscellany.* Taiwan. (February 1971) 30-38. In 1955, Wang visited Mises and Mises' NYU seminar in New York. This is a 15,000 word Chinese-language article about Mises' philosophy, economic theory, life, and career. Wang "believes that Dr. Mises' economic philosophy and analysis would provide Taiwan with the much-needed weapon in its struggle against Chinese Communism and would help pave the way for genuine freedom, voluntary cooperation and prosperity." The article also includes comments on Mises books: *The Theory of Money and Credit* (B-2), *Socialism* (B-4), *Bureaucracy* (B-13), *Human Action* (B-16), and *Theory and History* (B-20). Annotation based on summary supplied the compilers by Hsiao-Ming Peng, a Chinese student in the United States.

Wang, Fuchow, with other Chinese scholars. Essay in *Western Economics Encyclopedia.* Compiled by the Economic Research Department (Bank of Taiwan, 1971). Included is a biography of Mises, a review of *Socialism* (B-4) by Wang and reviews by other Chinese scholars of *The Theory of Money and Credit*

(B-2), *The Ultimate Foundation of Economic Science* (B-22), *Human Action* (B-16) and *Theory and History* (B-20).

Winterberger, Gerhard. "Gestalten der österreichischen Schule der Nationalökonomie" [The Austrian School of Economics]. *Der Bund.* Bern, Switzerland. 164 (July 18, 1971) 21. Reviews the history of the "School" in Vienna, its origin in Carl Menger's *Principles of Economics,* its inter-war peak, its many noted scholars, including Mises, and their emigration. Mises' private seminar is mentioned and its participants listed. Noted also is Mises' upcoming 90th birthday, to be celebrated in New York in September.

Mises' Ninetieth Birthday (September 29, 1971) Remembered:

R. A. "Zwei Neunzigjährige [Two Ninety-Year Olds]: Ludwig von Mises und Louis Koppel." *Aufbau.* 37:40 (October 1, 1971).

Greaves, Bettina Bien. "Ludwig von Mises: a tribute to a great man of ideas on his 90th birthday." *Human Events.* Washington, D.C. 31:39 (September 25, 1971) 12, 21. Reprinted in Colorado Springs *Gazette-Telegraph.* (November 21, 1971) 11-12C. Reprinted also in Mises' *The Anti-capitalistic Mentality* (B-19), 1972 & 1978 editions, pp.123-128. Published in abridged form to mark Mises' 100th anniversary: "Ludwig von Mises, Champion of Freedom." *Competition* (Washington, D.C.: Council for a Competitive Economy). 2:10 (September 1981) 12-13.

Neue Zürcher Zeitung. "Ludwig von Mises 90 Jahre alt" [Ludwig von Mises 90 years old]. 459 (No.270) (October 3, 1971) 19-20.

Schmölders, Gunther. "Für die Freiheit des Bürgers" [For Individual Freedom]. *Frankfurter allgemeine Zeitung,* Frankfurt-am-Main. No.225 (September 29, 1971) 17. Discusses Mises' birthday, his life and major works. "The old liberal von Mises projects into our changing age, like a hard stone of primitive volcanic rock, the jagged corners of which the years cannot wear down." (Translated from the German)

Zeitschrift für das gesamte Kreditwesen. "Ludwig von Mises." 24:19 (October 1, 1971) 868.

Toward Liberty: Essays in Honor of Ludwig von Mises on the Occasion of His 90th Birthday, September 29, 1971. 2 volumes. Menlo Park, Calif.: Institute for Humane Studies, 1971. I. xv:437. II.viii:454. Most contributors to this Festschrift, listed here alphabetically except for the authors of the front matter, were members of the Mont Pèlerin Society. Essays with little or no mention of Mises are listed but not annotated. This Festschrift was reviewed by John Chamberlain in *The Freeman* (Irvington, N.Y.), 22:2 (February 1972) 125-128, and by Murray N. Rothbard in *The Libertarian,* 3:11 (December 1971).

Harper, F. A., Secretary, "Introduction." I:v.

Velasco, Gustavo R. "On the 90th Anniversary of Ludwig von Mises." I:vi-viii. "Those of us who have had the undeserved good fortune of penetrating a little behind his reserve know that Mises is as cultured as he is witty and as sympathetic as he is kind and warmhearted." Reprinted in Velasco's *El Camino de la Abundancia.* Mexico, 1973. See "Books and Articles About Mises: 1973."

Harper, F. A. "Ludwig von Mises." I:ix-x. A brief survey of Mises' life.

Benegas Lynch, Alberto. "Property and Freedom." I:1-13. "Mises' teachings show the relevance of private property and individual freedom for the improvement of civilization . . . . ¶Professor

Ludwig von Mises has been preaching for a long time the right ideas for a prosperous social order . . . . [and] explaining clearly the dangers of government intervention, of nationalism, of protectionism, of inflation, of socialism and collectivism, all of which policies deteriorate private property and are contrary to the classical liberal capitalism which made possible the greatness of Western civilization." (pp.1, 13)

Berger-Perrin, René. "Pour éviter 'Une Collectivisation par Annuities'" [To Avoid Gradual, Year-by-Year, Collectivization]. I:94-96. Berger-Perrin first encountered Mises' work when writing a thesis on liberalism. At Mont Pèlerin meetings Berger-Perrin came to know Mises as a persistent critic of intervention. "Intransigent, an enemy of compromise, but one who knew how to use examples in an explanation. For instance: 'I am no more an enemy of the state than I would deserve to be called an enemy of sulphuric acid if I dared to claim that, useful as it may be for various purposes, it is not suitable for consumption or for washing one's hands." (p.96) (Translated from the French)

Bien [Greaves], Bettina. "Values, Prices and Statistics." II:53-65. "During the course of his New York University graduate seminar, Mises frequently criticized the propensity of the 'new economists' to compile historical data in numerical form . . . . When they [the students] asked his reasons for opposing statistics, he always denied that he was 'against statistics' in any way. But, he added, they should remember that statistics were *always* history, and *only* history. Statistics could in no way advance the understanding of economic theory." Prices and money, the building blocks of economic statistics, stem from subjective values and have no significance for economic reality when converted into numerical aggregates. "Subjectivity remains at the root of every human action."

Brownlee, Oswald. "The Tax System and a Free Society." II:66-74.

Buchanan, James M. "How 'Should' Common-Access Facilities Be Financed?" II:75-87.

Colberg, Marshall R. "Pitfalls in Planning: Veterans' Housing after World War II." II:88-100. "Von Mises called it a 'paradox of planning' that socialist economic calculation could to some extent rely on prices established under a previous regime of capitalism but that as conditions changed the planners would more and more grope in the dark." Gives the example of the "utter confusion which can attend the work of a government committee responsible for making materials allocations."

Cunningham, R. L. "Presents for the Poor." II:101-107.

Curtiss, W. Marshall. "Restrictions on International Trade: Why Do They Persist?" II:108-117. Opens with a quote from Mises' *Human Action.* Discusses some arguments given in favor of protection and how free trade can be achieved. Reprinted in *The Freeman.* Irvington, N.Y. 21:9 (September 1971) 554-561.

Dent, Ulysses R. "The Need to Make Cognizance [Understanding] Available." I:258-275. Dent writes about "the decisive influence of Professor Mises' writings and lectures" on the Centro de Estudios Económico-Sociales and other organizations in Guatemala with which Dent is associated. "Originators like Mises," he says, "influence more through the writings of their followers than they seem to do directly." Dent discusses also some of the disastrous consequences of government intervention in Latin America.

Diaz, Ramon. "The Political Economy of Nostalgia." II:441-454. There are some who yearn, , for a return to the world-view of the Middle Ages when, "in the words of R. H. Tawney, human society was 'a spiritual organism, not an economic machine'." (p.441) But this would mean "do[ing] away with all material progress" and Diaz says, as Mises pointed out in *Human Action,* this "would involve the curtailment of the population growth by the sheer starvation of millions." (p.449)

Duncan, George Alexander. "Growth Delusions." I:276-288.

Dykes, E. W. "Human Action." II:118-122. "My first and unforgettable meeting with Dr. Ludwig von Mises occurred at a cook-out at Leonard Read's Bronxville home. I was perhaps thirty-three at the time and a mere neophyte in libertarian matters. After supper, the group of a dozen or so casually divided itself into two smaller groups . . . . I had been pushing some point fairly successfully in my group when somehow there was a pause and suddenly . . . it became Dr. Mises versus Dykes. Practically paralyzed, I weakly defended my point. Dr. Mises said in clinching his argument, 'It is right because it works'. . . . That . . . part of the discussion ended as suddenly as it began. ¶But I was happy only in the thought that I could tell my grandchildren I had once debated Dr. Ludwig von Mises."

Erhard, Ludwig. "Das Ordnungsdenken in der Marktwirtschaft" [Order in the Market Economy]. I:121-137.

Eucken-Erdsiek, Edith. "Unsere Gesellschaftsordnung und die radikale Linke" [Our Social Order and the Radical Left]. I:138-163.

Ferrero, Romulo A. "La Integración Económica de America Latina" [The Economic Integration of Latin America]. I:393-408.

Fertig, Lawrence. "The Genius of Mises' Insights." II:123-131. "When Mises advanced the concept 'human action' (he terms this 'praxeology') as the basis of economics, he did as much to create a whole new world as did the explorers of the 15th and 16th centuries who discovered new continents." Discusses Mises' analyses of the "equalitarian state," socialism, marginal utility, "connexity" on the market, and the relationship of monetary policy to labor laws.

Fisher, Antony. "Protection for Farmers." I:46-62. In 1946, Fisher, disturbed at "the wrong direction in which British policies" were taking his country, asked Professor Hayek's advice. Hayek told Fisher "to keep out of politics and to set up an organisation to do independent economic research." So in 1955, Fisher founded the Institute of Economic Affairs. He sent a copy of an early study, "The Marketing of Milk" by Linda Whetstone, to Mises who commented that it was "precisely the kind of economic monograph that is badly needed in order to substitute a reasonable analysis of economic conditions for the uncritical repetition of the complaints and wishes of various groups of people who are merely interested in the creation or preservation of conditions that further their own interests at the expense of the consumer." (pp.52-56)

Frickhöffer, Wolfgang. "Privateigentum -- die für die Mitmenschen günstigste Lösung bei den Produktionsmitteln" [Private Property -- The Most Advantageous Solution for our Fellow Human Beings to the Problem of the Means of Production]. I:164-187.

Graaff, Andries de. "On the Entrepreneur." I:380-392. "We have a few definitions of the entrepreneur and his tasks, developed by von Mises, Schumpeter and Knight. But . . . literature on the entrepreneur himself is rare."

Grantchester, Lord. "For Philosophy of Choice." I:63. "Politics is the art of the possible . . . . No one has more clearly shown that short-cuts are deceptive, and von Mises did more than follow through with relentless logic the consequences of actions personal and governmental in the field of economics. He raised the study from a purely materialist and deterministic basis into the realm of a philosophy of choice, thus giving to it a place in our general concept of freedom."

Greaves, Percy L. Jr. "On Behalf of Profits." II:132-145. "As Mises has taught us, entrepreneurial profits are 'the prize' the market place awards to those who remove a maladjustment in production and thus satisfy consumers better than their competitors. Profits 'disappear as soon as the maladjustment is entirely removed'. . . . ¶In the words of Mises, the 'market is actuated and kept in motion by the exertion of the promoting entrepreneurs, eager to profit from differences in the market prices of the factors of production and the expected prices of products' . . . . ¶If there were no hope or anticipation of profits, there would be no entrepreneurs and no production . . . . Profits are thus the very lifeline of a continuing society or civilization."

Habsburg, Otto von. "Krise der Politischen Formen in Europa" [The Crisis of Political Structure in Europe]. I:241-257. Habsburg is the oldest son of Austrian Emperor Charles I, who was forced to abdicate after World War I. "Seldom is a prophet permitted to see the fulfillment of his predictions. Prof. Ludwig von Mises, whose anniversary we celebrate, is a happy exception . . . . Recognition that his thoughts, which were formerly in opposition to current fashions, have lasting validity and are constantly being vindicated by events is a most beautiful reward for the master's 90th birthday." The remainder of the paper deals with the information explosion, social regrouping, sovereignty, parlamentarianism, and economic policy. (Translated from the German)

Harris, Ralph. "The Surest Protection." I:64-71. Adapted from a Harris manuscript, "Return to Reality."

Harriss, C. Lowell. "Tax Reform: Two Ways to Progress." II:146-158. "If Professor von Mises were rewriting *Human Action* in the 1970's, he would doubtless give more space . . . to taxation . . . . One after another of his sentences could serve as the thesis for a full article. Yet the two subjects which I wish to examine briefly here go rather beyond any explicit discussions in *Human Action.* ¶For one thing, it seems to me, reliance upon the taxation of 'business' should be drastically reduced. For another, greater reliance ought to be placed upon the taxation of pure site or location (land) value . . . . ¶Taxes do *not* meet standards of *neutrality* which are endorsed in *Human Action* . . . . ¶For reasons which I have developed elsewhere, present property taxes as they fall upon buildings and other improvements have substantially undesirable results. One possible means of reducing them would be to raise the tax rates on land while lowering them on buildings."

Hayek, F. A. "Principles or Expediency?" I:29-45. Discusses the rule of law versus the rule of men. "Individual freedom, wherever it has existed, has been largely the product of a prevailing respect for such principles which, however, have never been fully articulated in constitutional documents . . . . ¶[T]he principles and preconceptions which guide the development of law inevitably come in part from outside the law and can be beneficial only if they are based on a true conception about how the activities in a Great Society can be effectively ordered." (p.44)

Hazlitt, Henry. "The Future of Capitalism." II:159-171. "Capitalism may be thought of as a combination of two institutions -- private property and the free market. Private property means that everyone is free to keep the fruits of his labor, or to put them to any use he sees fit, as long as he does not infringe the similar rights of others." Exchange, competition and prices permit capitalists to calculate. Capitalism "is a profit-*seeking* system . . . a profit-*and-loss* system . . . . a system of both incentives and deterrents. This system does not maximize incentives to *all* production; it maximizes incentives to the more *efficient* production of the goods that are most urgently wanted . . . . ¶Capitalism . . . is a great cooperative and creative system that has produced for our generation an affluence that our ancestors did not dare to dream of. Yet it is so little understood, it is attacked by so many and intelligently defended by so few, that the outlook for its survival is dark."

Heuss, Ernst. "Macht oder ökonomisches Gesetz" [Control or Economic Law]. I:188-202. Comments on Böhm-Bawerk's essay of the same title.

Horwitz, Ralph. "Towards the Just Society." I:72-83. Inspired by Mises' statement that "what is just and what is unjust invariably refers to interhuman social relations" (*Theory and History*, B-20). Reflects on the "just society." Comments on pre-Apartheid South Africa and post World War II England.

Hutt, W. H. "Reflections on the Keynesian Episode." II:13-37. A revised version of an essay published in Japanese in *Toyo Keizai*, Tokyo (1966). Hutt aims "to throw light on some of the causes which appear originally to have created, and since to have been perpetuating, the hold that neo-Keynesianism has acquired in academic circles."

Kemp, Arthur. "Prices and Property Rights in the Command Economy." II:172-186. Discusses the problem, to which Mises called attention, of economic calculation under socialism, paying special attention to the experience of the U.S.S.R. Mentions attempts by Yevsei G. Liberman and V. S. Nemchinov to introduce some measure of profitability. "In addition to the myth of the disappearance of scarcity to which socialist economists seem forever addicted, there is also the fond hope expressed over and over again that modern electronic computers will provide, *in the future,* the key element for solving the problems of economic calculation and rationalization in a socialist society. Such a belief, even if it turns out to be as patently impossible as Mises originally asserted, or as impracticable as both Vilfredo Pareto and Enrico Barone believed, cannot help but to delay movements toward markets and market data experiments within the socialist camps."

Kershner, Howard E. "The Inevitable Bankruptcy of the Socialist State." II:187-193.

Kiga, Kenzo. "Convergence Theories and Ownership of Property." I:304-321. "In 1920, when Ludwig von Mises wrote his first critical essay on the possibility of rational planning in a socialist economy, there were signs of economic collapse in Soviet Russia." Kiga explores the trend toward socialism in capitalist countries and the problems with socialism being encountered in the USSR. He asks, but does not answer, the question: is it inevitable that capitalism and socialism will converge into a third system?

Kirzner, Israel M. "Entrepreneurship and the Market Approach to Development." II:194-208. Kirzner distinguishes his view of the entrepreneur from "Schumpeter's vision of the entrepreneur as a spontaneous force pushing the economy *away* from equilibrium." (p.200) Reprinted in Kirzner anthology, *Perception, Opportunity, and Profit* (University of Chicago Press, 1979).

Klein, Guillermo Walter. "Technological Progress and Social Resistance." I:14-28. "Technological advance appears to be almost synonymous with expanded and intensified division of labour, as has been stressed, since Adam Smith, by all great economists, Professor von Mises not the least of them." (p.16)

Koether, George. "The New Science of Freedom." II:209-219. "There may be a science of politics -- a *political science* .... Government ... politics in action .... can never become a science, in my belief, until it embraces the praxeological principle which Ludwig von Mises has shown to be necessary to social order .... ¶Freedom, thanks to Ludwig von Mises, and the other economists upon whose efforts he founded his own great work, now rests upon the certitude of praxeological science. It does not depend upon the contradictory claims of parties or factions. ¶And if freedom can be thus scientifically defined, then on this foundation it may be possible to build a new Science of Freedom. As praxeology lifted economics out of the limited confines of 'economizing scarce means' and broadened it to a general theory of choice embracing all human action, so can praxeology, with the aid of economics, develop a Science of Freedom."

Lachmann, L. M. "Ludwig von Mises and the Market Process." II:38-52. "Thirty years ago Mises warned us of the futility of late classical formalism. Characteristically he thrust his blade into his opponents' weakest spot. He showed the inadequacy of the main tool of the formalists, the notion of equilibrium .... ¶In the 30 years which have now elapsed since Mises made his attack .... the notion of 'growth equilibrium' or 'steady state growth' has come to acquire a place of prominence in contemporary thought .... ¶In this essay we set ourselves two tasks: in the first place, to examine the question whether the new notion of equilibrium growth may be regarded as exempt from the criticism of the old variety of static equilibrium which Mises has presented. In the second place, Mises' hints about the Market Process as an alternative to equilibrium as a fundamental concept will have to be worked out more fully."

Leduc, Gaston. "En défense de l'économie liberale: réponse à quelques objections" [In Defense of the Economic Liberal: A Reply to Some Objections]. I:97-109.

Leffson, Ulrich (with Jörg Baetge). "The Reliability of Financial Statements." I:203-214.

Lhoste-Lachaume, Pierre. "L'Occident pour son malheur a choisi Keynes contre Mises" [To its Misfortune, The West Chose Keynes Over Mises]. I:110-120. Writing to Lhoste-Lachaume in 1959 about a French "Manifesto for a Free Society," Mises deplored that "all the plausible errors which were once taught by the German School of Social Policy and which led to the coming of Nazism, are being repeated by these pseudo-liberals. Unfortunately you are right in saying that their program reflects the dominant mentality of our controlling bourgeoisie, because it is just as true in the United States and England as it is in France." The remainder of the paper discusses the power of the market and a "true democracy" which protects individual rights, not group interests. (Translated from the French)

Machlup, Fritz. "Financing, Correcting, and Adjustment: Three Ways to Deal with an Imbalance of Payments." II:220-238.

Müller-Armack, Alfred. "Ist die Inflation unser Schicksal?" [Is Inflation To Be Our Destiny?]. I:215-226. Müller-Armack first encountered Mises' work during his student days. The author then reviews German monetary history from pre-World War I to the present, and the future prospects for inflation.

Murata, Toshio. "Soaring Urban Land Prices and Market Economy." I:322-333. "Whenever Professor Ludwig von Mises found any glimpse of an original idea in a student of his seminar class during discussion, he used to encourage the student by saying, 'Why not elaborate on it as a thesis?'. . . ¶The works by Professor Mises . . . are filled with many original and thought-provoking ideas . . . . ¶The purpose of the present essay is to demonstrate failures of government intervention in market prices of land and private ownership" with special reference to Japan.

Muthesius, Volkmar. "Der reiche Goethe und der arme Schiller" [The Rich Goethe and the Poor Schiller]. I:227-240.

Paarlberg, Don. "On Protecting One's Self from One's Friends." II:239-248. Writes of Mises' "brand" of economics, "the enterprise system," and describes the categories of people who are his "friends." "Is enterprise economics viable in our modern industrial world? A chorus of voices responds in the negative. Von Mises' brand of economics, it is said, appeared in England during the early stages of industrialization, when life was simple, when individual entrepreneurs were numerous, when wide disparities of wealth were tolerated . . . . Now all this is changed, it is said, and the economics of enterprise is outmoded. ¶If by this argument one means that the form of enterprise economics in the Twentieth Century must differ from its form during the late Eighteenth Century, then the contention is valid. Any effort to restrict enterprise economics to its original form is certain to fail. But the essence of enterprise economics is that while the central concepts are persistent, the form is fluid . . . . ¶Advocacy of enterprise economics should not be a doctrinaire position that renounces all the enlightened institutions that have developed since the turn of the century, though certain 'friends' take this position. Those who believe in enterprise economics should claim as part of their system all developments that lift the capacity for wise individual decision-making."

Papi, Giuseppe Ugo. "Ways to Communism." I:289-303.

Paton, William A. "Recollections Re a Kindred Spirit," II:249-267. Paton writes that he "didn't have the good fortune to be a pupil of that great scholar and teacher, Ludwig von Mises, but it was [his] privilege to study under a master logician . . . and an unexcelled expositor of the neoclassical position: Fred Manville Taylor." The remainder of the paper is a paean to Taylor, whose 1929 address as President of the American Economic Association was included in the Lippincott-Lange anthology, which was critical of Mises' 1920/1935 thesis concerning economic calculation in a socialist economy (*On the Economic Theory of Socialism* (see "Books and Articles About Mises: 1938," Lippincott).

Peterson, William H. "Ludwig von Mises." II:268-273. "A generation of students at New York University's graduate business school who took the economics courses of Ludwig von Mises remember a gentle, diminutive, soft-spoken, white-haired European scholar -- with a mind like a steel trap . . . . ¶Starting right after World War II, Mises gave three courses at NYU: Socialism and the Profit System, Government Control and the Profit System, and Seminar in Economic Theory . . . . ¶To be sure, many economists and businessmen have long felt that Mises is entirely too adamant, too unyielding. If that is a fault, he is certainly guilty. But Ludwig von Mises, the antithesis of sycophancy and expediency, the intellectual descendant of the Renaissance, believes in anything but moving with what he regards as the errors of the times . . . . He glories in the potential of reason and man. In sum, he stands for principle in

the finest tradition of Western Civilization. And from that rock of principle, during a long
and fruitful life, this titan of our time has never budged."

Petro, Sylvester. "The Economic-Power Syndrome." II:274-292. "Nature goes its own way, following
laws of its own, shaped by forces in which human action -- passion, will, thought -- is
irrelevant. Man's laws and man's societies are something else. The works of Ludwig von
Mises, summed up in the monumental *Human Action* (B-16), demonstrate more powerfully
than those of any other writer the role played by human will and human thought in the
universe which affects and is affected by human action . . . . ¶As a part of nature we share the
universal conatus, the striving to *be*. But our conatus is generic and undefined; we are more
than the birds and the bees, or perhaps less, but different, anyway. And our intelligence is
correspondingly different. We can kill ourselves, and we can err. ¶More strangely still, we
are capable through intellectual error of killing ourselves by policies which we believe
necessary to our survival. I believe that what I call here the 'economic-power syndrome'
constitutes one of the most destructive combinations of moral and intellectual error that
mankind has ever suffered, and I propose to disperse this dark syndrome with the aid of one of
Professor Mises' most brilliant contributions to the formulation of sound social policy: his
insistence upon a central role for the concept of consumer sovereignty . . . . ¶The significant
difference between economic and political power rests in the *purely* consensual character of
economic power as contrasted to the only partly consensual character of political power . . . .
¶The productive power of any business has its beginning in the man or men who found it and
who are able to convince others to invest their capital and their talents in it. However, the
business succeeds only if the consumers approve its production. In a market economy there is
no way for a firm to compel any one to deal with it or to purchase its goods and services. As
Ludwig von Mises has said so often, the consumers daily vote for and against the products of
American business." Reprinted in *The Freeman*. Irvington, N.Y. 22:4 (April 1972) 212-225.

Poirot, Paul L. "Ownership as a Social Function." II:293-298. Expands on Mises' assertion: "In the
market society the proprietors of capital and land can enjoy their property only by employing
it for the satisfaction of other people's wants." Poirot writes: "If one were obliged to list a
single cause of our age of revolution, it might be this: *the irresponsible use of private
property.*" He asks "whether or not the owner's right to his property carries with it any
corresponding duty or responsibility toward others. And the tendency of the law in the
nineteenth century was to say no; let the owner do with his property as he pleases so long as
he doesn't interfere with the property rights of others. ¶While such a view toward property
may be economically and morally sound, it probably reflects poor political strategy. There is
every logical reason, in a market-oriented economy, why decisions concerning the use of
property are best left to the owner. But the owner may properly be accused of negligence if he
relies heavily upon the government to defend his title . . . . ¶Established owners sometimes
seek governmental protection, to exclude would-be competitors from the market. Such
protectionism also curbs production and distorts or weakens the signals consumers send to
market . . . . ¶The market has been severely, and unjustly, condemned of late for allowing or
even encouraging the waste of natural resources and the serious pollution of air, water,
morals, and other requisites for clean living. But closer inspection will reveal that the
properties thus polluted are those not clearly subject to private ownership and control: the
atmosphere, rivers, lakes, oceans, parks, streets, schools, Appalachia, the body politic . . . .
Private ownership is a social function." Reprinted in *The Freeman*. Irvington, N.Y. 21:10
(October 1971) 599-604.

Powell, J. Enoch. "Size and Well-Being." I:84-93. Examines the argument that small countries cannot
achieve satisfactory economic growth.

Read, Leonard E. "To Abdicate or Not." II:299-302. A year or two after Mises arrived in the United
States, Read, then General Manager of the Los Angeles Chamber of Commerce, entertained
him in his home. The gathering included "renowned economists . . . and several

businessmen, . . . all first-rate thinkers in political economy . . . . ¶The final question was posed at midnight: 'Professor Mises, I agree with you that we are headed for troublous times. Now, let us suppose you were the dictator of these United States. What would you do?' ¶Quick as a flash came the reply, '*I would abdicate!*' Here we have the renunciation side of wisdom: man knowing he should not lord it over his fellows and rejecting even the thought . . . . ¶Professor Mises knows that he does not or cannot rule; thus, he abdicates from even the idea of rulership." Reprinted in *The Freeman.* Irvington, N.Y. 21:9 (September 1971) 562-565.

Regnery, Henry. "The Book in the Market Place." II:303-306. "Few would deny that any more profound, complete or persuasive exposition and defense of the free market has been written than Ludwig von Mises' *Human Action*." (B-16) Regnery then comments on "a flaw in the workings of the free market system . . . which . . . creates . . . the problem of the serious book . . . . ¶In this connection it is not amiss to point out that *Human Action* itself was originally published by a university press, by a publishing organization, therefore, neither subject to the disciplines of the market nor to the restrictions that purely market considerations impose . . . . ¶It is true, as Professor von Mises says, that 'publishers cater to the majority by publishing detective stories' but I am not at all sure that the minority interested in 'lyrical poetry and philosophical tracts' comes off quite so well." Three exceptions -- "not only *Human Action*, but Hayek's *Road to Serfdom* and Weaver's *Ideas Have Consequences*," all published by university presses, "were accidents. In the case of *Human Action*, the editor of the press possessed a degree of intellectual courage and independence not common in the academy; after his dismissal, the press let the book go out of print and was glad to cede the rights to a commercial publisher. *The Road to Serfdom* was originally published in this country, quite accidentally in a very small edition, as an import from England, and the Director of the press who brought out *Ideas Have Consequences* was soon after fired. So not much of a case for university presses [as publishers of serious books] can be made on the basis of these three books."

Reig, Joaquín. "En Torno a la Función del Capital" [Concerning the Role of Capital]. II:1-12. Reig quotes Mises on the entrepreneur, economic calculation under socialism, economic crises, intervention, workers and wages, capital and taxation. "These are a few of the many truths with which Mises increased our understanding. But over and above such invaluable examples, the great legacy of the master consists, I believe, in his having taught many of us to think, to speculate mentally with the greatest possible rigor given our respective personal limitations." (Translated from the Spanish)

Rothbard, Murray N. "Lange, Mises and Praxeology: The Retreat from Marxism." II:307-321. Oscar Lange, Mises' leading adversary in the economic calculation debate, goes a long way toward adopting the principles of praxeology and capitalism in his posthumously published *Political Economy*. "Thus, while Lange is willing to concede the universality of the economic principle, and the achievement of subjectivist economics in discovering a praxeology that can be applied to political economy and to other fields, he is of course not willing to concede that economics is exclusively praxeological. The remainder of Lange's discussion is an unsatisfactory attempt to outline what Marxism or any other economic theory might add to praxeology in the formation of economics . . . . ¶And so, as Marxian economic thought joins the actual economies of Eastern Europe in a headlong flight from Marxism and socialist central planning to Western and capitalistic modes of thought and economic systems, Oskar Lange's original irony is truly beginning to boomerang: Perhaps the free-market, capitalist economy of a future Poland will erect a statue of Lange alongside the monument to his old antagonist?" (pp.315, 318)

Rottenberg, Simon. "The Production and Exchange of Used Body Parts." II:322-333. Opens with a quote from Mises' *Human Action*. Asks if there is anything wrong with selling blood and kidneys rather than giving them away?

Rydenfelt, Sven. "Rent Control in Sweden: Lessons from a Thirty-Year Old Socio-economic Experiment." I:419-437. Opens with a quote from Mises' *Human Action.*

Salceda, Alberto G. "Jesus and the Question of Wealth." I:334-352. "Professor Ludwig von Mises . . . writes discerningly of the influence Christianity has had on the political and economic structure of our society . . . . [H]e holds that it is impossible to reconcile Christianity with a free social order based on private ownership of the means of production, adding that a living Christianity cannot, it seems exist side by side with Capitalism". . . . ¶I think, however, that an investigation showing that Jesus was a defender of personal liberty will be useful . . . . Since I feel this would please Professor Mises, I want to offer him . . . a synthesis of my investigations in this field." Salceda concludes: "Jesus did not advocate any political or economic system but from the moral principles that he preached, only one system can be derived, the one which goes hand in hand with a rational and free human nature, namely capitalism."

Schuettinger, Robert L. "The Education of Lord Acton," II:334-346.

Sennholz, Hans F. "Chicago Monetary Tradition in the Light of Austrian Theory." II:347-366. The Chicago School has "successfully reconstructed a version of the quantity theory of money and re-emphasized the importance of monetary policy." However, Sennholz says, their theory is "built on the quicksand of macro-economic analysis." (p.347) Sennholz discusses the Chicago School's intellectual predecessors -- William Stanley Jevons, Alfred Marshall, Ralph G. Hawtrey, Irving Fisher -- and Milton Friedman, whom he calls "the most influential economist of the Chicago tradition." (p.347) Sennholz then comments on "the essential differences between the monetary theories of the Chicago tradition, which Prof. [Milton] Friedman so brilliantly represents, and the subjective theories of the Austrian School of which Ludwig von Mises is its revered elder." (p.353) According to Chicagoans, "The problem of maintaining economic stability is far too complex to be left to fiscal finetuners. Therefore, Professor Friedman advocates a simple rule for steady monetary expansion . . . . a rate of increase of 3 to 5 percent per year for all currency plus all commercial bank deposits . . . . But there are also considerable time lags between monetary changes and their economic effects. (p.354-355) . . . ¶From Marshall to Friedman money has been criticized for its lack of stability (p.357) . . . . [W]hile the Keynesians recommend compensatory fiscal policies the Chicagoans realize the futility of continuous finetuning and therefore seek long-term stabilization through a steady 3 to 5 percent expansion of the money supply. In the light of Austrian theory such an expansion of the stock of money would suffice to generate some malinvestments and maladjustments . . . . Prof. Mises' trade cycle theory envisions economic booms and busts in every case of credit expansion from one percent to hundreds of percent (p.358) . . . . ¶The monetarists actually have no business cycle theory, merely a prescription for government to 'hold it steady'." (p.359) Reprinted in *Reason.* Santa Barbara, Calif., 3:7 (October 1971) 24-30; also in Sennholz's *Age of Inflation* (Belmont, Mass., 1979) pp.39-54.

Sirc, Ljubo. "Problems of Economic Responsibility and Initiative Re-emerging in Eastern Europe." I:409-418.

Spengler, Joseph J. "Hubris and Environmental Variance." II:367-374.

Tullock, Gordon. "An Application of Economics in Biology." II:375-391. Mises' pointed out that "economics can be expanded to deal with many areas outside of its traditional scope." So Tullock's "work in expanding economics into new areas was in a real sense, begun by my reading of *Human Action.*" In this article, he applies economic "externalities" to pollution and the environment.

Van Sickle, John V. "What Mises Did for Me." II:392-397. Assigned to post World War I Vienna as Assistant Secretary to the American Unofficial Delegation to the Austrian Section of the Reparations Commission, Van Sickle used the opportunity to write a doctoral thesis on a topic Mises suggested, "Direct Taxation in Austria," later published (*Harvard Economic Series.* Vol. 35, 1931) with a dedication to Mises. Van Sickle says that when he reviewed

Mises *Die Gemeinwirtschaft* [*Socialism,* B-4] in 1923, there "was (and there still is) a bit of the Fabian socialist in me." He acknowledges that Mises' "glimpses into the future have proved far more accurate than those inspired by my wishful thinking . . . . that the State, through taxing and spending . . . . can provide a guaranteed income for all." And he acknowledges that "if I survive to the ripe age of Professor Mises, I may well be forced to admit that his predictions of the consequences of political interventions with the market's allocative functions have again proved far more accurate than my wishful thinking."

Velasco, Gustavo R. "A Program for a Liberal Party." I:353-379. A condensation of (classical) liberal thought. Opens with a quote from Mises' *The Free and Prosperous Commonwealth* (B-6) and closes as follows: "Liberalism does not offer to transform man or to turn him into a superior being. It merely believes that it furnishes an opportunity for the development and realization of all our aptitudes and abilities . . . . Liberalism awaits [the future] fearlessly and confidently because it is sure that in the society erected on its bases man will find the best way of solving the problems he encounters, of rising as high as his purpose, and of achieving the happiness that is attainable on this earth." Reprinted in Spanish in *El Camino de la Abundancia* (Mexico, 1973).

Wiegand, G. C. "Economics in a Changing World." II:398-421.

Yeager, Leland B. "Can a Liberal Be an Equalitarian?" II:422-440.

1972

Bukharin, Nikolai. *The Economic Theory of the Leisure Class.*   Introduction by Donald J. Harris. New York: Monthly Review Press, 1972. This book, completed in 1914, was published in Russian in 1917, and in English translation in 1927 (International Publishers). Lenin is said to have called Bukharin "the most valuable and biggest theoretician" in the Bolshevik movement. (p.xv) Bukharin joined the Bolsheviks as a student, was arrested, sent to Siberia, escaped and made his way to Vienna, where he attended Böhm-Bawerk's seminar at the University of Vienna and studied the Austrian theorists. He was imprisoned in Austria just before World War I and deported, went to Switzerland and continued his study of marginal utility theory, then traveled to Sweden, Norway and the United States (pp.7-10). Bukharin returned to Russia in 1917, worked closely with Lenin, later defending Lenin's New Economic Policy (NEP), thus becoming an opponent of Stalin's. He was ousted from power in 1929, arrested in 1937, and tried in March 1938 (according to Stephen F. Cohen, writing in Bukharin's *Selected Writings* . . . . , 1983. pp.ix-xiv). He was executed on March 15, 1938 (see Harris' "Introduction," p.xv).

    Harris calls this book "a counteroffensive from the Marxist side" to Böhm-Bawerk's definitive critique of Marx. (p.xi) In this book, Bukharin wrote: "Karl Marx presented a classic example for the analysis of gold (in *Capital* and in his *Contribution to a Critique of Political Economy*) and those pages of his work concerned with the analysis of money are the finest things ever done in this field. As opposed to this work of Marx, the 'theory' of money advanced by the Austrian School plainly reveals the entire theoretical barrenness of all their constructions -- their complete theoretical bankruptcy."* (p.89)

    *One of the latest advocates of the Austrian School, a specialist in the theory of money, Ludwig von Mises, admits, in his book . . . (B-2), that the Austrian money theory is not satisfactory . . . . Mises attempts to eliminate this *circulus vitiosus* historically, somewhat after the same fashion as Böhm-Bawerk does in the section on substitution value, and of course with the same success." (p.198, n.100)

Burtt, Everett Johnson, Jr. *Social Perspectives in the History of Economic Theory.* New York: St. Martin's Press, 1972. Chapter 7, "Subjective Economics and the Conservative Reaction: Menger and the Austrian School," discusses Menger, Böhm-Bawerk, Schumpeter, Mises, Hayek and others: "As for the younger Austrians, Ludwig von Mises wrote at first on money and credit (1912), then turned to attacking the 'irrationality' of socialism (1922), and continued to develop Austrian subjectivism in the philosophical direction of extreme individualism and libertarianism, as typified in his *Human Action* (1949). Government economic control was anathema to him." (p.196)

Castorina, Camille. "Ludwig von Mises." *A is A Newsletter* (July 1972) 4. A brief overview of Mises and his work.

Feiwel, G. R. "On the Economic Theory of Socialism: Some Reflections on Lange's Contributions." *Kyklos.* 25 (1972) 614-616. Re the debate between Oskar Lange, the Polish economist, and Mises on the possibility of economic calculation under socialism, where prices are determined by the State instead of individuals.

Heiner, Ron. "American Competitivism: Cause or Result?" *The Freeman.* Irvington, N.Y. 22:3 (March 1972) 164-167. "From time immemorial, thinkers and philosophers have attributed . . . all of those noteworthy accomplishments achieved by various civilizations" to character, spirit, ethics. This view was challenged by Adam Smith's development of "an essentially new discipline . . . economics." Mises writes in *Human Action* that "there prevails a regularity of phenomena to which man must adjust his actions if he wishes to succeed." In other words, Heiner writes, "the belief in the sole primacy of ethics in social matters was fundamentally challenged: society could not be organized according to any set of ethical norms."

Johnston, William. *The Austrian Mind: An Intellectual and Social History, 1848-1938*. Berkeley: University of
     California Press, 1972. "The Austrian economists operated at a high level of abstraction, preferring
     examples drawn from preindustrial economies like that attributed to Robinson Crusoe. They all endorsed
     Menger's postulate that generalizations or idealizing assumptions are indispensable for organizing the data
     of social behavior. Except for Schumpeter and Mises, these theorists slighted mathematics. The school
     divided in evaluating socialism: Menger, Böhm-Bawerk, and Mises regarded any tincture of socialism as
     distorting the free-market economy, while somewhat halfheartedly Wieser and Schumpeter advocated a
     mixed economy (p.85) . . . . ¶For the invisible hand of Adam Smith, the economists substituted a
     Leibnizian premise of harmony between created nature and social law. No one carried faith in an invisible
     order underlying the market economy farther than Ludwig von Mises, who insisted that any meddling
     with the market can only disrupt it (p.86) . . . . ¶Refusal by nineteenth-century physicians to intervene
     in natural processes paralleled the reluctance of many Austrians to participate in politics. Likewise the
     preference of Carl Menger and Ludwig von Mises for an unimpeded market economy seemed to
     corroborate the medical dictum, 'The essential is to do no harm'." (p.229)

Napoleoni, Claudio. *Economic Thought of the Twentieth Century.* First published in Italian, 1961. Edited,
     expanded, translated and introduced by Alessandro Cigno. London: Martin Robertson, 1972. Chapter
     10, "The Theory of Economic Planning," discusses the criticisms of von Mises, Hayek and Robbins:
     "[I]f one accepts that the mechanism which determines the choices of the individuals . . . that generates
     relative prices, can be put in the form of a system of equations, then one has to accept, at least in
     principle, that given the terms of the problem the prices can be calculated without any need for a market
     . . . . If these data can be measured statistically the general equilibrium system will tell us what is the
     most efficient configuration. This point was realized by many economists who, nevertheless, followed
     von Mises in denying the possibility of a rational planned economy. The most important among them
     are Hayek and Robbins who, unlike von Mises, accepted that in principle an economy could be rationally
     planned, but denied that this could be done in practice for two reasons. Firstly, because the general
     equilibrium system of equations is too large and complex . . . . Secondly, because . . .the calculation
     would require such a long time that the statistical information . . . would be out of date by the time the
     results were found. ¶The position of these economists is therefore much less rigid than that of von
     Mises: for von Mises a planned economy is inconceivable; it is not even a proper economy but only an
     uncoordinated set of activities. For Hayek and Robbins, on the other hand, a planned economy is quite
     conceivable in theory but could not be put into practice." (pp.134-135)

Nove, Alec & D. M. Nuti, eds. *Socialist Economics*. Baltimore, Md.: Penguin Books, 1972. A collection of
     papers on central planning and the socialist calculation debate. Includes an excerpt from Mises' Article
     20.6 (English translation, Article 35.1).

Shackle, George L.S. *Epistemics and Economics: A Critique of Economic Doctrines*. Cambridge: Cambridge
     University Press, 1972. Discusses epistemology. Book not seen by the compilers.

1973

Block, W. "A Comment on 'The Extraordinary Claim of Praxeology,' by Professor Gutierrez." *Theory and Decision.* 3 (1973) 377-387. See Gutierrez, "Books and Articles About Mises: 1971." According to Stephan Boehm (*Method, Process and Austrian Economics.* Israel Kirzner, ed., 1982. p.49n), this paper deals with the current controversy concerning praxeology.

Browne, M. Steffy. *Wiener Freie Presse.* (February 17/18, 1973). A discussion of four post World War I groups in Vienna with which Steffy Browne was associated: one sparked by newspaper editor Paul Wittek; one by historian Heinrich Friedjung; one by Othmar Spann's students, Herbert Fürth and Friedrich Hayek; and one by Ludwig von Mises, i.e., his private seminar. Browne lists members of the Mises seminar and remarks: "Mises was by no means authoritative and he had absolutely no objection to being contradicted. However, his manner, like his intellectual character, was marked by a certain inflexibility; his liberalism or his individualism were not subject to compromise, any more than was his courage in the face of unpopularity." (Translated from the German)

Buchanan, James M. & G. F. Thirlby, eds. *L. S. E. Essays on Cost.* London School of Economics and Political Science. Weidenfeld & Nicolson, 1973; New York University Press, 1981. A collection of papers, most previously published. In Buchanan's "Introduction: L.S.E. Cost Theory in Retrospect," he writes: "[M]odern economic theorists measure their own confusion by the degree to which they accept the alleged Lange victory over Mises [in the debate concerning the possibility of economic calculation under socialism] (p.5) . . . . ¶[I]n Mises and his followers economic theory is explicitly acknowledged to be wholly non-objective." (p.9) Other mentions of Mises in papers by F. A. von Hayek (1937) and G. F. Thirlby (1952), listed by their original publication dates under "Books and Articles About Mises."

Coleson, Edward. "Capitalism and Morality." *The Freeman.* Irvington, N.Y. 23:10 (October 1973) 625-633. After quoting Mises' 1947 statement: "Nothing is more unpopular today than the free market economy, i.e. capitalism," Coleson traces anti-capitalistic ideas throughout history.

Crane, Jasper & Rose Wilder Lane. *The Lady and the Tycoon: Letters of Rose Wilder Lane and Jasper Crane.* Roger Lea MacBride, ed. Caldwell, Idaho: The Caxton Printers, Ltd., 1973. See Lane, below.

Economics '73-'74 Encyclopedia. Guilford, Conn.: Dushkin Publishing Group, 1973. Includes brief entry on Mises, p.157.

Gherity, James A. "von Mises." *McGraw-Hill Encyclopedia of World Biography.* (1973) 7:436-437. "One of von Mises' earliest publications and the one that solidly established his reputation as an economist was *The Theory of Money and Credit* (1912 [B-2]) . . . . ¶A theory of the business cycle grew out of von Mises' theory of money and was developed by him in detail by 1928 . . . . ¶Von Mises was known throughout his career as an uncompromising champion of laissez-faire."

Gonce, R. A. "Natural Law and Ludwig von Mises' Praxeology and Economic Science." *Southern Economic Journal.* 39:4 (April 1973) 490-507. Gonce concludes that "Mises' economic science is based on his natural law philosophy (p.503) . . . . ¶The parts of Mises' system fit together elegantly. From Epicurean foundations he proceeds by a method warranted by a rationalist theory of knowledge to build an individualistic secular natural law philosophy. Upon it he works out his version of Austrian economics. He uses it to justify liberalism and condemn its rivals." (p.504) For a critique of Gonce's position and an explanation of Mises' utilitarian, non-natural law, position, see Murray N. Rothbard, "Books and Articles About Mises: 1980."

Greaves, Percy L. Jr. *Understanding the Dollar Crisis.* Foreword by Ludwig von Mises (Article 73.1). Belmont, Mass.: Western Islands, 1973; 2nd ed. Dobbs Ferry, N.Y.: Free Market Books, 1984. Over a period of 22 years, through the NYU seminar and personal contacts, Greaves "developed a very close association with Mises." At one seminar session, Greaves writes: "Mises was asked by a graduate student what he would have the government do during a depression. Mises replied in his quiet manner by presenting his free market position . . . . The student, aghast, exclaimed: 'You mean the government should do nothing?' Mises leaned back . . . and said: 'Yes, but I mean the government should start doing nothing much sooner!'" (p.xxi) In this book Greaves simplifies Mises teachings with respect to human action, value, prices, money, and the boom/bust cycle. "[F]ree market economics is the only system of the division of labor that advances the general welfare of all the people. It is in accordance with the Golden Rule. We advance ourselves as we help others. The more we help others, the more we receive in return." (p.62)

Hazlitt, Henry. "Salute to von Mises: for 92 years he has fought the good fight." *Barron's National Business and Financial Weekly* (October 1, 1973) 7. Editorial commentary. "Last Saturday [September 29, 1973] marked the 92nd birthday of Ludwig von Mises, the greatest analytical economist of his generation . . . . one of this century's ablest champions of private enterprise and the free market . . . . ¶If ever a man deserved the Nobel Prize in economics, it is Mises . . . . ¶[T]he greatest difficulty to the realization of socialism, in Mises' view, is intellectual. It is not a mere matter of goodwill, or of willingness to cooperate energetically without personal reward. 'Even angels, if they were endowed only with human reason, could not form a socialistic community.' Capitalism solves this problem of economic calculation through money prices and money costs of both consumers' and producers' goods, which are fixed by competition in the open market." Reprinted in *The Freeman.* 23:12 (December 1973) 744-747. Inserted by Congressman John M. Ashbrook in *The Congressional Record.* 119:158 (October 18, 1973) E6628-6629. Reprinted also in *Planning for Freedom* (B-18), 3rd ed. (1974) 185-189; 4th ed. (1980) 271-275.

Hicks, J. R. & W. Weber, eds. *Carl Menger and the Austrian School of Economics.* Oxford: Clarendon, 1973.

High, Jack. Letter to the editor. *Barron's* (November 5, 1973). Comments on Hazlitt's article (*Barron's,* October 1, 1973), see above: "Later generations have often recognized and honored men of genius ignored by their own age. Future economists, if economics is to have a future as a science, will surely place Ludwig von Mises in this category."

Kirzner, Israel M. *Competition and Entrepreneurship.* Chicago: University of Chicago Press, 1973. Kirzner expands Mises' explanation of the role of the entrepreneur. He is critical of the emphasis of many economists "on the *values of the price and quantity variables,* and in particular on the set of values consistent with *equilibrium* conditions." According to Kirzner, "The market is still, of course, seen as made up of the activities of the market participants -- the consumers, producers, and factor owners. Their activities result from decisions to produce, to buy, and to sell commodities and resources. And once again there exists a pattern of decisions which are mutually consistent, so that all planned activities can be carried out without disappointment. Furthermore, this pattern of decisions is recognized as of very special interest because it makes up the state of equilibrium. *But it is not this equilibrium situation which is the focus of attention . . . .* ¶Rather, in the approach to price theory underlying this book, we look to price theory to help us understand how the decisions of individual participants in the market interact to generate the market forces which compel *changes* in prices, in outputs, and in method of production and the allocation of resources." (pp.5-6) Mises is cited throughout the section, "Misesian Entrepreneurship" (pp. 84-87).

Kuskey, Garvan F. Letter to the editor. *Barron's.* (November 13, 1973). "Henry Hazlitt's excellent commentary on Ludwig von Mises (*Barron's,* October 1, 1973) should have included the following quotation from Mises' 1956 book, *The Anti-Capitalistic Mentality* (B-19): 'The people of the United States are more prosperous than the inhabitants of all other countries because their government embarked later than the governments in other parts of the world upon the policy of obstructing business'."

Lane, Rose Wilder & Jasper Crane. *The Lady and the Tycoon: Letters of Rose Wilder Lane and Jasper Crane.* Roger
 Lea MacBride, ed. Caldwell, Idaho: Caxton Printers, 1973. Edited from some 4,000 pages of Lane-
 Crane correspondence (1946-1966). According to editor MacBride, Mrs. Lane "never suffered fools
 gladly." MacBride calls businessman Crane "one of the remarkable men of this century." Lane, a spicey
 and opinionated author, wrote about Mises that he "has prestige, and he is sound in economics, indeed a
 pioneer in that field; but in politics he is irrationally and obstinately a democrat. He ADVOCATES,
 passionately and fervently, 'the rule of the majority,' and every effort to discuss this with him, or to
 explain to him the American political principle of restriction of 'rule' has come up against his obstinacy."
 (p.78) "WHY does Ludwig von Mises do such a masterpiece of thought as *Human Action,* and then
 throw it all away by such crass idiocy as demanding 'democracy' and declaring that 'Any form of
 government will work well' if good men run it?" (p.183) "Seriously, it would be a treat if Herr von
 Böhm-Bawerk wrote as enthrallingly as Ludwig von Mises does, and did especially in *Human Action.*
 But somehow I doubt that." (p.252) On one occasion, Crane wrote Lane: "Your thought, expressed twice
 in these pages, that action only occurs when man expects to obtain a profit, is identical with von Mises'
 statement that man always acts to remove uneasiness, which, in those words or with such alteration in
 expression as may occur to you, might emphasize your thought of expectation to gain a profit. I think
 the removal of uneasiness is the lowest denomination, or the simplest, spring of action."(p.255)

Lukes, Steven. *Individualism.* Oxford: Basil Blackwell, 1973. Lukes' aim is to survey the meanings of
 "individualism," to isolate "the distinct unit-ideas (and intellectual traditions)" of the term, and to explore
 those relations and "show which elements of individualism hang together and which do not." (p.x) Lukes
 refers only once to Mises: "Perhaps the most systematic and sophisticated defenders of extreme economic
 individualism in our own day are economists such as Ludwig von Mises, Milton Friedman and F. A.
 Hayek." (p.92)

Meek, Ronald L. "Marginalism and Marxism." *The Marginal Revolution in Economics: Interpretation and
 Evaluation.* R. D. Collison Black, A. W. Coats and Craufurd D .W. Goodwin, eds. Durham, N.C.: Duke
 University Press, 1973. pp.233-245. Includes a discussion of Mises, Lange and Robbins on praxeology.

North, Gary. *An Introduction to Christian Economics.* [Nutley, N. J.]: Craig Press, 1973. An anthology of North
 articles, many from *The Freeman.* Many mention Mises. North asks: "Is there such a thing as a
 distinctively Christian economics? Yes." Then he explains the difference between Christian and secular
 economics. "The uniqueness of Christian economics is that the Christian economist has specific,
 concrete biblical revelation concerning the limits of economic theory and practice. A secular economist
 may see the relationship between monetary inflation and fraud, but he does not stand with the authority of
 the Bible behind him, and he is, in the mid-twentieth century, utterly unable to convince ninety-nine
 percent of his academic colleagues (and no minister of finance) of the validity of his critique. Thus, the
 monetary theories of a Mises or a Rothbard lie unused in academic circles (p.vii) . . . . ¶I have chosen to
 follow the lead of Mises and Rothbard in monetary theory, but it is my contention that the writings of
 Mises and Rothbard on monetary affairs are accurate because their presuppositions concerning the proper
 'givens' of economic analysis are in fact the same 'givens' set forth by the Scriptures." (p.xi)

Rothbard, Murray N. *The Essential von Mises.* Lansing, Mich.: Oakley R. Bramble Minibooks, 1973. 60pp. "In
 the world of politics and ideology, we are often presented with but two alternatives, and then are exhorted
 to make our choice within that loaded framework. In the 1930s, we were told by the Left that we must
 choose between Communism and Fascism: that these were the only alternatives open to us . . . .
 ¶Virtually forgotten is a third path, far above the petty squabbles over the monetary/fiscal 'mix' of
 government policy . . . . Here is the neglected path of the GENUINE free-market: a path that has been
 blazed and fought for all his life by one lone, embattled, distinguished, and dazzlingly creative economist:
 Ludwig von Mises." This minibook discusses the Austrian School of Economics, Mises' life and his
 contributions. Reprinted in Mises,' *Planning for Freedom,* 4th ed., 1980 (B-18) 234-270. Also reprinted

as a separate booklet (Auburn, Ala.: Ludwig von Mises Institute, 1983).

Spanish translation by Joaquín Albiol Reig: "Lo esencial de von Mises." Madrid: Union Editorial, 1974; 1985.

Spanish translation by Eduardo L. Suárez: "Ludwig von Mises, Su Esencia" in *Ludwig von Mises: Infatigable Luchador Contra la Economía Ficticia* [Ludwig von Mises: Indefatigable Fighter Against False Economics]. Mexico: Centro de Estudios en Economía y Educación, 1983. pp.19-52.

Norwegian translation by Arild Emil Presthus: "Ludwig von Mises - Hans Liv Og Laere." Published in four parts in *Ideer om Frihet* [Ideas on Freedom]. (July 1981, pp.15-18; Winter 1982, pp.12-15; Spring 1982, pp.19-21; and Winter 1983, pp.16-19).

Portuguese translation by Maria Luiza Borges, *O Essencial Von Mises*. Rio de Janeiro: Instituto Liberal, 1984; 1988.

_____. *For a New Liberty.* New York: Macmillan, 1973; revised edition, New York: Collier Books/Macmillan, 1978. On p.138, quotes Mises' statement on compulsory education (*Liberalism* (B-6), pp.114-115). In a section on "Ludwig von Mises and 'Value-Free' Laissez Faire" (pp.205-212) Rothbard questions whether any pronouncement on the basis of praxeological reasoning, for or against any policy, may be "value free" as Mises claims it can be. "For Mises must concede that no one can decide upon *any* policy whatever unless he makes an ultimate ethical or value judgment. But since this is so, and since according to Mises *all* ultimate value judgments or ethical standards are arbitrary, how then can he denounce these *particular* ethical judgments as 'arbitrary'? . . . ¶Thus, while praxeological economic theory is extremely useful for providing data and knowledge for framing economic policy, it cannot be sufficient by itself to enable the economist to make any value pronouncements or to advocate any public policy whatsoever." (p.212) This section not included in the 1978 revised edition.

_____. "Praxeology as the Method of Economics." *Phenomenology and the Social Sciences: Vol 2*. M. Natanson, ed. Evanston, Ill.: Northwestern University Press, 1973. pp.311-339. Includes several comments concerning Mises: "There is considerable controversy over the empirical status of the praxeological axiom. Professor Mises, working within a Kantian Philosophical framework, has maintained that, like the 'laws of thought,' the axiom is a priori to human experience and hence apodictically certain. This analysis has given rise to the designation of praxeology as 'extreme apriorism' (p.315) . . . .¶Only an individual has a mind; only an individual can feel, see, sense, and perceive; only an individual can adopt values or make choices; only an individual can *act* . . . . Ludwig von Mises points out that what differentiates purely individual action from that of individuals acting as members of a collective is the different *meaning* attached by the people involved." (p.336) Reprinted as "Praxeology as the Method of the Social Sciences." *Individualism and the Philosophy of the Social Sciences* (San Francisco: Cato Institute, 1979) pp.31-61. Also reprinted in *Austrian Economics I*. Stephen Littlechild, ed. (Aldershot, Hants, England; Brookfield, Vt: Edward Elgar, 1990) pp.452-480.

Sennholz, Hans. *Inflation, or Gold Standard*. Lansing, Mich.: Bramble Minibooks, 1973. 64pp. Expanded from the 32-page 1969 minibook of the same title. Includes further explanations of the pressures leading to inflation, plus predictions by the author.

Velasco, Gustavo R. *El Camino de la Abundancia: Una política social y económica para México* [The Road of Abundance: A Social and Economic Policy for Mexico]. Mexico: Editorial Humanidades, 1973. An anthology of lectures and essays, some in English, by a noted Mexican lawyer, banker, teacher, outspoken advocate of free markets and limited government, good friend of Mises, and translator of some of his writings into Spanish. In this collection, Velasco refers frequently to Mises.

_____. *Labor Legislation from an Economic Point of View.* Indianapolis: Liberty Fund, 1973. A critique of labor union privileges. Cites Mises on the effect of unionism on wages and employment.

Mises Dies October 10, 1973, at St. Vincent's Hospital in New York City. His ashes repose at Ferncliff Cemetery Mausoleum, Hartsdale, New York.

Obituaries:

The American Economic Review. "In Memoriam: Ludwig von Mises, 1881-1973." 64:3 (June 1974) 518. Drafted (but unsigned) by Fritz Machlup: "Mises was certainly not a popular economist; by his blunt criticism of popular views and policies, by his unrelenting attacks on inflationism, interventionism, and socialism, and by his uncompromising steadfastness in arguing the case for private enterprise and free markets, he acquired as many intellectual enemies and detractors as any of the renowned economists of the twentieth century. At the same time, Mises was a beloved teacher and friend of a host of students who came to appreciate the integrity and profundity of his teachings in courses and seminars but particularly in his private seminars."

Applied Christianity. "In Memoriam." 3:1 (January 1974) 47. "Few men have delved so profoundly into the motives of human beings and have explained so clearly the reasons for their actions . . . . ¶Only in his writings did his intellectual power and brilliant mastery of history shine forth with first magnitude intensity."

Austrian Information. "Ludwig von Mises." 26:7 (1973) 8. Death announcement.

Benegas Lynch, Alberto. "Von Mises ha muerto: sobreviven sus enseñanzas" [Von Mises has died: his teachings survive]. *La Prensa.* Buenos Aires. (October 20, 1973). "The pure intellectual honesty of Professor von Mises was one of the virtues which set him apart. That virtue, together with his acknowledged learning, justify the respect which it raised among those who knew him and could appreciate his moral integrity. His vast philosophical, legal, and economic erudition lent profundity to the knowledge others contributed to those disciplines." (Translated from the Spanish) Reprinted in *Ideas sobre la Libertad* (Centro de Estudios sobre la Libertad, Buenos Aires). 11:29 (December 1973) 6-10.

Bidinotto, Robert James. "Von Mises -- A Final Salute." *Unbound!* Boston: Individuals for a Rational Society. 2:1 (September-October 1973) 1-2. "Our age may well be labeled by future historians as 'the Age of Mediocrity.' Nothing is so characteristic of this century as the ever-shrinking stature of its men. Yet if these times are to be vindicated, it will be solely by the grace of a few lonely giants who stood tall and strode far, guided down unexplored paths by unflinching courage and unwavering vision. ¶On October 10, 1973, one of those giants fell . . . . ¶Dr. Ludwig von Mises is dead at the age of 92. And it is difficult to conceive of any person in our time who has given the world so much, yet been rewarded so little in return."

Chamberlain, John. "Unsung Economist Who Was Prophet." *Chicago Tribune.* Section 1 (October 13, 1973) 14. "Genuine innovators such as von Mises have to wait for death to gain their rightful recognition. It is all very unfair, but the truth does eventually catch up with the showmen, relegating them to the historical footnote positions where they belong . . . . ¶Von Mises' great work, *Human Action,* a study of the conditions needed to release an optimum amount of productive energy in a society . . . . will live long as a monument to von Mises."

Connell, Dennis. "Von Mises Dies in New York City." *Hillsdale Collegian.* Hillsdale, Michigan. 96:7 (October 25, 1973). "Professor Mises and a small group of distinguished colleagues, working up from the principles laid down by preceding generations of scholars, steadfastly defended the three pillars supporting western civilization: individual freedom, private property and a spiritual view of man. Moreover, Professor Mises played a leading role in the construction of a great intellectual dam, the purpose of which was to stem the rising tide of powerful currents generated by radical ideas."

Daily News. New York. "Ludwig Edler von Mises." (October 11, 1973) 106. Obituary.

D. Tel. (Daily Telegram, or Telegraph ?) U.K. "Ludwig von Mises." (October 11, 1973). "With the death of Prof. Ludwig von Mises yesterday, aged 92, the world's liberal economists lose their most prolific pen, and Austria loses the last lingering reminder of the intellectual pre-eminence of Vienna at the turn of the century . . . . ¶As an authoritative exponent of liberal economics he has enjoyed a popularity, never foreseen, in the Asian liberal economies of Japan, Hongkong and Formosa, and a respect, never foreseen, in the Communist countries, for his exposition of the impossibility of calculation in a full socialist society . . . . ¶The gentle, witty but tenaciously logical teaching of von Mises in Europe and America earned him a loyal army of auxiliary writers and pamphleteers."

Eick, Jürgen. "Ludwig von Mises; Ein Leben für die Freiheit des Burgers" [A Life for the Citizens' Freedom]. *Frankfurter Allgemeine Zeitung.* 259 (November 6, 1973) 13. "For liberals, reading Mises' books is always refreshing, even and especially in the world of today. Mises' monetary theory was the only powerful declaration of war against the collapse of money; the opposition of inflationism has gained thereby the power that can come only with intellectual clarity and incorruptibility of judgment. (Translated from the German)

Fertig, Lawrence. Remarks at Mises' memorial service, October 16, 1973. Multilithed by the Foundation for Economic Education (Irvington, N.Y.) 4-5. "Ludwig Mises was beyond doubt the leading exponent in the world in our time of the philosophy of the free market and the free society. In his world famous books he built his philosophy on the supremacy of the individual . . . . And it's interesting to note that this philosophy which permeated his writing and his life was clearly reflected in the character of this wonderful man. It was reflected in his integrity, in his staunch individualism, in his refusal to utter a word of complaint to any of his friends about the hostility he encountered among Establishment economists in his battle for human freedom."

_____. Tribute in *National Review.* 25:45 (November 9, 1973) 1245-1246. "Historians of the twenty-first century will surely be puzzled by the rankings accorded to economists in this era. ¶On the one hand they will note that academic honors, and in many cases substantial monetary rewards, were profusely showered on Establishment economists whose contributions were minuscule . . . . On the other hand they will note that the work of the colossus of that period -- Ludwig von Mises -- was largely neglected by Establishment economists, despite the fact that this great social philosopher had formulated a coherent and powerful general theory the likes of which the world had not seen for over a century."

Foundation for Economic Education (Irvington, N. Y.). "Ludwig Edler von Mises (1881-1973): In Memoriam." See separate entries for remarks by Percy L. Greaves, Jr. at Mises' commitment (October 13, 1973), Lawrence Fertig, Henry Hazlitt, and Leonard E. Read at his memorial service (October 16, 1973). 9pp.

The Franklin Auditor (1973). "Ludwig von Mises." "[I]n 1881 a giant was born at Lemberg, Austria, who would spend his life fighting the falsehoods inherent in Socialist doctrine."

The Gold Bug. New York: Committee to Reestablish the Gold Standard. "Von Mises Dies." 2:10 (October 1973) 1. "Von Mises was the great link between our age and the great age of classical liberalism . . . . ¶It is to von Mises that we owe the continued existence of a pro-gold movement in the United States."

Greaves, Percy L., Jr. "Ludwig Edler von Mises: In Memoriam." Remarks at Mises' commitment, October 13, 1973. Multilithed by the Foundation for Economic Education (Irvington, N. Y.) 1-4. "'God's magnificence' manifests itself 'in endowing His creatures with reason and the urge toward the pursuit of happiness' [Mises' *Human Action* (B-16), 3rd ed., p.147]. And so he [Mises] asked us to use our reason. Those of us here gathered together in his memory, strengthened by the vision and understanding that Mises has passed on to us, let us resolve to use our God-given reason to promote the immutable, irrefutable Mises message: Political interference produces results contrary to its purposes. It makes matters worse, not better, from the viewpoint of its sponsors." Inserted by Congressman Larry McDonald in the *Congressional Record.* 127:137 (September 29, 1981).

Hayek, F. A. "In Memoriam Ludwig von Mises 1881-1973." *Zeitschrift für Nationalökonomie.* 33 (Vienna) 1973.

_____. "Die Wiener Schule der Nationalökonomie: Der Beitrag von Ludwig Mises zu Problemen der Wirtschaftswissenschaft" [The Viennese School of Economics: Ludwig von Mises' Contribution to Economic Problems]. *Die Presse.* (October 22, 1973). "In his last decades, Mises was known above all as the old master of the reviving liberal movement. However, he will undoubtedly be assigned a lasting position in the history of economic science for his contributions to monetary and business cycle theory, to the theory of socialism and to the methodology of the social sciences." (Translated from the German)

_____. Tribute in *National Review.* 25:45 (November 9, 1973) 1244-1245. "The foundations of the great system of social thought that we now know as the work of Ludwig von Mises were laid half a century ago when he was a busy administrator for whom research and teaching could be only spare-time occupations."

Hazlitt, Henry. Remarks at Mises' Memorial service, October 16, 1973. 6-8. Multilithed by the Foundation for Economic Education (Irvington, N.Y.) 6-8. "His outstanding moral quality was moral courage, the ability to stand alone, and an almost fanatical intellectual honesty and candor that refused to deviate or compromise an inch. This often cost him personally dear, but it set an ideal to strengthen and inspire his students and all the rest of us who were privileged to know him."

_____. Tribute in *National Review.* 25:45 (November 9, 1973) 1244. "An incredible worker, he is the author of at least 19 books if one counts only first editions, and of perhaps double that number if one includes revised and expanded versions. He wrote hundreds of articles and monographs, and delivered countless lectures . . . . ¶Mises was not only a great thinker but a great man. I have never met anyone more completely dedicated to a life of the mind."

Huntington, Josh. Letter to the editor. *The Wall Street Journal.* (October 25, 1973). Comments on Peterson's tribute (*The Wall Street Journal,* October 12, 1973): "Dr. von Mises' great contribution is that . . . he saw that capitalism alone among economic systems is consistent with man's nature as a rational being."

International Herald Tribune. "Economist Ludwig von Mises; Advanced Libertarian Theory." (October 12, 1973) 5. "Mr. von Mises was recognized as a brilliant contributor to economic thought not only by his disciples but also by many who disagreed radically with his political and social philosophy."

Katz, Howard S. "Ludwig von Mises Dies at Age 92." *Rip-Off Resistance.* 1:4 (December 1973) 3. "If ever it could be said that one man stood against the ideological tide of an era, that was von Mises. But whether his efforts have turned that tide is a question to be resolved in the future by those who understood his economic theories and share his love of liberty."

Kirzner, Israel M. Memorial resolution. Graduate School of Business at New York University faculty meeting. October 24, 1973. 3pp. typed mss. "[I]t was perhaps in these years at G. B. A. [NYU Graduate School of Business Administration] that his students and colleagues saw before them the fullest extent of Mises' intellectual courage, integrity, and dedication. An outspoken exponent of the free market system, Mises came to this country at a time when his ideas were profoundly unpopular in academic as well as in lay circles. Suffering for a long time unfortunate neglect by the economics profession, Mises patiently and without bitterness pursued his tasks of writing and teaching with incorruptible consistency."

_____. Tribute in *National Review.* 25:45 (November 9, 1973) 1246, 1260: "To those who knew him, Ludwig Mises was, in the face of shocking neglect by so many of his contemporaries, a living exemplar of incorruptible intellectual integrity, a model of passionate, relentless scholarship and dedication. It will not be easy to forget these stern lessons which he so courageously personified."

McFalls, John, investment advisor. "The Passing of Ludwig von Mises." Broadcast memorial to Ludwig von Mises, October 14-16, 1973, during Value-Action radio programs: "Mises was a master of synthesis. He brought wholeness out of the fractured field of economics. He was a scholar of great patience and integrity who believed that the movement toward collectivism and state intervention posed a grave threat to Western civilization."

Milwaukee Sentinel. "Wise Economist." (date ?). "In a world in which freedom is at a premium, his [Mises'] great works, such as *Human Action,* will stand as beacons to those who still seek that most precious right."

Monatsblätter für Freiheitliche Wirtschaftspolitik. "Der letzte Liberale" [The last liberal]. 11 (November 1973) 645. "With the passing of 'the last liberal,' a liberal of the old school who occasionally said, 'Liberalism, that is what I am,' the last survivor of the epoch-making Viennese School of Economics is gone at 92 years of age. Now honored by a diminishing band of followers, he has almost become a legend, on the one hand in the field of money and business cycle theory, and on the other hand and above all in the world of economic and political theory." (Translated from the German)

Mont Pèlerin Society. *Newsletter.* "Ludwig von Mises." 4 (October 1973) 1. Death notice.

_____. "In Memoriam: Tribute to Ludwig von Mises." 5 (May 1974) 2-3. Short tributes by Henry Hazlitt, F. A. Hayek, Lawrence Fertig, Israel Kirzner, William H. Peterson.

National Review. "Tribute to von Mises." 25:45 (November 9, 1973) 1244-1246, 1260. Four-part tribute; see separate entries for Hazlitt, Hayek, Fertig, and Kirzner. Inserted by Congressman Jack F. Kemp in the *Congressional Record.* 119:166 (November 1, 1973) E6947-6949.

Neue Zürcher Zeitung. "Ludwig von Mises gestorben" [Ludwig von Mises has died]. (October 13, 1973).

New York Post. "Ludwig von Mises, 92." (October 11, 1973) 62. Obituary.

New York Times. (October 11, 1973). Death notice.

Northway, Martin E. "Ludwig von Mises, R.I.P." *Chicago rap* (A University of Chicago and Hyde Park community newspaper). (October 15, 1973). "Professor von Mises stood as almost a lone sentry against the wave of statism which swept Europe since before World War I . . . . ¶Yale Brozen, University of Chicago professor of business economics, has evaluated Professor von Mises' contribution in this way: 'Professor von Mises . . . . inspired many generations of students . . . . Management action must be future-looking, and von Mises taught us that there is no way to motivate such action without tying management's rewards to the outcome of management's decisions. That, of course, is the profit system. He was a marvelous man.'"

Opitz, Edmund A. Eulogy at the Foundation for Economic Education Board of Trustees meeting, December 3, 1973. 2pp. typed mss. "Greatness is not to be measured by a popularity contest. Mises never courted public acclaim, nor did he solicit the approval of his own profession. He pursued his studies and set forth his conclusions with no motive but to forward the truth by his efforts."

The O-T-C Market Chronicle. New York. "Between the Bull and the Bear." 7:43 (October 25, 1973) 1, 3. "Mises was an outspoken critic of government intervention in the free market place, and probably for this reason, he did not command the public attention that the liberal-minded economists of the modern era received. But his published economic theories are recognized as classics among the noted economists of the world."

Peterson, William H. "Ludwig von Mises: In Memoriam." *The Wall Street Journal.* (October 12, 1973). "Mr. von Mises believed in choice. He believed that choosing among options determines all human decisions and hence the entire sphere of human action . . . . ¶While man could destroy himself and civilization, he could also ascend -- in a free society, i.e., a free economy -- to undreamed-of cultural, intellectual and technological heights. In any event, thought would be decisive. Mr. von Mises believed in the free market of not only goods and services but of ideas as well -- in the potential of human intellect . . . . ¶He held that a free society and a free market are inseparable. He gloried in the potential of reason and man. In sum, he stood for principle in the finest tradition of Western Civilization."
Inserted in the *Congressional Record* by:
    Congressman Jack F. Kemp. 119:158 (October 18, 1973) H9277-H9278.
    Congressman Philip M. Crane. 119:159 (October 23, 1973) E6695-6696.
    Senator William E. Brock. 119:164 (October 30, 1973) S19654-S19655.
    Senator James L. Buckley. 119:168 (November 5, 1973) S19961-19962.
Spanish translation: "En Conmemoración de Ludwig von Mises" [In Commemoration of Ludwig von Mises]. *Tópicos de Actualidad.* Guatemala: Centro de Estudios Económico-Sociales. 15:310 (January 15, 1974) 13-20.
Expanded version, which draws heavily on Peterson's contribution to *Toward Liberty,* the Festschrift in honor of Mises' 90th birthday (see "Books and Articles About Mises, 1971"), reprinted in *The Intercollegiate Review.* 9:1 (Winter 1973-1974) 37-41.

La Prensa. Buenos Aires. "Ludwig von Mises: Murió en Nueva York" [Ludwig von Mises: Died in New York]. (October 18, 1973). "Mises' life, his works and his conferences were all dedicated to rounding out the thesis that men are not automatons; they act rationally and the ideas that motivate them are the original cause of the course of history. His concepts make clear that government intervention leads inevitably not only to conflicts within a country, but also to international conflicts." (Translated from the Spanish)

Rampart College Newsletter (Santa Ana, Calif.). "Ludwig von Mises 1881-1973." (November 1973) 4. Ludwig von Mises "was an illuminating example of individualistic integrity."

Read, Leonard. Remarks at memorial service, October 16, 1973. 8-9. Multilithed by the Foundation for Economic Education (Irvington, N.Y.) 8-9: "Ludwig Mises is truly -- and I use this in the present tense -- a Teacher. More than two generations have studied under him and countless thousands of others have learned from his books. Books and students are the enduring monuments of a Teacher and these monuments are his. This generation of students will pass away but the ideas set in motion by his writings will be a fountain source for new students for countless generations to come."

Ross, Warren. "Von Mises: In Memoriam." *Ergo.* [Boston]. (October 17, 1973) 1, 3. Mises "has stood for reason, individualism and economic freedom for longer than the Keynesian theories have existed . . . . It is for his intransigent devotion to his principles and his unerring economic ability that Ludwig von Mises will live on in the memories of all those who seek rationality in economics and all those who seek ammunition to fight the current ever-increasing trend toward statism and collectivism."

Rothbard, Murray N. "Ludwig von Mises: 1881-1973." *Human Events.* Washington, D.C. (October 10, 1973) 847. "Readers of Mises' majestic, formidable and uncompromising works must have often been surprised to meet him in person. Perhaps they had formed the image of Ludwig Mises as cold, severe, austere, the logical scholar repelled by lesser mortals, bitter at the follies around him and at the long trail of wrongs and insults that he had suffered. ¶They couldn't have been more wrong; for what they met was a mind of genius blended harmoniously with a personality of great sweetness and benevolence. Not once has any of us heard a harsh or bitter word escape from Mises' lips. Unfailingly gentle and courteous, Ludwig Mises was always there to encourage even the slightest signs of productivity or intelligence in his friends and students . . . . ¶And always there as an inspiration and as a constant star." Inserted by Philip M. Crane in *Congressional Record.* 119:159 (October 23, 1973) E6696-6697.

_____. "Ludwig von Mises 1881-1973." *Free Libertarian.* New York: Free Libertarian Party. 2:11 & 12 (November-December 1973) 2. "[I]n his mighty canon of work as well as in his life, Ludwig von Mises was an inspiration to every libertarian."

_____. "Ludwig von Mises, RIP." *The Libertarian Forum.* New York. 5:11 (November 1973) 1-2. Expanded version of Rothbard's obituary in *Human Events* (see above).

St. John, Jeffrey. Remarks on his "Spectrum" broadcast (CBS Radio Network). (October 18, 1973). "'To defeat the aggressors is not enough to make peace durable,' wrote the economist Ludwig von Mises. 'The main thing is to discard the ideology that generates war'. . . . ¶History, I believe, will come to regard him [Mises] as the de Tocqueville of 20th century economics . . . . ¶The genius of von Mises was in his perception of the basic unit of all human action: the individual. He was the first modern economist to recognize and construct a workable economic theory that held that all human action begins and ends with the desires and wants of the subjective individual."

St. Petersburg (Florida) *Times.* "Ludwig von Mises, Economist." (October 12, 1973) 11-B. Death announcement.

San Francisco Chronicle. "Ludwig Edler von Mises." (October 11, 1973). Death announcement.

Schaller, François. "Ludwig von Mises ou la fin d'une époque" [Ludwig von Mises or the End of an Era]. Source not identified (1973). "The blunt, often extreme, position that von Mises adopted at first, promptly dismissed all forms of religion, especially Christianity . . . . He wasted no effort in pointing out it made no sense to argue for the legitimacy of prices on the basis of morality. Market prices based on costs are not, and can never be, either 'moral' or 'immoral'. From the moment that von Mises took efficiency as the only criterion for justifying a liberal economy, considerations for a 'just price' could not but appear spurious to him. For him, religious faith and economic science are on two different planes . . . . Don't Christians reproach capitalism for favoring speculation? 'But exactly what is speculation?' Mises asks. If speculation from which all action starts were to come to a halt, from that very moment on no economic activity would be possible." (Translated from the French)

Scheps, Samuel. "Décès d'un grand économiste: Ludwig von Mises, le dernier des 'vrais' libéraux" [The Death of a Great Economist: Ludwig von Mises, the Last of the "True" Liberals]. *Journal de Genève.* 245 (October 20-21, 1973). "Von Mises gave a new direction to the quantity theory of money. According to him, the idea of a level of prices was too abstract and could not serve as a measure of money's purchasing power. It is not the quantity of money that influences the development of prices but the subjective judgments of individuals . . . . This idea surely influenced John Maynard Keynes, since he stressed liquidity preference . . . . ¶To be sure, the rigidity of his [Mises'] attitude did not permit him to follow the development of Röpke or the path of Keynes which broke with classical economic thought and that of the 19th century. But Ludwig von Mises created, over a period of many years, an extremely propitious atmosphere for the discussion of the problems of liberty." (Translated from the French)

320

Silk, Leonard. "Ludwig von Mises, Economist, Author and Teacher Dies at 92: Champion of the Libertarian View
Developed Theory of Subjective Value." *The New York Times.* (October 11, 1973) 48. "Professor von
Mises was best known in this country as a champion of libertarian economics -- the doctrine that regards
with intense suspicion any intervention in the economy by government . . . . ¶[He] was credited with
helping to revive respect for free-market economics in Europe (he was considered by some the intellectual
godfather of the German postwar 'economic miracle')." Inserted by Senator James L. Buckley in
Congressional Record. 119:168 (November 5, 1973) S19962-S19963.

Society for Individual Liberty News. Philadelphia, Penna. "Ludwig von Mises: R.I.P." 4:11 (November 1973) 1.
"If capitalism becomes the economic system of the future it will largely be due to the scholarship of Dr.
von Mises and the inspiration of his students."

Time. "Milestones." (October 22, 1973) 87. Death notice.

Times (London).   "Prof. L. von Mises: Libertarian Economist." (Date, ?). "Von Mises acquired his first
recognition for his *The Theory of Money and Credit* [B-2], published in German in 1912. In it he
developed the theory of subjective value to explain the demand for cash balance as a basis for expansions
and contractions in economic activity . . . . ¶He set out his critique of collectivist economics in
Socialism: an Economic and Sociological Analysis [B-4], which had a considerable impact on socialist
thinking."

Velasco, Gustavo R. "Ha muerto Ludwig von Mises" [Ludwig von Mises Has Died]. *El Heraldo de México.*
(November 16, 1973). "Mises was not only a great theoretical economist, but also an ardent and noted
defender of the social order most favorable for social cooperation. In this area, his name must be added to
the large number of eminent thinkers who originated and perfected the doctrine of liberalism such as
Hume, Smith, Burke, Humboldt, Tocqueville, and Acton." (Translated from the Spanish)

The Washington Post. "Ludwig von Mises, Economist, Author." (October 11, 1973) C13. AP obituary.

Zeitschrift für das gesamte Kreditwesen. "In Memoriam: Ludwig von Mises." 5 (November 1, 1973). "Ludwig
von Mises was a most faithful guardian of the old liberal tradition and reason, one of the defenders of
'laisser faire' ideas on a firm intellectual basis. As such he will be held by his friends in deep and loving
memory." (Translated from the German)

Zürcher Zeitung. "Ludwig von Mises: Engagement für Freiheit und Laisser-faire" [Commitment to Freedom and
Laissez-faire]. (October 1973). "The politico-economic idea from which Mises never departed is clearly
expressed in *Die Ursachen der Wirtschaftskrise* [The Causes of the Economic Crisis (B-9)]. He was
convinced that there was only *one* way out of the crisis: 'Forego every attempt to prevent market prices
from impacting production. Give up the pursuit of policies which seek to establish interest rates, wage
rates and commodity prices different from those the market indicates.'   Von Mises followed the liberal
tradition, to be sure, for the 'continuous intervention of an invisible hand' in the realm of money, and he
advocated strict Laisssez-faire, rejecting, for example, proposals for preventing employment by
stimulating consumption and investment." (Translated from the German)

1974

Brandenburg, Howard. *Economics and Marx: The Fraudulent Antagonists.* San Mateo, Calif.: Hillsdale Press, 1974. A critique of Marxist logic, reasoning, epistemology, "scientific socialism." Attacks the idea that economics is 'empirical,' i.e., based on historical data and statistical aggregates. "People throw dice," he writes, "but *people are not dice.*" (pp.71-72) He cites Mises frequently.

Braun, Marcus R. "Speaking the Public Mind: Stop the Press." *Kansas City Star.* (September 25, 1974). "In 1920, Ludwig von Mises, the world renowned economist, was called upon by frantic government officials to give his remedy for the ever-worsening Austrian inflation. ¶He agreed to meet with them on one condition -- that it was to be at midnight on a certain street corner in Vienna. ¶Although government officials were baffled by his request, they nevertheless agreed. When they met, it was quiet except for the continuous noise of machinery in an adjacent building. ¶When officials asked von Mises how to solve their foremost economic problem, he simply pointed to the noisy building and said, 'First and foremost, you must stop that noise.' ¶The building was the government printing plant, and the sound was the printing of money 24 hours a day . . . . ¶If Ludwig von Mises were alive today and the U. S. Treasury Department asked him a similar question about stopping our inflation, would he suggest that the noise of our government presses that print money and U. S. bonds to cover our deficit spending also be stopped?"

Brown, Susan Love; Karl Keating; David Mellinger; Patrea Post; Stuart Smith; and Catriona Tudor. *The Incredible Bread Machine.* San Diego: World Research, 1974. Six young people rewrote in modern vernacular Richard Grant's 1966 book of this same title. Chapter 2, "The Sun Sinks in the Yeast," presents a brief, highly readable summary of Mises' theory of "the great depression." (For Grant's version, see "Books and Articles About Mises: 1966.")

Business Week. "The Austrian School's Advice: 'Hands Off!'" (August 3, 1974) 40-41. "The U. S. Branch of the Austrian School traces its origins to Friedrich von Hayek and the late Ludwig von Mises, both highly articulate preachers on laissez-faire principles." The article lists their disciples' beliefs as being related to morality, inflation, the gold standard, depression, monopoly, and the free market.

Engel-Janosi, Friedrich. *. . . aber ein stolzer Bettler: Erinnerungen aus einer verlorenen Generation.* [Once More a Proud Beggar: Reflections of a Lost Generation]. Austria: Verlag Styria, 1974. Engel-Janosi describes four intellectual circles in Vienna during the 1920s and 1930s, each centered around a prominent personage: (1) historian Paul Wittek, (2) economist Ludwig von Mises, (3) historian Heinrich Friedjung and (4) students of Othmar Spann (Herbert Fürth and Friedrich Hayek): "The Mises seminar, whose members had at least a doctorate, met about once a month in Mises' Chamber of Commerce office. After an approximately two-hour discussion, they went for at least that long to the 'Ancora Verde' [a restaurant]. Mises was proud of his seminar." Engel-Janosi recalled it as "a training ground for precise thinking. It was by no means political. The conversations at the 'Ancora' were just as interesting as those at the Chamber of Commerce. In neither place was Mises in any way authoritarian; he raised absolutely no objection to opposition. However, his intellectual character, like his manner, was marked by a certain inflexibility; his liberalism like his individualism was not open to compromise. Similarly, his courage in the face of unpopularity. And one suspects that even if the subject was a question of historical understanding, his disposition was definitely set." (p.112) (Translated from the German)

Friedman, Milton. "Schools at Chicago." *The University of Chicago Magazine.* 67:1 (Autumn 1974) 11-16. "The homogeneity and provincialism of the New York intellectual community made them pushovers in discussions about Goldwater's views . . . . [T]his kind of intellectual homogeneity is destructive of tolerance. It is no accident that in the New York -- or more generally, the eastern -- environment, divergent views take the form of cults, not schools. One of the great economists of all time, Ludwig von Mises

. . . was barely tolerated for years in a peripheral academic position at New York University. He was never accepted as being in the intellectual mainstream, even though he had a far greater influence than all but a handful of the more prestigious professors of economics at Columbia, Yale, Princeton, or Harvard. Mises had disciples but few students because of the overpowering and stultifying intellectual atmosphere of New York." (p.16)

Greaves, Percy L., Jr. "In Memoriam, Ludwig von Mises: An Economic Giant." *New Guard.* Sterling, Va.: Young Americans for Freedom. 14:8 (October 1974) 20-22. Greaves reflects on his years of attendance at Mises' NYU seminar and mentions some of Mises' homey illustrations. Commenting on his first article on the monetary problem (1907), Mises said a former Austrian Finance Minister "chided him for thinking that inflation would ever again be a serious problem. The elderly statesman told him the gold standard was here to stay and that no great nation would ever again resort to inflation." At one of Mises' last seminars, he spoke of the government's "paper gold" scheme: "If a government took a piece of paper and marked it CHEESE and then called it 'cheese,' if the government then said that this paper could be offered in satisfaction of a contract calling for the delivery of cheese, you would know something was fishy." Inserted by Larry McDonald in the *Congressional Record.* 127:137 (September 29, 1981).

_____. *Mises Made Easier: A Glossary for Ludwig von Mises' Human Action.* Dobbs Ferry, N. Y.: Free Market Books, 1974; 2nd edition, Irvington, N. Y.: Free Market Books, 1990. Defines, explains, interprets and translates the difficult, unfamiliar terms and foreign phrases in *Human Action* (B-16), permitting readers to grasp Mises' fine points. Foreword by Mrs. Ludwig von Mises. Includes a translation from the German by Bettina Bien Greaves of "A Critique of Böhm-Bawerk's Reasoning in Support of His Time Preference Theory," an excerpt from Mises' *Nationalökonomie* (B-11, pp.439-444).

Grinder, Walter E. "In Memoriam: Ludwig von Mises." *Laissez-Faire Review.* New York. (September-October 1974). "[S]igns around us make it seem likely that Mises' influence will be stronger in years to come than it ever was during his lifetime. Both the present frightening objective conditions and the current subjective malaise make it clear that Ludwig von Mises' ideas are more desperately needed now than at any time since the Great Depression of the 1930's." Reprinted in *Laissez-Faire Free Market Economics & Investment Catalog* (1975) 2-3; also in *Laissez-Faire Books Catalog* (Fall 1981) 34-35.

Hillsdale College. *Champions of Freedom: The Ludwig von Mises Lecture Series.* Hillsdale, Mich.: Hillsdale College Press, 1974. First in a series of annual compilations of Ludwig von Mises Lecture Series.
> Bleiberg, Robert M. "Wage and Price Controls." 111-131.
> Hazlitt, Henry. "The Future of Money." 7-23.
> Kirzner, Israel M. "Capital, Competition and Capitalism." 69-91.
> Petro, Sylvester "Labor-Service Agencies in a Free Society." 93-109.
> Read, Leonard E. "The Miracle of the Market." 49-67.
> Roche, George. "Introduction." 1-4. Includes a few remarks about Mises.
> Rogge, Benjamin A. "Will Capitalism Survive?" 25-47. Reprinted in Rogge's *Can Capitalism Survive?* (Indianapolis: Liberty Fund, 1979) 15-36.

Kuehnelt-Leddihn, Erik von. *Leftism: From de Sade and Marx to Hitler and Marcuse.* New Rochelle, N. Y.: Arlington House, 1974. The author describes the founding in 1946 of the Mont Pèlerin Society by post-World War II "liberal scholars . . . . Almost all of them, as far as economics go, had been inspired by Ludwig von Mises." (p.197) He quotes Mises on the over-optimism of liberals who "fell prey . . . to the irresistible power of reason . . . and to the divine inspiration of majorities." (p.513n.1)

Liggio, Leonard P. "Mises and History." *The Libertarian Forum.* New York. (January 1974) 3-4. Liggio attended Mises' seminar at NYU while Mises was working on *Theory and History* (B-20): "One of the important causes of the decline of liberalism, Mises believed, was the illusion that society would necessarily continue to accept and perfect its ideas . . . . [A]s classical liberalism came closer to realization, it was necessary for its advocates not to rest, but to increase their activity and perfect the theoretical base of classical liberalism . . . . ¶However, the wedge of Ricardian concepts of disharmony of interests in a perfect capitalist society, and the existence of special interest political parties in societies claiming to be capitalist, permitted the socialists to appear the champions of the abolition of privilege, of a classless society resulting from the withering away of the state . . . . Through the dominant position socialism gained at the Universities, it was able, in Mises' view, to gain the sincere, honest, and best minds among the youth. In many ways, the success of socialism was due to its ability to appear to be what liberalism actually is."

Maybury, Rick. Letter to the editor. *Business Week.* (July 20, 1974) 10. "Von Mises never learned to speak in political euphemisms. Where a Keynesian might describe the cause of inflation as 'the creation of excess demand,' and a monetarist might describe it as 'the creation of excess liquidity,' von Mises would describe it as 'the printing of too much paper money.'"

Mont Pèlerin Society. *Tribute to Mises (1881-1973).* Chislehurst, Kent, England: Quadrangle Publications, 1974. Remarks dedicated to the memory of Ludwig von Mises delivered at the Society's session at Brussels, September 13, 1974.

Shenfield, Arthur (President) and Joaquin Reig (Chairman, Commemoration meeting). "Foreword."

Hayek, F. A. "The Courage of His Convictions." 2-7. "Like all leading figures among the intellectuals, Ludwig Mises at the turn of the century, when still a student and publishing his first articles, clearly shared the prevailing prejudices and leant towards what we now regard as the left. And then, entirely on his own, rather shocking his contemporaries who were of a mild Fabian-socialist persuasion, he discovered for himself the ideas of classical liberalism and devoted his life to rebuilding and reviving that tradition."

Iwai, Yujiro. "Defender of Freedom." 7-9. When Iwai first acquired a copy of *Human Action*, he "opened it almost with a sense of reverence . . . . It was a revelation . . . . *Human Action* gave me hope and consolation. It made me less despairing of mankind's future . . . . ¶Afterwards I had the opportunity of meeting him [Mises] in person and was impressed to find a man whose mild exterior as a German professor concealed an uncommonly sharp mind, keen wit and wry humour. He also seemed utterly unconcerned with fame and fortune."

Machlup, Fritz. "His Work Lives." 10-16. Machlup spoke of Mises' "gift of prophecy," anticipating as early as 1924, the 1931 collapse of the Kreditanstalt, and in 1927, "the end of freedom in Central Europe and the impossibility for us to go on living in Austria." Mises had then speculated in jest as to the jobs for which his friends and students would be qualified, "as actors, singers, waiters, hostesses, and bar-keepers" in a night club, for instance. As for himself, Mises had said, "unfortunately" he was "not good as a dancer or singer," and he did not think he could be a good waiter; he would "have to be the doorman in a uniform in front of the place."

Mises, Margit von. "My Husband: A Gentleman." 25-27. "I have a very good friend who used to say: 'What a gentle man your husband is'. . . . Of course, he was always gentle with me: he was a gentleman. But he was not gentle. He had a mind like a blade of steel, and he had a will of iron. From time to time I called him stubborn. Once I told this to Fritz Machlup, and his answer was: 'With a man like Ludwig von Mises you don't call it stubborn -- you call it character.' There, I had learned another lesson."

Roche, George III, "Man of Integrity." 23-24. "When I first went to the Foundation for Economic Education some years ago, I immediately discovered the force and presence of Ludwig von Mises both in his intellect and, perhaps more important, in his character. He so transcendently typified the man of integrity in academic affairs . . . that it was impossible to be near him . . . without immediately sensing that quality. He was a remarkable human being."

Rothbard, Murray. "Devotion to Truth." 19-22. "Professor Mises' great achievement was to give us a mighty structure of economic thought: the level of integration was absolutely fantastic compared to anything else that the twentieth century has produced. He wrote a mighty series of integrated works covering not only economics itself, but also philosophy, methodology and the whole compass of the social sciences, including history . . . . ¶Unfortunately, he wrote this mighty structure of thought in an age when mighty structures have become unfashionable for various reasons. Very few people can absorb -- or even be informed of -- all the disciplines . . . . In that sort of academic intellectual atmosphere . . . it became almost impossible for his work to achieve the recognition and honour it merited."

Velasco, Gustavo. "Intellectual and Moral Giant." 16-19. Velasco first encountered Mises through his uncle, Luis Montes de Oca, who arranged Mises' visits to Mexico. Velasco and his uncle translated into Spanish several of Mises' works, including *Socialism* (B-4). What Velasco most admired in Mises was "his steadfastness, his adherence to the principles and ideas which he believed were true and advantageous to the human race. For Mises, the greatest sin was to compromise. He never deviated, in spite of the fact that his great achievements were only tardily and incompletely recognized."

North, Gary. "Magic, Envy and Economic Underdevelopment." *The Journal of Christian Reconstruction.* Woodland Hills, Calif. 1:2 (Winter 1974) 149-161. In discussing envy, North denies "that we are hurt by our neighbor's advantages." According to North, Mises calls this fallacy the "Montaigne dogma" and "correctly argues that this doctrine [the mercantilist concept that one man's gain in trade is another man's loss] is at the bottom of all theories of class conflict." *Human Action* (B-16) p.664. Reprinted in *The Freeman.* 25:2 (February 1975) 80-87.

Nozick, Robert. *Anarchy, State, and Utopia.* New York: Basic Books, 1974. "Our account of the state involves less intentional coordination of action with some other individuals," Nozick says, "than does Mises' account of a medium of exchange." (p.344 n.14)

Osterfeld, Dave. "Marx, Mises and Socialism." *The Freeman.* Irvington, N.Y. 24:10 (October 1974) 605-611. "No sooner had Mises written [his critique of socialism, 1922] than his theory received dramatic confirmation." Discusses Oskar Lange's 1937 "attempt . . . to demonstrate the viability of socialism" and the claim of Paul Sweezy, "[p]erhaps the pre-eminent American Marxist . . . that a non-market economy is possible." (For Lange article, see "Books and Articles About Mises: 1936.")

Paul, Jeffrey Elliott. "Individualism, Holism, and Human Action: An Investigation into Social Scientific Methodology." Ph.D. dissertation, Brandeis University, 1974. Discusses the individualism of Mises, Hayek, Robbins and Watkins as well as the thought of some non-individualists, such as Mandelbaum, Gellner, Lukes, Danto, Goldstein and Brodbeck. "In what follows I hope to demonstrate that the contemporary arguments both for and against methodological individualism ultimately fail. In addition, I outline a possible defense of the principle and consider why such a defense has hitherto not been given. Finally, I produce that defense in detail and, subsequently, provide illustrations of properly structured and correctly adduced social theories as suggested by that defense." (p.8)

Peterson, William H. "Mises and Fisher on Theory and History." *The Freeman.* Irvington, N.Y. 24:6 (June 1974) 323-326. Discusses Mises' *Theory and History* (B-20) and Antony Fisher's *Must History Repeat Itself?* (Churchill Press, 1974). Fisher pioneered mass-production of broilers and "dramatically reduced the price of chicken to the British consumer while making record profits." Fisher then founded the Institute of Economic Affairs. "So, as doer and thinker, Antony Fisher has been something of a one-man Manchester School . . . . ¶[He] reflects the free market thinking of Ludwig von Mises . . . . [and] calls for ending all government monopoly and control."

Petro, Sylvester. "Civil Liberty, Syndicalism, and the NLRA." *The University of Toledo Law Review.* 5:3 (Spring 1974) 447-513. Petro cites specific legal cases and explains the economic reasons for "the incompatibility of the National Labor Relations Act [NLRA] with any coherent conception of civil liberty." (pp.447-448) He cites Mises on the harm done by the NLRA's invasions of freedom "to the market economy in general and to the interests of workers and consumers in particular." (p.481)   Petro also cites Mises on the importance of leaving entrepreneurs free to negotiate, the ability of the market economy "to allocate resources more efficiently than command economies" (p.483), the effects of union power "to exclude competition" (p.484), and the dependence of labor productivity on "the tools which savers, investors, and engineers design and provide." (pp.510-511)

_____. "Competition, Monopoly, and the Role of Government." *The Freeman.* Irvington, N.Y. 24:2 (February 1974) 91-100. "The more one examines American labor law the more one becomes convinced of the validity of Professor Mises' theory that no abusive monopoly is possible in a market economy without the help of government in one form or another. If employers were permitted to band together peacefully in order to *resist* unionization, as unions are permitted to engage in coercive concerted activities in order to *compel* unionization, it is probable that the purely economic (nonviolent) pressures of unions would not be as effective as they have been in increasing the size and power of the big unions." (pp.95-96)

_____. "Feudalism, Property, and Praxeology." *Property in a Humane Economy: A Selection of Essays Compiled by the Institute for Humane Studies.* Samuel L. Blumenfeld, ed. LaSalle, Illinois: Open Court, 1974. pp.161-180. Petro reviews the history of land law in England from the Norman Conquest to the 17th century in the light of the "current of thought [which] is moving powerfully and swiftly toward ever more extensive and more pervasive qualifications" of the right to own property. (p.161) He refers to the economic calculation debate raised by Mises to show that "private property is the indispensable feature of the market" (p.163) and he closes by referring to Mises' *Human Action* (B-16) which "both explains and is itself illuminated by the history. we have just surveyed." (p.178)

_____. "Sovereignty and Compulsory Public-Sector Bargaining." *Wake Forest Law Review.* 10:1 (March 1974) 25-165. Concerning "the role of sovereignty in a laissez faire society," Petro says (p.70): "laissez faire . . . cannot exist except under the protection of a sovereign government; it is not to be confused with anarchy" and he footnotes Mises' *Human Action.* (B-16)   Petro distinguishes, as Mises does, between two forms of interpersonal cooperation, "the way of agreement, and the way of command" (p.91), and he quotes (pp.91-92 and 102) from Mises' *Bureaucracy* (B-13).

Read, Leonard E., compiler. *The Free Man's Almanac.* Irvington, N. Y.: Foundation for Economic Education, 1974. Includes four quotes from Mises' works, pp.46, 77, 180 and 231.

_____. "Who Is A Teacher?" *Notes from FEE.*   Irvington, N.Y.: Foundation for Economic Education. (March 1974). "We are pursuing Truth when searching for a Teacher; we stray far from it when promoting ourselves as teachers . . . . let us mark the distinction by using "teacher" and Teacher! The first is what millions of classroom instructors call themselves; the second is a tribute one person pays to another . . . . Ludwig Mises is truly . . . a Teacher. More than two generations have studied under him and countless thousands of others have learned from his books." Reprinted in Read's *Castles in the Air* (Foundation for Economic Education, 1975) 150-154.

Szasz, Thomas. "A Synoptic History of the Promotion and Prohibition of Drugs." *Ceremonial Chemistry: The Ritual Persecution of Drugs, Addicts, and Pushers.* Garden City, N. Y: Doubleday, 1974. Quotes Mises' statement on drugs from *Human Action* (1st ed., pp.728-729; 2nd ed., p.734; 3rd ed., pp.733-734). Entire "Synoptic History . . ." reprinted in Wallechinsky, David & Wallace Irving. *The People's Almanac* (Garden City, N. Y.: Doubleday, 1975) 1075-1084.

1975

Bettleheim, Charles. *Economic Calculation and Forms of Property: An Essay on the Transition between Capitalism and Socialism.* Translated by John Taylor. New York: Monthly Review Press, 1975.

Galbraith, John Kenneth. *Money: Whence It Came, Where It Went.* Boston: Houghton Mifflin, 1975. Referring to the Austrian inflation of the 1920s, Galbraith states: "The inflation was experienced or remembered by the men who were to compose the world's most distinguished coterie of conservative (in the European sense, liberal) economists of the next generation -- Friedrich von Hayek, Ludwig von Mises, Gottfried Haberler, Fritz Machlup and Oskar Morgenstern, all of whom also moved eventually to the United States. All shared with Schumpeter a profound mistrust of any action that seemed to risk inflation along with an even greater distaste for anything that seemed to suggest socialism. All were influential." (p. 152)

Greaves, Bettina B. *Free Market Economics: A Syllabus.* Irvington, N.Y.: Foundation for Economic Education, 1975. A free market guide for the high school teacher, written from the Austrian perspective. Includes frequent references to, and quotes from, Mises. An accompanying volume, *Free Market Economics: A Basic Reader,* reprints six articles by Mises.

Greaves, Percy L. Jr. "The Wolf Is Now At The Door." *The Review of the NEWS.* Belmont, Mass. 11:11 (March 12, 1975) 31-40. An analysis of the government's deficit: "[L]eft alone, the market system flows smoothly. As the late Professor Ludwig von Mises has clearly demonstrated, every political interference with market processes only makes matters worse. Every political interference helps a few temporarily at the expense of the many, until the system eventually breaks down."

Hayek, F. A. "Inflation, the Misdirection of Labour, and Unemployment." *Full Employment at Any Price?* (Occasional Paper 45). London: Institute of Economic Affairs, 1975. pp.15-29. Lecture delivered February 8, 1975 to the Convegno Internazionale: Il Problema della Moneta Oggi, organized in commemoration of the 100th birthday of Luigi Einaudi by the Academia Nazionale dei Lincei at Rome, and published in the proceedings of that congress. "I do not want to leave this recollection of the great inflation [in Germany and Austria during the 1920s] without mentioning that I have probably learnt at least as much as, if not more than, I learnt from observing the actual facts of the great inflation by being taught to see -- largely by my teacher, the late Ludwig von Mises -- the utter stupidity of the arguments which were then, especially in Germany, propounded to explain and justify the increases in the quantity of money. Most of these arguments I am now encountering again in countries which then seemed economically more sophisticated and whose economists rather looked down at the foolishness of the German economists." Reprinted, slightly revised, in Hayek's *New Studies in Philosophy, Politics, Economics and the History of Ideas* (Chicago: University of Chicago Press, 1978) pp.197-209. Passage quoted from p.198 of that Hayek anthology. Also included (pp.3-17) in *The Essence of Hayek.* Chiaki Nishiyami & Kurt R. Leube, eds. (Stanford, Calif.: Hoover Institution Press, 1983).

Hillsdale College. *Champions of Freedom: The Ludwig von Mises Lecture Series.* Hillsdale, Mich.: Hillsdale College Press, 1975. Volume II in the on-going Ludwig von Mises Lecture Series. References to Mises in the following addresses:
>   Roche, George Charles III. "Introduction."
>   Davenport, John. "The Market and Human Values." 1-12.
>   Exter, John. "Money in Today's World." 33-58.
>   Shenfield, Arthur. "Must We Abolish the State?" 13-32.
>   Sparks, Bertel M. "Retreat from Contract to Status." 59-82.

L'Informateur. Lyon (?). c.1974-5. "Quelques Leçons de Ludwig von Mises" [Some Lessons from Ludwig von Mises]. Consists of several short articles about Mises -- one titled "Ludwig von Mises et W. Roepke," another "La chaîne sans fin des interventions économiques" [The Endless Chain of Economic Interventions] -- plus reprints of a couple of Mises' articles and short extracts from *Bureaucracy* (B-13) and *Socialism* (B-4).

Jefferson, Michael. "Ludwig von Mises: Anti Anti-capitalist." *Prophets of Freedom and Enterprise.* Michael Ivens, ed. London: Kogan Page for Aims of Industry, 1975. pp.52-59. "In keeping with his intention of placing economics within a broader framework of human action, of the whole range of choices a human being can make, von Mises covers an enormous canvas with confidence and insight. He discusses philosophical matters at one moment and pricing policies or interest rates at another. And not surprisingly, if you know your man, socialism comes under heavy fire . . . . ¶Von Mises places great faith in the power of human reasoning, and one reason for his individualist beliefs is that individuals have the power to think while 'the State' or 'Society' does not . . . . ¶The weakness of von Mises' position lies here, and he recognised it. He could not extricate himself from the dilemma he posed: 'the illusion of the old liberals.' The social philosophy of the Enlightenment, he records, failed to see the dangers that the prevalence of unsound ideas could engender. The classical economists and the Utilitarians . . . . overlooked the fact that public opinion could favour spurious ideologies whose realization would harm welfare and well-being and distintegrate social cooperation . . . . ¶Perhaps one of the more extraordinary characteristics of von Mises was that, while he noted these depressing features of modern society, he remained an almost incurable optimist."

Maling, Charles E. "Austrian Business Cycle Theory and Its Implications." *Reason Papers.* No. 2 (Fall 1975) 65-90. (Not seen by the compilers)

McDowell, Edwin. "Free Enterprise's Moveable Mountain." *The Wall Street Journal.* (September 5, 1975). "Ludwig von Mises' death . . . . removed one of the world's most influential libertarian theorists and the oldest living member of the MPS [Mont Pèlerin Society]." Several MPS members who had been influenced by Mises were specifically mentioned as being in attendance at the Society's 1975 meeting at Hillsdale College: Toshio Murata, economist from Japan, Joaquin Reig, lawyer from Spain, and Manuel F. Ayau, Guatemalan businessman and rector of the Universidad Francisco Marroquín. This MPS meeting "amounted virtually to a verbal *Festschrift*" to F. A. Hayek, "a student and disciple of Mises," the Society's founder and honorary President who had just been named co-winner of the 1974 Nobel Prize for economics.

Raico, Ralph. "Ludwig von Mises." *The Alternative: An American Spectator.* Bloomington, Indiana. (February 1975) 21-23. "It is said that . . . when Bill Buckley was at the beginning of his career of college-speaking, he once wrote two names on the blackboard . . . . The name of the defender of democratic socialism (I think it was Harold Laski, possibly John Dewey) was recognized by most of those present. The name of Ludwig von Mises was entirely unknown to them . . . . How has it been possible that the great majority of economics and social science students, even at elite American universities, are completely unfamiliar with Mises?" Mises was "even more than a great economist," Raico says; he played "the key role" in the discussion of the viability of central economic planning. He attributes the widespread neglect of Mises to his "intransigence", his refusal to compromise. Raico reviews Mises important contributions, one of which, he says, is Mises' criticism of the idea commonly found among American conservatives that "there is an intimate relationship between commitment to a free society and faith in Christianity."

Read, Leonard E. "Right Now!". *Notes from FEE.* Irvington, N.Y.: Foundation for Economic Education. (May 1975) 3. "Never once did I know him [Mises] to equivocate. Always, he spoke and wrote what he believed to be right -- no heed whatsoever to the approval of anyone." Recalling the founding meeting

(1947) of the Mont Pèlerin Society: "Mises presented what he believed to be right . . . . Later, I overheard Professor Wilhelm Roepke, one of the most notable among the founders, vigorously express his disapproval of Mises' views. Two years later, I was invited to dine with Professor and Mrs. Mises, [was told] that they 'had a guest from Europe.' Who did the guest turn out to be? Roepke! In this brief period, Professor Roepke had come to share the view of Mises -- philosophically, the two had become substantially one." Reprinted in *The Love of Liberty* (Foundation for Economic Education, 1975) 154-155.

Sennholz, Hans F. (ed.) *Gold I$ Money.* Westport, Conn.: Greenwood Press, 1975. Only two of the nine papers mention Mises:

> Sennholz, Hans F. "No Shortage of Gold." 41-60. The regression analysis, "first developed by Ludwig von Mises, endeavors to explain the first emergence of a monetary demand for a commodity that hitherto was used for industrial purposes only. It explains how the present purchasing power of money emerged as the result of both kinds of demand, monetary as well as industrial." (p.52)
>
> Sparks, John A. "The Legal Standing of Gold -- Contract vs. Status." 77-103. "No less an economist than Ludwig von Mises has supported the traditional prerogative of state mintage in the *limited sense* prescribed by the U. S. Constitution . . . . [M]anufacturing coins with similarity of appearance, weight, and fineness 'was and still is the premier task of state monetary activity'." (pp.82-83)

Symms, Steve (Idaho First District Congressman). *H.R. 8358.* (94th Congress, 1st Session, June 26, 1975). "A BILL To provide a new United States gold coinage . . . . This coin shall bear a portrait of the late economist Ludwig von Mises on one side and the seal of the United States of America on the other." Joining Mr. Symms in introducing this Bill were Congressmen Richard H. Ichord of Missouri, Larry McDonald of Georgia and John H. Rousselot of California; it was referred to the Committee on Banking, Currency and Housing; it was not passed.

Vanberg, V. *Die zwei Soziologien: Individualismus und Kollektivismus in der Sozialtheorie* [The Two Sociologies: Individualism and Collectivism in Social Theory]. Tübingen: Mohr, 1975. Assesses Mises' contributions to epistemology and methodology.

1976

Dolan, Edwin G. (ed.). *The Foundations of Modern Austrian Economics.* Kansas City [Mission, Kansas]: Sheed & Ward, 1976. The following essays mention Mises:

   Dolan, Edwin G. "Austrian Economics as Extraordinary Science." 3-15. "From the earliest days, the hallmark of Austrian work [on the theory of money and economic fluctuations] ... has been a microeconomic approach to macroeconomic problems. Ludwig von Mises's *Theory of Money and Credit* (B-2) ... , a pioneering contribution, identified the lack of coordination between individual expectations and the supply of money and credit as a prime cause of economic disturbance."

   Kirzner, Israel M. "Equilibrium versus Market Process." 115-125. "[E]conomists of sharply differing persuasions within the Austrian tradition all display a characteristic disenchantment with the orthodox emphasis on both equilibrium and perfect competition. Thus Joseph A. Schumpeter's well-known position on these matters is remarkably close to that of Ludwig von Mises (p.115) .... ¶Mises's concept of human action embodies an insight about man [that he is not only a calculating agent but is also *alert to opportunities*] that is entirely lacking in a world of Robbinsian economizers . . . . Misesian theory of human action conceives of the individual as having his eyes and ears open to opportunities that are 'just around the corner'." (p.119) Reprinted (pp. 115-125) in Kirzner anthology, *Perception, Opportunity, and Profit* (University of Chicago Press, 1979) pp.3-12.

   _____. "Philosophical and Ethical Implications of Austrian Economics." 75-88. "In the writings of Ludwig von Mises the *Wertfreiheit* tradition [objectivity, or freedom from value judgments] was vigorously upheld" (p.77) Kirzner then asks, "can we reconcile Mises's strong normative position in economics with his declared insistence on *Wertfreiheit?*" Kirzner believes that we can. He compares Mises with the scientist whose research into the causes of a dread disease can be "entirely *wertfrei.* . . . what motivates a scientist to dedicate his life to such research may be his wish to free mankind from the scourge . . . . ¶Mises the defender of the free market and Mises the economic scientist were indeed one and the same individual . . . . [O]ne who wishes to promote a free society with unhampered markets may legitimately cite the conclusions of economic science with respect to the coordinative-allocative properties of competitive markets."

   _____. "The Theory of Capital." 133-144. Kirzner asks how can we reconcile the impossibility of aggregate capital measurement with the frequent references in Mises "to the consequences of the fact that one country possesses a greater quantity of capital (or a greater quantity of capital per worker) than a second country." The answer, Kirzner says, is due to the fact that an *individual* may estimate the value of the aggregate worth of his own stock of capital goods. "Individual forward-looking measurement is both possible and feasible." (p.142)

   _____. "On the Method of Austrian Economics." 40-51. "Hayek asserted (in a footnote reference to the work of Ludwig von Mises) that every important advance in economic theory in the preceding century had been a result of the consistent application of subjectivism." (p.46) Reprinted in *Austrian Economics: I.* Stephen Littlechild, ed. (Aldershot, Hants, England; Brookfield, Vermont: Edward Elgar/Gower Publishing Company, 1990) pp.313-323.

   Lachmann, Ludwig M. "On the Central Concept of Austrian Economics: Market Process." 126-132. In discussing his view of expectations as equilibrating devices, Lachmann refers to Mises' explanation of how planners learn from experience: "unsuccessful planners make capital losses and thus gradually lose their control over resources and their ability to engage in new enterprises; the successful are able to plan with more confidence and on a much larger scale." Reprinted in *Austrian Economics: III.* Stephen Littlechild, ed. (Aldershot, Hants, England; Brookfield, Vt.: Edward Elgar, 1990) pp.80-86.

O'Driscoll, Gerald P. Jr. & Sudha R. Shenoy. "Inflation, Recession, and Stagflation." 185-211. "Carl Menger provided the theoretical framework for explaining why a medium of exchange was used. Then, after Knut Wicksell drew attention to the failure of the classical quantity theory to explain how changes in the money supply affect prices, Mises, building on Menger and Wicksell, showed more completely how money could be integrated into general economic theory." (p.194)

Rothbard, Murray N. "The Austrian Theory of Money." 160-184. "The Austrian theory of money virtually begins and ends with Ludwig von Mises's monumental *Theory of Money and Credit* (B-2), published in 1912." Rothbard then proceeds to present Mises' explanation of the value of money on the basis of the theory of marginal utility, his development of the regression theorem, his rejection of Walrasian general equilibrium, his position on free banking, and his analysis of inflation and credit expansion.

_____. "New Light on the Prehistory of the Austrian School." 52-74. "Kauder perceptively pointed out that in contemporary economics, 'only von Mises, the most faithful student of the three [Austrian] pioneers, maintains the ontological character of economic laws'." (p.70)

_____. "Praxeology: The Methodology of Austrian Economics." 19-39. "Praxeology is the distinctive methodology of the Austrian school . . . first applied to the Austrian method by Ludwig von Mises, who was not only the major architect and elaborator of this methodology but also the economist who most fully and successfully applied it to the construction of economic theory . . . . ¶Praxeology rests on the fundamental axiom that individual human beings *act*, that is, on the primordial fact that individuals engage in conscious actions toward chosen goals (p.19) . . . . ¶It should be noted that for Mises it is only the fundamental axiom of action that is a priori; he conceded that the subsidiary axioms of the diversity of mankind and nature, and of leisure as a consumers' good, are broadly empirical." (p.27) According to Rothbard, Mises made "the outstanding contribution" to the relationship between theory and history, pointing out that "economic theory does not need to be 'tested' by historical fact but also that it *cannot* be so tested." For a fact to be usable for testing theories, "it must be a simple fact, homogeneous with other facts in accessible and repeatable classes." As every historical fact is heterogeneous, it "cannot be used either to test or to construct laws of history, quantitative or otherwise . . . . ¶Mises's radically fundamental opposition to econometrics now becomes clear." (pp.32-33)

_____. "Praxeology, Value Judgments, and Public Policy." 89-111. "[O]f all the economists in the twentieth century, [Mises was] the most uncompromising and passionate adherent of laissez-faire and at the same time the most rigorous and uncompromising advocate of value-free economics and opponent of any sort of objective ethics. How then did he attempt to reconcile these two positions? ¶Essentially, Mises offered two very different solutions to this problem. The first is a variant of the unanimity principle . . . . [I]f a given policy will lead to consequences, as explained by praxeology, that *every one* of the supporters of the policy will agree is bad, then the value-free economist is justified in calling the policy a 'bad' one." (pp.100-101) Rothbard refers to the example of government-imposed price controls, which Mises cites. "But how could Mises know that some advocates of price control do not want shortages? (p.102) . . . . ¶Mises's attempt to advocate laissez-faire while remaining value-free, by assuming that all of the advocates of government intervention will abandon their position once they learn of its consequences, falls completely to the ground . . . . Mises conceded that the economic scientist cannot advocate laissez-faire but then added that as a *citizen* he can do so." (p.104) Rothbard admits that Mises' second attempt to escape "the self-contradiction of being a value-free praxeologist advocating laissez-faire," was more successful. "[H]e took his stand as a citizen willing to make value judgments . . . . But for Mises the utilitarian, ... he was only willing to make *the one* value judgment that he joined the majority of the people in favoring their common peace, prosperity, and abundance." (p.105)

Hayek F. A. *Law, Legislation and Liberty, 2: The Mirage of Social Justice.* Chicago, University of Chicago Press, 1976. In this book, which presents "a new statement of the liberal principles of justice and political economy," Hayek refers several times to Mises.

_____. "Einführung zur Neuauflage von 1976" [Introduction to the new 1976 edition], *Kritik des Interventionismus* (B-8). Darmstadt: Wissenschaftliche Buchgesellschaft, 1976. "Mises was known not only as an extremely sharp critic, but also as a pessimist. And only too often, unfortunately, he was right. Other contemporaries may survive who will recall an occasion in September 1932 when a committee of the Verein für Sozialpolitik [Society for Social Policy] meeting in Bad Kissingen was taking tea in a garden with the members of a larger group. Suddenly Mises asked whether we realized that we were gathered together for the last time. The remark caused surprise at first, then laughter when Mises explained that twelve months from then Hitler would be in office. That appeared unlikely to the others present. But even so, they thought, why shouldn't the Verein meet again after Hitler had come to power? -- As it turned out, the Verein did not meet again until after the end of World War II." (p. vii) (Translated from the German)

Hill, Lewis E. & Gene C. Uselton. "The Economic Epistemology of Ludwig von Mises." *Reason Papers: A Journal of Interdisciplinary Normative Studies.* 3 (Fall 1976) 64-82. After reviewing Mises' epistemology and methodology, the authors ask if his economic analysis was "consistent with his stated views on epistemology and methodology?" They find "only one apparent inconsistency," Mises' statement in *Human Action* (p.10) that Western civilization "owes its material wealth to the implementation of laissez faire economic policies." (p.72) The authors believe that Mises did not clearly explain here his reasoning process. They ask: "But is praxeology the only legitimate approach to economic epistemology and methodology? Our answer is that von Mises has found an important part of the truth but something less than the whole truth in at least two respects. First, von Mises erred in rejecting the logical validity of inductive reasoning. Second, he was mistaken to the extent that he denied the need for and practical usefulness of verification procedures in economic analysis (p.74) .... ¶The problem with von Mises's system, it seems to us, is that his legitimate distrust of empirical verification of formal economic models led to an illegitimate rejection of all empirical work." (p.77)

Hillsdale College. *Champions of Freedom: The Ludwig von Mises Lecture Series, III.* Hillsdale, Mich.: Hillsdale College Press, 1976. Introductory remarks about Mises by Margit von Mises. Only other mention of Mises in this volume by Antony Fisher in his "Must History Repeat Itself," pp.101-130.

Keckeissen, Joseph Edward. "The Meanings of Economic Law." Ph.D. dissertation. New York University, 1976. A comparison of (1) economics "without law" (i.e. economics based on generalizations, guesses, complex phenomena), (2) economics with "weak" laws (i.e., empirical, quantitative, historical laws), (3) economics based on natural law, and (4) economics based on "strong economic laws" (i.e. Marxian assumptions and Austrian-Misesian *a priori* laws).

Lachmann, Ludwig M. "From Mises to Shackle: An Essay on Austrian Economics and the Kaleidic Society." *Journal of Economic Literature.* 14:1 (March 1976) 54-62. Lachmann compares L. S. Shackle's "*kaleidic society*, a society in which sooner or later unexpected change is bound to upset existing patterns" with Mises' "market process kept in motion by the flow of events." Lachmann concludes Mises and Shackle "share a common outlook on the foundations of our discipline." However, Lachmann says, Shackle (1) extends "the scope of subjectivism from tastes to expectations" (2) discusses the way the market process helps to coordinate divergent expectations, and (3) questions whether the market process can be viewed as "potentially terminating in a state of long-run general equilibrium." Reprinted in *Austrian Economics*, *I.* Stephen Littlechild, ed. (Aldershot, Hants, England; Brookfield, Vt: Edward Elgar, 1990) pp.325-333.

Landauer, Carl. "Recent German Literature on Gemeinwirtschaft." *Social Research.* Berkley: University of California. 43:2 (Summer 1976) 295-321. Presents pro-interventionist, anti-market arguments. A report on the literature of German social scientists who have tried to counter Mises' glorification of the free market. Mises labeled this school the school of Gemeinwirtschaft [socialism].

Latsis, Spiro J., ed. *Method and Appraisal in Economics.* Cambridge: Cambridge University Press, 1976. Several contributors mention Mises:
>   Hicks, J. R. "'Revolutions' in Economics." 212-213. Refers to Mises' use of the term "catallactics."
>   Hutchison, T. W. "History and Philosophy of Science and Economics." Comments (p.201) on Samuelson's assertion concerning "the exaggerated claims . . . in economics for the power of deduction and *a priori* reasoning" made by such persons as Carl Menger, Lionel Robbins, Frank Knight and Ludwig von Mises. Hutchison quotes Samuelson: "Fortunately we have left that behind us."
>   Latsis, Spiro J. "A Research Programme in Economics." Discusses (pp.7-13) Mises' defense of the rationalistic approach via his aprioristic methodology. "An important merit of von Mises' methodology has been to alert us to the fact that some position on these problems . . . must be adopted even before we embark on the explanation and prediction of economic and social phenomena."

Machlup, Fritz, ed. *Essays on Hayek.* Foreword by Milton Friedman. New York: New York University Press, 1976; Hillsdale (Mich.) College Press, 1976; London: Routledge & Kegan Paul, 1977. Papers at Mont Pèlerin Society meeting, Hillsdale College (Hillsdale, Mich.) August 24-28, 1975. Contributions by William F. Buckley, Jr., Gottfried Dietze, Ronald Max Hartwell, Shirley Robin Letwin, Fritz Machlup, George C. Roche III, and Arthur Shenfield. Only a few brief mentions of Mises by Roche (pp.6 & 9), Machlup (pp.31 & 34), Buckley (pp.102 & 103) and Shenfield (p.173). Machlup's paper, "Hayek's Contribution to Economics," reprinted from *The Swedish Journal of Economics* (December 1974).

Mises, Margit von. *My Years With Ludwig von Mises.* New Rochelle, N.Y.: Arlington House, 1976; 2nd enlarged edition: Cedar Falls, Iowa: Center for Futures Education, 1984. An account of Margit's life with Ludwig, their meeting, marriage in Switzerland, and years in New York. Chapter 8 deals with the unfortunate second (1963) Yale edition of *Human Action.* Hayek's 1956 tribute to Mises and Mises' 1962 tribute to Hayek are reprinted in appendices.
>   German translation by Margit von Mises: *Ludwig von Mises: Der Mensch und sein Werk.* Munich: Philosophia Verlag, 1981.
>   Reviewed by:
>>   Brown, Susan Love. *World Research INK* (San Diego). 1:8 (May 1977) 5.
>>   Buckley, Priscilla. *National Review.* (May 13, 1977) 567.
>>   John Chamberlain. *The Freeman.* 27:2 (February 1977) 125-128.
>>   _____. *The Freeman.* 34:10 (October 1984) 635-637.
>>   _____. "The Scholar from Vienna Who Battled Karl Marx." *Barron's.* (February 7, 1977).
>>   Cooper, Richard A. *Humanist Century.* (November 1986).
>>   Ebeling, Richard M. "Life with Mises." *The Libertarian Forum.* (January 1977) 3.
>>   Evans, Medford. *American Opinion.* 20:2 (February 1977) pp.67ff.
>>   Friedman, Milton. *The New American Review.* (November 1977) 35.
>>   Jolly, Ellen Roy. "Reminiscence: Story of Economist Introduces His Work." *Sunday Advocate* (Baton Rouge, La.). (May 15, 1977) 2-E.
>>   Mann, Amy. *The Academic Reviewer.* (Spring-Summer 1979) 1-2.
>>   Peterson, William H. "The Way of the Prophet." *Modern Age.* 21:3 (Summer 1977) 320-323.
>>   Pietrusza, David A. *Reason.* (February 1978) 45.
>>   Rothbard, Murray N. "The Human Side of von Mises." *Human Events.* (December 25, 1976) 988-989.
>>   _____. *Libertarian Review.* (January-February 1977) 4.

R.J.R. [Rousas J. Rushdooney]. *Chalcedon Report* #183. (November 1977).

Spangler, Mark. *The Entrepreneur* (Grove City College, Grove City, Penna.). 2:3 (May 1977).

Moss, Laurence S., ed. *The Economics of Ludwig von Mises: Toward a Critical Reappraisal.* Kansas City [Mission, Kansas]: Sheed and Ward, 1976. Papers presented November 15, 1974 at the Southern Economic Association meeting, Atlanta, Georgia. Book includes a chronology of the major events in Mises' life, and a list of his major translated works.

Baumgarth, William. "Ludwig von Mises and the Justification of the Liberal Order." 79-99. Quotes many pertinent passages from Mises' *The Free and Prosperous Commonwealth* or *Liberalism* (B-6).

Kirzner, Israel M. "Ludwig von Mises and the Theory of Capital and Interest." 51-65. Contrasts Mises' theory with the productivity theory of interest held by Frank H. Knight and shows Knight's theory to be holistic, mechanical and, thus, inconsistent with modern subjective value theory. Reprinted in the Kirzner anthology, *Perception, Opportunity, and Profit* (1979); also in *Austrian Economics II.* Stephen Littlechild, ed. (Aldershot, Hants, England; Brookfield, Vt.: Edward Elgar, 1990) pp.93-107.

Machlup, Fritz. "Opening Remarks: Mises, Keynes, and the Question of Influence." 9-12. Machlup says Keynes credits Mises with having first introduced (1912) into the economic literature the distinction which he, Keynes "made between Savings and Investment." Yet, Machlup says, Keynes later confessed to an inability to comprehend ideas expressed in the German language. (p.10)

_____. "Closing Remarks." 111-116.

Moss, Laurence S. "Introduction." 1-8.

_____. "The Monetary Economics of Ludwig von Mises." 13-49. Much of this lengthy paper is phrased in the terminology of mechanics and 'aggregate' economics. Moss misrepresents Mises' position in several respects.

Rothbard, Murray N. "Ludwig von Mises and Economic Calculation under Socialism." 67-77. Reviews the history of the debate concerning the possibility of economic calculation under socialism. Compares a completely socialist world with a world "under the exclusive, monopolistic control of One Big Firm."

Vaughn, Karen I. "Critical Discussion of the Four Papers." 101-110.

Nash, George H. *The Conservative Movement in America: Since 1945.* New York: Basic Books, 1976. Although admittedly Mises was not a "conservative," Nash notes that his anti-socialist, laissez-faire, pro-capitalist writings "did not go unnoticed." (p.12)   "Single books usually do not instantly turn ideological tides. Still, it would be difficult to exaggerate the contributions of Friedrich Hayek and Ludwig von Mises to the intellectual rehabilitation of individualism in America at the close of World War II. One right-wing journalist, William Henry Chamberlin, called the redoubtable Mises (whom he knew personally) 'a true St. George fighting the dragon of collectivism'." (p.13)

New Libertarian Weekly. "Libertarians Have Own Money Now!" 47 (November 7, 1976) 1. Announces production by the Ludwig von Mises Mint (Ft. Collins, Colorado) of Mises "Barter Medallions" with Mises' profile on the front, available in silver, gold and platinum. The coins are called "medallions" because only the U.S. government can mint "coins."

North, Gary. "The Austrian School of Economics." *Fall Notes: 1976.* H. F. Langenberg, Reinholdt & Gardner, St. Louis, Mo. 32 (1976) 49-55. North contrasts the Chicago and Keynesian schools with the Austrian School. "The tiny Austrian School is the most rapidly growing intellectual force among modern economists (p.50) . . . . ¶The most famous 'Austrian' is the 1974 co-Nobel Prize winner, F. A. Hayek . . . . Other living economists who are traditional Austrian School representatives are Israel Kirzner (the inheritor of Ludwig von Mises' mantle), Ludwig Lachmann, Hans Sennholz, William Peterson . . . .

also several journalists and other social scientists who are favorable to Austrian economics, such as Percy Greaves, William F. Rickenbacker, Harry Browne, and many of those in the 'gold bug' financial newsletter camp. Of course, the staff of the Foundation for Economic Education (FEE) in Irvington-on-Hudson, New York, are pro-Mises, but FEE is concerned with the transmission of introductory economic ideas rather than front-line economic research. ¶My list has not included Murray Rothbard. Dr. Rothbard affirms the basic methodology of the Austrian School, and he has done the best work in clarifying, popularizing, and applying the ideas of the late Ludwig von Mises, the 'dean' of the Austrian School until his death in 1973. But Prof. Rothbard is a philosophical anarchist, unlike the traditional Austrian School members . . . . Only Prof. Kirzner is 'respectable' within academic circles (p.51) . . . . ¶[T]he Austrians produce no statistical monographs (p.53) . . . . ¶Professional Austrian economists simply refuse to make specific economic predictions, except as personal recommendations . . . . ¶The great strength of the Austrian School is its readability. Intelligent laymen, given enough time and effort can master the language and logic of Austrian economics. The mathematics is simple or nonexistent; the equations are verbal, and not really equations anyway; the perspective -- anti-socialistic, anti-inflationist -- is correct; and the system can be taught without computer-laden academic programs." (p.55)

_____. "Monetary Deflation." *Remnant Review*. 3:10 (May 19, 1976) 57-58. "One of the basic tenets of Prof. Ludwig von Mises' monetary theory was that government policies of monetary inflation eventually produce the boom-bust cycle. Yet a less well known aspect of Mises' *practical application* of his theory was his advocacy of stable money, i.e, anti-monetary deflation . . . . Mises also recommended free banking, i.e., commercial banking unprotected by government licensing of fractional reserves. In fact, he once admitted that government-mandated 100% reserve banking would be preferable to what we have now. (*Human Action*, 1949 ed., p.439)."

Reason. Santa Barbara, Calif. "Austrian Economic Conferences." Frontlines column. (June 1976) 120-121. Discusses "the Austrian road show," Joey Rothbard's term for the conferences held in Virginia, New Jersey, Connecticut, Vermont and Wisconsin, all with essentially the same cast of speakers. In Milwaukee, "James Buchanan told the conference that the idea of economic harmony is a quasi-religious concept . . . . ¶Mario Rizzo. . . argued that it was extremely important for Austrian economists to steer clear of any quasi-religious or normative claims, even though these might be quite effective with some people. As a scientific paradigm, Rizzo asserted, the epistemology of Austrian economics is just as valid -- if not more valid -- than the paradigm of the Chicago school, or 'positive economics.' It would be harmful in both the long and short run if economic 'scientists' were able to use Buchanan's argument against him, to dismiss Austrian theory as mere economic 'religion.' ¶Mises would have been proud."

Robbins, Lord. *Political Economy: Past and Present. A Review of Leading Theories of Economic Policy*. New York: Columbia University Press, 1976. "There is a passing reference in a review by Mill [to planning production under collectivism] . . . . It was not until the early 1920s that the problem attracted wide attention when von Mises, the Austrian economist, in his famous work on Socialism, *Die Gemeinwirtschaft* (B-4), boldly asserted that economic calculation would be out of the question in communities where there existed no markets in services and other means of production and that therefore, in such conditions, rational production would be impossible (*unmöglich*). ¶As might be expected, this contention aroused much debate . . . . But its insolubility was denied, and various solutions were suggested . . . . ¶Now impossible (*unmöglich*) is a strong word; and I have no doubt at all that von Mises deprived his position of much of its force by using it. It is true that he was using it in regard to what he called rational production, production which responded as nearly as possible to the demands of consumers and investors . . . . But be that as it may, the use of such a word in a world in which Collectivist systems were churning out vast quantities of stuff which, whether or not it corresponded to the von Mises ideal of rationality, had *some* use for *some* purposes, was bound to give rise to scepticism. This was a pity because there is much more substance in the von Mises position than is usually supposed." (pp.143-144)

Schultz, Helen E. *Economic Calculation Under Inflation.* Indianapolis: Liberty Fund, 1976. Papers presented at a
   Liberty Fund conference, February 1975. Two brief mentions of Mises, as follows:
   Fabricant, Solomon. "Economic Calculation Under Inflation: The Problem in Perspective." 21-63. "[I]n
      a free society, as was pointed out above all by Mises and Hayek, individuals have the authority
      and the incentives to use the particular knowledge which they -- and only they -- possess to
      adapt most economically to the incessant changes that go on in a dynamic world.*" (p.30)
         *"Many people are familiar with the idea that capitalism is efficient and free, at any rate
         relative to other systems, but not with the idea that capitalism is efficient in substantial part
         because it is free. The idea helps us to understand the difficulties encountered by Soviet Russia
         in its effort to reach a 'Western' -- a capitalistic -- level of economic efficiency . . . . ¶The
         analysis by Mises . . . was made shortly after World War I, in the course of a theoretical
         examination of the possibility of rational economic calculation in a socialist economy.
         Soviet Russia's experience since then has provided some concrete information on the relation
         between rational economic calculation and economic and political freedom, something that
         Hayek also had very much in mind, and to which Burns referred in his warning of the menace of
         inflation. Understanding has grown in Russia of the limitations of a centralized planning
         agency in acquiring and utilizing effectively all the information about consumer demand and
         production possibilities that is needed for the efficient allocation of resources. There has
         consequently been a good deal of discussion there about the desirability and feasibility of a
         system of decentralized decisions, and even some hesitant movement towards something like a
         profit incentive and freer price system. The trend has been hesitant because it is also realized
         that such a move would lead to, and its success require, a degree of economic freedom
         incompatible with the tight control Party stalwarts feel to be essential." (p.30n)
   Fletcher, William H. "Economic Calculation by Capital Intensive Industries During Periods of
      Inflation." 217-246. "The late Ludwig von Mises, modern leader of the Austrian school of
      economics, seems to indicate that all indices are imperfect. The preparers of indices change
      the basis of computation from time to time, and it is probable that indices controlled by
      political bodies are biased by political considerations." (p.224)

White, Lawrence H. "Entrepreneurship, Imagination, and the Question of Equilibration." Unpublished 1976 paper.
   15pp. White argues "that the pervasive uncertainty faced by entrepreneurs, stressed by Mises but
   deliberately downplayed in Kirzner, suggests speculation or *imagination* more than alertness to be
   characteristic of entrepreneurship." Reprinted in *Austrian Economics: III.* Stephen Littlechild, ed.
   (Aldershot, Hants, England; Brookfield, Vt.: Edward Elgar, 1990) pp.87-104.

World Research, Inc. *The Incredible Bread Machine Study Guide.* San Diego, Calif., 1976. 263pp. A study guide
   for the film based on the 1974 book, *The Incredible Bread Machine* (see "Books and Articles About
   Mises: 1974," Brown). Mises is cited on pp.45-46, 89 and 131.

Wriston, Walter B. "Blue Eagles and Déjà Vu." *Politics vs. Prosperity.* V. Orval Watts, ed. Midland, Mich.: Pendell
   Publishing Co., 1976. pp.19-26. "There is no case of government planning not implemented in the end
   by coercion. ¶If proponents of central planning came right out and said they wanted to create an
   economic police state, their cause would never get off the ground. So, they resort to 'doublespeak,' as
   Mario Pei so aptly called it, the usual camouflage for the ultimate use of force against the individual.
   ¶Ludwig von Mises summed it up when he wrote: 'All this talk: the state should do this or that
   ultimately means: the police should force consumers to behave otherwise than they would behave
   spontaneously. In such proposals as: let us raise farm prices, let us raise wage rates, let us lower profits
   . . . the *us* ultimately refers to the police. Yet, the authors of these projects protest that they are planning
   for freedom and industrial democracy.'" (p.23)

Yeager, Leland B. "Toward Understanding Some Paradoxes in Capital Theory." *Economic Inquiry.* 14 (September
   1976) 313-346.

1977

Aldcroft, Derek H. *From Versailles to Wall Street 1919-1929.* Allen Lane [University of California Press], 1977. Referring to Murray N. Rothbard's stand that the banking system was responsible for the 1930s depression and that the economy could best adjust without government interference: "It is hard to believe that as late as the 1960s such an anti-Keynesian stance could be adopted. Rothbard's thesis is based on the Austrian theory of the trade cycle and his great mentor is Ludwig von Mises." (p.276n.)

Block, Walter. "Austrian Monopoly Theory -- A Critique." *Journal of Libertarian Studies.* Oxford, England; Elmsford, N.Y.: Pergamon Press. 1:4 (Fall 1977) 271-279. An analysis of the "two views of monopoly within what might be called the broad Austrian camp," i.e. the Mises-Kirzner and the Rothbard views. Block is critical of the Mises-Kirzner view principally because "there is simply no scientific way of establishing whether any given price that exists on the market is a monopolistic price, or not." (p.279) Block notes what he considers inconsistencies in Mises and Kirzner statements.

Cook, James R. "The Teacher." *The New Agora.* (January 14, 1977). Discusses Mises' accomplishments. Reprinted in *IRI Insights* (Minneapolis, Minn.). 1:2 (January/February 1981) 12-14.

Ebeling, Richard M. "On the Theory of Costs." *Austrian Economics Newsletter.* New York: Center for Libertarian Studies. 1:1 (Autumn 1977) 8-9. Credits Mises with recognizing "the link between subjectivism and opportunity cost." Reprinted in *Austrian Economics: I.* Stephen Littlechild, ed. (Aldershot, Hants, England; Brookfield, Vt.: Edward Elgar, 1990) pp.253-254.

Freeman, Roger A. "The Growth of American Government: a Lecture." The Ludwig von Mises lecture series. Stanford: Hoover Institution, Stanford University, 1977. 19pp.

Friedman, Milton. *The New American Review.* (November 1977) 34-35. In a review of Margit von Mises' *My Years with Ludwig von Mises* (1976): "A coin has two sides. Von Mises' greatness as an economist, his extraordinary influence on a wide range of followers, the hero worship he attracted -- all these derived from his inflexible honesty, with the 'inflexible' element as important as the 'honesty' element. But the other side of that coin was intransigence, even dogmatism, that bordered on intolerance for anyone who did not wholly agree with him. He was a cultivated and civilized person who was, except for . . . occasional outbursts . . . uniformly polite, so his intolerance never took personally objectionable form, but it was there and has been magnified -- as unfortunate traits so often are -- in some of his disciples."

Greaves, Bettina Bien. "Persona Grata: An Interview with Margit von Mises (March 21, 1977)." *World Research INK.* San Diego. 1:8 (May 1977) 7-9, 12. For annotation, see below: Mises, Margit von.

_____. "Mises Misunderstood." *Occasional Review: A Journal of Contemporary Thought in the Humanities, Arts & Social Sciences.* San Diego, Calif.: World Research, Inc. 6 (Summer 1977) 95-110. A review of *The Economics of Ludwig von Mises.* Laurence S. Moss, ed. (see "Books and Articles About Mises: 1976"). "The papers vary tremendously in quality," the reviewer writes. She then devotes most space to the longest paper in the anthology, the editor's "The Monetary Economics of Ludwig von Mises." Moss undoubtedly admires Professor Mises, she says, "and in some passages he reveals a fair understanding of some of Mises' work." However, she states: "Much of Moss' paper is phrased in the terminology of mechanics and 'aggregate' economics, which Mises criticized so rigorously."

Grinder, Walter E. "In Pursuit of the Subjective Paradigm." *Capital, Expectations, and the Market Process: Essays on the Theory of the Market Economy* by Ludwig M. Lachmann. Kansas City [Mission,

Kansas]: Sheed Andrews and McMeel, 1977. pp.3-24. In this Introduction to the Lachmann anthology, Grinder reviews the important events in Lachmann's life and intellectual development. It is "the thoroughgoing subjectivism of Menger, Mises, and, interestingly enough, Max Weber that Lachmann identified as the true heritage of the Austrian school." (p.4) Grinder points to Lachmann's agreements and disagreements with Mises. Lachmann's essays in this anthology that refer to Mises are cited and annotated in this bibliography under "Books and Articles About Mises" in the year in which they first appeared.

Hayek, Friedrich. "Persona Grata: Interview." *World Research INK.* San Diego. 1:12 (September 1977) 7-9. Hayek was interviewed by a group of young people at World Research. Although Hayek had his "old friend Mises" and one or two other friends with similar beliefs, he had generally felt alone, "isolated from the world," even after the publication in 1944 of his *The Road to Serfdom.* As a young man, after two years in the army, dissatisfaction with society had led him to study economics, which soon convinced him that his plans for social reform wouldn't work. He "had the good fortune of getting in an office, a temporary wartime office, to settle prewar private debts between the countries in the war, and my supervisor became Ludwig von Mises." Then "at a very decisive phase of my development, 1922 when I was 23, Mises' book on socialism came out and that cured me forever. However I must say, that while Mises was absolutely convincing in his conclusions, I never found his argument perfectly satisfactory."

High, Jack. "From Realistic Theory Comes Sensible Advice." *Barron's.* (July 11, 1977). A review of *The Foundations of Modern Austrian Economics.* Edwin G. Dolan, ed. (See "Books and Articles About Mises: 1976," Dolan.) "At the turn of the century, Austrian economists were amicably debating the English and French schools, and were bitterly disputing German Socialists. During the next three decades, the Austrians won many of their points, and younger members of the class -- notable Ludwig von Mises and F. A. von Hayek -- introduced several new ideas . . . . In 1930, the success of this school seemed assured; by 1950, the school was nearly extinct, ¶Causes of its death were largely political. The Austrians had demonstrated that intervention would lead to chaos. Naturally, then, Hitler's take-over of Austria made these economists unwelcome in their homeland (Mises' library was seized and destroyed by the Nazis) . . . . ¶In 1950, few traces of Austrian influence were to be found in economic theory. Moreover, neither Mises nor Hayek, leaders of the school, had a respected academic position from which to extend his influence. Prospects were bleak. ¶Publication of *The Foundations of Modern Austrian Economics* is an event no one would have imagined 25 years ago."

Kregel, J. A. "On the Existence of Expectations in English Neoclassical Economics." *Journal of Economic Literature.* 15:2 (1977) 495-500. Comments on Ludwig M. Lachmann's "From Mises to Shackle" (for annotation of Lachmann's article, see "Books and Articles About Mises: 1976").

Lavoie, Don C. "From Hollis and Nell to Hollis and Mises." *Journal of Libertarian Studies.* Oxford, England; Elmsford, N.Y.: Pergamon Press. 1:4 (Fall 1977) 325-336. A review-essay of *Rational Economic Man* (Cambridge, 1975) by Martin Hollis and Edward J. Nell who, Lavoie says, are respectively rationalist philosopher and orthodox Marxian economist. "Hollis and Nell demonstrate that economics must be a deductive science . . . . In making this claim [they] align themselves with a point of view that has been completely neglected by the economic Establishment: the praxeological approach of Ludwig von Mises and the Austrian school." Lavoie agrees with Hollis' and Nell's critique of positivism and their "dissection of positivist methodology." But he finds that the authors, especially Nell, go astray in other respects.

Littlechild, Stephen C. "Change Rules O.K.?" Inaugural Lecture, University of Birmingham, England, May 28, 1977. Published in *Austrian Economics: I.* Stephen Littlechild, ed. (Aldershot, Hants, England; Brookfield, Vt.: Edward Elgar, 1990) pp.150-165. Mentions Mises as a member of the "second generation" of the Austrian School. "Since not all Austrians are enthusiastic about the use of mathematics, it is worth pointing out that Mises believed such imaginary constructions, albeit unrealistic, were both appropriate and indispensable for treating certain problems." Littlechild calls "received economic theory" deficient in that it is "a static equilibrium theory which fails to accommodate change." He points to "exciting new possibilities for research and teaching in economics, and for the conduct of industrial policy."

Mises, Margit von. "Persona Grata: An Interview (March 21, 1977)" by Bettina Bien Greaves. *World Research INK.* San Diego. 1:8 (May 1977) 7-9, 12. Mrs. Mises reminisced about her life with Mises along the lines of her 1976 book. Concerning their early years in the States: "It wasn't easy in the beginning. Henry Hazlitt was a big help. Lu had been in touch with Hazlitt before as a result of the review that Harry wrote for the *New York Times* of the English edition of Lu's *Socialism* (B-4) . . . . ¶Of course, he [Mises] knew English. He lectured once in a while in English and he had written some English articles. But he never knew English as well as he did French. French he really *did* know very well. And he spoke it well! He didn't have that strong accent which he had in English . . . . ¶[H]e read for an hour in the morning. He read the *New York Times* very, very thoroughly. And then he read the *Wall Street Journal.* He always bought a paper at night also, when there were evening papers. But he didn't keep any clipping files, just books and pamphlets. History and the development of political events . . . were two of his greatest loves."

Nozick, Robert. "On Austrian Methodology." *Synthese.* 36 (November 1977) 353-392. According to Block, Nozick "focuses on four main tenets of Austrianism, or praxeology: methodological individualism, the *a priori* nature of human action, and the concepts of indifference and time-preference (p.397) . . . . ¶Nozick objects to Mises's supposed contention that acting man will always act rationally (p.413). . . . ¶Nozick goes on to consider and criticize Mises's views on time-preference (p.432)." And more in the same vein. Comments quoted from Block's "On Robert Nozick's 'On Austrian Methodology'." *Inquiry.* 23 (December 1980) 397-444.

O'Driscoll, Gerald P. Jr. *Economics as a Coordination Problem: The Contributions of Friedrich A. Hayek.* Foreword by F. A. Hayek. Kansas City [Mission, Kansas]: Sheed Andrews and McMeel, 1977. Based on O'Driscoll's Ph.D. dissertation. Refers briefly to Mises. For instance: "Hayek constructed his monetary theory upon the foundations laid by early British monetary theorists and Knut Wicksell and Ludwig von Mises. (p.37) . . . ¶In an odd way the success of Mises's work hurt it. As Robbins noted, the ideas worked their way slowly into Anglo-Saxon monetary theory, despite the wide currency of his ideas on the Continent. By the 1930s English-speaking economists could no longer recognize the revolutionary character of *The Theory of Money and Credit.* ¶Mises extended the Wicksellian theory by explicitly examining the differential impact on demand for consumption and capital goods brought about by a divergence between loan and natural interest rates. (p.45) ¶Hayek referred to Mises's theory as the Wicksell-Mises's theory." (pp.46)

Reason. Santa Barbara, Calif. Trends column: "J. M. Keynes, R.I.P." (February 1977) 11-12. "The idea that government fiscal and monetary policies can significantly alter GNP and employment has been an article of faith for most of the past several decades . . . . The principal dissenters . . . have been the monetarists, led by Milton Friedman, and the Austrians, such as Ludwig von Mises and F. A. Hayek . . . . ¶This Austrian insight has suddenly become the hottest new theoretical development in economics, thanks to Robert E. Lucas, Jr. . . . , Neil Wallace and Thomas J. Sargent," whose "rational expectations" theory is discussed in *Business Week* (November 8, 1976).

Skousen, Mark. *Economics of a Pure Gold Standard* (1977). 2nd ed. Auburn, Ala.: Praxeology Press, Ludwig von Mises Institute, 1988. Reviews the history of money and banking throughout the ages. Then discusses proposals for 100% specie reserves, a pure specie standard, and free banking. Quotes Mises frequently: "Mises sees no fraudulent behavior in the development of fractional reserve banking (p.84) . . . . ¶Ludwig von Mises, perhaps the most vocal supporter of 'free banking' in this century, maintains that privileged monopolistic banks, under state charters, are responsible in the main for over-issue, bank runs and economic disasters . . . . ¶According to Mises, there are two natural forces which limit the increase in fiduciary media: first, suspicions of the public which would increase redemptions and a possible run on the bank; and second, too rapid a rise in prices causing a move into 'real values'." (p.90)

_____. *Playing the Price Controls Game: How Some People Will Profit from the Coming Controls.* New Rochelle, N.Y.: Arlington House, 1977. "Government has never been inclined to sit idly by and watch the unwelcome effects of its policies take hold. Instead, it seeks to deal with shortages, black markets, quality deterioration, distortions, and queues of angry consumers by extending even further its arm of authority . . . . ¶Ludwig von Mises was one of the first economists to recognize this universal tendency of gradual government expansion of its powers under economic controls." (pp.121-122) Skousen then quotes at length from Mises' "Middle-of-the-Road Policy Leads to Socialism" (Article 50.4).

Spangler, Mark. "Remembering Ludwig von Mises." *The Entrepreneur.* Grove City, Penna.: Grove City College. 2:2 (January 1977) 2-3. "Truths are not determined by popularity contests. Columbus was ridiculed for concluding the earth was spherical as was Copernicus for thinking the sun is the center of the solar system, yet this knowledge is valid. Mises' writings cannot be dismissed as invalid simply because they are unpopular. Mises' contributions to economic knowledge deserve to be remembered. Even more, can they be ignored without bringing economic ruin to mankind?"

Summers, Brian. "The Economics of Ludwig von Mises." *World Research INK.* San Diego. 1:8 (May 1977) 3, 11. "Mises was able to see farther than others because while other economists examined aggregates . . . Mises consistently focused his attention on individuals. By considering the goals, plans, and actions of individuals, Mises was able to develop economics into the coherent science he described in *Human Action* (1949) -- the first general treatise on economics to be published since World War I."

White, Lawrence H. *Methodology of the Austrian School* (Occasional Paper #1). New York: Center for Libertarian Studies, 1977. Includes sections on Menger, Wieser, Böhm-Bawerk, Mises, Hayek, Lachmann, Kirzner and Rothbard. "What unifies this school of thought . . . is the methodological outlook of its members: subjectivism." (p.4) "Following his teacher [Böhm-Bawerk] on many facets of theory, Mises nonetheless developed an entirely different epistemological defense for his views. A neo-Kantian, he denied the possibility of arriving at laws by induction and defended the possibility of a purely *a priori* system of economic theory which he labelled 'praxeology.'" (p.15) Reprinted as *The Methodology of the Austrian School Economists.* (Auburn, Ala.: Ludwig von Mises Institute, 1984). Also reprinted in *Austrian Economics, I.* Stephen Littlechild, ed. (Aldershot, Hants, England; Brookfield, Vt.: Edward Elgar, 1990) pp.371-407.

Wolf-Thieberger, Therisia. "Should Old Acquaintance . . ." *World Research INK.* San Diego. 1:14 (December 1977) 4. Mises' secretary in Vienna (1910 to October 1934) comments on the interview with Professor Hayek (*World Research INK*. September 1977) annotated above. She was "surprised" that Hayek did not mention how his friendship with Mises developed. "Professor Hayek was a pupil of Professor Mises." Austria-Hungary had lost World War I. "In the following years," she said, "it was very hard to get any job. To enable Hayek to get one, Prof. Mises, who was already famous all over Europe and had great influence . . . . founded the 'Österreichisches Konjunkturinstitut' (Austrian Institute for Business Cycle Research) . . . And it was Professor Mises who appointed Hayek as director of this Österreichisches Konjunkturinstitut. Prof. Mises, of course, remained the head of it."

1978

Browne, Harry. *New Profits from the Monetary Crisis.* New York: William Morrow, 1978. Browne's Suggested
    Readings include books by Mises and Misesians. In Browne's "Acknowledgments": "[A] lot of what I
    understand about economics has come from the late Ludwig von Mises. I sometimes think he's the only
    man who ever lived who was capable of understanding the whole world. His books, while not easy to
    read, provide the ultimate explanation of human action. ¶I began reading the books of von Mises only in
    the last few years. Prior to that, I had been exposed to his ideas through the works of his intellectual
    descendants -- particularly Murray N. Rothbard, Henry Hazlitt, and Alvin Lowi." (p.453)

Ebeling, Richard M. & Gary G. Short. "An Interview With Ludwig Lachmann." *Austrian Economics Newsletter.*
    New York: Center for Libertarian Studies. 1:3 (Fall 1978) 1-2, 11, 15. For annotation, see Lachmann
    below.

_____ & Don Lavoie. "Equality, Planning, and the Market Economy: An interview with Austrian economist
    Ludwig Lachmann." *Libertarian Review.* San Francisco. (April 1978) 17-22. For annotation, see
    Lachmann below.

Greaves, Percy L., Jr., "Ludwig von Mises on Currency Depreciation and Gold." *Gold Newsletter.* New Orleans:
    National Committee for Monetary Reform. 7:4 (April 1978) 1. "Over the years our leaders in academia,
    the mass media and both major political parties have been swept off their feet by the mad delusion that
    paper money can buy permanent prosperity. Their self-deception now exceeds that of the 14th and 15th
    century alchemists, the 16th century tulipomaniacs and the early 18th century followers of John Law.
    There was one man who kept his feet on solid ground and his mind on sound money -- the very essence
    of a market system, the only practical process for raising mass living standards. That man was Ludwig
    von Mises. He devoted his long life to detecting and dissecting the major economic problem of our
    century."

Grice-Hutchinson, Marjorie. *Early Economic Thought in Spain: 1177-1740.* London: George Allen & Unwin,
    1978. "John Law (1671-1729) was recognised by L. Mises as a forerunner of the Austrian school on
    account of his subjective theory of value, which he applied to money as well as goods." (p.114)

Hanusch, Horst, pub. *Der Betriebswirt: Theorie und Praxis für Führungskräfte* [The Business Manager: Theory
    and Practice for Leadership]. Concerning the posthumous publication of *Im Namen des Staates oder die
    Gefahren des Kollektivismus* (B-25), the early German-language version of *Omnipotent Government* (B-
    12): "In our fast moving time of ever increasing knowledge, names fade very fast, even the names of
    those whose ideas have influenced their generation. Among these names is that of von Mises. To many
    who have dealt with economics the name of this great liberal economist who has embodied the tradition
    of the Austrian School and enlightened liberalism is known only through the history of economic
    principles and ideas. Now, more than five years after his death, it is surprising that it is not his major
    work, *The Theory of Money* (B-2) that appeared in 1912 and which is no longer available, that has
    been published again . . . . but rather a manuscript von Mises wrote in 1939 at the Graduate Institute for
    International Studies in Switzerland." (Translated from the German)

Hayek, F. A. "Coping With Ignorance." *Imprimis.* Hillsdale, Mich.: Hillsdale College. 7:7 (July 1978). An
    address in the Ludwig von Mises Lecture Series. "It was essentially his [Mises'] second great work, *Die
    Gemeinwirtschaft* of 1922, which appeared in English translation only fifteen years later as *Socialism* (B-
    4), that completely won me over to his views. And then in his *Privatseminar*, as we called the little
    discussion group which met at his office, I became gradually intimately familiar with his thinking . . . .
    ¶I have perhaps most profited from his teaching because I was not initially his student at the university,

an innocent young man who took his word for gospel, but came to him as a trained economist, trained in a parallel branch of Austrian economics from which he gradually, but never completely, won me over. Though I learned that he usually was right in his conclusions, I wasn't always satisfied by his arguments, and retained to the end a certain critical attitude which sometimes forced me to build different constructions, which however, to my great pleasure, usually led to the same conclusions . . . . ¶It is the obscuring of the empirical fact of people learning what others do by a process of communication of knowledge which has always made me reluctant to accept von Mises' claim of an *a priori* character of the whole of economic theory." Reprinted in *Champions of Freedom*, 5. Cheryl A. Yurchis, ed. Hillsdale, Michigan: Hillsdale College Press, 1979) pp.13-28.

_____. *New Studies in Philosophy, Politics, Economics and the History of Ideas.* Chicago: University of Chicago Press, 1978. A collection of Hayek papers. Mentions Mises as follows:

"The Errors of Constructivism." 3-22. Lecture at University of Salzburg (January 27, 1970): "The recognition of the defects of these [socialist] plans is now generally and justly ascribed to the great discussion which was started in the 1920s by the writings of Ludwig von Mises. But we should not overlook how many of the important points had been clearly seen earlier by some economists." Hayek then quotes from a German-language (1879) article by Erwin Nasse. (p.15n) This lecture previously published only in German as "Die Irrtümer des Konstruktivismus und die Grundlagen legitimer Kritik gesellschaftlicher Gebilde" (Munich, 1970; reprinted Tübingen, 1975).

"Personal Recollections of Keynes and the 'Keynesian Revolution'." 283-289. Keynes "did not read any foreign language except French -- or, as he once said of himself, in German he could understand only what he knew already. It is a curious fact that before the First World War he had reviewed L. von Mises' Theory *of Money* for the *Economic Journal* . . . without in any way profiting from it." (p.284) N.B.: Keynes' review of *The Theory of Money and Credit* (B-2) reprinted above in Book Review section, pp.182-183. This essay by Hayek previously published in *Oriental Economist*. Tokyo. (January 1966).

"Socialism and Science," 295-308. Lecture to the Canberra Branch of the Economic Society of Australia and New Zealand (October 19, 1976): "What play has not been made with occasional passages in the work of the greatest scientific critic of socialism, Ludwig von Mises, in which he described socialism as 'impossible'; Mises obviously meant that the proposed methods of socialism could not achieve what they were supposed to do! (p.297) . . . ¶The founders of socialism, including Marx and Engels, did not even understand that any central direction of the machinery of production owned by society required, if resources were to be effectively used, calculations in terms of value . . . . Even when discussion of the problem was seriously started, immediately after the First World War, it was caused by the social science expert among the Vienna school of logical positivists claiming that all calculations of the efficiency of social production could be carried out *in natura* . . . . It was against this position that Ludwig von Mises and some of his contemporaries (including Max Weber) developed the first decisive critique of the socialist position . . . . ¶So the first attempt by the socialists to answer the critique by Mises and others soon collapsed." (pp.301-303) This lecture previously unpublished. Reprinted in *The Essence of Hayek.* Chiaki Nishiyama & Kurt R. Leube, eds. (Stanford, Calif.: Hoover Institution Press, 1984) pp.114-127.

"Inflation, the Misdirection of Labour, and Unemployment." 197-209. For annotation of this lecture, see "Books and Articles About Mises: 1975," Hayek.

_____. "Can We Still Avoid Inflation?" *The Austrian Theory of the Trade Cycle and Other Essays* (Occasional Paper No. 8). New York: Center for Libertarian Studies. (1978) 35-44. Lecture delivered May 18, 1970, in Tarrytown, N. Y., before the Board of Trustees and guests of the Foundation for Economic Education. "The whole conventional analysis reproduced in most textbooks proceeds as if a rise in average prices meant that all prices rise at the same time by more or less the same percentage, or that this at least was true of all prices determined currently on the market, leaving out only a few prices fixed by decree or long term contracts, such as public utility rates, rents and various conventional fees. But this is not true or even possible. The crucial point is that so long as the flow of money expenditure continues to grow and prices of commodities and services are driven up, the different prices must rise, not at the same time but *in succession*, and that in consequence, so long as this process continues, the prices which rise first must all the time move ahead of the others. This distortion of the whole price structure will disappear only sometime after the process of inflation has stopped. This is a fundamental point which the master of all of us, Ludwig von Mises, has never tired from emphasizing for the past sixty years." (p. 36) Entire booklet, with this Hayek lecture plus papers by Rothbard, Haberler, and Mises (Article 36.6), reprinted 1983 (Ludwig von Mises Institute, Auburn, Ala.).

_____. "Einleitung" [Foreword], (May 1977, Lisbon). *Erinnerungen von Ludwig von Mises*, 1978 (German version of *Notes and Recollections*. B-23) xi-xvi. "Certainly the reasons why Mises never received a regular professorship at a German language university during the 1920s, or before 1933 . . . were rarely objective. His employment would have benefited any such university. Yet the ordinary professors felt instinctively, and with some justification, that Mises would not completely blend into their circle. His knowledge of professional science went beyond that of most occupants of professorial chairs, to be sure, but he was never a true departmental specialist . . . . ¶In spite of his exquisite courtesy in social intercourse and his generally substantial self-control -- Mises *could* explode occasionally -- he was not a person who could successfully conceal his contempt. This drove him into an ever-increasing isolation from specialists, even from those in local Viennese circles with whom he was scientifically and professionally associated. The distance between him and his contemporaries and his students increased when he disassociated himself from the social and political ideas that were coming into prominence . . . . ¶[A] fellow student of Mises . . . . wanted to warn me against betraying the 'social' values in a similar way and against showing too much sympathy for 'discredited' liberalism . . . . [A] Jewish intellectual who justified capitalism was considered some sort of a monstrosity, something unnatural that no one knew how to classify or cope with." (Translated from the German) Another translation of Hayek's Foreword by Hans-Hermann Hoppe in *Austrian Economics Newsletter* (Ludwig von Mises Institute, Auburn, Ala.). (Fall 1988) 1-3.

Kirzner, Israel M. "The Perils of Regulation: A Market-Process Approach" (Law and Economics Center Occasional Paper). Coral Gables, Florida: University of Miami School of Law, ©1978. Discusses the economic calculation debate and comments on the socialist calculation literature: "The textbook literature did not so much ignore the arguments of Mises and Hayek *as it failed to understand the view of the market process, which underlies their critique of socialist calculation* . . . . ¶Lange's response to Mises placed much emphasis on the *'parametric function of prices,* i.e., on the fact that . . . each individual separately regards the actual market prices as given data to which he has to adjust himself'. . . . ¶Mises and Hayek, by contrast, saw the price system under capitalism from a totally different -- an Austrian -- perspective. For these writers, the essence of the market process lies not in the 'parametric' function of price, and not in the perfectly competitive state of equilibrium, but in the rivalrous activity of entrepreneurs taking advantage of disequilibrium conditions." (pp.126-129) Reprinted as Chapter 6 in Kirzner's *Discovery and the Capitalist Process* (University of Chicago Press, 1985) 119-149, from which this passage was quoted. Included in *Austrian Economics: III*. Stephen Littlechild, ed. (Aldershot, Hants, England; Brookfield, Vermont: Edward Elgar, 1990) 211-220.

Kristol, Irving. *Two Cheers for Capitalism*. New York: Basic Books, 1978. Quotes Mises as saying: "Economics . . . abstains from any judgment of value. It is not its task to tell people what ends they should aim at." (pp.59-60) This chapter reprinted in *The Portable Conservative Reader*. Russell Kirk, ed. (Penguin Books, 1982).

Lachmann, Ludwig. "An Interview With . . ." by Richard M. Ebeling & Gary G. Short. *Austrian Economics Newsletter.* New York: Center for Libertarian Studies. 1:3 (Fall 1978) 1-2, 11, 15. Lachmann first read one of Mises methodological articles in the late 1920s and "found it most interesting. In particular the Austrian economics Mises espoused seemed to be something rather different from what I knew from the textbooks."

_____. "Equality, Planning, and the Market Economy: An interview with Austrian economist Ludwig Lachmann" by Richard Ebeling & Don Lavoie. *Libertarian Review.* San Francisco. (April 1978) 17-22. Lachmann studied under Hayek at the London School of Economics in the 1930s. Lachmann states: "I came across one or two of his [Mises'] articles in the late 1920s, read them, and found them fascinating, so I read more of them. It was through reading Mises that I first came across Hayek in German, too." (p.18)

Leube, Kurt R. "Wer sind die 'Austrians"?" [Who are the Austrians?]. *Wirtschaftspolitische Blätter* (1978).

Littlechild, Stephen C. *The Fallacy of the Mixed Economy: An 'Austrian' Critique of Conventional 'Mainstream' Economics and of British Economic Policy"* (Hobart Paper 80). London: Institute of Economic Affairs, 1978. An historical sketch of the Austrian School and a discussion of economic planning, nationalization of industries and restrictions on monopoly in Britain from the "Austrian" viewpoint. Mises is cited. Revised for American readers and reprinted as *The Fallacy of the Mixed Economy: An 'Austrian' Critique of Conventional Economics and Government Policy* (CATO Paper No. 2). San Francisco: CATO Institute, 1979).

Machlup, Fritz. *Methodology of Economics and Other Social Sciences.* New York: Academic Press, 1978.

Monatsblätter für freiheitliche Wirtschaftspolitik. Volkmar Muthesius, ed. "Randnoten: Ludwig von Mises" [Marginal Notes]. 24:6 (November/December 1978) 405. A very brief overview of Mises' contributions. Cites the characterization of Mises by his friend and student, F. A. Hayek, as "one of the most original thinkers in the field of economic and social philosophy." Quotes Otto von Habsburg's comment on *Notes and Recollections* (B-23), to the effect that it deals "not so much with recollections of the past as with instructions for the future." According to the commentator (Muthesius ?), this is even more true of the recently published *Im Namen des Staates oder die Gefahren des Kollektivisumus* (B-25), a German-language version of *Omnipotent Government* (B-12). (Translated from the German)

Moorhouse, John C. "The Mechanistic Foundations of Economic Analysis." *Reason Papers.* 4 (Winter 1978) 49-67. Moorhouse contrasts "neoclassical" methodology in economics and the use of mathematics and statistics with Mises' views: "Mises argues that economics is a purely a priori science. Its theorems, like those in mathematics, are logically deduced from a few fundamental axioms . . . . ¶Statistical studies, however useful, represent history, not economics, according to Mises . . . . ¶In spite of the growing interest in Austrian economics . . . these methodological views have not as yet had a significant impact on the discipline. The vast majority of economists continue to reject what T. W. Hutchison refers to as 'the dogmatic and extreme apriorism of Professor Mises' (pp.50-51) . . . . ¶[S]urely the hallmark of an economic process is adaptive, purposive behavior; and that of an economic system, evolutionary change. As Mises and then Hayek have so cogently argued, new knowledge generated as an economic process unfolds implies that initial conditions can never be restored even if an elaborate effort is made to replicate the initial incentive structure." (p.57) Economists should not become "so wedded" to classical mechanics and physics, Moorhouse concludes, as to ignore "the critical insights" the Austrian school can provide toward explaining the "real economic problem . . . the coordination of the bits and pieces of knowledge held by different participants in the market process." (p.64)

Müller-Armack, Alfred. Foreword. *Im Namen des Staates, oder die Gefahren des Kollektivismus* (1978, B-25) 11-15. "Ludwig von Mises has published extensively and enjoyed German and international renown since the beginning of our century. It is a remarkable stroke of luck that a new book, written by him in the German language in Geneva in 1938-9, can now be published in its original text . . . . The book, completed in the spring of 1939 and supplemented in the fall by another chapter, was not published. In 1940 Mises migrated to the United States. The basic ideas it contained were in his first successful English-language book, *Omnipotent Government* (B-12)." (Translated from the German)

Pasour, E. C. Jr. "Cost and Choice -- Austrian vs. Conventional Views." *The Journal of Libertarian Studies.* Oxford, England; Elmsford, N.Y.: Pergamon Press. 2:4 (Winter 1978) 327-336. The "primary purpose" of this paper was "to contrast Austrian and conventional concepts of cost. Cost in the logic-of-choice context of conventional neoclassical economic theory is contrasted with subjective cost relevant to individual decision-making. The Austrian subjectivist concept of cost is shown to be sound as it relates to individual choice." Pasour cites Mises and a number of "latter-day Austrians."

Petro, Sylvester. "Injunctions and Labor-Disputes: 1880-1932." *Wake Forest Law Review.* Winston Salem, N.C. 14:3 (June 1978) 341-576. Discusses Mises' theory of catallactic competition and entrepreneurship. Concerning labor disputes: "A better archetype than class-struggle for the labor-disputes we are investigating would be what Ludwig von Mises calls *catallactic competition*: which is to say, *market-competition*, competition between persons offering largely interchangeable goods and services; competition, in brief, which occurs within rather than between classes." (pp.418-419)

Rothbard, Murray N. Letter to the Editor. *Business Week.* (January 16, 1978) 7. Commenting on Seymour Zucker's "Economic Diary" (December 12) concerning interest rates: The Keynesian and Fisher-Friedman monetarist views are not the only ones, Rothbard says. "There is a third point of view: the Mises-Hayek, or 'Austrian,' position. Austrians fully acknowledge that expectations are not automatic and that an easy money policy will indeed affect real economic activity. ¶But the impact of easy money, according to the Austrians, is radically different from the Keynesian scenario. It is precisely because bank credit expansion and artificially low interest rates are not instantly discounted away that these policies lead to unsound investments that will be seen to be losing investments when the camouflage of credit expansion slows down or ends. In short, easy money policies create, not real economic growth, but malinvestment and the tragedies of the boom-bust business cycle."

Spadaro, Louis M. ed. *New Directions in Austrian Economics.* Kansas City [Mission, Kansas]: Sheed Andrews & McMeel, 1978. Papers presented at a September 1976 Symposium, Windsor Castle, in celebration of the centennial of the "marginalist" revolution in economic theory. Brief mentions and bibliographical citations of Mises by Ludwig Lachmann (pp.10, 12), John B. Egger (pp.19-20, 24-27), Mario J. Rizzo (p.56), S. C. Littlechild (p.81), Gerald P. O'Driscoll (p.123), Roger W. Garrison (pp.169, 173, 176), and Louis M. Spadaro (pp.207-208). Lachmann's contribution reprinted in *Austrian Economics: I.* Stephen Littlechild, ed. (Aldershot, Hants, England; Brookfield, Vermont, 1990); Garrison's paper reprinted as *Austrian Macroeconomics: A Diagrammatical Exposition.* (Institute for Humane Studies, Menlo Park, Calif., 1978). More incisive references to Mises in:

Kirzner, Israel M. "Economics and Error." 57-76. Discusses the views of Mises, Benedetto Croce, Harvey Leibenstein, George Stigler, Alfred Marshall, Lionel Robbins, and others, with respect to error, ignorance, and rationality.

Moss, Laurence S. "The Emergence of Interest in a Pure Exchange Economy: Notes on a Theorem Attributed to Ludwig von Mises." 157-166. Uses formulae representing utility functions and preferred allocations, in his attempt to show "that much of the misunderstanding regarding Mises' interest theory has to do with the special meaning Mises attached to the term *time preference.*"

Rothbard, Murray N. "Austrian Definitions of the Supply of Money." 143-156. Deals with the various categories of money that constitute the "money supply."

Steele, David Ramsay. "Lange's Theory of Socialism After Forty Years." *Austrian Economics Newsletter.* New York: Center for Libertarian Studies. 1:3 (Fall 1978) 4, 12, 14. After discussing the economic calculation debate, Steele concludes: "Lange's scheme was first presented as above all a practical suggestion. Yet it has never been tried and very likely never will be . . . . Today the two most commonly cited refutations of Mises are Lange and the Soviet Union. But the Soviet Union is not practicing the Lange system. We therefore have a 'socialist' society without any satisfactory theoretical explanation, and an allegedly practical theory with no real-world application."

Van Til, L. John, cataloguer. *Inventory of the Private Papers of Ludwig von Mises.* Grove City, Penna.: Grove City College, 1978. Catalogue of Mises' private papers in the Grove City College library. Part I describes pamphlets, reprints, book reviews, etc., collected by Mises; Part II itemizes Mises' personal files--letters, clippings, reprints, reviews, addresses, etc. Includes five pages of biographical information.

Wilczynski, J. *Comparative Monetary Economics: Capitalist and Socialist Monetary Systems and their Interrelations in the Changing International Scene.* Oxford University Press, 1978. "Although in many Western economists' view (such as R. G. Hawtrey, J. M. Keynes, L. von Mises, W. Röpke), business cycles are caused and can be cured by monetary factors, Marxist writers emphatically insist that the sources of capitalist fluctuations are more deep-rooted, going to the very foundations of capitalism -- viz. the private ownership of the means of production, the 'anarchical' market mechanism and the 'antagonistic' production and social relations." (p.216)

1979

Andelson, Robert V., ed. *Critics of Henry George: A Centenary Appraisal of Their Strictures on PROGRESS AND POVERTY*. Rutherford, N.J.: Fairleigh Dickinson, 1979. Two contributors in this anthology refer to Mises: C. Lowell Harriss, in his "Rothbard's Anarcho-Capitalist Critique," identifies Rothbard as "a leading libertarian and student of Ludwig von Mises" (p.354); Oscar B. Johannsen criticizes George Oser's 1974 study of Henry George ("Oser: Reservations of a Friendly Commentator") for his use of statistics and cites Mises on the impossibility of using statistics "to prove or disprove economic principles." (p.372)

Bradley, Robert, Jr. "Compliment to Mises." Letter to the Editor. *Reason*. 11:8 (December 1979) 12. "It is discouraging to see that after all the effort in recent years . . . to raise the level of scholarship regarding the crucial Austrian-Chicago methodological debate, we are back to first base. It is discouraging because Dr. Diamond, in his review of Mises's *Ultimate Foundations* [see "Book Reviews: *The Ultimate Foundation* . . .], ignores the Austrian objections against the Chicago method . . . . ¶As all the positivists before him, Dr. Diamond unwittingly uses the Austrian method to make his points against the very same method . . . . So even though the book review if highly critical of Mises, Dr. Diamond has given the dean of the Austrian economists a backdoor show of support."

Buchanan, James. *What Should Economists Do?* Indianapolis: Liberty Fund, 1979. Only brief references to Mises. Buchanan characterizes Mises' *"general* theory of human action, or choice" as "nonoperational and empirically empty." (p.65)

Davis, John F. (Rev. Msgr.). *This Priest Is Thankful*. Boston: St. Paul Editions, 1979. Davis attended NYU Graduate School of Business Administration. Mises "was pleased to see a priest pursuing a business degree" and encouraged Davis to earn his M.B.A. "Had it not been for von Mises," Davis wrote, "I never would have finished that thesis ["The Monetary Proposals of Major Douglas and the Alberta Experiment in Social Credit"] or received the degree . . . . ¶But it was, as always, a *person* who inspired those years of study and Professor von Mises brought alive the world of economics and especially the free market." (pp.69-70)

Drucker, Peter F. *Adventures of a Bystander*. New York: Harper & Row, 1979. Austrian-born Drucker reminisces about individuals he had known in Vienna. According to Drucker, Annette, a classmate of Mises, was the first woman in Austria to go into economics. "Annette by common consent was the superstar, equally gifted in theory and in mathematical analysis. Even Mises, who was no feminist and did not suffer from undue modesty, admitted her superiority. Years later in the 1950s when Mises was old and very famous, he and I were colleagues at New York University. We did not see much of each other -- Mises considered me a renegade from the true economic faith (with good reason). But one day going down in the elevator together, he turned to me and said: 'You knew Annette, didn't you? If she'd been a man and encouraged to go on, she would have been the greatest economist since Ricardo'." (p.50)

East, John P. "American Conservative Thought: the Impact of Ludwig von Mises." *Modern Age*. Bryn Mawr, Penna.: Intercollegiate Studies Institute. 23:4 (Fall 1979) 338-350. Reviews Mises' contributions and influence: "Out of an eminent group of economists, Ludwig von Mises and his former student, Friedrich A. von Hayek, have emerged as the key economic theorists of American conservative thought since World War II . . . . ¶From the vantage point of Mises' [classical] liberalism, 'The key stone of Western civilization is the sphere of spontaneous action it secures to the individual'. . . . ¶In Mises' analysis the principal enemies of liberalism were positivism, socialism, and interventionism." East quotes Mises' warning that "our civilization is beginning to scent a whiff of death in the air" because of the government intervention. However, East wrote that Mises "quickly counseled, 'Yet, this outcome is not inevitable. It is the goal to which the prevailing trends in our contemporary world are leading. But trends can change and hitherto they always have changed . . . . To accomplish such a change is the task of the rising generation'." Inserted by Senator Jesse Helms in the *Congressional Record,* September 29, 1981 (Vol. 127, No. 137, S10689-91) as a tribute to Mises on the 100th anniversary of his birth. Reprinted in John P. East, *The American Conservative Movement: The Philosophical Founders.* Chicago: Regnery Books, 1986. pp.209-231.

Garrison, Roger W. "In Defense of the Misesian Theory of Interest." *The Journal of Libertarian Studies.* New York: Center for Libertarian Studies. 3:2 (Summer 1979) 141-150. A critique of Laurence S. Moss' "The Emergence of Interest in a Pure Exchange Economy: Notes on a Theorem Attributed to Ludwig von Mises" in *New Directions in Austrian Economics.* Louis M. Spadaro, ed. (See "Books and Articles About Mises: 1978," Spadaro). According to Garrison, Moss' paper "is thoroughly neoclassical rather than Austrian in substance and in form, and hence does not do justice to Mises' theory of interest, which was developed within the context of his own praxeological framework of analysis . . . . ¶[T]he Moss paper starkly points up the fact that if they [present-day economists schooled in the neo-classical tradition] wish to embark on new directions in *Austrian* economics, they had better adopt the Austrian tradition as their point of origin." (p.141)

Gross, David C. "Unsung hero? If Germany had heeded von Mises' theories in 1920s, would Nazism have arisen?" *The Jewish Week-American Examiner.* (Week of June 24, 1979) 38. "One man *can* change the world, and sometimes there are men who might have changed the world, but did not, for a series of reasons that have little or nothing to do with the individual's abilities or genius. One such man was the little known economic thinker, Ludwig von Mises, the grandson of a rabbi, who died in obscurity in New York at the age of 92, virtually unknown to the wide general public, but revered by many leaders of the science of economics . . . . ¶Throughout his lifetime he . . . . preached strongly against inflationism, socialism, interventionism, and won the enmity of many intellectuals, and at the same time the loyalty of many followers who agreed with him that the greatest threat to Western civilization was the shrinking and eventual cessation of the free market . . . . ¶One wonders *if* only Germany had emulated Austria in the 1920s and stopped inflation in its tracks, as taught by the grandson of a rabbi."

Hayek, F A. *Law, Legislation and Liberty 3: The Political Order of a Free People.* Chicago: University of Chicago Press, 1979. Hayek quotes a passage from p.54 of Mises' *Theory and History* (B-20): "The ultimate yardstick of justice is conduciveness to the preservation of social co-operation. Conduct suited to preserve social co-operation is just, conduct detrimental to the preservation of society is unjust." Hayek then comments: "Though this is more rationalistically formulated than I would care to do, it clearly expresses an essential idea. But Mises was of course a rationalist utilitarian in which direction, for reasons given, I cannot follow him." (pp.204-205, n.51).

Hummel, Jeffrey Roger. "Problems With Austrian Business Cycle Theory." *Reason Papers.* 5 (Winter 1979) 41-53.

Hutt, W. H. *The Keynesian Episode: A Reassessment.* Indianapolis: Liberty Fund, 1979. A substantial revision of *Keynesianism -- Retrospect and Prospect,* 1963. (See "Books and Articles About Mises: 1963," Hutt.) Four chapters were omitted, two drastically curtailed, and three new chapters added. References to Mises throughout. "Ludwig von Mises' contention that 'inflation is the fiscal complement of statism and arbitrary government . . . a cog in the complex of policies and institutions which gradually lead toward totalitarianism' has been confirmed by one who might be wrongly interpreted as welcoming this result. Martin Bronfenbrenner has argued that through the Keynesian influence upon policy -- through the consequent secular inflation -- the 'peaceful acceptance' of Marxian aims has been secured. Where the drastic measures which Marx himself contemplated would have failed, Keynesian methods have quietly succeeded." (p.131)

Kemp, Jack. "The Political Relevance of Ludwig von Mises." *Champions of Freedom: 5. The Ludwig von Mises Lecture Series.* Cheryl A. Yurchis, ed. Hillsdale, Mich.: Hillsdale College Press, 1979. pp.89-104. At a time when "Governments almost everywhere were intervening increasingly in economics affairs . . . . the grounds for pessimism seemed realistic. ¶Yet Mises argued ["The Political Chances of Genuine Liberalism," Article 51.3] that the opposite was true; that genuine liberalism had a good chance for success, if its defenders would recognize the nature of the adversary and learn to relate capitalism's strengths to the people, to their opportunities for more jobs, better wages, and lower prices." (p.89) Kemp then argued for lower tax rates.

McClain, Stephen Michael. "The Political Thought of the Austrian School of Economic." Ph.D. dissertation. Johns Hopkins University, 1979. The premise of this dissertation is that capitalism, as a social system, requires and entails the projection of a political theory and that Mises and Hayek fashioned a comprehensive political theory for capitalism. It deals with Mises' philosophical base, his views on socialism and interventionism, and his political thought (pp.115-272) and compares Mises and Hayek. (pp. 443-446)

Nove, A. "Marx, the Market and 'Feasible Socialism'." *Wirtschaft und Gesellschaft. Festgabe für O. Sik.* U. Gärtner and J. Kosta, eds. Berlin: Dunker und Humblot, 1979. Reviews attempts to solve the problem of socialist economic calculation in the Soviet Union in 1919-1920.

Paul, Ron. "Capitalism." *Congressional Record.* Extension of Remarks (December 6, 1979) E5970-5973. Mentions Mises' 1959 Argentine lectures, published as *Economic Policy* (B-27), and reprints the chapter on "Capitalism" from *The Freeman* (December 1979). Paul comments: "[S]ome honest intellectuals who oppose the free market apparently do so under the impression that top businessmen control the economy when the Government does not. But this is far from the truth. In a free market, it is the consumer who is king. The consumer's desires are what determine every economic activity. Businessmen succeed only to the extent that they are able to satisfy consumer needs and wants . . . . ¶[T]hese lectures are even more relevant to the 1980s than they were to the 1950's." (p.E5970).

Petro, Sylvester. "A Strategy for the War of Ideas." *The Freeman.* Irvington, N.Y. 29:6 (June 1979) 323-333. "It has taken me a long time fully to absorb the meaning and implications of Mises' frequent exhortation: 'write books!' A solid scholarly work on an important subject has a much longer life and greater influence than any living person has . . . . ¶Any decent scholarly work will be purchased by all the great university and public libraries . . . . Its silent and passive look on the shelves is deceptive, for no decent scholar will write a serious work without at least consulting the library card-catalogues available to him . . . . I first ran across Henry Hazlitt's writing in a card-catalogue. I encountered Mises' *Human Action* by chance in another card-catalogue. Life has never been the same for me. Books are not passive." (pp.329-330)

Powell, Jim. "Where to Turn in Ruff Times." *The New York Times.* (November 11, 1979) III:9. Howard J. Ruff, financial newsletter writer, "is widely viewed as king of the gold bugs . . . . ¶Critics dwell on Mr. Ruff's lack of academic credentials in finance. 'Look,' he retorts, 'the so-called experts helped bring us chronic inflation and runaway taxes. I'm a guy with a wife, nine kids and a mortgage, trying to beat inflation plus a little. ¶The basis of my thinking is the free-market economics of scholars such as Ludwig von Mises and the Nobel laureate Friedrich Hayek. Their theories show what caused evils like inflation, recession and shortages. I use their theories to make practical decisions for the average guy who wants to protect his savings'."

Quayle, Dan. "Von Mises Looks at Congress." *Champions of Freedom: 6. The Ludwig von Mises Lecture Series*: Ronald L. Trowbridge, ed. Hillsdale, Mich.: Hillsdale College Press, 1979. pp.1-11. "Since Professor Ludwig von Mises' death in 1973, the Congress, the country, and the world have changed . . . . If von Mises were to revisit Congress today, he would observe a much different one than five years ago . . . . ¶Von Mises surely would feel Congress' excessive spending practices to be a disappointment. He would lament how his adopted country was apparently going the way of his Austrian homeland . . . . ¶Though the overall record of Congress has been dismal, we can see the flickering of the spirit of von Mises. Surely he must have looked down on the big dome in Washington and smiled as airline deregulation was voted in. An $18 billion tax break was given to the Americans. The first significant steps were taken to control the bureaucracy through civil service reform. We also witnessed the rare termination of a government bureau, the Renegotiation Board . . . . ¶We do not have an easy road to travel. Von Mises understood what we must now understand if our economy is to make the changes necessary for its survival. Economic freedom . . . . is the freedom to own property, to enter into business transactions, to grow and to prosper. We must learn again -- and the whole world with us -- that economic freedom is the indispensable prerequisite for individual political freedom. You cannot have one without the other."

Randerson, Roger. "Hayek -- Scholar, Teacher, Liberal." *Social Justice, Socialism & Democracy: Three Australian Lectures by F. A. Hayek.* Centre for Independent Studies, Australia. (1979) 47-52. Discusses Hayek's relationship to Mises during the Vienna years.

Reekie, W. Duncan. *Industry, Prices and Markets.* New York: John Wiley, 1979. Discusses Mises' views on entrepreneurship, the exchange process (catallactics) and the evenly rotating economy.

Reisman, George. *The Government Against the Economy.* Ottawa, Ill: Caroline Publishers, 1979. Refers to Mises' insight on the "harmony of interests between the consumer and the producer under capitalism." (p.84) Cites price controls as an illustration of Mises' thesis that government programs intended to help consumers wind up hurting them. Discusses Mises' views on socialism.

Rizzo, Mario J., ed. *Time, Uncertainty and Disequilibrium: Exploration of Austrian Themes.* Lexington, Mass.: D. C. Heath, 1979. Papers presented at the Conference on Issues in Economic Theory: An Evaluation of Current Austrian Perspectives, at New York University, January 7-8, 1978, plus a paper by G. L. S. Shackle, who had been unable to attend, and S. C. Littlechild's comment on Shackle. Brief mentions of Mises as follows:
> S. C. Littlechild compares Shackle's views with those of Mises and Kirzner. (pp.32-49)
> Sir John R. Hicks finds it difficult to accept Mises' dismissal of models. (p.55)
> Murray N. Rothbard comments briefly on Mises' position on "nonaction." (p.94)
> Israel M. Kirzner stresses the importance for Mises of action and purposefulness. (p.146-147)
> Richard E. Wagner recognizes Mises' contribution, in his work on socialism, to the importance of knowledge. (p.180)
> Leland B. Yeager, in spite of the praise accorded Frank A. Fetter and Mises, "cannot believe that the Austrians have a *pure* time-preference theory of interest." (p.208)
> Roger Garrison, commenting on Yeager's views on interest theory, discusses the "extremely radical subjectivist position" attributed to Fetter, Mises, Rothbard, and Kirzner. (pp.219-220)

Schuettinger, Robert L. & Eamonn F. Butler. *Forty Centuries of Wage and Price Controls: How Not To Fight Inflation.* Wash., D.C.: Heritage, 1979. Quotes Mises' "Inflation and Price Control" (Article 45.4).

Sennholz, Hans F. *Age of Inflation.* Belmont, Mass.: Western Islands, 1979. In reviewing this book, George Koether writes: "Ludwig von Mises said it almost seventy years ago: 'State regulation . . . in the sphere of banking, as everywhere else . . . has been a failure.' ¶Now one of Mises' most eminent and articulate disciples, Professor Hans Sennholz of Grove City College, has restated that principle much more forcefully . . . . ¶This book deals with fundamentals . . . . ¶He challenges the Chicago School's Nobel-prize winner, Milton Friedman, with a frontal attack on Friedman's monetary theory . . . . ¶Sennholz's castigation of the Federal Reserve System is unreserved and devastating." (*The Freeman*, January 1980).

Tuchtfeldt, E. "Wilhelm Röpke: Einleitende Bemerkungen zur Neuausgabe seiner Werke" [Introductory Remarks to the New Edition of Röpke's Works]. *Wilhelm Röpke: Die Lehre von der Wirtschaft* [The Works of Wilhelm Röpke: Theory and Economy]. Bern & Stuttgart: Paul Haupt, 1979. pp.v-xxxvi. "[T]he history of neo-liberalism begins with three groups that developed the liberal tradition during the first third of the 20th century. The earliest group was led by E. Cannan at the London School of Economics (Th. Gregory, L. Robbins, F. C. Benham, W. H. Hutt and F. W. Paish). The second group developed out of the circle around Ludwig von Mises in Vienna. Mises, arising out of the Austrian School tradition, had already begun, with his book *Nation, State, and Economy* (1919) [B-3], to erect a consistent structure of liberal thought. This was followed in the 1920s and 1930s by a series of unusually original and stimulating publications which continued when he moved to Geneva and New York . . . . Out of the famous Mises' seminar in Vienna came M. St. Braun, G. Haberler, F. A. von Hayek, F. Machlup, O. Morgenstern, R. Strigl, and many others . . . . Mises' strict logic strongly influenced not only the London group but also the third group in Chicago." xxxiii-xxxiv. (Translated from the German)

Van den Haag, Ernest. "Libertarians & Conservatives." *National Review.* 31:23 (June 8, 1979) 725-739. An attack on the libertarian ideology and libertarian movement, directed mainly at Murray Rothbard: "[N]ew-style anarchists --libertarians -- take their cue from Ayn Rand; or (via Murray Rothbard) from Ludwig von Mises; or finally, via some of his Chicago disciples, from Friedrich von Hayek. Oddly enough, none of these would agree with the libertarian (anarchist) development of his doctrine. ¶Thus, von Mises wrote: 'Government as such is not only not an evil but the most necessary and beneficial institution, as without it no lasting cooperation and no civilization could be developed or preserved'." (p.726)

Van Dun, Frank. "Het Epistemologisch Statuut van de Wetenschappen van het Menselijk handelen: de bijdrage van Ludwig von Mises" ["The Epistemological Status of the Sciences of Human Action: The Contribution of Ludwig von Mises"]. *Tijdschrift voor Sociale Wetenschappen* 24:2 (April-June 1979) 181-192. *Dialog Information Services* printout says this doctoral thesis summarizes Mises' exposition of the historical and praxeological methods, discusses the subjective judgments in historical explanations and defends Mises' insistence that praxeology be put into a category distinct from the formal and practical sciences. Published in Belgium in Dutch; hard copy from University Microfilms [137725 83N2264].

Williams, Philip M. *Hugh Gaitskell: A Political Biography.* London: Jonathan Cape, 1979. The author describes Gaitskell's impressions of Mises: "The advanced foreign students were among the chosen few invited by Ludwig von Mises to his private seminar or 'inner circle'. In this select gathering, Gaitskell noted (with some exaggeration, for argument was lively): 'there is no discussion. He is just incapable of it. There's one exception -- the *English* are allowed to speak . . . but if any Austrian or German student raises his voice Mises shuts him up at once.' Gaitskell took advantage of the exception, volunteering almost at the first meeting to present -- in German -- a paper refuting Mises's own recent book arguing that a Socialist state could not have a rational pricing system: 'I was a little nervous for, of course . . . Mises is not exactly good at taking criticism. However, it went off better than I expected. He was very polite, and Haberler and Strigl both came firmly to my rescue.' A visiting American economist recalls that Mises thanked the speaker only for his excellent German, though he himself had found the paper 'a quite convincing demonstration of a workable price system under socialism . . . a compelling piece of argumentation.' It was a bold undertaking for a young man of twenty-seven, and after the ordeal was over Hugh wrote to his brother that he was 'feeling very happy and relieved and lazy'." (p.53)

1980

Bartlett, John. *Familiar Quotations: A collection of passages, phrases and proverbs traced to their sources in ancient and modern literature.* 15th ed., rev. & enl. Emily Morison Beck, ed. Boston: Little, Brown, 1980. Includes four Mises quotations.

Blaug, Mark. "Economic Methodology in One Easy Lesson." *British Review of Economic Issues.* 2:10 (May 1980). According to Stephan Boehm, Blaug rejects Mises' methodology: "This school of so-called 'modern Austrian economics' has interesting things to say about the study of competitive processes, as distinct from the properties of final equilibrium states, but its methodological ideas are a throwback to the Neanderthal 'essentialism' of yesterday." (See Boehm's "The Ambiguous Notion of Subjectivism" in *Method, Process, and Austrian Economics: Essays in Honor of Ludwig von Mises.* Israel M. Kirzner, ed. 1982, p.49 n.5)

_____. *The Methodology of Economics.* Cambridge: Cambridge University Press, 1980. According to Stephan Boehm, Blaug dismisses Mises' methodological writings as "so cranky and idiosyncratic that we can only wonder that they have been taken seriously by anyone." (See Boehm's "The Ambiguous Notion of Subjectivism" in *Method, Process, and Austrian Economics: Essays in Honor of Ludwig von Mises.* Israel M. Kirzner, ed. 1982, p.42)

Block, W. "On Robert Nozick's 'On Austrian Methodology'." *Inquiry.* 23 (December 1980) 397-444. A careful theoretical reply to Robert Nozick's "On Austrian Methodology" (*Synthese.* 36 (1977) 353-392). In support of his criticism of Nozick, Block quotes Mises, Rothbard, et al, on Austrian methodological individualism, a priori, indifference, and time preference. For annotated Nozick entry, see "Books and Articles About Mises: 1977."

Cave, Martin. *Computers and Economic Planning: The Soviet Experience.* Cambridge: Cambridge University Press, 1980. Apparently one of the "refutations" of Mises' thesis that economic calculation is impossible under socialism, claiming that the advent of computers and cybernetics makes such planning possible. Discusses the Soviet experience. Not seen by the compilers.

Cordato, Roy E. "The Austrian Theory of Efficiency and the Role of Government." *The Journal of Libertarian Studies.* New York: Center for Libertarian Studies. 4:4 (Fall 1980) 393-403. "To truly understand the Austrian point of view, it is necessary to understand the concept of human action as the Austrians define it. Simply stated, human action is viewed as 'purposeful behavior'. . . . the application of specific means to achieve desired ends. This concept of human action has been developed, with respect to economics, most thoroughly in the writings of economist Ludwig von Mises." In developing his thesis, Cordato quotes Kirzner most frequently.

Ebeling, Richard M. & Joseph T. Salerno. "An Interview with Professor Fritz Machlup." *The Austrian Economics Newsletter.* New York: Center for Libertarian Studies. 3:1 (Summer 1980) 1, 9-12. For annotation see Machlup (below).

High, Jack. "Maximizing, Action, and Market Adjustment: An Inquiry into the Theory of Economic Disequilibrium." Ph.D. dissertation. UCLA, 1980.

Hillsdale College. *Champions of Freedom: 7. The Ludwig von Mises Lecture Series.* Ronald L. Trowbridge, ed. Hillsdale, Mich.: Hillsdale College Press, 1980. Two contributions mention Mises:

Evans, M. Stanton. "Unlearning the Liberal History Lesson: Some Thoughts Concerning
    Conservatism and Freedom," 1-18. Evans spoke "as a former student of Ludwig von Mises."
    "[T]he first thing Prof. Mises tried to teach us in his seminar was the science of
    epistemology: the science, that is, of how we know things."
Watrin, Christian. "A Critique of Macroeconomic Planning from a Misesian-Hayekian Standpoint,"
    59-81. Watrin opens with a discussion of the economic calculation debate and then applies the
    Misesian-Hayekian arguments to centralized economic planning.

Katouzian, Homa. *Ideology and Method in Economics*. New York: New York University Press, 1980. Katouzian
    considers Ludwig von Mises the "most dogmatic expositor" of the position that "the methodology of
    natural science was inapplicable to economics" and that "economic theory could nevertheless be
    completely value-free." Concerning Mises' position on *a priori:* "[H]e goes on to argue at length that
    therefore 'no kind of experience can ever force us to discard or modify *priori* theorems; they are logically
    prior to it and cannot be either proved by corroborative experience or disproved by experience to the
    contrary'.   And if this does not do sufficient justice to a full exposition of the phantasmagoria of von
    Mises's *a priorism,* the reader may take some joy (or horror) from the following statement: 'If a
    contradiction appears between a theory and experience, *we must always assume* that a condition pre-
    supposed by the theory was not present, or else that there is some error in our observation' . . . . [p.30,
    Epistemological Problems . . . (B-10)] In other words, if reality is in conflict with your ideas, do not
    adjust your views because reality must be at fault!" (pp.39-40)

Kirzner, Israel M. "The 'Austrian' Perspective on the Crisis." *The Public Interest: Special Edition. The Crisis in
    Economic Theory.* New York: National Affairs, 1980. pp.111-122. "The term 'Austrian' economics . . . .
    refers to the work now being done in this country by a group of younger economists who have
    discovered, especially through the work of Mises and Hayek, the value and fruitfulness of certain insights
    basic to the earlier school of Austrian economics, originating in the 1870's with Carl Menger in Vienna."
    (p.111n) Kirzner examines "from the Austrian perspective" neo-classical fallacies, especially the concept
    of equilibrium. Reprinted in *Austrian Economics: I.*   Stephen Littlechild, ed. (Aldershot, Hants,
    England; Brookfield, Vt: Edward Elgar, 1990) pp.191-202.

Littlechild, S. C. & G. Owen. "An Austrian Model of the Entrepreneurial Market Process." *Journal of Economic
    Theory.* 23 (December 1980) 361-379. Not seen by the compilers.

Machlup, Fritz. "An Interview" by Joseph T. Salerno and Richard M. Ebeling. *Austrian Economics Newsletter.*
    New York: Center for Libertarian Studies.   3:1 (Summer 1980) 1, 9-12. Machlup discusses his
    association with Mises and Austrian economics: "Well, deductive is fine, *a priori* is something else . . . .
    [Y]ou can deduce things from statements whether they are *a priori* or *a posteriori.* Now, Mises gave us
    his views on his *a priori* ideas and they were criticized by Kaufmann, Schutz and others, but . . . it isn't
    really necessary to criticize these terms because . . . even in an entirely empirical science, you could
    construe an abstract, internally consistent system of propositions . . . . So one does not have to take the
    aprioristic position of Mises so seriously as he himself has done."

_____. "My Early Work on International Monetary Problems." *Quarterly Review.*   Rome: Banca Nazionale del
    Lavoro. 133 (June 1980) 113-146. "My first publications were in this field . . . . ¶The Europe of 1914
    had 10 currencies, all with fixed gold parities and fixed exchange rates. The Europe of 1920 had 27 paper
    currencies, none with a gold parity, none with fixed exchange rates, and several of them in various stages
    of inflation or hyperinflation . . . . ¶Monetary 'experts' everywhere were raising questions about the best
    techniques of stabilization and, possibly, of a return to the gold standard . . . . Very little was known
    about the gold standard without gold coins, and when Professor Mises proposed to me to investigate it,
    historically as well as theoretically, I went to work." (pp.115-116)

McKenzie, Richard B. "The Neoclassicalists vs. the Austrians: A Partial Reconciliation of Competing Worldviews." *Southern Economic Journal.* 47:1 (July 1980). Not seen by the compilers.

Meyer, W. "Erkenntnistheoretische Orientierungen und der Charakter des ökonomischen Denkens" [Directions of Knowledge Theory and the Character of Economic Thought]. *Zur Theorie marktwirtschaftlicher Ordnungen.* E. Streissler & Ch. Watrin, eds. Tübingen: Mohr, 1980. Assesses Mises' contributions to epistemology and methodology. Not seen by the compilers.

Mises, Margit von. "When Keynes' Influence Began." *The City Recorder.* Kent (England). (July 24, 1980). Mrs. von Mises corrects Penrose for having cited in his June 12 column (see below) erroneous publication dates for Mises' books; then she adds: "Long before Hitler came to power in 1933, he [Mises] was on the blacklist not only of the Nazis but also of the Russians. I myself consider this an honor. Not only for him, but for the thousands of courageous men and women fighting abroad . . . who had recognized that the disappearance of the free market would also mean the disappearance of individual liberty."

O'Driscoll, Gerald P., Jr. "Frank A. Fetter and 'Austrian' Business Cycle Theory." *History of Political Economy.* 12:4 (1980) 542-557. Not seen by the compilers.

Opitz, Edmund A. "The Philosophy of Ludwig von Mises." *The Freeman.* Irvington, N.Y. 30:7 (July 1980) 430-442. "Classical liberalism," Opitz writes, "presupposes a religious philosophy which regards man as a created being who bears a unique relation to God . . . . This free being is under the moral law laid down in the original constitution of things, responsible for discovering this law and obeying it . . . . ¶Now, some critics of classical liberalism have judged it to be crass, too neglectful of man's higher nature. Not so, says Mises: 'The critics who speak in this vein show only that they have a very imperfect and materialistic conception of these higher and nobler needs'." Opitz then quotes Mises' tribute in *Bureaucracy* to the "elite" whose "heroism and self-sacrifice" made the present civilization possible: "Every step forward on the way toward an improvement of moral conditions has been an achievement of men who were ready to sacrifice their own well-being, their health, and their lives for the sake of a cause that they considered just and beneficial."

Pasour, E. C. Jr., "Benevolence and the Market." *Modern Age.* Bryn Mawr, Penna.: Intercollegiate Studies Institute. 24:2 (Spring 1980) 168-178. "Conservative and libertarian defenders of the market, epitomized by Wilhelm Roepke and Ludwig von Mises, agree that capitalism is the most productive economic system. However, there is . . . a basic conflict in the views of Mises and Roepke toward the appropriate criteria for evaluating the market . . . . ¶Whereas Mises defended free markets on utilitarian grounds, . . . Roepke based his defense on ethical grounds, regarding the market as a necessary but not sufficient condition for the attainment of the 'good society' (pp.168-169) . . . . ¶Although a great deal of effort has been devoted to a utilitarian defense of the market, the relationship of the market to ethical or moral considerations has been given short shrift. Yet, free institutions have value beyond their ability to increase material output." (p.176)

Penrose, Harry. "Around the City" column. *The City Recorder.* Kent (England). (June 10, 1980). This column not available, but apparently it referred to Ludwig von Mises and his writings. (See Mises, Margit von, above).

_____. "Around the City" column. *The City Recorder.* Kent (England). (July 10, 1980). Penrose quoted Mises on the situation in Switzerland. It is "a small country . . . which nature has endowed very poorly . . . . But its people, over the centuries, have continually pursued a capitalistic policy. They have developed the highest standard of living in continental Europe." Other countries could attain the same high standard of living "after some years of good policies. But," Mises emphasized, "the policies must be good."

Perroux, François. "Peregrinations of an Economist and the Choice of his Route." *Quarterly Review.* Rome: Banca Nazionale del Lavoro. 133 (June 1980) 147-162. "There was an ardent pursuit of research in the seminars of Ludwig von Mises whom a certain ostracism kept at a distance from the University. ¶These meetings . . . were thronged by an international audience, attracted by his books and gripped by his lectures . . . . ¶I recall lively discussions between Ludwig von Mises and our common friend, Hugh Gaitskell, who was one day to become Chancellor of the Exchequer and who at that time was modestly pursuing his studies in advanced economics side by side with us. ¶Whereas von Mises stigmatized the inevitable unemployment caused by the excess of the supply of labour over the demand or pointed out the long list of disequilibria and compensations which were unavoidable in the abstract, the future leader of the Labour Party stressed the margin for manoeuvre by acting on profit . . . . 'What can you expect?' insinuated von Mises with a feigned indulgence, the sincerity of which was not quite above reproach. 'He is bent on a socialist career'." (pp.147-149)

Reese, Alan David. "Alienation and Economics in Karl Marx." Ph.D. dissertation. Virginia Polytechnic Institute and State University, 1980. According to dissertation abstract: "Ludwig von Mises's claim that socialism is the 'abolition of rational economy'. . . . amounts to a fundamental and unanswered critique of Marxian socialism and makes, at the very least, a prima facie case for the impossibility of Marxian socialism."

Rothbard, Murray N. "Ludwig von Mises and Natural Law: A Comment on Professor Gonce." *The Journal of Libertarian Studies.* New York: Center for Libertarian Studies. 4:3 (Summer 1980) 289-297. Rothbard argues that Mises was a utilitarian, not a natural law theorist, as R. A. Gonce maintained in "Natural Law and Ludwig von Mises' Praxeology and Economic Science." (*Southern Economic Journal.* April 1973. 39:490-507). Rothbard writes: "We conclude that in each and every one of the references which Gonce cites in support of his contention that Mises upholds and grounds himself on the natural law philosophy, and indeed uses it as his 'magistral principle,' not a single reference bears out Gonce's position . . . . We are forced to conclude that either Professor Gonce has willfully distorted Mises' position to support his own 'ideological' dislike of Mises' classical liberal views, or that he is woefully ignorant of the polar difference between natural law and its mortal enemy, utilitarianism." (p.295) (For annotated Gonce entry, see "Books and Articles About Mises: 1973.")

_____. "Mises' Regression Theorem." *The Essence: Series 5.* Menlo Park, Calif.: Institute for Humane Studies. (August-November 1980). "Ludwig von Mises solved the problem of the Austrian Circle . . . . [i]n his Regression Theorem . . . . ¶Mises' Regression Theorem showed that logically the demand for money can be pushed back to the day *before* gold began to be used as a medium of exchange, when it was demanded purely for its consumption."

Salerno, Joseph T. & Richard M. Ebeling. "An Interview with Professor Fritz Machlup." *The Austrian Economics Newsletter.* New York: Center for Libertarian Studies. 3:1 (Summer 1980) 1, 9-12. For annotation, see Machlup (above).

Siegel, Marjorie. "Leading Gurus of Gold-Backed Money." *Dun's Review.* (April 1980) 64-65. Includes brief biographies and photos of Mises, Hazlitt, Rueff and Rees-Mogg. Not seem by compilers.

Taylor, Thomas C. Jr. "Accounting and Austrian Economics." *Austrian Economics Newsletter.* New York: Center for Libertarian Studies. 3:1 (Summer 1980) 6-9. "Mises, in positing accounting as a major facet of monetary calculation, recognized its role in capital and income determinations . . . . ¶Mises divided monetary calculation into two classifications, retrospective and anticipatory, and relegated the accounting for profit and loss to the retrospective domain . . . . ¶One of the great contributions of Austrian economics is its recognition of the problems of knowledge and coordination and the function of the price system in telecommunicating monetary signals so that these problems are alleviated . . . . Over several decades now there has been an increasing promulgation of mandatory accounting rules and procedures . . . . Could it be that this direct government intervention into accounting is potentially more serious than many other forms of government obstruction of the entrepreneurial market process? . . . ¶In the final analysis, the most valuable Austrian insight into the problems of accounting could well be an argument that the accountant is a special and indispensable kind of entrepreneur engaged in developing and offering accounting services in a competitive market, and that any interference into this discovery process is likely to result in hazardous unforeseen consequences to the development of sound accounting methods."

Vaughn, Karen I. "Does It Matter That Costs Are Subjective?" *Southern Economic Journal.* 46 (Summer/January 1980) 702-715. Not seen by compilers.

_____. "Economic Calculation under Socialism: the Austrian Contribution." *Economic Inquiry* 18 (October 1980) 535-554. Paper presented at The Southern Economic Association meetings (1977) revised. "Economic theories of socialism during the 1930's were based on Walrasian general equilibrium models in which the central planning board was to function as the auctioneer . . . . The Austrians, Ludwig von Mises and Friedrich Hayek, argued that even market socialism would fail to achieve the efficiency of real market capitalism because Walrasian models used to construct the economic theory of socialism left out important features of real markets that generate efficient outcomes. Specifically, the entrepreneurial nature of the adjustment process, the importance of decentralized information and the role of incentives under varying institutional settings (p.535) . . . . ¶During the 1920's there was a genuine debate between Mises and the German and Austrian socialists, but by the 1930's, Mises had finished with the issue and it was Friedrich Hayek who took upon himself the role of critic of socialism in England . . . . Occasionally, Hayek's criticisms were noted in scholarly articles . . . . Mostly, Mises was ridiculed, and Hayek, on this issue seen as little more than Mises' apologist, was ignored." (p.537)   Vaughn then summarizes the major points in Mises' and Hayek's analysis and examines the work of H. D. Dickinson, Oskar Lange and Abba Lerner, which she categorizes as "naive at best." (p.550) Reprinted in *Austrian Economics: III.* Stephen Littlechild, ed. (Aldershot, Hants, England; Brookfield, Vt: Edward Elgar, 1990) pp.332-351.

1981

Barry, Norman P. "Austrian Economists on Money and Society." *National Westminster Bank Quarterly Review.* (May 1981). 20-31. Not seen by compilers.

_____. "Restating the Liberal Order: Hayek's Philosophical Economics." *Twelve Contemporary Economists.* J. R. Shackleton and Gareth Locksley eds. London: Macmillan, 1981. pp.87-107. Reportedly contains discussions of Hayek's views on a number of topics, including the calculation debate. Not seen by compilers.

Browne, Harry & Terry Coxon. *Inflation-Proofing Your Investments.* New York: William Morrow, 1981. Browne dedicates this book to "Ludwig von Mises, Henry Hazlitt, Murray N. Rothbard, and Milton Friedman, for helping us to understand how the world works." Mises is credited (p.44n) with having been the first to point out in 1912 that deflation can be caused by an increase in the demand for money as well as by a decrease in the quantity of money without a corresponding decrease in demand for it. Commenting on Mises' *Human Action* (B-16), "Harry Browne's thinking has been influenced more by Ludwig von Mises than by any other economist." (p.476)

Bush, Paul D. "'Radical Individualism' vs. Institutionalism: Parts I & II." *American Journal of Economics and Sociology* 40:2 & 3 (April & July 1981) 139-147 & 287-298. A 2-part analysis of David Seckler's *Thorstein Veblen and the Institutionalists.* Part I (April) is sub-titled "The Division of Institutionalists Into 'Humanists' and 'Behaviorists'." Bush approves of Seckler's criticizing Veblen, even if he does not agree with Seckler's criticism: "Institutionalists finally have been given the kind of critical attention that is so vital to intellectual progress. Criticism is the catalyst of a vigorous intellectual existence; it is being ignored that is deadly." (I:142) Part II (July), sub-titled "Philosophical Dualisms as Apologetic Constructs Based on Obsolete Psychological Preconceptions," discusses the influence of Mises' work on Seckler who was, according to Bush, "completely persuaded by the whole pantheon of classical philosophical dualisms which find their expression in such methodological prescriptions as Ludwig von Mises' 'insurmountable methodological dualism'." (II:287)

Chafuen, Alejandro A. "Los Fundamentos Escolásticos de la Economía de Mercado" [The Scholastic Foundations of the Market Economy]. *Pensamiento Económico.* Buenos Aires: Cámara Argentina de Comercio. #425 (2nd quarter 1981) 14-16. Quotes Mises' book on money.

Chilton, David. *Productive Christians in an Age of Guilt Manipulators: A Biblical Response to Ronald Sider.* Tyler, Texas: Institute for Christian Economics, 1981; 2nd ed., 1982; 3rd ed., 1985. A pro-free market book, a fundamentalist Christian's slant on subjectivist economics. Cites Mises on savings, investment, profits, socialism, etc.

Collins, Robert M. *The Business Response to Keynes, 1929-1964.* New York: Columbia University Press, 1981. "Some segments of the business community" refused to go along with the Keynesian consensus "in accepting the primacy of the federal government's role in economic stabilization and in forsaking the orthodoxy of the annually balanced budget. The NAM [National Association of Manufacturers], for example, continued to view compensatory economics with distaste. The Association's postwar position was epitomized in its study of *The American Individual Enterprise System.* Published in 1946, this two volume treatise was the culmination of six years of work by an 'Economic Principles Commission' which included among its members Ludwig von Mises, an expatriate Austrian already famous as an archfoe of 'statism'." (p.170)

Dyke, C. *Philosophy of Economics.* Englewood Cliffs, N.J.: Prentice-Hall, 1981. Chapter 4, "Two Alternative Theories of Economic Value," contrasts the views of Mises, who "asks us to think of human beings as creatures with wants, needs, and intelligence," (p.68) with the views of Karl Marx who "gives us the picture of groups of people working together for the mutual achievement of their destiny as human beings." (p.72)

Evans, Rowland & Robert Novak. *The Reagan Revolution.* New York: E. P. Dutton, 1981. Evans interviewed Ronald Reagan: "[W]hat philosophical thinkers or writers most influenced your conduct as a leader, as a person?" Reagan: "Well, . . . I've always been a voracious reader -- I have read the economic views of von Mises and Hayek, and . . . Bastiat . . . . I know about Cobden and Bright in England -- and the elimination of the corn laws and so forth, and the great burst of economy or prosperity for England that followed." (p.229)

Fuerle, Richard D. "Praxeology: A Restatement. The Study of the Logical Implications of the Existence of Volitional Action." Ph.D. dissertation. Los Angeles: International College. September 1981. 199pp. Supervised by Dr. Hans F. Sennholz (Grove City College, Grove City, Penna.). This thesis expanded and published as a book, *The Pure Logic of Choice* (New York: Vantage Press, 1986).

Garrison, Roger W. "The Austrian-Neoclassical Relation: A Study in Monetary Dynamics." Ph.D. dissertation. University of Virginia, 1981. Wicksell's economic theories formed the basis for the development of the Austrian and neoclassical schools, both of which proceeded to develop Wicksellian themes in different directions. Garrison inquires into the nature and significance of this difference. Patinkin and Mises are on opposite ends of an analytical spectrum in macroeconomics, the contrast of which is considered worthwhile; locating Keynes on the Patinkin-Mises spectrum yields a new perspective on Keynesian macroeconomics.

Gilder. George. *Wealth and Poverty.* New York: Basic Books, 1981. "The more important charge of the intellectual consensus is that capitalism is morally vacant . . . . The great Austrian political economists Friedrich von Hayek and Ludwig von Mises, like Milton Friedman in *Capitalism and Freedom*, are all eloquent in their critique of collectivism and their celebration of liberty, but they are uncertain of what it is for: their argument tends to be technical and pragmatic. Freedom is good in itself and also makes us rich; collectivism compounds bondage with poverty. None of these writers sees reason to give capitalism a theology or even assign to its results any assurance of justice." (p.6)

Greaves, Bettina Bien. "The Tragedy of Inflation: *Much More Than Higher Prices.*" *The Freeman.* Irvington, N.Y. 31:10 (October 1981) 598-605. Discusses the effects of government-created monetary expansion, i.e. of inflation, to which Mises called attention -- illusory profits, production shifts, malinvestment, clusters of errors and economic waste, discouragement of saving, etc. "[I]f government continues to offer benefits to some at the expense of others, financing them through higher taxes and monetary expansion, serious economic disaster must be expected. New evidence will then demonstrate once more the truth of Ludwig von Mises' statement that government interference with the economy, no matter how well intentioned 'produces results contrary to its purpose, that it makes conditions worse, not better, from the point of view of the government and those backing its interference'."

Hazlitt, Henry. "Understanding 'Austrian' Economics." *The Freeman.* Irvington, N.Y. 31:2 (February 1981) 67-78. Summarizes the major tenets of the "Austrian" school of economics, as they stemmed from Menger, Wieser, and Böhm-Bawerk, and have been passed along through Ludwig von Mises to the present generation of "Austrians." Mises' *Human Action* (B-16) "still stands as the most complete, powerful, and unified presentation of Austrian economics in any single volume."

Hutchison, T. W. *The Politics and Philosophy of Economics: Marxians, Keynesians and Austrians.* New York University Press, 1981. A collection of essays on philosophical and political aspects of economics. In a review of this book Don Lavoie writes that Hutchison says "most Austrians rely on an 'infallibilist' methodology that insulates itself from all criticism and therefore necessarily tends to degenerate into a rigid dogmatism." Lavoie holds that "It is particularly inappropriate to charge Mises and Hayek with infallibilism because the content of their economic analysis has *always* been primarily concerned with showing that all human action . . . is necessarily fallible . . . . ¶Hutchison quotes several passages in which Mises appears to suggest that economic reasoning is beyond tests of any kind." Lavoie claims, this misinterprets Mises. "Mises specifically argued that 'Man is not infallible' and that consequently economists employing the deductivist method must always scrupulously examine the steps of their reasoning for possible errors." Quoted from Lavoie's review in *Market Process.* Fairfax, Va.: Center for the Study of Market Processes, George Mason University. 2:1 (Winter 1984) 10-13)

Johannsen, Oscar B. "Ludwig von Mises: Praxeologist Supreme." *Fragments.* Floral Park, N.Y. 19:1 (January-March 1981) 1. "Long before I met Mises, I had read most of his major works . . . . ¶As a Georgist, I would have liked to argue with him about the treatment of land, but unfortunately, at his advanced age, because of his impaired hearing, it was difficult to communicate with him. However, I had the pleasure of listening to a learned scholar, who at all times was the epitome of a 19th century gentleman, expound on the virtues of the free market and, indirectly, on individualism . . . . ¶If Mises taught me nothing else, he did teach me by his example to stand up and fight for what I believe in, regardless of the cost, but always with due regard for the views of those opposing me, and with that respectful courtesy which distinguishes a gentleman from a boor."

Journal of Libertarian Studies. New York: Center for Libertarian Studies. 5:1 (Winter 1981). A collection of "articles on central economic planning, covering some theoretical disputes . . . as well as some historical instances of attempts to put it into practice." Introduction by Don Lavoie.

Bradley, Robert, Jr. "Market Socialism: A Subjectivist Evaluation," 23-39. A survey of the economic calculation debate, quoting Mises, Hayek, Lange, Kirzner, Rothbard, Harvey Leibenstein, P. C. Roberts, et al. An attempt, Bradley says, "to string together the far-ranging criticisms of market socialism, laying to rest the widespread belief that, while the insights of Austrians were valid against Marxian socialism, they lose their theoretical sting against market socialism."

Lavoie, Don. "A Critique of the Standard Account of the Socialist Calculation Debate," 41-87. Analyzes various critics of Mises' position in the economic calculation debate, notably Joseph Schumpeter, Abram Bergson, Benjamin Ward, Benjamin E. Lippincott, Alan R. Sweezy, Maurice Dobb and Frank Knight. According to Lavoie, "In all of these accounts we repeatedly find the same neoclassical misinterpretation of Mises' challenge." (p.72)

    Summarized in *Literature of Liberty.* Menlo Park, Calif.: Institute for Humane Studies. 5:1 (Spring 1982) 76-77.

    Spanish translation: "Crítica de la interpretación corriente del debate sobre el cálculo económico socialista." *Libertas.* Buenos Aires: ESEADA. 4:6 (May 1987) 3-71.

    Opening sections (pp.41-46) reprinted in *Austrian Economics: III.* Stephen Littlechild, ed. (Aldershot, Hants, England; Brookfield, Vt.: Edward Elgar, 1990) pp.352-357.

Richman, Sheldon L. "War Communism to NEP: The Road from Serfdom," 89-97. An historical study. Richman quotes Trotsky's admission that "Reality came into increasing conflict with the [planned economic] program of war communism." In other words, his planning didn't work. Richman points out that, although it seems paradoxical, "a centrally directed economy is the least fit for organizing production . . . . [T]he 'planned economy' cannot plan. ¶This was the insight of 'Austrian' economist Ludwig von Mises in his pioneering work of the 1920's." (p.91)

Steele, David Ramsay. "The Failure of Bolshevism and Its Aftermath," 99-111. One section (pp.105-106) asks "Does Russia Refute Mises?" "Mises claimed that socialism was impossible. Socialism exists in Russia. Therefore Mises was undoubtedly mistaken." Steele discusses Mises' response to this apparent dilemma, namely that "Russia is dependent on the market system in the rest of the world." (p.105)

_____. "Posing the Problem: The Impossibility of Economic Calculation under Socialism," 7-22. Hermann Heinrich Gossen (1854), Nikolaas G. Pierson (1902), Boris Brutzkus (1920), Max Weber (1920), and Mises (1920) all dealt with the problem of socialism and calculation. However, "the outstanding figure was undoubtedly Mises. His statement was published first [Article 20.6], it was soon incorporated into a comprehensive critique of socialism in all its aspects [B-4], . . . it quickly reached a wide audience of socialists and was so stinging and provocative that it could not be ignored." (p.16)

Martin, Paul C. "Von Faulen & Fleissigen" [The Lazy and the Industrious]. *Welt am Sonntag.* 30 (July 26, 1981) 9. Review of anthology (*Grundtexte zur Sozialen Marktwirtschaft - Zeugnisse aus zweihundert Jahren ordnungspolitischer Diskussion* [Fundamentals of the Social Market Economy - Witnesses to 200 Years of Political Discussions]. Stuttgart/New York: Gustav Fischer, 1981) which reprints Mises' "Interventionismus" (Article 26.5). The reviewer quotes Mises: "If the power of the labor unions were not real, the unemployment would act on the market to push the artificially high wage down once more to the natural rate . . . The long term unemployment of millions . . . is the consequence of interventionism: the artificial holding up of wages through unions and unemployment insurance." (Translated from the German)

Mises, Margit von. Letter to the editor. *The Wall Street Journal.* (January 29, 1981). Comments on Leopold Tyrmand's speculation (*Wall Street Journal,* January 20, 1981; see below) as to whether President Ronald Reagan had read Mises. Mrs. von Mises told of meeting Reagan. "I am honored to meet you," he had said. "You don't know how often I consult the books of your husband before I make a speech."

Randerson, Roger. "Ludwig von Mises -- the master of economics, and Fearless Champion of Freedom." *Independent.* Western Australia. (June 28, 1981) 14. Discusses Mises' thought and influence; an introduction to Mises' six (1959) Argentinean lectures, scheduled to be serialized in the *Independent* starting the following Sunday.

Reagan, Ronald. "Fellow Conservatives: Our Moment Has Arrived." *Human Events.* (April 4, 1981) 7. "There are so many people and institutions who come to mind for their role in the success we celebrate tonight. Intellectual leaders like Russell Kirk, Friedrich Hayek, Henry Hazlitt, Milton Friedman, James Burnham, Ludwig von Mises. They shaped so much of our thoughts."

Rothbard, Murray N. "The Myth of Neutral Taxation." *The CATO Journal.* San Francisco: Cato Institute. 1:2 (Fall 1981) 519-564. Recognizing, with Mises, that there is no such thing as a "neutral tax," Rothbard concludes: "That neutral taxation is an oxymoron; that the free market and taxation are inherently incompatible; and that therefore either the goal of neutrality must be forsaken, or else we must abandon the institution of taxation itself."

Scott, Gilbert Mason. "Liberalism and the Austrian School of Economics." M.A. thesis. Western Michigan University, 1981. 56 pages. Not seen by the compilers.

Seldon, James R. "The Relevance of Subjective Costs: Comment." *Southern Economic Journal.* 48 (July 1981) 216-221. Not seen by compilers. See Vaughn, "Does It Matter That Costs Are Subjective?" ("Books and Articles About Mises: 1980."). See also Vaughn (below).

Shackle, G. L. S. & Alex H. Shand. *Subjectivist Economics: The New Austrian School.* Oxford: The Pica Press, 1981. Not seen by the compilers.

Tetley, John T. Letter to the Editor. *Fragments.* Floral Park, N.Y. 19:2 (April-June 1981) 11. "I was . . . present at the Henry George School, one evening, when Mises condescended to state his opinion of the views of Henry George. Unfortunately, he gave no definite answers to questions put to him. All I can remember Mises saying was that if Henry George's proposals were put into effect in the nineteenth century, the West would never have been settled."

Tyrmand, Leopold. "The Conservative Ideas in Reagan's Victory." *The Wall Street Journal.* (January 20, 1981). "Many names could be cited, but five should be mentioned as perhaps having a pervasive influence in the formation of future answers to the complexity of social and moral concerns. Those are Ludwig von Mises, Richard Weaver, Leo Strauss, Gordon Keith Chalmers and John Hallowell . . . . ¶With books such as *Human Action,* von Mises devoted his life to proving that capitalism and free enterprise are sources of humanity and virtue (which makes him an ancestor of supply-side microeconomics), and that any form of collectivism and statism must end in totalitarian oppression." See comments by Margit von Mises (above) and Vandersteel (below).

Vandersteel, William. "Letter to the Editor." *Wall Street Journal.* (January 29, 1981). Tyrmand (see above) "mentions five people who were influential in the formation of future answers to the complexity of social and moral concerns. Of these five, Ludwig von Mises was certainly the most influential but the remaining four are of much less significance than either Ayn Rand or Friedrich von Hayek . . . . ¶It should be noted, however, that in many areas libertarian principles are in direct conflict with some of Reagan's conservative ideas and it will be interesting to see where the future takes us."

Vaughn, Karen I. "Introduction," ix-xxxvii. *Economic Calculation in the Socialist Society* by Trygve J. B. Hoff Indianapolis: Liberty *Press*, 1981. Vaughn surveys the debate on economic calculation under socialism; comments on several pro and con articles that are not easily accessible in libraries. "While the early socialist writers had simply asserted the superiority of their system by claiming its historic inevitability, the genuine debate about the problem of economic calculation began in 1920 with the publication of Ludwig von Mises' article, 'Die Wirtschaftsrechnung im sozialistischen Gemeinwesen'." (Article 20.6). For annotated entry of the English translation of Hoff's Norwegian-language 1938 book, see "Books and Articles About Mises: 1949."

_____. "The Relevance of Subjective Costs: Reply." *Southern Economic Journal.* 48 (July 1981) 222-226. See Seldon (above). Not seen by compilers.

Waring, Edward. "The Architect of a Free Society - Von Mises." *The Southern Libertarian Messenger.* 10:5 (September 1981) 7. A brief description of Mises' contributions.

Zanotti, Gabriel J. "Los Fundamentos Metafísico-Antropológicos de la Praxeología" [The Metaphysical-Anthropological Fundamentals of Praxeology]. *Pensamiento Económico.* Buenos Aires: Cámara Argentina de Comercio. #425 (2nd quarter 1981) 20-21. Argues that Mises' views on praxeology do not contradict those of Aquinas.

100th anniversary   of Ludwig   von Mises' birth (September 29,   1881) commemorated.

Austrian Information. New York. "President Reagan Honors Ludwig von Mises." 34:9 (1981) 8. Quotes from the telegram read at the centennial dinner given in Mises' honor December 7, 1981 by the Center for Libertarian Studies. See Reagan (below).

Bethell, Tom. "Ludwig von Mises: a Centenary." *National Review.* 33:19 (October 2, 1981) 1143-1144. "All his life Mises reasoned that *agreement* both materially and morally improved mankind. But the Misesian remedy -- voluntary exchange, free prices, limited government -- was no match for the terrible plague of socialism that spread across the world in the course of his lifetime. The ideas of liberty and voluntarism that he espoused, ideas that one might imagine would have some appeal for university professors and intellectuals in an age of supposed enlightenment, to this day have remained partially concealed in the shadows of command and coercion -- ideas that are far more appealing to the intelligentsia. Why this should be remains perhaps the greatest intellectual conundrum of our era."

Buckley, William F. Jr. "Kick the Machine?" *National Review.* 33:21 (October 30, 1981) 1296-1297. "The ongoing rhetoric about Reagan's 'favoring' of the rich reminds me of envy, which reminds me that Ludwig von Mises would have been 100 years old last month, which reminds me that von Mises wrote a book about envy, which reminds me that Whittaker Chambers wrote me a letter denouncing his [Mises'] thesis: 'Von Mises's point is that the anti-capitalist mentality is the product of envy. Hitler explained it differently. He said the Devil in history is the Jew. Envy is von Mises's Jew. It is always more painful to think than to use stencils. It is extremely difficult for conservatives to think. Who does not suspect that everyone is envious? There is something we can deal with -- the veritable Jew. Only, it isn't true'." Reprinted from Buckley's syndicated column.

P.C. "Ludwig von Mises: Honderdste verjaardag von zijn geboorte. Vrijheid als Hoogste Ekonomisch Goed." [Ludwig von Mises: Hundredth Anniversary of his Birth. Freedom as the Highest Economic Good]. *Standaard.* The Netherlands. (September 29, 1981).

Center   for Libertarian Studies. New York. *In Pursuit of Liberty: The Newsletter of the CLS.* 5:2 (February 1982) 1, 3-4. For details, see Petersen, Dyanne. "The Mises Centennial Celebration" (below).

Chapman, Stephen. "Centennial of a Prophet." *Chicago Tribune.* Section 2 (September 27, 1981) 12. "Poland's economy is in chaos. But contrary to popular belief, the problem did not begin with the severe labor unrest, the unpopularity of the current regime, or the growing pressure from the Soviet Union. In fact, Poland's economic malady has such deep roots that it was foreseen sixty years ago by a now-forgotten professor at the University of Vienna. ¶Ludwig von Mises, who was born one hundred years ago this Tuesday, was the first theorist to point out that in the absence of prices established by the free interplay of market forces, socialist planners would have no way to know what to produce, how to produce it, and how much to produce . . . .   ¶By any measure, Mises was one of the most important economists of the twentieth century . . . . ¶So how does it happen that Mises has declined into oblivion, his memory kept alive only by a coterie of free-market economists . . . and other apostles of laissez-faire? . . . ¶Mises' unfashionable advocacy of unfettered capitalism, coupled with his extreme pugnacity, made him anathema in the academy."

Chattanooga News-Free Press. "Ludwig von Who?" (September 29, 1981). "We all need to be introduced . . . to Ludwig von Mises . . . . ¶Mises may not be well known to the man on the street, but he is well known to those who form economic policy. And to help make him better known throughout the nation, today is being noted as the 100th anniversary of the birth in Austria of Ludwig von Mises."

Cook, Jim. "Interviews Percy *and* Bettina Greaves." *IRI Insights.* Minneapolis, Minn.: Investment Rarities. 1:5 (Fall 1981) 32-37. See Greaves (below).

J.J.D. [James J. Drummey]. "Ludwig von Mises: Centennial Profile of the Great Economist of Liberty." *The Review of the News.* Belmont, Mass. 17:40 (October 7, 1981) 63-64. "It is impossible to overstate the extraordinary contribution which Mises made to the understanding of Free Market economics through 19 books and the powerful lectures he gave to outstanding students in Vienna, Geneva, and New York over more than half a century."

Ebeling, Richard M. "Method, Money and State." *Laissez Faire Books Catalog & Review.* New York. (Fall 1981) 37. "It is easily forgotten that just twelve years ago, when at the age of 89 he retired from teaching at New York University and just eight years ago when he died at the age of 92, Ludwig von Mises was viewed by most economists as an intellectual relic from the dustbin of the history of economic thought, condemned to an intellectual purgatory. What was his sin? He questioned the three gods of the post-World War II economics profession: prediction, planning and inflation."

Feder, Don. "A Happy 100th to the Greatest Economist of All." *Journal-American.* (September 29, 1981) A6. "Ludwig von Who, you might well ask? His name is hardly a household word. Contemporary culture has not treated this great scholar kindly. *The Encyclopedia Britannica* devotes a miserly 83 words to von Mises, compared to more than 400 verbs and adjectives lavished on that prophet of pop economics, John Kenneth Galbraith . . . . ¶Von Mises viewed the free market as the great liberator of mankind. In just a generation it had lifted the common man out of his natural state of poverty. In socialism, and its welfare state variant, he perceived a revolt against the modern age."

Foundation for Economic Education. Irvington, N.Y. *The Freeman.* (September 1981). "The Wisdom of Ludwig von Mises." Excerpts from *Human Action,* selected by George Koether, published as a tribute to Mises on the 100th anniversary of Mises' birth. For annotation, see Article 81.1, Posthumous Publications. Included in this issue of *The Freeman* is "*Human Action* Reappraised" by John Chamberlain; for annotation of Chamberlain review, see "Book Reviews: *Human Action.*"

Frankfurter Allgemeine Zeitung. "Ludwig von Mises." #227 (September 30, 1981). Excerpts from Mont Pèlerin Quarterly articles by Wilhelm Röpke, Henry Hazlitt, Lawrence Fertig, Albert Hunold and Gottfried Haberler.

Graber, Karl. *Die Presse.* Vienna. (November 23, 1981) 7. A review of *Nationalökonomie,* plus notice of Mises' 100th anniversary. (See "Book Reviews: *Nationalökonomie.* ")

Greaves, Bettina Bien. "Mises's New York University Seminar (1948-1969)." *The Libertarian Review.* Washington, D.C. 10:9 (September 1981) 23-25. Describes topics covered at the seminar; quotes several of Mises epigrammatic remarks. "Mises understood very well that the fate of the world depends on the ideas men hold. He found little in the daily papers to give him hope that the inflation would soon be halted. Thus, he was inclined to be pessimistic. Yet he told us on occasion that he was becoming more optimistic about the future, for he had confidence in 'the genius of the people'."

_____. "Ludwig von Mises: Champion of Freedom." *Competition.* Washington, D.C.: Council for a Competitive Economy. 2:10 (September 1981) 12-13. Abridged version of "Ludwig von Mises: A Tribute to a Great Man of Ideas on his 90th Birthday" in *Human Events,* September 25, 1971; see "Books and Articles About Mises: 1971," B.B.Greaves, p.299 above.

Greaves, Percy and Bettina. "Jim Cook Interviews . . ." *IRI Insights.* Minneapolis, Minn.: Investment Rarities. 1:5 (Fall 1981) 32-37. "Percy and Bettina Greaves are a unique couple who have worked tirelessly in their efforts to create an awareness and a better understanding of the great economist Dr. Ludwig von Mises and the ideas he espoused . . . . ¶As we commemorate the 100th birthday of Ludwig von Mises on September 29, 1981, we welcome the ideas of two of his closest and most devoted students."

Grinder, Walter E. "In Memoriam: Ludwig von Mises." *Laissez Faire Books Catalog and Review.* New York. (Fall 1981) 34-35. Reprint of Grinder essay in *Laissez Faire Books Catalog, 1974;* see "Books and Articles About Mises: 1974."

Helms, Jesse. "The Centennial of the Birth of Ludwig von Mises." *Congressional Record.* 127:137 (September 29, 1981) S10689-10691. Pays tribute to Mises on the 100th anniversary of his birth. Quotes Mrs. Ludwig (Margit) von Mises' January 29, 1981 *Wall Street Journal* letter (see above) and reprints John P. East's "American Conservative Thought: The Impact of Ludwig von Mises," 1979; see "Books and Articles About Mises: 1979," East.

Hillsdale College. *Homage to Mises: The First Hundred Years.* Foreword by George C. Roche III. John K. Andrews, Jr., ed. Hillsdale, Mich.: Hillsdale College Press, 1981. Papers commemorating the centenary of the birth of Ludwig von Mises, delivered at Hillsdale College September 10-11, 1981.

Ebeling, Richard M. "Ludwig von Mises and Some Contemporary Economic Themes." 38-44. Compares Mises' teachings with those of the Keynesians, monetarists, and "supply-siders." "The Austrian tradition, which has found its most developed formulation in the writings of Mises . . . . comes closest to finding the elusive microeconomic foundations to macroeconomic phenomena that has become the quest of a growing number of economists. This celebration of Ludwig von Mises' centenary may serve as an important instrument in directing the economic profession in the right direction." (p.44)

Haberler, Gottfried von. "A Vienna Seminarian Remembers: A Letter." 49-52. "[T]he famous 'Privatseminar' of Professor Ludwig von Mises . . . . met twice a month, on Fridays at 7:00 p.m. in Mises' office in the Chamber of Commerce; Mises sat at his desk, and the members of the group around him. The meeting would begin with a talk by Mises himself or with a paper by another member . . . . The always lively discussion lasted until close to 10:00 p.m. when the group walked over to the Italian restaurant 'Ancora Verde'. . . where dinner was taken. There the discussion continued . . . and later in the evening usually took on lighter tones . . . . At 11:30 p.m. or so those members who were not yet exhausted went to the Café Kuntsler . . . . Mises was always among the hardy ones who went to the Café Kunstler, and was the last one to leave for home, never before 1:00 a.m. The next morning he would be at his office at 9:00 a.m., fresh as a daisy. He kept to his habit of working late and rising early well into his eighties." Reprinted in *Wirschaftspolitische Blätter* (see below); also in *Austrian Economics: I.* Stephen Littlechild, ed. (Aldershot, Hants, England; Brookfield, Vt.: Edward Elgar, 1990) pp.108-111.

Hazlitt, Henry. "An American Admirer Remembers: A Letter." 53-54. Unable to visit Hillsdale due to "age and health," Hazlitt wrote a few words about his association with Mises.

Kirzner, Israel M. "Mises and the Renaissance of Austrian Economics." 14-18. "For Mises economic science is very definitely *wertfrei* . . . . ¶For Mises the systematic search for economic truths is an activity that is eminently worthy of human endeavor. This sense of worth had its source in Mises' passionate belief in human liberty and the dignity of the individual. For Mises the preservation of society in which these values can find expression depends, in the last resort, upon the recognition of economic truths. But, paradoxically enough, Mises was convinced that these deeply held values can be promoted, through the advancement of social science, only if scientific activity is itself conducted as an austerely dispassionate undertaking . . . . The values to be achieved by economics require value-freedom [*Wertfreiheit*] in economic investigation (pp.14-15) . . . . ¶The historic contribution of Mises, I submit, was represented not so much, perhaps, by the magisterial works that he produced in 1912, or 1922, in 1933, or 1940, -- as by his courageous, lonely vigil during the arid decades of the Forties, Fifties and Sixties, a vigil marked by a stream of unpopular books and papers, and by patient, unperturbed teaching and lecturing to whomever he was able to influence. It was this painful, unappreciated work which kept Austrian ideas alive during the years of eclipse." (p.16) Reprinted in *Austrian Economics: I.* Stephen Littlechild, ed. (Aldershot, Hants, England; Brookfield, Vt.: Edward Elgar, 1990) pp.113-117.

Machlup, Fritz. "Ludwig von Mises: A Scholar Who Would Not Compromise." 19-27. "I count myself as one of his [Mises'] sincere admirers. Yet, because I have not been an uncritical admirer, I have sometimes been charged with being 'unfaithful' to the master. So strong was his hold on the minds of many of his students that they regarded me as a heretic, or even a traitor if I disavowed any of the master's revealed truths." Machlup said he had been criticized for questioning Mises' methodological apriorism, for his "insistence that the libertarian position was firmly based on value judgments," for his "reluctance to accept without qualifications Mises' theory of consumer sovereignty," and for his "disavowal of some of [Mises] convictions related to the desirability and feasibility of a restoration of the gold standard." (pp.24-25) To this, Machlup replied: "Admiration for a great man and his important work does not presuppose uncritical acceptance of all his views. The fact that I could take exception to some of Mises' teaching does not make me an apostate. It should prove, instead, that the great teacher had produced students with open and critical minds." (p.26). Reprinted in Hillsdale College's *Champions of Freedom: The Ludwig von Mises Lecture Series, 9.* (1982) 1-16.

Mises, Margit von. "Ludwig von Mises, the Man." 10-13. "All through my husband's work there are four topics which -- like a leading melody in a symphony by Mozart or Beethoven -- were the subjects of most of his writings. He fought against *Communism,* he fought against *inflation,* he fought for *freedom of the individual,* and he fought for *free enterprise.* And the more my husband wrote, the harder he fought for his ideas, and the more admirers and enemies he got." (p.11) Reprinted as a pamphlet: Ludwig von Mises Institute, Auburn, Ala:, n.d.

Peterson, William H. "Mises and Keynes." 28-38. "I remember Lu Mises in three courses I took under him at New York University's Graduate School of Business Administration in the early 1950s . . . . In each course he carefully established, in a Mengerian methodological sense, the primacy of the individual and the indispensability of freedom in the marketplace. His focus was ever on social cooperation springing from *individual human action,* in turn springing from subjective ends and limited means. He denied the implied concept in so much of modern macroeconomic theory of standardized, homogenized human beings, of human beings amounting to interchangeable integers or virtual automatons in many macro calculations and derivations such as the Gross National Product, M1B, and the Consumer Price Index." (p.29)

Roche, George C. III. "Ludwig von Mises, Mentor and Teacher." 6-9. Dr. von Mises "warned that the greatest danger to Western society would come from the increasing concentration of political and economic power in the hands of the State. ¶No one sounded the alarm more clearly, warning of the ravages of hyperinflation and the dangers of the welfare staate. Perhaps, in time, his warnings will be heeded and the headlong rush to destruction will be reversed. When that time comes, the ideas of this titan of our age will be accorded their proper recognition. ¶When that understanding of freedom arrives, many of the books which showed the way will have been Mises' own, charting for us the course away from collectivism and statism toward individualism and freedom." (p.8)

Shenfield, Arthur. "Capitalism Under the Tests of Ethics." 55-65. Discusses the "knee-jerk reactions of those who see only monopoly and power in every capitalist cupboard." Mises is not mentioned.

Siegel, Barry. "Austria Comes to Oregon." 45-48. Describes Siegel's personal journey from Keynesian to free marketer, via a year as a Fulbright lecturer in Yugoslavia, and his efforts to introduce "Austrian economics" into his college curriculum. "Needless to say, Austrian ideas are now present in every course I teach (p.46) . . . . ¶[M]y personal ambitions for reforming the study of economics at the graduate and undergraduate level go beyond merely introducing Austrian concepts into the standard curriculum. In my opinion, Ludwig von Mises, Friedrich Hayek, and the younger members of the Austrian school, as well as those in the associated field of public choice, have revived the field of political economy -- or at least begun its recapture from the Marxists. This is certainly evident in von Mises' work on omnipotent government, on bureaucracy, socialism, liberalism, and so forth." (p.48)

Indianapolis Star. "A Guidelight Mind." (September 16, 1981) 12. A brief overview of Mises and his work on his hundredth anniversary. "A central element of von Mises' thinking is the immense significance of the role of choice in economic activity and all human conduct. It is a role that some self-proclaimedly 'scientific' views reject. Yet it is the key to freedom and, it appears, economic success as well."

Juárez-Paz, Rigoberto. "Centenario, Ludwig Edler von Mises (1881-1981)" [Centennial]. *Tópicos de Actualidad.* Guatemala: Centro de Estudios Económico-Sociales. 22:496 (October 15, 1981) 130-138. Probably first given as an address in 1980. After summarizing Mises' major contributions, Juarez-Paz comments on Mises' statement: "The Austrian School of Economics was peculiarly Austrian in the sense that it grew in the soil of an Austrian culture, which Nazism later crushed . . . . In Austria the air was free from the specter of Hegelian dialectics." (p.39, *Notes and Recollections,* B-23) Juarez-Paz speculates: "In an environment dominated by a collectivist philosophy, such as Hegelianism . . . neither the freedom philosophy nor Austrian economics could arise (p.134) . . . . ¶Because of the collectivism that has dominated social thought in our time, Mises' contributions have not received the recognition they deserve. ¶However, I want to say in concluding that in Guatemala, at least at the Universidad Francisco Marroquín, Ludwig von Mises is studied and admired, in part because we are convinced of the falseness of collectivist doctrines, in part because no student of economics can ignore one of the most profound economists of the 20th century, and in part because his life, dedicated as it was to scientific and philosophical investigation and to the defense of liberty, presents a noble example for our university youth." (p.138) Reprinted in *Condiciones del Diálogo y Otros Ensayos.* Guatemala: Universidad Francisco Marroquín, 1982. pp.83-91. (Translated from the Spanish)

Koether, George (compiler). "The Wisdom of Ludwig von Mises (1881-1973)" For annotated entries, see Foundation for Economic Education (above) or Article 81.1: Posthumous Publications.

Lavoie, Don. "Mises and the Next Generation." *The Libertarian Review.* Washington, D.C. 10:9 (September 1981) 20-21. "There is an old cliché that great men of ideas seldom live to enjoy the fruits of their fame and influence, but in the case of Ludwig von Mises, it must have been still more frustrating -- he began his career with a splash, as one of the most prominent young students of a world-renowned economist, Eugen von Böhm-Bawerk, only to watch his influence wane steadily throughout his very productive career . . . . ¶In an age of infatuation with the application of sophisticated mathematical techniques to economic theory, there seemed to be no room for such an early and vociferous critic of this trend as Mises . . . . ¶It is as astonishing as it is ironic that, in the brief span of eight years between Mises's death and the hundredth anniversary of his birth, we have seen his influence not only stop its tragic decline, but increase to a degree far higher than it ever has been in this country."

Leube, Kurt R. "Begreifen und Verstehen: Zum 100. Geburtstag von Ludwig von Mises" [Conception and Understanding: On the 100th Birthday of Ludwig von Mises]. *Orientierungen.* Bonn (West Germany). 10 (December 1981) 29-31. Discusses Mises' books and thought. Reprinted in part: "Zum 100. Geburtstag Ludwig von Mises'" [On the 100th Birthday of Ludwig von Mises]. *Monatsblätter für freiheitliche Wirtschaftspolitik.* Frankfurt a.M (West Germany). 28 (1982) 45-48.

_____. "Die Visionen haben sich erfüllt: Ludwig von Mises und die Renaissance der Österreichischen Schule" [The Visions Have Been Fulfilled: Ludwig von Mises and the Renaissance of the Austrian School]. *Die Industrie.* 39:25 (September 1981) 8-10. After reviewing Mises life and contributions, Leube speaks of the Austrian Institute for Business Cycle Research which Mises and Hayek founded. "It is thanks especially to Mises, the intellectual mentor and organizer of this economically and politically important institution, that it was completely independent of the state and other economic organizations." (Translated from the German)

Levatter, Ross. "Remembering von Mises." *Reason.* Santa Barbara, Calif. 13:6 (October 1981) 37. A brief survey of the high points in Mises' life.

The Libertarian Review. Washington, D.C. "Mises Himself." 10:9 (September 1981) 26-27. A collection of quotes from Mises' books.

La Libre économique et financière. Belgium. "Il y a cent ans, naissait: Ludwig von Mises, l'inspirateur des économistes 'libertariens'" [Born 100 Years Ago: Ludwig von Mises, Inspiration of "Libertarian" Economists]. (October 3/4, 1981). "As an Austro-Hungarian, Ludwig von Mises was influenced . . . by Eugen Böhm-Bawerk and, especially, by Carl Menger. ¶We owe to C. Menger the first true analysis of marginal utility and the theory of subjective value . . . . the foundation of the modern microeconomic approach . . . . ¶Professor Mises was especially concerned with the disruption of the market by political intervention. Analyzing in the early 1920s the socialist policies which were entrancing Europe, he demonstrated that socialism, or 'dirigisme,' lacks the economic indicator provided by a system of free market prices, which is indispensable for directing production. Thus it has no valid guide for planning production. That means that for a market price system to function, individuals must be free to own and to trade their property as they choose." (Translated from the French)

McDonald, Larry. "Happy Birthday Ludwig von Mises." *Congressional Record.* 127:137 (September 29, 1981) E4477-4479. "He, above all others, would appreciate what the President is attempting to do in righting our economy. He would be delighted to read about the dollar getting stronger and discussions in the daily papers concerning reductions in big Government." Also inserted here in the *Congressional Record* is Percy L. Greaves, Jr.'s "Ludwig von Mises: An Economic Giant," 1974; see "Books and Articles About Mises: 1974," P.L.Greaves.

_____. "Ludwig von Mises: In Memoriam." *Congressional Record.* 127:137 (September 29, 1981). "Ludwig von Mises was one of the great economists of our age. His influence is felt now among policymakers in the present administration. His views, those of the Austrian school, have had a positive effect on our Nation and our economists." Also inserted here in the *Congressional Record* is Percy L. Greaves, Jr.'s remarks at Mises' commitment, October 13, 1973; see "Books and Articles About Mises: 1973: Obituaries," P.L.Greaves.

Morris, Victor F. "Letter to the Editor." *National Review*. 33:21 (October 30, 1981) 1238, 1240. Commenting on Bethell (see above): "It is true that at NYU's Graduate School of Business Administration in the closing years of his career von Mises was 'surrounded largely by time-serving, uncomprehending majors in accounting or business finance,' as Murray Rothbard wrote. But some of us were impressed (circa 1948) and the others were at least respectful. At the unnamed 'prestigious academic centers' Rothbard referred to, however, von Mises would have encountered hostility, even ridicule."

Petersen, Dyanne M. "The Mises Centennial Celebration." *In Pursuit of Liberty.* New York: Center for Libertarian Studies. 5:2 (February 1982) 1, 3-4. "On December 7, 1981 the Center for Libertarian Studies honored the great champion of economic and individual liberty Ludwig von Mises on the 100th anniversary of his birth." The speakers included CLS President David Padden, Robert Bleiberg, CLS

Board member Murray Rothbard, Professor Israel Kirzner, Ron Paul, Harvard Professor Robert Nozick, and Mrs. Ludwig (Margit) von Mises. Friedrich A. Hayek was scheduled to speak, but was unable to attend due to illness. A telegram from President Ronald Reagan was read at the dinner (see below). Petersen quotes several of the speakers:

Kirzner, Israel. Mises' "finest hour," according to Kirzner, was "not as an internationally famed scholar at his prestigious university position in Geneva, but as an old man whose ideas were treated by the economics profession with contempt and disdain and tolerated with barely disguised embarrassment;" this was the time of "his courageous, lonely vigil during the arid decades of the 1940's, 50's and 60s." (p.1)

Mises, Mrs. Ludwig von (Margit).   "This Centennial Celebration indicates a turning point in the political and cultural history of this century. Twenty years ago my husband's defense of liberty, his fight for freedom of the market, was a lonely voice in the wilderness, a voice in the past. Finally the time has come when Ludwig von Mises will not be 'treated as a second-class citizen by the university,' as Murray Rothbard once wrote. Finally he will receive the place in the history of economic thought he deserves." (p.3)

Nozick, Robert. "In 18 years of teaching at Princeton and Harvard, I never encountered any professor teaching a seminar where non-degree-seeking adults would continue to attend year after year." Mises' evening seminars were "unique in attracting mature minds without demanding discipleship." What drew Mises' adult listeners was the "content of his ideas and their power and lucidity." (p.3)

Paul, Ron. Paul spoke of the "immorality of inflation," the "moral nature of money," the necessity of returning to the gold standard, and how Mises' writings helped him to understand "the importance of economics outside the classroom." (p.1)

Raico, Ralph. "The Legacy of Ludwig von Mises: A Centennial Celebration." *The Libertarian Review.* Washington, D.C. 10:9 (September 1981) 18-22. Essentially the same as Raico's February 1975 article in *The Alternative: An American Spectator* (Bloomington, Ind.); see "Books and Articles About Mises: 1975," Raico.

Reagan, Ronald (U. S. President). *In Pursuit of Liberty.* 5:2 (February 1982) 4. Telegram to Center for Libertarian Studies (New York) on the occasion of their dinner (December 7, 1981) commemorating the 100th anniversary of Mises' birth: "Not since the enlightenment has such a finely developed mind focused on the intellectual underpinnings of the free society. Through his works, von Mises rekindled the flames of liberty in new generations of thinkers. As a wise and kindly mentor he was quick to encourage all those who sought to understand the meaning of freedom. He was a teacher's teacher who taught many of our century's great economic thinkers, including Nobel Laureate F. A. von Hayek. We owe an incalculable debt to this dean of the Austrian School of Economics for expanding our knowledge and inspiring a new vision of liberty in our age. His humanity, combined with his unique understanding of the essential elements on which human advancement depends, was the basis of his dream of a free and prosperous commonwealth." Quoted in *Austrian Information.* New York; see above.

Reisman, George. "Ludwig von Mises, Defender of Capitalism." *The Intellectual Activist.* New York. 2:8 (August 15, 1981) [2-5]. "Von Mises challenged everyone's basic assumption. He showed that *capitalism operates to the material self-interests of all,* including the non-capitalists -- the so-called proletarians ... . ¶Von Mises was not primarily anti-socialist. He was *pro*-capitalist. His opposition to socialism, and to all forms of government intervention, stemmed from his support for capitalism and from his underlying love of individual freedom and conviction that the self-interests of free men are harmonious -- indeed, that one man's gain under capitalism is not only not another's loss, but is actually others' *gain.*" Reprinted in *The Freeman.* Irvington, N.Y. 32:7 (July 1982) 432-439.

Richman, Shel[don]. "Ludwig von Mises: Sage of Liberty." *Individual Liberty.* Warminster, Penna.: Society for Individual Liberty. 12:9 (September 1981) 1, 5. "This anniversary is an opportune time for us to rededicate ourselves to the struggle for liberty, trade and peace, the things Mises struggled for all his life -- without bitterness, pessimism or compromise."

Rothbard, Murray N. "The Laissez-Faire Radical: A Quest for the Historical Mises." *The Journal of Libertarian Studies.* New York: Center for Libertarian Studies. 5:3 (Summer 1981) 237-253. In the "light of the recent Mises centennial year," Rothbard attempts "to rescue the real, 'historical' Mises from the image which has been generally formed of him . . . . as a quintessential *National Review* conservative." Rothbard finds "a proclaimed pacifist, who trenchantly attacked war and national chauvinism, a bitter critic of Western imperialism and colonialism; a believer in non-intervention with regard to Soviet Russia; a strong proponent of national self-determination, not only for national groups, but for sub-groups down to the village level -- and in theory, at least, down to the right of individual secession, which approaches anarchism; someone so hostile to immigration restrictions that he almost endorsed war against such countries as the United States and Australia to force them to open up their borders; a believer in the importance of class conflict in relation to the State; a caustic rationalist critic of Christianity and of all religion; and an admirer of the French Revolution."

Seuss, Wilhelm. "Mahner vor den Feinden der Freiheit: Zum 100. Geburtstag von Ludwig von Mises" [Warning to the Enemies of Freedom: On the 100th Birthday of Ludwig von Mises]. *Frankfurter Allgemeine Zeitung.* 225 (September 29, 1981) 13. "Post World War II students have looked on the name of Ludwig von Mises as the name of someone out of the past. The books by this scholar of the "Austrian School" of economics that were known in this country, date from 1912 (*Theory of Money and Credit*) [B-2] and 1922 (*Socialism*) [B-4]. In the days when the German Republic was developing the social market economy from out of the wreckage, Mises' name was connected with a type of liberalism which was not suited to the time and which certainly could hardly offer anything for the future, that is as an "old liberal" . . . . ¶Mises, who for decades had debated with the historical school of economics and positivism, takes up once more in *Human Action* [B-16] thoughts presented in *Socialism* [B-4] and formulates an independent theory of social cooperation that rests on exchange among individuals (methodological individualism). ¶*Nationalökonomie* [B-11] and *Human Action* [B-16] are the 'summit' of a mighty intellectual structure developed over decades. Many of his friends do not even share his view of the *a priori* character of economics . . . . However, seldom have such strong arguments in the defense of human freedom emerged from profound abstract thought based on fundamental principles, as they have in the case of Mises." (Translated from the German)

Silverman, Paul. "Zum 100. Geburtstag von Ludwig von Mises: Renaissance eines liberalen Denkers" [On the 100th Birthday of Ludwig von Mises: Renaissance of a Liberal Thinker]. *Neue Zürcher Zeitung.* 223 (September 27/28, 1981) 17-18. (Translated into German from the English by Kurt R. Leube). Describes Mises' books, the theories he expounded, and the turning point in world events that has directed the interest of economists toward Mises.

Strother, Eric G. "Scholars Honor Mises Centennial." *Hillsdale Collegian.* Hillsdale, Mich. 105A:3 September 17, 1981) 1.

Wirtschaftspolitische Blätter: "*Ludwig von Mises--Seine Ideen und Seine Wirkung*" [Ludwig von Mises -- His Ideas and His Influence]. 28:4 (1981) Festschrift issue published on 100th anniversary of Mises' birth. Essays in German or English, each with a summary in the other language.
    Baltzarek, Franz. "Ludwig von Mises und die österreichische Wirtschaftspolitik der Zwischenkriegszeit" [Ludwig von Mises and the Austrian Economic Policy Between the Wars]. 127-139. Mises' contention in his *Notes and Recollections* (B-23) that "he had prevented Austria from entering upon a bolshevistic experiment . . . . is overdrawn."

Mises "played an important role in the reconstruction of the Austrian currency . . . . In the long run, [however] his arguments against reduction of subsidies were without effect . . . . ¶Today, no one in Austria holds such an extreme liberal view of the role of the market. Following World War II . . . the so-called global steering of economics had become [a] task of the state." (English summary, p.139)

Browne, Martha Steffy. "Erinnerungen an das Mises-Privatseminar" [Reminiscences of Mises' Private Seminar]. 110-120. Browne claims that Mises' *Notes and Recollections* (B-23), written in 1940, reflects not only pessimism but also optimism. "Whoever reads his reminiscences carefully will see that Mises by no means describes only the 'decline' of civilization but also expresses faith and hope. I think especially of his report on his private seminar. The work of the participants of this seminar has not only justified, but far surpassed, the optimism and confidence to be found in his remarks. Most of the 26 students listed as participants have become recognized specialists in their respective fields, and a surprising number have received worldwide acclaim." (p.110) (Translated from the German)

Ebeling, Richard M. "Mises' Influence on Modern Economic Thought." 15-24. "Social science, . . . according to Mises, is grounded at its start in methodological individualism and methodological subjectivism. The alpha and omega of social phenomena is the subjective world of acting man . . . . ¶Within this Misesian schema are to be found all the dynamic elements that have become the intellectual spearheads at the frontiers of contemporary economic analysis: imperfect knowledge, time, process and change, expectations and foresight . . . . (p.16) ¶The 'acid test' of an economist's contribution is not only . . . . that it can be expressed in a single achievement. Many are the economists during the last two hundred years who have proposed 'systems.' Equally, if not more importantly, is the capacity of that contribution to appear alive, fresh and relevant to generation after generation of thinkers and scientists. By this latter 'acid test,' the contributions of Ludwig von Mises have more than proven their timeless value to the sciences of man." (p.23) Summarized in *Literature of Liberty.* Menlo Park, Calif.: Institute for Humane Studies. 5:1 (Spring 1982) 77-78.

Haberler, Gottfried von. "Mises's Private Seminar." 121-126. Same as Haberler's article in Hillsdale College's *Homage to Mises* (see above) with the addition of three of Felix Kaufmann's German-language lyrics about the Mises seminar.

Hörtlehner, Alexander. "Ludwig von Mises und die österreichische Handelskammerorganisation" [Mises and the [Austrian] Chamber of Commerce]. 140-150. Mises' "influence on the chamber's opinions, memoranda, and recommendations to the government was considerable. Despite his reputation, he never aspired to a top position in the chamber; he was satisfied with being the 'economic conscience' of the chamber and of Austrian Economic Policy." (English Summary, p.149)

Kirzner, Israel M. "Mises on Entrepreneurship." 51-57. "Of course Mises never falls into the error of treating the market as if it has attained the unrealizable state of equilibrium. But neither does he fail to stress the systematic manner in which entrepreneurial profit-motivated endeavor works to discover and eliminate the maladjustments which constitute the state of disequilibrium. Perhaps the most encouraging intellectual development in economics in the last few years has been a growing appreciation -- even if still all too limited -- of the profound insights embodied in the Misesian understanding of the entrepreneurial character of the market process." (p.57)

Lavoie, Don. "Mises, the Calculation Debate, and 'Market Socialism'." 58-65. According to Lavoie, Mises did more than "forc[e] the advocates of central planning to examine their proposals, and in particular to recognize the indispensable function of prices in any technologically advanced economy." He also "anticipated the essential tenets of the market socialists." (p.58)

Machlup, Fritz. "Ludwig von Mises: The Academic Scholar Who Would Not Compromise." 6-14. Essentially the same as the article in Hillsdale College's 1981 *Homage to Mises;* see above.

März, Eduard. "Die Bauer-Mises-Schumpeter-Kontroverse" [The Bauer-Mises-Schumpeter-Debate]. 66-79. Mises' 1920 article was addressed, März says, to Otto Bauer's "Der Weg zum Sozialismus" [The Road to Socialism] which "led to the founding of an abortive 'Socialization Commission.' Joseph Schumpeter "opposed Bauer on several issues, especially on the program of socialization'." However, Schumpeter's "Sozialistische Möglichkeiten von Heute" [Today's Socialist Possibilities] (1921) "shows clearly that he did not categorically oppose a socialization program." Oskar Lange "constructed the model of a socialist market economy and demonstrated its theoretical consistency . . . . ¶The Bauer-Mises-Schumpeter-debate of the interwar period leads us into the tenaciously conducted present day debate on socialism. That socialism is a thoroughly functional system, as Schumpeter stressed, seems in no need of special proof today." (English summary, pp.78-79)

Meyer, Willi. "Ludwig von Mises und das subjektivistische Erkenntnisprogramm" [Ludwig von Mises and the Research Program of Subjective Economics]. 35-50. "Mises the economist who tried to explain the facts of a market society did not follow all the postulates of Mises the epistemologist who tried to give the social sciences an apriori and unshakable foundation. The remarkable thing is that Mises' central idea of the nature of human action is the link between the successful and the less successful part of his research program. This idea made him believe that economic knowledge could be absolutely certain but it made him also aware that the analysis of the generation of information and expectations will be fundamental for a proper understanding of the market process. If one deletes his apriorism one retains a promising research program." (English summary, pp.59-40)

Moss, Laurence S. & Stephen C. MacDonald. "An Economical or a Secure Currency? Ludwig von Mises and the Defense of the Gold Standard." 98-109. "Perhaps, Mises was correct after all. Domestic monetary autonomy . . . is not a reform at all. Insofar as it allows political leaders to manipulate national currencies for narrow, partisan ends, it is a retreat from constitutionalism and its ideal of limited responsible government." (p.108)

Neudeck, Werner. "Der Einfluss von Ludwig von Mises auf die österreichische akademische Tradition gestern und heute" [Mises' Influence and the Austrian Academic Tradition]. 25-33. Neudeck reviews Mises' contributions. "In the late thirties Mises and his circle left Austria for political or economic reasons. They never came back. We thus find a curious break in economic tradition in 1938. After 1945 Austrian economic teaching espoused Keynesianism, thereby blatantly rejecting the principles of the Mises-School: Macroeconomic concepts were used, the Keynesian explanation of the cycle replaced the 'Austrian theory of the trade cycle', and political interventions were proposed and carried out. The main reason for this rise of 'Austro-Keynesianism' was the great success of Keynesian policies in Austria . . . . ¶This is why Mises' influence on the Austrian academic tradition of today is relatively small." (English summary, p.34)

Silverman, Paul. "Society as Factory and Society as Norm: Kelsen and Mises on the Problem of Social Control." 80-97. The careers of Hans Kelsen and Ludwig von Mises paralleled each other to a striking degree. Both were born in the same year, studied at the same schools, taught at the same schools, migrated to Switzerland, then to the U. S., and both died in the U. S. in the same year. Silverman recognizes also "an affinity between the theoretical work of the two men . . . . This relationship is actually a quite wide reaching one, stretching from questions of method to political philosophy." In this article, Silverman considers only "the independent responses of Kelsen and Mises to related projections of the socialist society of the future." (p.81) In his Ph.D. thesis (University of Chicago, 1984) Silverman deals with the ideas of these two men in some detail.

INDEX

373

INDEX

INDEX

INDEX

INDEX

INDEX

INDEX

INDEX